TIME SANCTIFIED

The Book of Hours in Medieval Art and Life

TIME SANCTIFIED

The Book of Hours in Medieval Art and Life

ROGER S. WIECK

WITH ESSAYS BY

Lawrence R. Poos
Virginia Reinburg, John Plummer

GEORGE BRAZILLER, INC., NEW YORK
IN ASSOCIATION WITH
THE WALTERS ART MUSEUM, BALTIMORE

First published in 1988 in the United States of America by George Braziller, Inc., New York, in association with The Walters Art Gallery, Baltimore, on the occasion of the exhibition organized by The Walters Art Gallery, "Time Sanctified: The Book of Hours," 23 April–17 July, 1988

For information, please address the publisher:
George Braziller, Inc.
171 Madison Avenue
New York, NY 10016

Library of Congress Cataloging-in-Publication Data:
Wieck, Roger S.
Time sanctified: The Book of Hours in Medieval Art and Life.
Catalog of an exhibition.
1. Hours, Books of—Exhibitions. I. Poos, Lawrence R. II. Reinburg, Virginia.
III. Plummer, John. IV. Walters Art Museum (Baltimore, Md.) V. Title.
BX2080.W54 1988 242 87-15084
ISBN 0-8076-1498-X (pbk.)

Major funding for the original publication was provided by the National Endowment for the Humanities, a federal agency, and by a grant from the Marion I. and Henry J. Knott Foundation of Baltimore. A generous donation from Bruce Ferrini and Michael Greenberg Rare Books of Akron, Ohio, also made the publication possible. Support for the revised edition was provided by Octavo Plus, the friends of the Department of Manuscripts at The Walters Art Museum.

Design by Vincent Torre

Printed and bound in Japan by Toppan Printing Company

Second edition

Contents

Foreword, by Gary Vikan 7

Acknowledgements 9

The Miniatures of Walters 288 11

THE BOOK OF HOURS IN MEDIEVAL LIFE

CHAPTER I

Introduction, by Roger S. Wieck 27

CHAPTER II

Social History and the Book of Hours, by Lawrence R. Poos 33

CHAPTER III

Prayer and the Book of Hours, by Virginia Reinburg 39

THE BOOK OF HOURS AND MEDIEVAL ART

by Roger S. Wieck

CHAPTER IV

Calendar 45

CHAPTER V

Gospel Lessons 55

CHAPTER VI

Hours of the Virgin 60

CHAPTER VII

Hours of the Cross, Hours of the Holy Spirit 89

CHAPTER VIII
"Obsecro te" and "O intemerata" 94

CHAPTER IX
Penitential Psalms and Litany 97

CHAPTER X
Accessory Texts 103

CHAPTER XI
Suffrages 111

CHAPTER XII
Office of the Dead 124

THE BOOK OF HOURS AND ITS TEXT

CHAPTER XIII
"Use" and "Beyond Use," by John Plummer 149

APPENDIX
Texts and Prayers of the Book of Hours, by Roger S. Wieck 157

Catalogue of Manuscripts, by Roger S. Wieck 169

Concordance 226
Books for Further Reading 228
Index of Artists 230

Foreword

Henry Walters is celebrated as one of the greatest art collectors in American history. The comprehensiveness and quality of the collection he bequeathed to the city of Baltimore in 1931, and which now forms the core of The Walters Art Museum, is well known to the art world. Unique among our country's foremost art museums, the Walters has a major library of illuminated manuscripts and incunabula, testimony to Mr. Walters' role as a bibliophile and to his interest in viewing the art of the book as part of the continuum of artistic creation.

Of the approximately six hundred western European medieval and Renaissance manuscripts in the Walters collection, nearly half are Books of Hours, the most popular book of the Middle Ages. This assemblage of Books of Hours is one of the largest in the Western Hemisphere; its size approaches that of the great collection at the Bibliothèque Nationale de France in Paris. The Walters Books of Hours range from the late thirteenth through the early sixteenth century and originate in all of the major manuscript-producing centers of Europe. It is thus highly appropriate that *Time Sanctified: The Book of Hours in Medieval Art and Life* tells the story of the Book of Hours relying on examples drawn primarily from the Walters collection.

Time Sanctified was first published in conjunction with an exhibition of the same name held at the Walters in 1988. The mastermind behind that exhibition, and this publication, was Roger S. Wieck, then curator of the Walters manuscript collection, now Curator of Medieval and Renaissance Manuscripts at the Pierpont Morgan Library in New York. It was he who recognized the potential of the museum's holdings for explicating the Book of Hours, who conceived the character of this book, and who wrote most of it. Other contributions are by Professor Lawrence R. Poos of the Catholic University of America, Professor Virginia Reinburg of Boston College, and John Plummer, emeritus curator at the Morgan Library.

Time Sanctified has become the standard reference work on Books of Hours for scholars, students, and collectors. It has been out of print for several years, and the time is right for an updated edition. Since it was first published, the bibliography on individual manuscripts has rapidly expanded. Many of the manuscripts discussed here have now been catalogued by Lilian M. C. Randall in her monumental three-volume study, *Medieval and Renaissance Manuscripts in the Walters Art Gallery*, published between 1989 and 1997. The first volume of her catalogue was in press at the time of the exhibition. Now, all of the French and Flemish manuscripts in the Walters collection have been described in comprehensive detail, and references are made to them in the updated bibliography of each manuscript in the catalogue at the end of this publication. Moreover, this new edition of *Time Sanctified* coincides with the reopening of the medieval galleries of the Walters, now The Walters Art Museum, and the collection of manuscripts will be on regular display to even greater advantage than had previously been possible.

The wonderful production of this volume is due to the continued partnership of George Braziller, still America's preeminent name in the field of publications on illuminated manuscripts. This revised edition could not have been carried out to such a high standard if it were not for the support of Octavo Plus, the friends of the Department of Manuscripts at the Walters. We are most grateful to them for their loyal support of the collection of manuscripts, in all its endeavors.

Gary Vikan, Director
The Walters Art Museum

NOTE TO THE SECOND EDITION

A baker's dozen years have passed since *Time Sanctified* originally appeared in 1988. Since then, numerous important books and articles, containing valuable information on the particular manuscripts included here, have been published (or are about to be). Foremost among the new books are the three magisterial volumes (in no less than five parts) on the illuminated manuscripts housed by the Walters Art Museum; because these publications by Dr. Lilian M. C. Randall (cited in the revised bibliography on p. 170) offer exhaustive descriptions of the Walters codices, it would have been silly not to have provided the reader with citations to them. Thus I have reviewed the bibliographies for the complete suite of 119 catalogue entries (pp. 171–225), almost all of which have now been updated or amended. Furthermore, I have also reviewed my attributions and dating, and have used this opportunity to offer some corrections or readjusments. Finally, "Books for Further Reading" (pp. 228–29) includes references to new publications, appearing since 1988, that significantly expand our knowledge of Books of Hours.

R.S.W.

Acknowledgements

(TO THE FIRST EDITION)

Time Sanctified was made possible only because a number of people, over a long period of time, supported my work. Marsha Semmel of the National Endowment for the Humanities was an early believer in my idea and approach; her support became the foundation upon which I was able to plan the entire project. A generous grant from the National Endowment for the Humanities made the execution of these plans possible. This grant provided essential funding for all aspects of the project: research, catalogue, and exhibition. The Marion I. and Henry J. Knott Foundation of Baltimore, likewise, was a primary source of the funding for *Time Sanctified*. Further essential support came from Bruce Ferrini and Michael Greenberg Rare Books of Akron, Ohio.

The assistance of the staff of The Walters Art Gallery during the preparation for the catalogue and exhibition was an essential component for the project's success. Robert P. Bergman, Director, and Gary Vikan, Assistant Director for Curatorial Affairs/Curator of Medieval Art, provided continuing encouragement. Beth Dettelbach, Eric Zafran, and Ellen Reeder, museum colleagues, offered much moral support. Lilian M. C. Randall, Curator of Manuscripts and Rare Books at the Walters, was generous with her heart—as well as her mind. The first volume of Dr. Randall's catalogue, *Medieval and Renaissance Manuscripts in the Walters Art Gallery,* is in press, and I frequently consulted it and her volumes in preparation. Dr. Madeleine McDermott made a painstaking iconographic tabulation of the Books of Hours in the Bibliothèque Nationale in Paris based on Leroquais' catalogue; the conclusions I offer in Chapters IV through XII incorporate her statistical analysis of this large group of manuscripts. Dr. McDermott also assisted me on the Latin translations. Carla Brenner, Troy Moss, Muriel Toppan, and Helen Tigertt provided editorial assistance, and Walters photographer Susan Tobin, assisted by Sara Glik and Stephen Szymanski, was responsible for the museum's photographs.

This study would not have been possible without access to the manuscripts in other major American collections. The following curators and their staff members kindly gave me that access as well as much of their time and expertise: John Plummer, William M. Voelkle, and Gregory Clark of the Pierpont Morgan Library; William Matheson and Kathleen T. Mang of the Library of Congress; Rodney G. Dennis, Eleanor M. Garvey, and Nancy Finlay of the Houghton Library of Harvard University; Thomas Kren, Ranee Katzenstein, William Diebold, and Peggy J. Roberts of the J. Paul Getty Museum; Ann Percy and Francesca Consagra of the Philadelphia Museum of Art; Stephen Parks of the Beinecke Rare Book and Manuscript Library of Yale University; and Marie E. Korey of the Philadelphia Free Library. My history of the Book of Hours would have been incomplete without my consulting the manuscripts of these institutions and including seventeen of them in this study and exhibition.

There are many people outside museums whose involvement with *Time Sanctified* was also essential to its success. Contributing authors Lawrence R. Poos, Virginia Reinburg, and John Plummer were the most perfect of collaborators. James H. Marrow, Barbara Shailor, and Judith Oliver kindly gave me access to their research in progress or in press. James Marrow was especially generous in sharing his expertise on the Dutch *Horae* included here. Knud Ottosen shared a copy of his research on the Office of the Dead with the Walters, a study I frequently consulted. Kathleen Sweeney performed the word processing of the catalogue entries with uncanny accuracy. The faith of George Braziller in this volume and the enthusiasm of his editor, Beatrice Rehl, were a continuous source of encouragement.

Finally, I dedicate this volume to its *sine qua non,* Jean-François Vilain.

R. S. W.

Acknowledgements

(TO THE SECOND EDITION)

Gary Vikan was my boss at the Walters when I first wrote *Time Sanctified;* for his support then as well as now, as the museum's director, I salute him. Friend and colleague William Noel, Walters's Curator of Manuscripts and Rare Books, spearheaded this second edition. George Braziller recognized the opportunity to bring the book up to date and allowed for the revisions; my editor, Mary Taveras, kindly held my hand. Gregory Clark convinced me of some important changes of attribution.

Over the past years certain invitations to mount exhibitions or conduct research have granted me exposure to even more Books of Hours. These opportunities have afforded me growth and I am grateful to William Voelkle for the idea to present the exhibition, "Medieval Bestseller: The Book of Hours," at the Morgan Library in 1997; and to Charles E. Pierce, Jr., for allowing me to curate the show, also at the Morgan Library, "Jean Poyet: Artist to the Court of Renaissance France," in 2001. James Tanis kindly invited my participation for the Philadelphia Museum of Art's exhibition,"Leaves of Gold: Treasures of Manuscript Illumination from Philadelphia Collections," also in 2001. And, finally, three collectors have generously granted me frequent access to their private collections: Jeanne Blackburn, Bernard Breslauer, and Scott Schwartz.

I dedicate this edition to Lilian Randall, to honor her work and her friendship.

R. S. W.

The Miniatures of Walters 288 by the Master of the Munich *Golden Legend*

France, Paris, ca. 1425-30 (Cat. No. 34)

The complete cycle of miniatures from one of the most important and beautiful Books of Hours in The Walters Art Museum (MS W.288) is reproduced in its entirety in the following twelve color plates. The manuscript was created during a period—the first third of the fifteenth century—and in a place—Paris—when manuscript illumination reached one of its effervescent climaxes. The miniatures are the work of one of the leading illuminators of the early fifteenth century, a painter christened the Master of the Munich *Golden Legend* (a name based on a manuscript of this text that he painted and that is now housed at the Bavarian State Library in Munich). Their fine quality, their deep and pure colors, their attention to detail, and their nearly perfect state of preservation make these miniatures remarkable. But they are even more so because of the rich array of events and scenes that the pictures unfold for us. Twelve monumental miniatures illustrate the standard prayers of a Book of Hours: the Hours of the Virgin, the Penitential Psalms, the Hours of the Cross, the Hours of the Holy Spirit, and the Office of the Dead. These miniatures are accompanied by no fewer than forty-two medallions in the borders. This total of fifty-four different pictures, all between the covers of one book, constitutes a veritable medieval encyclopaedia of all the important events in the life of Christ and the Virgin Mary. The cycle is also linked to the Old Testament by the inclusion of episodes from the career of King David, and it poignantly makes its final point by reminding us, in the last miniature of a medieval funeral, of the ultimate test we all must one day face.

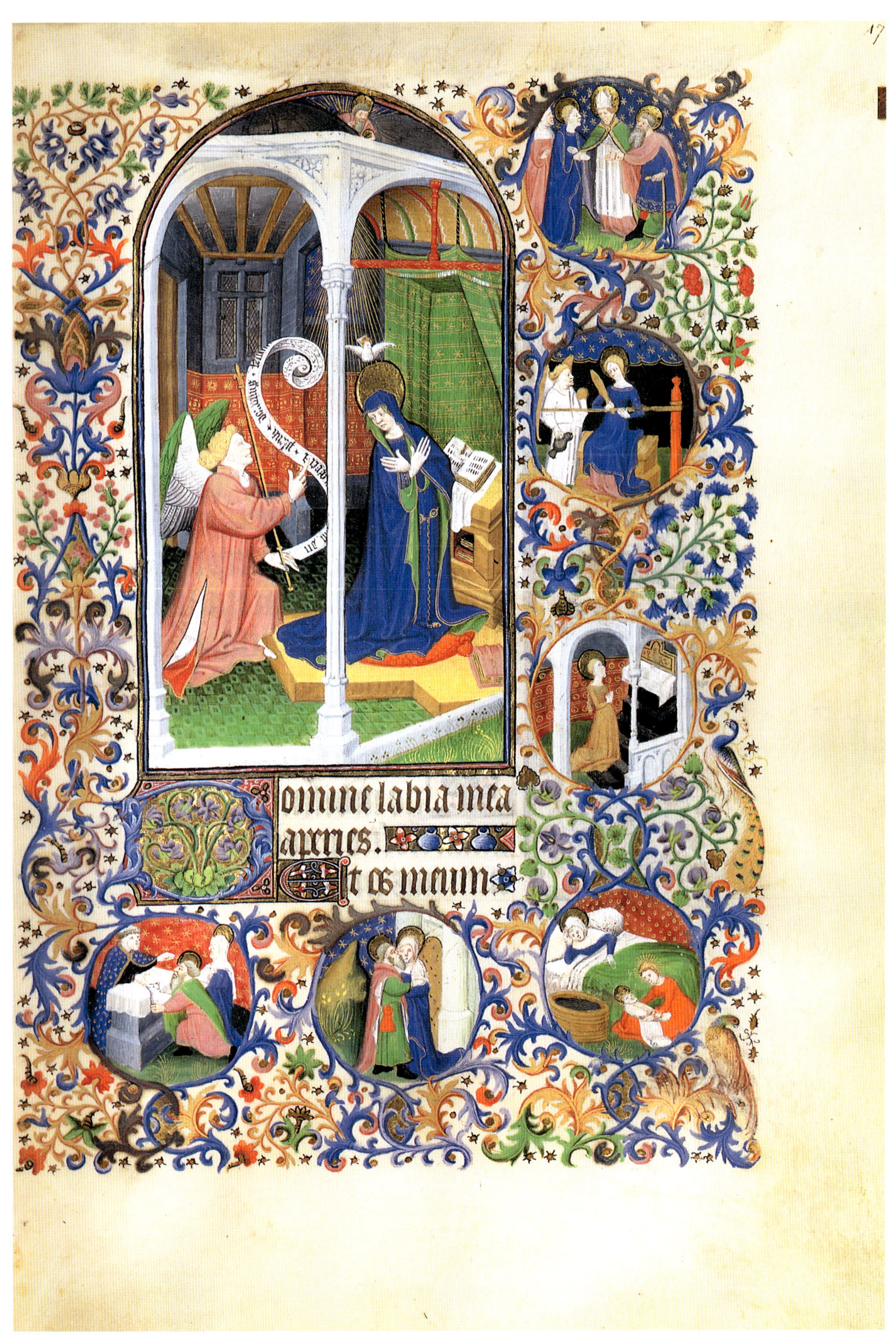

Pl. 1. *Annunciation*, border: *Sacrifice of Joachim and Anne; Meeting at the Golden Gate; Birth of the Virgin; Virgin Praying in the Temple; Virgin Weaving; Marriage of the Virgin* (Hours of the Virgin: Matins; fol. 17).

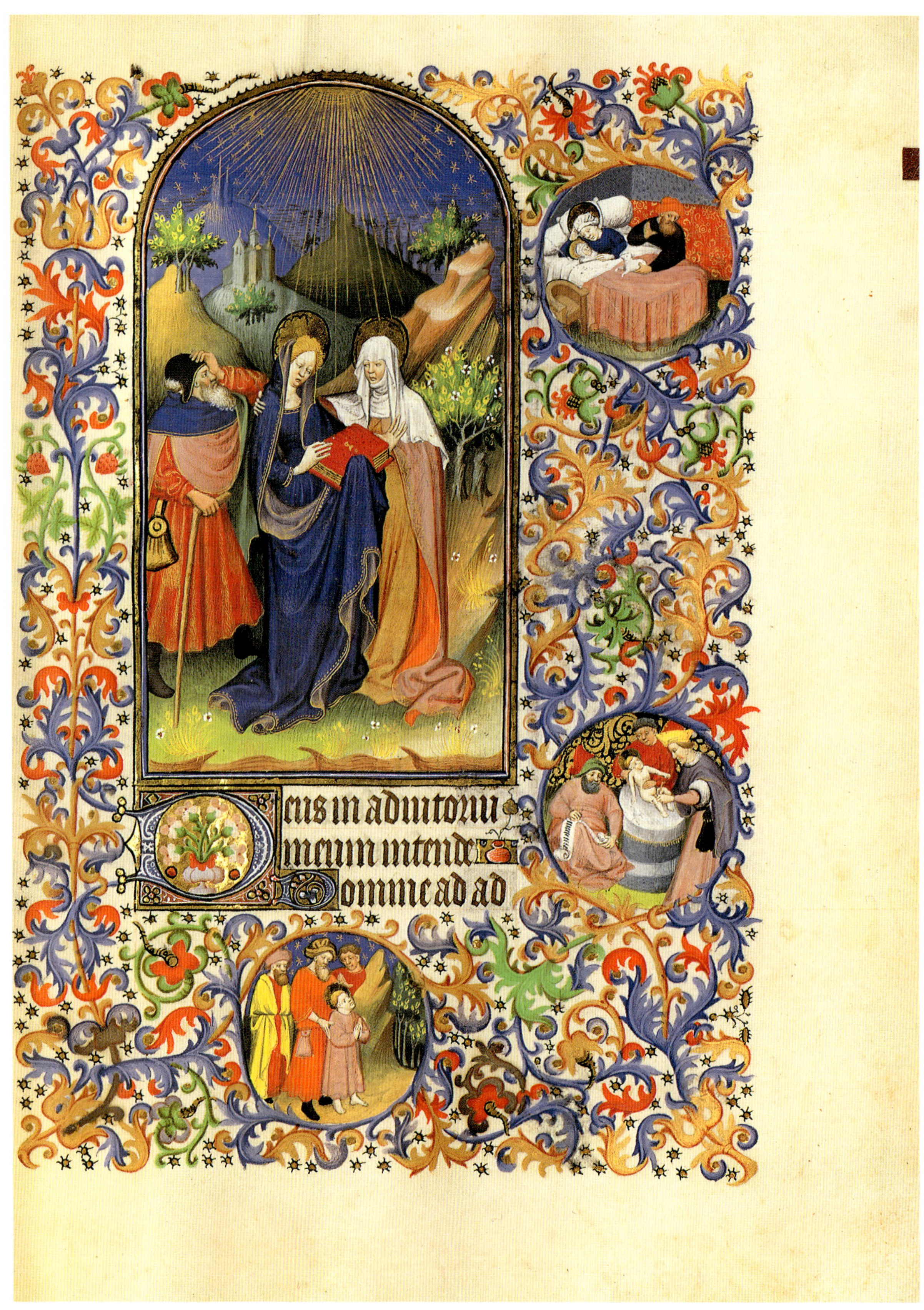

Pl. 2. *Visitation*, border: *Birth of John the Baptist; Circumcision and Naming of John the Baptist; John the Baptist Entering the Wilderness* (Hours of the Virgin: Lauds; fol. 41).

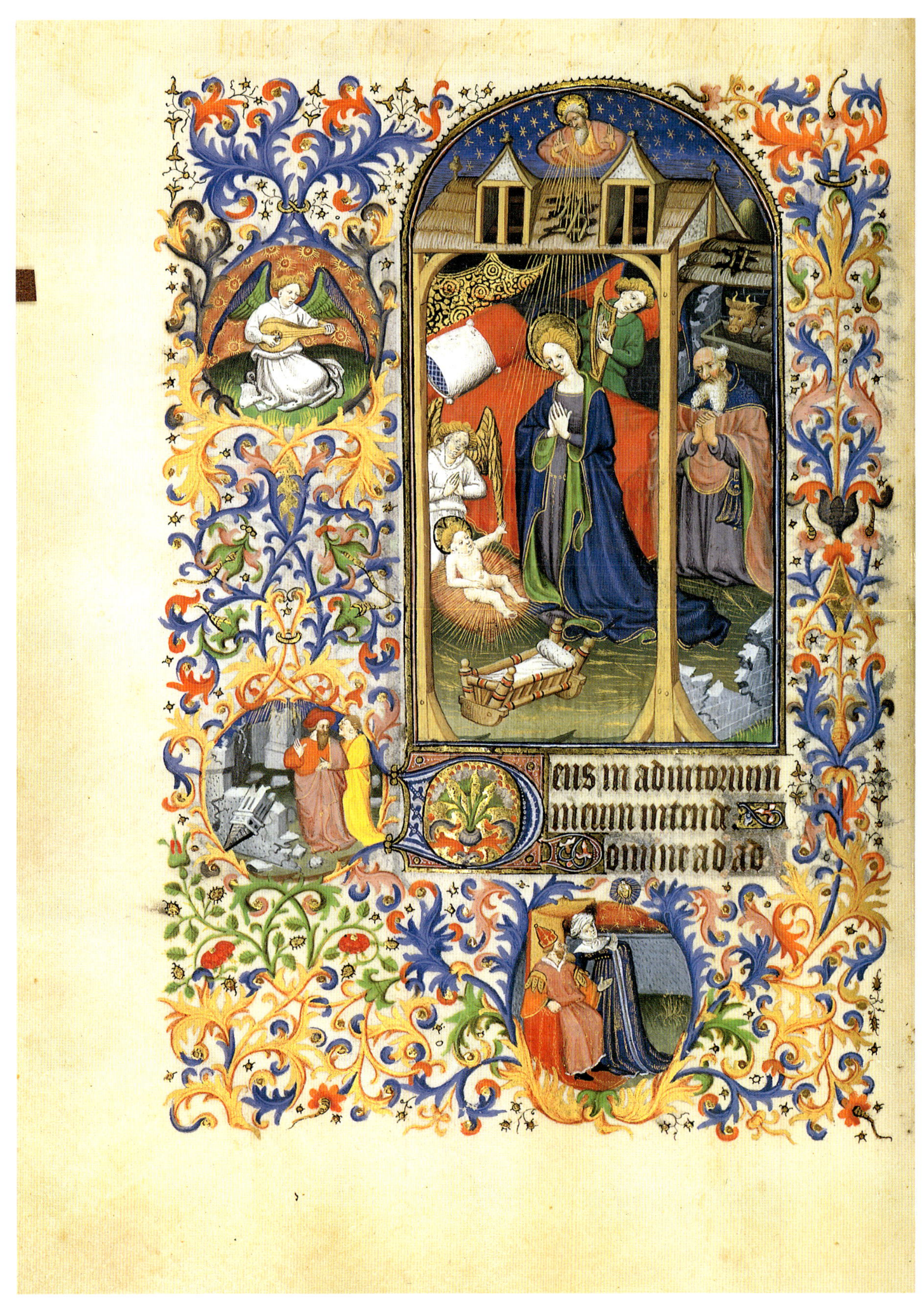

Pl. 3. *Nativity*, border: *Angel Playing Lute; Fall of the Temple of Peace; Augustus and the Tiburtine Sibyl* (Hours of the Virgin: Prime; fol. 52v).

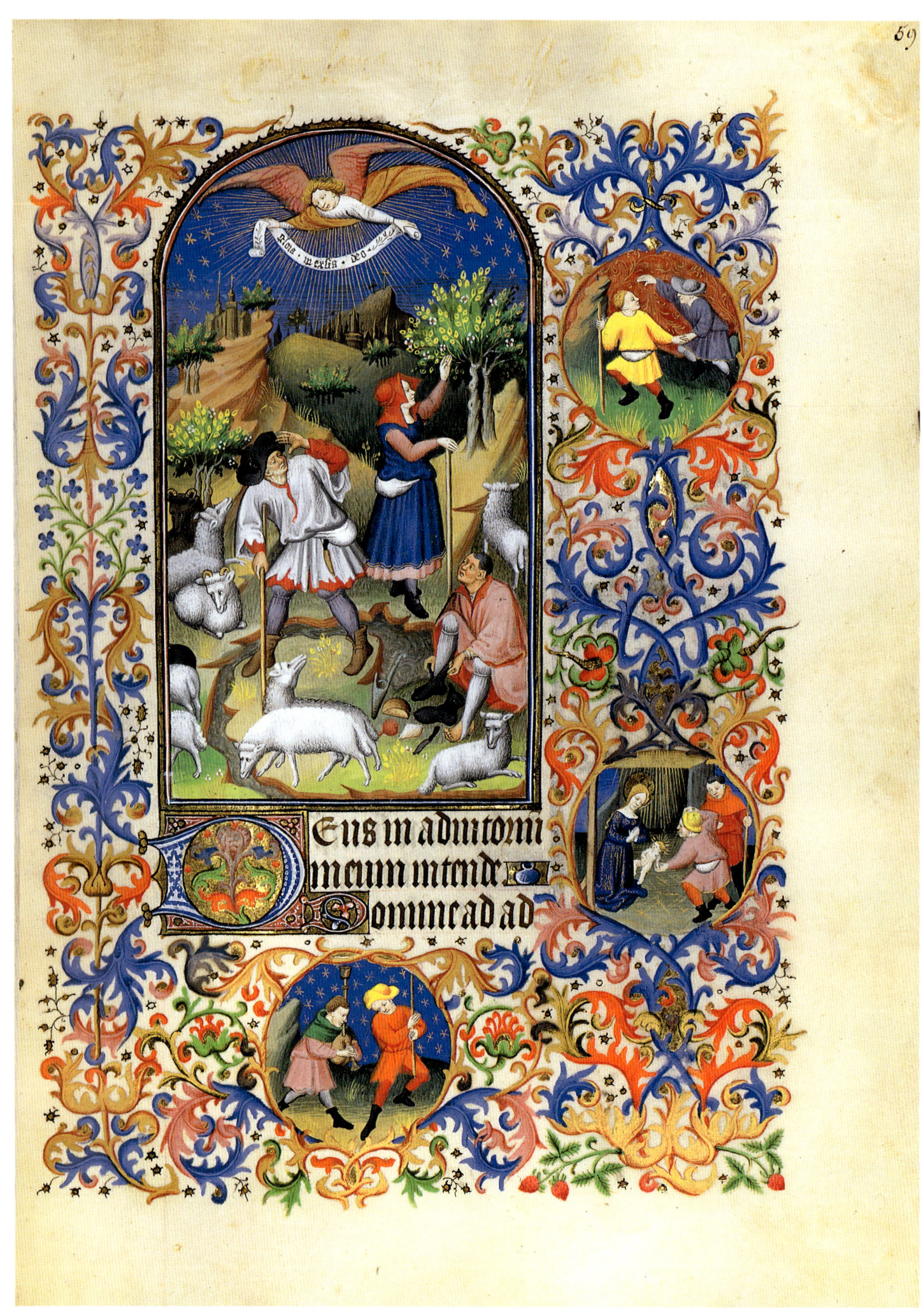

Pl. 4. *Annunciation to the Shepherds,* border: *Shepherds Dancing; Adoration of the Shepherds; Shepherds Journey to Bethlehem* (Hours of the Virgin: Terce; fol. 59).

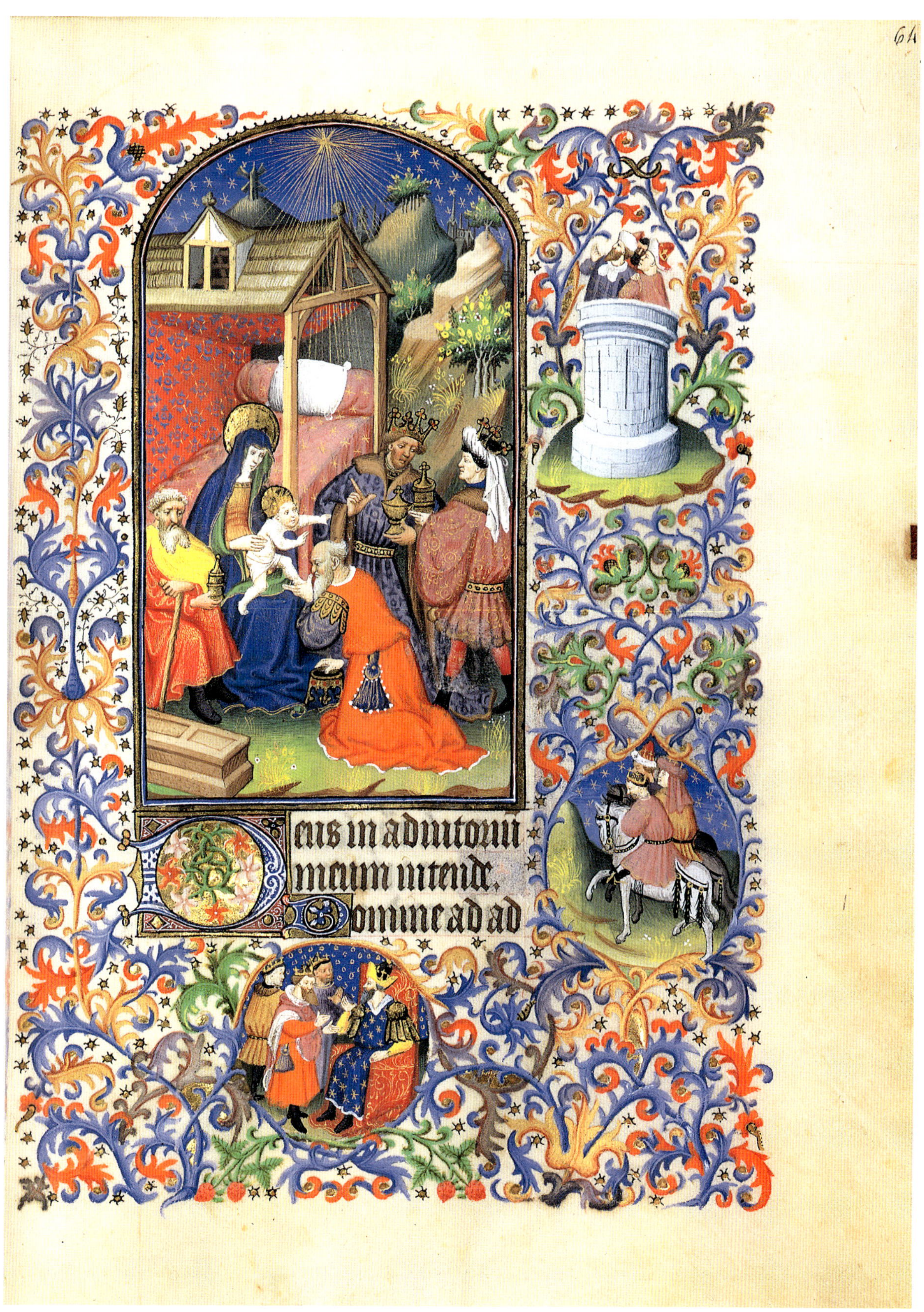

Pl. 5. *Adoration of the Magi*, border: *Magi in Observation Tower; Magi Journey to Bethlehem; Magi before Herod* (Hours of the Virgin: Sext; fol. 64).

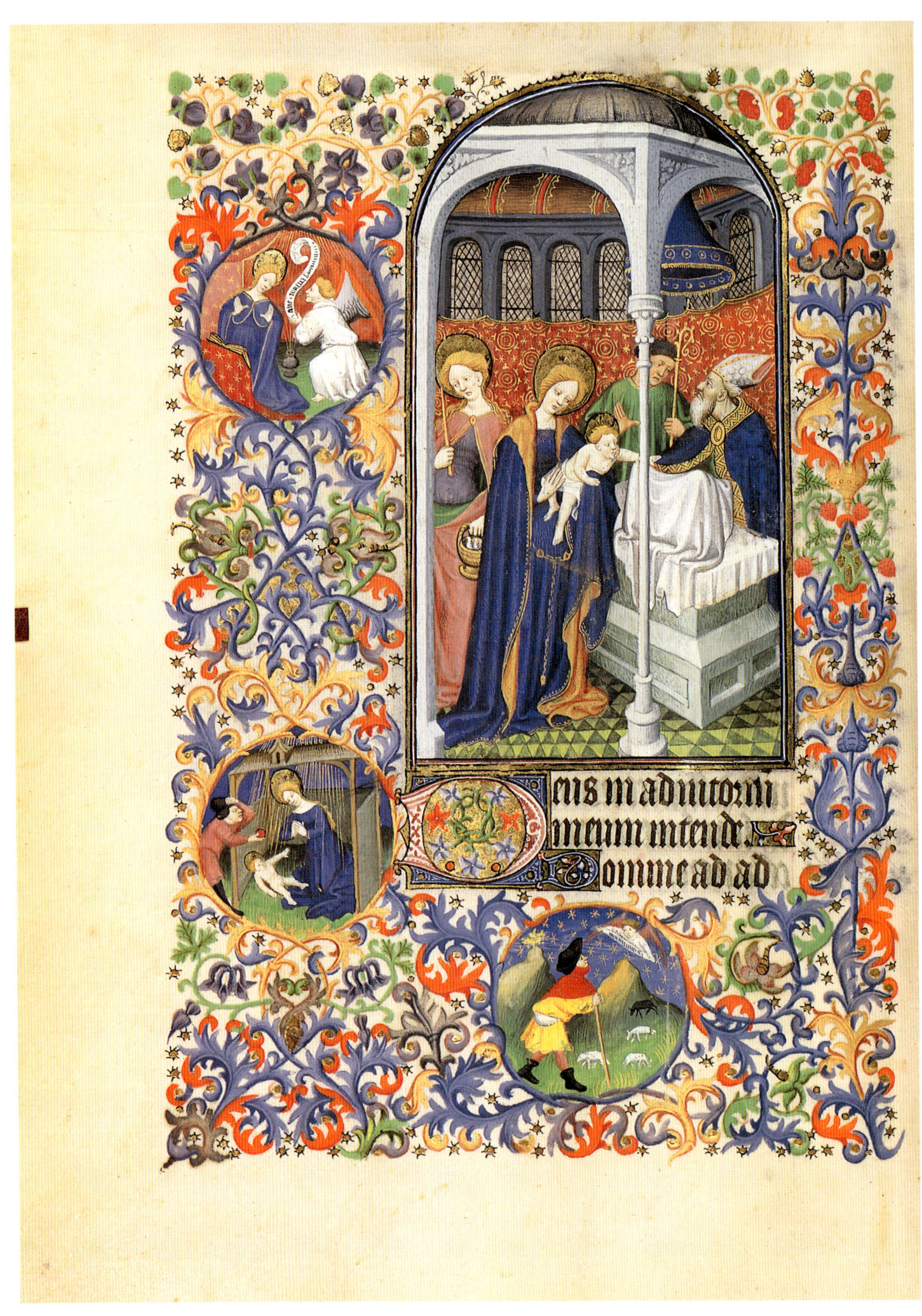

Pl. 6. *Presentation in the Temple,* border: *Annunciation; Nativity; Annunciation to a Shepherd* (Hours of the Virgin: None; fol. 68v).

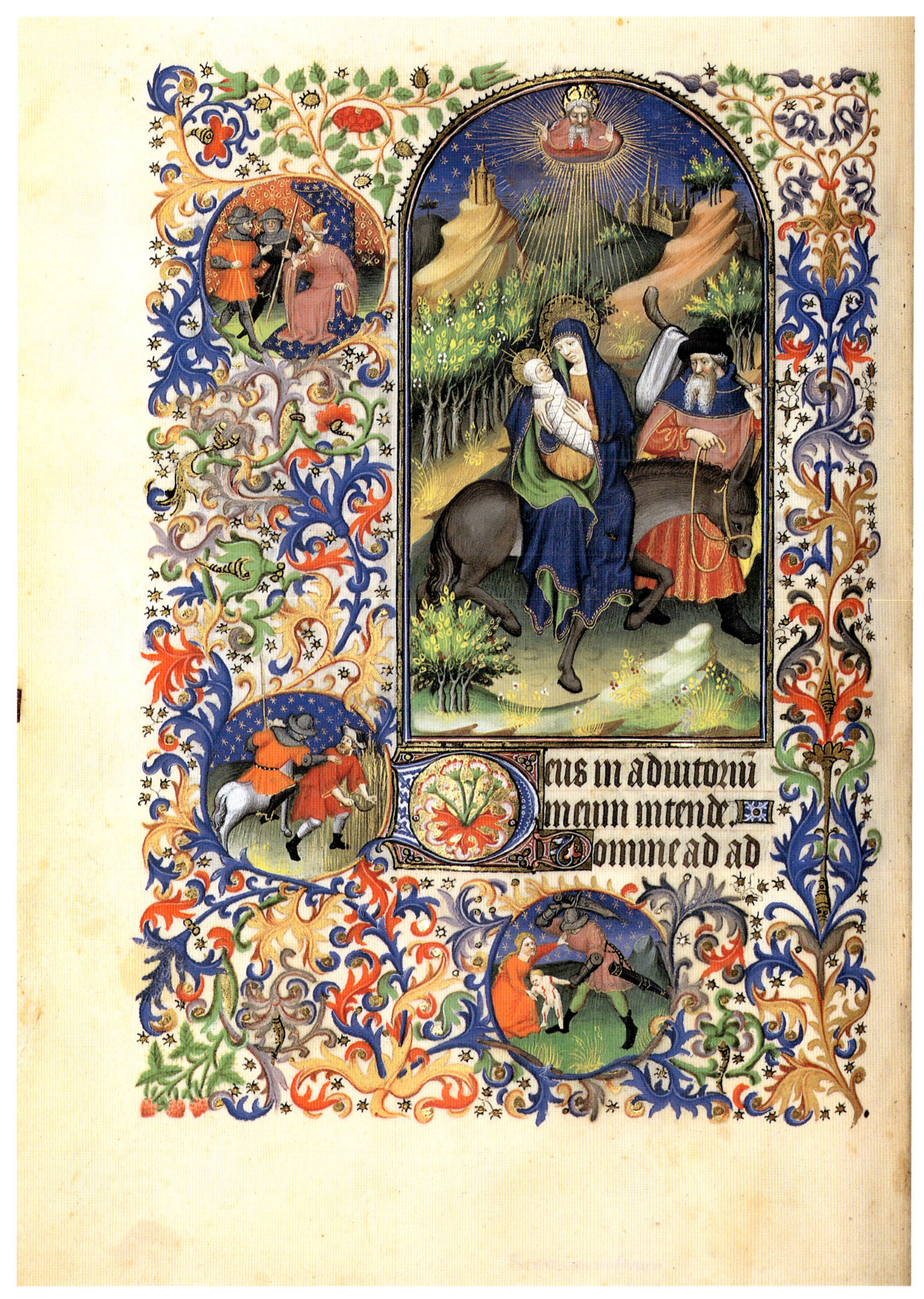

Pl. 7. *Flight into Egypt*, border: *Herod Commanding Soldiers; Soldier Questioning Farmer; Massacre of the Innocents* (Hours of the Virgin: Vespers; fol. 73v).

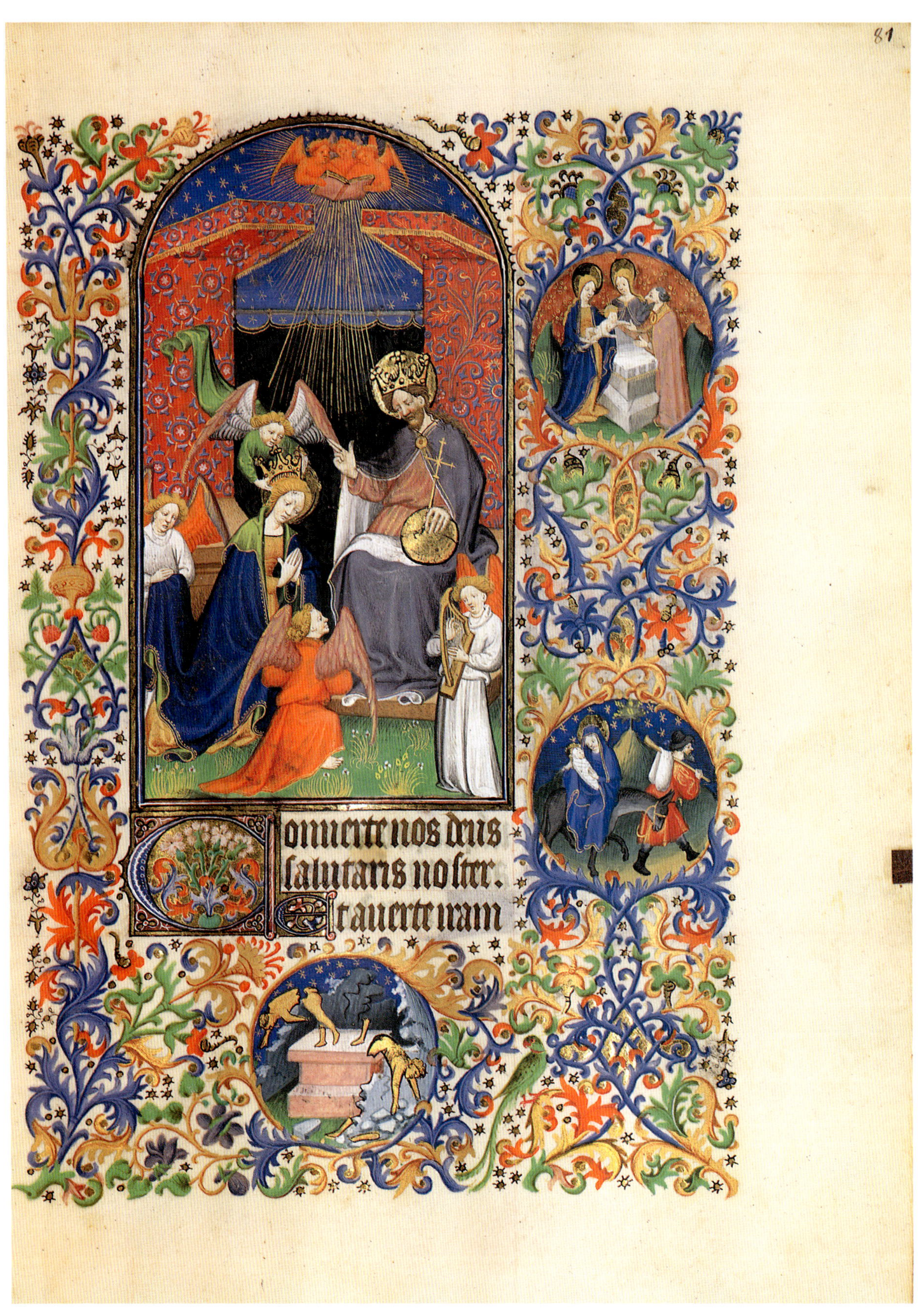

Pl. 8. *Coronation of the Virgin,* border: *Presentation in the Temple; Flight into Egypt; Fall of the Idols* (Hours of the Virgin: Compline; fol. 81).

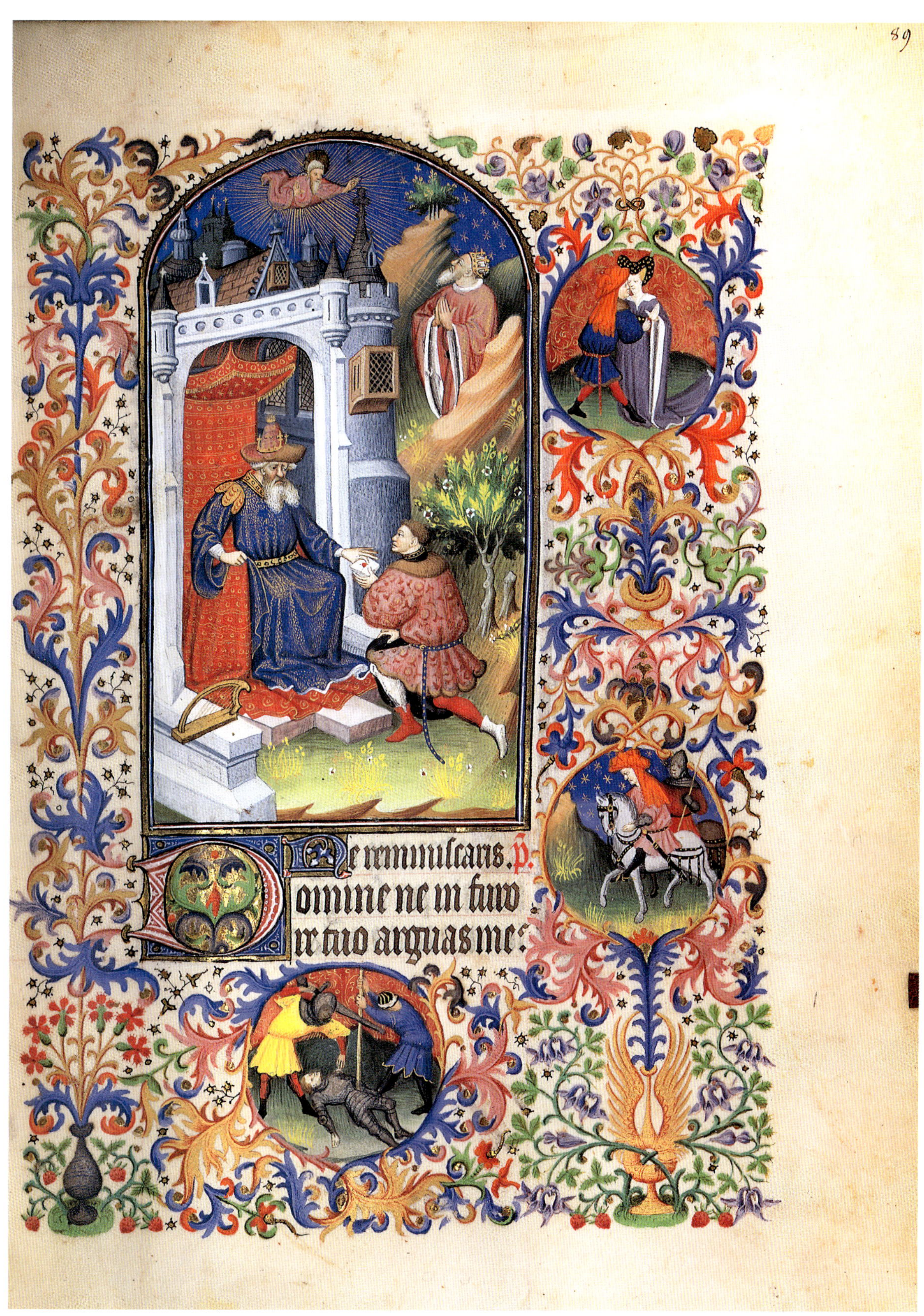

Pl. 9. *David and Uriah,* border: *Uriah Kisses Bathsheba Goodbye; Uriah Riding to Battle; Uriah Slain* (Penitential Psalms; fol. 89).

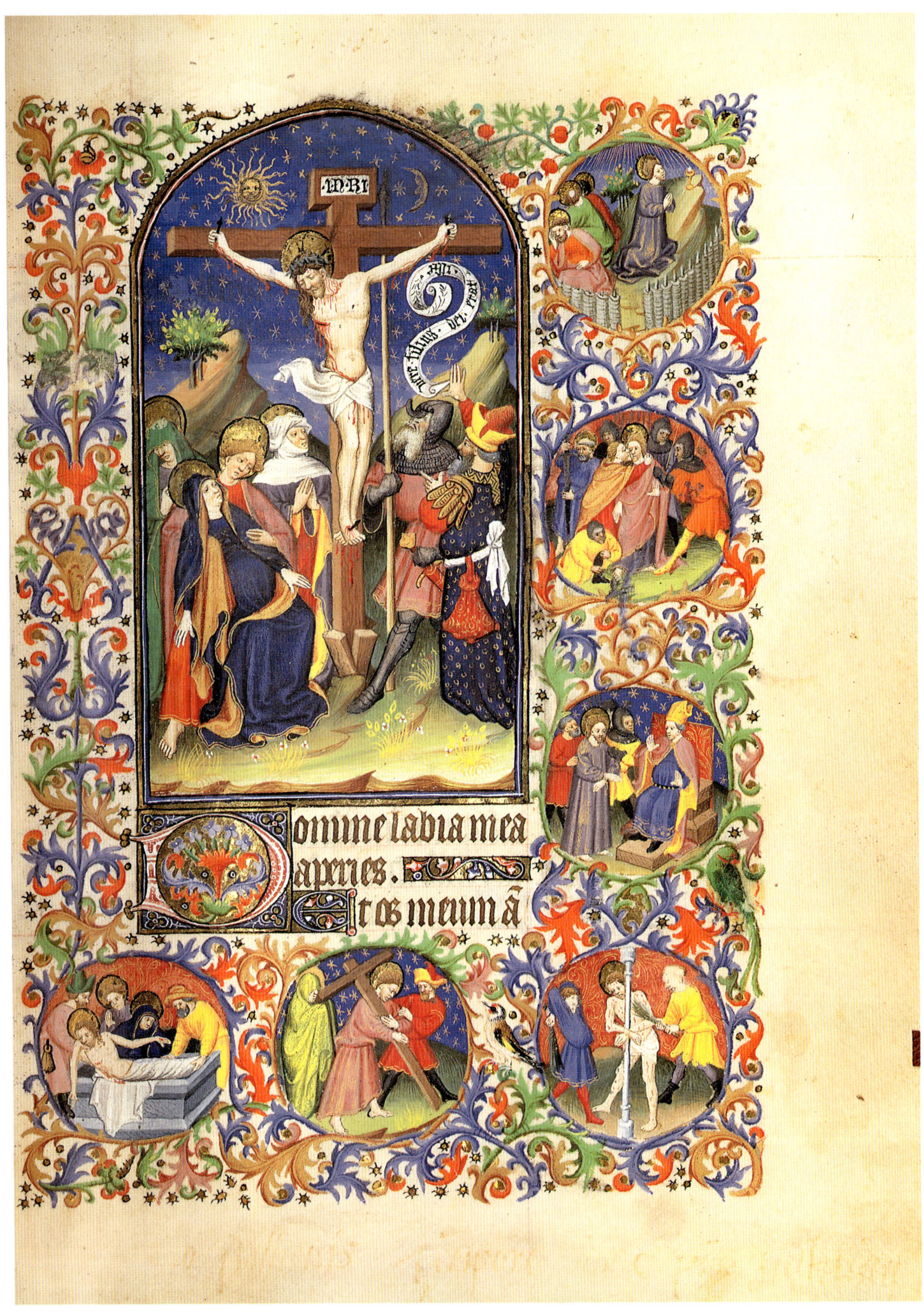

Pl. 10. *Crucifixion*, border: *Agony in the Garden; Betrayal; Christ before Caiaphas; Flagellation; Christ Carrying the Cross; Entombment* (Hours of the Cross; fol. 108).

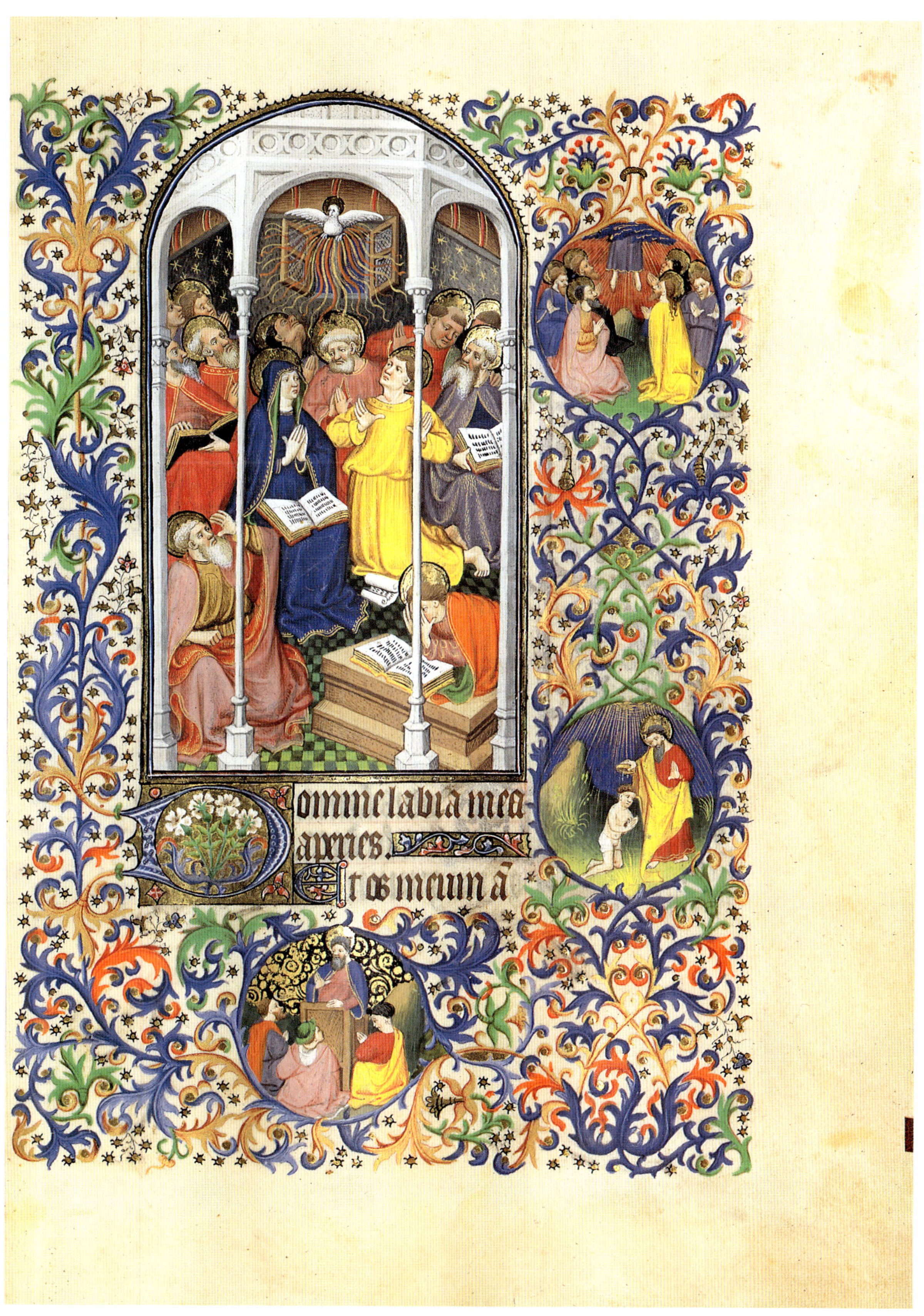

Pl. 11. *Pentecost,* border: *Ascension; Apostle Baptizing; Apostle Preaching* (Hours of the Holy Spirit; fol. 117).

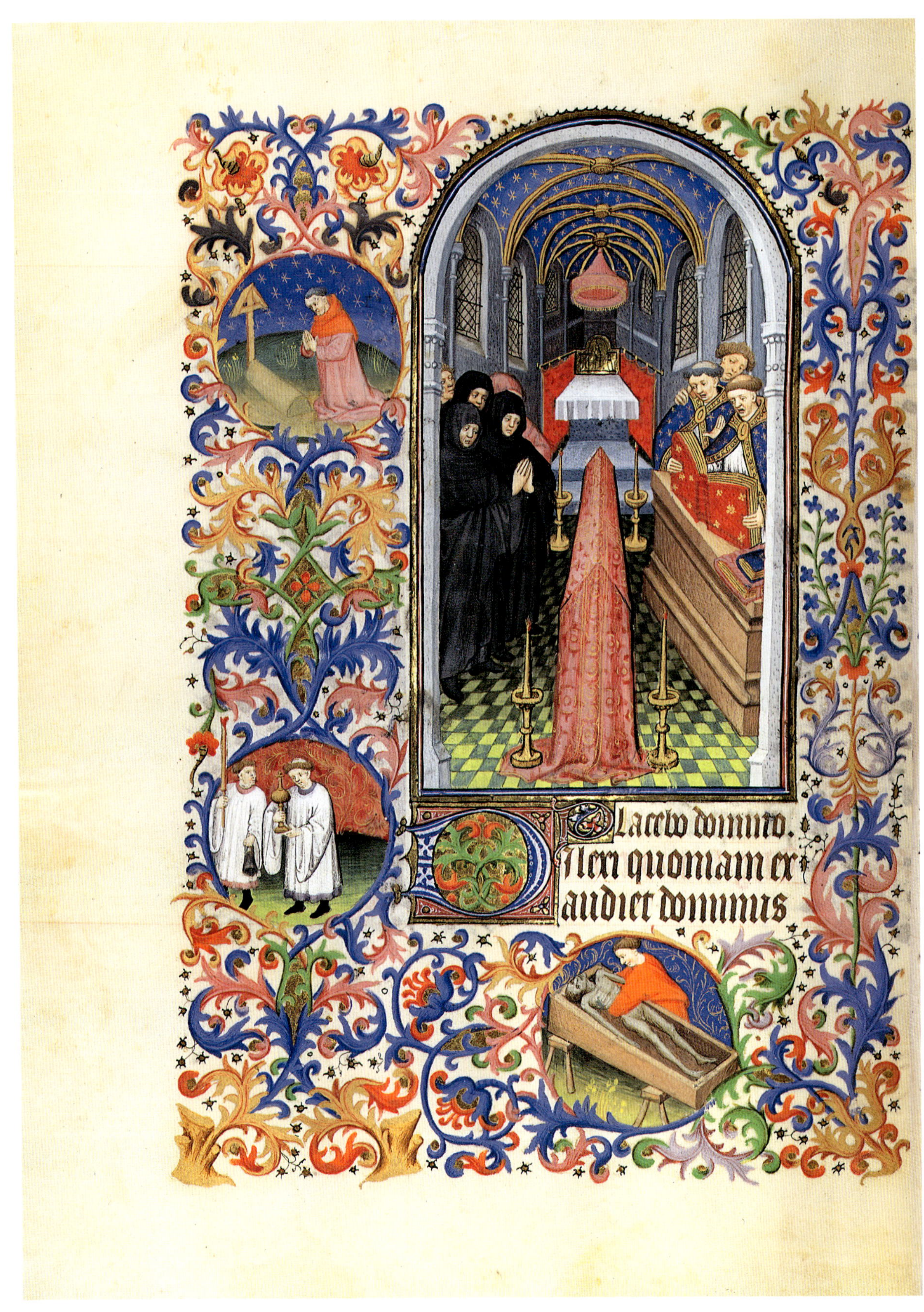

Pl. 12. *Funeral Service,* border: *Man Placing Corpse in Coffin; Funeral Procession; Man Praying at Grave Site* (Office of the Dead; fol. 124v).

TIME SANCTIFIED

CHAPTER I

Introduction

"And what is the use of a book without pictures or conversations?" mused Alice on the first page of *Alice's Adventures in Wonderland.* The men and women of the late Middle Ages would have agreed with Alice that such books were boring. Like her, they were attracted to books that both delighted the eye and stimulated the mind. From the late thirteenth to the early sixteenth century, the Book of Hours was *the* medieval best-seller, number one for nearly 250 years. More Books of Hours, in manuscript and, at the end of the Middle Ages, in printed editions, were produced during this period than any other single type of book, including the Bible. Why was this so? Because it was on the pages of Books of Hours that the best artists created some of the most beautiful pictures of the period, and because the words that were also on these pages offered their medieval reader an intimate conversation with one of the most important people in his or her life: the Virgin Mary.

A Book of Hours is a prayer book. It is a prayer book, however, intended to be used not by priests, or monks, or nuns, but by ordinary people, the lay men and women of the Middle Ages. God's ordained were required by the Church to recite daily the Divine Office, a complicated series of prayers that changed every day. Priests, monks, and nuns fulfilled this obligation by singing from large choir books, antiphonaries, or reciting their prayers from books called breviaries. One factor behind the emergence of the Book of Hours as a popular book for the laity was their desire, in an era of increasing secularization, to imitate the clergy. The laity coveted both the clergy's prayers and their books. Lay men and women also envied their intimate, and direct, relationship with God. They sought a series of prayers like the clergy's, but less complex, and a type of book like the breviary, but easier to use and more pleasing to the eye. The Book of Hours, by which secular time was sanctified for lay men and women of the Middle Ages, was that book.

There is a second factor that helps explain the emergence and subsequent popularity of the Book of Hours: the cult of the Virgin. Emblematic of this devotion to Mary, the Mother of God, in whose honor so many Gothic cathedrals were built during the 250 years under discussion, were the Hours of the Virgin. The Hours of the Virgin, an ancillary devotion that had been added a century or two earlier to the breviary, were extracted from this book and became the focus, the main altar as it were, around which was constructed an elaborate Gothic cathedral of prayers and pictures. Instead of portal sculpture, a high altar, stained glass windows, and a cemetery, the Book of Hours had a Calendar, the Hours of the Virgin, Suffrages, and an Office of the Dead. A Book of Hours is a "Notre Dame" that can be held in the hands. Like a cathedral it was expensive to produce, but was a source of pride and pleasure, as well as a means of obtaining salvation. Like a cathedral that formed an important part of a community's culture and heritage, a Book of Hours was a treasure handed down from parent to child, a part of family history.

The contents of a Book of Hours vary from volume to volume, but typically a *Horae* (the Latin plural of "hour," originally referring to the Hours of the Virgin but used now to signify the entire book) consists of eight parts: 1) a Calendar; 2) the four Gospel Lessons; 3) the Hours of the Virgin; 4) the Hours of the Cross and Hours of the Holy Spirit; 5) two prayers to the

Virgin known as the "Obsecro te" and the "O intemerata"; 6) the Penitential Psalms and Litany; 7) the Office of the Dead; and 8) numerous Suffrages. Each of these prayers and texts has a rich pictorial tradition. The beginning of each section of text presented the artist with the opportunity for a picture, or a whole cycle of pictures, provided the patron's pocketbook could match the painter's imagination. These illustrations acted as bookmarks, offered a feast for the eye, and aided meditation. Pictures were an intrinsic component of the Book of Hours. They were, in fact, one of the reasons behind the popularity of these manuscripts, and rare indeed is the unillustrated *Horae*.

The core of any Book of Hours, and the text after which it receives its name, is the series of prayers called the Hours of the Virgin (or, the Little Office of the Blessed Virgin Mary). This series of prayers is made up of eight Hours: Matins, Lauds, Prime, Terce, Sext, None, Vespers, and Compline. Each Hour is composed of psalms, hymns, canticles (liturgical songs derived from the Bible), lessons (readings from the Bible, found in Matins only), prayers ("orationes"), and "little chapters" ("capitula"), with a generous sprinkling of ejaculatory phrases—antiphons, versicles, and responses. Ideally, these eight Hours were to be recited at seven different times throughout the course of each day:

Matins and Lauds:	daybreak
Prime:	6:00 a.m.
Terce:	9:00 a.m.
Sext:	noon
None:	3:00 p.m.
Vespers:	sunset
Compline:	evening

These times more or less follow the canonical hours, the traditional times of the day when, according to the rule (or "canon") of the Church, the clergy were to pray. Lay people of the Middle Ages did not live in an ideal world, however, and evidence suggests that people used their *Horae* mostly at home in the morning or in church at Mass.

Before they became popular with the laity, the Hours of the Virgin formed an important part of the clergy's liturgical prayer. Traces of a special votive Office to the Virgin can be found as far back as the eighth or ninth century. By the tenth century it appears that the Hours of the Virgin formed an ancillary devotion to those required prayers that were already read as part of the Divine Office and that they were recited throughout much of northern Europe.

Actual manuscripts containing the Hours of the Virgin can be found as early as the eleventh century. During the course of the twelfth and thirteenth centuries, the Hours of the Virgin became attached for a time to the psalter, the prayer book commonly used by the laity during those two hundred years, and formed a type of book called the Psalter-Hours. By the late thirteenth century, however, Psalter-Hours began to lose the lengthy and cumbersome psalter. With the psalter dropped, the Hours of the Virgin, embellished by a Calendar, the Penitential Psalms, a Litany, and the Office of the Dead (all liturgical elements extracted from the breviary), became the central and most important feature of the type of manuscript we call the Book of Hours. This book would remain the preferred prayer book for the laity for nearly 250 years and, as mentioned above, would be the most popular book of its time.

France was the leader for the entire two and a half centuries of the Book of Hours' history, a dominance reflected in the fact that almost two thirds of the *Horae* included here are French and the manuscripts span, in date, the third quarter of the thirteenth century to 1524. The consistent vitality and sheer beauty of French illumination during these two and a half centuries are nothing less than astounding. At the end of the thirteenth century, illuminators in Paris and northern France, heirs to the spare but refined Court Style of St. Louis, applied themselves to the decoration of Books of Hours, then just coming into fashion (Cat. Nos. 1–5; Figs. 3, 37, 40, 48, 56). Jean Pucelle, the dominant artistic personality of the first half of the fourteenth century, is represented here by the Savoy Hours (Cat. No. 11; Fig. 1). Pucelle's style delicately grafts an Italianate sense of three-dimensionality onto an inherently cool, High Gothic elegance. In the second half of the century, the Savoy Hours received miniatures by the most important illuminator of the court of King Charles V of France, the Master of the Bible of Jean de Sy (Fig. 2). The hand of the second most influential artist of Charles' reign, the Master of the *Livre du Sacre de Charles V*, can be seen in the exquisite Edith G. Rosenwald Hours (Cat. No. 13; Fig. 43). Both artists painted in a style still infused with Gothic elegance, but now more naturalistic and earthier than their predecessors'.

The early fifteenth century in France witnessed an enormous explosion of artistic output, a great deal of it centering on those artists patronized by Jean, duc de Berry, and other members of the French and Burgundian courts. Many of the most important artists, working in what is called the International Style, are included here: the Luçon Master (Cat. Nos. 19–21; Pl. 24, Fig. 83) and the Master of Berry's *Cleres Femmes* (Cat. Nos. 21–23; Pls. 16, 32, Fig. 111), the two "jewellers" of the International Style whose paintings are extremely

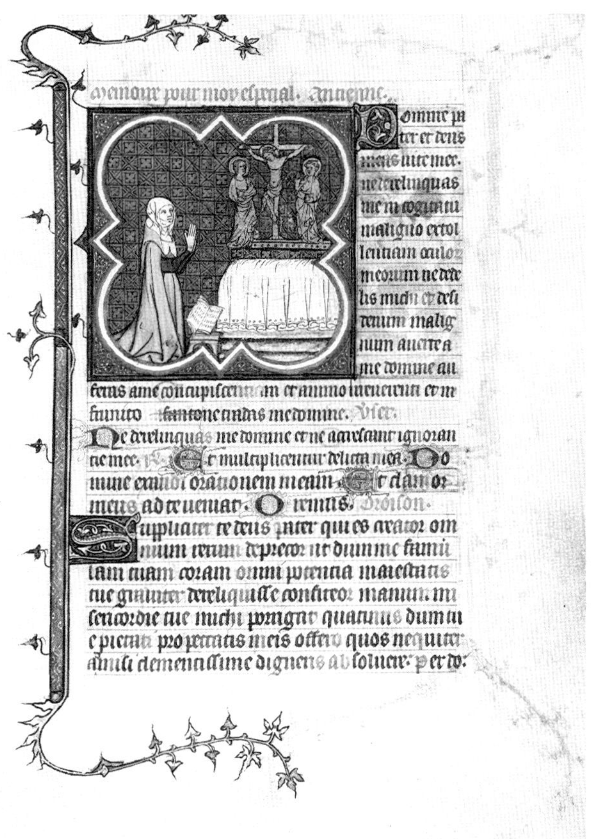

Fig. 1. *Blanche of Burgundy Praying for Herself before an Altar* (Suffrage), France, 2nd quarter of the 14th century, by the workshop of Jean Pucelle (Yale, Beinecke 390, fol. 25; Cat. No. 11).

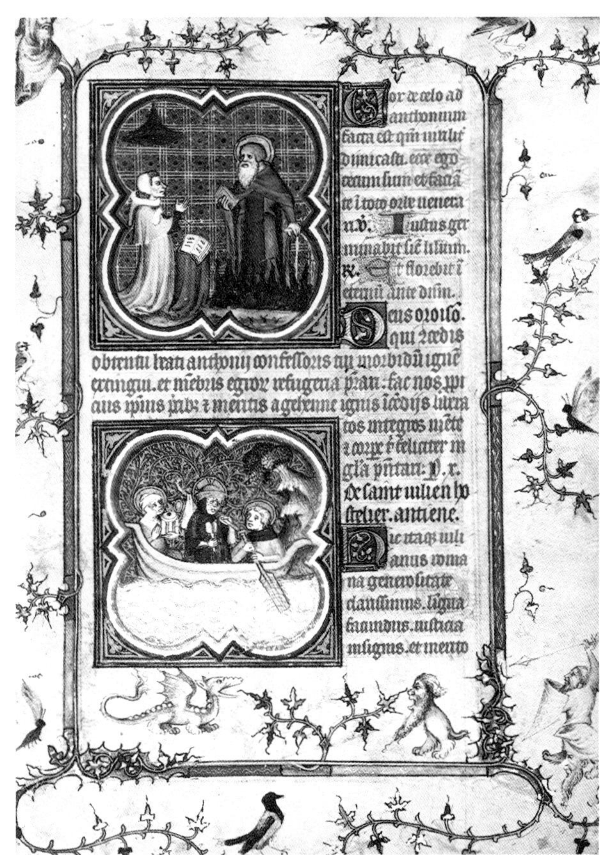

Fig. 2. *Anthony with Kneeling King Charles V of France; Julian the Hospitaller in a Boat* (Suffrages), France, ca. 1370, by the Master of the Bible of Jean de Sy (Yale, Beinecke 390, fol. 4; Cat. No. 11).

precious and gemlike; the Boucicaut Master (Cat. Nos. 24–28; Pl. 25, Figs. 54, 57, 73), who defined space for three generations of northern painters, and his most important follower, the Master of the Harvard Hannibal (Cat. Nos. 29–30; Pls. 18, 34, Figs. 29, 87, 88, 107); and, finally, the Rohan Master (Cat. No. 31; Fig. 116), whose interests in the emotional and the lugubrious contrast sharply with those of his contemporaries. Anyone who was anyone in the early fifteenth century owned not just one Book of Hours, but a few, and the demand made this genre of manuscripts one of the period's primary vehicles of artistic expression. The paintings of the second generation of fifteenth-century French illuminators, beginning about 1425–30, are executed in a less ethereal style and incorporate much more detail from the observable world. The chief exponents of this style are the Bedford Master (Cat. Nos. 33, 50; Pl. 31, Fig. 14), the Master of the Munich *Golden Legend* (Cat. No. 34; Pls. 1–12), and the Master of Walters 281 and his followers (Cat. Nos. 35–37; Pls. 17, 33, Figs. 34, 60, 118).

In the third quarter of the century, and continuing into the 1480s, a period of transition for France from the late Middle Ages to the early Renaissance, there emerges a group of disparate artists with markedly distinguishable artistic personalities. Nicknames, the various "Masters of the So-and-So," begin to recede and actual names begin to emerge. In the 1460s, the Coëtivy Master, probably the artist Henri de Vulcop (Cat. No. 42; Pl. 38, Figs. 13, 102, 106), still works in a late medieval manner, but his interest in representing readable space and volume separates him from the preceding generation. An interest in volume and pictorial depth also characterizes the style of Jean Colombe (Cat. Nos. 55–57; Pls. 30, 40, Fig. 32), although the output of his large workshop is at times facile or seems hurriedly done. This is similarly the case with the two other major artists of the period, the Maître François (Cat. Nos. 50–52; Figs. 59, 127) and the Master of the Geneva Latini (Cat. Nos. 58–61; Figs. 30, 52, 61, 117, 120, 128). The demand for Books of Hours was reaching its second peak of the century, and both the Maître

Francois, working in Paris, and the Latini Master, in Rouen, met this accelerated demand by establishing factory-like shops that turned out *Horae* in large numbers. Like the girl in the nursery rhyme, their work, when it was good, was very, very good, but when it was bad it was horrid.

The Renaissance proper in France, accompanied by renewed court patronage, witnessed a revival of truly first-rate illumination in the hands of Jean Bourdichon and Jean Poyet. The latter is especially well represented here in a group that includes the Cumberland Hours, a manuscript that is easily Poyet's masterpiece (Cat. Nos. 67–70; Pl. 20, Figs. 67, 96, 123). Mannerism also finds its way into French manuscript illumination, and one of the most glorious examples is the Hours of Jean de Mauléon, executed by artists of the so-called 1520s Hours Workshop (Cat. No. 77; Pl. 15, Figs. 8, 17). The painters of this group skillfully integrate influences from such different sources as Germany, Italy, and Antwerp, and, uniting them in a process whereby the resulting art still appears inherently French, produce a pyrotechnic finale of manuscript illumination in France.

The area that is now modern Belgium was the second largest producer of Books of Hours and this leadership, especially from about 1430 to the early sixteenth century, is reflected among the many Flemish *Horae* included here. The Master of Guillebert de Mets (Cat. Nos. 83–85; Pls. 35, 36, Fig. 108) is represented in three manuscripts, including the important Hours of Daniel Rym that, datable to the late 1420s, forms an anchor for the dating of this painter's work. Like the second-generation illuminators of fifteenth-century France, the Mets Master mixes the elegance and the penchant for gemlike colors he inherited from the International Style with a desire to represent aspects of the tangible world. His successor, the Master of the Ghent Privileges, who worked until about 1460, painted two Books of Hours included here (Cat. Nos. 85–86; Pl. 27, Fig. 93), one of which reveals the collaboration between him and the older Mets Master (or at least his workshop). The style of the Ghent Privileges Master leans toward the decorative: colors, especially blue, are very pure and figures quite doll-like. Contemporaneous with the Master of the Ghent Privileges is a large number of illuminators who, based in Bruges and all painting in a similar style, are gathered together into what is called the Gold Scrolls group (Cat. Nos. 87–90; Figs. 45, 64, 76, 77, 110). They produced great quantities of Books of Hours, both for local consumption and export. Some work by these illuminators can be quite routine, but certain members were highly gifted and achieved a striking sense of realism in their miniatures that rivals that produced by their colleagues who were painting panels. Like the Maître François in France, Willem Vrelant (Cat. Nos. 91–95, 109; Pls. 21, 29, 39, Figs. 10, 11, 46, 58, 82, 86, 92, 99), in the third quarter of the fifteenth century, headed a large workshop specializing in the mass production of Books of Hours. The other important and prolific Flemish illuminator of this period, Loyset Liédet, hardly ever painted Books of Hours, but one of the rare ones he did execute is included here (Cat. No. 96; Fig. 104). The work of another illuminator who rarely painted *Horae*, the Master of Edward IV (Cat. No. 102; Fig. 124) active in the 1480s, can also be seen in a manuscript from his shop. The rugged features and scraggly beards of his figures contrast with the attractive, if somewhat uniformly so, figures that populate the worlds of Vrelant and Liédet. A follower of Simon Marmion (Cat. No. 101; Figs. 75, 131), master of a shop painting both panels and illumination, is represented here by a Book of Hours of about the 1480s in which he employs his characteristic "dramatic close-up."

The most distinguishing feature of the so-called Ghent/Bruges school of illumination of the late fifteenth and early sixteenth centuries (Cat. Nos. 99–100, 103–105; Figs. 15, 24, 84, 100) is the *trompe-l'oeil* border. Fruit and flowers, on which insects, butterflies, or dragonflies have alighted, are painted as if they had been casually sprinkled across the pages of the open book. Finally, Simon Bening (Cat. No. 106; Fig. 19), the last great master of Flemish illumination, is represented by the splendid Calendar illustrations in the Da Costa Hours of about 1515.

The select group of four Dutch *Horae* included here demonstrates the high quality of Netherlandish illumination during the first half of the fifteenth century, while, at the same time, revealing an esthetic approach quite different from that of both France and Flanders. The paintings of the Masters of Zweder van Culemborg (Cat. Nos. 108–109; Figs. 50, 113) and the Master of Catherine of Cleves (Cat. No. 110; Fig. 69) might never be called pretty, but the works have a kind of power and straightforwardness found in no other illumination.

In England, iconoclastic attitudes and royal proclamations of the Reformation did not look kindly upon "papist" prayer books and, as a result, English Books of Hours survive in fewer numbers than their continental sisters. The four examples included are too few, but they do demonstrate two important aspects of English illumination: high quality charged with an independent spirit and idiosyncratic bent during the thirteenth and fourteenth centuries (Cat. Nos. 111–112; Pl. 13, Figs. 70, 95), and a waning, in the fifteenth century, coupled with a reliance on Flemish models and style (Cat. Nos. 113–114; Figs. 47, 122).

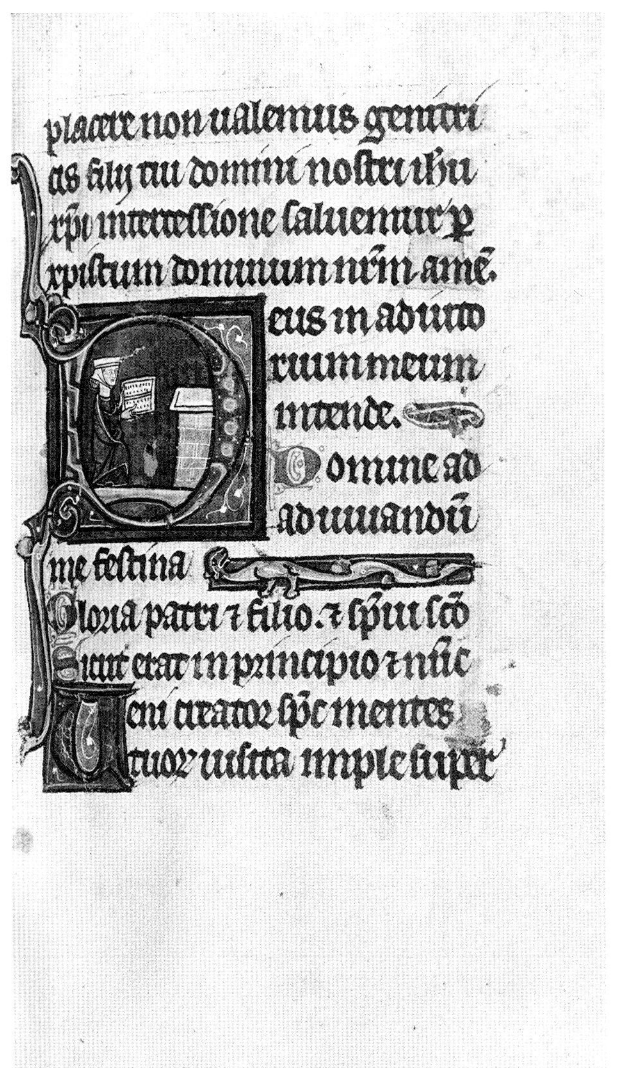

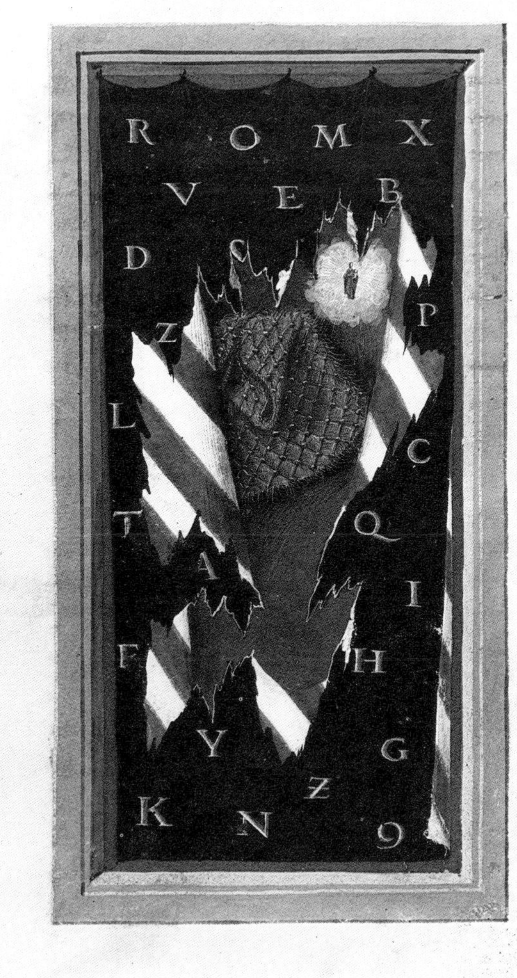

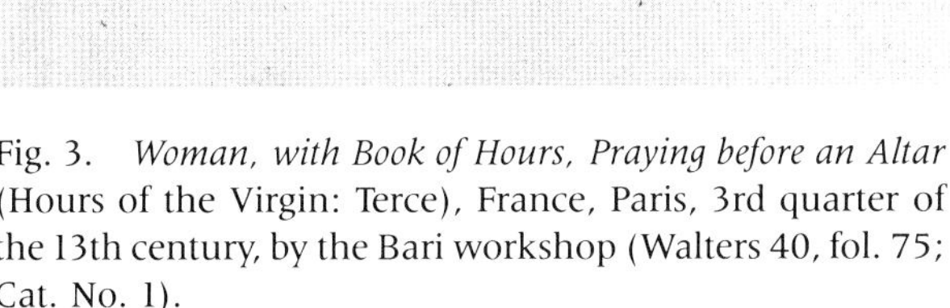

Fig. 3. *Woman, with Book of Hours, Praying before an Altar* (Hours of the Virgin: Terce), France, Paris, 3rd quarter of the 13th century, by the Bari workshop (Walters 40, fol. 75; Cat. No. 1).

Fig. 4. *Hair Shirt and Madonna Seen through Torn Curtain* (Hours of the Virgin: Matins), France, Tours or Bourges, ca. 1510–20 (Walters 446, fol. 15v; Cat. No. 75).

In Italy, Spain, and Germany, the Book of Hours was on foreign soil and the manuscripts reflect this. While the history of northern European illumination could be written based solely on pictures found in Books of Hours, this is not the case with Italy. Stunning examples, of course, exist (Cat. Nos. 115–117; Figs. 65, 101, 130), but as a genre, the Book of Hours did not interest patrons of the Italian Renaissance. Spain and Germany also produced relatively few Books of Hours (Cat. Nos. 118–119; Figs. 20, 103). They preferred to import Flemish *Horae*, or, failing that, produce books in imitation of this highly admired style.

The primary focus of this study is not on style, however, but on the iconography of the pictures in Books of Hours and their relationship to the texts they accompany. Other aspects of the manuscripts—provenance and patronage—can receive but little attention. Only original owners of the manuscripts, or a few early ones who altered the books or left their names or inscriptions in them, are cited in the catalogue entries. The omission of the complete provenance for each manuscript can obscure some important information concerning the evolution of the Book of Hours in general or the fate of one in particular. Consider the Savoy Hours, mentioned earlier (Cat. No. 11). This manuscript was commissioned by Blanche of Burgundy, granddaughter of St. Louis, in the second quarter of the fourteenth century from the workshop of Jean Pucelle, the most highly regarded painter in France at the time. It was an extremely luxurious production containing no fewer than 167 miniatures, many of which included a portrait of Blanche (Fig. 1). By about 1370 the manuscript was in the hands of King Charles V, who, at that time, added a number of prayers and an extra sixty-eight miniatures! Not to be outdone by Blanche, Charles hired the best artist of his generation, the Master of the Bible of Jean de Sy, and incorporated portraits of himself into most of the added miniatures (Fig. 2). The book, so rich in its illumination and so full of portraits, must have impressed one of the most voracious consumers of manuscripts at the time, Jean, duc de Berry. In the 1380s he commissioned the *Petites Heures,* a manuscript whose text and iconography are so similar to the Savoy Hours that the latter must have influenced the former. It seems likely that, in any case, the Savoy Hours helped show the duke what a glorious vehicle for both art and self-aggrandizement a Book of Hours could be. Jean de Berry must have continued to admire the book because in 1409 his nephew, the crazy King Charles VI, gave it to him. Hundreds of years later, the manuscript was the property of the National Library in Turin where it was destroyed by fire in 1904. Six years after the fire, twenty-six leaves from the Savoy Hours, which had been detached before the conflagration, were discovered in the library of Portsmouth Cathedral in England. In 1941 this library was dispersed and the leaves went to the Presbytery at Winchester from which they were stolen but later found, lying open, in some bushes. The leaves were bought in 1967 by the twentieth century's most famous bookseller, H. P. Kraus, who, two years later, sold them to Edwin Beinecke, who in turn gave them to Yale. *Habent sua fata libelli* ("Books have their own fate"). Each Book of Hours in this study has its own story, but space did not allow relating more than its early stages.

Patronage, related to provenance, is another aspect of the Book of Hours, discussed by others, that is given limited space in these pages. Each manuscript included here, of course, was commissioned or specially bought by someone and was thus the beloved possession of a patron. Each book has something to tell us, by itself, or as part of a group, about patronage. Compare, for example, Walters 40, a Parisian Book of Hours from the third quarter of the thirteenth century and the earliest manuscript included here (Fig. 3), with one of the latest, a Book of Hours commissioned by Jean Lallemant le Jeune in the second decade of the sixteenth century (Fig. 4). The anonymous female patron of Walters 40, kneeling humbly before an altar as she prays from her Book of Hours, is a different kind of patron from Jean, whose miniature concerns itself with his mysterious and purely personal devices and reduces the figure of the Madonna to the size of a fly—and this in the illustration for the Hours of the Virgin itself! The honest piety of the earlier, medieval patroness stands in stark contrast with Jean's proud painted boast; the early manuscript is God-centered, the later one man-centered. The dividing line between the Middle Ages and the Renaissance is sometimes difficult to locate, but it definitely separates these two patrons.

In the two essays that follow, Lawrence R. Poos and Virginia Reinburg conjure up the people who once held these books in their hands. Both authors explore avenues by which one can "read" the Book of Hours and learn about medieval patrons: their literacy, their funerary practices and attitudes toward death, their social climbing, their piety in general and practices of prayer in particular, their attitudes toward labor, and their family relations. The insights and observations offered here place the Book of Hours in its cultural context. In another approach to the Book of Hours, John Plummer, in the last chapter, describes a new method for localizing the manuscripts, that is, for determining where they were produced. Plummer includes evidence for localizing an important but previously elusive group of *Horae,* those illuminated by the Gold Scrolls group, to Bruges, and publishes here, as the result of his research, a prototypical Bruges Calendar.

It is Chapters IV through XII, however, that form the core of this study. In these discussions I focus on the pictures painted in Books of Hours, their iconography and changing traditions, and their relationship to the texts they accompany. The particular manuscripts illustrated and discussed have not been randomly selected, but are typical examples. Each picture represents a traditional iconographic type and stands for hundreds of similar miniatures that could have been chosen. My observations and conclusions, varying at times from those of previous authors, are based on a statistical analysis of almost a thousand Books of Hours: the nearly three hundred *Horae* in The Walters Art Museum, the over three hundred in the Bibliothèque Nationale in Paris, and a nearly equal group made up of the Books of Hours in the seven major American collections cited in the Acknowledgements. The relationship between the pictures and their texts is an important part of these discussions, so in the Appendix I offer the reader commentaries, references to published sources, textual outlines, or translations—the tools, in other words, I have found particularly useful in understanding not only what is painted in a Book of Hours but also what is written on its pages.

CHAPTER II

Social History and the Book of Hours

For historians in all fields, the fourteenth and fifteenth centuries are commonly regarded as a transitional period of great significance for Western European society. Many dichotomies of "before" and "after" can be drawn. In political history, the feudal monarchies of the high Middle Ages became absolutist states (or, in the case of England, the Tudor constitutional monarchy). Economic life witnessed a change from a peasant, agrarian system, through a severe demographic and economic collapse, to the beginnings of early-modern commercial agriculture and mercantile trade. European Christianity was shaken from its flourishing medieval vigor by challenges of schism and dissent, with important implications for the Reformation of the sixteenth century. In artistic and intellectual life, early Renaissance thought and style emanated northward from Italy, ultimately to transform the face of Western culture.

It would be remarkable to the social historian if such wide-ranging changes in European society did not reverberate in one of the most distinctive religious and artistic artifacts of that era: the Book of Hours. Indeed, if for no other reason than the sheer number of surviving examples, Books of Hours are an impressive relic of late medieval culture. No other type of medieval book survives in such quantity, even discounting the many Books of Hours that have disappeared or were cut to pieces for the sake of their individual illustrations. In fact, these books speak volumes to the social historian about the society in which they were created, both directly—in their depictions of people and activities—and more obliquely—in the clues that their contents, production and marketing, and patterns of ownership provide about the attitudes and mentality of the period.

One of the most immediately intriguing points raised by Books of Hours is their very existence. Medieval Europe was a largely illiterate society. Even by 1500, persons who could read were a small fraction of most nations (the more advanced of the early-Renaissance Italian towns were perhaps the only exceptions). However, by the fourteenth century, at least rudimentary literacy had become commonplace among two small but powerful sections of lay European society: the nobility, whose experience of legal and political affairs and participation in polite society necessitated familiarity with the written word, and the emerging urban middle classes, for whom trade and business demanded the same. For this audience, new types of books gained a widely increased circulation, including etiquette manuals, travel accounts, and both romantic and more earthy literature.

Books of Hours are prayer books intended for the lay reader and were acquired in huge numbers by these nobles and urban people. Thus they reflect this slowly expanding literacy, and this is true despite the fact that the bulk of the prayers, scriptural excerpts, and other texts in these books remained in ecclesiastical Latin rather than the vernacular languages that were the native tongues of the books' owners. For the first time since classical antiquity, the most common book being produced was intended to remain in non-clerical hands. Moreover, although modern eyes are understandably drawn to the most lavishly and beautifully illustrated of these books (which for that reason are the most likely to have escaped destruction in the intervening centuries), the most commonplace Books of Hours were virtually mass-produced from standard exemplars. It was this more mundane, less lavish, version that was manufactured and owned in the largest numbers. This meant that more than just the very wealthy could aspire to book ownership, though, of course, ownership remained financially impossible for the mass of ordinary peasants and urban workers.

Books of Hours reflect at the same time lay religious piety and the pride, or possibly conspicuous acquisitiveness, of ownership. It is not too cynical to point out that medieval piety incorporated a substantial element of public display. More than one satirical broadside aimed at the social pretensions of the urban middle class singled out the vogue for carrying about richly adorned Books of Hours. As especially valuable possessions, these books commonly figured in the wills and testators' inventories of wealthy persons. Nonetheless a sufficiently impressive body of anecdotal evidence survives to indicate that genuinely felt private prayer and devotion incorporating use of these books was widespread among their patrons.

Pride of ownership is visually reflected in many Books of Hours. Owners often had their coats-of-arms included in their books' illustrations. The portrait that Adolph of Cleves and La Marck had painted in his Book of Hours is awash not only with Adolph's coats-of-arms, but also with his mottos and monograms (Fig. 5). Isabelle de Coucy incorporated her arms, as well as her husband's, no fewer than ten times in her Book of Hours (Fig. 6). In fact, they are used as "illustrations" in place of the traditional scenes from the Infancy of Christ. This interest in heraldry is not chronologically coincidental. It was only in the fourteenth and fifteenth centuries, when Books of Hours reached the height of their popularity, that heraldry, the science of genealogical identification and a means of precise recognition for individual knights, came into its

Fig. 5. *Adolph of Cleves and La Marck Kneeling in Prayer* ("Obsecro te"), Belgium, ca. 1480 (Walters 439, fol. 13v; Cat. No. 98).

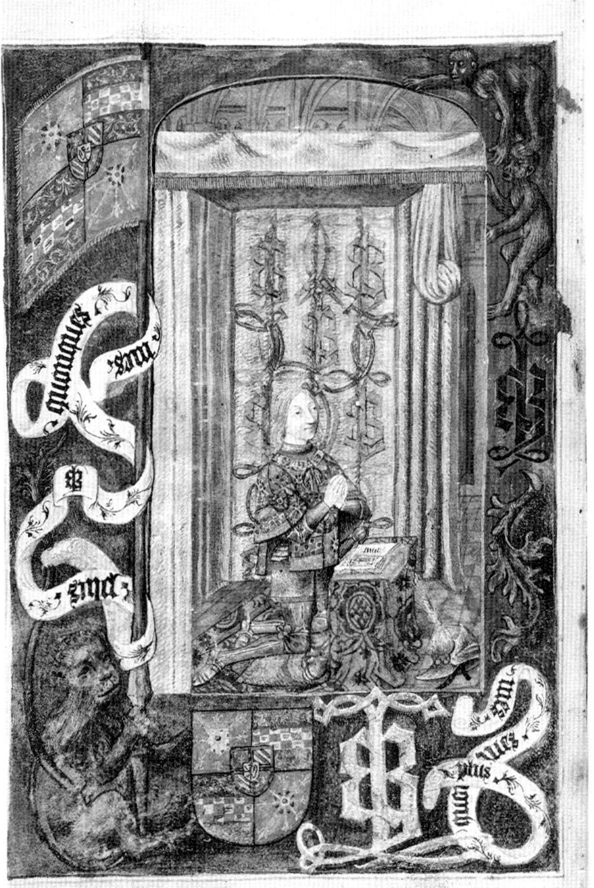

Fig. 6. *Madonna with Kneeling Isabelle de Coucy*, border: Coucy Arms (Prefatory miniature), France, Paris, ca. 1380, by the Master of the *Rational des divins offices* (Walters 89, fol. 3v; Cat. No. 14).

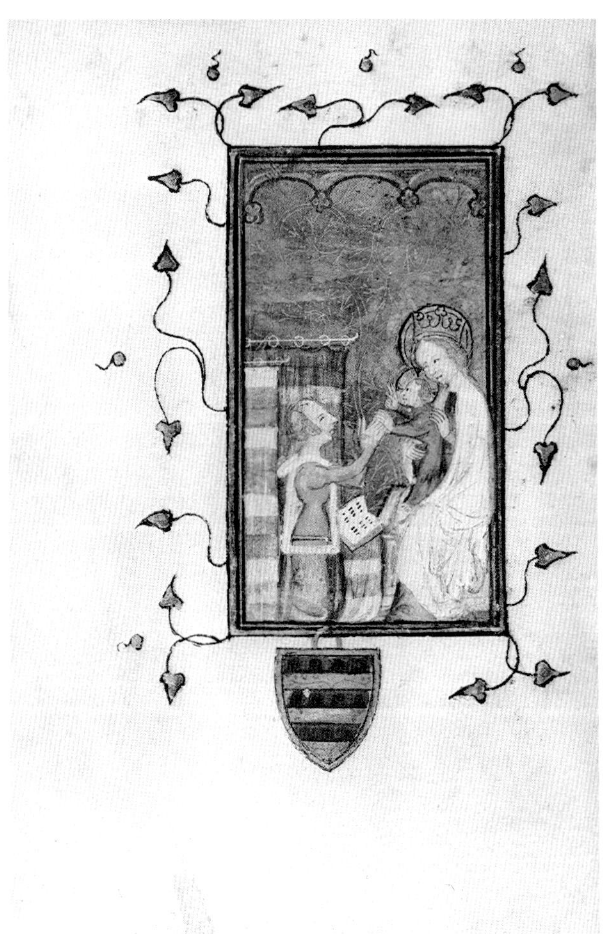

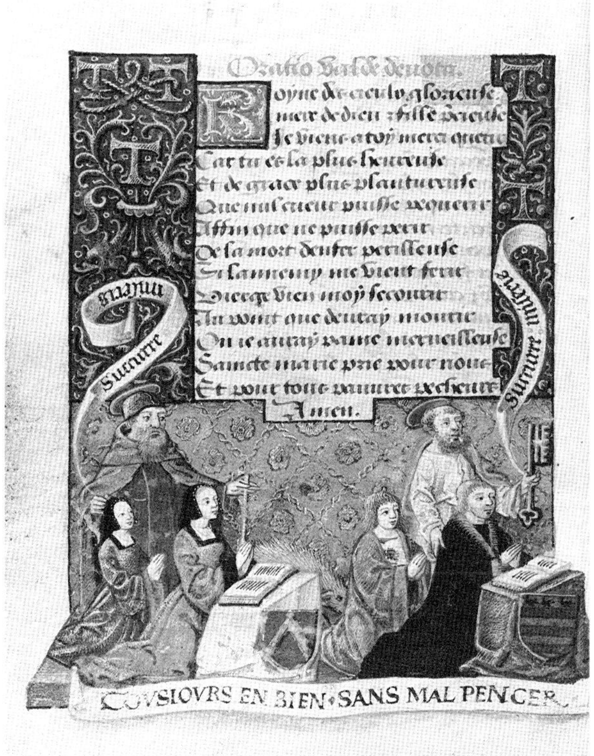

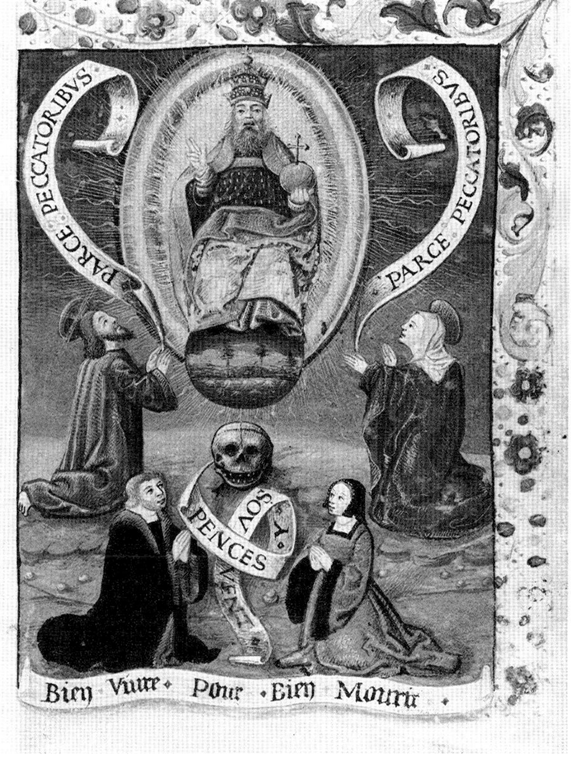

Fig. 7. a) *Tourotte Family Praying, with Sts. Anthony and Peter;* b) *God with Christ and the Virgin Interceding for the Tourottes* ("Domine Iesu Christe . . ."), France, early 16th century (Walters 222, fols. 1v-2; Cat. No. 45).

own in Western European noble society. In the later Middle Ages every kingdom had groups of heralds, experts knowledgeable in the arms and feats of great families, and armorial shields proliferated in the homes and on the possessions of powerful lords and ordinary knights. In these social circles, a coat-of-arms was nearly as distinctive a mark of one's individuality as a personal portrait.

Portraits of the owners of Books of Hours also appear among the illuminations, sometimes as family portraits. This too reflects a developing sense of individuality among wealthy Europeans, as does the more realistic, individualized portraiture that was increasingly appearing on tombs, that other stage for lasting aristocratic self-depiction. In the prayer books, patrons were usually depicted in poses of conventional piety —often kneeling before an open Book of Hours, as in the family portrait added by the Tourottes to a Book of Hours they came to possess in the early sixteenth century (Fig. 7).

Especially suggestive is the obvious prominence of women in these scenes (Figs. 6, 7; see also Pls. 13, 14, Figs. 9, 11, 12). For much of the Middle Ages the experiences, religious or otherwise, of women in European society are a subject of conjecture from sources largely silent as to female viewpoints. This changed somewhat in the late medieval period, as women's lives are made known from a widening range of narrative, legal, and other sources. It would appear that at least rudimentary literacy was not uncommon for women at the highest levels of society by the fifteenth century. Women are also known to have participated in many of the new religious movements and modes of spirituality evolving at the time. That they owned, and appeared in, Books of Hours in large numbers is thus another distinctive sign of the era in which they lived.

The illustrations contained in Books of Hours, particularly those dealing with other than strictly religious themes, also provide the most tangible evidence of late medieval life and the attitudes or mental world of their patrons and artists. Yet one must be cautious in drawing inferences about contemporary society from these depictions. Accurate or "journalistic" reporting in the modern sense was far from the primary objective of illustrators whose main concern was, rather, to augment the books' religious content in a manner pleasing to their customers. Despite the high artistic achievements of many painters (most notably in specially commissioned works that undoubtedly embodied much accurate observation), a large number of Books of Hours were illustrated with stock, almost stereotypic images. But ultimately these depictions of everyday life and ordinary people must reflect the artists' and patrons' perceptions of their world to some degree, whether these derive from acutely realistic observation or a more idealized view.

The most obvious examples of this reflection are found in illustrations accompanying the Calendars. The individual months of these Calendars were often decorated with scenes of the seasons' work, especially depictions of agricultural labor. This motif was by no means unique to the later Middle Ages, since examples from other types of manuscripts can be found from much earlier centuries. Since the overwhelming majority of European people were employed in, and the bulk of medieval wealth was produced by, agriculture, the rhythms of the farming year were much more deeply implanted into people's consciousness than the modern audience can perhaps appreciate. So these agricultural scenes are a natural reflection of medieval perceptions of the changing seasons.

The eyes for which these illustrations were intended were, however, not those of the people who actually participated in this work. More genteel pursuits, such as hawking or "May-ing" in springtime (Fig. 8a), that reflect aristocratic patrons' modes of life (or perhaps those to which slightly less exalted patrons aspired), did find their way into Calendars. By contrast, another arena of everyday working experience, one of growing importance to the economy of Europe in the later Middle Ages—the bustle, tumult, and industry of medieval city life with its craftsmen and artisans,

Fig. 8. a) *Making Music* (Calendar: May); b) *Shearing Sheep* (Calendar: June), France, Tours?, 1524, by the 1520s Hours Workshop (Walters 449, fols. 6v, 7v; Cat. No. 77).

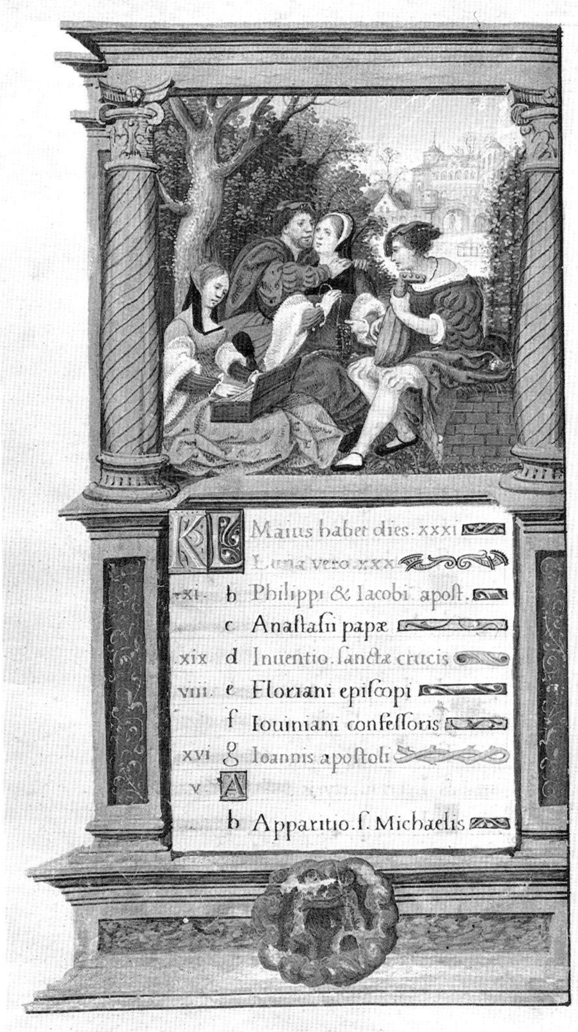

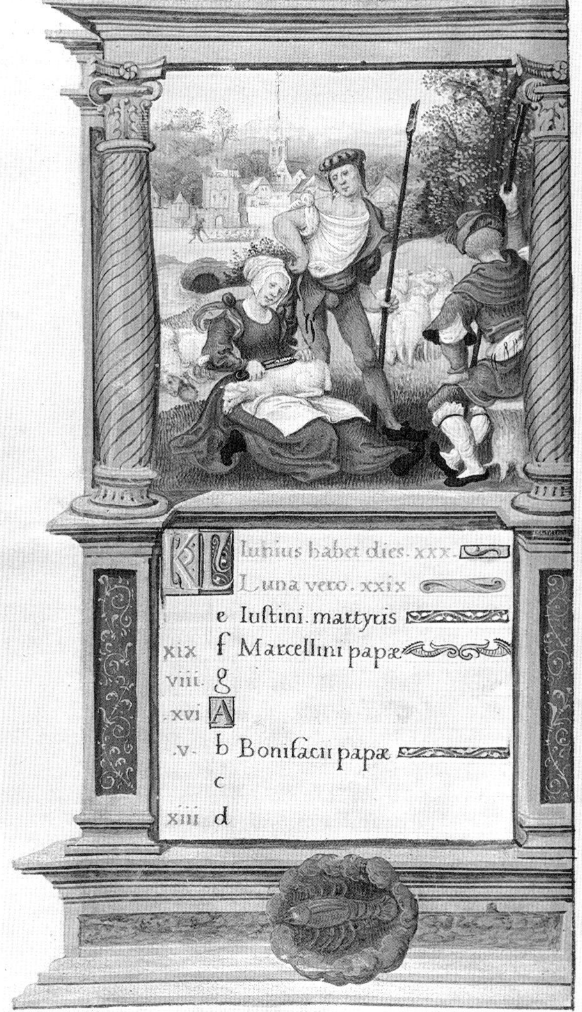

among whom were the scribes and artists who produced Books of Hours—is conspicuous by its near total absence from the books' illustrations. It is, in fact, difficult to find images of urban work and everyday town life depicted. No doubt this reflects the traditional nature of the rural motifs, but it is intriguing in view of the fact that urban mercantile wealth purchased many Books of Hours. As in other periods of European history, it was the lordly, aristocratic way of life to which the middle classes of the towns aspired, and which they preferred for illustration in their books.

Virtually by definition, medieval nobles were lords of manors and thus of peasants; the rent and other dues they collected from their manors and peasants formed the foundation of their wealth. Therefore, the ways in which rural people and their occupations were depicted are a potential clue to the perceptions of their social betters concerning what rural life was like, or ought to be. There is a consistent sense in these scenes of a placid, bucolic, unchanging world, into which there seldom penetrates any of the hard work and harsh poverty that was the reality of this life (Fig. 8b). Literary scholars have commented upon a similar tone in courtly or aristocratic poetry of the fifteenth century: a rise (or perhaps a revival, in different guise, from classical literature) of an idealized, idyllic, and unrealistic vision of the simple rustic life.

An historian with a psychoanalytic bent might be tempted to apply the concept of cognitive dissonance to this vision. At the time when Books of Hours were most popular, Western Europe had been convulsed by rapid change and occasional violent outbursts of protest by peasants, laborers, and artisans. The later fourteenth century in particular witnessed the first widespread revolts of the common people in medieval history. The English revolt of 1381 paralyzed a large area of the country for several weeks as rural and urban rebels burned the legal records of manorial lords, vandalized London and provincial towns, and killed two of the royal government's highest officials. The *Jacquerie* of 1358 was the bloodiest peasant revolt in medieval French history. Flanders and Florence were shaken by urban unrest at about the same time, and Spain had prolonged rural uprisings through much of the fifteenth century. In the long run these revolts would help bring serfdom, one of the main underpinnings of medieval feudalism, to an end. In the process, these outbursts also provoked mistrust and, occasionally, fear of the common people on the part of feudal lords and urban oligarchs. Considered against this social background, the peaceful vision of rural life in Books of Hours strikes the social historian as even more of an idealization.

Another aspect of European society equally linked to changing events of the later Middle Ages, and providing equally fertile ground for conjecture about the mental world of the period, concerns its attitudes toward death. By modern standards, medieval life was appallingly short and fragile, because of violence, but even more, because of disease. The late Middle Ages, furthermore, were devastated by a new and terrible mortality. In late 1347, ships brought to southern Italy from the Middle East the agent of this calamity: plague. The resulting epidemic, the Black Death, spread throughout Western Europe in the next three years and, by the best modern estimates, killed roughly one third of the European population in that short time. Equally disastrously, plague remained a recurring fact of the demographic experience in Western Europe for at least three centuries thereafter.

Against a background of an already fragile life, plague's novelty was its ability to strike suddenly, without warning, and to kill many very quickly. To make things worse, the later Middle Ages saw the introduction into Europe of several other diseases, including syphilis, new strains of influenza, and probably typhus. Life expectancy in early Renaissance Florence, outside the period of the Black Death itself, has been estimated as well under one half that of the United States in the 1980s. The European population continued to remain extremely low for the rest of the Middle Ages, and the economic consequences of this demographic stagnation were far-reaching.

The emotional or psychological impacts of this dangerous new environment were equally profound, if less readily grasped by modern sensibilities. Historians have long recognized a new concern with death and dying in late medieval religious and cultural attitudes. One result of this concern was a heightened sense of the carnal aspects of life and death. In Books of Hours this resulted in especially vivid illustrations accompanying the Office of the Dead, the section containing prayers for funerals and commemorations. These depictions offered particularly wide scope for originality on the part of illuminators, and modern eyes are especially drawn to this originality, even grisliness. Scenes include deathbed gatherings, funeral processions and burials, depictions of the naked soul before God or in judgement, and horrifying personifications of death itself (see the illustrations of Chapter XII).

There is more to this than mere obsessive morbidness. One aspect of this preoccupation was an intensified awareness of the suddenness and unexpectedness of death: one never knew when it might come, so one always had to be prepared. One particularly popular theme, both for illustrations in Books of Hours and in various literary forms, was the story, "The Three Living and The Three Dead." Three young men in the prime of life out riding one day suddenly encounter three hideous corpses; upon questioning, the dead reveal themselves to be the young men themselves, as they were soon bound to become (Fig. 128). Other portions of Books of Hours also reflect this foreboding imminence. Many of the popular prayers in these books appear to play a role that to modern perceptions lies in the gray area between religion and superstition. Special prayers invoked particular saints for aid in warding off the hazards common to medieval life: plague, of course, but also more mundane afflictions like toothaches and bedbugs. The very presence of the Office of the Dead in all Books of Hours implies that lay people read it regularly, as a protection against dying unprepared. The "Obsecro te," the universally popular prayer to the Virgin Mary, asks specifically that death not come suddenly or unexpectedly.

Another lesson drawn from this material is death's leveling effect. *Piers Plowman,* a late fourteenth-century English poem combining religious allegory with sympathetic social observation, expressed this attitude: "It is very hard to tell a knight from a serf when he comes to lie in the church vaults." The sentiment was pictorially expressed in some Books of Hours by juxtaposing the symbols of earthly power—bishops' miters, monarchs' crowns—with skulls or by making use of the theme of the Dance of Death whereby all levels of society are ultimately affected (see the border medallions in Fig. 128).

This is an appropriate metaphor upon which to conclude these comments on the social world lurking behind the Book of Hours. Western Europe at the end of the medieval era was far removed from modern democracy. But Books of Hours, it can be argued, reflect some significant developments in European society. As artifacts of a devotion based upon reading by the laity, they betoken a movement—as yet, admittedly, only glacial—towards a mode of religious experience that expressed itself, at least in part, in the personal, private actions and internalized mentality of believers. At the same time the production of these sacred books was an essentially secular process, carried out by nonclerical, largely anonymous, and mostly fairly humble scribes, illuminators, and artisans in the towns. The products of their labors offer a wealth of pictorial detail from the fourteenth, fifteenth, and early sixteenth centuries, a wealth that social historians have barely begun to tap. When read perceptively, the underlying attitudes, preconceptions, and fears of medieval Europeans implicit in their books are as revealing as the pictures.

CHAPTER III

Prayer and the Book of Hours

Books of Hours are splendid objects of art. For men and women of the fourteenth, fifteenth, and early sixteenth centuries, however, they were also prayer books, and prayer was as central to medieval life as art was. Books of Hours tell us much about the art and material culture of the world that produced them, but for twentieth-century viewers they are also windows onto the interior, spiritual lives of ordinary lay people of the late Middle Ages.

The many pages of Latin text inside a Book of Hours contain prayers: Offices or Hours (special versions for lay people of the clergy's required daily devotions), and numerous other prayers to God, the Virgin Mary, and saints. Even the beautiful illuminations for which these manuscripts are justly famous were often aids to prayer for their medieval owners. Who were the owners of Books of Hours and how might they have prayed from their books?

We know a great deal about some of these people. Queens, dukes, and noblemen ordered their manuscripts directly from well-known artists, and had them designed according to their own artistic and devotional tastes. Sometimes their faces appear in the prayer books they left behind. The Hours of Mary of Burgundy contains a mysterious portrait of its owner in prayer before the Madonna (Fig. 9). In the Savoy Hours, commissioned by Blanche of Burgundy, there were no fewer than twenty-five pictures of Blanche herself portrayed in various pious poses. Among the prayers she might read from her book we find a "Prayer for Myself" (Fig. 1). Clearly Blanche's *Horae* was designed for her exclusive use. A similar effort to personalize a Book of Hours, albeit on a much reduced scale, can be seen in Walters 98, a thirteenth-century French manuscript from Rheims (Cat. No. 5). The owner's name is unknown but she is seen kneeling before the Madonna in two historiated initials. Several prayers in this book are written for a woman (suggested by the feminine form of Latin pronouns), and in place of the usual "Pray for us" in the Litany we read "Pray for your handmaiden."

Mary, Blanche, and the anonymous woman from Rheims hailed from the privileged classes of late medieval society. Who else but the wealthy and well-connected could pay famous artists to paint their portraits in the most fashionable style? Who else could pay clerics to compose prayers especially for them, or even scribes to modify standard prayers to include their names? For the first 150 years of its life, the Book of Hours was a luxury, a work of religious art ordered to taste and bought at great cost. But during the fifteenth century, changes in both manuscript production and the structure of northern European society made it possible for non-noble people to acquire them. Scribal shops began to turn out large numbers of mass-produced Books of Hours, which urban dwellers, now endowed with cash, could afford. Merchants, shop owners, and lesser rural landowners purchased their own prayer books from shops in Paris, Bruges, and other cities. Like Ogier Bénigne and Marie Caillet of Dijon in Walters 291 (Cat. No. 62), they proudly inscribed their names inside Books of Hours that they bought or inherited. Or like the Tourotte family, they had their portraits added to the book's existing illuminations (Fig. 7).

Although neither a prince nor a duke, Ogier Bénigne was still a man of sufficient social status to be appointed a minor, part-time royal official. The price of

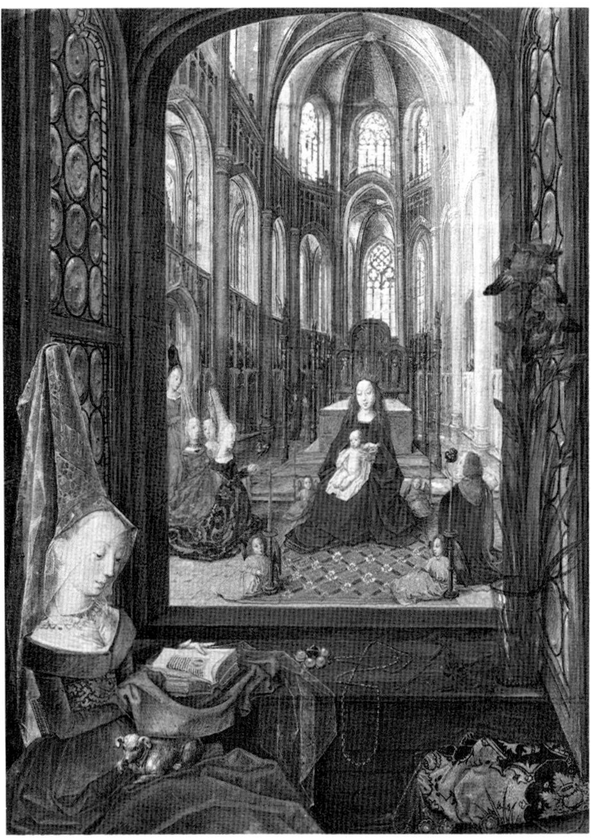

Fig. 9. *Mary of Burgundy Praying from her Book of Hours* (Accessory Text: 7 Joys of the Virgin), Belgium, ca. 1480, by the Master of Mary of Burgundy (Vienna, Österreichische Nationalbibliothek, Cod. 1857, fol. 14v).

manuscripts did not fall so dramatically that members of every social class could afford them. Peasants and laborers never numbered among the owners of Books of Hours, not only because their income was too low, but also because they were almost always illiterate. The Book of Hours was, after all is said about its artistic importance, primarily a book of Latin prayers.

Who in the fifteenth century could read prayers in Latin? This is a difficult question to answer precisely. We can probably assume that most priests were familiar with the Church's official language for liturgy, scholarship, and business. But what about lay people? Literacy in the European vernacular languages (French, Flemish, German) reached into the merchant and artisan classes, because their work required some of these people to read and write. It is difficult to say with any assurance how much Latin people like Ogier Bénigne and Marie Caillet knew. As they were neither priests nor scholars, they probably never studied Latin formally. Yet a lifetime of immersion in the Church's liturgy and sacraments gave them a practical education in Latin that most twentieth-century observers would find alien. Imagine Ogier's son Bernard saying the Office of the Dead for the repose of his father's soul. Perhaps Bernard mouthed the Latin psalms from his father's prayer book at the same time he heard his parish priest recite the same benedictions, rites, and prayers. Lacking a scholar's knowledge of Latin grammar would not prevent a lay person from praying fervently nor prevent his understanding the comforting opening antiphon of the Office of the Dead: "Placebo Domino in regione vivorum" ("I will please the Lord in the land of the living," Psalm 114:9).

For many owners, the Book of Hours was a prized possession, dear for reasons beyond artistic merit. Like family Bibles of more recent times, family history might be passed down through the Book of Hours—as can be seen in that belonging to the Bénigne family or the Doffinnes family of Flanders (Cat. No. 107), where family diaries are penned onto flyleaves and in margins. Owners signed their names, inked in coats-of-arms, indicated how the book came into their hands, added favorite prayers—in short, whatever necessary to make the book their own. A hint of owners' feelings about their Books of Hours comes to us from inventories drawn up after death. Doubtless, most people were like Catherine Rousseau, the widow of a sixteenth-century French royal official, who kept her prayer book not on a shelf with other books, but rather in a little cabinet with her jewelry, rosaries, and religious medallions.

For owners like Catherine Rousseau, the Book of Hours was a cherished possession lovingly cared for, added to, worked on. And this loving care goes beyond the obviously material, into the spiritual world. The Book of Hours was a veritable jewel box of devotion. Devout medieval people collected prayers the way twentieth-century cooks collect recipes. The variety of texts and images found in these manuscripts is staggering. Consider Walters 237, a fifteenth-century Book of Hours from Avignon (Cat. No. 17). In addition to the usual Offices and prayers to the Virgin and saints, we find the popular "Charlemagne Prayer," a series of blessings said to have been given to Charlemagne by Pope Leo to protect him from the Saracens. Whoever said, heard, saw, or wore this prayer daily was promised protection from almost every earthly peril. Blanche of Burgundy might leaf through the numerous prayers in her *Horae*, searching for special intentions, as she might rummage through her jewel case for just the right necklace. The devotional riches of the Book of Hours easily matched its artistic ones.

Did people actually use Books of Hours for prayer?

Evidence is fragmentary and scattered. Some late medieval treatises of religious counsel recommended that lay people say Offices, especially the Little Office of the Blessed Virgin Mary, which is the heart of any Book of Hours. French theologian Jean Quentin advised lay people to say "matins, prime, and hours if you can" upon waking, before leaving the bedchamber. Sources suggest that some followed this advice. An anonymous Parisian merchant wrote an advice book for his wife that took careful account of her spiritual life. He took pains to explain the concept of "the artificial day," as he called it: while laywomen are not required to pray on an hourly schedule, practicing a modified version of this method of prayer would help them dedicate ordinary daily existence to God. An early fifteenth-century English priest urged a merchant who consulted him for spiritual guidance to retire to "a secret place" in his house and say Matins and Vespers of Our Lady.

This desire to sanctify even lay time, to render it holy, explains the laity's attraction to the Little Office of the Blessed Virgin Mary. Priests and monks who recited the Divine Office "prayed without ceasing," in the words of St. Paul. The medieval laity were taught to see everything about clerical life as holy: a priest's business was to administer eternal salvation; a life of chastity and prayer was spiritually superior to mere secular existence. Is it any wonder that lay people would want access to the clergy's method of prayer? Reciting the Hours of the Virgin represented an avenue into a world of personal religious experience formed by centuries of Church tradition. By praying from a Book of Hours a lay person enjoyed spiritual privileges usually reserved for the clergy.

Saying the Hours of the Virgin with complete absorption could be like entering a cloister, a cloister of prayer. The opening prayer itself invites intimacy with God: "Lord, open my lips, and my mouth shall proclaim your praise. God, come to my assistance." Imagine the devout reader of Jean Quentin's treatise, reciting Lauds before leaving his bed at daybreak, coming upon the opening line from Psalm 62: "O God, my God, I watch for you at dawn."

Psalms, the most ancient and beloved of Judeo-Christian prayers, were, seemingly, intended to be read aloud. The Little Office's rhythm of psalm and antiphon recalls the alternation of voices heard in the monastic recitation of the Divine Office. In fact, the Hours of the Virgin were probably read aloud, even by solitary devotees. The historian Jean Leclercq has described the reading of religious works in the Middle Ages as a reflective, active process—"listening to the voices of the page" with eyes, ears, and lips. People read slowly

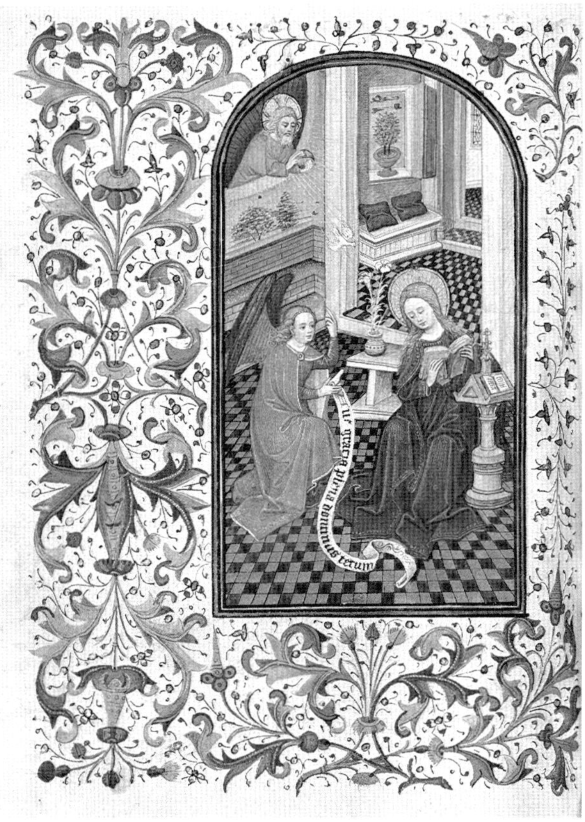

Fig. 10. *Annunciation* (Hours of the Virgin: Matins), Belgium, Bruges, 1450s, by Willem Vrelant (Walters 240, fol. 167v; Cat. No. 92).

and carefully, ruminating about every word. Murmuring or mouthing the words of psalms helped lay people to understand Latin words they knew from the liturgy, and perhaps reminded them that they shared the world of the clergy, those who prayed without ceasing.

Books of Hours themselves reveal something about the medieval experience of absorbed prayer. In miniatures of the Annunciation the angel Gabriel interrupts Mary's devotions to bring her the good news. Mary is often shown praying from a Book of Hours, kneeling in a private chapel or chamber (Fig. 10; see also Pls. 1, 18). Other images suggest to us the gestures, feeling, and interiority of perfect prayer: Mary of Burgundy serenely following the words of her prayer with her finger; Isabelle de Coucy and Adolph of Cleves lost in meditative prayer (Figs. 5, 6); the anonymous man kneeling beside his bed in Rosenwald 9 (Fig. 84).

Most men and women of the Middle Ages—even devout ones—did not have the leisure time necessary to say lengthy Offices. This was the privilege of the elite, of duchesses and wealthy merchants who hired

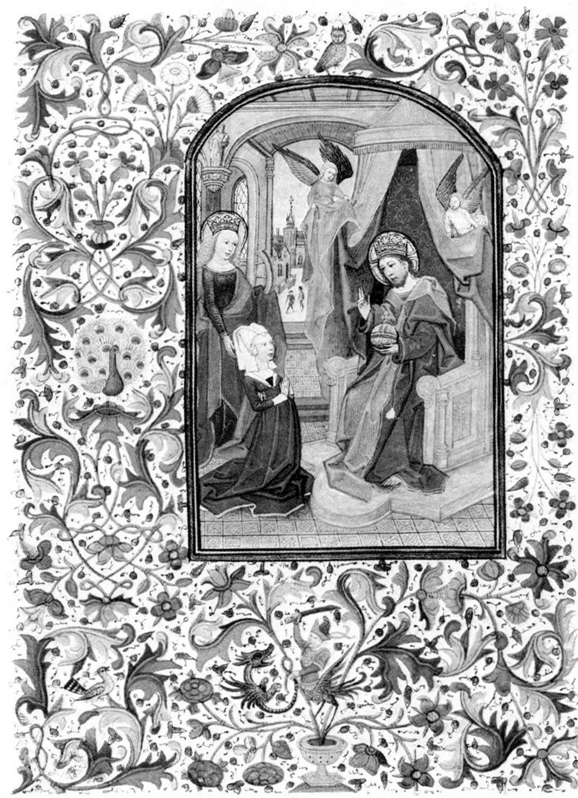

Fig. 11. *Catherine Presenting a Patroness to Christ* (Suffrage), Belgium, Bruges, ca. 1450, by Willem Vrelant (Walters 220, fol. 150v; Cat. No. 91).

servants to cook and clean. But the beauty of the Book of Hours from the devotional point of view was its ability to provide something for every literate owner. Even those who flipped past the Hours of the Virgin might well use their prayer book for private prayer during the official, public prayer of the medieval Church—Sunday Mass. An early sixteenth-century manual of spiritual advice for French laywomen, for example, recommended copying out prayers for Mass onto a slip of paper to be inserted "inside the Book of Hours you bring to church." We have ample pictorial evidence that lay people took prayer books to Mass. The miniature in the Savoy Hours depicting the celebration of Mass shows Blanche of Burgundy clasping her open Book of Hours (Cat. No. 11, folio 10v). The Buves Hours includes a depiction of a funeral service in which lay mourners are clearly praying from books (Fig. 114). The climactic moment of the Mass, the elevation of the Eucharist, is the subject of a remarkable picture in the fourteenth-century Butler Hours, a picture no less remarkable for its fine family portrait of the Butlers themselves (Pl. 13). Such miniatures within Books of Hours offer pictorial confirmation that these manuscripts frequently accompanied their owners to church.

Furthermore, many Books of Hours include prayers an owner might read at important moments of the Mass, especially at the elevation of the host and the reception of Holy Communion. The variety of texts is interesting. While most Books of Hours offer a few brief prayers to say while gazing upon the host as the priest holds it up, a few unusual *Horae* include long devotions a person might read throughout the entire Mass.

Ordinary owners of Books of Hours, however, were probably more attracted to short prayers addressed to the Virgin Mary and saints than they were to long Offices and prayers for Mass. In fact, most of the prayers in Books of Hours appeal to the Virgin and saints. As God's chosen ones, members of the court of heaven, they were believed willing to listen to the prayers of human beings who lacked the courage to speak directly to the heavenly King himself. Among the saints, the Mother of God had special status. In the words of the medieval theologian Jean Gerson, God anointed Mary the "treasury of grace, mother of mercy, advocate, and counselor." An early fifteenth-century *Blessed Life of Our Lady* identified Mary as the one "by whom the world is sustained, and by whom all grace and all goods are given to us." By the late Middle Ages, an elaborate cult had developed around the Virgin as co-redemptrix of humanity, as Mary was sometimes called.

Within many Books of Hours, themselves an outgrowth of the cult of Mary, is the expressive prayer called the "Obsecro te." It begins by listing, in litany-like fashion, the Virgin's attributes: "I beseech you, Mary, holy lady, mother of God, most full of piety, daughter of the greatest king, most glorious mother, mother of orphans, consolation of the desolate, the way for those who stray, salvation for those who hope in you . . . " (the complete prayer is found in the Appendix). The devotee appeals to Mary not only as co-redemptrix, but also because of the motherly qualities she displays toward human beings: she guides, she nurtures, she consoles. As the prayer continues the devotee cites significant episodes in Mary's life, contemplating the physical and emotional experiences of each.

The "Obsecro te" illustrates several important characteristics of late medieval piety. The devotee tries to create an intimate relationship with the supernatural person being addressed, in this case Mary as mother. The prayer uses a repertoire of sensory experiences to create this bond. Mary felt her own as well as her son's pain during the Crucifixion; thus she can re-

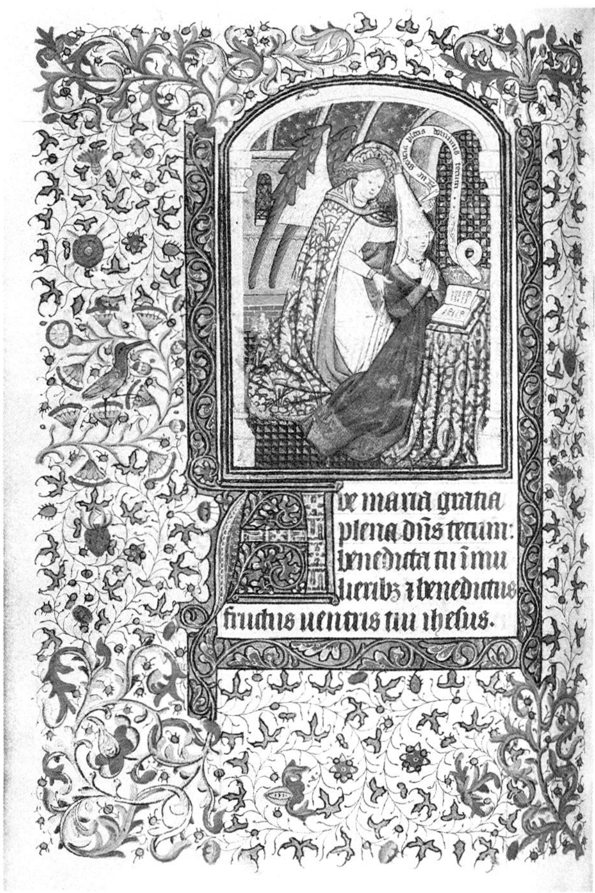

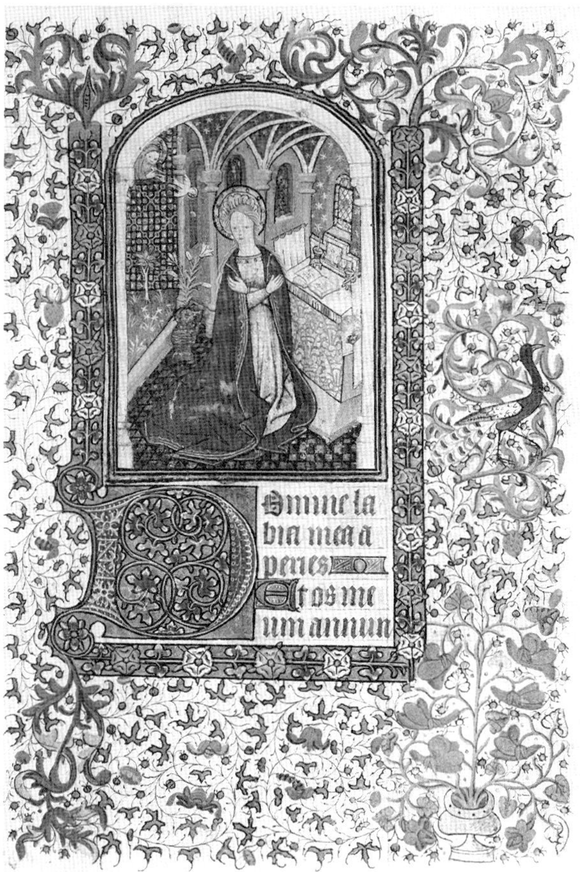

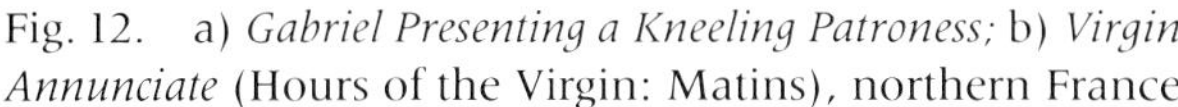

Fig. 12. a) *Gabriel Presenting a Kneeling Patroness;* b) *Virgin Annunciate* (Hours of the Virgin: Matins), northern France or southern Belgium, 1450s (Walters 267, fols. 13v–14; Cat. No. 40).

spond sympathetically to the devotee's suffering. Frequently the "Obsecro te" is accompanied by an illustration of the Madonna. In some of these pictures, as in Walters 220 (Pl. 29), a lay person kneels before the Virgin. Seeing an image of the Madonna portrayed in a familiar setting—a chapel, a kitchen, a bedchamber—and meditating on the picture could help the person praying to envision and feel the intimacy with Mary that the "Obsecro te" encourages.

If prayers addressed to Mary invariably establish a mother-child relationship between Mary and the devotee, prayers to the saints reveal the wide variety of possible human-supernatural relations,which is another interesting feature of late medieval piety. Northern Europe at this time was a social world of kinship and patronage. Men and women of every social class depended on family and patrons for economic and emotional sustenance. The kin and patron-client relations that prevailed in secular life were mirrored in spiritual life. People chose personal patron saints to protect and guide them in both this world and the next. The owner of Walters 284 (Cat. No. 60) evidently had a personal devotion to St. John, for her prayer book includes a special prayer to him with an image of herself praying to him. The Tourotte Hours contains several portraits of the Tourottes and their special saints in which human and supernatural persons seem to mingle (Fig. 7a). Saints Anne, Peter, Anthony, and Clare are included in the illustrations almost as friends of the family.

Devotees might pray to personal patrons in heaven, but for particular intentions they also turned to specialists. St. Sebastian cared especially about the problems of plague victims, a large population in the era of the Black Death (Fig. 93; see also the text of the Suffrage to Sebastian in the Appendix). St. Margaret, an early Christian martyr, was the patron for pregnancy and childbirth. She is usually shown emerging unharmed from the belly of a dragon that had swallowed her (Figs. 105, 106). According to some prayers, Margaret's terrible sufferings at the hands of her tormentors rendered her sympathetic to the pain and anxiety of mothers-to-be.

The revealing miniature of St. Catherine in Walters 220 offers a pictorial explanation of how the saint helps her protégée (Fig. 11). As the woman kneels in prayer before Christ, Catherine stands behind her, resting a hand on her shoulder. The woman has the courage to approach the Savior himself, depicted as King, because of the support and encouragement she receives from her patron Catherine.

Perhaps the owner of this prayer book found the image of St. Catherine more compelling than the Latin prayer it accompanied. Indeed, one of the virtues of the Book of Hours as a guide to devotion was that anyone—even a busy or marginally literate person —was able to use images to inspire prayer. In fact, some images could serve as aids to contemplation without a text. A good example is Veronica's Veil, the image of Christ's face that was imprinted on the saint's kerchief on the way to Calvary. The veil was preserved as a relic in St. Peter's in Rome. The legend of the veil was widely repeated during the late Middle Ages, and two popes granted indulgences to pilgrims who saw the relic or even a representation of it. The prayer to Christ's face, "Salve sancta facies," is found frequently in Books of Hours, and often accompanied by miniatures (Fig. 76). Images of the Mass of St. Gregory possessed similarly redemptive qualities. This legend told how Christ had miraculously appeared in the flesh on the altar as St. Gregory said Mass, thus demonstrating concretely the real presence of Christ in the consecrated bread (Fig. 79). Like most medieval Christians, owners of Books of Hours probably believed that gazing upon images of the Mass of St. Gregory or Veronica's Veil was itself a form of prayer.

Images in Books of Hours could also help a devotee visualize the process of prayer. As mentioned above, many depictions of the Annunciation portray Mary's quiet acceptance, her humility, as she communicates with God. Books of Hours also frequently contain images of David in fervent prayer (Pl. 31). Some of the most powerful images of prayer are those showing devotees before the Madonna. The fifteenth-century Buves Hours contains a surprising portrait of its female owner (Pl. 14, Fig. 12). Here a standard Annunciation is transformed by the presence of a lay woman kneeling between Gabriel and Mary. Perhaps for owner and artist the Annunciation simply provided another opportunity for a noble lady's portrait. But might it also have had devotional significance? Perhaps visualizing herself present at the most intimate physical and spiritual moment of the Virgin's life helped the devotee create the intimacy essential for true dialogue with Mary and God.

In the portrait of Mary of Burgundy at prayer the medieval devotional imagination is well displayed (Fig. 9). Mary prays from her Book of Hours in her oratory, before a window opening onto a Gothic chapel. The Madonna sits before an altar inside the chapel, adored by angels and several lay people —including Mary of Burgundy herself. Mary's eyes focus on her book, not on the scene beyond her window. What we see is Mary's visualization of the act of prayer. Through prayer Mary imagines herself in the Madonna's presence. Mary of Burgundy's closeness to the Virgin grows out of absorbed contemplation. Her Book of Hours creates a physical and psychic space for solitude and contemplation. The Virgin becomes her mother, her friend, a confidante to whom she can disclose herself, her pain, her joy.

If we were able to ask medieval men and women themselves why they prayed, they would probably not articulate the stillness, attentiveness, and peace we see in these images. They would probably not mention the personal closeness between human and supernatural beings that we find so compelling. They would reply that the goal of prayer was salvation, for themselves and others for whom they prayed. They knew that prayer redeemed them and saved their souls. It was this that gave the Book of Hours its ultimate, lifesaving significance.

CHAPTER IV

Calendar

We tend to call the twenty-fifth day of the last month of the year not December 25, but Christmas. And the day before this holiday is not so much December 24th as it is Christmas Eve. We celebrate New Year's Day, not January 1. The fourteenth of February is, of course, Valentine's Day, named, not after a greeting card, but after the Roman saint whose martyrdom is celebrated on this day. Children trick-or-treat on Halloween not because it is October 31, but because this day is the "hallowed eve" before the Feast of All Saints (which we call November 1). The names by which these days are referred to are a remnant of the medieval manner of telling time. With these few exceptions we of the twentieth century refer to the day of the year by the numerical sequence within which it falls in each of twelve months. In the Middle Ages, by contrast, each day commemorated an event in the life of Christ or a saint, usually the day he or she died, and it was this religious significance, and not its numerical designation, that gave the day its real meaning.

The Calendar is the first section of a Book of Hours. It is a list of the 365 feast days of the year, divided into the twelve months. In some Books of Hours, especially the earliest ones, the lesser feasts were written in black ink and the more important ones in red—hence the expression, "red-letter days." In lavish manuscripts blue or gold replaces the red for these major feasts. Calendars also contain, at the left, a column composed of a series of numbers, called the Golden Numbers, and a second column of letters, called the Dominical Letters. The latter helped one locate Sundays throughout the year, and together both columns were used to find the date of Easter, the Church's most important feast. Calendars from early Books of Hours also contain the ancient Roman calendar system, an extremely confusing way of telling time that continued throughout much of the Middle Ages and was finally abandoned in the Renaissance. (Easter computations and the Roman calendar are explained in the Appendix.) Some Calendars also contain designations in the form of a large "D" for the "dies egyptiaci" (or "dies mali," from which our adjective "dismal" is thought to derive). These are bad luck days, of which there were two per month. Finally, Calendars also at times had pictures, and it is these that are our primary concern here.

Calendars, when illustrated, contain representations of the signs of the zodiac and of the labors of the months. Both of these traditions are old, the former with roots in Mesopotamia and the latter going back to classical antiquity. Calendars in Books of Hours are actually illustrated less than half of the time, even in manuscripts with otherwise lavish cycles of miniatures. The Calendar miniatures from the Duc de Berry's *Très Riches Heures* are the most famous such pictures and are among the best-known paintings from all the Middle Ages. This cycle of large miniatures was painted by the best artists of the time, the Limbourg brothers, and for the most cultivated patron of this or nearly any other period, Jean, duc de Berry. But, as one author has recently commented, the *Très Riches Heures* is really something of a freak and its full-page Calendar illustrations unique at their time. Calendars in the majority of Books of Hours are not illustrated at all, and those that are usually have only small or half-page miniatures, historiated borders, or vignettes in the margins. Like the portal of a Gothic cathedral carved with the signs of the zodiac and the labors of the months,

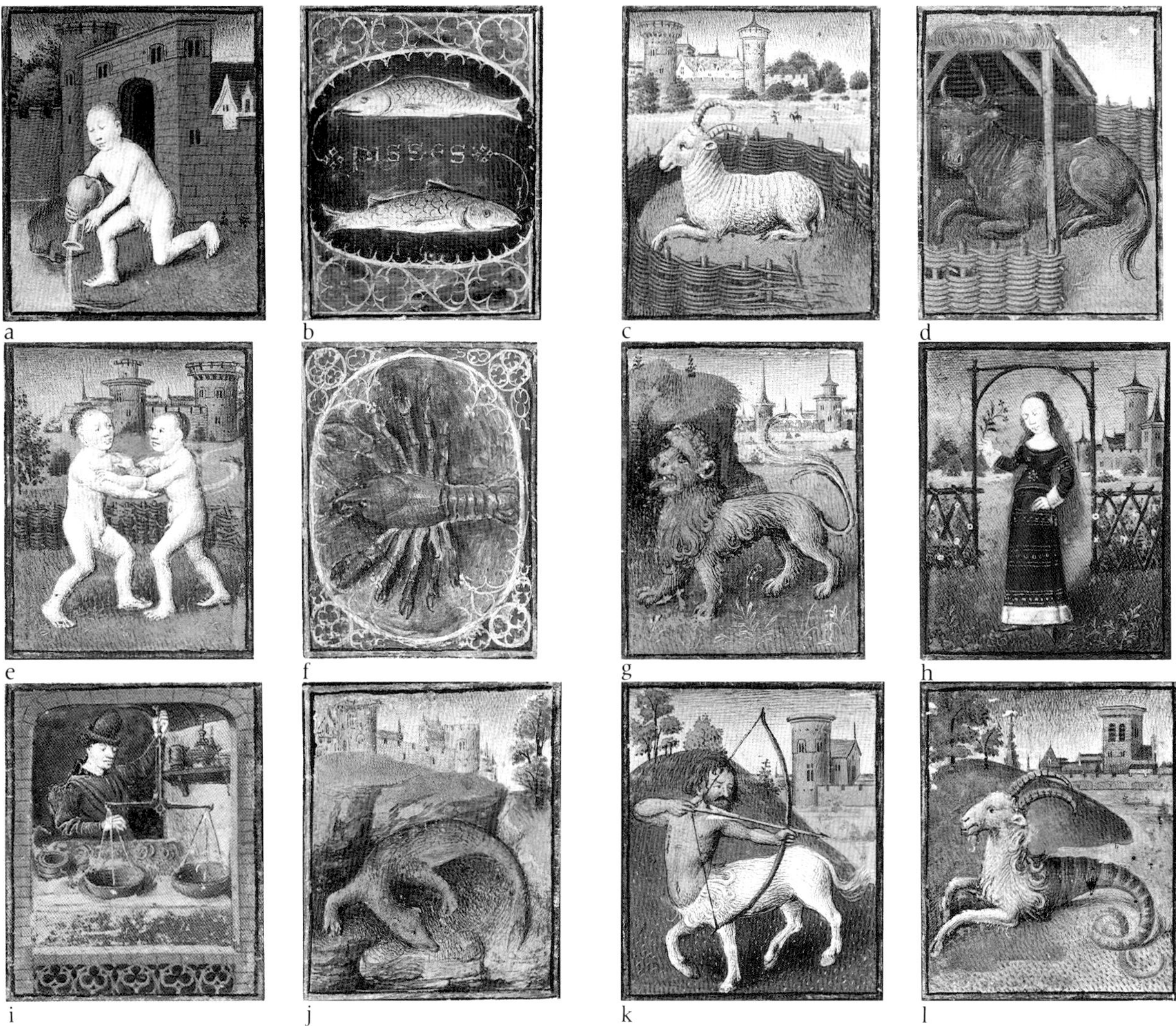

the Calendar is that part of the Book of Hours concerned with the here and now, the visible world. As with the portal, the Calendar, consulted quickly, allows the reader to pass to the prayers within the book itself, the prayers that, like the liturgical ceremonies enacted within a church, bring him into contact with God. The typical medieval reader would have found full-page pictures in a Calendar not only distracting but also inappropriate. Only in the sixteenth century do Calendars with large-scale cycles begin to appear with regularity.

The astrological signs of the zodiac were thought to influence the make-up of one's personality and to control specific areas of the human body. For example, Aries governed the head and face, Cancer the breast and stomach. The zodiac had to be consulted prior to bleeding, performed for medicinal purposes, since each sign exerted a good, bad, or indifferent influence on this surgical practice.

In Walters 274, a richly illuminated Book of Hours painted (for the most part) by the Coëtivy Master, two vignettes, one with the labor of the month, the other with the zodiacal sign, accompany each month (Fig. 13). The sequence adheres to the following traditional assignments:

January:	Aquarius, the Water Carrier
February:	Pisces, the Fish
March:	Aries, the Ram
April:	Taurus, the Bull
May:	Gemini, the Twins
June:	Cancer, the Crab
July:	Leo, the Lion
August:	Virgo, the Virgin

Fig. 13. Zodiacal Signs, France, Angers?, 1460s, by the Coëtivy Master (Henri de Vulcop?), with some 16th-century retouching (Walters 274; Cat. No. 42).

a) January: *Aquarius* (fol. 1v)
b) February: *Pisces* (fol. 2v)
c) March: *Aries* (fol. 3v)
d) April: *Taurus* (fol. 4v)
e) May: *Gemini* (fol. 5v)
f) June: *Cancer* (fol. 6v)
g) July: *Leo* (fol. 7v)
h) August: *Virgo* (fol. 8v)
i) September: *Libra* (fol. 9v)
j) October: *Scorpio* (fol. 10v)
k) November: *Sagittarius* (fol. 11v)
l) December: *Capricorn* (fol. 12v)

Fig. 14. Labors of the Months, France, Paris?, ca. 1430, by a follower of the Bedford Master (Walters 285; Cat. No. 50).

a) January: *Janus Feasting* (fol. 4v)
b) February: *Keeping Warm* (fol. 5v)
c) March: *Pruning* (fol. 6v)
d) April: *Picking Flowering Branches* (fol. 7v)
e) May: *Hawking* (fol. 8v)
f) June: *Mowing* (fol. 9v)
g) July: *Reaping* (fol. 10v)
h) August: *Threshing* (fol. 11v)
i) September: *Treading Grapes* (fol. 12v)
j) October: *Sowing* (fol. 13v)
k) November: *Thrashing for Acorns* (fol. 14v)
l) December: *Slaughtering a Pig* (fol. 15v)

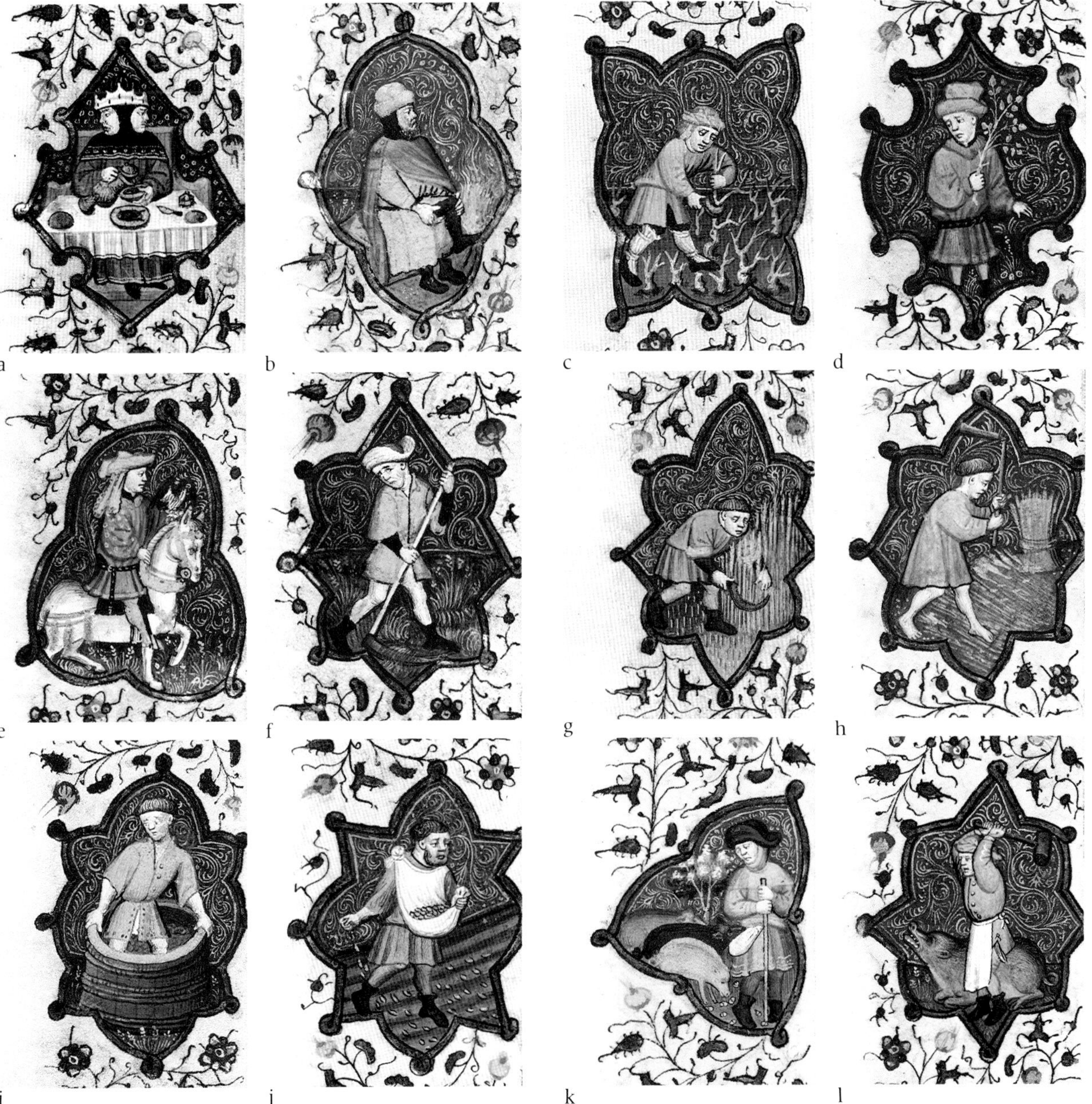

September: Libra, the Balance
October Scorpio, the Scorpion
November: Sagittarius, the Archer
December: Capricorn, the Goat

With few exceptions, the Coëtivy Master places the animals and people representing the signs of the zodiac in deep, finely rendered landscapes. Although they sometimes receive treatment equal to that of the labors in early Books of Hours, zodiac signs generally do not receive such careful attention. Through the course of the fifteenth and early sixteenth centuries the signs are not forgotten, but they do assume an ancillary role to the labors of the months.

The labors, and a few leisures, of the months follow the rural peasant activities dictated by the seasons and the work to be done in each. The following list gives the traditional task for each month; the first activity is the standard one and those in parentheses represent frequently found variations:

January: Feasting (or, Janus Feasting, Keeping Warm)
February: Keeping Warm (or, Chopping Wood, Pruning, Breaking Ground, Feasting)
March: Pruning (or, Breaking Ground)
April: Picking Flowers (or, Hawking)
May: Hawking (or, Riding, Courting, Making Music)
June: Mowing (or, Shearing Sheep)
July: Reaping (or, Mowing)
August: Threshing (or, Reaping, Winnowing)
September: Treading Grapes (or, Harvesting Grapes, Sowing, Ploughing)
October: Sowing (or, Treading Grapes, Harvesting Grapes, Ploughing, Thrashing for Acorns)

Fig. 15. Labors of the Months, Belgium, early 16th century (Walters 425; Cat. No. 105).

a) January: *Keeping Warm and Feasting* (fol. 1)
b) February: *Pruning and Splitting Wood* (fol. 2)
c) March: *Breaking Ground* (fol. 3)
d) April: *Planting* (fol. 4)
e) May: *Riding* (fol. 5)
f) June: *Mowing* (fol. 6)
g) July: *Reaping* (fol. 7)
h) August: *Threshing* (fol. 8)
i) September: *Ploughing* (fol. 9)
j) October: *Treading Grapes and Making Wine* (fol. 10)
k) November: *Slaughtering a Pig* (fol. 11)
l) December: *Throwing Snowballs* (fol. 12)

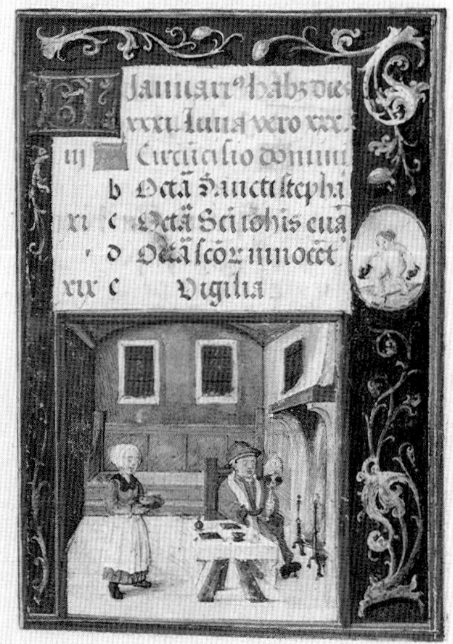

a

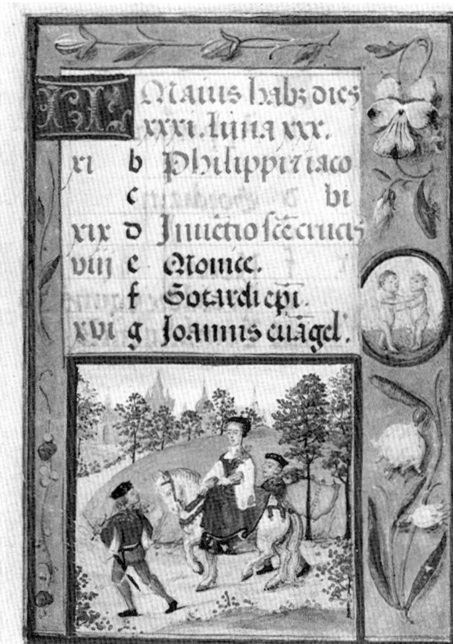

e

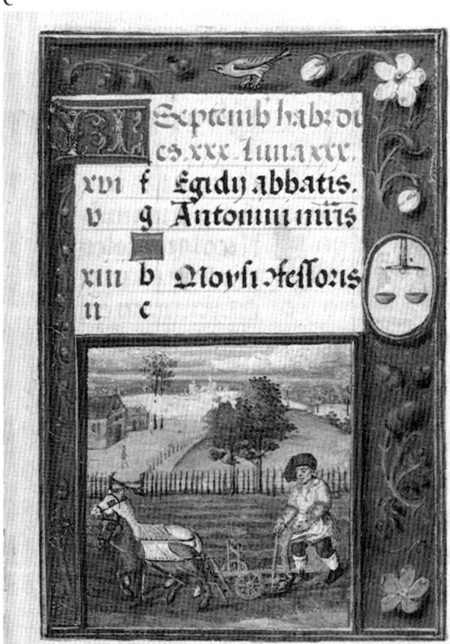

i

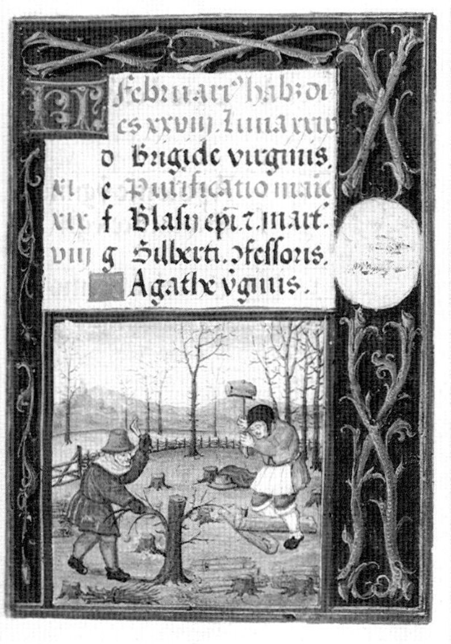

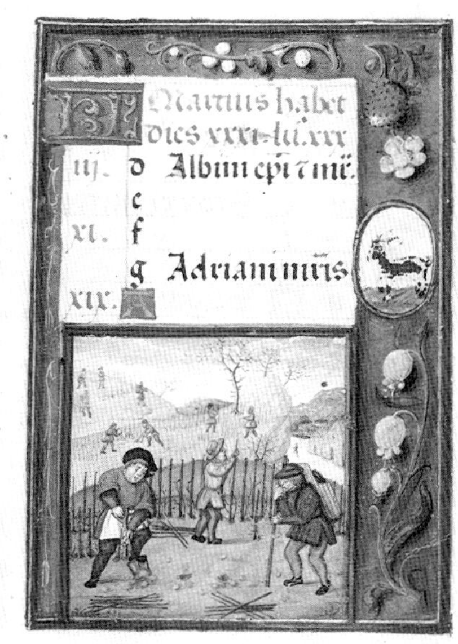

c

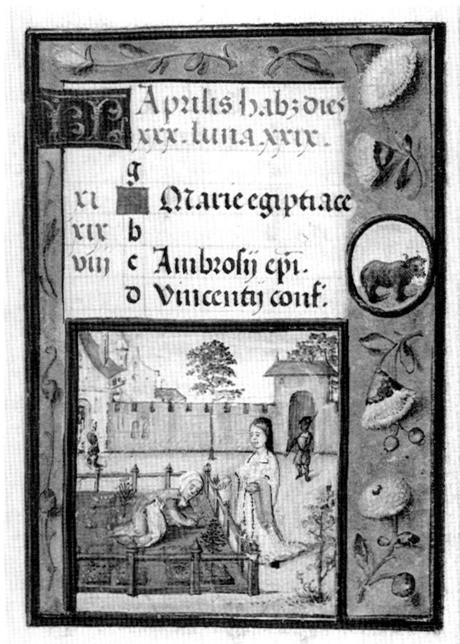

d

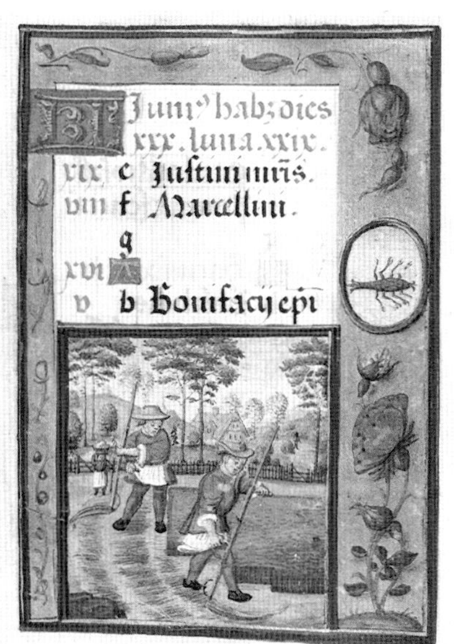

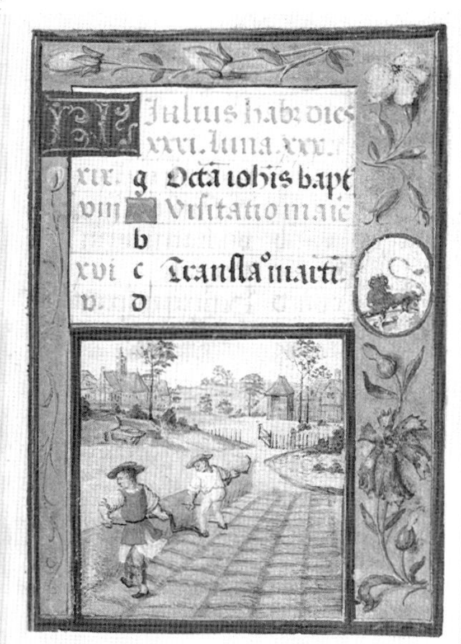

g

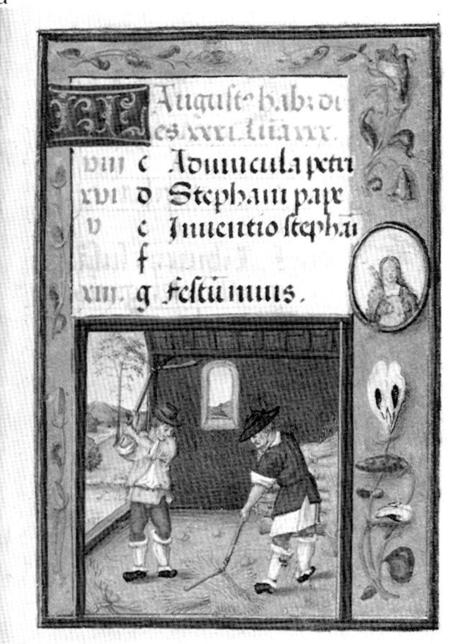

h

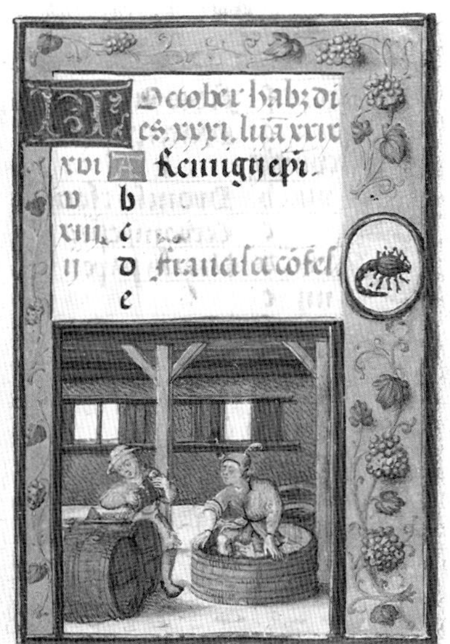

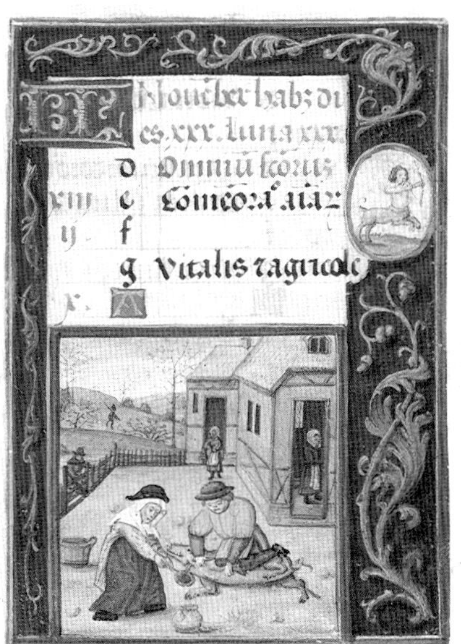

k

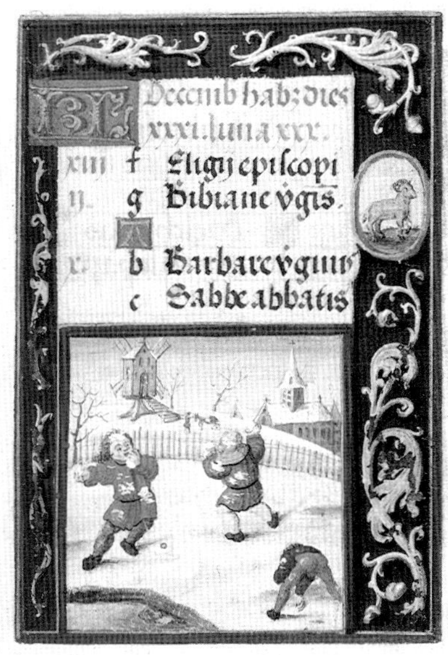

l

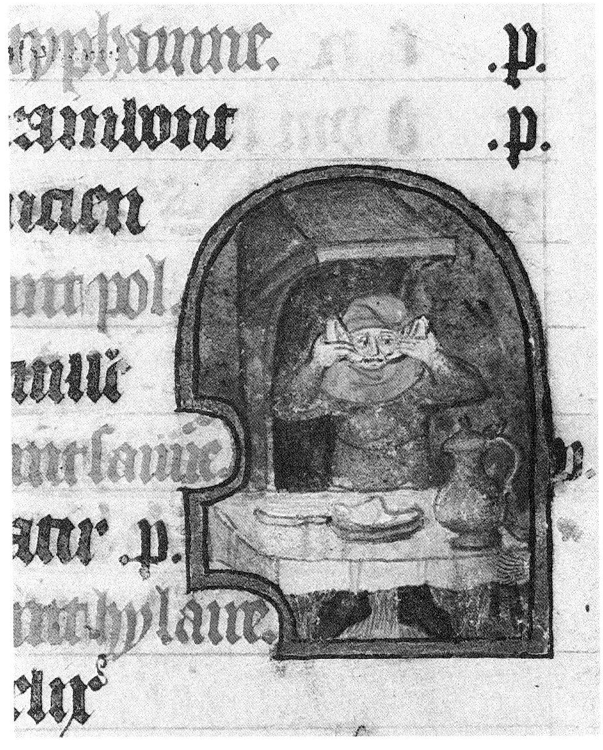

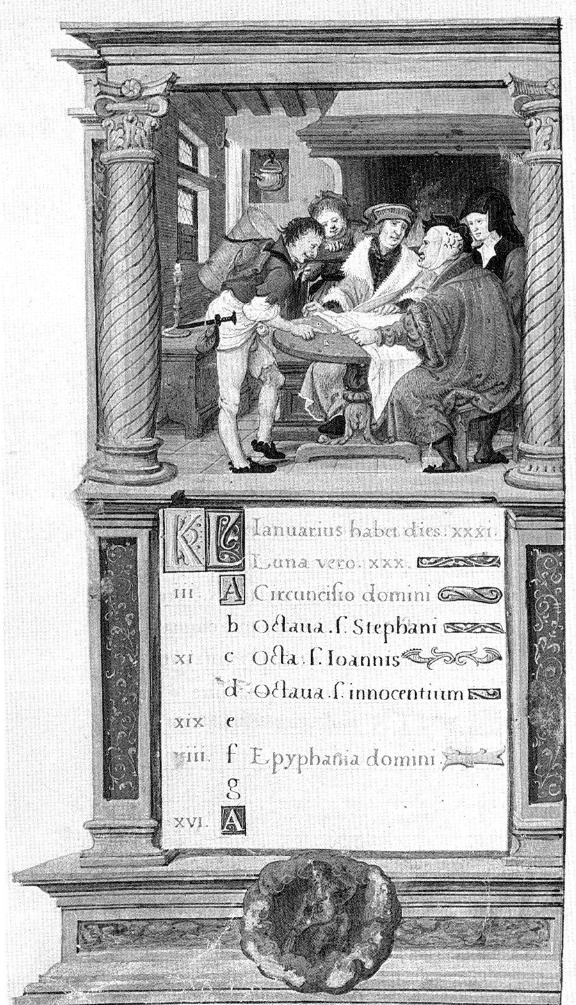

November: Thrashing for Acorns (or, Slaughtering a Pig, Slaughtering an Ox, Baking)
December: Slaughtering a Pig (or, Baking, Roasting Pigs)

Two cycles of typical Calendar illustrations are reproduced in these pages. The first consists of vignettes painted about 1430, probably in Paris, by a follower of the Bedford Master (Fig. 14). The second sequence is from an early sixteenth-century Flemish *Horae* and consists of half-page miniatures (Fig. 15). Both cycles are iconographically and stylistically typical of illustrated Calendars.

Winter is mostly spent indoors. As the cycles reveal, the typical labor for January is eating, preferably fireside. The diner in the January vignette from the fifteenth-century manuscript is the two-faced Janus, the Roman god of the new year who looked both back into the past and forward into the future (Fig. 14a). This type of double-faced eater inspired the depiction of the hungry man in a January vignette of an early fifteenth-century Book of Hours from the workshop of the Luçon Master (Fig. 16). The artist has eliminated one of the faces but retains the two cups, from both of which the man drinks at the same time! A rare, perhaps even shocking, miniature for January is that from the Hours of Jean de Mauléon, a manuscript by the 1520s Hours Workshop (Fig. 17). To help while away their winter time and improve his own pecuniary position, a poor but cocky tradesman has challenged his employers to a game of dice. The February illustrations from the two cycles depict the common activities for this month: keeping warm and chopping wood (Figs. 14b, 15b). This last task leads to the outdoors and to spring.

The major task of March, the first month of spring, is pruning (Fig. 14c). Ground breaking, along with planting, are also often shown, as in the March scene from the Flemish cycle (Fig. 15c) or the elaborate historiated border from an early sixteenth-century French manuscript (Fig. 18). In April, the nobles who kept warm and well fed in January and February come outdoors. Illustrations for this month show well dressed young men and women picking flowers (Fig. 14d), making flower wreaths, flirting, or hawking. The lat-

Fig. 16. January: *Feasting*, France, Paris, 1400–10, by the workshop of the Luçon Master (Walters 103, fol. 1; Cat. No. 20).

Fig. 17. January: *Playing Dice*, France, Tours?, 1524, by the 1520s Hours Workshop (Walters 449, fol. 2v; Cat. No. 77).

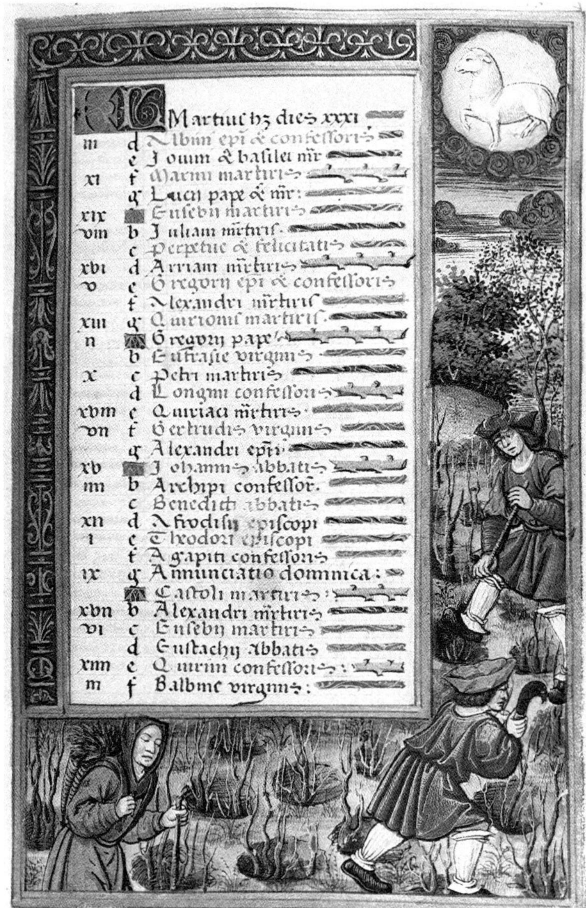

Fig. 18. March: *Pruning and Breaking Ground,* France, early 16th century (Walters 451, fol. 5; Cat. No. 76).

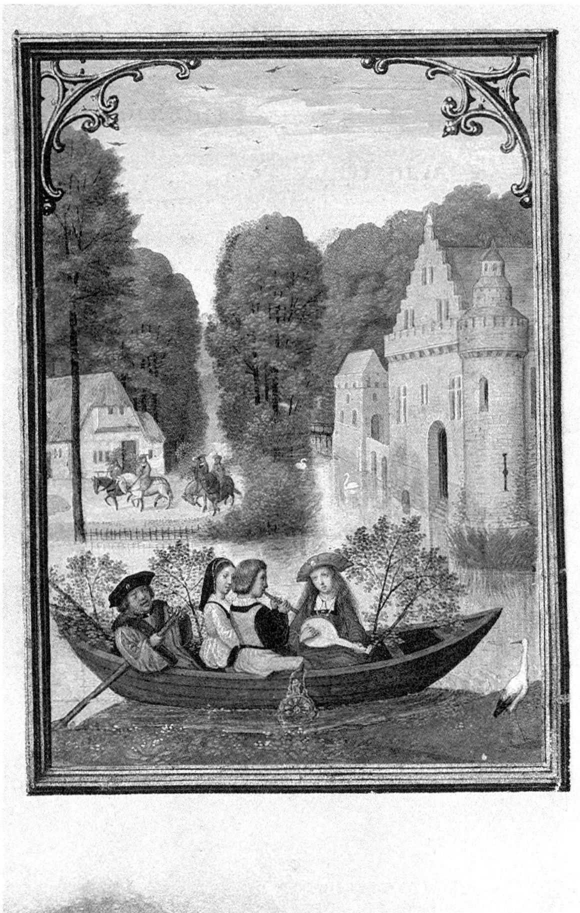

Fig. 19. May: *Courting,* Belgium, Bruges?, ca. 1515, by Simon Bening (Morgan M.399, fol. 6v; Cat. No. 106).

ter is the principal pleasure for May (Fig. 14e), while "May-ing," taking rides to pick budding branches, as the Flemish cycle shows, was also popular (Fig. 15e). Courting accompanied by music is also a popular pastime during this month. May from the famous Calendar series by Simon Bening in the early sixteenth-century Da Costa Hours offers an idyllically rendered version of this amorous theme (Fig. 19). A group of young men and women slowly glide on the quiet canals of Bruges, entertaining themselves with music as their wine cools over the side of the boat. Musical entertainment seems to have encouraged the amorous interests of one of the male listeners in the May miniature of the Hours of Jean de Mauléon (Fig. 8a).

As the illustrations in the two cycles reveal, June, the first month of the summer, is spent mowing hay (Figs. 14f, 15f). This arduous duty is performed not, of course, by flirtatious nobles, but by workers who wield long-handled scythes. In the June miniature from an early sixteenth-century Book of Hours from Strassburg, a tired peasant warily eyes a sinister-looking lobster lurking in the nearby waters (Fig. 20). The animal is actually the Crab of the zodiac that, like all the signs in this Calendar, and as is typical with some manuscripts, has been incorporated within the space of the miniature itself. Sheep shearing is another June labor that finds its way frequently into Calendar miniatures. The Hours of Jean de Mauléon has a charming depiction of this task, a perhaps overly bucolic image of peasant life (Fig. 8b). The traditional task of July is reaping. In both cycles workers are seen cutting wheat with sickles (Figs. 14g, 15g). Mowing, June's labor, is sometimes continued in July, as in the border vignettes for July in an early fourteenth-century Flemish Book of Hours (Fig. 21). The illuminator took advantage of the double-page arrangement of the Calendar to expand upon each month's activity. For July he has depicted one mower busy at work, but he forgot to paint the hay the man is cutting; the artist's attention seems

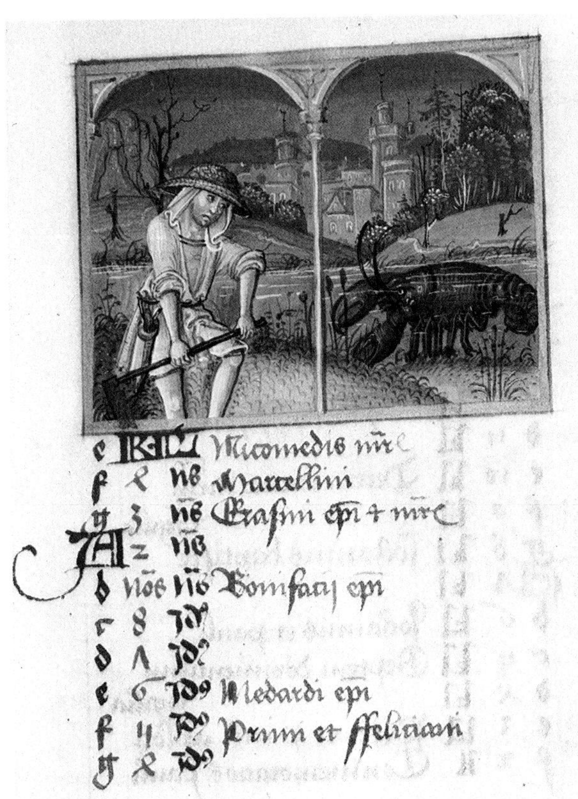

to have been distracted by his second mower who, instead of working, is flirting with a female co-worker. The wheat that is harvested in July is threshed in August. In the two cycles workers beat the stalks of wheat with flails to loosen the grain from its husk (Figs. 14h, 15h). The reaping that did not get finished in July is sometimes continued in August, as is the case in the Hours of Jean de Mauléon (Pl. 15a).

September, the first month of fall, is the time for the grape harvest. The task normally symbolizing this month, as in the French cycle, shows a man treading grapes (Fig. 14i). In some cases the man treading grapes is shown eating some or partaking of a sample of the liquid he is working so hard to produce (Fig. 22). Other tasks involved with the harvest, such as picking the grapes or storing the freshly squeezed juice in large barrels, also appear in the illustrations. Sowing and

Fig. 20. June: *Mowing,* Germany, Strassburg, early 16th century (Getty, Ludwig IX.16, fol. 6; Cat. No. 119).

Fig. 21. July: *Mowing and Mowers Flirting,* Belgium, Cambrai?, early 14th century (Walters 88, fols. 9v–10; Cat. No. 80).

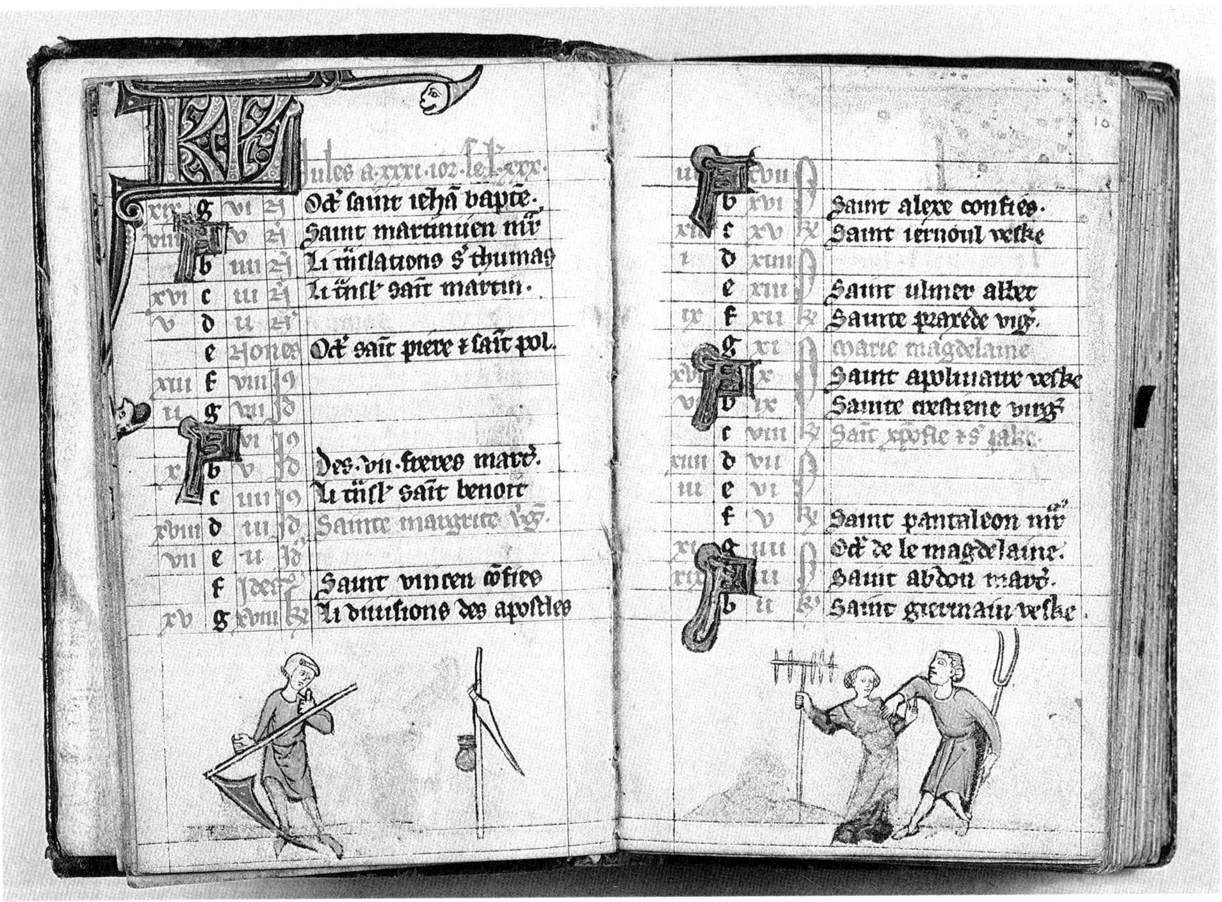

ploughing, though they figure as September labors in the Flemish cycle (Fig. 15i), are more frequently performed in October. A sower casting seeds onto a freshly ploughed field is the subject of the French cycle (Fig. 14j). In another French *Horae*, painted about 1490 by a follower of Jean Bourdichon, the October sower is followed by a team of horses that pulls a harrow to mix the seeds into the freshly ploughed earth (Fig. 23). In some areas, wine making does not take place until October and it is assigned to this month about as frequently as sowing. We see this in the Flemish cycle (Fig. 15j), as well as in the Hours of Jean de Mauléon

Fig. 22. September: *Treading Grapes,* Belgium, Huy, ca. 1300–10 (Walters 37, fol. 7; Cat. No. 79).

Fig. 23. October: *Ploughing and Sowing,* France, Tours?, ca. 1490, by a follower of Jean Bourdichon (Walters 227, fol. 7v; Cat. No. 65).

Fig. 24. December: *Roasting a Pig,* Belgium, Bruges?, ca. 1500 (Walters 428, fol. 12v; Cat. No. 104).

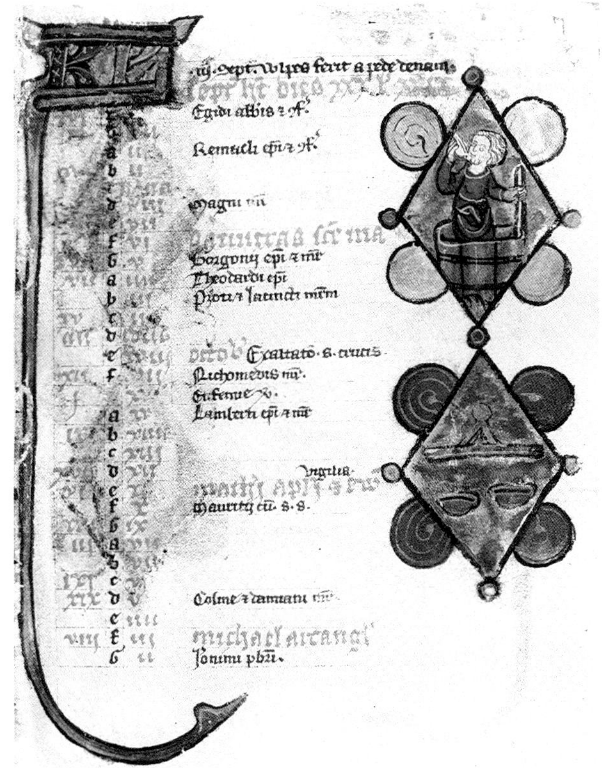

22

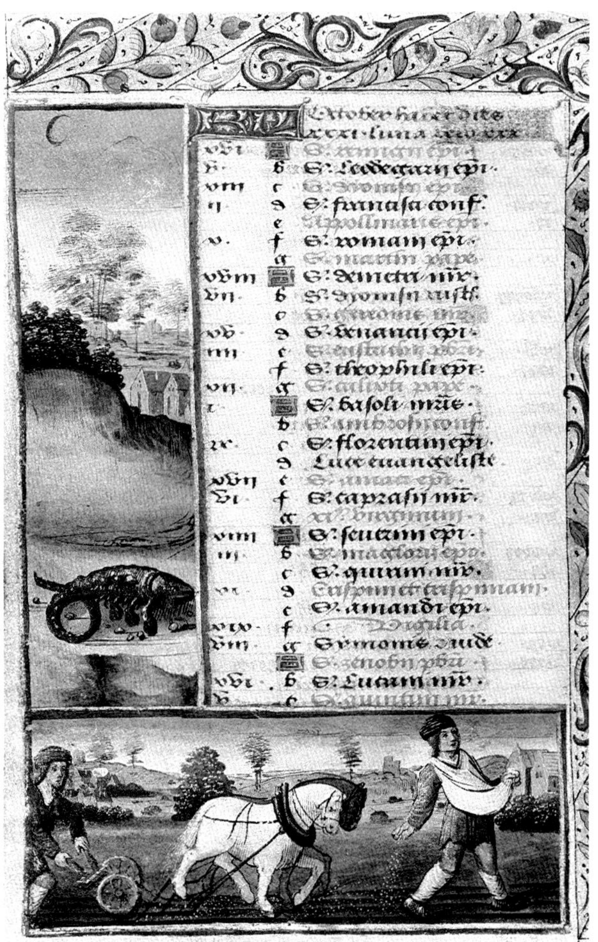

23

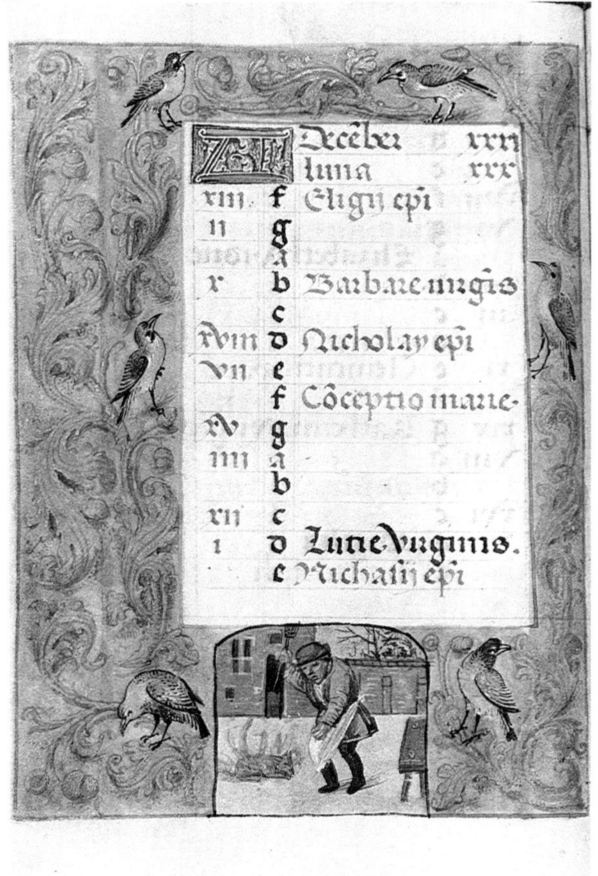

24

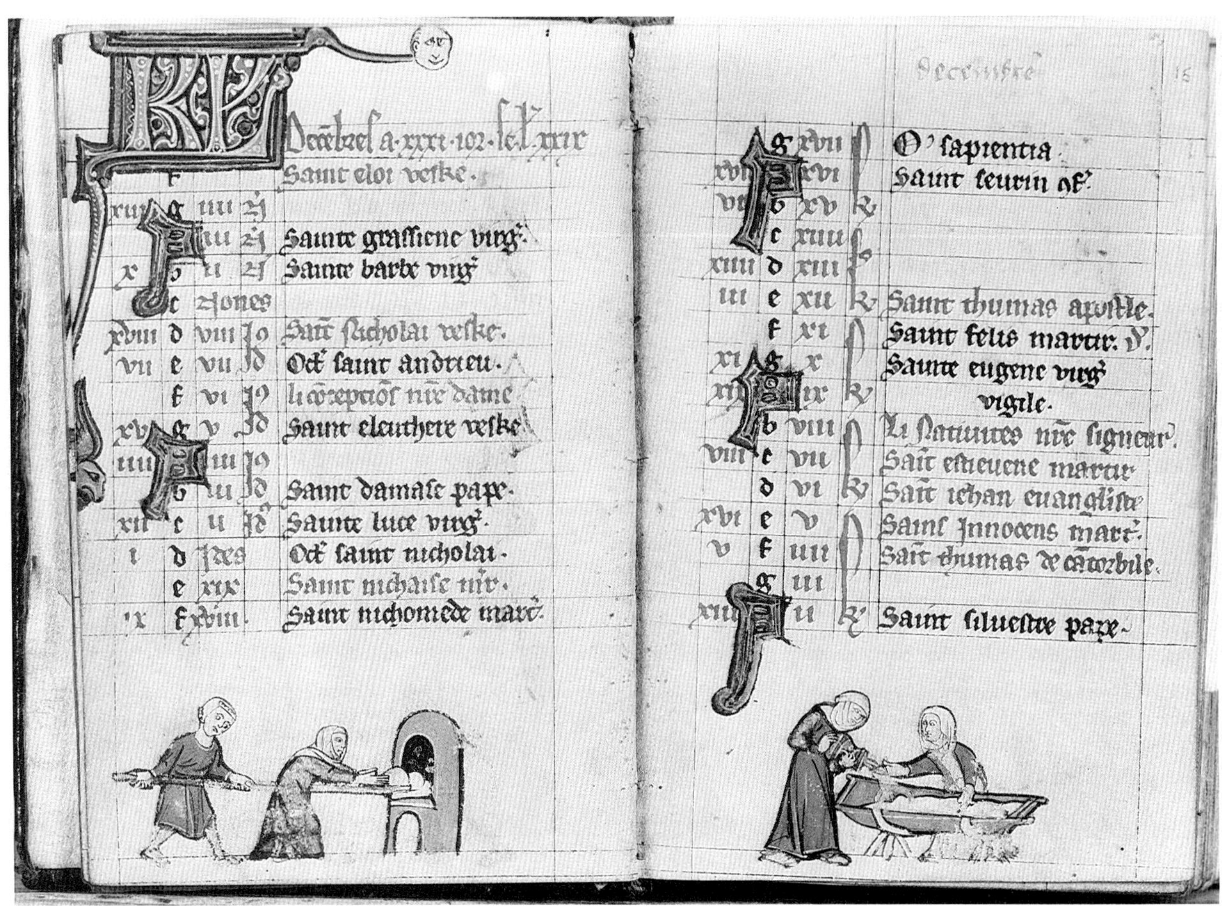

Fig. 25. December: *Baking Bread and Making Dough,* Belgium, Cambrai?, early 14th century (Walters 88, fols. 14v–15; Cat. No. 80).

(Pl. 15b). November is spent in the forests where peasants thrash oak trees or throw sticks into their branches to harvest the acorns as food for their pigs (Fig. 14k). Some illustrations for this month, as in the Flemish cycle, show the slaughtering of a fattened pig (Fig. 15k). The animal's neck is slashed and the blood drained into a pan.

The butchering of the pig, however, is most frequently found illustrating December, the first winter month. The last month of the year from the French cycle is illustrated with this theme, although the vignette shows a slight variation with the man's not slitting the pig's throat but stunning the animal first with a large mallet (Fig. 14*l*). A Flemish *Horae* of ca. 1500 features, instead of the slaughter, the subsequent roasting of the pig (Fig. 24). The slaughter and roasting of the pig provided meat for the long winter months—for those January feasts that began this discussion. The same is true for the other major labor associated with December, baking. The marginalia from the early fourteenth-century Flemish Book of Hours that provided us with the flirtatious mowers illustrate this month with a group of men and women mixing a large batch of dough in a trough and placing the loaves into an oven (Fig. 25). Children's games were sometimes used as ancillary scenes in Calendars. The subject of the December miniature from the Flemish cycle, however, is as rare as it is charming (Fig. 15*l*). The labor for this month consists of throwing snowballs!

CHAPTER V

Gospel Lessons

By the beginning of the fifteenth century the Gospel Lessons had become a regular feature of the Book of Hours. Traditionally these lessons follow the Calendar as the second part of the manuscript. This section is usually, but not always, illustrated, but more often than the Calendar, especially in manuscripts whose other texts contain cycles of miniatures.

Typically, the illustration of the Gospel Lessons consists of a cycle of four portraits of the evangelists, one placed at the beginning of each reading. The sequence, as follows, is: John, Luke, Matthew, and Mark. Reproduced here are a *John on Patmos* from the second decade of the fifteenth century by an artist related to the Parisian Master of Berry's *Cleres Femmes* (Pl. 16); a *Luke* from another Parisian *Horae* of about 1420 by a follower of the Boucicaut Master (Fig. 26); a *Matthew* from a manuscript of about 1470 and probably from Troyes (Fig. 27); and, finally, a *Mark* from an early sixteenth-century Rouen Book of Hours by a follower of the Master of Morgan 85 (Fig. 28). Miniatures like these follow a tradition from classical antiquity (and kept alive during the Middle Ages) of placing an author's portrait at the beginning of his text. These four pictures follow the iconography conventional for Books of Hours by showing the evangelists in the act of composing their texts on scrolls or writing them directly into bound codices. The practices and equipment of medieval scribes are reflected in these miniatures, such as the lectern in the miniature of Mark (Fig. 28), and the desks with tilted surfaces on which Luke and Matthew write (Figs. 26, 27). In the latter the illuminator has delighted in depicting the straps with weighted ends used in the Middle Ages to hold down the scrolls or pages of the book from which the scribe was copying.

In most miniatures for the Gospel Lessons, the evangelists are often accompanied by their symbols, as in each of the examples reproduced: the eagle for John, the ox for Luke, the angel for Matthew, and the lion for Mark. In a few rare cases, such as an early fifteenth-century Book of Hours from the area of Flanders and northern France (Cat. No. 81), the evangelists themselves are omitted and their symbols alone are used to identify their texts.

While the other three evangelists are normally shown at work in a scriptorium or study, John is nearly always shown seated on Patmos, the island to which he was banished by the Roman emperor Domitian and where, tradition has it, he wrote the Book of Revelation. Appropriately, the Virgin of the Apocalypse or the Beast of the Apocalypse appears in the background of a few representations of John seated on this desolate island. To these miniatures a playful motif is also sometimes added—a mischievous devil who tries to thwart the young evangelist's efforts at composition by stealing or overturning his ink well. This devil, lurking behind the trees in our miniature (Pl. 16), holds the ink pot in his claws, but his dark form is difficult to perceive amongst the shadows. A much larger and more visible devil hovers behind John in a miniature by the Master of the Harvard Hannibal (Fig. 29). Undetected by the evangelist, the devil has just grabbed the author's pen case, causing the contents of the attached ink well to spill on the ground. The devil in this miniature has been smudged—out of superstition demons and executioners in Books of Hours were sometimes defaced by later owners.

The four author portraits comprising the normal cycle for the Gospel Lessons are usually all the same size. In

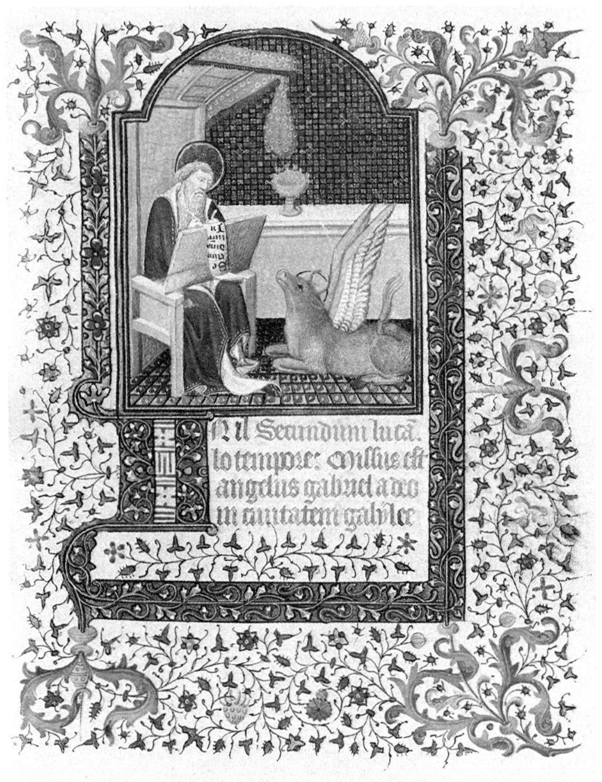

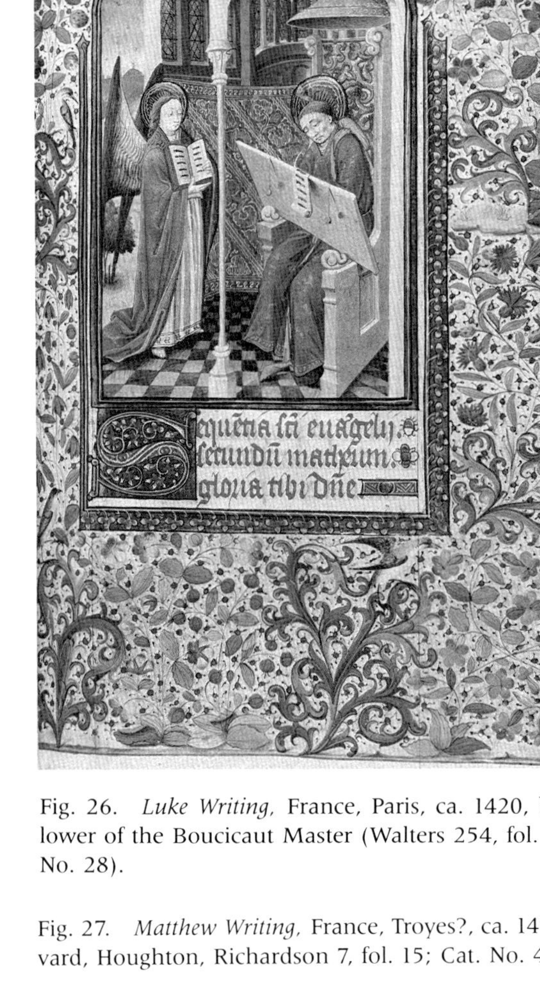

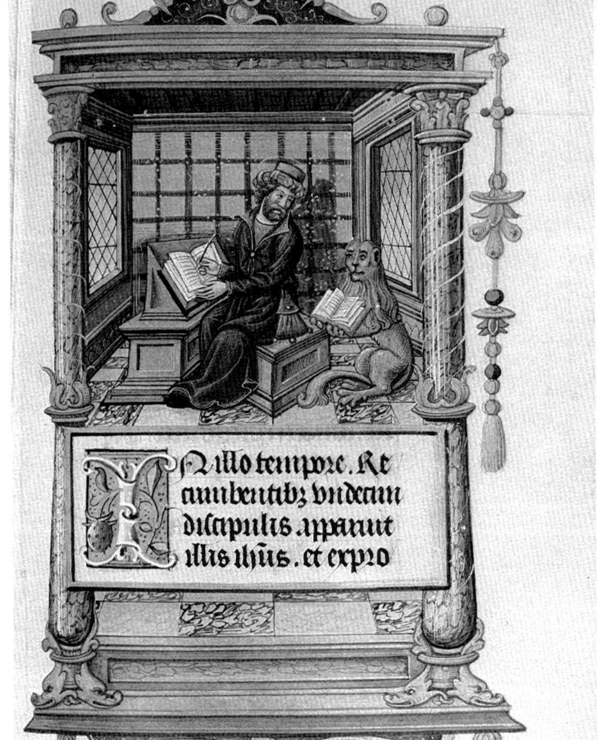

Fig. 26. *Luke Writing,* France, Paris, ca. 1420, by a follower of the Boucicaut Master (Walters 254, fol. 22; Cat. No. 28).

Fig. 27. *Matthew Writing,* France, Troyes?, ca. 1470 (Harvard, Houghton, Richardson 7, fol. 15; Cat. No. 48).

Fig. 28. *Mark Writing,* France, Rouen?, early 16th century, by a follower of the Master of Morgan 85 (Walters 455, fol. 22; Cat. No. 73).

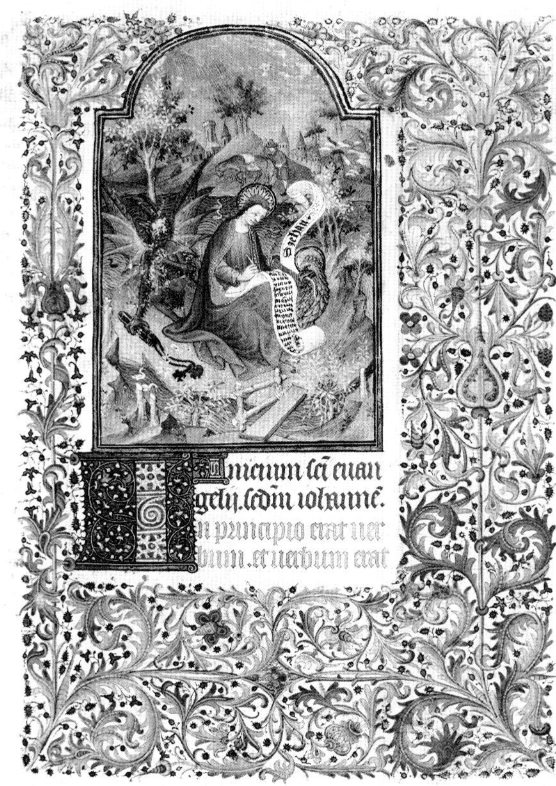

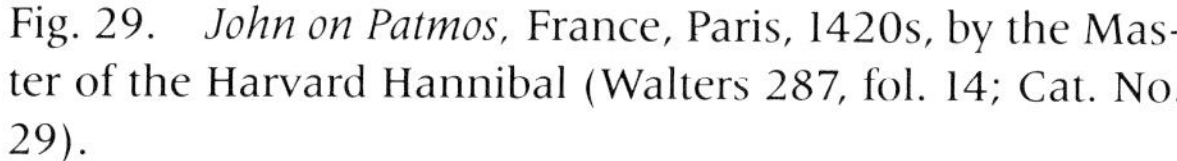

Fig. 29. *John on Patmos,* France, Paris, 1420s, by the Master of the Harvard Hannibal (Walters 287, fol. 14; Cat. No. 29).

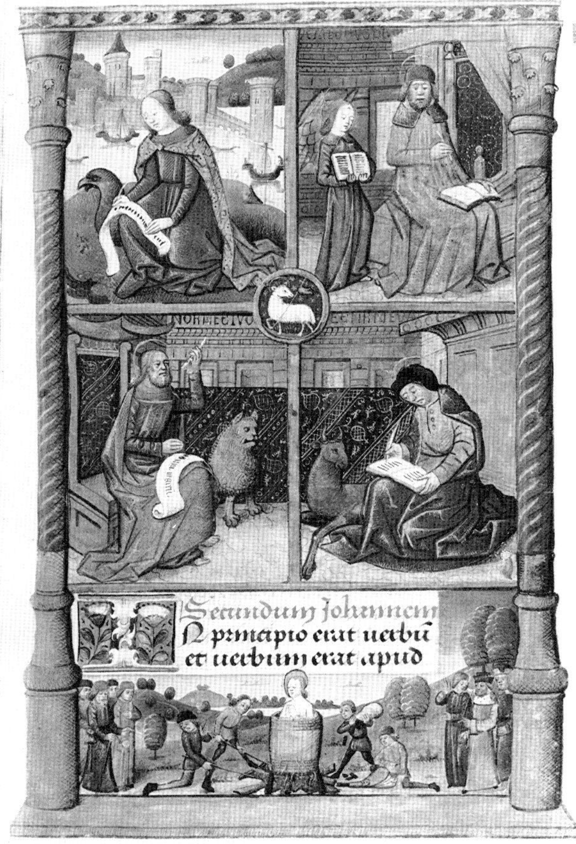

Fig. 30. *John on Patmos, Matthew Writing, Mark Examining Pen, Luke Writing,* border: *John Boiled in Oil,* France, Rouen, ca. 1480, by the Master of the Geneva Latini (Walters 224, fol. 7; Cat. No. 58).

some manuscripts, however, the first miniature, John on Patmos, is large, and the three following made smaller or reduced to historiated initials. In another solution to illuminating the Gospel Lessons that is frequently encountered, a single miniature of John is placed at the beginning of all four lessons.

Yet another manner in which artists treated this section was to provide one miniature that included all four evangelists. The Master of the Geneva Latini, working in Rouen in the second half of the fifteenth century, frequently employed this device (Fig. 30). Bored with the repetitiveness that an arrangement of four writing authors can produce, the Latini Master varies the evangelists' activities. While John and Luke write, Matthew reads and Mark examines the point of his pen. In other manuscripts the authors are shown sharpening their pens or quietly collecting their thoughts. Since the texts these men write relate the history of Christ's life on earth, the design by the Latini Master incorporates a medallion of the Lamb of God placed at the center of the quadripartite miniature like a boss, the central keystone, in a Gothic vault. John is given prominence by the inclusion, in the border, of the episode from his life when the Emperor Domitian attempted, unsuccessfully, to execute the saint by boiling him in oil.

Episodes from the lives of the evangelists are sometimes used for the Gospel Lessons instead of the more simple portraits. The most popular is Luke Painting the Virgin. According to medieval tradition, Luke was not only the composer of one of the Gospels, but also a painter who executed a portrait of the Virgin Mary. A miniature in Walters 281 is one of the earliest representations of this subject (Pl. 17). This Book of Hours, of the early 1430s, is the masterpiece and eponymous manuscript of the Master of Walters 281. Like portraits of the evangelists that unveil details of medieval scribal practices, representations of Luke as a painter often offer fascinating insights into artists' practices and techniques of the late Middle Ages and Renaissance.

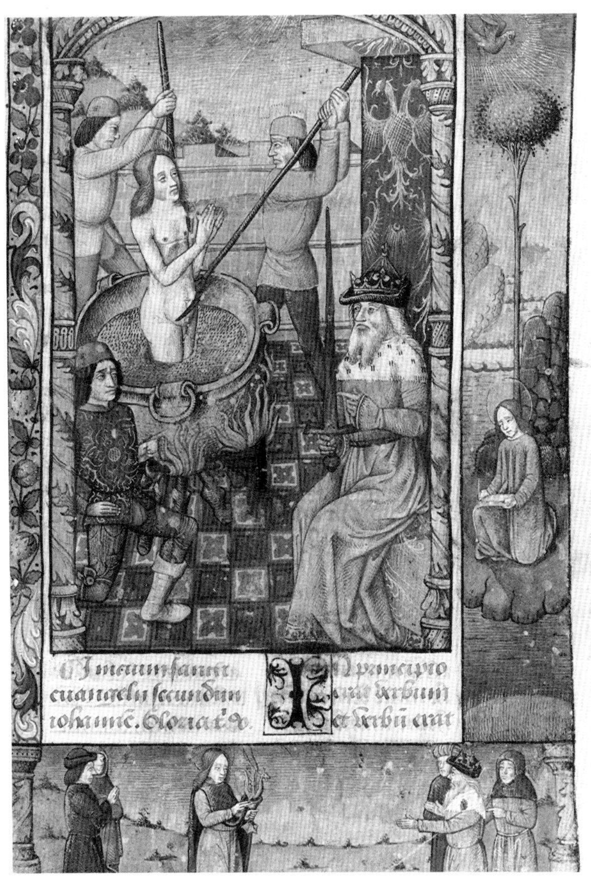

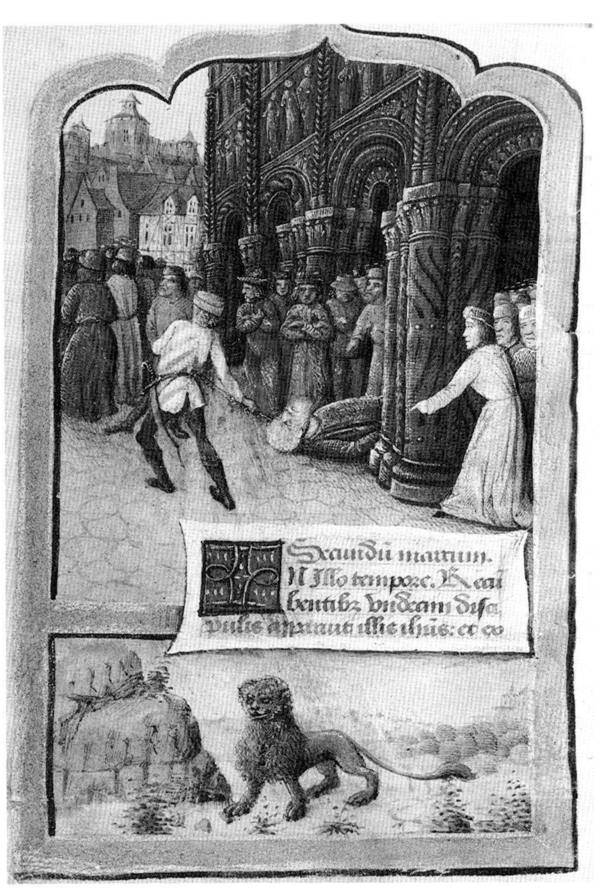

Fig. 31. *John Boiled in Oil,* border: *John on Patmos, John with the Cup of Poison,* France, mid-1480s (Walters 245, fol. 63; Cat. No. 64).

Fig. 32. *Mark's Body Dragged through the Streets of Alexandria,* France, Bourges?, late 1480s, by Jean Colombe (Walters 445, fol. 23v; Cat. No. 57).

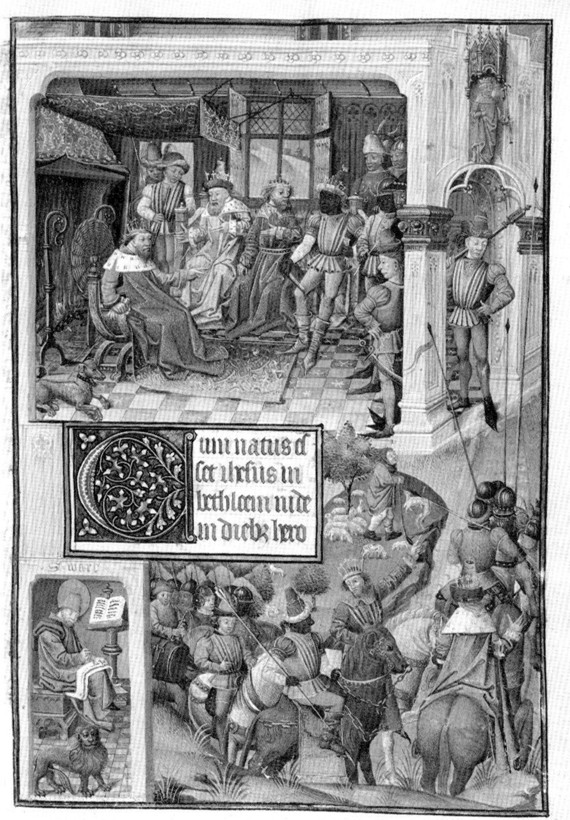

Fig. 33. *Magi before Herod,* border: *Magi Travelling, Matthew Writing* (mistakenly given Mark's attribute), France, Paris, or eastern France?, ca. 1465, by the Master of Jacques de Luxembourg (Morgan M.1003, fol. 16; Cat. No. 43).

This miniature shows, for example, the rectangular shape of the medieval palette and reveals that the picture's frame was an integral part of the panel's construction, decorated at the same time as the rest of the painting.

John Boiled in Oil, which was used as a border motif by the Master of the Geneva Latini, is sometimes the subject of a large miniature for his lesson. A dramatic depiction of this scene occurs in a richly illuminated Book of Hours from the mid-1480s (Fig. 31). While Domitian directs the torture from his imperial throne, his henchmen vainly try to expedite the saint's execution by pushing his body below the surface of the boiling oil. In the lower border, thwarting yet another attempt on his life, John blesses a cup of poison that the high priest Aristodemus (looking rather much like Domitian) challenged him to drink without harm. John's imbibing the poison with no ill effect converted the high priest, the local proconsul, and the latter's whole family. The right margin shows John banished to the island of Patmos where his eagle, his divine inspiration, appears in the sky above his head.

In a Book of Hours illuminated by Jean Colombe and filled with unusual iconographic features, the first miniature for the Gospel Lessons also illustrates Domitian's attempt on John's life. Instead of the torment itself, however, Colombe chose the anxious moments preceding it when John is led to the boiling cauldron. The other three miniatures in this cycle are equally unusual, but the most dramatic is that of Mark (Fig. 32). The picture shows his martyrdom at the hands of Alexandria's angry inhabitants who drag the aged apostle from the church in which he was celebrating Easter Mass.

The author portraits accompanying the Gospel Lessons in a Book of Hours illuminated by the Master of Jacques de Luxembourg are relegated to minor roles in the lower margins while the three large miniatures of the cycle (Luke's is missing) are devoted to rare illustrations closely related to the Gospel Lessons themselves. John's Gospel has a Last Supper that includes a dramatic encounter between Judas and a statue of *Ecclesia* decorating the portal of the building from which the traitor departs. Mark's Gospel is accompanied by a depiction of the Ascension, the subject of the text, that takes place in an expansive landscape. The miniature for Matthew's Gospel, which is read on the Feast of the Epiphany, illustrates the events related in that passage (Fig. 33). The Magi are shown first on their journey and then being interviewed by the suspicious Herod. Matthew, at the lower left, has mistakenly been given Mark's attribute.

CHAPTER VI

Hours of the Virgin

The heart of the Book of Hours is the devotional series of prayers known as the Little Office of the Blessed Virgin Mary, more commonly called the Hours of the Virgin. As the cult of the Virgin developed during the thirteenth century, this set of prayers, extracted from the breviary, grew in importance as it was embellished with other prayers and texts to form the popular prayer book known as the Book of Hours. If the Book of Hours can be compared to a Gothic cathedral, the Hours of the Virgin would be its high altar, placed at the center of the choir and surmounted by an elaborately carved and painted altarpiece on top of which would be mounted, at a height close to the soaring vaults of the church, a radiant statue of the Virgin Mary holding the Christ Child.

The Hours of the Virgin comprise eight separate sections, called Hours: Matins, Lauds, Prime, Terce, Sext, None, Vespers, and Compline. Each Hour consists of various combinations of psalms, hymns, prayers, and, in Matins, lessons, plus innumerable short ejaculations known as antiphons, versicles, and responses. (An outline of the Hours of the Virgin is given in the Appendix.) Early in the development of the Book of Hours, it became the tradition for the Hours of the Virgin to be accompanied by a series of pictures, either miniatures or historiated initials, devoted to those joyous events in the Virgin's life surrounding the infancy of Christ. The standard cycle, with common variations, is as follows:

Matins:	Annunciation
Lauds:	Visitation
Prime:	Nativity
Terce:	Annunciation to the Shepherds
Sext:	Adoration of the Magi
None:	Presentation in the Temple
Vespers:	Flight into Egypt (or, Massacre of the Innocents)
Compline:	Coronation of the Virgin (or, Flight into Egypt, Massacre of the Innocents, Assumption of the Virgin, Death of the Virgin)

The cycle of eight miniatures from the Book of Hours illuminated by the Master of Walters 281 is reproduced in its entirety (Fig. 34). During the following discussion the reader will be referred to this cycle as well as to that of Walters 288, a *Horae* illuminated by the Master of the Munich *Golden Legend*, reproduced in color (Pls. 1–8). These two cycles have been chosen because they follow the traditional iconography and because the quality of their illumination is very high.

Matins is accompanied by the Annunciation. As the miniatures in the two cycles show, the angel Gabriel delivers the message, that she has been chosen to be the Mother of God, to the Virgin who kneels at prayer in her private bedroom or a chapel (Pl. 1, Fig. 34a). In Walters 281, the Virgin prays in the nave of a church before the rood screen that encloses the main altar; in a Book of Hours that is one of the masterpieces by the Master of the Harvard Hannibal, Mary kneels directly in front of the altar in a small private chapel (Pl. 18). In all these miniatures the volume from which the Virgin prays is clearly meant to be a Book of Hours. Mary is, of course, a model of piety for the reader, but she is also, as depicted, a reflection of contemporaneous devotional practices. In most representations of the Annunciation Gabriel's opening words, "Ave Maria, gratia plena, Dominus tecum" ("Hail Mary, full of grace, the Lord is with you"), are written on a scroll. The "Ave Maria" prayer was to be recited before the Hours of the Virgin itself. The devotee reads Gabriel's joyful greeting and, aided by the words, gains spiritual intimacy with the Mother of God. This prayer, memorized by all medieval Christians in childhood, is hardly ever found actually written as a preface to the Hours themselves; a rare exception is Walters 267, where the "Hail Mary" is provided on the page facing the opening words of Matins (Pl. 14, Fig. 12).

Lauds is illustrated with the Visitation. The meeting of the Virgin and her cousin Elizabeth takes place in a hilly landscape through which, according to the Bible, Mary journeyed to the house of Elizabeth and Zacharias. In the *Visitation* from the cycle of Walters 281 (Fig. 34b) and another from a late fourteenth-century Book of Hours by the workshop of the Pseudo-Jacquemart de Hesdin (Fig. 35), Elizabeth gently touches the Virgin's swollen stomach, emphasizing the words she uttered upon seeing Mary, "Blessed are thou among women and blessed is the fruit of thy womb." In another late fourteenth-century *Horae,* this one painted by followers of Jacquemart de Hesdin, the older woman reverently kneels as she touches the Virgin's stomach (Pl. 19). In Walters 288, illuminated by the Master of the Munich *Golden Legend,* medallions in the border contain ancillary episodes relating to Elizabeth's own son: the birth, the circumcision and naming of John the Baptist, and his entering the wilderness (Pl. 2).

The miniature for Prime is the Nativity. The depiction in a French Book of Hours of the early fourteenth century shows the Virgin resting on her bed, tended by a tired Joseph, as the ox and ass guard the Christ Child (Fig. 36). The Nativities reproduced in the cycles show a dramatic change in the iconography of Christmas Day (Pl. 3, Fig. 34c). In both miniatures, as well as in a *Nativity* from a late fifteenth-century Book of Hours by Jean Poyet (Pl. 20), Mary and Joseph kneel in adoration of the newborn Christ. This change is related to a detailed account of the Nativity seen in visions by the fourteenth-century saint, Bridget of Sweden. These visions, which describe the adoration of the Savoir by his parents, exerted a lasting influence on the art of the fifteenth century, as these and innumerable other miniatures testify.

Terce is accompanied by the Annunciation to the Shepherds. The historiated initial from a small French Book of Hours from the late thirteenth century already contains many of the motifs that will continue to appear throughout the next two hundred years (Fig. 37). In a rural landscape two shepherds, whiling away their time with bagpipes, are surprised by the sudden appearance in the sky of the angel announcing the birth of mankind's Savior. The theme of the interruption of the shepherd's humble concert also appears, again with bagpipes, in the illustration from the cycle by the Master of Walters 281 (Fig. 34d). In a miniature for Terce from a Flemish Book of Hours illuminated by Willem Vrelant, it is a very lively group of shepherds dancing in a circle whose attention the angel attracts with his announcement (Pl. 21). In the miniature by the Master of the Munich *Golden Legend,* the standing shepherd, the older of the two with his gray beard, shields his squinting eyes from the bright and startling rays of the angel's glory (Pl. 4). His younger companion, his meal interrupted, hurries to put on his shoes. The border medallions continue with their activities: they race off to the manger, shyly pay their respects to the Christ Child, and, at bottom, depart in a joyful celebration of these wondrous events.

The miniature for Sext is the Adoration of the Magi. That by the Master of Walters 281 shows one Magus doffing his crown, another opening the lid of his luxurious offering, and the third and eldest kneeling to kiss the Savior's foot as the latter sits, as if enthroned, on the Virgin's lap (Fig. 34e). The Sext miniature in Walters 288 is accompanied by border motifs showing the three kings tracking the bright star's course from the top of an observatory, their journey, and, at the bottom, their interview with Herod (Pl. 5). The journey of the Magi also appears in the historiated border of a Book of Hours illuminated by a follower of the Masters of Morgan 96 and 366 (Pl. 22). In the *Adoration of the Magi* from a charming Flemish *Horae* illuminated by a follower of the Master of Anthony of Burgundy (Philippe de Mazerolles?), an embarrassed Joseph shyly peers at his distinguished visitors from behind a curtain (Fig. 38).

The Hour of None is accompanied by the Presentation in the Temple. In a tiny (2¼ x 1¾") Book of Hours from France of about 1360, a nervous and shivering Christ is presented by his mother to the high priest Simeon (Fig. 39). This motif of a frightened Christ appears in other depictions of the Presentation. In each of the miniatures from the two cycles (Pl. 6, Fig. 34f), a handmaiden carries a basket of turtle doves, the sacrificial offering, and either she or Joseph holds a candle for the procession of lights following the ceremony (from which we derive the name Candlemas). Some miniatures conflate the Presentation of Christ to Yahweh with the Savior's Circumcision, the Jewish rite that, according to tradition, was performed a week after Christ's birth (and celebrated on January 1st). A clear allusion to the Circumcision is made by the prominent knife resting on the altar in the *Presentation* of the Flemish Book of Hours by the Master of Anthony of Burgundy follower (Pl. 23). The blood that Christ shed

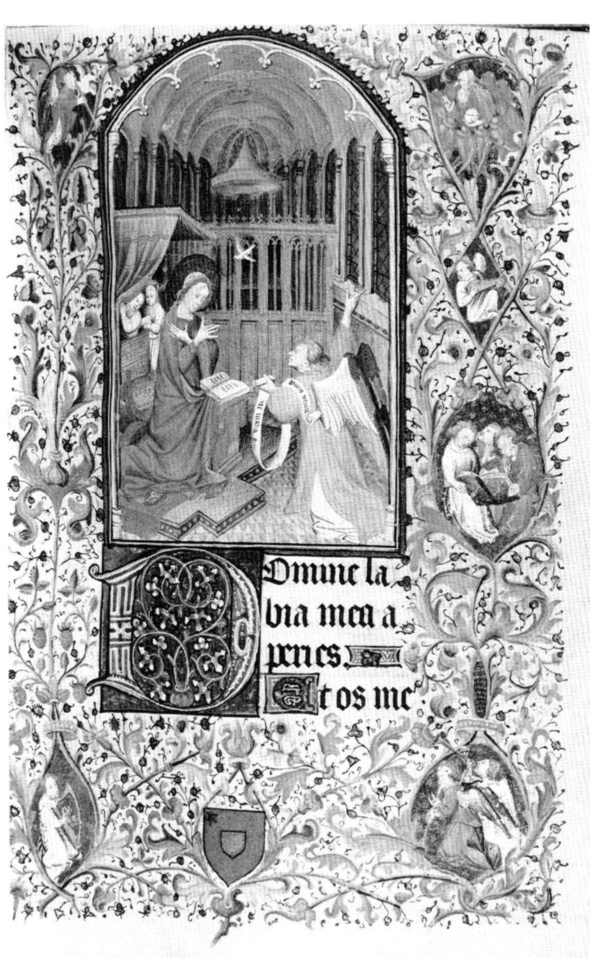
omine la
bia mea a
peries.
t os me

a

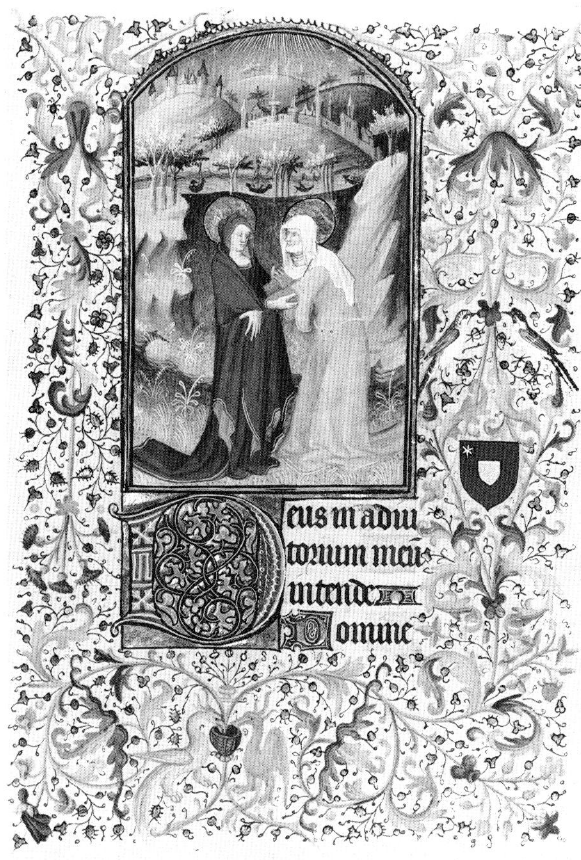
eus in adiu
torium meu
intende
omine

b

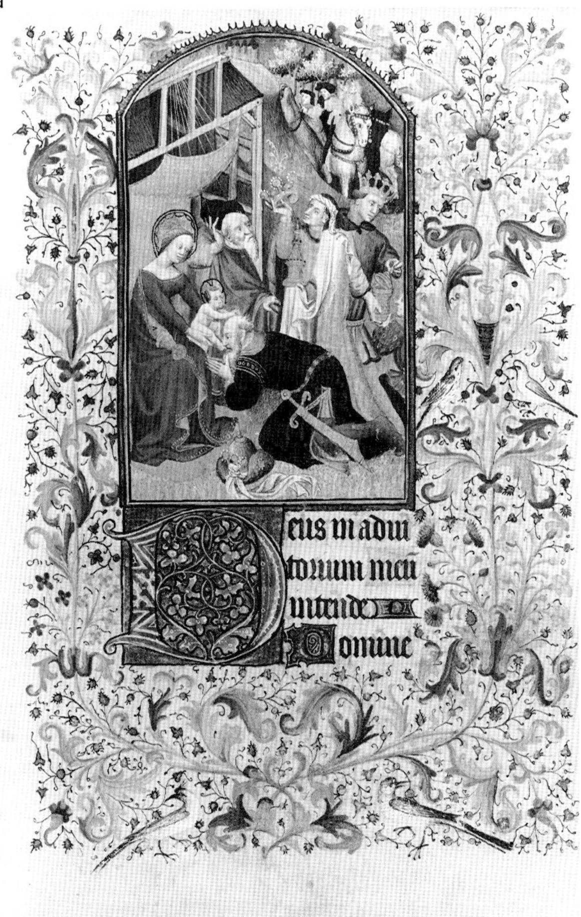
eus in adiu
torium meu
intende
omine

e

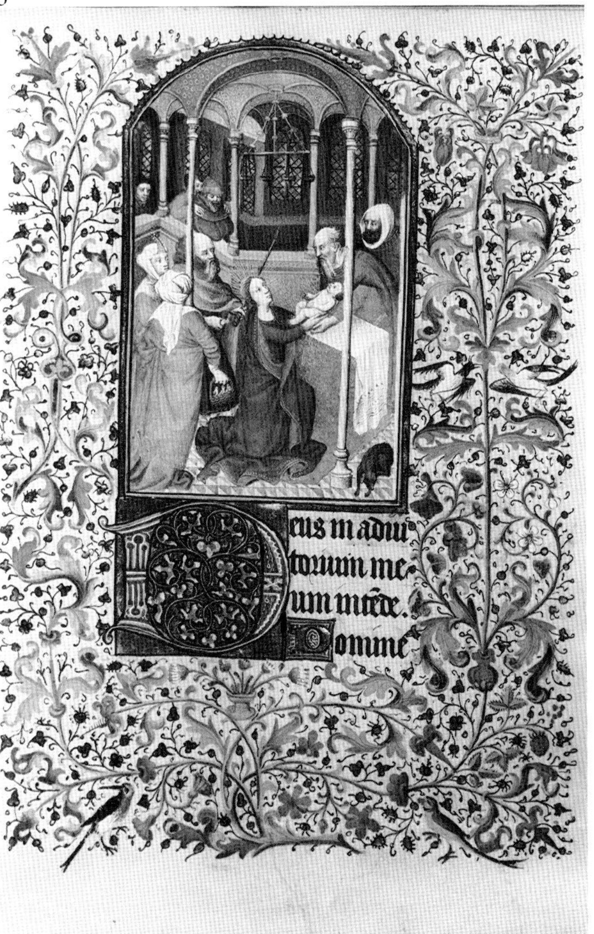
eus in adiu
torium me
um intende.
omine

f

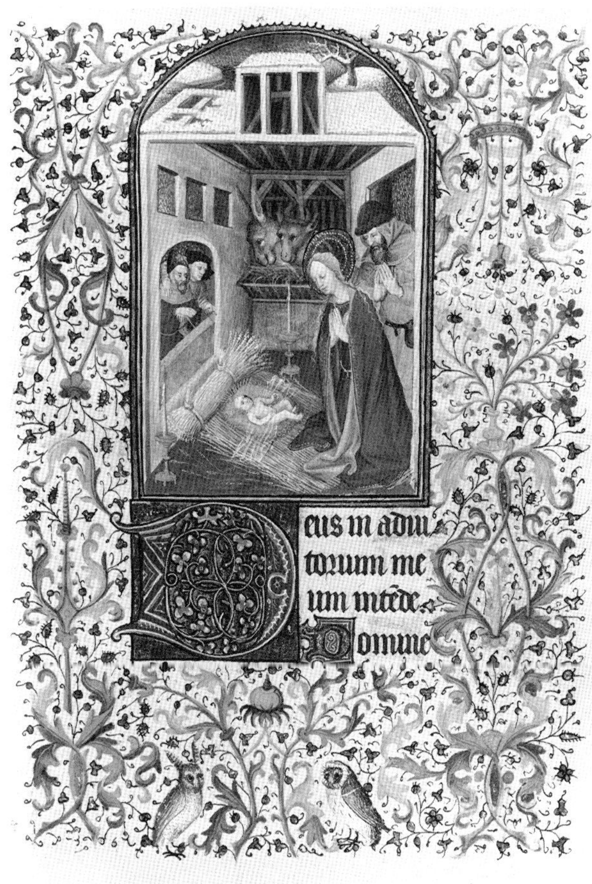

c

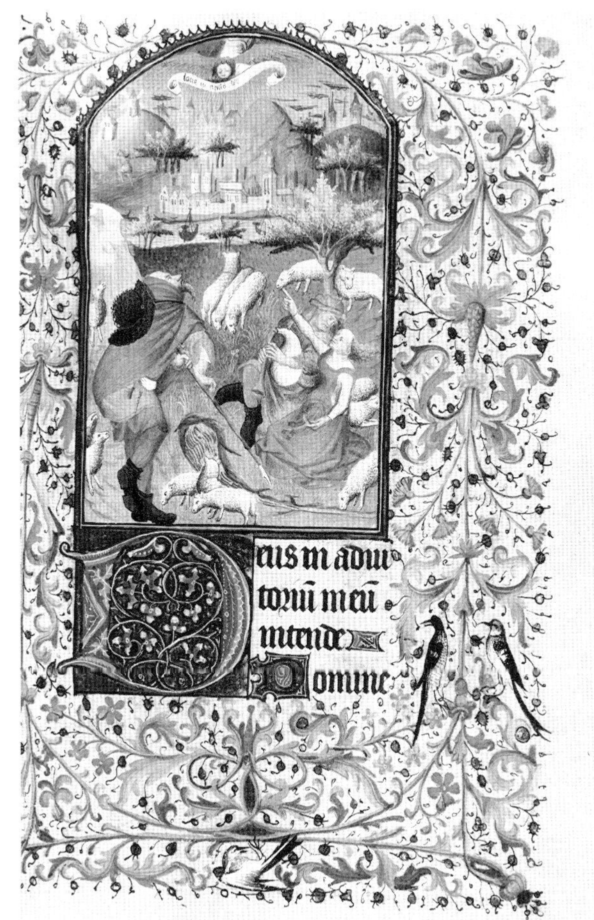

d

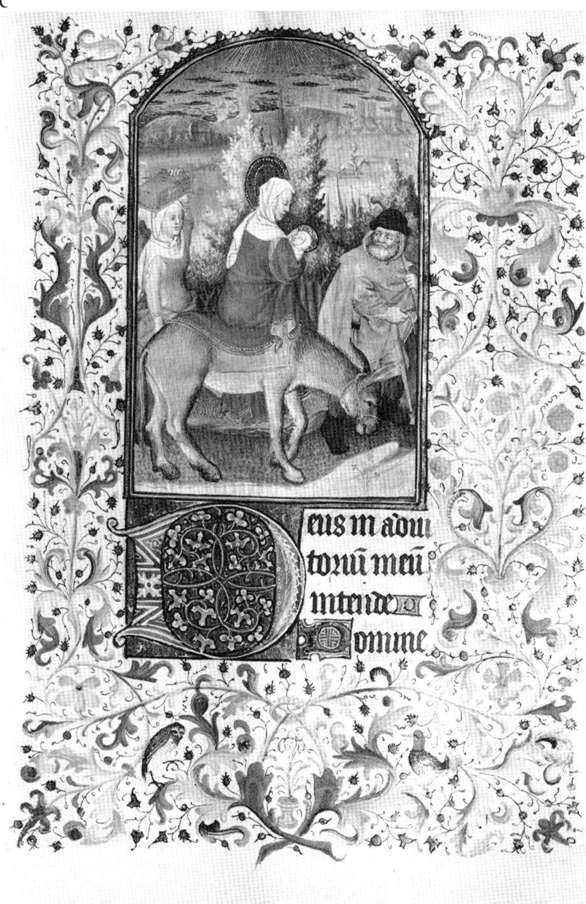

g

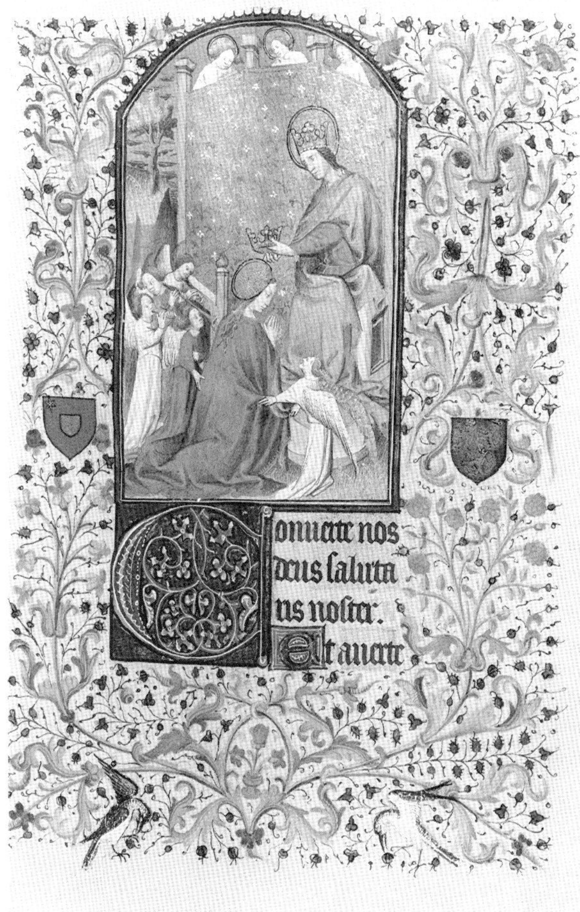

h

PREVIOUS PAGES

Fig. 34. Infancy Cycle, northern France or Belgium, Tournai, ca. 1430–35, by the Master of Walters 281 (Walters 281; Cat. No. 35).

a) *Annunciation* (Matins, fol. 31)
b) *Visitation* (Lauds, fol. 64)
c) *Nativity* (Prime, fol. 79)
d) *Annunciation to the Shepherds* (Terce, fol. 85)
e) *Adoration of the Magi* (Sext, fol. 91)
f) *Presentation in the Temple* (None, fol. 97)
g) *Flight into Egypt* (Vespers, fol. 103)
h) *Coronation of the Virgin* (Compline, fol. 112)

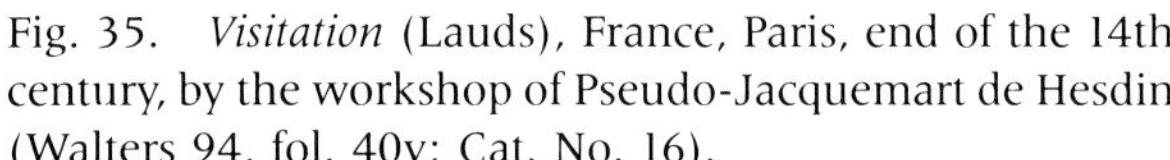

Fig. 35. *Visitation* (Lauds), France, Paris, end of the 14th century, by the workshop of Pseudo-Jacquemart de Hesdin (Walters 94, fol. 40v; Cat. No. 16).

Fig. 36. *Nativity* (Prime), northern France, early 14th century (Walters 90, fol. 61v; Cat. No. 7).

Fig. 37. *Annunciation to the Shepherds* (Terce), northern France, late 13th century (Walters 39, fol. 91; Cat. No. 3).

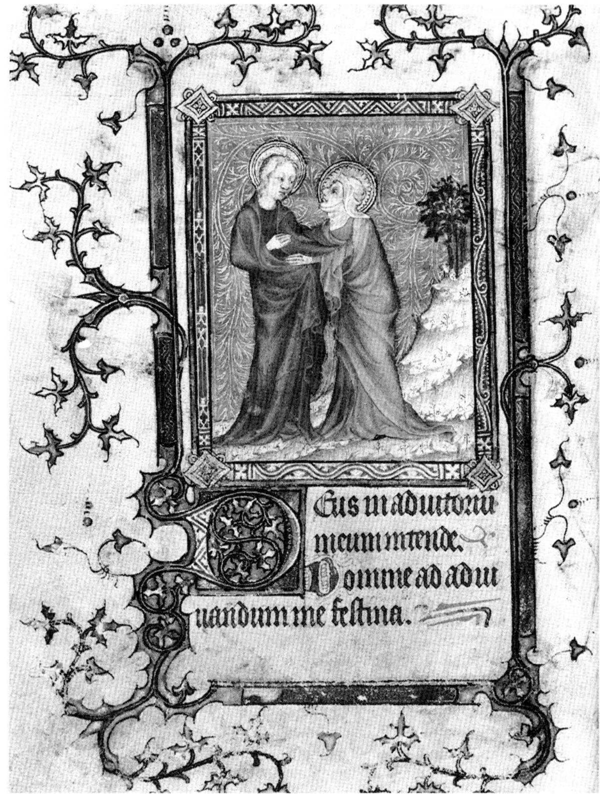

35

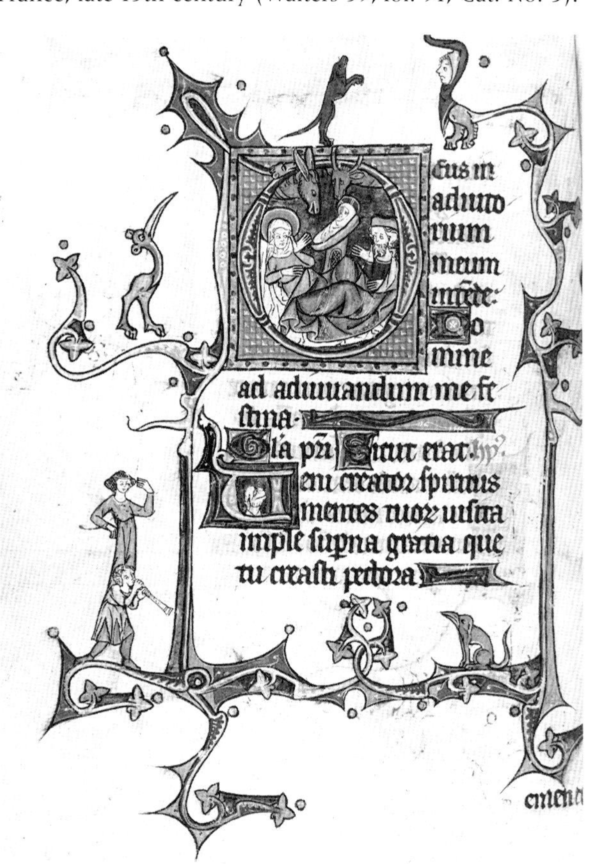

36

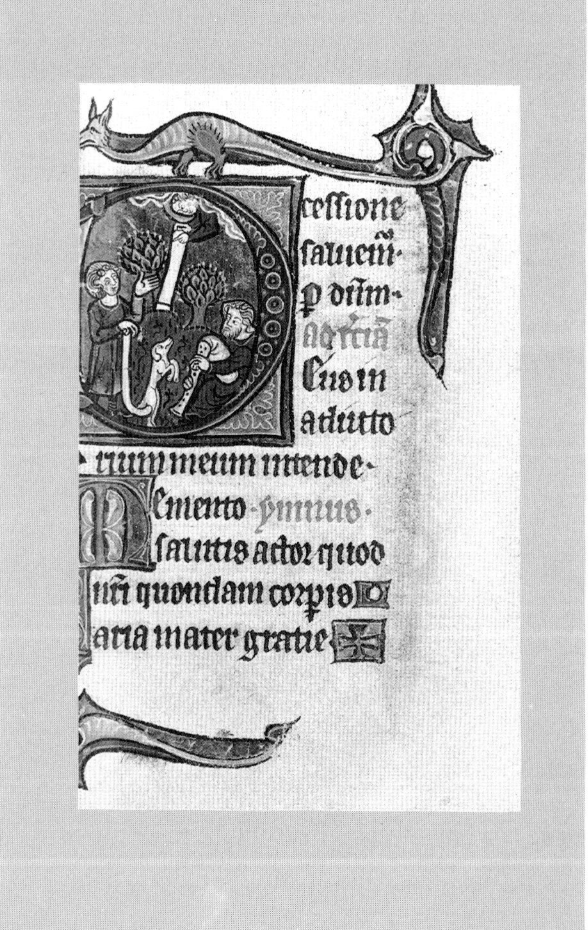

37

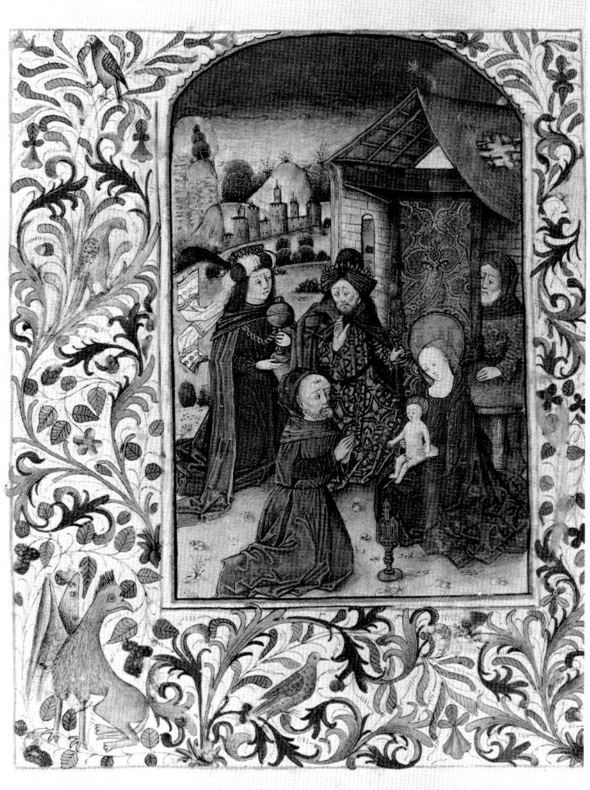

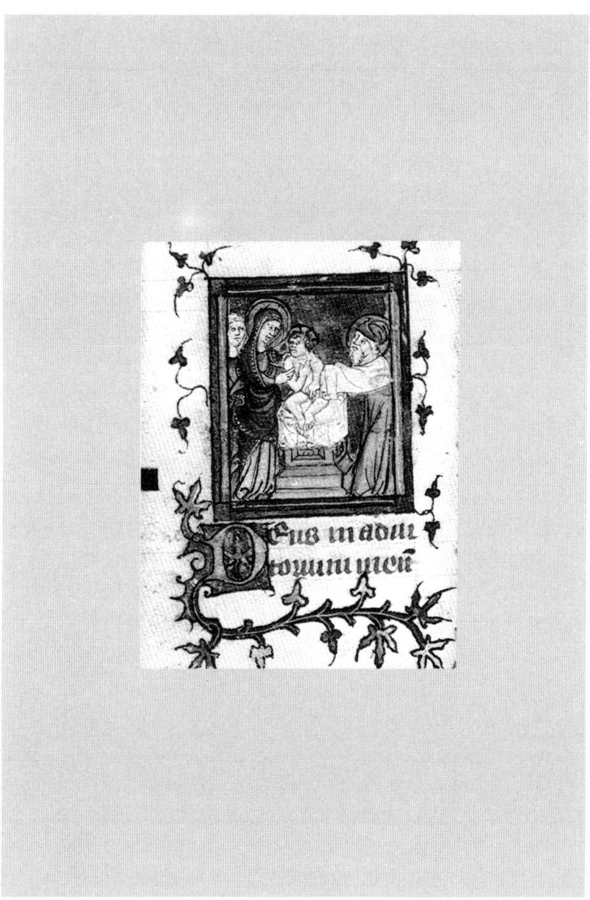

at his circumcision was interpreted as the first he offered for mankind's salvation and the event was viewed as an allusion to his Passion.

Vespers is most frequently illustrated with the Flight into Egypt. The finely wrought example by the Luçon Master shows only the Holy Family as they emerge from behind a hill (Pl. 24). The *Flight* by the Master of Walters 281 includes a handmaiden balancing luggage on the top of her head (Fig. 34g). In the miniature by the Master of the Munich *Golden Legend*, God the Father looks down protectively from the sky over the Holy Family's flight (Pl. 7). The bottom border medallion depicts the *Massacre of the Innocents*, the terrible event from which the family flees. A second roundel shows a soldier questioning a farmer who is cutting wheat with a sickle. This motif is given greater prominence in the background of the *Flight into Egypt* in the Flemish Book of Hours by the follower of the Master of Anthony of Burgundy, two of whose miniatures we have already touched on (Fig. 42). The story, typical of those fanciful legends of which the Middle Ages were so fond, relates that the Holy Family, in their flight, passed a farmer sowing his field. The Virgin told the farmer that, should anyone ask, he was to tell the truth, that he saw them at the time of sowing. In a miraculous flash, the wheat grew and ripened so that when Herod's soldiers were told that the persons they sought had passed at the time of sowing, they turned back thinking that this had been some months before.

Sometimes Vespers is illustrated by the Massacre of the Innocents, as in Walters 86, a late thirteenth-century French Book of Hours, that has a particularly dramatic depiction (Fig. 40). A towering soldier, huge sword in hand, is seconds away from killing a baby as the mother tries to pull the child to safety. At the left a second mother, in a gesture of horror, brings her hands to her face. In another early manuscript, produced in Lorraine in the early fourteenth century and with unusual stencil-cut borders, the massacre is over and a pair of soldiers, looking rather distraught, stands on top of a pile of bleeding babies (Fig. 41).

Compline, the last of the Hours of the Virgin, was also at times illustrated by the Flight into Egypt, as in the Edith G. Rosenwald Hours of the Library of Congress (Fig. 43). This tiny, jewellike manuscript was painted by the Master of the *Livre du Sacre de Charles V*, one of the most important illuminators of the second half of the fourteenth century and one who, as his

Fig. 38. *Adoration of the Magi* (Sext), Belgium, Bruges?, by a follower of the Master of Anthony of Burgundy (Philippe de Mazerolles?) (Walters 272, fol. 86v; Cat. No. 97).

Fig. 39. *Presentation in the Temple* (None), northern France, ca. 1360 (Walters 84, fol. 81v; Cat. No. 12).

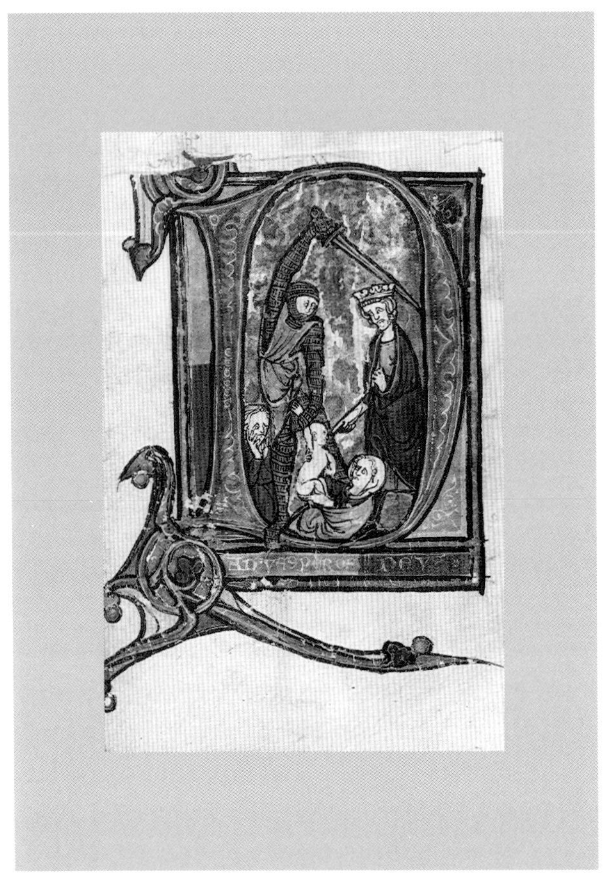

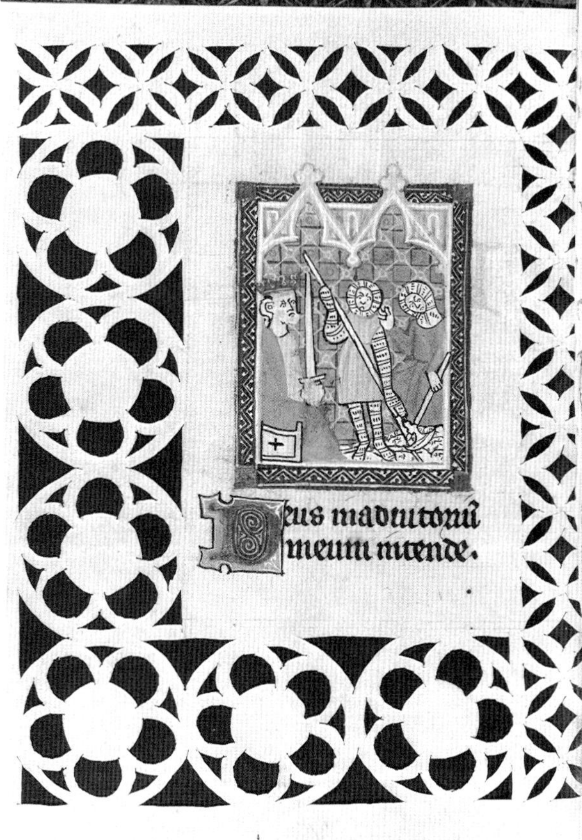

name indicates, worked for King Charles of France.

The most frequent illustration for Compline, however, as both cycles show, is the Coronation of the Virgin (Pl. 8, Fig. 34h). Angels hold the Virgin's cloak or supply music as she receives the crown as Queen of Heaven from her son the King. The Assumption of the Virgin is also used for Compline in some Books of Hours. This motif appears in the side border in Walters 223, a manuscript already mentioned, where the miniature itself is of the *Coronation* (Fig. 44). The bottom border of this page is illustrated with the *Death of the Virgin*, another theme that is sometimes used for Compline, albeit rarely. The Virgin's death is the subject of the large Compline miniature in a Book of Hours from the workshop of the Boucicaut Master (Pl. 25). Mary has just died; her soul, in the form of a small child, rests on Christ's left arm. The apostles gather around the bed to mourn and pray—we recognize the beardless John at the top of the bed and Peter, dressed in a black cope, sprinkling the Virgin's body with holy water.

The traditional Infancy cycle for the Hours of the Virgin is sometimes supplanted, or accompanied, by another cycle, that of the Passion of Christ. The Passion series was a frequent alternative to the Infancy cycle in the fourteenth century, losing popularity, especially in France, by the fifteenth. Passion cycles are frequently found in the fifteenth century, however, in Flanders, the Netherlands, in England and in manuscripts made for English use, and also in France at the turn of the sixteenth century. The usual sequence of episodes illustrated is as follows:

Matins:	Agony in the Garden
Lauds:	Betrayal
Prime:	Christ before Pilate
Terce:	Flagellation
Sext:	Christ Carrying the Cross
None:	Crucifixion
Vespers:	Deposition
Compline:	Entombment

Matins is usually illustrated with the Agony in the Garden, as in the example from a Bruges Book of Hours illuminated by a painter of the Gold Scrolls group (Fig. 45). In this manuscript, as is the case with some Books of Hours, each of the eight large Passion miniatures is

Fig. 40. *Massacre of the Innocents* (Vespers), northeastern France, late 13th century (Walters 86, fol. 88v; Cat. No. 4).

Fig. 41. *Massacre of the Innocents* (Vespers), France, Lorraine, early 14th century (Walters 93, fol. 81v; Cat. No. 6).

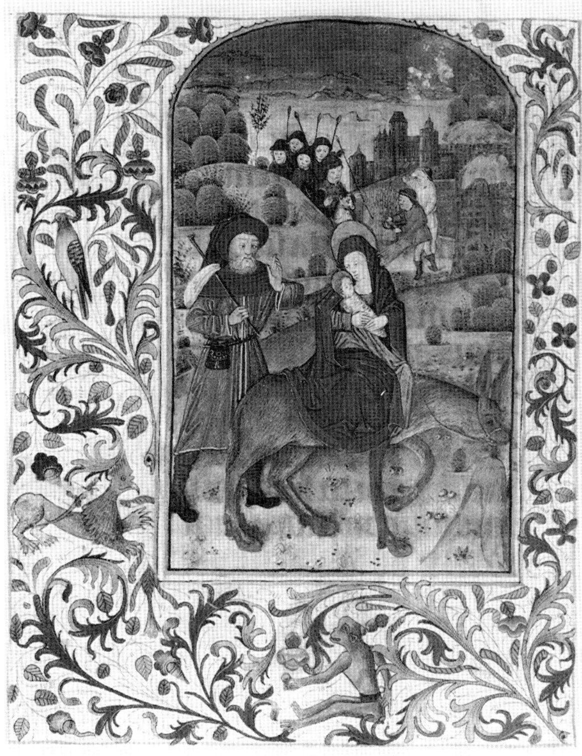

Fig. 42. *Flight into Egypt* (Vespers), Belgium, Bruges?, by a follower of the Master of Anthony of Burgundy (Philippe de Mazerolles?) (Walters 272, fol. 96v; Cat. No. 97).

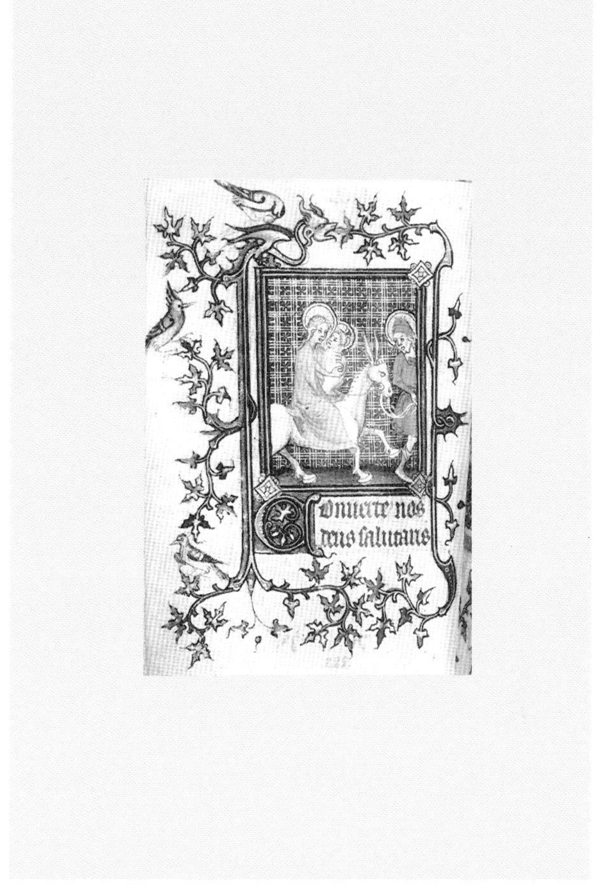

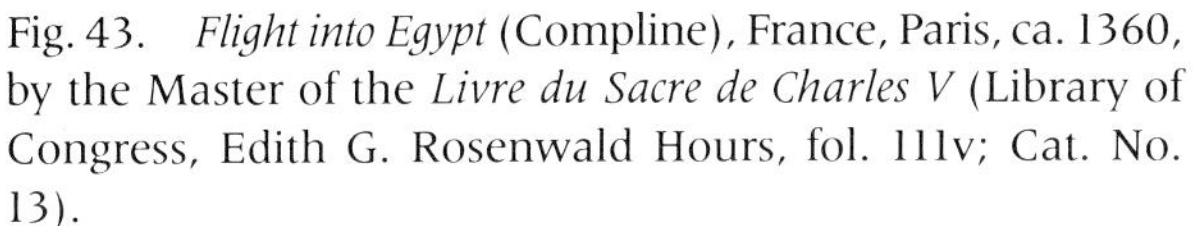

Fig. 43. *Flight into Egypt* (Compline), France, Paris, ca. 1360, by the Master of the *Livre du Sacre de Charles V* (Library of Congress, Edith G. Rosenwald Hours, fol. 111v; Cat. No. 13).

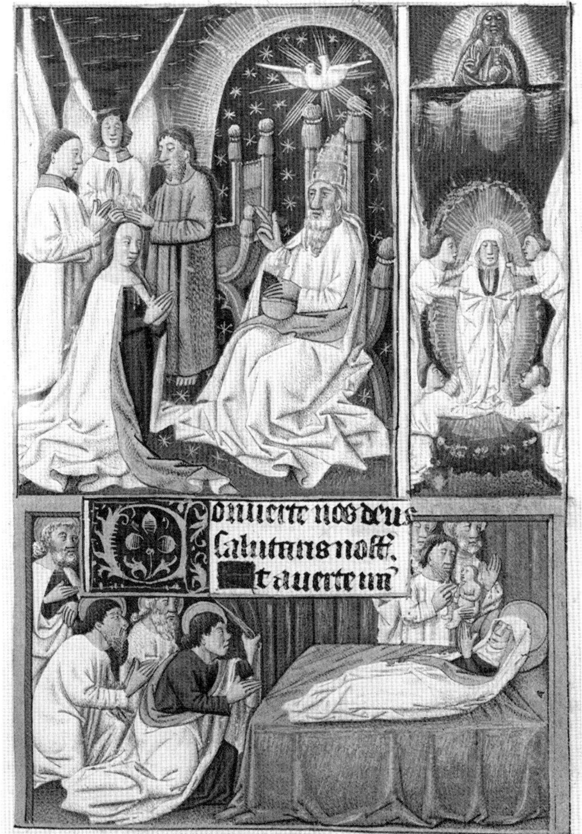

Fig. 44. *Coronation of the Virgin*, border: *Death and Assumption of the Virgin* (Compline), France, probably Poitiers, 1460s, by a follower of the Masters of Morgan 96 and 366 (Walters 223, fol. 76; Cat. No. 46).

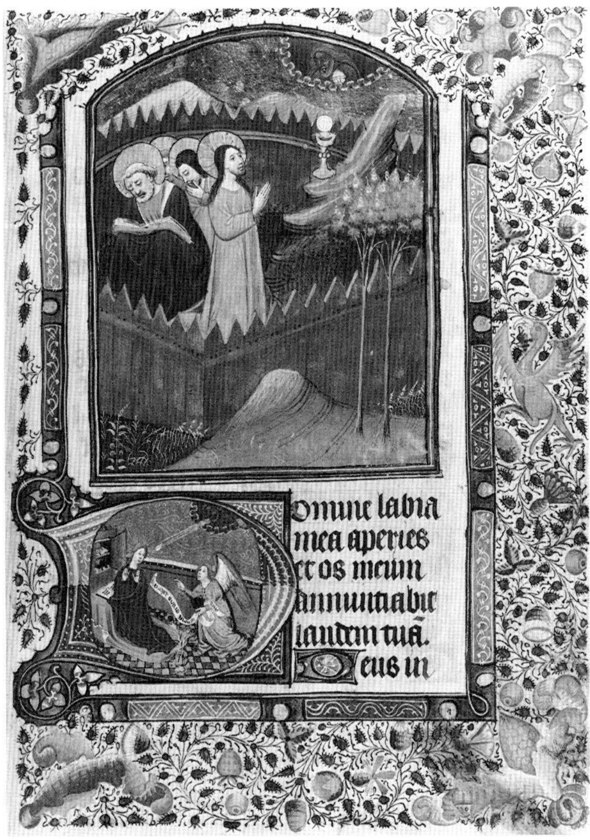

Fig. 45. *Agony in the Garden,* initial: *Annunciation* (Matins), Belgium, Bruges, 1440s, by a painter of the Gold Scrolls group (Walters 173, fol. 26; Cat. No. 89).

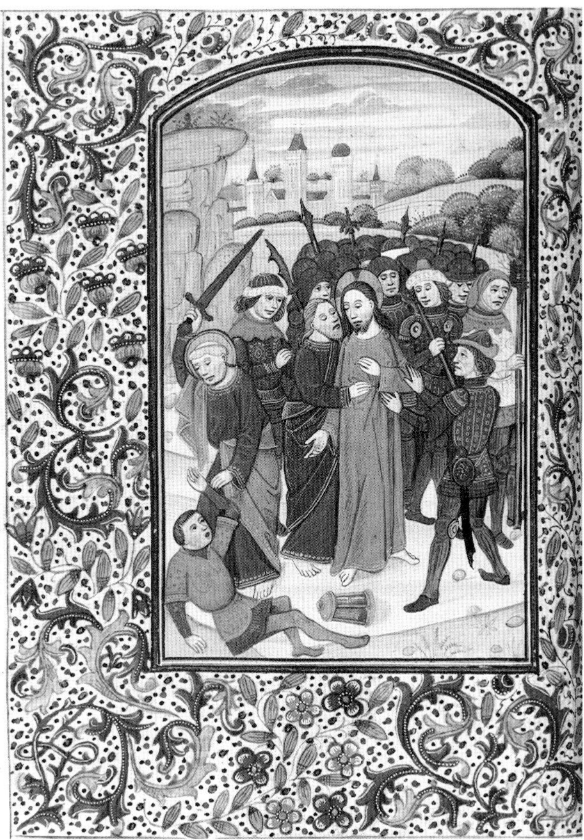

Fig. 46. *Betrayal* (Lauds), Belgium, Bruges, ca. 1470, by the workshop of Willem Vrelant (Walters 195, fol. 31v; Cat. No. 95).

also accompanied by the traditional scene from the Infancy cycle; the *Annunciation*, here, is depicted below the miniature in a large historiated initial.

Lauds is accompanied by the Betrayal, as in a *Horae* of about 1470 from the workshop of Willem Vrelant, one of the most prolific Flemish illuminators and one whose shop produced scores—the latest tabulation reaches sixty—of Books of Hours (Fig. 46). In the Lauds miniature Judas leans towards Christ to plant his traitor's kiss on the Savior's cheek. Christ, already resigned to the forthcoming events, gestures towards the fallen Malchus whose ear he will restore after the blow from Peter's sword.

The miniature for Prime shows Christ before Pilate, illustrated here by a miniature from a Dutch Book of Hours of the second decade of the fifteenth century (Pl. 26a). The book itself is small, not even four inches tall, and the miniatures even smaller, but the delicate figures are painted with great power and dignity. Christ, his hands bound, looks down at the floor while Pilate, his eyes also cast down in a look of resignation, reaches

Fig. 47. *Flagellation* (Terce), England, ca. 1470 (Harvard, Houghton, Richardson 34, fol. 37v; Cat. No. 114).

Fig. 48. *Christ Carrying the Cross* (Sext), France, Paris, last quarter of the 13th century (Walters 97, fol. 40; Cat. No. 2).

Fig. 49. *Crucifixion* (None), southern Belgium, ca. 1300 (Walters 85, fol. 32; Cat. No. 78).

Fig. 50. *Deposition* (Vespers), Holland, ca. 1435, by one of the Masters of Zweder van Culemborg (Walters 188, fol. 71; Cat. No. 108).

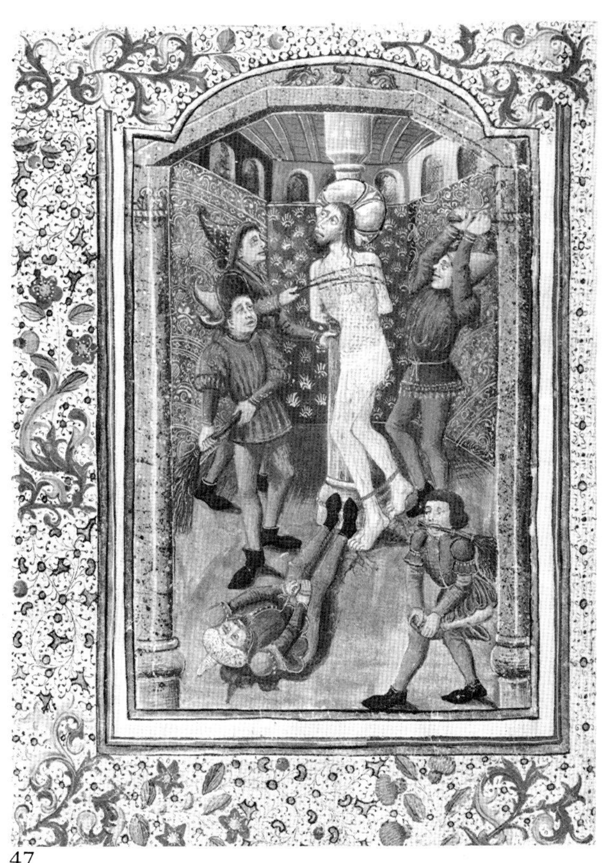

47

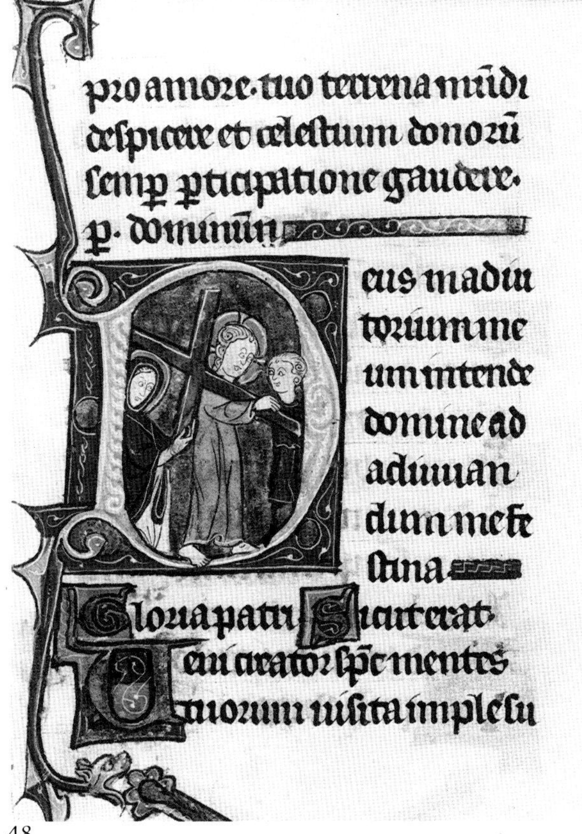

48

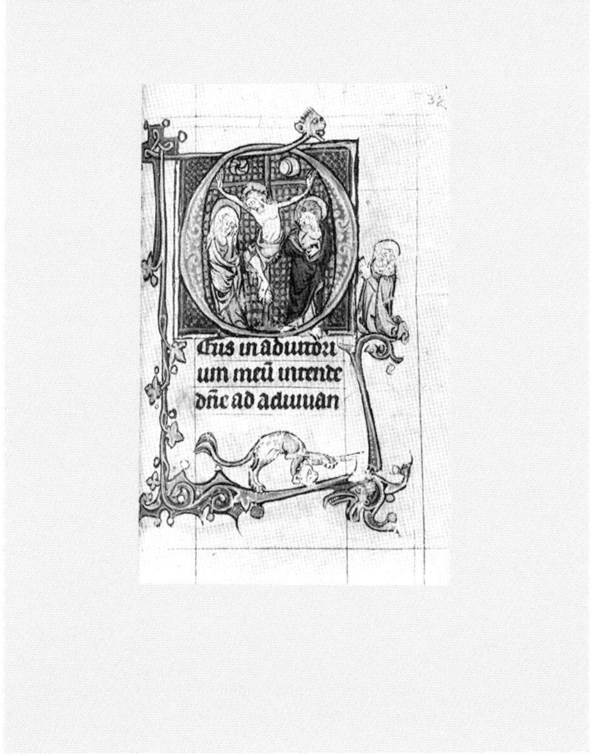

49

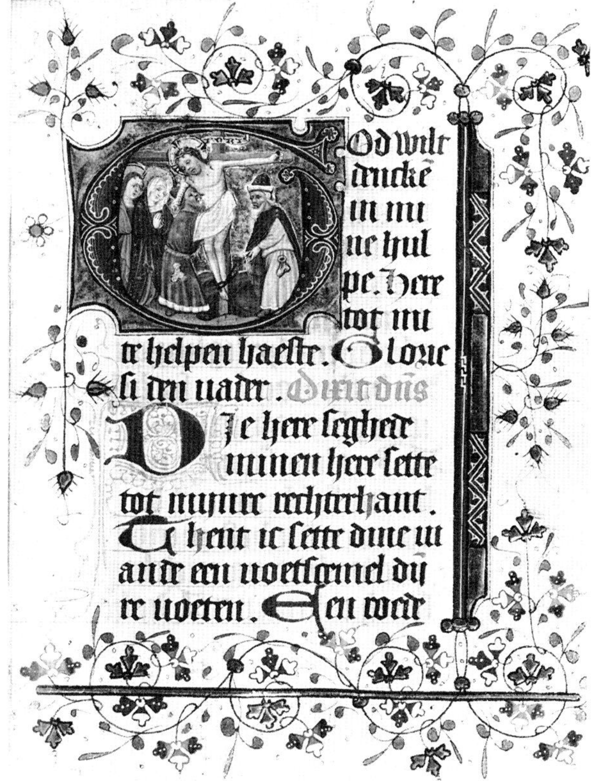

50

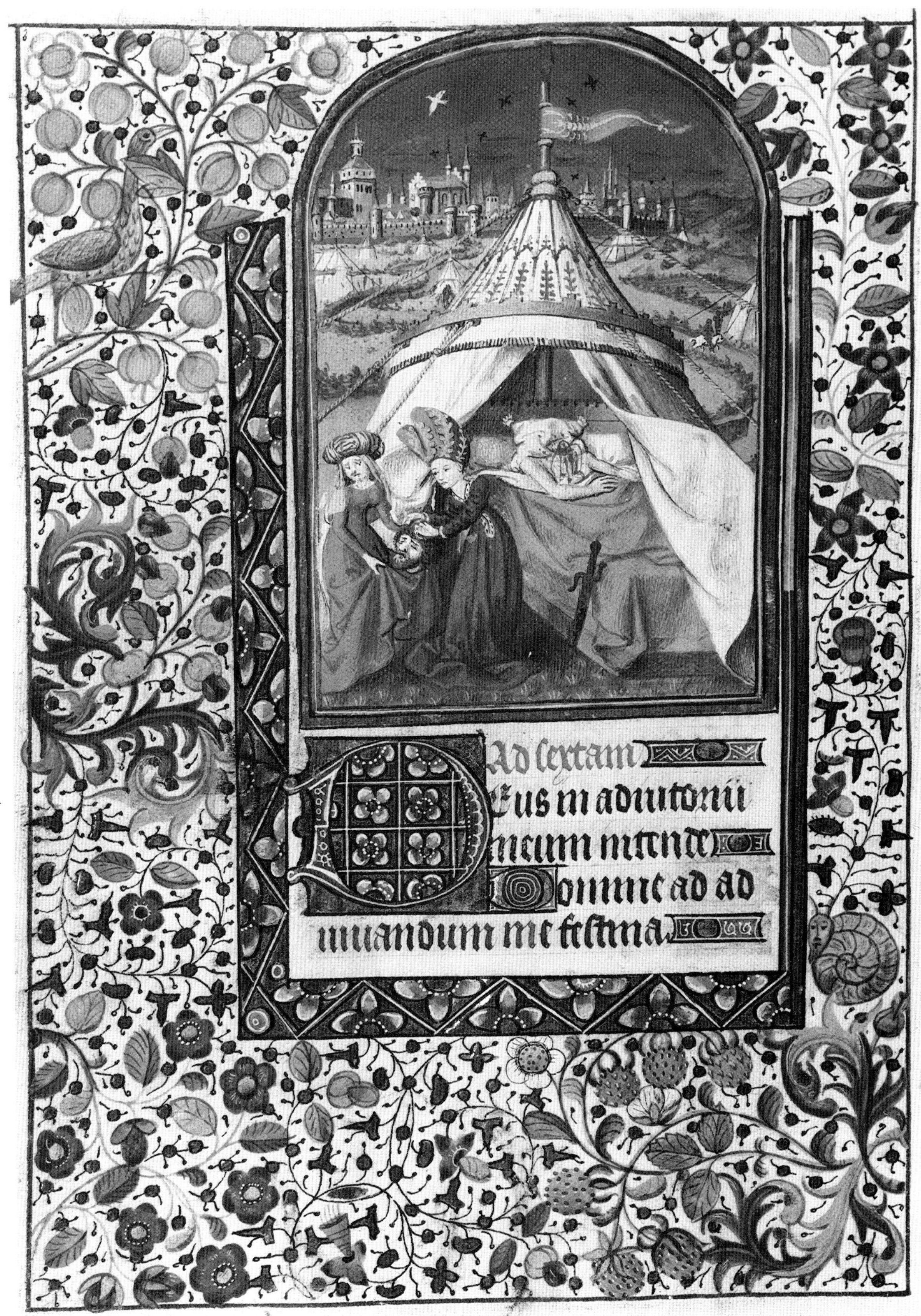

Fig. 51. *Judith Decapitating Holofernes* (Sext), France, Savoy, ca. 1465–70, by an artist of the Hours of Louis de Savoie (Walters 292, fol 59v; Cat. No. 44).

toward the basin of water to wash his hands. (Of the four Dutch *Horae* included in this study, Cat. Nos. 107–110, all but one have Passion cycles illustrating their Hours of the Virgin.)

Terce is illustrated with the Flagellation. The miniature from the same manuscript shows a Christ whose greenish and emaciated body is covered with bleeding wounds (Pl. 26b). One torturer attacks the Savior with bound sticks and the other with a cat-o'-nine-tails. This painting, gruesome as it is, is almost sweet when compared to the *Flagellation* in an English Book of Hours of about 1470 (Fig. 47). In this picture Christ receives the ministrations of five brutes who attack their victim with obvious relish. Their lashings leave patterned trails on Christ's body and raise so much blood that it runs down his body in rivulets onto the floor. The young tormentor at the lower right rolls his hose down to his knees; looser clothes (in addition to exposing his behind shamelessly) will offer the youth greater agility and more efficient use of his energies.

Sext is usually accompanied by a miniature of Christ Carrying the Cross, as in an early Parisian Book of Hours from the last quarter of the thirteenth century (Fig. 48). The Virgin, in her compassionate role as coredemptrix, lifts the end of the cross in an attempt to ease her son's burden. The Passion cycle in this *Horae*, as is sometimes the case in manuscripts whose Hours of the Virgin are illustrated with a Passion cycle, is introduced by a Marian subject; in this book the opening miniature depicts a Madonna with a kneeling patroness.

None, the hour of Christ's death, is illustrated with a Crucifixion, as seen in a minute Book of Hours (only 2⅝" tall) dating to about 1300, the earliest Flemish manuscript in this study (Fig. 49). Christ, suspended on the cross in the twisted but elegant form characteristic of Gothic art, is flanked by the Virgin and John. In the border, on a delicately spiraling tendril, kneels the patroness of the book.

Vespers is accompanied by the Deposition, as shown in a small but finely painted historiated initial by one of the Masters of Zweder van Culemborg from a Dutch Book of Hours of about 1435 (Fig. 50). The Virgin and John watch sorrowfully while Joseph of Arimathaea embraces the dead body of Christ as it falls forward; Nicodemus, having removed the nail from the Savior's right hand, pulls out the one securing his feet. The Gospels relate that Joseph wrapped Christ's body in a linen shroud before burial, and it is this cloth that is draped over Joseph's arm as he leans forward to support the collapsing body.

Compline, the last of the Hours of the Virgin, is illustrated with the Entombment, here found in Walters 172, a luxurious *Horae* of about 1440 illuminated by the Master of the Ghent Privileges, a gifted painter from the second quarter of the fifteenth century, and the workshop of the Master of Guillebert de Mets. The Passion cycle in this manuscript consists of eight full-page pictures that are accompanied, on facing pages, by large historiated initials illustrated, as was the Gold Scrolls *Horae* that began this discussion, with traditional Infancy scenes. The large Compline miniature of the Entombment (Pl. 27) is complemented by an initial of the Massacre of the Innocents. In the miniature the Virgin, comforted by John, turns her gaze from the scene as Joseph of Arimathaea (with the beard) and Nicodemus (applying ointment), assisted by two other men, place Christ's body inside the sarcophagus. The large open arcade of the tomb itself provided the Ghent Privileges Master with an excuse for including in his composition a spacious landscape with rolling hills, a distant city whose towers are reflected in the calm river, and (one of the artist's specialties) a deep blue, star-filled sky.

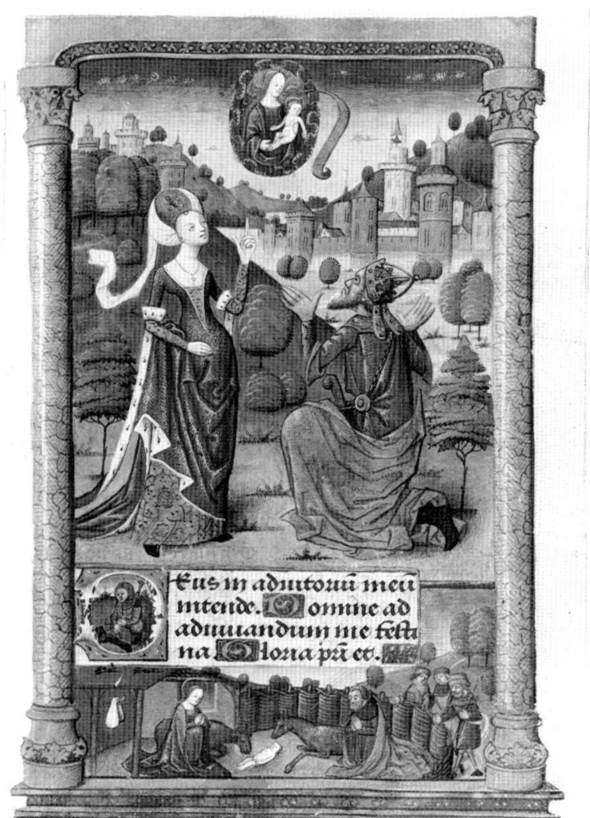

Fig. 52. *Augustus and the Tiburtine Sibyl*, border: *Nativity* (Prime), France, Rouen, ca. 1480, by the Master of the Geneva Latini (Walters 224, fol. 30; Cat. No. 58).

Not all Hours of the Virgin are illustrated with Infancy or Passion cycles; there are some fascinating and instructive exceptions. In Walters 40, a French Book of Hours from the third quarter of the thirteenth century, and the earliest manuscript included in this study, the Hours of the Virgin are marked by a series of historiated initials showing a woman, and in one case a man, kneeling in prayer before an altar (Fig. 3). One reason for this somewhat repetitive series can be found in the presence of a long cycle of prefatory miniatures (originally with no textual accompaniment), containing both Infancy and Passion illustrations, that forms a sort of elaborate frontispiece to the whole volume. The presence of such a cycle precluded duplication of these themes within the Hours themselves. Indeed, at this early date in the development of the Book of Hours, large pictures had not yet made the move from the front of the book into the body of the text itself.

The patron who commissioned Walters 219 (portrayed kneeling before the Madonna in one of the miniatures) obviously wanted something out of the ordinary in his prayer book (Cat. No. 32). The Hours of the Virgin are illustrated with a cycle that includes such scenes as *David Excising the Tongue of Goliath, Death Invading a Garden Party,* and the *Crossing of the Red Sea.* The keys to these iconographic puzzles are to be found written on the scrolls unfurled by the figures in the initials below the miniatures: quotations on these banderoles, taken from the psalms contained in the Hours themselves, suggested themes or provided images for this unique cycle.

The Marescalci Hours, illuminated in Savoy in the late 1460s, is the work of an artist of the Hours of Louis de Savoie, a highly inventive painter whose stylistic and iconographic repertoire broke all late medieval conventions. Eschewing New Testament iconography for the Hours of the Virgin altogether, the artist offers a cycle of Old Testament heroes and heroines depicted at climactic moments of their careers. These include Abel being murdered in a particularly bloody manner, Noah welcoming the grand procession of animals into the ark, Moses presenting the Tablets of the Law and, in a second miniature, turning his rod into a snake before a terrified pharaoh, and, in the most dramatic miniature of all, Judith absconding with the decapitated head of Holofernes (Fig. 51).

In a Rouen Book of Hours of about 1480 painted by the Master of the Geneva Latini, the usual scenes from the Infancy of Christ have been relegated to minor roles in the bottom border of each page while the large miniatures have been given over to Old Testament or pagan prefigurations of these New Testament events. At Prime, for example, the traditional *Nativity* is placed in the lower margin while the *Vision of the Ara Coeli,* the Tiburtine Sibyl's interpretation of Augustus' heavenly vision of a mother and child as a reference to the forthcoming Savior, is the subject of the main miniature (Fig. 52). A similar rich cycle of Old Testament typological scenes (events believed to foreshadow those in the New Testament) illustrates the Hours of the Virgin in a *Horae* illuminated by Jean Colombe (Cat. No. 57). Here, in addition to those for the Hours of the Virgin, prefigurations are also used for the Hours of the Cross and the Hours of the Holy Spirit (providing an extra fourteen miniatures) that have been interspersed within the Hours of the Virgin themselves. Both of these Books of Hours reveal the influence of typological treatises such as the *Biblia pauperum* and the *Speculum humanae salvationis.* These two texts were widely circulated during the fifteenth century in manuscript, blockbook, and incunabular editions, and their iconographic schemes, which flank a New Testament event with two from the Old Testament or pagan antiquity, were very influential.

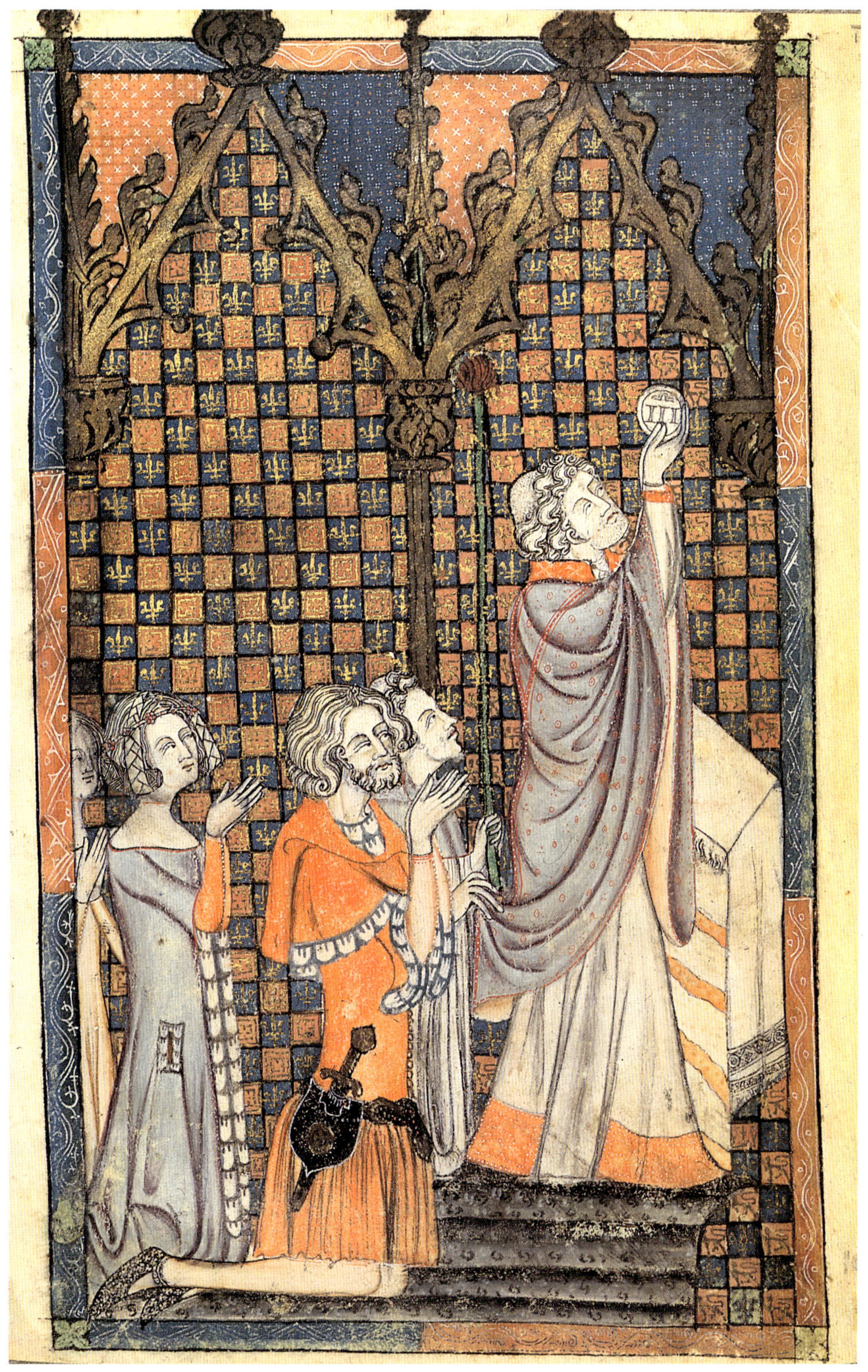

Pl. 13. *Butler Family at Mass* (Prefatory miniature), England, ca. 1340 (Walters 105, fol. 15; Cat. No. 112).

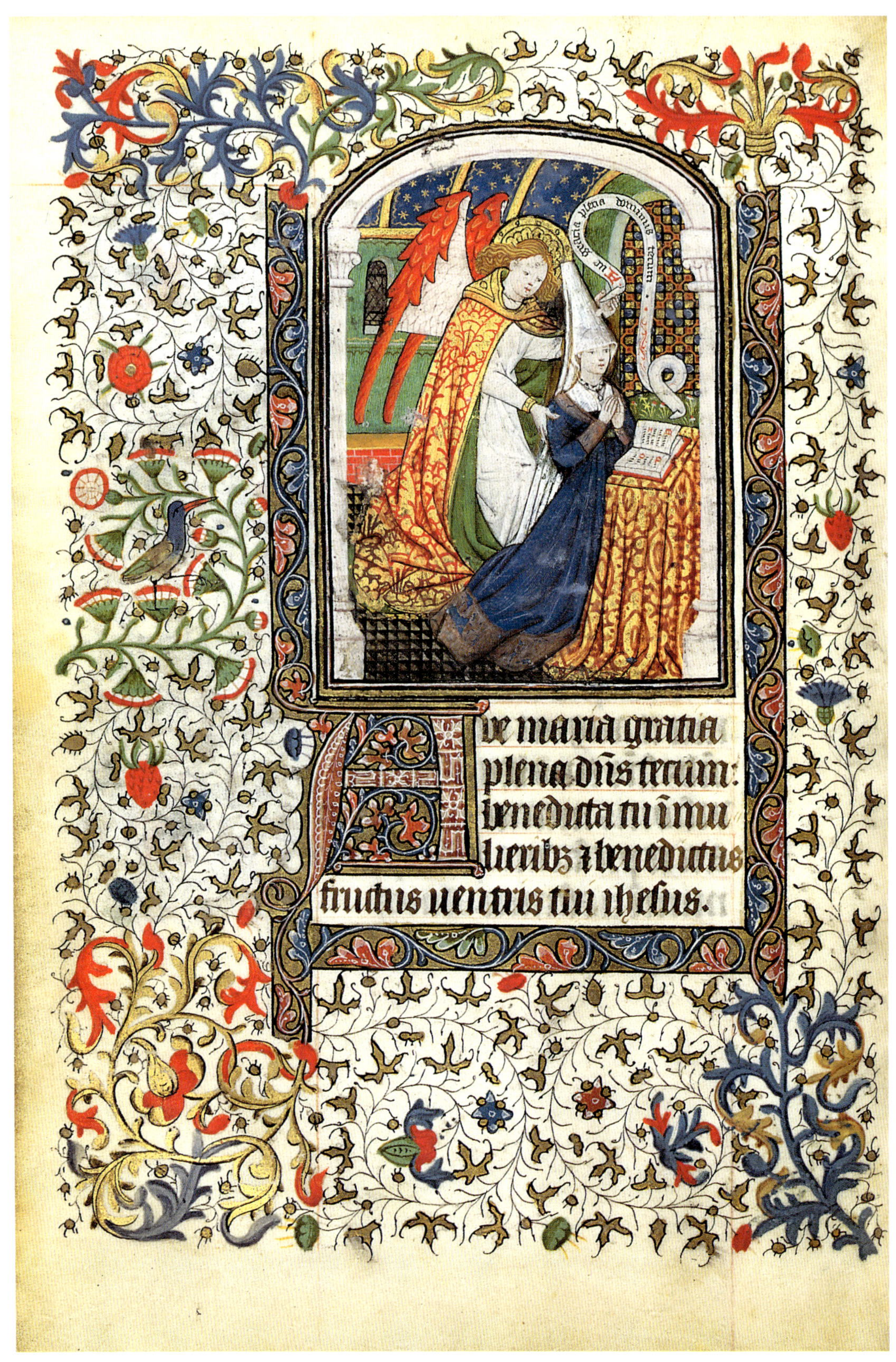

Pl. 14. *Gabriel Presenting a Kneeling Patroness* (Hours of the Virgin: Matins), northern France or southern Belgium, 1450s (Walters 267, fol. 13v; Cat. No. 40).

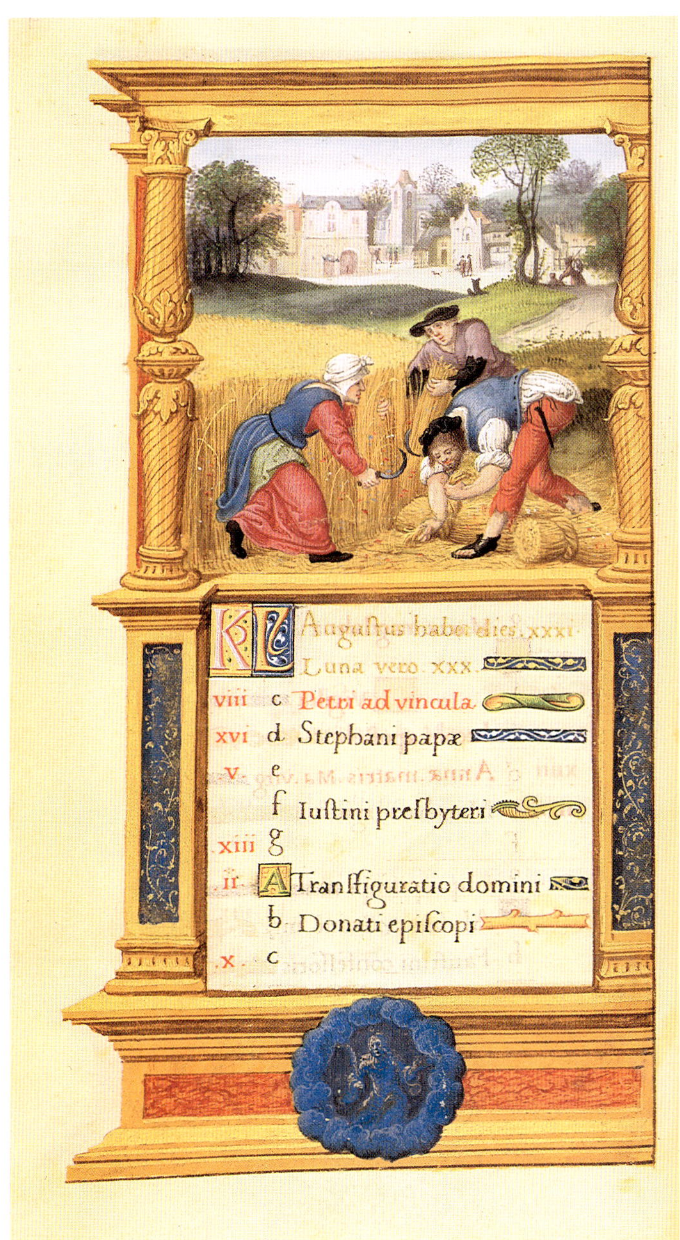

KL Augustus habet dies. xxxi
Luna vero. xxx.
viii c Petri ad vincula
xvi d Stephani papæ
.v. e
f Iustini presbyteri
xiii g
ii A Transfiguratio domini
b Donati episcopi
.x. c

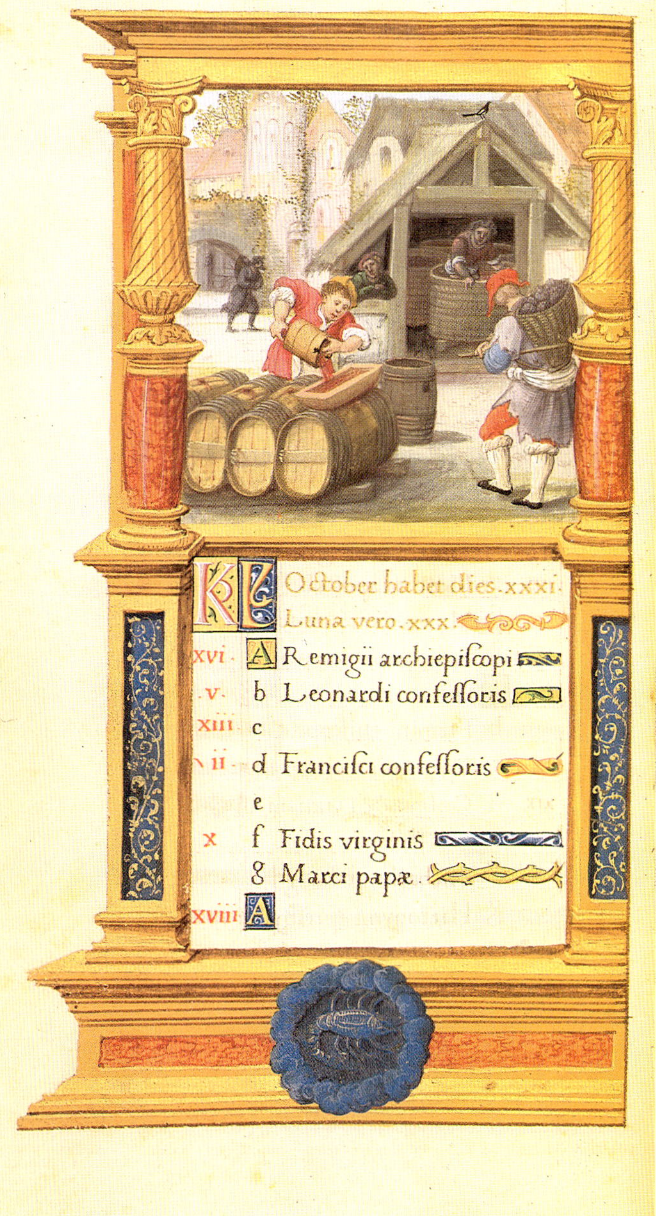

KL October habet dies. xxxi
Luna vero. xxx.
xvi A Remigii archiepiscopi
.v. b Leonardi confessoris
xiii c
ii d Francisci confessoris
e
x f Fidis virginis
g Marci papæ
xviii A

Pl. 15. a) *Reaping* (Calendar: August); b) *Making Wine* (Calendar: October), France, Tours?, 1524, by the 1520s Hours Workshop (Walters 449, fols. 9v, 11v; Cat. No. 77).

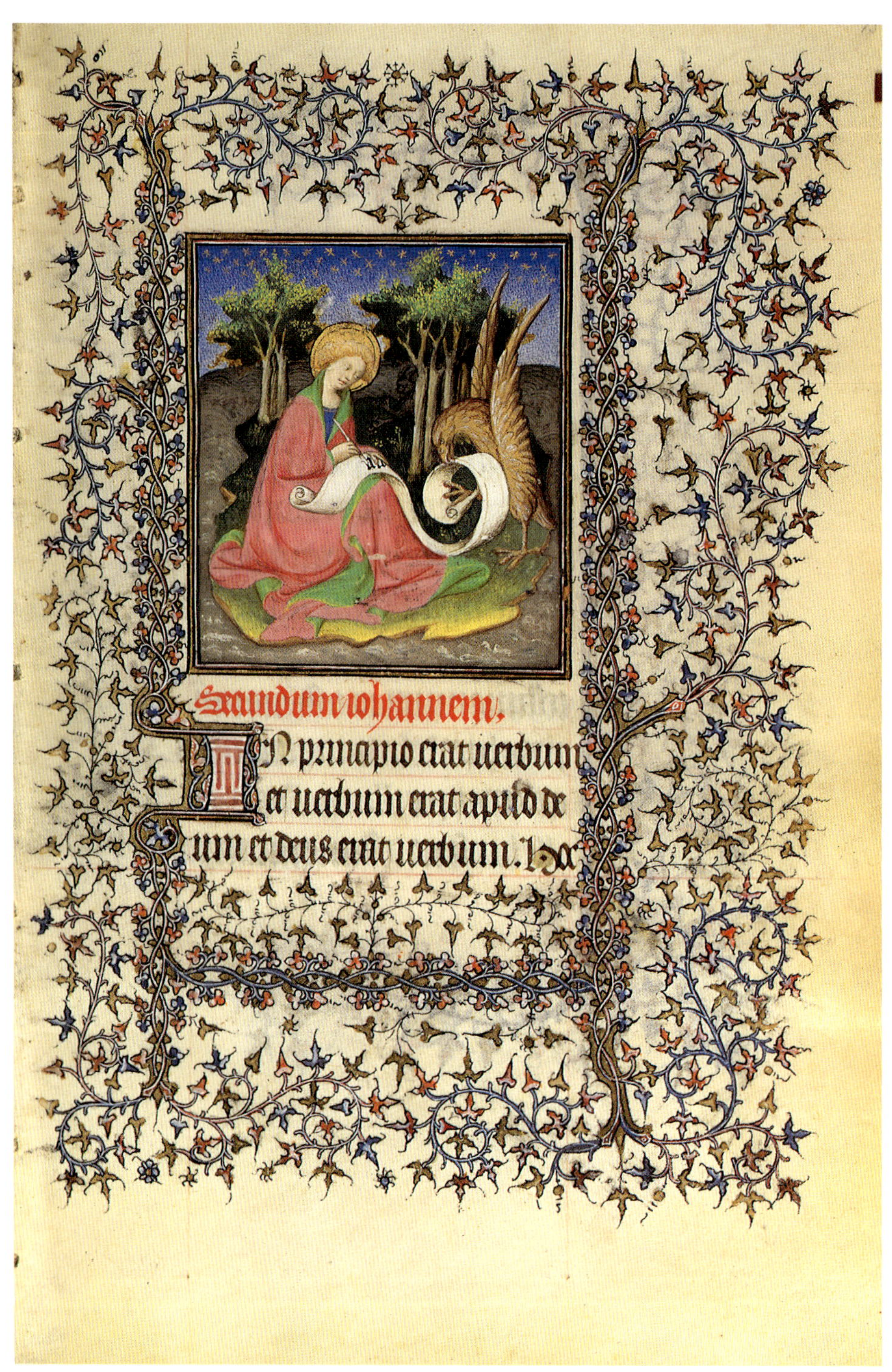

Pl. 16. *John on Patmos* (Gospel Lessons), France, Paris, ca. 1410–20, by an artist related to the Master of Berry's *Cleres Femmes* (Walters 265, fol. 15; Cat. No. 23).

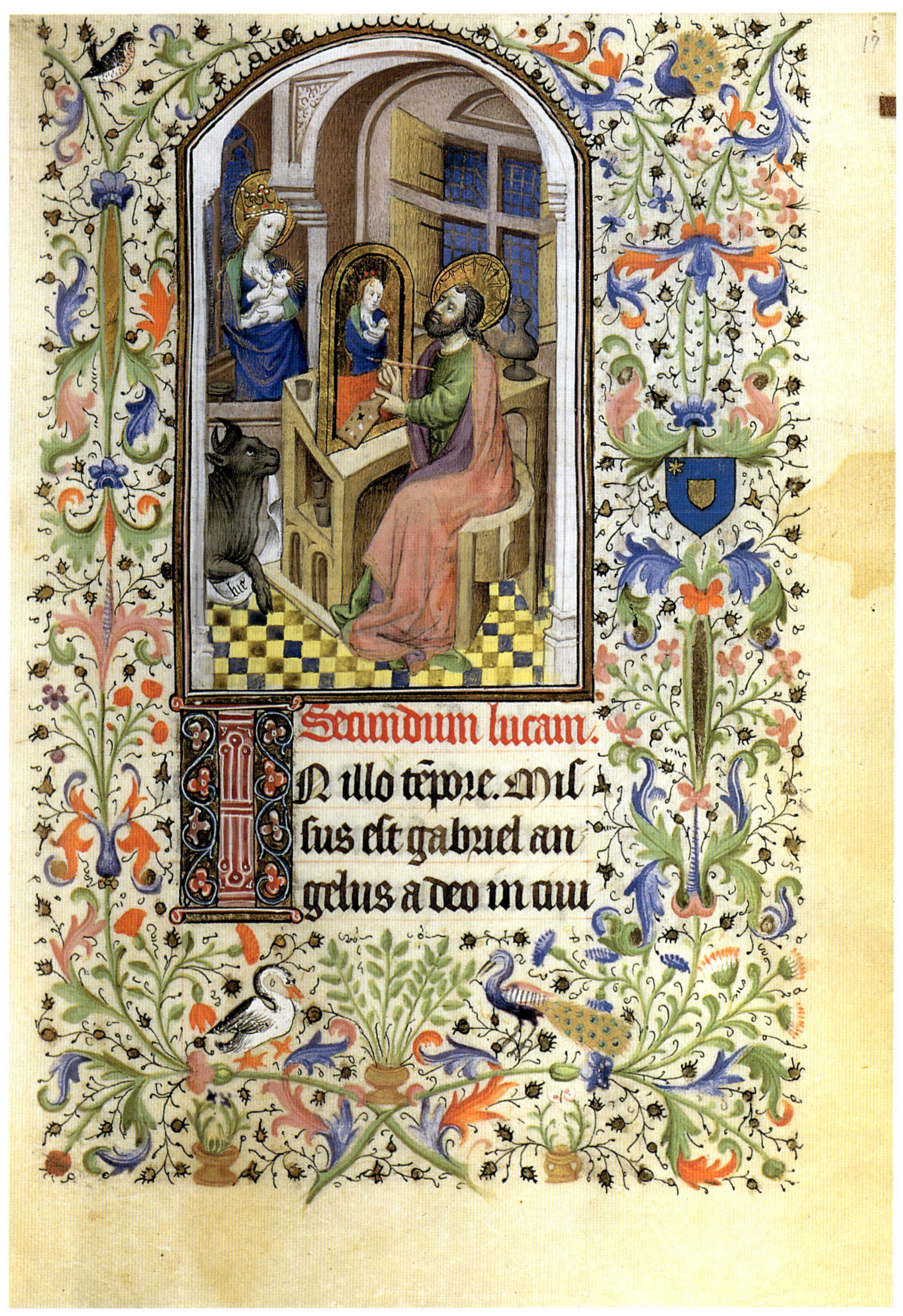

Pl. 17. *Luke Painting the Virgin* (Gospel Lessons), northern France or Belgium, Tournai, ca. 1430–35, by the Master of Walters 281 (Walters 281, fol. 17; Cat. No. 35).

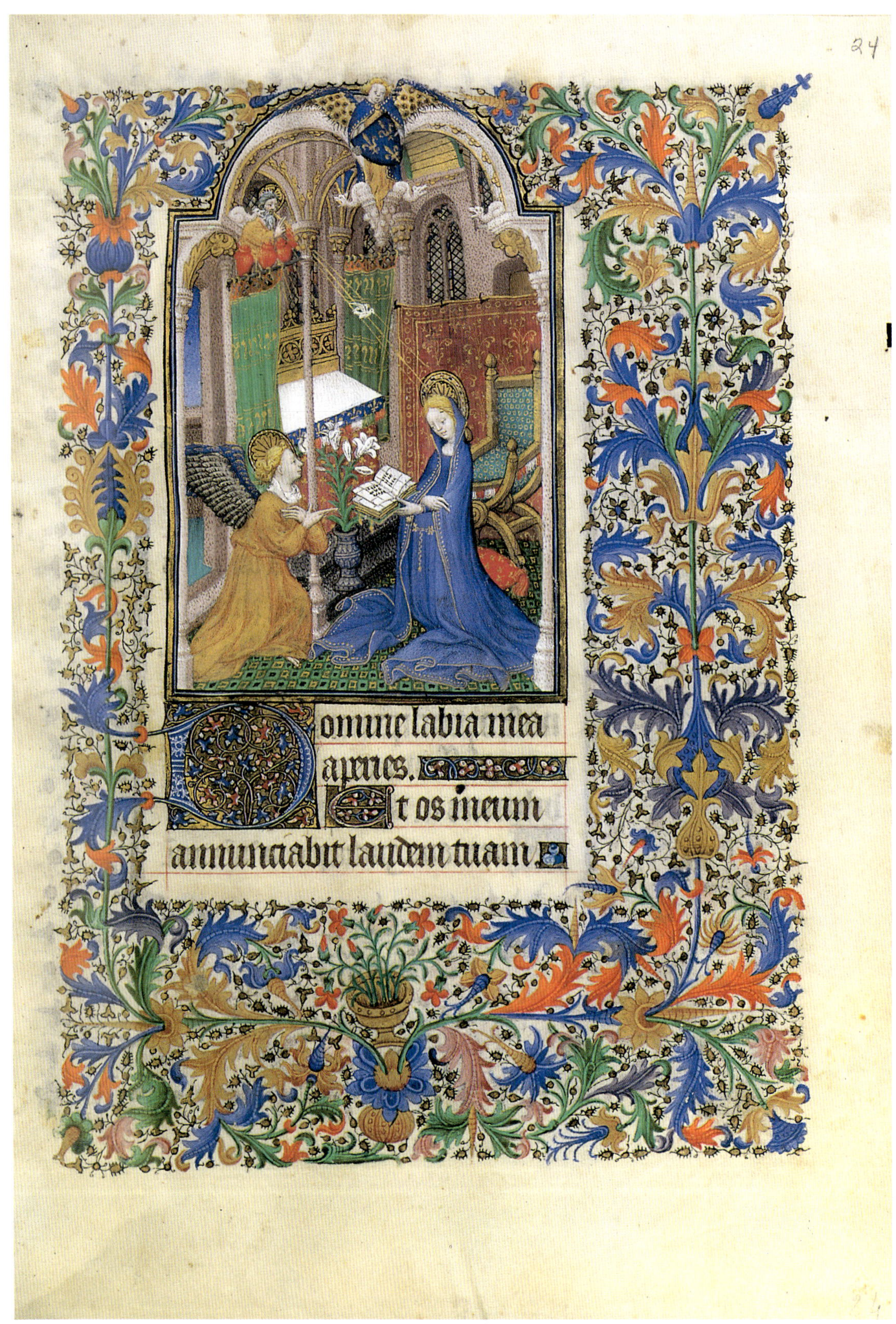

Pl. 18. *Annunciation* (Hours of the Virgin: Matins), France, Paris, 1420s, by the Master of the Harvard Hannibal (Walters 287, fol. 24; Cat. No. 29).

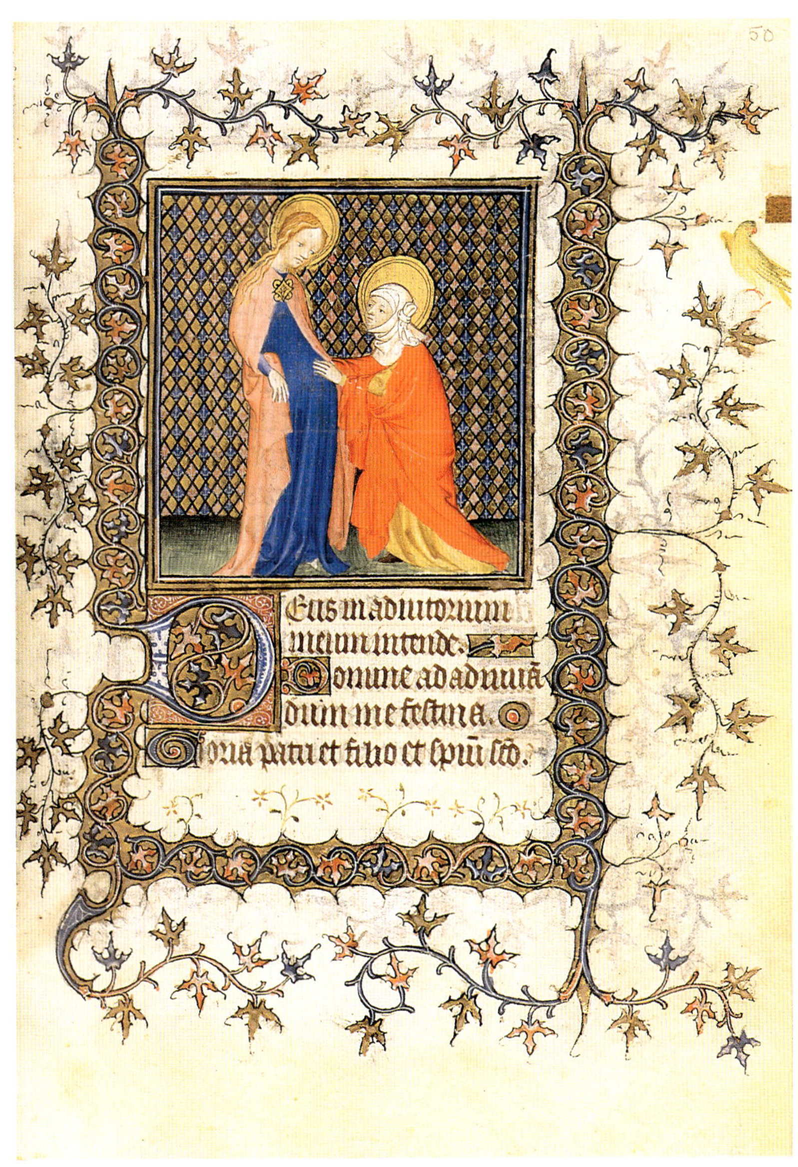

Pl. 19. *Visitation* (Hours of the Virgin: Lauds), France, Paris, ca. 1390, by a follower of Jacquemart de Hesdin (Walters 96, fol. 50; Cat. No. 15).

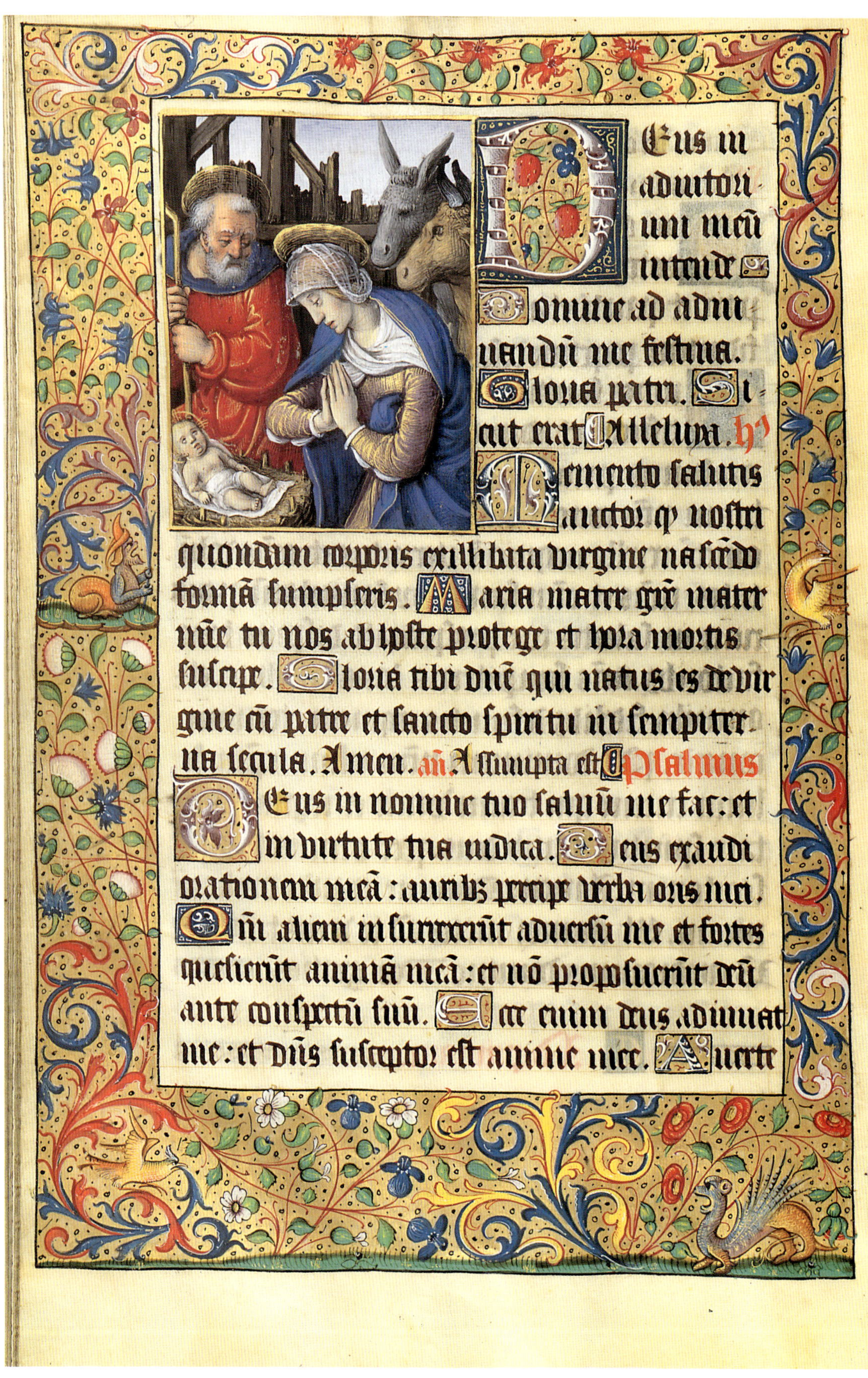

Pl. 20. *Nativity* (Hours of the Virgin: Prime), France, Tours, late 15th century, by Jean Poyet and his workshop (Walters 295, fol. 20v; Cat. No. 67).

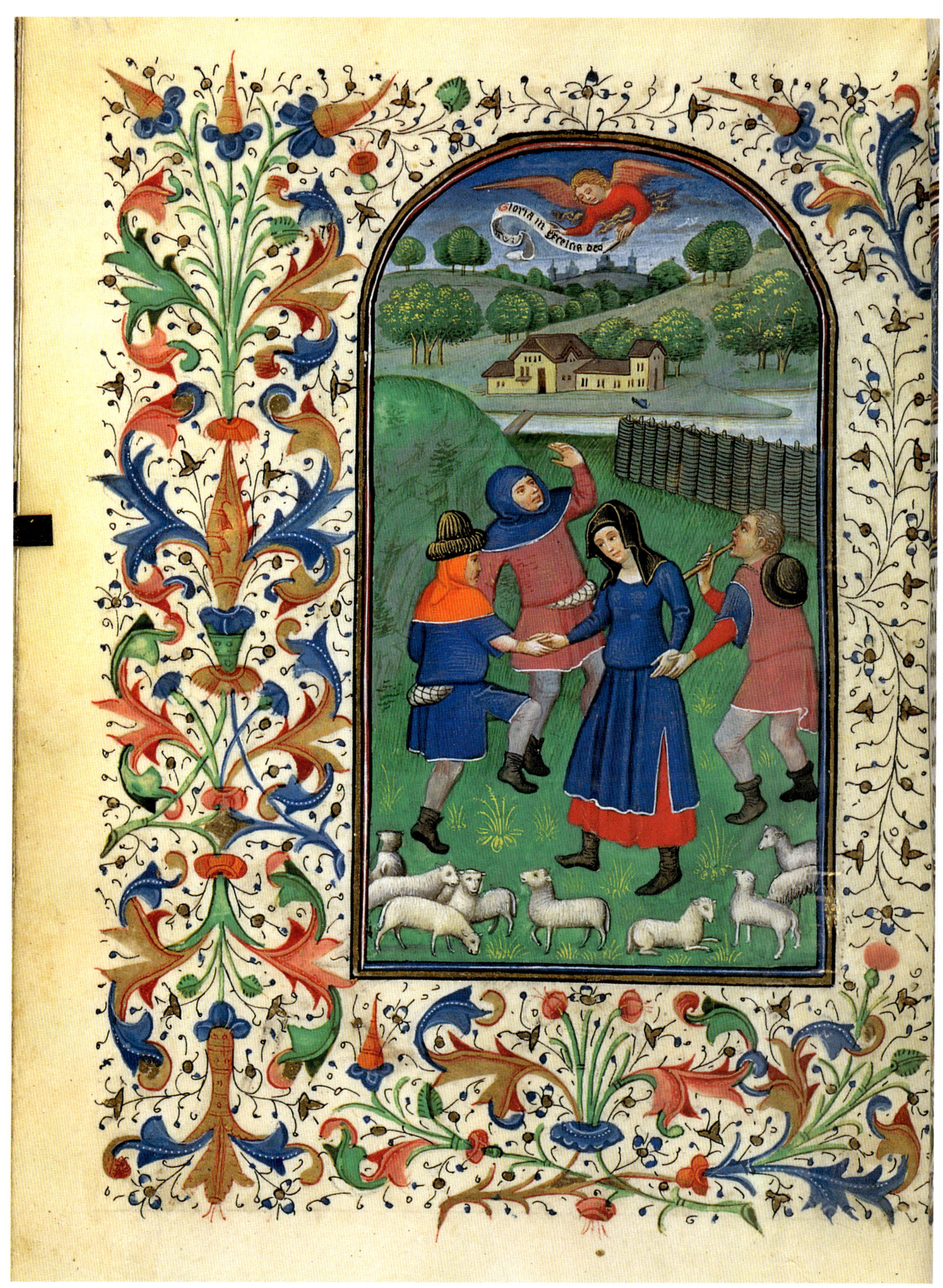

Pl. 21. *Annunciation to the Shepherds* (Hours of the Virgin: Terce), Belgium, Bruges, 1450s, by Willem Vrelant (Walters 240, fol. 198v; Cat. No. 92).

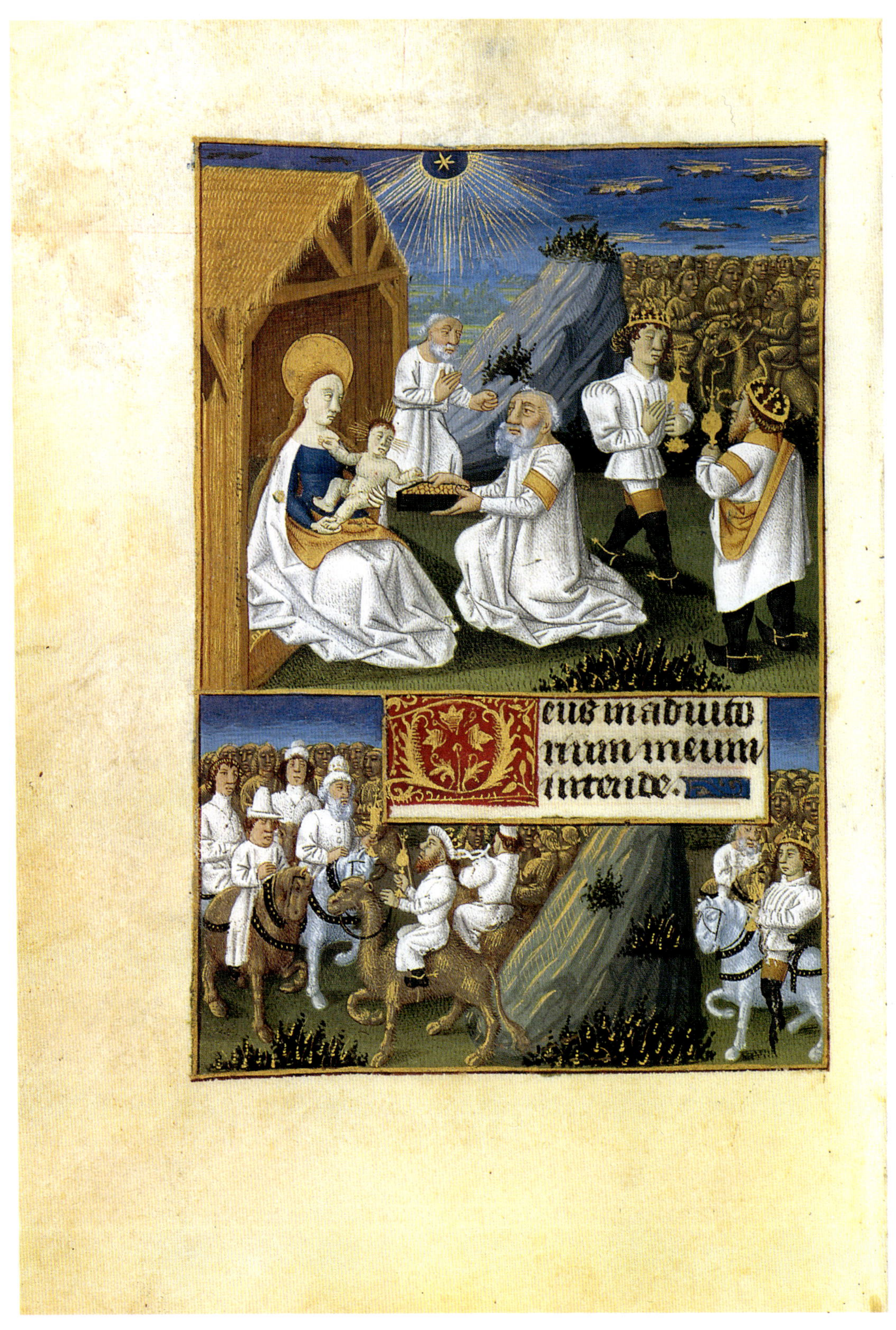

Pl. 22. *Adoration of the Magi,* border: *Journey of the Magi* (Hours of the Virgin: Sext), France, probably Poitiers, 1460s, by a follower of the Masters of Morgan 96 and 366 (Walters 223, fol. 62v; Cat. No. 46).

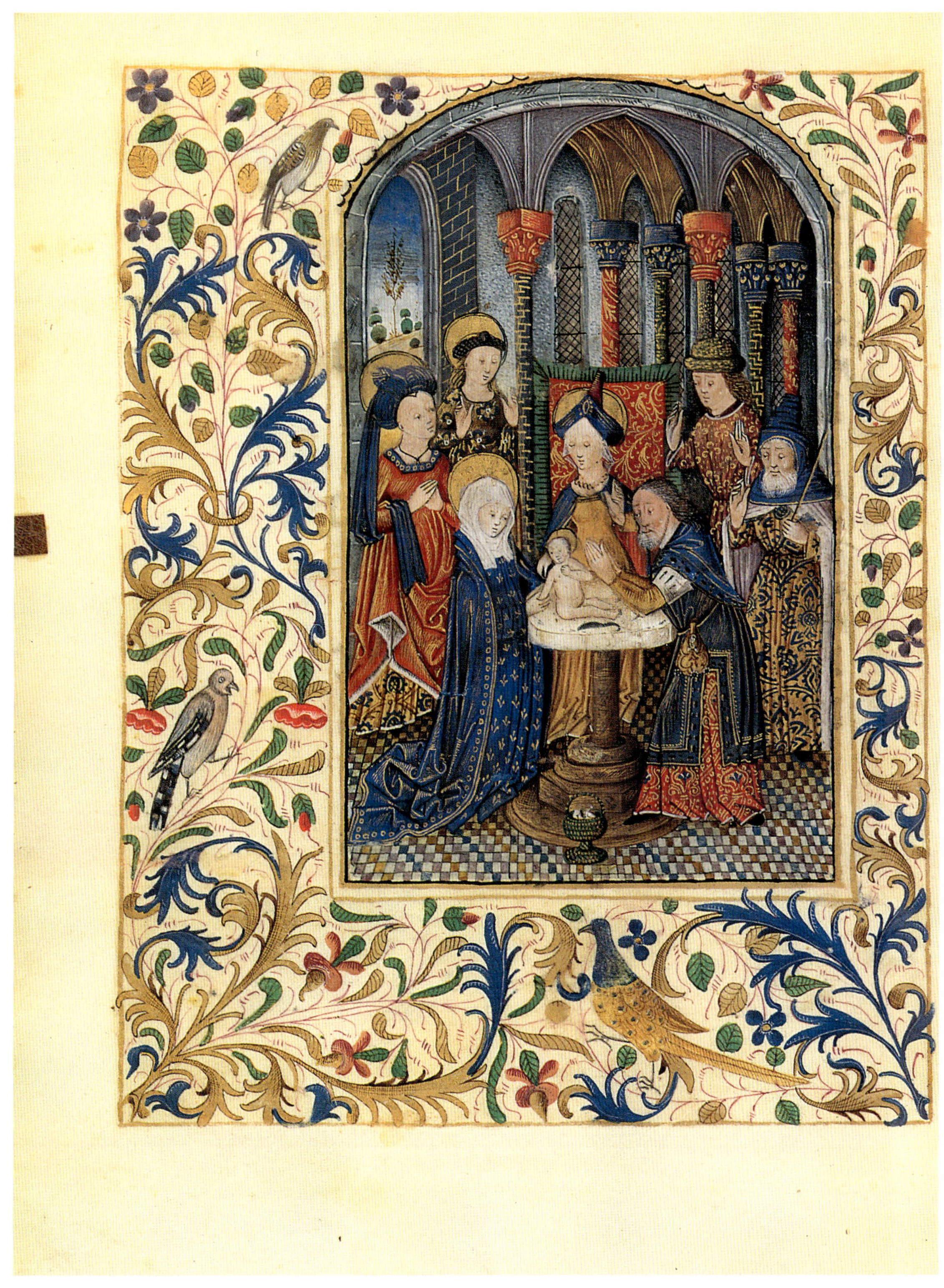

Pl. 23. *Presentation in the Temple* (Hours of the Virgin: None), Belgium, Bruges?, 1470s, by a follower of the Master of Anthony of Burgundy (Philippe de Mazerolles?) (Walters 272, fol. 91v; Cat. No. 97).

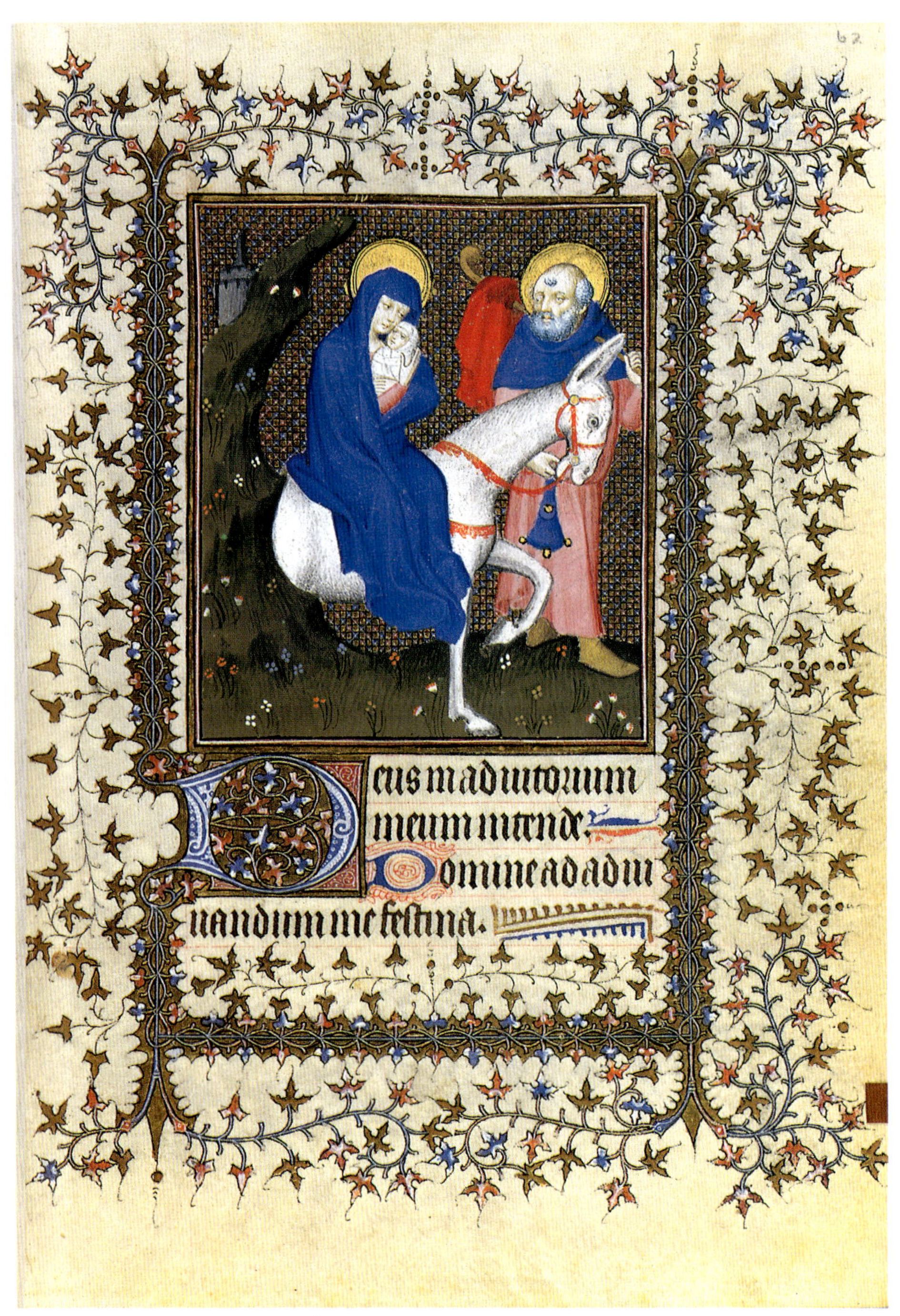

Pl. 24. *Flight into Egypt* (Hours of the Virgin: Vespers), France, Paris, ca. 1405, by the Luçon Master (Walters 231, fol. 62; Cat. No. 19).

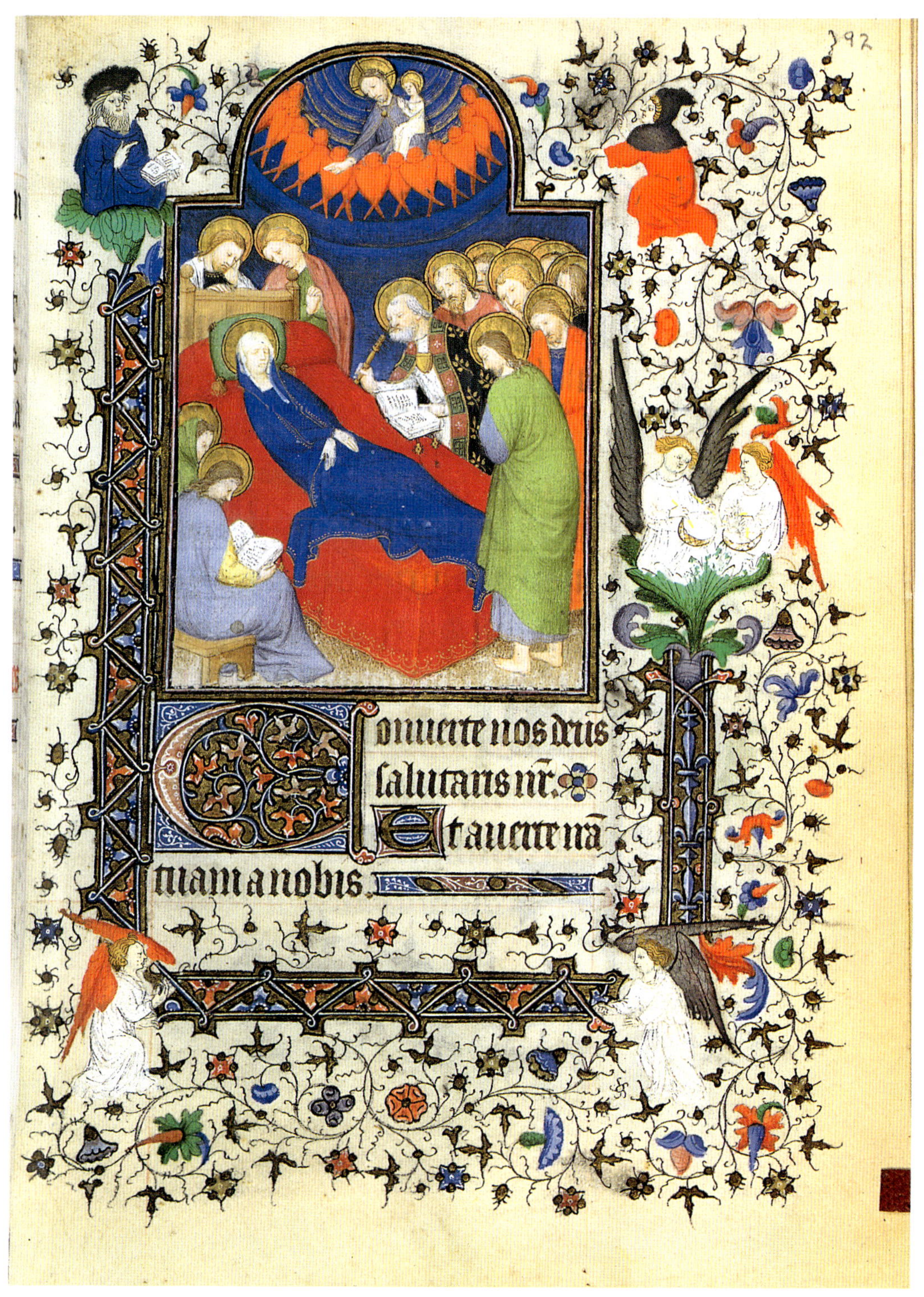

Pl. 25. *Death of the Virgin* (Hours of the Virgin: Compline), France, Paris, ca. 1415, by the workshop of the Boucicaut Master (Walters 260, fol. 92; Cat. No. 26).

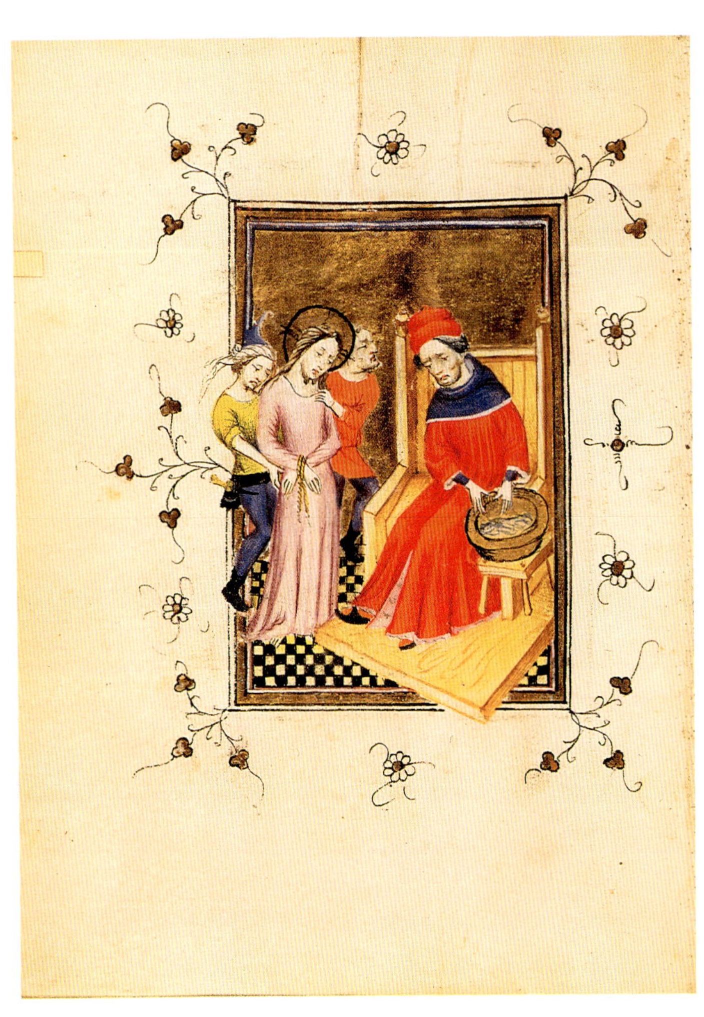

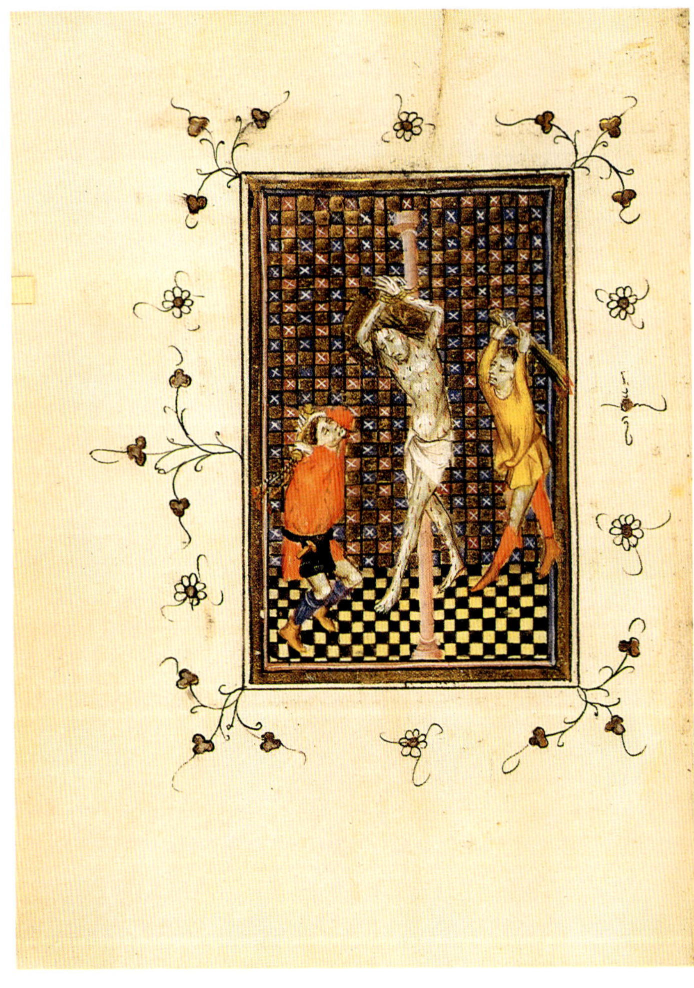

Pl. 26. a) *Pilate Washing his Hands* (Hours of the Virgin: Prime); b) *Flagellation* (Hours of the Virgin: Terce), Holland, ca. 1410–15 (Walters 185, fols. 49v, 58v; Cat. No. 107).

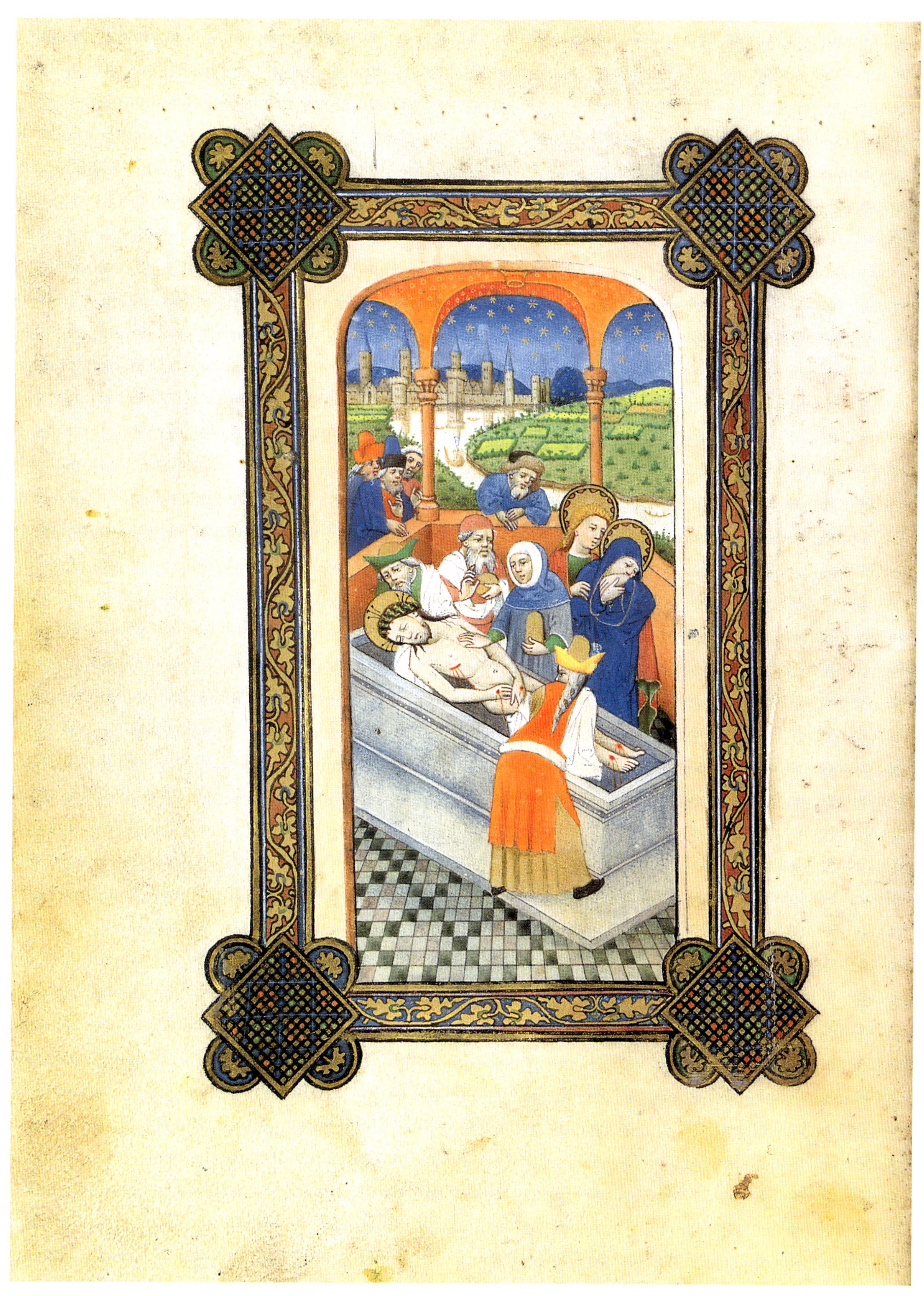

Pl. 27. *Entombment* (Hours of the Virgin: Compline), Belgium, ca. 1440, by the Master of the Ghent Privileges (Walters 172, fol. 46v; Cat. No. 85).

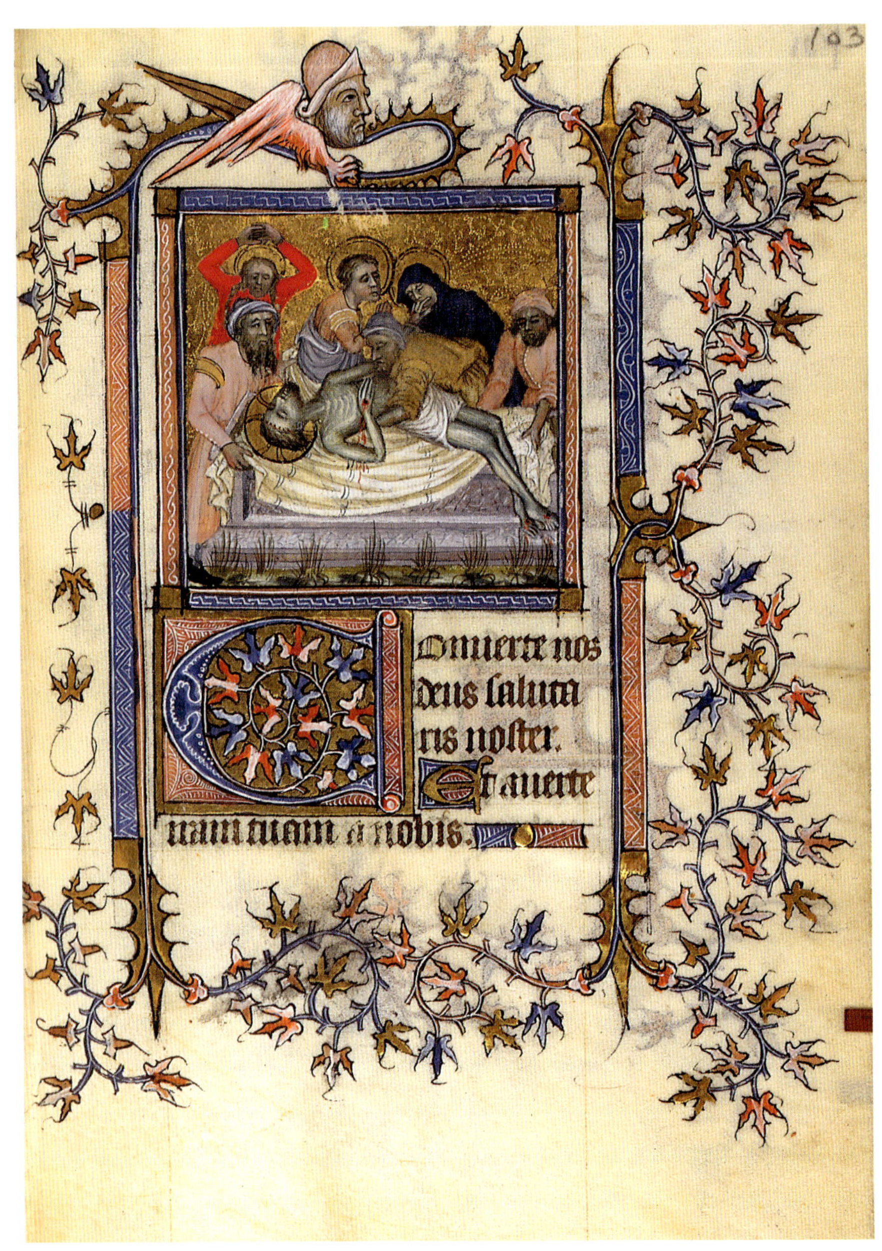

Pl. 28. *Entombment* (Hours of the Cross: Compline), France, Avignon, ca. 1400 (Walters 237, fol. 103; Cat. No. 17).

CHAPTER VII

Hours of the Cross, Hours of the Holy Spirit

Among the many additional Hours or Offices that appear in Books of Hours, two are found with great frequency: the Hours of the Cross and the Hours of the Holy Spirit. (Some other additional Hours are discussed in Chapter X.) In many manuscripts, the Hours of the Cross and the Hours of the Holy Spirit follow one right after the other, together forming a kind of unit. Their placement within a Book of Hours is not fixed but they often come immediately after the Hours of the Virgin, and it seems clear that this arrangement encouraged, time permitting, the reader to pray these two Hours right after finishing those devoted to Mary. The practice, or at least the desire, to read the Hours of the Virgin along with those of the Cross and the Holy Spirit is reflected too in what are called "mixed" Hours. In these instances, Matins of the Cross and Matins of the Holy Spirit are inserted immediately after Matins and Lauds of the Virgin, Prime of the Cross and of the Holy Spirit after Prime of the Virgin, Terce of the two additional Hours after Terce of the Virgin, etc., through Compline. Abbreviated "mixed" Hours also occur where, instead of the complete Hours of the Cross and Hours of the Holy Spirit interspersed within the Hours of the Virgin, only Matins from the two additional Hours is included, inserted after Matins and Lauds of the Virgin. Other manuscripts omit the Hours of the Holy Spirit and mix in only the Hours of the Cross. Still other rare *Horae* insert a third series of Hours, such as those of St. Catherine, in addition to the Hours of the Cross and of the Holy Spirit. (All of these various arrangements, not easy to describe, can be easily understood by a glance at the entries in the Catalogue of Manuscripts; see Nos. 45, 57, 64, 69, 71, 74, 112.)

Both the Hours of the Cross and the Hours of the Holy Spirit are relatively short texts. However, longer versions of them also appear in some Books of Hours. The longer version of the Hours of the Holy Spirit, which is designated here the Office of the Holy Spirit (also called the Long Hours of the Holy Spirit), is infrequently found and its illustration need be discussed only briefly. The longer version of the Hours of the Cross, which is here designated the Hours of the Passion (also called the Long Hours of the Cross, or Office of the Passion), is often found in the manuscripts. The terminology for these various texts was inconsistent in the Middle Ages and remains so today; the names used here reflect the most common medieval usages. The following chart may prove useful in the discussion below:

Additional Hours found in many Books of Hours:	Longer versions of these Hours found less often:
Hours of the Cross	Hours of the Passion
Hours of the Holy Spirit	Office of the Holy Spirit

As might be expected, the miniature accompanying the Hours of the Cross is almost always a Crucifixion. One example that stands for hundreds is the *Crucifixion* for the Hours of the Cross in a *Horae* illuminated by the Master of Jean Rolin II (Fig. 53). Its iconography is particularly rich. Below the profusely bleeding Savior, the Virgin faints into John's arms, an action that reveals how the Virgin shared Christ's suffering in her role as co-redemptrix of mankind. Medallions in the border illustrate the other major events of Christ's Passion: the *Agony in the Garden*, *Betrayal*, *Pilate Washing his Hands*, *Christ Carrying the Cross*, *Deposition*, and *Entombment*. In this book, the border illustrations surrounding the *Crucifixion* parallel those used around the *Annunciation* for the Hours of the Virgin, the only other place in this manuscript where medallions occur. These additional small pictures highlight these two sections of the book, underscoring their importance. Of course, not all Books of Hours have borders filled with such an elaborate array of additional scenes.

While the Crucifixion is the usual subject for the miniature at the Hours of the Cross, other episodes from the Passion are also used. These subjects include: the Agony in the Garden, the Betrayal, Christ Carrying the Cross, or the image of Christ as the Man of Sorrows.

While the Hours of the Cross normally receive only the one miniature, there are exceptions. In some Books of Hours there is a cycle of seven pictures (one for each Hour, Matins through Compline with no Lauds) illustrating the Passion of Christ. The typical series is nearly identical to that accompanying the Hours of the Virgin when the latter receive a Passion cycle (see Chapter VI). The following table gives the traditional iconography for the Passion cycle for the Hours of the Cross; variations appear in parentheses:

Matins:	Betrayal
Prime:	Christ before Pilate (or, Christ Mocked, Flagellation)
Terce:	Flagellation (or, Christ Crowned with Thorns, Christ Buffeted, Christ Carrying the Cross)
Sext:	Christ Carrying the Cross (or, Christ Nailed to the Cross, Crucifixion)
None:	Crucifixion
Vespers:	Deposition
Compline:	Entombment

The Hours of the Cross in a Book of Hours from Avignon of about 1400 are illustrated with a cycle that follows this scheme, including some of the variations. In typical fashion it begins with the *Betrayal* and ends with the *Entombment* (Pl. 28). Both the style and iconography of this manuscript are characteristic of Avignon illumination of the late fourteenth and early fifteenth centuries and betray a strong Italian influence and reliance on southern models. In the *Entomb-*

Fig. 53. *Crucifixion* with border vignettes (Hours of the Cross), France, Paris, ca. 1450, by the Master of Jean Rolin II (Walters 251, fol. 109; Cat. No. 39).

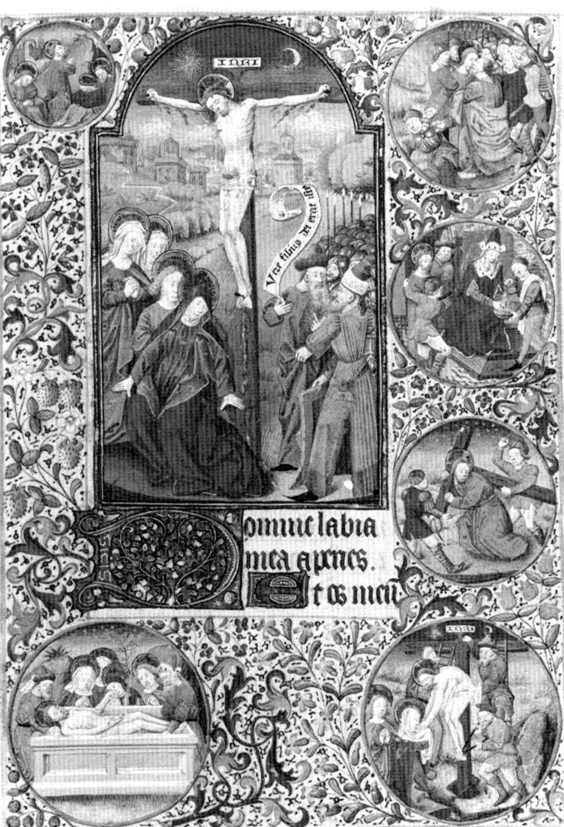

Fig. 54. *Helena Excavating the True Cross* (Hours of the Cross), France, Paris?, early 15th century, by a follower of the Boucicaut Master (Walters 271, fol. 110v; Cat. No. 24).

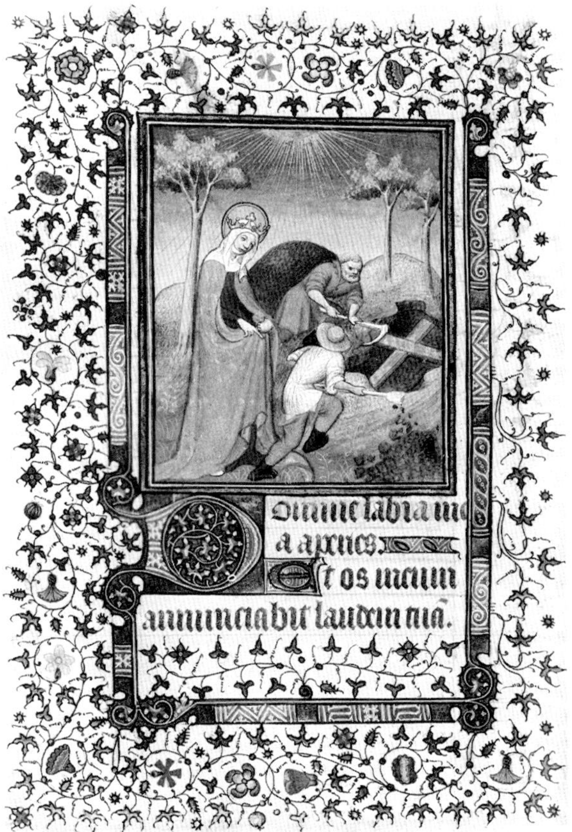

ment these Italianate features include the stiff green corpse of the Savior, the hot orange of Mary Magdalene's dress, and the dramatic mourning gestures of both the Magdalene, who wrings her hands over her head, and the Virgin, who gives the pierced hand of her Son a final kiss.

Sometimes, albeit rarely, the miniature accompanying the Hours of the Cross emphasizes the cross on which Christ died, an object that was believed to have survived in the form of relics distributed throughout Christendom. One cross, or sometimes three, or angels displaying a cross are all subjects of miniatures. Helena, the mother of Constantine, the first Christian emperor, or her archaeological search for the True Cross is also a theme for the Hours of the Cross, as in an early fifteenth-century Book of Hours illuminated by a follower of the Boucicaut Master (Fig. 54). In this finely painted miniature, Helena is depicted directing two laborers who uncover the True Cross with pick and shovel.

The much longer Hours of the Passion do not find their way into manuscripts with the same frequency as the shorter Hours of the Cross. When present, their illustration parallels that of the Hours of the Cross: a single miniature of the Crucifixion or a cycle of Passion illustrations. The Hours of the Passion from the *Horae* just mentioned are accompanied by a series that begins with the *Betrayal* and ends with the *Deposition* (the final miniature, probably the *Entombment*, is missing). Since the Hours of the Passion, almost by necessity, are illustrated with Passion episodes, the presence of these Hours within a book also containing the Hours of the Cross challenged artists to come up with imaginative ways to avoid duplicating subjects, as reflected in this manuscript. The use of a Passion cycle for the Hours of the Passion precluded a redundant theme for the Hours of the Cross, so for the latter text the illuminator used the less common, but appropriate, scene of Helena's excavating the True Cross. Another characteristic cycle for the Hours of the Passion is found in an early fourteenth-century Book of Hours from northern France. The series, composed of eight large historiated initials, begins with the *Betrayal* (Fig. 55) and continues through the Passion until the *Deposition*. The

Fig. 55. *Betrayal* (Hours of the Passion: Matins), northern France, 1310–20 (Walters 38, fol. 118; Cat. No. 10).

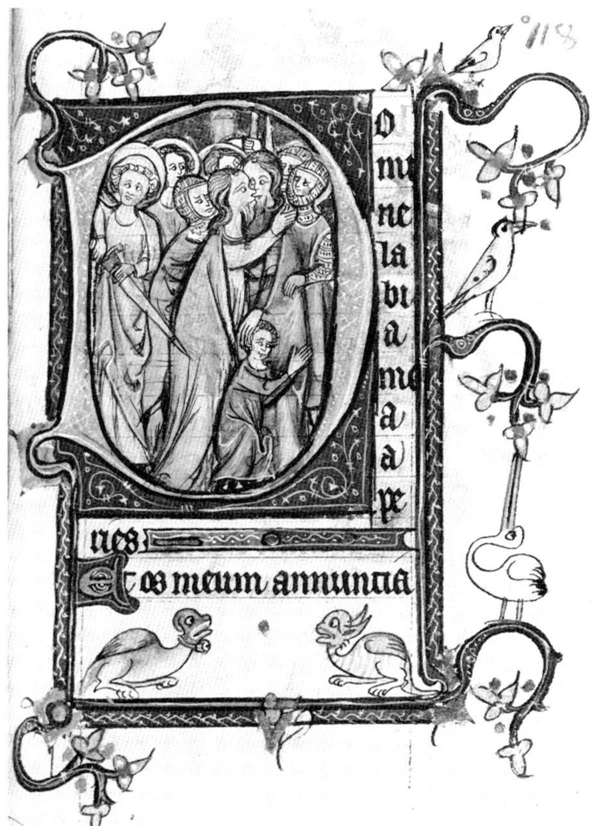

Fig. 56. *Battle of Constantine* (Hours of the Passion: Matins), France, Rheims, end of the 13th century (Walters 98, fol. 95; Cat. No. 5).

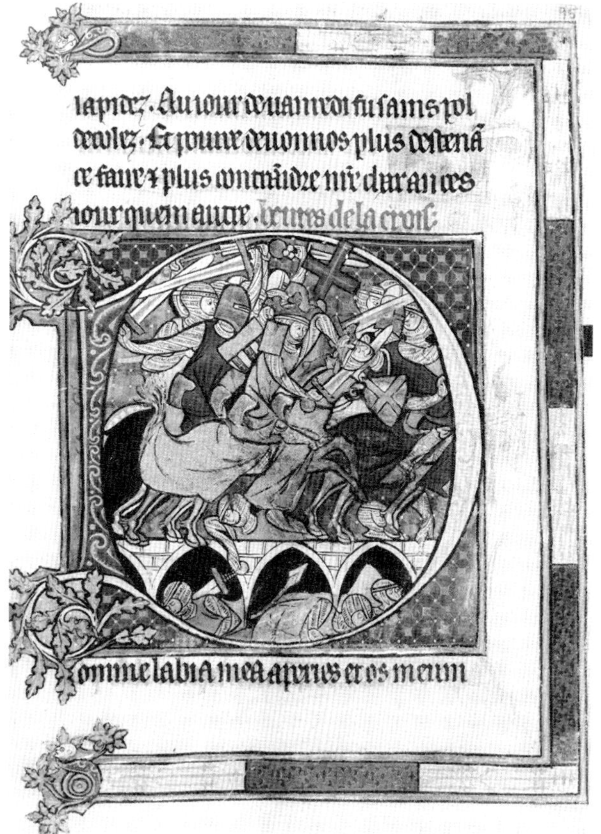

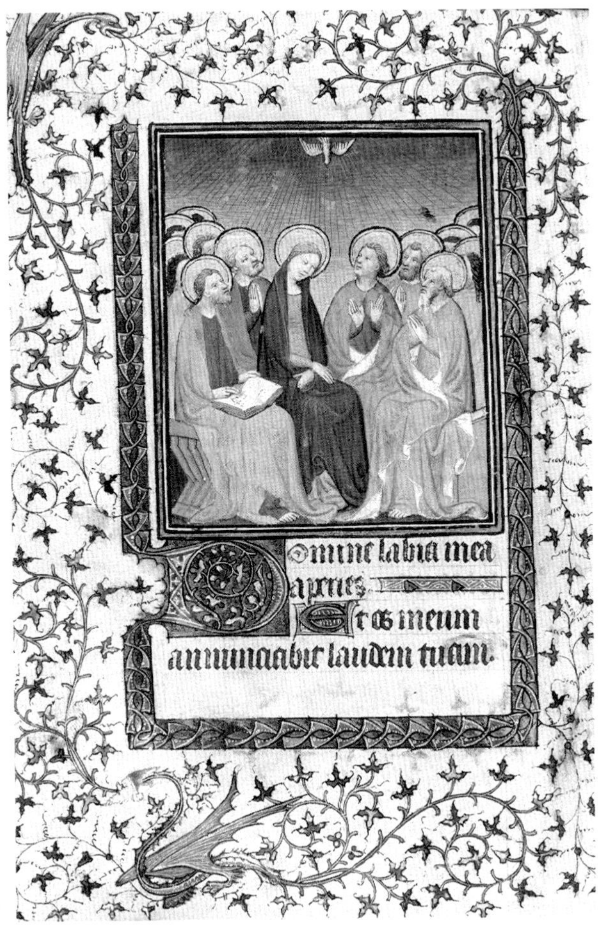

Fig. 57. *Pentecost* (Hours of the Holy Spirit), France, Paris, ca. 1412, by the workshop of the Boucicaut Master (Walters 238, fol. 82v; Cat. No. 25).

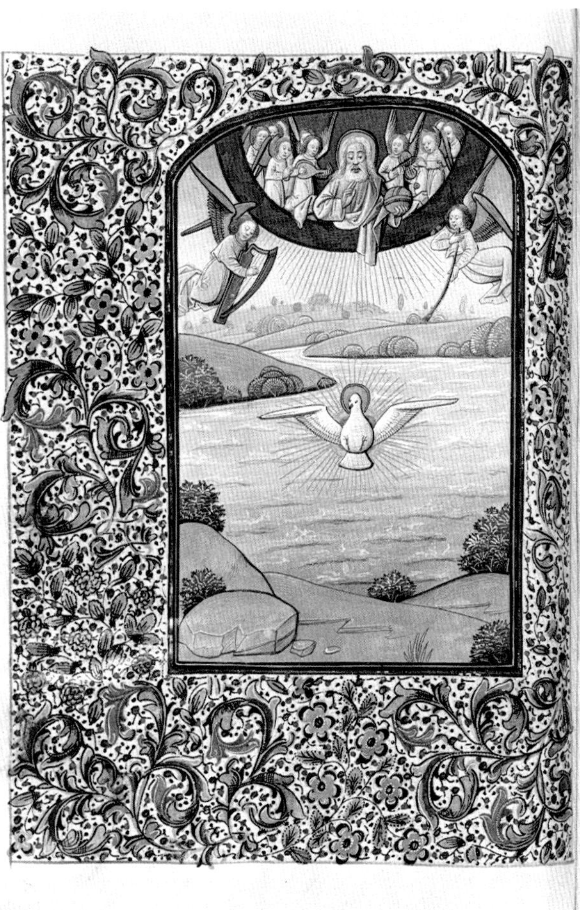

Fig. 58. *Holy Spirit Hovering over the Earth* (Hours of the Holy Spirit: Terce), Belgium, Bruges, ca. 1470, by the workshop of Willem Vrelant (Walters 196, fol. 30v; Cat. No. 94).

cycle ends, however, with the rarely depicted *Noli me tangere,* the name given to depictions of Christ's appearance to Mary Magdalene on Easter Sunday when he told her, "Do not touch me."

In another, a late thirteenth-century *Horae* from Rheims, the Hours of the Passion, which are called the "Heures de la croix" in this manuscript, are illustrated with an unusual cycle tracing the history of the True Cross. The series, which includes episodes of Helena's excavating, finding, and testing the True Cross, begins with the *Battle of the Milvian Bridge* (Fig. 56). Emperor Constantine, at the center of the picture and identifiable by his crown, decapitates Maxentius under the victorious emblem of the cross.

The most frequent illustration for the Hours of the Holy Spirit is Pentecost. In a miniature from a Book of Hours of about 1412, made in the workshop of the Boucicaut Master, the Virgin sits in the center of the surrounding apostles under the descending rays of the Dove of the Holy Spirit (Fig. 57). Behind Mary, to the left, Peter is recognizable and, to the right, the beardless John the Evangelist. In other manuscripts the miniature for the Hours of the Holy Spirit might be the Trinity or the Baptism of Christ.

The Hours of the Holy Spirit and the rarer, and longer, Office of the Holy Spirit are, like the Hours of the Cross or the Hours of the Passion, accompanied at times with cycles of miniatures. However, the Hours or Office of the Holy Spirit have no established set of traditional subjects. The Hours of the Holy Spirit from a *Horae* of about 1470 illuminated by the workshop of Willem Vrelant contain the following pictures: *David Receiving the Holy Spirit, Holy Spirit Hovering over the Earth* (Fig. 58), *Baptism of Christ, Apostles Blessing, Christ Appearing to the Apostles,* and *Pentecost.* These subjects are among the many episodes that appear in cycles for the Hours or Office of the Holy Spirit in other manuscripts. The Baptism of Christ or Pentecost, events where the

Holy Spirit manifests himself, were also popular. The mission of the apostles, after the descent of the Holy Spirit at Pentecost, to convert and save the world is also a theme in the Vrelant cycle that is repeated in other manuscripts. The illustration of the Dove hovering over the earth also appears in other cycles; the image refers to the spirit of God hovering over a newly created world and, indeed, some Hours of the Holy Spirit are accompanied by a series of Creation pictures (see, for example, Cat. No. 10).

The coupling of the Hours of the Cross and the Hours of the Holy Spirit formed a unit encouraging the reader to continue praying from one to the other. These two Hours are sometimes also joined pictorially. In some *Horae*, themes that are begun in the Hours of the Cross are continued and completed in the Hours of the Holy Spirit, as in the elaborate Hours of Anne of France (Cat. No. 55). Here, the series of pictures of the Hours of the Cross, which begin with the *Agony in the Garden* and end with Christ's *Entombment*, is picked up in the Hours of the Holy Spirit with the *Resurrection*, and continues with the *Ascension*, *Pentecost*, and scenes of the proselytizing of Peter. In other manuscripts, the unification of the Hours of the Cross and the Hours of the Holy Spirit is accomplished by means of historiated borders or vignettes in the margins. Examples of this solution are found in the Book of Hours illuminated by the Master of the Munich *Golden Legend* (Pls. 10, 11) and other manuscripts described in the catalogue entries (see Nos. 43, 49).

If early *Horae*, like the massive Savoy Hours (Cat. No. 11), can be viewed as compilations or as composites of various Hours, Offices, and numerous prayers, later Books of Hours tend to be more thematically unified. The sequence composed of the Hours of the Virgin, followed by the Hours of the Cross, and then the Hours of the Holy Spirit tells the story of those events that granted mankind salvation, events related in the chronological sequence in which they occurred.

CHAPTER VIII

"Obsecro te" and "O intemerata"

Of the innumerable optional prayers that owners of Books of Hours requested for their prayer books, the "Obsecro te" ("I beseech you") and the "O intemerata" ("O immaculate virgin") were the two most popular. Both prayers are addressed to the Virgin and seek her aid as intercessor to God for the benefit of the sinner. (Translations of both prayers are provided in the Appendix.) By the early fifteenth century these two prayers, the one usually following the other, become a fairly standard feature of the Book of Hours and, when included, are illustrated about two thirds of the time. Unlike the Calendar, the Gospel Lessons, or the Office of the Dead, texts whose positions within a Book of Hours are nearly constant, the placement of the "Obsecro te" and "O intemerata" was not fixed. Frequently, however, they are found following the Gospel Lessons and preceding the Hours of the Virgin. The Mother of God, usually with her Son, is the traditional subject of the miniatures accompanying these two prayers, miniatures painted to inspire these appeals.

The Virgin alone is sometimes the subject of the miniature for the "Obsecro te," but since the prayer appeals to Mary's role as an intercessor, this is iconographically not the most appropriate, and Mary by herself actually makes rare appearances in the miniatures. The first part of the "Obsecro te" emphasizes the Virgin's special role in the Incarnation and reminds her of the joys of motherhood. The majority of miniatures for the "Obsecro te" thus include a Madonna, that is, the Virgin with the Christ Child. There are numerous variations. The Virgin is sometimes shown seated on the floor in an iconographic type known as the Madonna of Humility. In another variation, Mary, as the *Virgo Lactans*, is shown nursing her Son. In other miniatures, the Virigin offers Christ flowers or fruit—an apple, an allusion to the serpent's offering in the Garden of Eden and cause of mankind's Fall, or a grape, a reference to the Eucharist and Christ's bloody sacrifice on the cross. In a small Book of Hours painted by the Maître François, a hungry Christ reaches toward the apple that Mary, aware of its portentous symbolism, holds beyond her Child's grasp (Fig. 59). Angels, as they do in many miniatures for the "Obsecro te," take up the role of courtly musicians. The Holy Family—the Virgin and Christ Child with St. Joseph—also appears in these illustrations. A delightful depiction of medieval domesticity is found in the "Obsecro te" miniature of the Collins Hours, a manuscript painted in Amiens or Bruges around 1440 (Fig. 60). The Virgin sits at her loom, busy at work, while her Son, to the dismay of the angel standing nearby in the hallway, pesters his mother for attention. The look on the Virgin's face reflects the sorrow, not yet accompanied by resignation, caused by the knowledge of what her Son's growing up will mean for him.

Unlike the various Hours or Offices in a Book of Hours, the "Obsecro te" is not a composite of psalms or other extracts from the Bible but a single prayer in which the reader addresses the Virgin directly, in plaintive tones and in the first person. The miniatures of the Madonna that accompany this prayer became, therefore, a favorite place for the men and women who owned these prayer books to assert as well as insert themselves via portraits. The miniature for the "Obsecro te" from Walters 220, painted in Bruges by Willem Vrelant, includes the patron of the manuscript (Pl. 29; the patron's wife appears in the miniature reproduced in Fig. 11). The Virgin gently tends

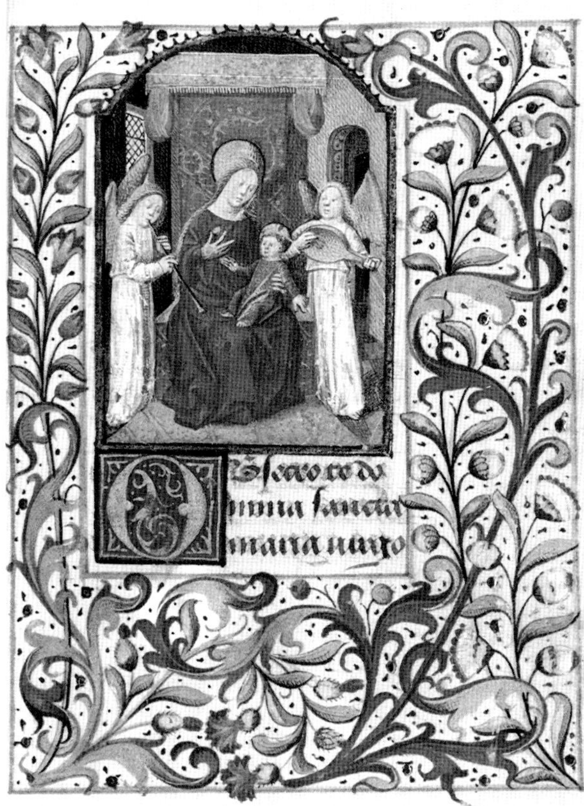

Fig. 59. *Madonna Enthroned, Serenaded by Angels* ("Obsecro te"), France, Paris, 1470s, by the Maître Francois (Walters 800, fol. 288; Cat. No. 52).

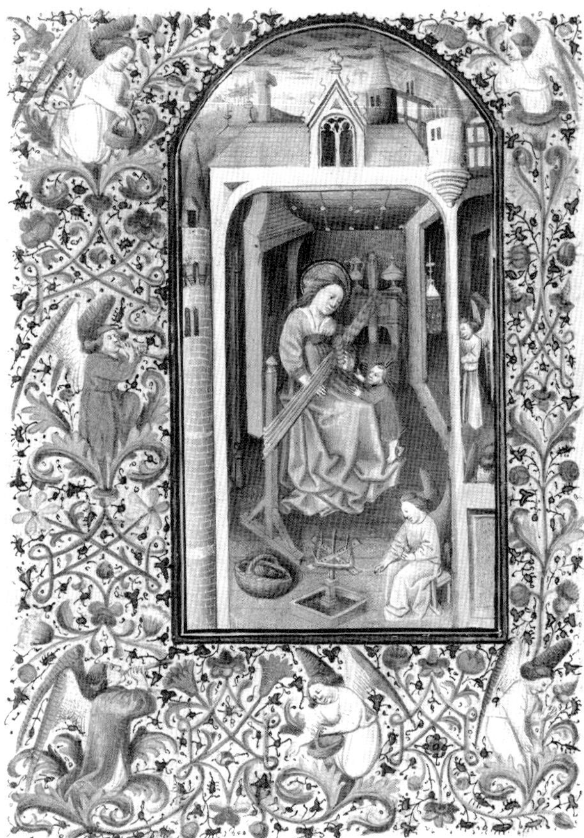

Fig. 60. *Virgin Weaving* ("Obsecro te"), France, Amiens, or Belgium, Bruges, ca. 1440, by the Master of the Collins Hours (Philadelphia Museum of Art, 1945-65-4, fol. 173v; Cat. No. 37).

the Christ Child, keeping him balanced on her lap and offering him fruit, while he turns to the kneeling patron and offers him a blessing of forgiveness. It is somewhat difficult to determine, exactly, who is visiting whom in the miniature. Has the man come to the Virgin's house to pay his respects or has the Virgin miraculously descended to the man's home? The miniature should be read on two levels simultaneously: while it depicts what the patron sees in his own mind's eye while praying, it also shows what he hopes to experience, in the eternity of heaven, as the result of the very prayer he recites.

A Rouen Book of Hours by the Master of the Geneva Latini contains a rare, but iconographically appropriate, subject for the "Obsecro te": the Mother of God as the Virgin of Mercy (Fig. 61). Her protective blue mantle is able to shield all those, even the inhabitants of the whole earth, who seek the Virgin's aid. The secular world, headed by a king, kneels under her left arm while the ecclesiastical, within which we can make out a bishop, a cardinal, and a pope, kneels at her right. As a sign of ownership, as well as a means to make their own personal prayer heard, the man and wife who owned this Book of Hours had themselves depicted in the lower margin, kneeling before the Madonna. The couple is dressed in Renaissance costume of about 1500, revealing that they are most likely the second-generation owners of this particular manuscript that had been produced about twenty years earlier. The couple had their portraits painted over those of the manuscript's original owners. Such alterations of portraits, arms, or mottos by later owners occur frequently in Books of Hours.

After reminding the Virgin of the joys she experienced as the Mother of God, the "Obsecro te" moves quickly on to her compassionate role as co-redemptrix of mankind through her empathetic experience of Christ's Passion. This theme, too, finds its way into the miniatures via depictions of the Lamentation or the Pietà.

The Pietà, however, is more usually the subject of the miniature for the second prayer, the "O intemerata," as in Walters 294, a French Book of Hours from the end of the fifteenth century (Fig. 62). Like a great number of Books of Hours from the fifteenth and early sixteenth centuries, this manuscript restricts the use of large miniatures for the more important texts (the Gospel Lesson of John, the eight Hours of the Virgin, the Hours of the Holy Spirit) and marks secondary texts with smaller pictures (the Gospel Lessons of the three other evangelists, the "Obsecro te," the "O intemerata," and the Suffrages). Also like many *Horae*, this manuscript uses a Madonna for the first prayer, the "Obsecro te," and a Pietà for the second, the "O intemerata." Reciting both prayers, one after the other, the reader is reminded by the illustrations of the two major themes of these prayers, the Virgin's joy and her sorrow. With the *Madonna* first and the *Pietà* second, these pictures record both the high point and the low in the Virgin's life, presented in chronological order. Walters 294 retains its original (or nearly so) soft velvet binding. The long, protective folds of this type of binding are often clearly depicted in miniatures that show people praying with their Books of Hours (Figs. 5, 9, 10).

The Pieta, or its slightly expanded version, the Lamentation, although the most common subject for the "O intemerata," is not the only one. All the themes cited above as subjects for the "Obsecro te" are also used for the "O intemerata," only less frequently so. In increasing order of popularity, these include the Holy Family, the Virgin (with a book, crowned, or weaving), and the Madonna. The last, as with the miniatures accompanying the "Obsecro te," has numerous variations, including the addition of patrons or angels. An example of the latter is found in a manuscript illuminated by Jean Colombe (Pl. 30). The Virgin (whose rounded features and bowed head are typical of Colombe), with her Son, is attended by a court of adoring angels whose multiple wings reveal their great number. The Mother of God wears her crown, an indication, along with the angels and the rays of God's approval shining from above, that the scene depicted takes place in heaven. This vision of celestial paradise offers the viewer a Mary who could not fail to present his requests to her Son and a Christ who could not refuse his mother anything.

Fig. 61. *Virgin of Mercy,* border: *Madonna Flanked by Patron and Patroness* ("Obsecro te"), France, Rouen, ca. 1480 (border retouched ca. 1500), by the Master of the Geneva Latini (Walters 224, fol. 10v; Cat. No. 58).

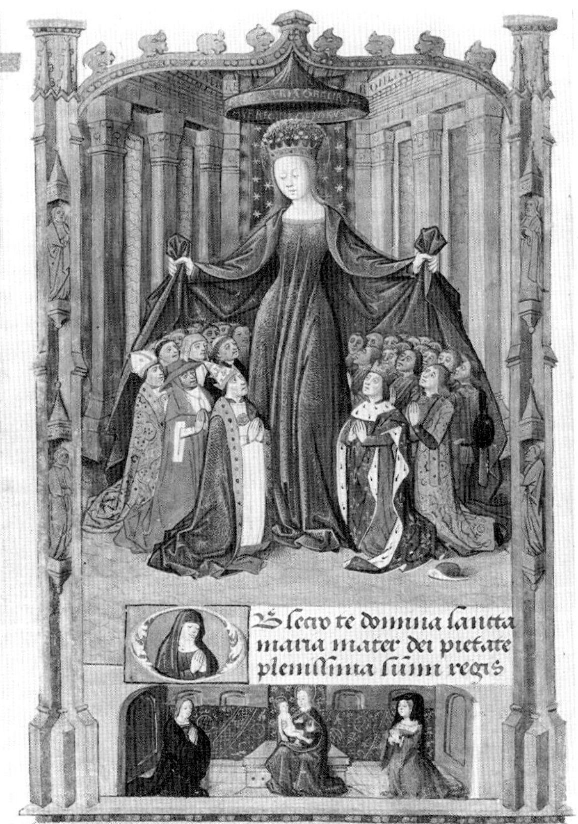

Fig. 62. *Pietà* ("O intemerata"), France, end of the 15th century (Walters 294, fol. 10; Cat. No. 66).

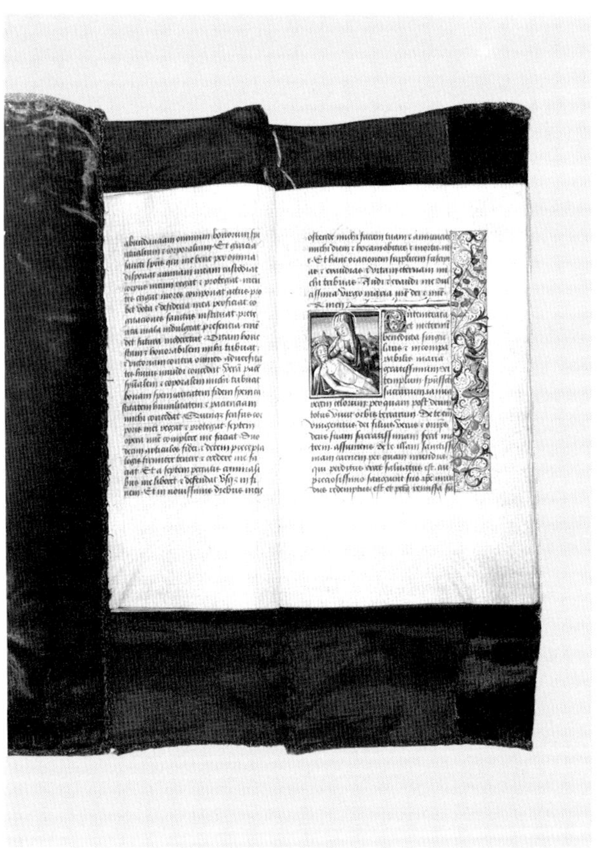

CHAPTER IX

Penitential Psalms and Litany

The seven Penitential Psalms traditionally have one miniature that marks the beginning of this section of text. While the usual subject, especially in the fifteenth century, is David in Prayer, this was preceded by an earlier tradition. In the thirteenth and fourteenth centuries (and in some areas continuing into the first half of the fifteenth) the traditional image for the Penitential Psalms is Christ as Judge at the end of the world or as the King of Heaven (the latter also called a *Salvator Mundi*, or Savior of the World, because Christ holds the globe of the world in his hands). Both types of images portray Christ as the final judge to whom man must account for his life, or, more particularly, for the sins he has committed during his life. Since Christ is the final arbiter of man's fate, it is to him that these Psalms of atonement are addressed and it was therefore fitting that Christ appear in the miniatures.

Walters 99 is an early fifteenth-century French Book of Hours executed in conservative style and iconography, and its miniature for the Penitential Psalms, *Christ Enthroned*, is representative of the traditions of the previous century (Fig. 63). The enthroned Christ blesses with his right hand and holds the orb of the world in his lap. Flanking him, as is sometimes the case in these miniatures, are the Eucharist, represented by a host and chalice, and the Tablets of the Law. Christ, the New Testament fulfillment of the Old Testament, is the unifying bridge between the two. Other manuscripts present the enthroned Savior in an iconographic type called Christ in Majesty in which the symbols of the four evangelists are set into the corners of the miniature. In rare manuscripts, God the Father will sit in for his Son in miniatures for the Penitential Psalms. Like Christ, he is shown enthroned, blessing, or surrounded by the evangelists' symbols.

In early Books of Hours, Christ is more frequently depicted as the Judge of the Second Coming than as the enthroned King. As Judge, he is shown seated and dressed in a loose robe exposing the wound in his side while he holds up his arms to display the wounds in both hands. More popular is an expanded version, the Last Judgement, that includes some or all of the following: the Virgin and John acting as intercessors, angels sounding trumpets, the resurrection of the dead. Popular everywhere in the thirteenth and fourteenth centuries, this tradition was replaced in France by scenes relating to David, but it had a healthy continued life in Belgium and Holland. A typical example is found in a Book of Hours executed by an artist of the Gold Scrolls group (Fig. 64). Seated on a rainbow with the world at his feet, Christ displays his wounds while seraphim wake the dead with blasts from their trumpets. Interceding on behalf of the dead are John and the Virgin who bares her breast to remind her Son of the nurturing kindness she bestowed on him as a child. The dead, fearful of Christ's justice but hopeful of his mercy, peer timidly from their freshly opened graves.

However, it is the life of David, who according to tradition was the author of the psalms, that dominates the miniatures for the Penitential Psalms. A survey of these illustrations unfolds the pivotal episodes of the career of this Old Testament king. David's boyhood as a simple shepherd is sometimes depicted in small border vignettes. His anointment by Samuel as the future king of Israel also appears, although rarely, as the subject of the large miniature itself. More frequent are images of David slaying Goliath, the military triumph that represents the dramatic beginning of David's career. The Adimari Hours, illuminated by the Florentine artist Zanobi Strozzi, uses this subject for its

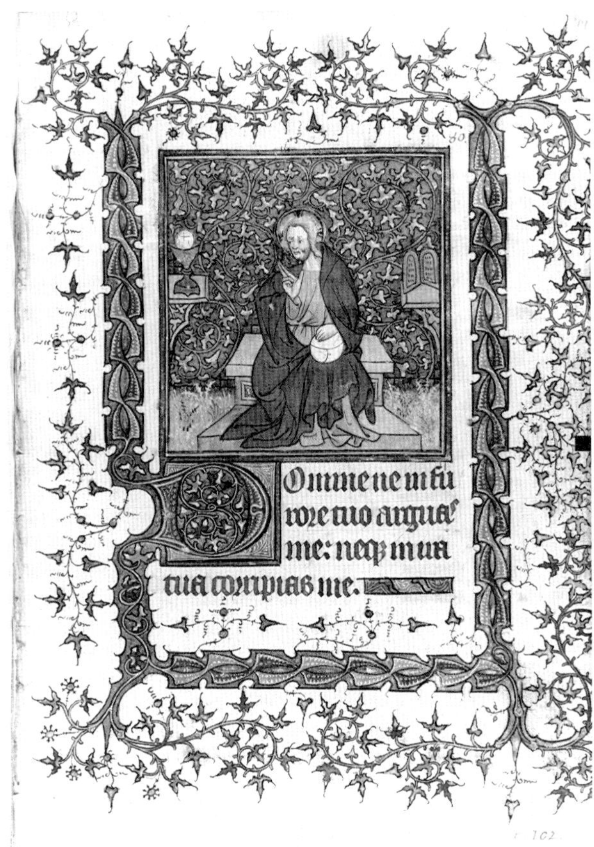

Fig. 63. *Christ Enthroned between the Eucharist and the Tablets of the Law* (Penitential Psalms), northern France, early 15th century (Walters 99, fol. 79; Cat. No. 18).

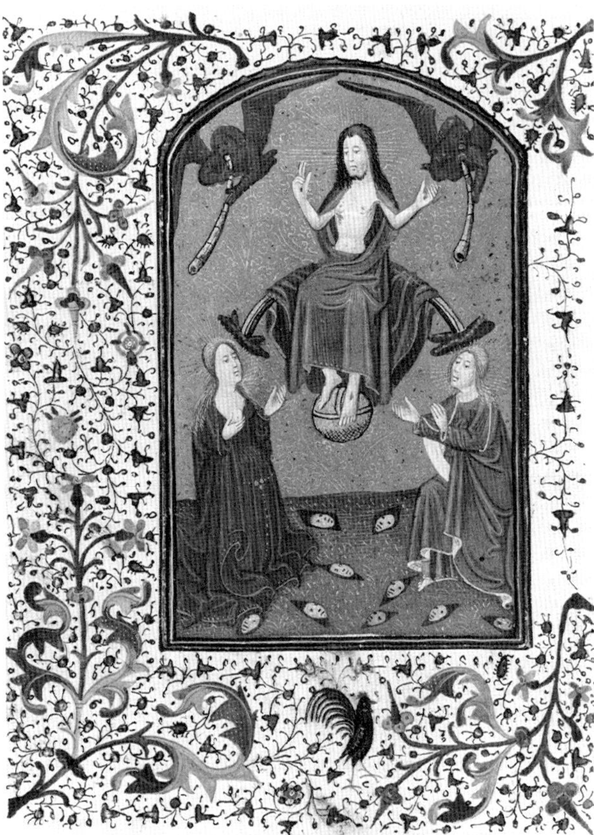

Fig. 64. *Last Judgement* (Penitential Psalms), Belgium, Bruges, ca. 1445, by a painter of the Gold Scrolls group (Walters 246, fol. 88v; Cat. No. 90).

Penitential Psalms (Fig. 65). A blond and youthful David stands upon the Philistine giant's body; in his right hand, he holds a sling and bloody sword, and in his left, Goliath's head, dripping blood from the wound in the forehead. David's presentation of Goliath's head to Saul is sometimes used for the Penitential Psalms, but more popular are pictures showing the boy, waving the head of the enemy from the end of the sword, received in triumph by the women of Israel.

These images of a good and youthful David stand in contrast to those of the sinful adult. Arising from an afternoon nap one day, the king looked out from the top of his palace and espied the beautiful Bathsheba, the wife of Uriah, at her bath. David lost no time in having the woman brought to him and sleeping with her. In a Bruges Book of Hours of about 1500, Bathsheba exposes her lower legs while she wets her feet in the pool of a delicate Renaissance fountain (Fig. 66). An excited David leans far out of his palace window. Here the aquatic theme of the miniature inspired the large fountain, with its many decoratively carved columns, that occupies the border surrounding the miniature as well as the text on the facing leaf.

Bathsheba conceived a child by David, so the king, to conceal his paternity, had Uriah called back to Jerusalem from the war so that the husband could have a conjugal visit with his wife. Uriah, however, returned to duty without seeing her. David then arranged to have Uriah put at the front line of the battle where the enemy killed him. The husband eliminated, David took Bathsheba as his wife. In a Book of Hours painted by a follower of Jean Poyet, the miniature for the Penitential Psalms shows the episode from this part of the tale most frequently illustrated (Fig. 67). In a courtyard of the royal palace, David hands Uriah the message he is to deliver to his commander Joab. Unbeknownst to him, Uriah holds his own death sentence. It is a dramatic moment in which Uriah's youthful innocence and trust are juxtaposed to David's adulterous machinations. In the Book of Hours by the Master of the Munich *Golden Legend,* the age difference between king and subject is even greater than in the book just mentioned and the portrayal of David is that of a lecherous old man (Pl. 9). The border vi-

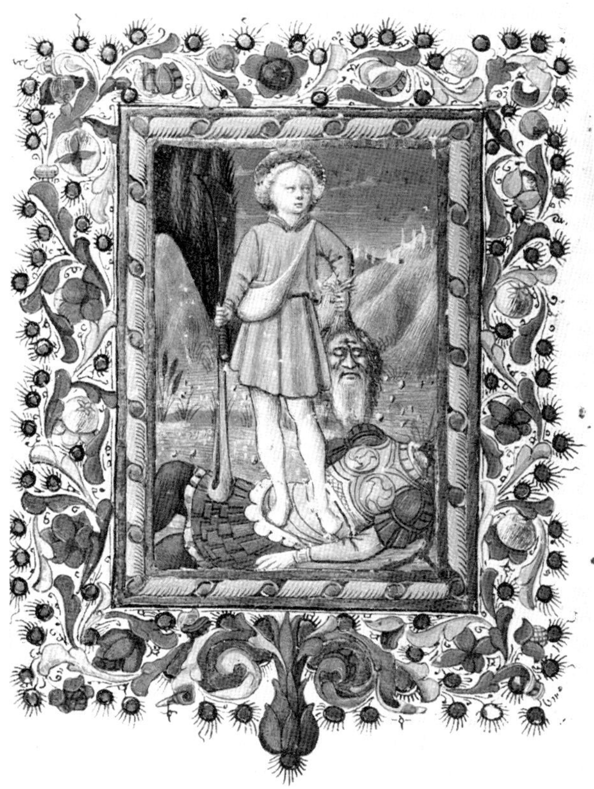

Fig. 65. *David and Goliath* (Penitential Psalms), Italy, Florence, early 1460s, by Zanobi Strozzi (Walters 767, fol. 169v; Cat. No. 116).

gnettes on the page tell the rest of the story: Bathsheba, her hand raised in a gesture of alarm, receiving a farewell kiss, Uriah marching off to battle, and Uriah's death. In some manuscripts the death of Uriah, instead of being an ancillary motif, is the subject of the large miniature itself. Following the events just described, an angry God sent Nathan to chastise David. Some miniatures for the Penitential Psalms illustrate this event with a sorrowful King David on his knees before the indignant prophet.

David's penance before God is the last event in this sketch of his career and it is the subject that is most frequently used for the Penitential Psalms. As a proud and powerful king who flagrantly committed both adultery and murder, David was struck down and reprimanded by God. The Penitential Psalms themselves, especially Psalm 50, are associated with his penance for these sins. A penitent David appears in the background of the miniature by the Master of the Munich *Golden Legend* (Pl. 9), but more characteristic is the miniature by the workshop of the Bedford Master where David in Prayer is the main subject of the miniature (Pl. 31). David, his rich robes lined with royal ermine, kneels on the ground, his hands crossed in humility across his chest; he directs his appeal for forgiveness to God who, with shining rays of light, looms like a large sun in the sky. God's avenging angel, red sword in hand, stands on a nearby hill. (In other miniatures this angel holds the three arrows of famine, war, and plague, the afflictions with which God threatened to punish David and his people.) David performs his act of contrition in a landscape whose depth and curvature gives the scene a sense of universality and timelessness. David, a great king but also a great sinner, is the model penitent.

Some Books of Hours relate more than just one episode from the life of David, such as the *Horae* by the Master of the Munich *Golden Legend,* already discussed. The Hours of Anne of France, lavishly illuminated by Jean Colombe, contains numerous unusual and unusually elaborate cycles of pictures for its various texts (Cat. No. 55). Instead of a single miniature for all the Penitential Psalms, each of the seven is given its own picture: *Bathsheba at her Bath, Bathsheba Brought to David, David and Uriah, Uriah Returning to Battle, Uriah's Dead Body Carried to Camp, Nathan Admonishing David,* and, as the culmination, *David Kneeling in Prayer.*

Cassiodorus, the sixth-century Roman author and monk who first enumerated the Penitential Psalms, referred to them as seven means of obtaining forgiveness. The number of the Psalms and that of the Deadly Sins being the same, the former, in the Middle Ages, became the weapons with which one did battle with the latter. A direct connection between the Penitential Psalms and the seven Deadly Sins is made in some Books of Hours. In Walters 240, a *Horae* rich in both texts and pictures, prayers against the Deadly Sins, each citing a specific one, are interspersed within the Penitential Psalms (Cat. No. 92). In other manuscripts, albeit rather rarely, the juxtaposition of Psalm and Sin takes on visual form, as in a Book of Hours of about 1475 with elaborate miniatures attributed to Robinet Testard. Seven pictures, one for each Psalm, form an unusual cycle in which personifications of each of the Deadly Sins, carrying various attributes, ride appropriate symbolic beasts. Gluttony, for example, rides a hog and has onions under his belt, a ham in his left hand and, in his right, a jug of wine (Fig. 68). In his eagerness to partake of the liquor the glutton spills most of the jug's contents down the front of his shirt. In the margin below is an orgy of eating and drinking with, at left, the devil Berich who holds his nose at the vomiting man at the end of the table. In the last miniature of the cycle, Lust, personified as a foppishly dressed youth, rides a goat, one of whose phallic horns he gently strokes. In the margin of this page the devil

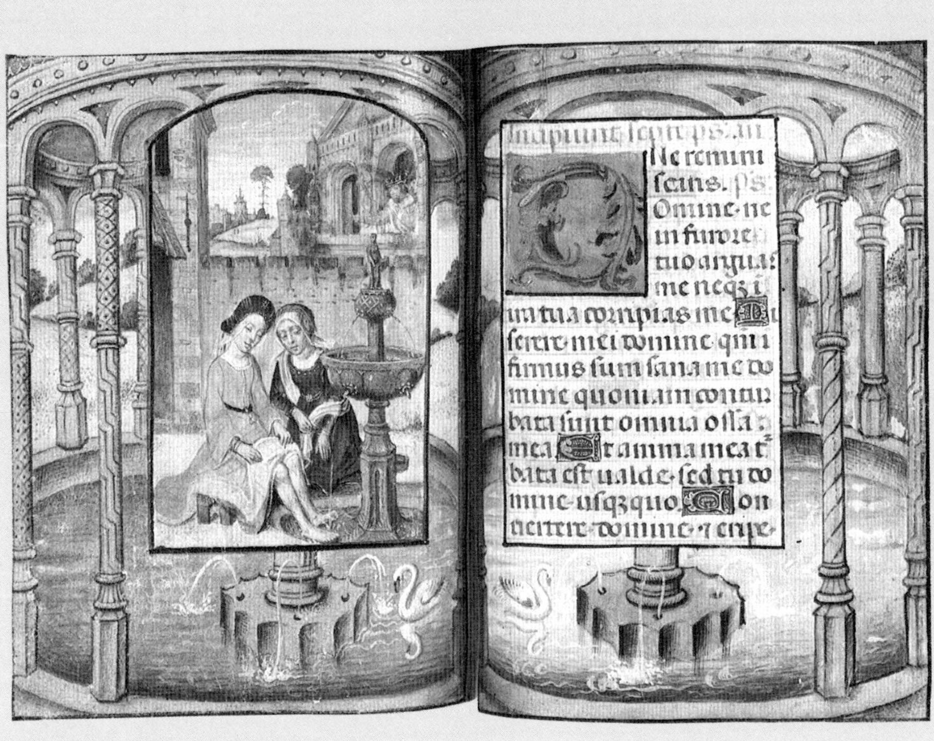

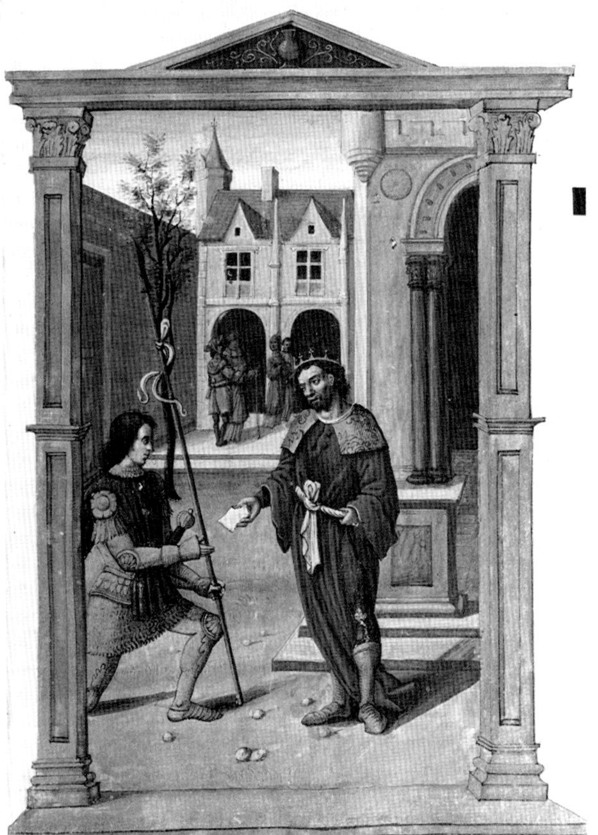

Asmodeus enjoys watching a young girl tempt three youths while a fourth aggressively puts his hand beneath another woman's dress.

The ultimate result of the inability to resist the seven Deadly Sins is sometimes, although rarely, illustrated in the Penitential Psalms. A graphic representation of this fatal result appears in an historiated initial in a Book of Hours executed by the workshop of the Master of Catherine of Cleves (Fig. 69). A devil gleefully pulls into the omnivorous mouth of hell the terrified soul of a foolish sinner who failed to heed the message of the Penitential Psalms. Seashells in the border, one mounted with a pilgrim's badge of Santiago de Compostella, the Spanish cathedral that was the goal of the medieval pilgrimage routes, allude to one

Fig. 66. *Bathsheba at her Bath* (Penitential Psalms), Belgium, Bruges?, ca. 1500 (Walters 427, fols. 133v–134; Cat. No. 103).

Fig. 67. *David and Uriah* (Penitential Psalms), France, Tours, ca. 1500, by a follower of Jean Poyet (Walters 454, fol 67; Cat. No. 69).

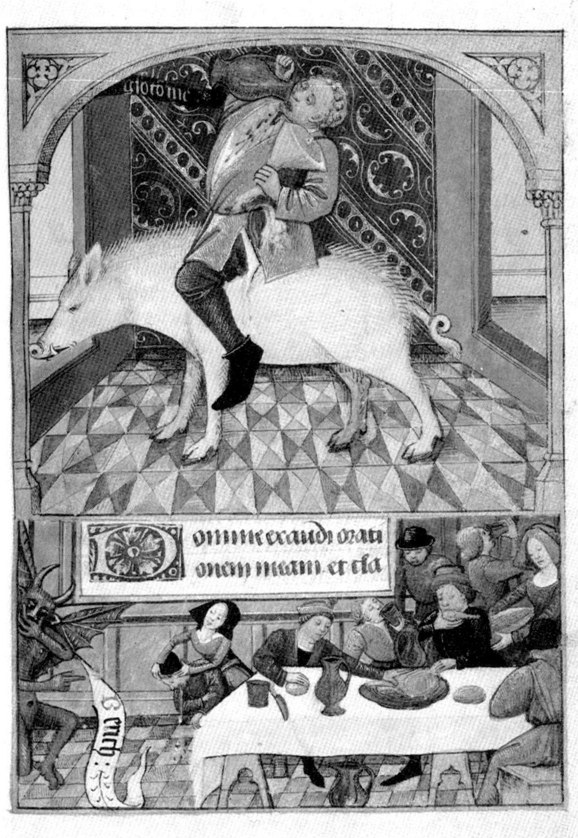

Fig. 68. *Gluttony Riding a Pig*, border: *Berich and a Gluttonous Feast* (Penitential Psalms), France, Poitiers, ca. 1475, attributed to Robinet Testard (Morgan M.1001, fol. 94; Cat. No. 53).

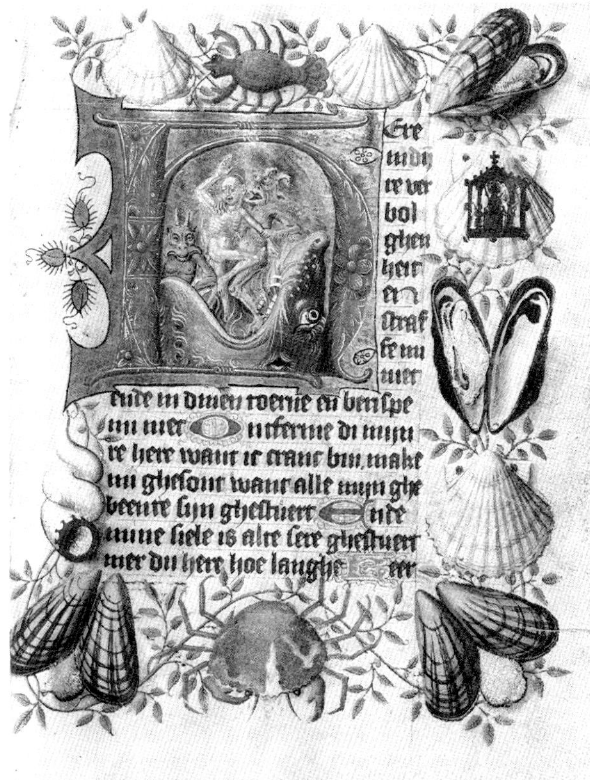

Fig. 69. *Souls Tormented by Devils in Hell* (Penitential Psalms), Holland, 1440s, by the workshop of the Master of Catherine of Cleves (Walters .782, fol. 113; Cat. No. 110).

manner of atoning for one's sins before it is too late.

The Litany is a list of saints with each invocation followed by "Ora pro nobis"—"Pray for us." In a Book of Hours it normally followed immediately after the Penitential Psalms and was recited with them. It is hardly ever illustrated. Some interesting exceptions, however, deserve mention. Walters 102 is an extremely idiosyncratic English Book of Hours from the late thirteenth century. For example, a scribe who executed pen-work initials could not resist the temptation to add numerous grotesques in variously colored inks. Some of them, a crucified Christ with the head of a chicken and a youth committing the sin of Onan, border on the obscene. The illustrations that fill blank spaces in the Litany of this manuscript, while not naughty, are certainly eccentric. A woman being swallowed by a dragon could be St. Margaret, but, curiously, she is not even invoked in the Litany. If there is a connection between the hermit saints addressed in the line below a picture of the she-wolf suckling Romulus and Remus, it is certainly a tenuous one. The tradition of depicting St. Stephen with a bleeding head wound, a reference to the lapidation by which he died, helps explain the image of the martyr's portrait included next to his name, but giving the head the cruciform halo that Christ alone wears is close to sacrilege (Fig. 70). The chess players, one dressed only in his underclothes, are equally baffling.

In the Ruskin Hours, a French Book of Hours from the early fourteenth century, the Litany was planned for illustrations, something that cannot be affirmed for the English *Horae* just described. In the French manuscript, each invocation was written on three lines, instead of the usual one, thus creating enough space for a series of small square miniatures for each saint (Fig. 71). The saints are given attributes, and Agnes can be recognized with the *Agnus Dei* and Catherine with sword and, beneath her feet, the Emperor Maxentius. Other saints are shown at particularly significant moments in their lives: Agatha, for example, is shown courageously undergoing the removal of her breasts.

Elaborately illustrated Litanies like those in Walters 102 and the Ruskin Hours are, however, rare. Occasionally, a single miniature or historiated border is used

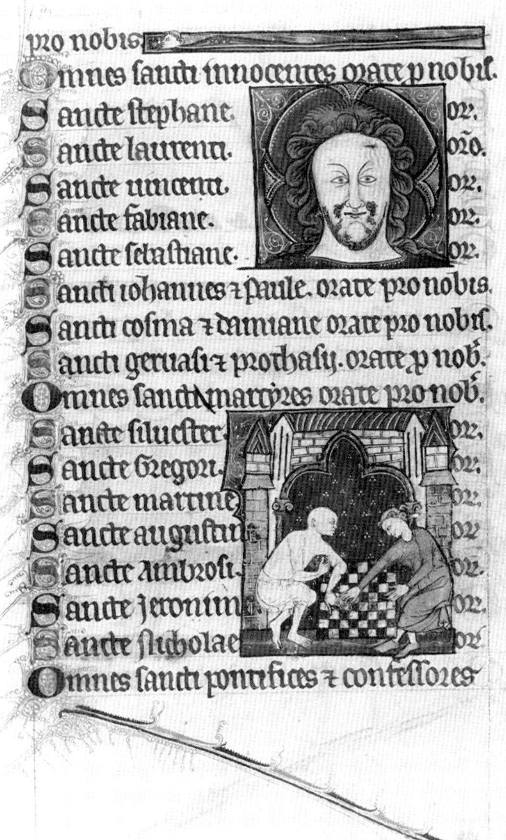

70

to mark the beginning of the Litany and thus separate it from the Penitential Psalms. In some early *Horae,* when the Litany does not immediately follow the Psalms and is thus a unit unto itself, it will be provided with a miniature like all the other important texts. This is the case in an early fourteenth-century Book of Hours produced most probably in Arras (Fig. 72). A miniature of three chanting monks is placed at the top of the Litany while figures of the apostles, standing on bits of foliage that sprout from the frame, are sprinkled in the border. On the facing page is a second miniature, filling a bit of blank space, of the Madonna; her help, as well as that of the numerous adoring angels that surround her, is sought in the Litany.

Fig. 70. *Head of Christ/St. Stephen, Chess Game* (Litany), England, end of the 13th century (Walters 102, fol. 29; Cat. No. 111).

Fig. 71. *Martyrdom of Agatha; Agnes; Cecilia; Lucy; Catherine* (Litany), northern France, early 14th century (Getty, Ludwig IX.3, fol. 105v; Cat. No. 9).

Fig. 72. *Three Monks Chanting,* border: *Saints* (Litany), France, probably Arras, early 14th century (Walters 104, fol. 71; Cat. No. 8).

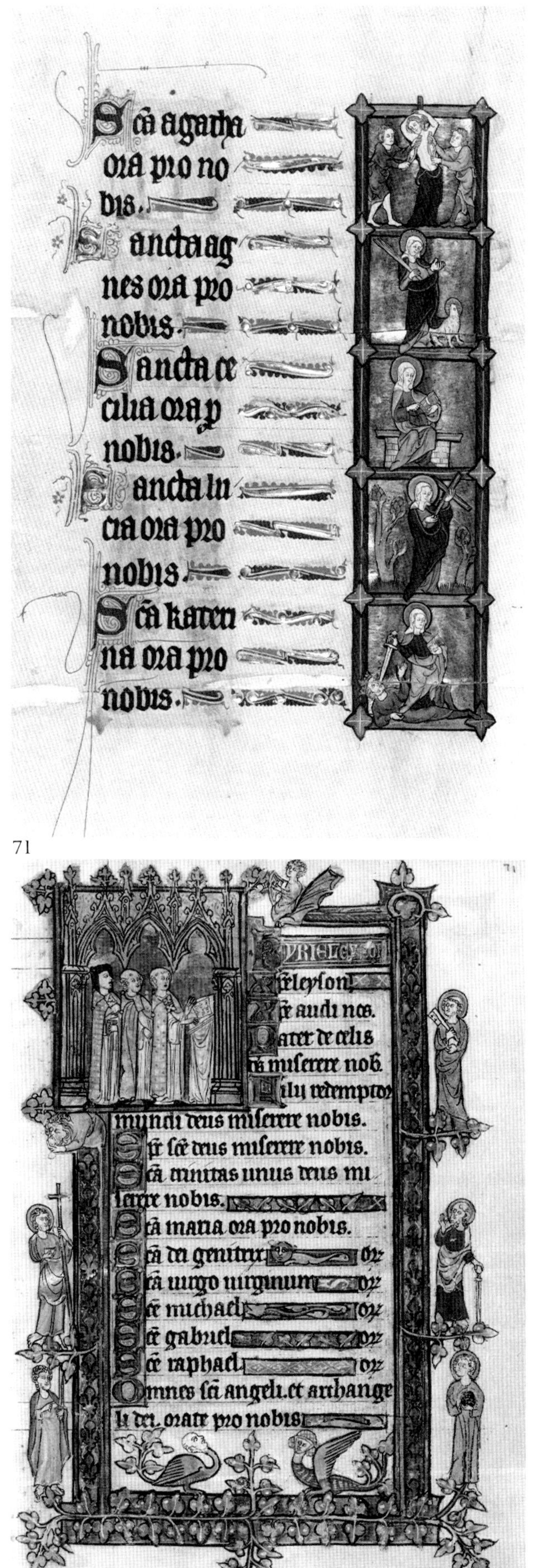

71

72

CHAPTER X

Accessory Texts

In addition to the more or less standard texts of a Book of Hours, a great number of accessory texts and prayers are also frequently found. A survey of the contents of a large body of Books of Hours reveals that owners felt free to insert any number of prayers, which were sometimes very personal, and that they exercised this freedom liberally. From these innumerable addenda there emerges a group of about fifteen prayers that enjoyed special popularity. Of these, about a dozen regularly received miniatures.

The commemoration of the Fifteen Joys of the Virgin is the most popular of all the accessory prayers, especially in fifteenth-century France. (Fifteen is the usual number of the Joys, but five, seven, and nine also appear.) The prayer celebrates the joyous moments of the Virgin's life: the Annunciation, Visitation, Conception of Christ, Nativity, Adoration of the Shepherds, Adoration of the Magi, Presentation of Christ in the Temple, Christ among the Doctors, Marriage Feast at Cana, Multiplication of the Loaves, Passion of Christ, Resurrection, Pentecost, Ascension, and Assumption of the Virgin. Nearly all miniatures for the Joys have the Virgin and Child as their subject, thus emphasizing the joys of motherhood in a manner similar to miniatures for the "Obsecro te" (see Chapter VIII). In a Parisian Book of Hours of about 1410, a *Virgo Lactans*, the nursing Madonna, is used for the Joys of the Virgin (Pl. 32). The miniature, by a follower of the Master of Berry's *Cleres Femmes*, shows Mary as the Virgin of Humility, seated, with the comfort provided by a few cushions, on the ground. The garden, filled with fruit trees and numerous flowers, refers to the "hortus conclusus," the enclosed garden that symbolizes Mary's virginity. The Virgin wears her crown as Queen of Heaven, and, indeed, in some miniatures for the Fifteen Joys she is shown enthroned. There are other numerous variations among these Madonnas used for the Joys. Angels frequently accompany Mary and the Christ Child, offering fruit or flowers, or playing musical instruments, at times with the Savior himself lending a hand. As with the miniatures for the "Obsecro te," owners sometimes had themselves included, kneeling in prayer before Christ and his mother.

The prayer that often immediately follows the Joys of the Virgin, as it does in the Parisian *Horae* just discussed, is the series of Seven Requests to Our Lord. It was nearly as popular in fifteenth-century France as the Joys of the Virgin. The prayer seeks God's pity by reminding him of those times or of those people upon which or on whom, in the past, he bestowed his kindness: at the Annunciation, at the Incarnation, on his disciples, on Peter at his denial, on the women on the road to Calvary, on the Virgin and John at the foot of the cross, and on the Good Thief. The Trinity appears in many miniatures of the Seven Requests, the inspiration for which was provided by the opening lines of the prayer that address the Trinity directly. Most miniatures, however, show Christ. While he is sometimes shown blessing or represented as the Man of Sorrows, the most frequently encountered image is Christ as Judge or Christ of the Last Judgement, often with the resurrection of souls. An example of the former can be found in Walters 260, a French Book of Hours painted by the workshop of the Boucicaut Master (Fig. 73). Christ sits on a rainbow and raises his arms to expose the bleeding wounds in his hands while opening his mantle to show the wound in his side; behind him angels carry the instruments of the Passion. The ico-

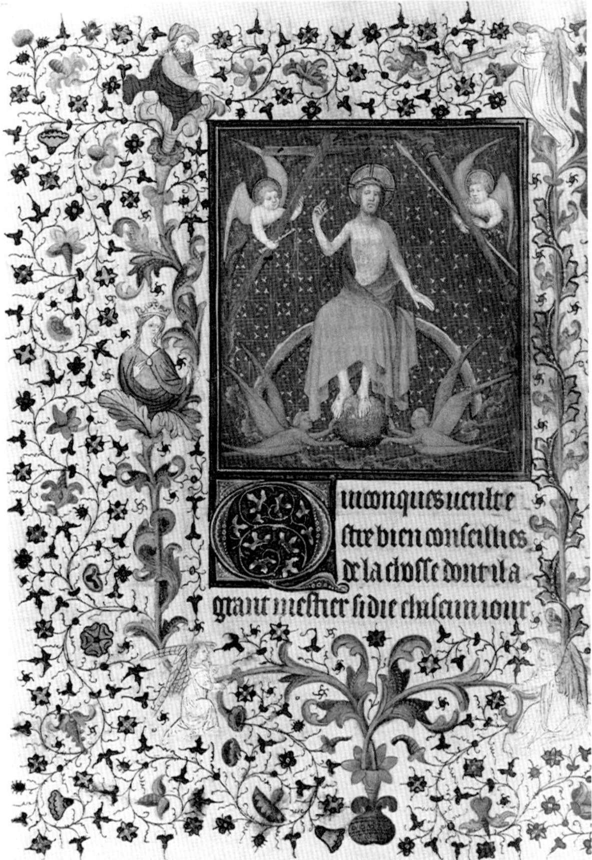

Fig. 73. *Christ as Judge* (7 Requests to Our Lord), France, Paris, ca. 1415, by the workshop of the Boucicaut Master (Walters 260, fol. 223v; Cat. No. 26).

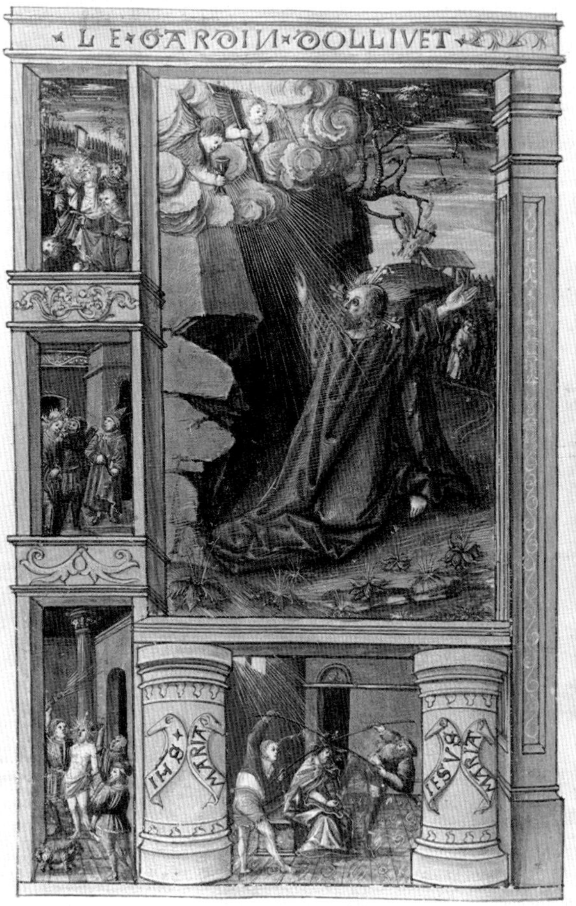

Fig. 74. *Agony in the Garden* with border vignettes (Passion according to John), France, Burgundy (Dijon?), ca. 1480 (Walters 291, fol. 19v; Cat. No. 62).

nography for the Seven Requests follows that of the early tradition for the Penitential Psalms (see Chapter IX). The general adoption in the fifteenth century of David's penance as the usual theme for the Psalms, however, eliminated duplication and permitted these illustrations of Christ to become the standard for the Seven Requests.

The biblical account of Christ's Passion often appears in Books of Hours, and the version used most frequently is John's. The evangelist's story begins with Christ's going forth with the disciples to the Garden of Gethsemane. Appropriately, Christ's Agony in the Garden is the subject painters used most for the miniature placed at the beginning of the text. A dramatic example can be found in the Hours of Ogier Bénigne, a Burgundian manuscript executed about 1480 (Fig. 74). In the main scene angels present a cross and chalice to a reluctant Savior whose outstretched arms seem too weak even to raise the weight of his heavy robe. In the background, in the fading twilight, Judas and soldiers have arrived. Vignettes in the border continue the story: the *Betrayal, Christ before Caiaphas,* the *Flagellation,* and *Christ Crowned with Thorns.* The Betrayal, here used as a vignette, is also frequently the main subject of the miniature introducing the Passion, but almost any episode from the Passion can be found here: the Flagellation, the *Ego Sum* (when Christ's response, "I am the one," to the soldiers who sought him caused them to fall to the ground in amazement), Christ Carrying the Cross, the Crucifixion, the Pietà, and, occasionally, the Man of Sorrows. In rare instances, John, the author of the Passion, is shown writing his text on Patmos.

The emotional intensity, rhythm, and rhymes of the "Stabat mater" made this prayer extremely popular in the Middle Ages. While a Crucifixion or a Lamentation is sometimes used to accompany this text, it is the Pietà that one encounters most frequently. This theme, of course, allowed painters to focus, as does the prayer itself, on the Virgin's overwhelming sorrow at the suffering of her Son. A late fifteenth-century Book of Hours by a follower of Simon Marmion contains a moving *Pietà* for its "Stabat mater" (Fig. 75). Marmion's use of the dramatic close-up serves him particularly well for this, the last time Mary will hold her Son. Our attention, like the Virgin's, focuses on the body of Christ. Although the wounds in his hands, side, and around his head still drip with blood, Christ's cheeks, lips, and the numerous cuts and bruises on his arms and torso have already assumed a death-like, blue pallor. His pupils float upward in slits of eyes that are swollen and red. While the Pietà is the usual subject for the "Stabat mater" others include the Man of Sorrows, the Virgin in Prayer, or the Virgin and John the Evangelist Mourning.

The prayer to the Holy Face of Christ, "Salve sancta facies," appears in many fifteenth-century Flemish Books of Hours. Christ as the *Salvator Mundi* and bust-length "portraits" of Christ are both found in miniatures for this prayer. More popular, however, is Veronica with her Veil, an image to which there were often generous indulgences attached if one recited the "Salve sancta facies" while looking at the picture. Walters 211, a Flemish Book of Hours painted by an artist of the Gold Scrolls group, contains a large variety of accessory prayers, including one series with, among other prayers, the Joys of the Virgin and the "Stabat mater." The "Salve sancta facies" heads the whole group and it is marked by a miniature of Veronica with her Veil (Fig. 76).

The Gold Scrolls *Horae* just mentioned also contains a series of optional Hours that find their way frequently into fifteenth-century Books of Hours, especially in Flanders. These are the Weekday Hours: Sunday Hours of the Trinity, Monday Hours of the Dead, Tuesday Hours of the Holy Spirit, Wednesday Hours of All Saints, Thursday Hours of the Holy Sacrament, Friday Hours of the Cross, and the Saturday Hours of the Virgin. Early Christians had retained from Jewish observance the dedication of a day of rest, but had transferred this to Sunday, which became the Lord's Day. The Jewish fast of Thursday was moved to Friday, the day of the Crucifixion. Other medieval traditions associated Monday with All Souls and Saturday with the Virgin. Each of the Weekday Hours in the Gold Scrolls *Horae* is pre-

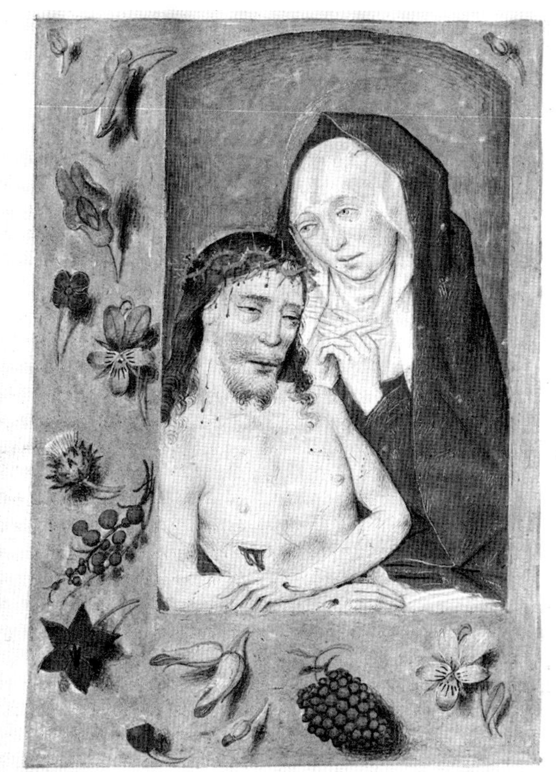

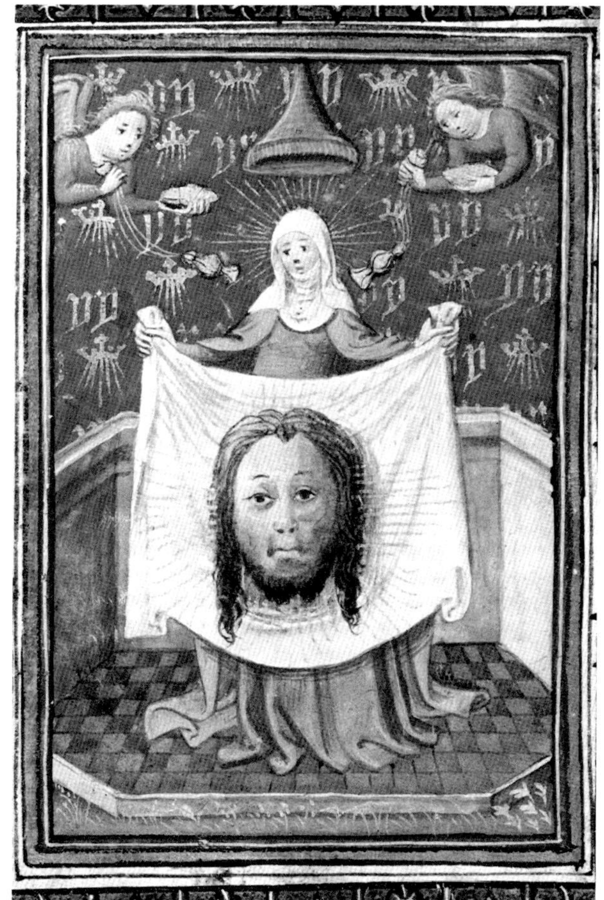

Fig. 75. *Pietà* ("Stabat mater"), Belgium, ca. 1480s, by the Master of Antoine Rolin (Walters 431, fol. 77v; Cat. No. 101).

Fig. 76. *Veronica with her Veil* ("Salve sancta facies"), Belgium, Bruges, ca. 1440, by a painter of the Gold Scrolls group (Walters 211, fol. 82v; Cat. No. 88).

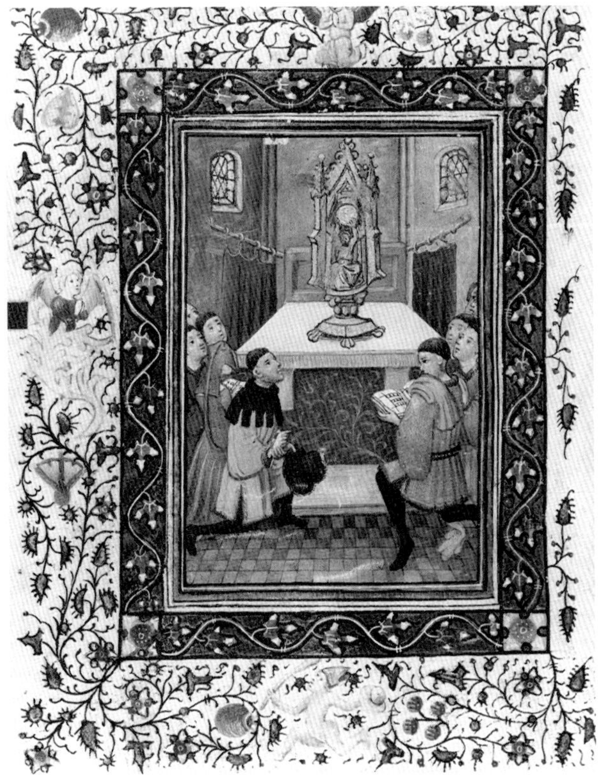

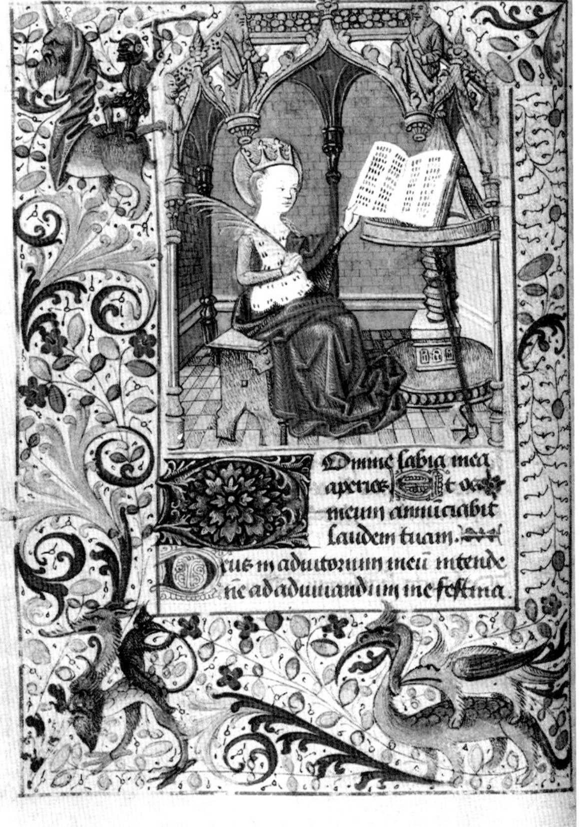

ceded by its own picture. The Thursday Hours of the Holy Sacrament have a representation of the Adoration of the Eucharist (Fig. 77). A group of men and women, two of whom pray from Books of Hours, kneel before an altar on which rests a large gold monstrance containing a consecrated host. The medieval desire to see the consecrated host, a desire that had, earlier on, given birth to the practice of elevating the wafer after the consecration at Mass (as in Pl. 13), also led to the practice of exhibiting the Eucharist in church for public prayer and adoration outside of Mass.

In the Gold Scrolls *Horae* just discussed, each of the Weekday Hours is accompanied by the appropriate Votive Mass. These Masses include those texts that change from one Mass to another—the Introit, Collect, Epistle, Gradual, Gospel, Offertory, Communion, and Postcommunion—as well as some standard texts—the Credo, Sanctus, and Agnus Dei. Books of Hours often had these special Masses, although they were not always combined with the Weekday Hours. Votive Masses were sometimes collected together into a group that included the Masses of the Holy Spirit, of the Virgin, and of the Dead. A Pentecost, a Madonna, and a Funeral Service are the usual subjects of the miniatures that sometimes accompany these Masses. The Mass of the Virgin is the one that most often appears in Books of Hours. While a Madonna is the usual image, the *Virgo Lactans*, Death of the Virgin, and Coronation of the Virgin are also found. For the Mass of the Virgin, as well as for the other Votive Masses, an image of a priest celebrating Mass is also used.

In addition to the Weekday Hours, a number of other optional Hours are found in *Horae*, often accompanied by miniatures. The most frequently encountered of these include the Hours of the Conception of the Virgin, the Hours of the Compassion of the Virgin, the Hours of Eternal Wisdom (a specialty of Dutch *Horae*), and a variety of Hours devoted to favorite saints. These include Joseph, John the Baptist, Agatha, Mary Magdalene, Barbara, and Catherine. The latter is sometimes considered the most popular saint of the Middle Ages and the frequency of the Hours of St. Catherine in Books of Hours tends to confirm this. In the Tourotte Hours, produced in Poitiers around 1465, a miniature of St. Catherine in her Study by the Master of Walters 222 precedes the Hours dedicated to her (Fig. 78). The

Fig. 77. *Adoration of the Eucharist* (Thursday Hours of the Holy Sacrament), Belgium, Bruges, ca. 1440, by a painter of Gold Scrolls group (Walters 211, fol. 45v; Cat. No. 88).

Fig. 78. *Catherine in her Study* (Hours of St. Catherine), France, Poitiers, ca. 1465, by the Master of Walters 222 (Walters 222, fol. 30v; Cat. No. 45).

image is iconographically very rich. Catherine wears royal ermine and a crown, for she is the daughter of King Costus; she holds a palm, the standard symbol of martyrdom, while reading from a book, the latter a reference to her great learning (for which she became the patron of students). On the floor lies a broken wheel, the instrument of torture with which the Emperor Maxentius vainly tried to execute the saint, and, leaning against the lectern, is the sword by which she finally met her end. A testimony to the high esteem in which Catherine was held in the Middle Ages can be gleaned from this Book of Hours. In a manner that is most unusual for Hours devoted to a saint, the Hours of St. Catherine have been interspersed within the Hours of the Virgin along with the Hours of the Cross and those of the Holy Spirit. Other episodes from the virgin saint's life are also the subject of miniatures preceding her Hours: Catherine Confounding the Doctors or Catherine Saved from the Wheel.

The Seven Prayers of St. Gregory, a series of seven short ejaculations addressed to the crucified Christ, often appears in Books of Hours. Tradition attributes this prayer to St. Gregory, the sixth-century pope and a Father of the Church, and it is always accompanied by a miniature depicting the Mass of St. Gregory. According to one legend, Gregory was celebrating a Mass during which one of his assistants doubted the real presence of Christ in the Eucharist. During the Mass, Christ himself appeared on the altar, allaying any doubts as to the real nature of the Communion wafer. Our example, typical of many, is from a French Book of Hours of the 1480s (Fig. 79). Gregory is shown genuflecting just after the Transubstantiation, the moment when the bread of the wafer becomes the body of Christ; he is about to stand and elevate the consecrated host, aided by the two assistants who will lift his chasuble. Above the chalice, at the exact position where the raised host would be, Christ appears, as the bleeding and crowned Man of Sorrows. Behind the Savior is the cross, along with the ladder, bag of coins, and Christ's robe; the rest of the *Arma Christi*, the instruments of the Passion, fill the border of the page. The manuscript contains, as is often the case with this prayer, a long rubric outlining the steps necessary to receive the indulgence attached to it—46,000 years in this case. One requirement of the indulgence, like that attached to "Salve sancta facies," is that the prayer be recited before a picture of Gregory's vision.

In addition to the texts of various Masses that occur in Books of Hours, as discussed above, there are also numerous prayers to the Eucharist to be said during Mass. As accompanying rubrics make clear, there are specific prayers to be recited before, during, and after

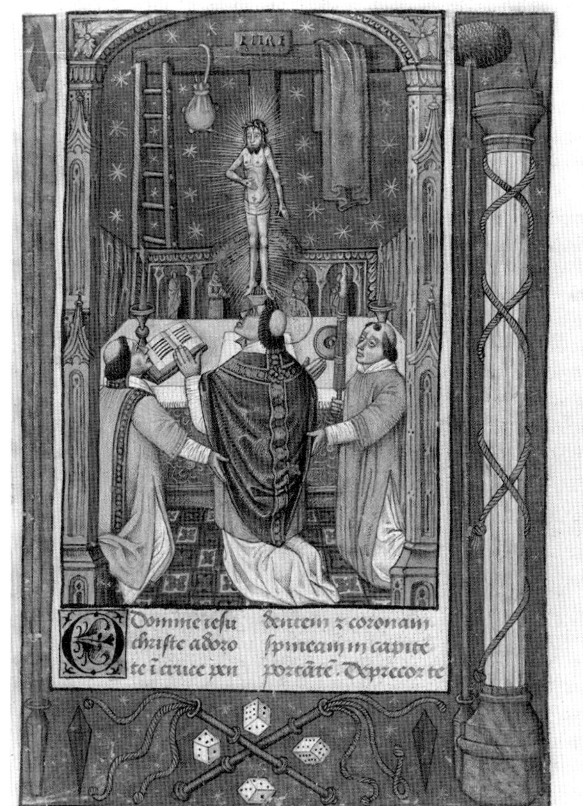

Fig. 79. *Mass of St. Gregory*, border: *Arma Christi* (7 Prayers of St. Gregory), France, mid-1480s (Walters 245, fol. 62; Cat. No. 64).

Communion. There are also specific prayers to be said at the elevation of the host by the priest. Most of these prayers do not receive miniatures. The "O salutaris hostia" is occasionally illustrated, albeit rarely. In 1433 Pope Eugene IV presented Duke Philip the Good of Burgundy with a precious relic, a miraculous Communion wafer. According to legend, this host, stamped with an image of Christ as Judge, had been subjected to desecration by a Jew and had miraculously begun to bleed. The duke had the relic installed in the Sainte Chapelle of the Chartreuse de Champmol, the Carthusian monastery that Philip's grandfather, Philip the Bold, had founded in Dijon as a mausoleum for himself and his heirs. In 1454 Philip's wife, Duchess Isabelle of Portugal, presented the canons of the Sainte Chapelle with a silver-gilt monstrance for displaying the relic. A few Books of Hours with connections to Dijon or the Burgundian court contain rare representations of this sacred host. The Hours of Ogier Bénigne belongs to this select group (Fig. 80). The image of Christ, arms outstretched and flanked by the instruments of

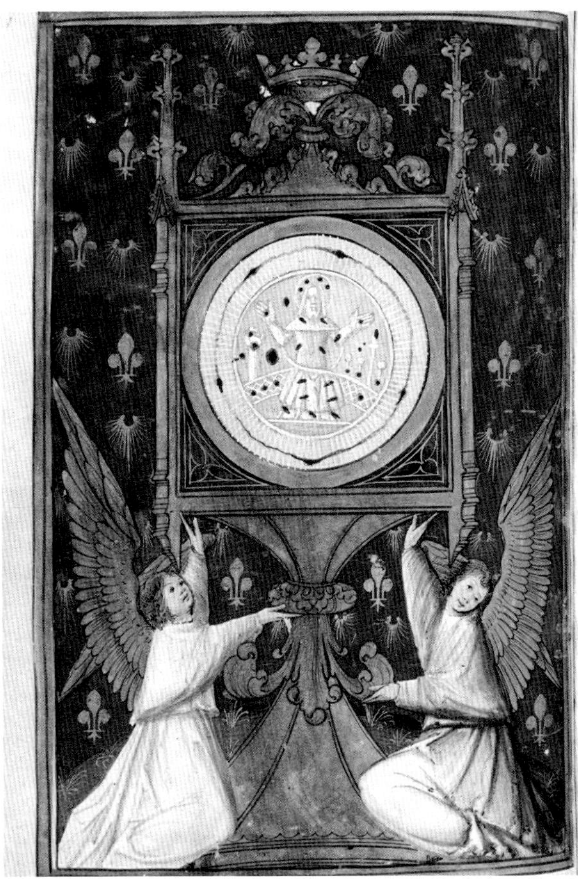

Fig. 80. *Miraculous Bleeding Host of Dijon* ("O salutaris hostia"), France, Burgundy (Dijon?), added ca. 1500 (Walters 291, fol. 17v; Cat. No. 62).

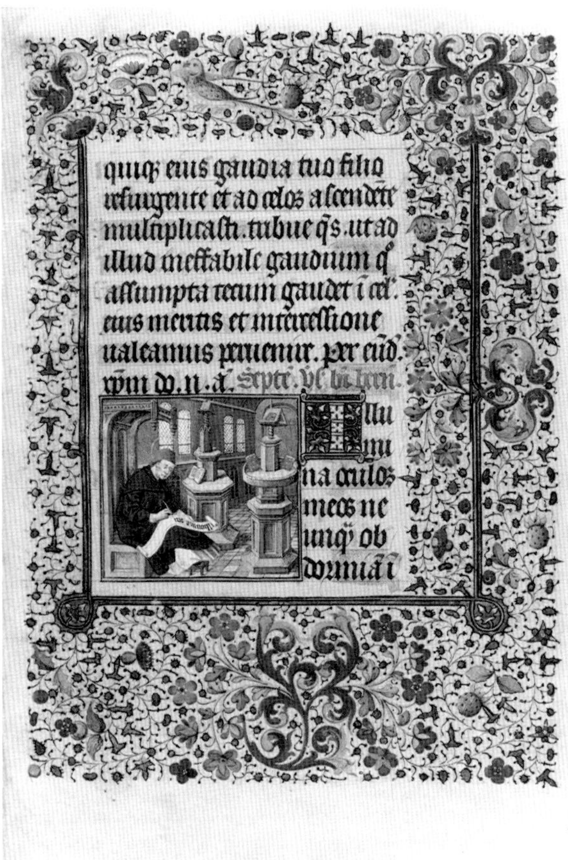

Fig. 81. *Bernard in his Study* (7 Verses of St. Bernard), France, Paris? and/or Loire region?, ca. 1470, by the Master of Jean Rolin II (Walters 285, fol. 100; Cat. No. 50).

the Passion, has been carefully painted by the illuminator. Painted with equal care are the miraculous drops of blood that appeared on the host after its mutilation; they spot the surface like wounds from a scourging and form a ring, like a crown, around the perimeter. Details of Isabelle's monstrance, destroyed during the Revolution (like so much of France's medieval art) but known from other sources, are also reflected in the miniature: the square form of the capsule, the base with two angels, and the top surmounted by pinnacles.

The Seven Verses of St. Bernard commemorate a humorous medieval legend. According to the story, the devil approached the famous Cistercian and told him that he knew of seven verses from the psalms that, if recited daily, would guarantee salvation. When the devil refused to reveal which seven verses these were, Bernard replied that he would simply recite the entire psalter each day. Horrified, the devil, who could think of no more efficacious means to salvation than praying all the psalms, identified the specific verses. The Hours of Pope Leo X contains a small miniature by the master of Jean Rolin II for the Verses of St. Bernard (Fig. 81). Surrounded by multi-tiered lecterns, Bernard sits in his study; on the scroll in his lap he writes the opening words of the first verse, "Illumina ocu(los)." Other miniatures for the Verses illustrate the episode related above, showing the devil in debate with the learned author.

A few other accessory prayers sometimes received miniatures as well. The Seven Last Words of Our Lord, a prayer constructed around the final utterances of the Savior, sometimes has a Crucifixion or Resurrection. The Psalter of St. Jerome, a sort of abbreviated psalter consisting of about two hundred shortened verses from the psalms, receives, when illustrated, a miniature of St. Jerome in his Study. In Walters 240 the miniature shows Jerome's removing a thorn (rather large in this case) from the paw of the lion that, henceforth, would become his faithful companion and, in art, his pictorial attribute (Fig. 82).

The early fifteenth-century Parisian *Horae*, whose

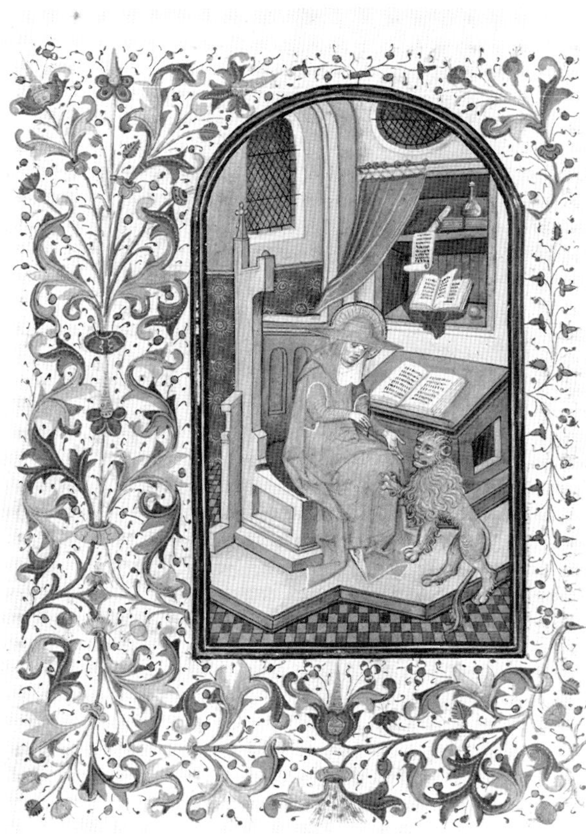

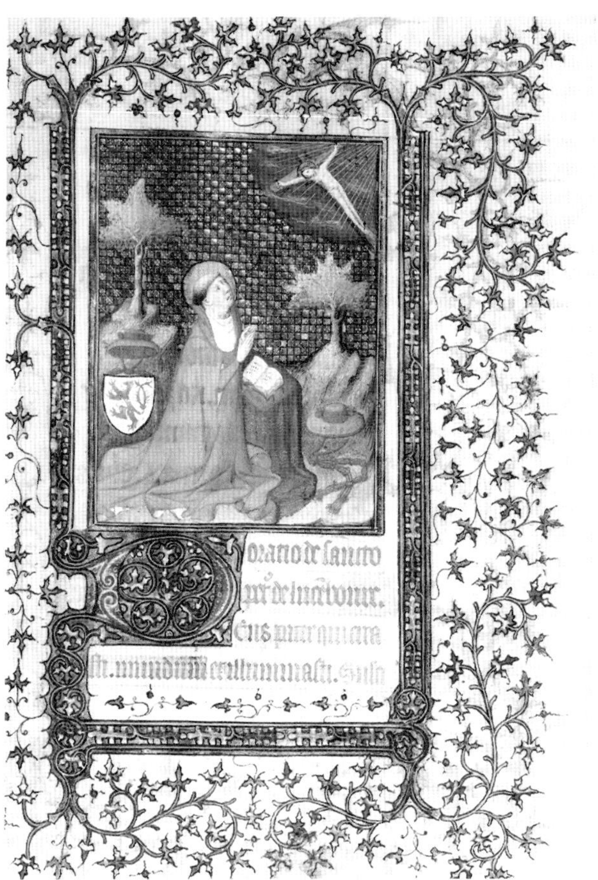

Fig. 82. *Jerome Removing the Lion's Thorn* (Psalter of St. Jerome), Belgium, Bruges, 1450s, by Willem Vrelant (Walters 240, fol. 304v; Cat. No. 92).

Fig. 83. *Peter of Luxembourg Kneeling before a Vision of the Crucifixion* (Prayer of Blessed Peter of Luxembourg), France, Paris, ca. 1410, by the Lucon Master (Walters 232, fol. 93; Cat. No. 21).

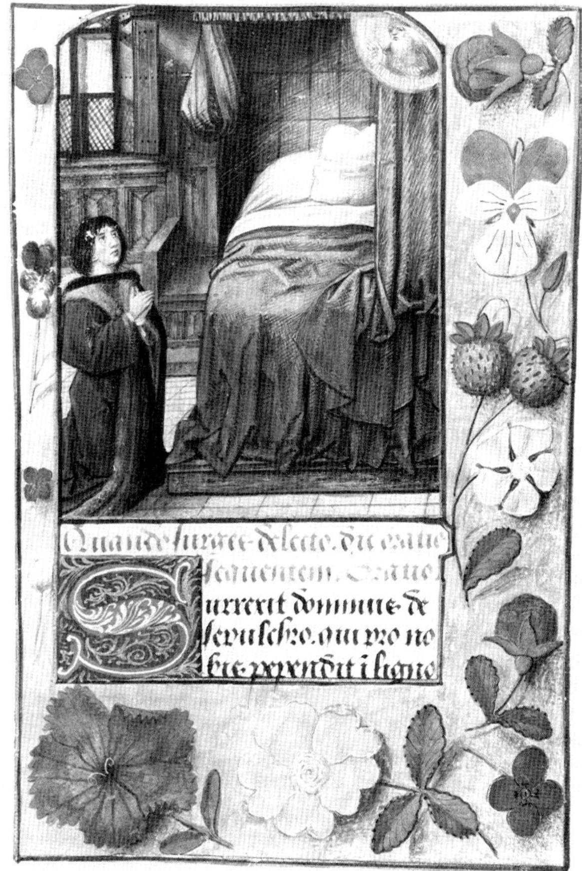

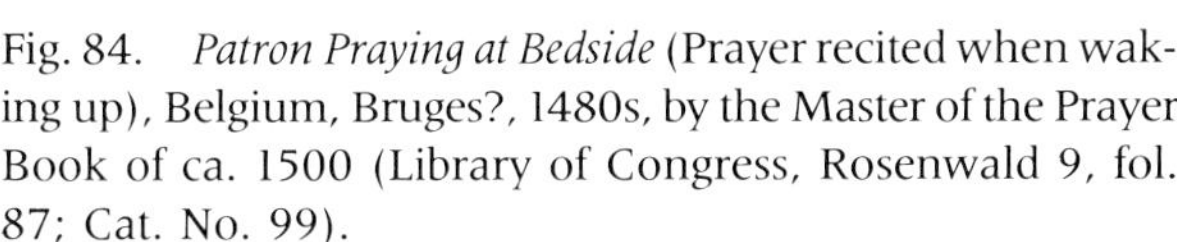

Fig. 84. *Patron Praying at Bedside* (Prayer recited when waking up), Belgium, Bruges?, 1480s, by the Master of the Prayer Book of ca. 1500 (Library of Congress, Rosenwald 9, fol. 87; Cat. No. 99).

miniature of the *Virgo Lactans* began this discussion of accessory prayers, also contains a miniature for the prayer attributed to Peter of Luxembourg (Fig. 83). Bishop at the age of fifteen, cardinal at seventeen, Blessed Peter of Luxembourg's career in the Church was meteoric even by medieval standards. Peter died in 1387 at the age of eighteen. Declared blessed and sometimes called a saint, he has yet to be canonized. As is typical with miniatures of this figure, Peter is dressed in his cardinal's robes and kneels in prayer before a vision of the crucified Christ.

Numerous Books of Hours contain prayers to be recited before going to bed (the ancestors of our "Now I lay me down to sleep") or upon waking up. These prayers are not usually illustrated, but sometimes they are. Among the many miniatures added by King Charles V of France to the Savoy Hours, Blanche of Burgundy's extremely rich prayer book, was a miniature, accompanying a prayer to be recited upon rising, representing the king in bed praying (Cat. No. 11; unfortunately this miniature is among the many from this manuscript destroyed by fire in 1904). A Flemish Book of Hours with miniatures by the Master of the Prayer Book of ca. 1500 also contains an illustrated morning prayer (Fig. 84). The picture represents the medieval Christian ideal: immediately upon waking and after getting dressed, but even before making one's bed, one dedicated the day to God.

CHAPTER XI

Suffrages

If the Book of Hours were a Gothic cathedral, its main altar dedicated to the Virgin Mary, the Suffrages would be its stained glass. Like stained glass windows, Suffrages are filled with images of popular or local favorite saints and episodes from their colorful lives. They usually appear at the end of a Book of Hours where a reader might turn to them somewhat leisurely, much as the visitor to a cathedral, his devout attention previously focused on the main altar, studies the colored windows while making his unhurried departure.

Suffrages, also called Memorials (*memoriae*), are primarily short prayers to saints. There can be a handful or, depending on the piety or pocketbook of the patron, a very large number. Blanche of Burgundy had eighty-three Suffrages included in her Book of Hours (Fig. 1, see Cat. No. 11). This, however, was not sufficient for King Charles V of France; when, later in the fourteenth century, Charles came to own Blanche's prayer book, he added thirty-two more (Fig. 2).

The saints commemorated in the Suffrages are usually arranged in an order reflecting the celestial hierarchy of heaven. God, of course, is invoked first, followed by the Virgin, Michael the Archangel, and John the Baptist. The Suffrages for the apostles are given next, followed by male martyrs and confessors. Female virgin martyrs are then listed, followed by widows. A typical sequence, as found in Walters 257 (Cat. No. 38), is: the Trinity, the Virgin, Michael, John the Baptist, Peter and Paul, John the Evangelist, Andrew, James, Stephen, Lawrence, Christopher, Dennis, Sebastian, Nicholas, Anthony, Maurus, Mary Magdalene, Catherine, and Margaret.

Suffrages, however, are not always illustrated. In some manuscripts the prayers receive no pictures; in others, a few favorite saints are given an illustration while those to whom the owner obviously felt less devoted are not. The saints are often shown standing, their attributes in hand, or they are depicted in one of the more dramatic moments of their lives.

In Walters 257, an example that can stand for many such *Horae*, the numerous Suffrages in the book are provided with but one picture, a *Trinity*, that marks the beginning of this section of the book (Fig. 85). God the Father supports a pathetically shriveled Christ who, without such help, would collapse to the floor.

Michael the Archangel is included among the many Suffrages in Walters 281, illuminated by the Master of Walters 281. Michael, the most popular angel in the Middle Ages, was the leader of the good angels who quashed Lucifer's revolt and sent the rebels to hell. In the miniature he is shown battling an energetic band of five devils (Pl. 33).

Walters 220, an extremely fine *Horae* by Willem Vrelant, contains a Suffrage to John the Baptist (Fig. 86). John, wearing the rough clothes of a hermit, stands among the trees and animals of a wilderness that is far from the towns seen in the background. John, the precursor of Christ, directs our attention to a lamb, the *Agnus Dei*, the symbol of Christ as the sacrificial victim.

Peter, the first pope, chosen by Christ as the leader of his followers, is usually the first of the apostles commemorated in the Suffrages. In a miniature from the workshop of the Master of the Harvard Hannibal, Peter is easily recognizable by his unique physiognomy (bald pate, short gray beard, and square jaw) as well as his attribute, the keys to the kingdom of heaven, dangling from his left hand (Fig. 87). Behind Peter is a large chair, resembling an episcopal throne. Set behind the

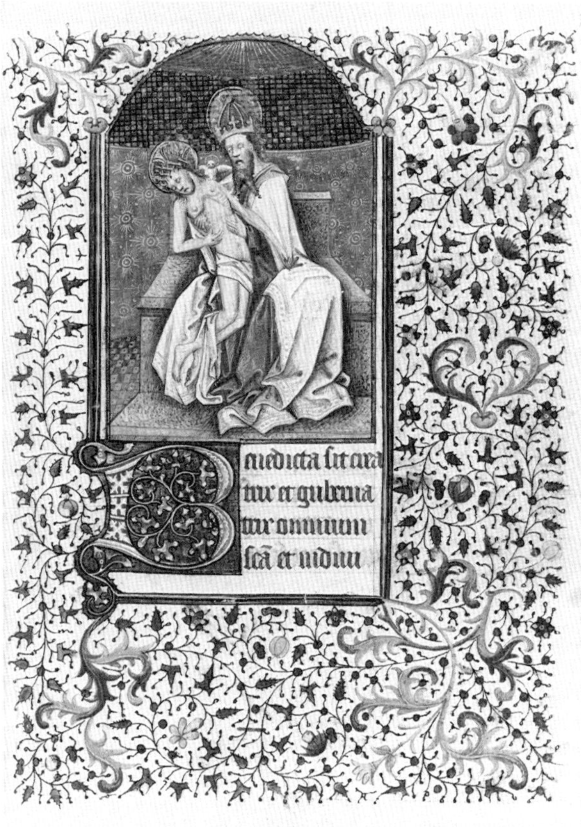

Fig. 85. *Trinity,* France, Paris?, mid-1440s (Walters 257, fol. 204; Cat. No. 38).

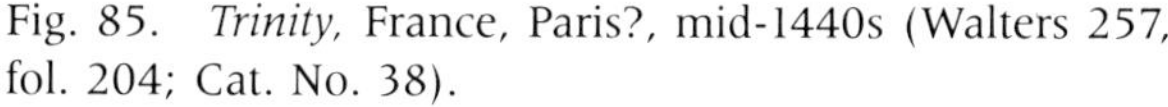

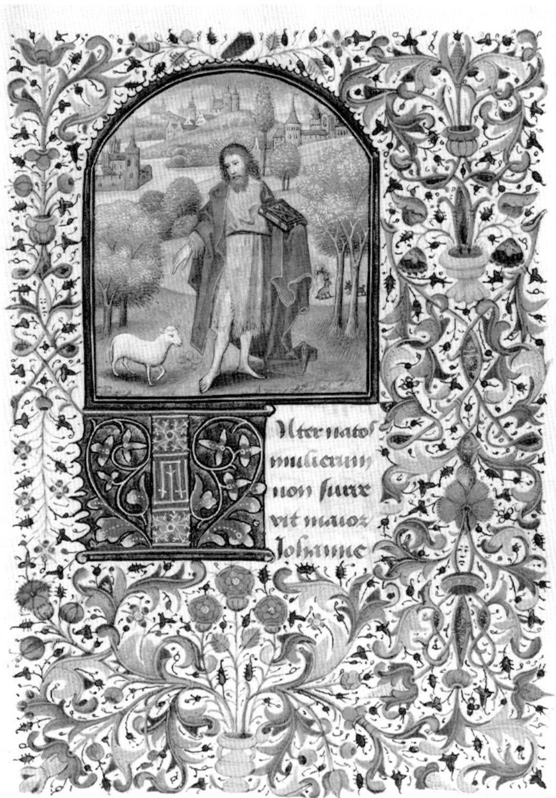

Fig. 86. *John the Baptist,* Belgium, Bruges, ca. 1450, by Willem Vrelant (Waters 220, fol. 148; Cat. No. 91).

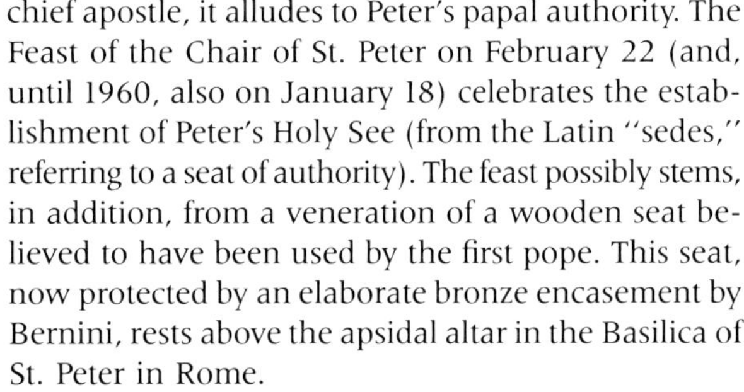

chief apostle, it alludes to Peter's papal authority. The Feast of the Chair of St. Peter on February 22 (and, until 1960, also on January 18) celebrates the establishment of Peter's Holy See (from the Latin "sedes," referring to a seat of authority). The feast possibly stems, in addition, from a veneration of a wooden seat believed to have been used by the first pope. This seat, now protected by an elaborate bronze encasement by Bernini, rests above the apsidal altar in the Basilica of St. Peter in Rome.

The Suffrage to Paul, Peter's companion in the conversion of the Romans, is also frequently illustrated. Walters 287, a masterpiece by the Master of the Harvard Hannibal, contains an elaborate series of twenty-two large and handsome Suffrage miniatures. The miniature of Paul is typical of the series in which the painter is able to combine statuesque, yet extremely elegant figures with interiors filled with minute, if at times fussy, detail (Fig. 88). Paul, like Peter, has a distinctively recognizable physiognomy: bulbous forehead and a long, pointed beard. In the miniature he carries the sword by which he met his martyrdom.

John the Evangelist follows Peter and Paul in the Suffrages. The Buves Hours contains an image of the evangelist holding one of his attributes, a chalice from which a small dragon emerges (Fig. 89). As the reader may recall from Chapter V, the high priest Aristodemus had challenged John to drink a cup of poison and remain unharmed. The apostle blessed the container and a serpent emerged, the miracle testifying to his direct access to divine powers. John stands before an altar on which rests a small retable painted with a

Fig. 87. *Peter,* France, Paris, 1420s, by the workshop of the Master of the Harvard Hannibal (Walters 259, fol. 79; Cat. No. 30).

Fig. 88. *Paul,* France, Paris, 1420s, by the Master of the Harvard Hannibal (Walters 287, fol. 129; Cat. No. 29).

Fig. 89. *John the Evangelist,* northern France or southern Belgium, 1450s (Walters 267, fol. 178v; Cat. No. 40).

Fig. 90. *Crucifixion of Andrew,* France, Paris? and/or Loire region?, ca. 1470, by the Master of Jean Rolin II (Walters 285, fol. 90; Cat. No. 50).

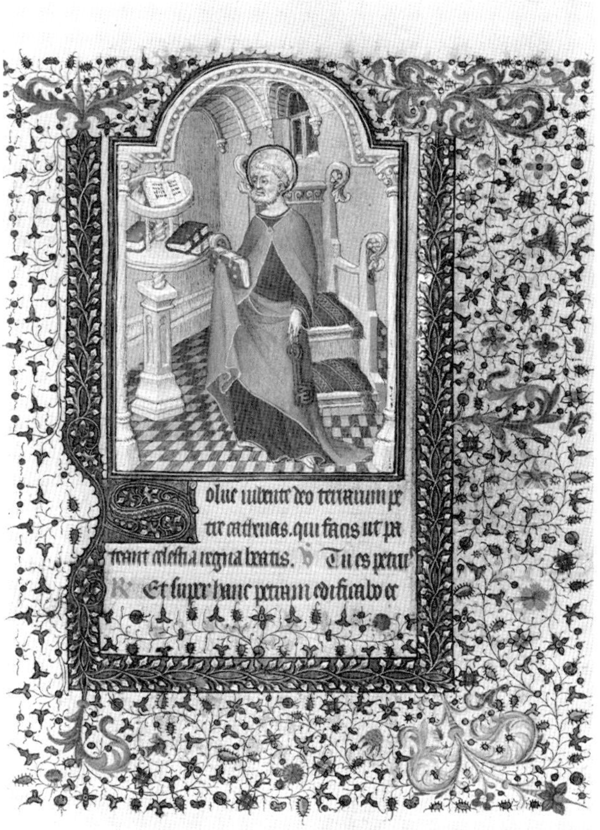

87

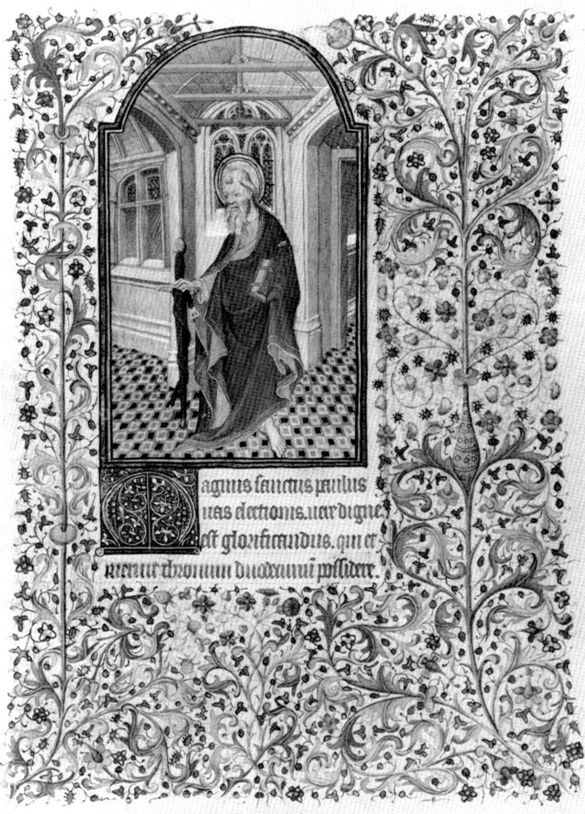

88

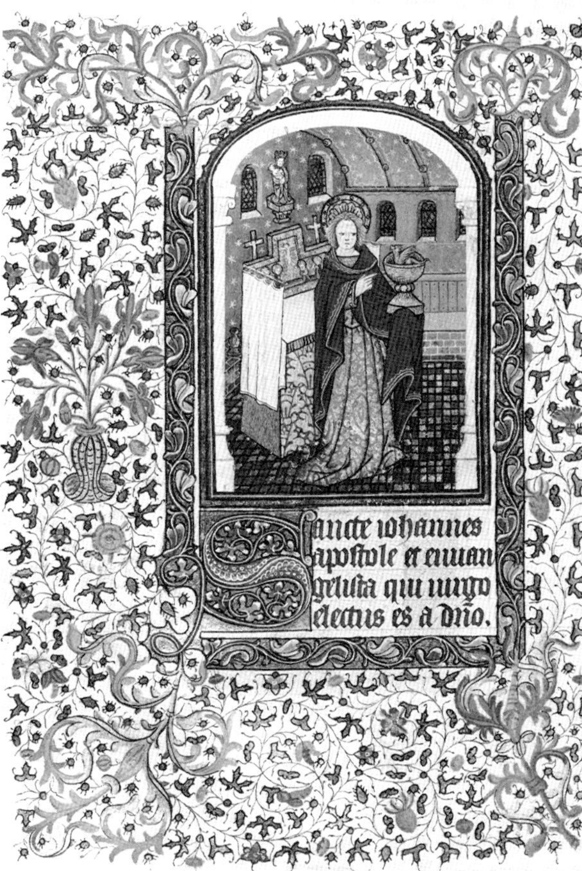

89

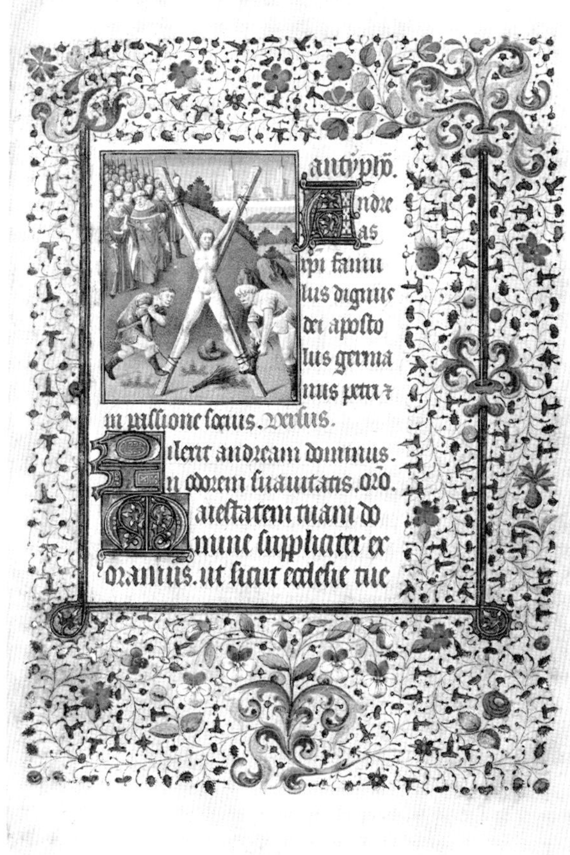

90

Crucifixion that includes both the Virgin and John himself standing below the cross. Affixed to the back wall of the apse is a statue of the Virgin whose welfare was entrusted to John by Christ from the cross.

The Hours of Pope Leo X contains an illustration for the Suffrage to St. Andrew by the Master of Jean Rolin II (Fig. 90). The brother of Peter and the first-chosen of Christ's disciples, Andrew was then among the first four whom Christ made his apostles. Late medieval tradition has it that Andrew was martyred by being tied to an X-shaped cross from which he was able to preach for two days before expiring.

Martyrs follow the apostles in the Suffrages. Stephen, the first Christian to die for his faith (and whose feast is celebrated the day after Christmas), holds a prominent position among martyrs. An early fifteenth-century Book of Hours from Flanders or northern France contains a dramatic depiction of the saint's painful death (Fig. 91). Three foppishly dressed youths fling rocks at the helpless deacon with a ferocity that requires their arms to extend beyond the frame of the miniature. While it was common, especially from the beginning of the fifteenth century on, for the Suffrages in a Book of Hours to be collected together at the end of the volume, there are numerous exceptions. Some manuscripts place Suffrages after Lauds of the Hours of the Virgin when they were meant to be recited. In this Book of Hours, groups of Suffrages follow not only Lauds, but also, in an unusual arrangement, each of the remaining six Hours of the Virgin (Prime through Compline).

Christopher has always been one of the Church's most popular saints, although he is not usually remembered as a martyr. He was the patron of travelers and, until his recent removal from the liturgical calendar, of motorists as well. Walters 240, a *Horae* by Vrelant, contains a typical representation of the best-known episode from this saint's life (Fig. 92). Christopher, a man of great size, was told by a hermit that he could best serve God by ferrying travelers across a dangerous river. A small child strangely proved to be his heaviest burden and the saint nearly drowned in his efforts to reach the river's shore. Setting the boy down, Christopher (whose name means "Christ-bearer") was told that his shoulders had supported not only the whole world, but also Him who had created it. (A translation of the Suffrage to Christopher from this manuscript is given in the Appendix.)

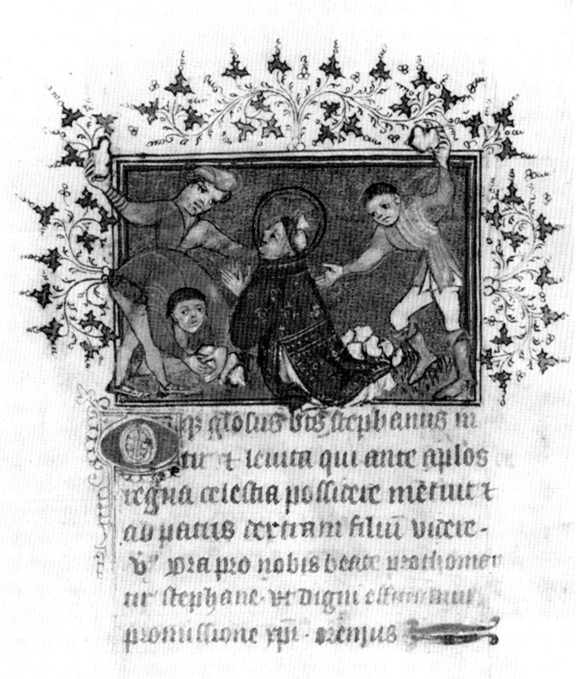

Fig. 91. *Lapidation of Stephen*, southern Belgium or northern France, early 15th century (Walters 215, fol. 65v; Cat. No. 81).

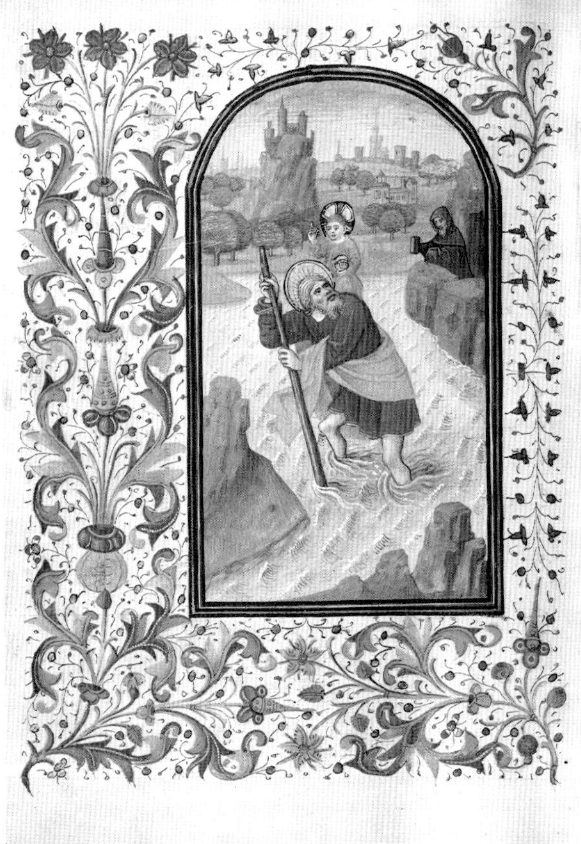

Fig. 92. *Christopher Carrying Christ*, Belgium, Bruges, 1450s, by Willem Vrelant (Walters 240, fol. 322v; Cat. No. 92).

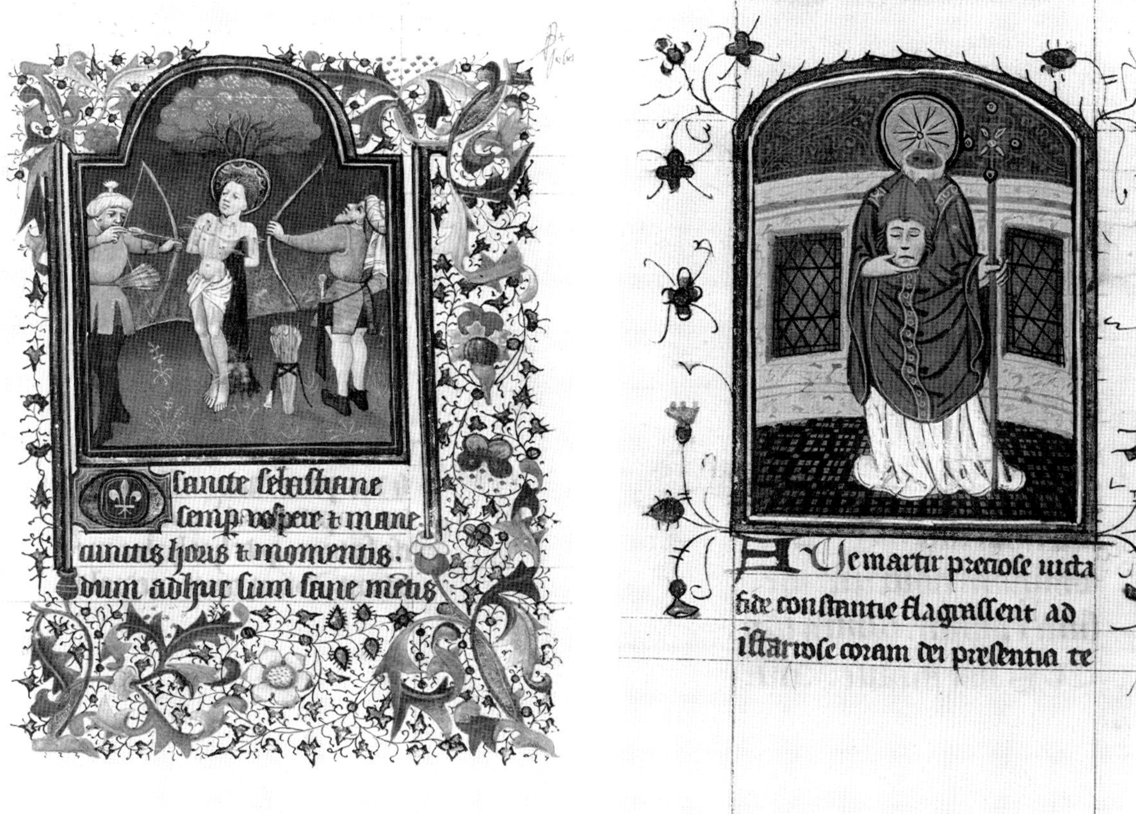

Fig. 93. *Sebastian Shot with Arrows,* Belgium, ca. 1440, by the Master of the Ghent Privileges (Walters 719, fol. 134; Cat. No. 86).

Fig. 94. *Nicasius,* Belgium, 1430s (Walters 164, fol. 173v; Cat. No. 82).

Along with Christopher, one of the most universally popular of all Christian martyrs is Sebastian. When it was discovered that the third-century captain in Diocletian's body guard was a Christian, the emperor handed him over to archers who shot his body full of arrows and left him for dead. The Master of the Ghent Privileges' representation of this event from the Egmont Hours is typical with the naked youth's body, pierced and bleeding, receiving further shots from archers who, as in all representations of the subject, tend to stand not too far away (Fig. 93). (Sebastian did not die from this torture: St. Irene removed the arrows and nursed him back to health. Sebastian returned to work for the emperor who promptly had him clubbed to death.) Sebastian's popularity in the late Middle Ages is due in great part to the bubonic plague of the fourteenth century and its later recurrences throughout the next. Sebastian was the patron saint of plague victims (he is invoked repeatedly in this capacity in the Suffrage from this manuscript provided in translation in the Appendix). The opportunity that Sebastian provided for portraying a beautiful nude youth ensured his popularity among artists and many of their clients. For this reason the nude Sebastian remained a popular subject from the late Middle Ages, through the Renaissance, to the nineteenth century.

Cephalophoric saints represent a particular kind of martyr of which the Middle Ages were particularly fond. Cephalophoric means "head carrying" and refers to those martyrs who, after being decapitated, picked up their heads and carried them for a while. Beheaded saints who might not have actually transported their heads anywhere, but are represented in art holding them, are also thrown into this group. Nicasius, a fifth-century bishop of Rheims, is a member of the latter type of cephalophoric saint (Fig. 94). The saint lost his head defending his city against barbarian invaders. Legend has it that he was in the middle of chanting a psalm when the fatal blow hit and that his severed head finished the interrupted verse. In this Flemish Book of Hours from the 1430s the saint, holding his head, recalls the arresting statue of Nicasius from the north portal of Rheims cathedral, carved almost exactly two hundred years before our miniature was painted. As is frequently the case in these paintings, the miniaturist has delighted in depicting the details of the severed arteries.

The most famous cephalophoric martyr was Dennis (Dionysius). This third-century saint was sent from his native Italy to Paris by Pope Fabian on the dangerous mission of restoring faith to the Gauls. The heathen Parisians tried to discourage his efforts by means of wild beasts, fire, and crucifixion. Finally, they were able to make him desist by beheading him on the site in Paris still called Montmartre. The headless body, however, rose to its feet, picked up its head and, guided by angels, walked the two miles from Montmartre to where the abbey church of St. Denis now stands on the site of the saint's collapse and later burial. The *Horae* by the Master of the Harvard Hannibal has a dramatic miniature for St. Dennis (Pl. 34). His two deacon companions, Rusticus and Eleutherius, look on miserably while Dennis kneels in calm acceptance of the sword's imminent blow. The executioner, grinning with sadistic delight, has knocked Dennis' miter down on his forehead and pushed its lappets forward in order to effect a clean cut.

International politics, conflicts between Church and State, and the clash of two dynamic personalities make the story of the career and martyrdom of Thomas Becket as fascinating to us in the twentieth century as it was to people of the twelfth. Henchmen for King Henry II slew the Archbishop of Canterbury in his own cathedral on December 29, 1170, scattering his brains on the church floor. Thomas was canonized a little more than two years later, an extraordinarily brief span of time for what was usually a lengthy process. Among the prefatory miniatures in the Butler Hours, an English *Horae* of the 1340s, is a miniature of the martyrdom of the archbishop (Fig. 95). Henry's soldiers slice through the crown of Thomas' head and injure the monk Edward Grim as he attempts to ward off blows with his cross. This miniature is remarkable not only for its drama and quality, but also for the fact that it exists at all. Images of Thomas Becket in English medieval art are rare since Henry VIII, in a proclamation of 1538, decreed that "his ymages and pictures, through the hole realme, shall be putte downe and auoyded out of all churches, chapelles, and other places, and that from hense forthe, the dayes vsed to be festiuall in his name, shall be not observed, nor the seruice, office, antiphones, collettes, and prayers in his name redde, but rased and put out of all the bokes." English prayer books that survived the establishment of the Church of England usually lack any image of Thomas,

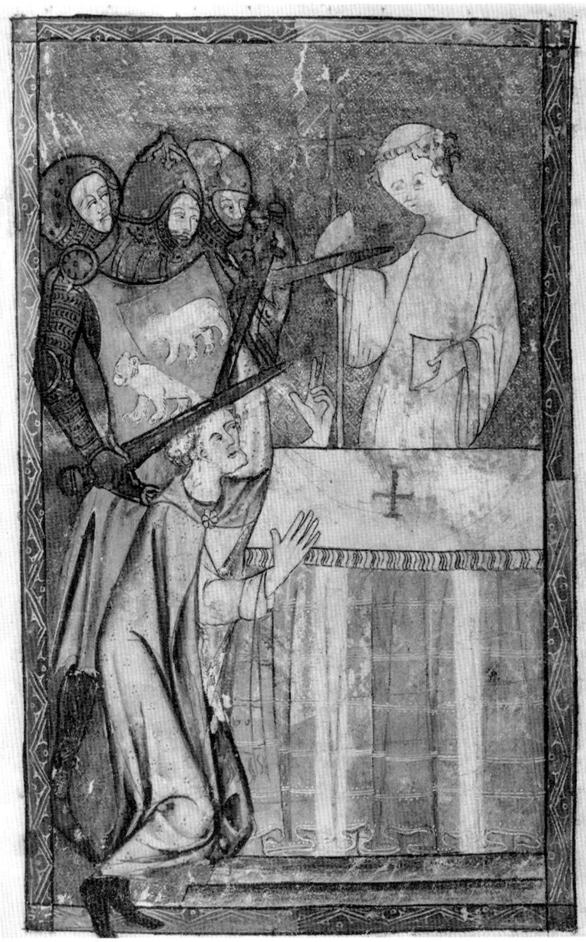

Fig. 95. *Martyrdom of Thomas Becket*, England, ca. 1340 (Walters 105, fol. 14; Cat. No. 112).

and his name, as well as that of any pope, is erased or crossed out.

A damsel in distress, a fire-breathing dragon, and a knight in shining armor—these are three motifs that characterize, for many people, their romantic vision of the Middle Ages. All three elements derive from the story of St. George, the early Christian soldier-martyr popular in both the Christian East and West and throughout the entire Middle Ages. Legend has it that George came upon a city named Sylene that had been terrorized by a fierce dragon. The inhabitants were in the habit of feeding sheep to the monster to appease its fury. Soon, however, they ran out of sheep, and the town's young sons and daughters were substituted as food. George chanced upon the scene the day on which the lottery had selected the king's own daughter as the sacrifice. Most depictions of George slaying the dragon show the youth on horseback as he, almost effortlessly, kills the beast. In a miniature by a follower of the Master of Guillebert de Mets, George has been forced to

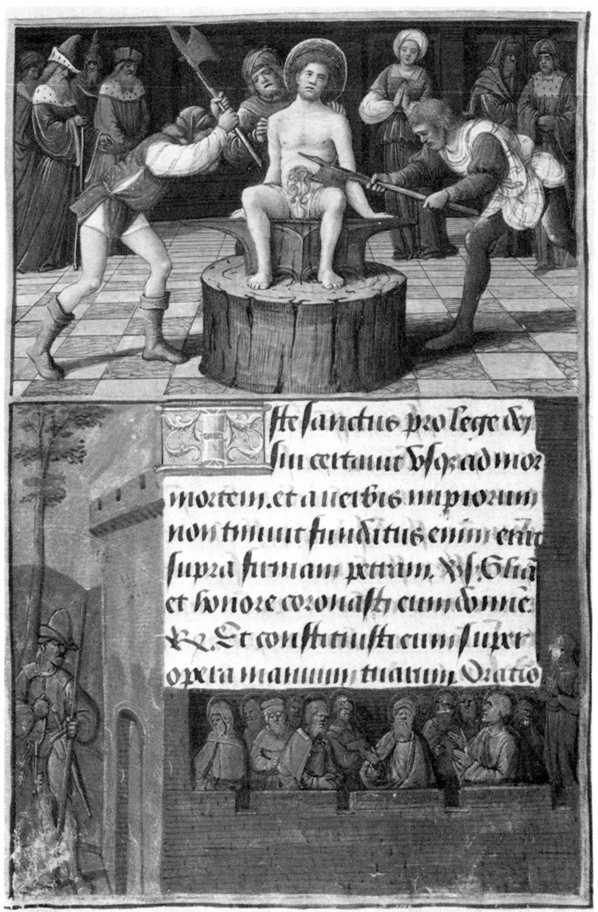

Fig. 96. *Martyrdom of Adrian,* border: *Christians in Prison,* France, Tours, ca. 1500, by Jean Poyet (Morgan H.8, fol. 181v; Cat. No. 70).

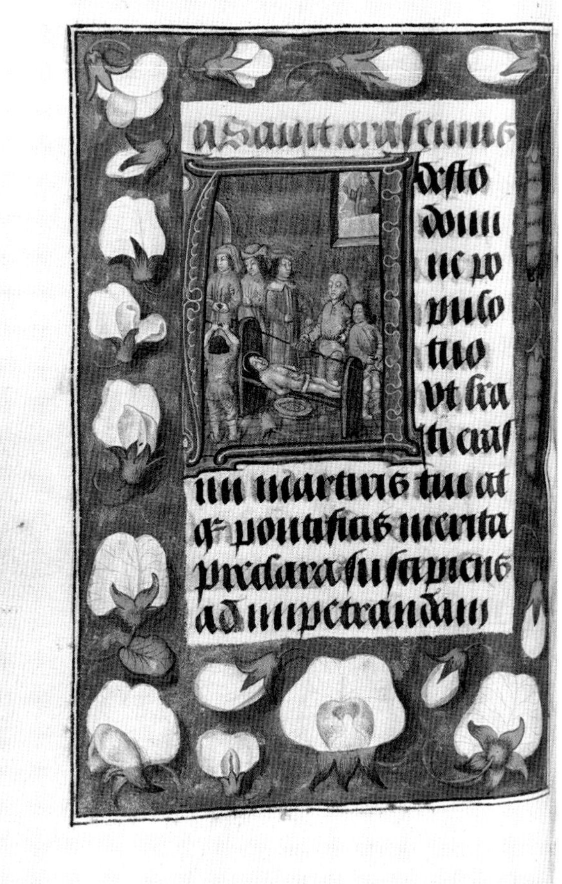

Fig. 97. *Evisceration of Erasmus,* Belgium, ca. 1480 (Walters 439, fol. 69v; Cat. No. 98).

put up more of a fight (Pl. 35). With broken bits of the saint's lance in its mouth (and on the ground), the dragon lashes out at George with fiery breath. Forced to abandon his mount, George attacks with his sword, his last weapon.

Adrian typifies those martyrs whose particularly painful and especially bloody deaths greatly excited the medieval imagination. For his conversion to the forbidden faith of Christianity, the fourth-century military officer was eviscerated, the bones of his arms and legs were broken, and his hands and feet cut off. Among the twenty-three Suffrages in the Cumberland Hours, the masterpiece of Jean Poyet, is a miniature of the martyrdom of Adrian, one of the more arresting miniatures in the book (Fig. 96). Against the light background of pale skin, the saint's vivid red and pink intestines spill out from his stomach over his loincloth. He sits weakened but serene as executioners hack off his legs with halberds. In the background, Natalia, Adrian's wife, calmly prays for her husband—after his death she secures one of Adrian s severed hands as a relic. In the border of the page is the prison filled with Christians whose unshakable faith during scourging had been the catalyst for Adrian's conversion.

Erasmus (also called Elmo) is another saint who suffered a gruesome evisceration, at least according to popular French and Flemish traditions. This fourth-century bishop died after having his intestines unwound and coiled around a windlass. Among the numerous historiated initials introducing Suffrages in the Hours of Adolf of Cleves and La Marck is one showing the saint's death (Fig. 97). Because of the method of his martyrdom, Erasmus is the patron of cramps and intestinal troubles. He is also the protector of sailors since the electrical discharges, called St. Elmo's fire and sometimes seen on the masts of ships following a storm, were viewed as a manifestation of his protection.

Confessors, saints who were not martyred and thus died natural deaths, are placed after martyrs in the hierarchical arrangement of Suffrages. One of the fore-

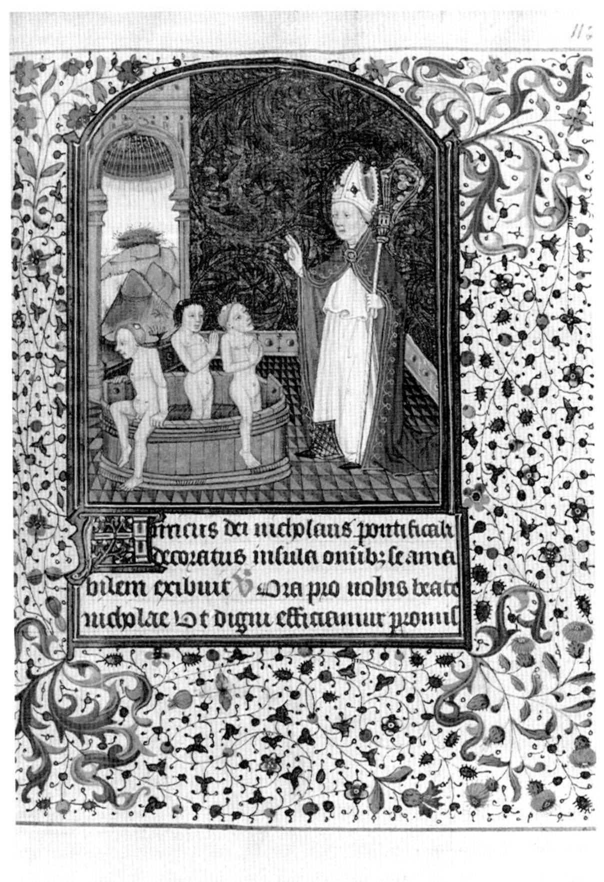
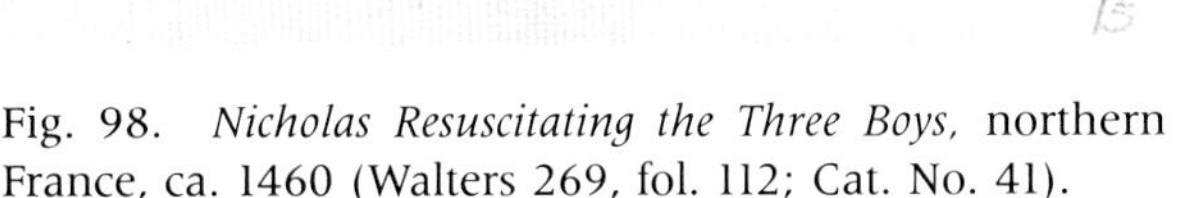

Fig. 98. *Nicholas Resuscitating the Three Boys,* northern France, ca. 1460 (Walters 269, fol. 112; Cat. No. 41).

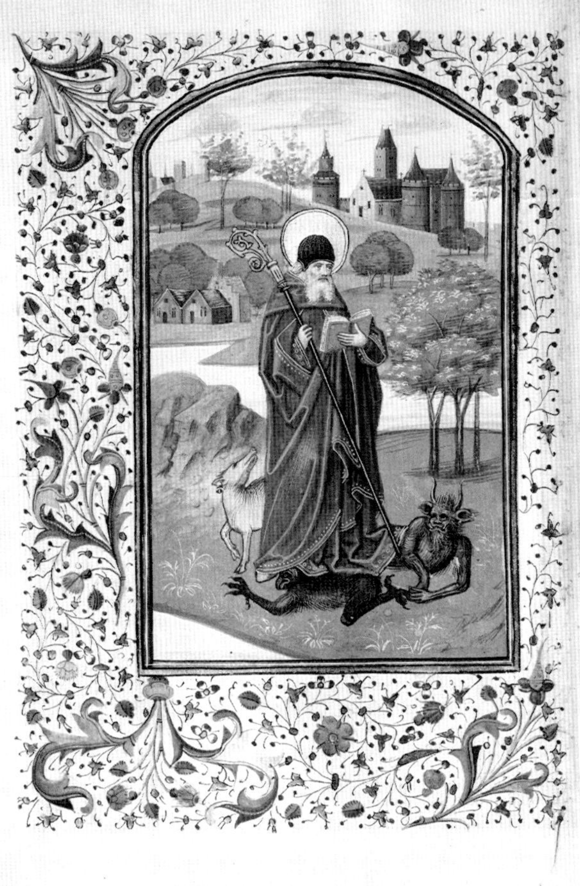

Fig. 99. *Anthony,* Belgium, Bruges, ca. 1460, by Willem Vrelant (Walters 197, fol. 16v; Cat. No. 93).

most confessors is Nicholas of Myra and Bari, the most popular saint in all of Christendom. Although known as Santa Claus and recognizable today by his big bag of toys and bright red suit trimmed with white fur, the fourth-century bishop had quite different attributes in the Middle Ages. One of the best known of these, and one that survives, for example, in modern Belgium, is a barrel of three naked boys. A Suffrage miniature from a northern French Book of Hours of about 1460 is typical (Fig. 98). A surly innkeeper had killed and dismembered three schoolboys, throwing their mutilated bodies in a pickling tub as food for his guests. Nicholas blessed the tub and the three boys were miraculously brought back to life.

Anthony, like Sebastian, is a patron against the plague, but also syphilis, as well as erysipelas, the contagious inflammation of the skin known as St. Anthony's fire. The founder of Christian monasticism, Anthony spent much of his life as a hermit in the desert where he was frequently set upon and tempted by devils. A large and extremely handsome Book of Hours by Willem Vrelant contains a cycle of eleven large Suffrage miniatures, among which is one of Anthony (Fig. 99). Devils vainly try to distract a calm and statuesque Anthony from his meditations. The saint holds a crozier, symbol of his abbatial authority, and is accompanied by a pig, whose lard was thought to be efficacious against St. Anthony's fire. The bell earring worn by the animal refers to the privilege granted to some of the Hospital Brothers of St. Anthony whose pigs, in certain areas, were permitted to forage freely in the woods in gratitude for the charity the monks performed. One attribute missing here is the fire in which Anthony often stands. These flames, an allusion to his patronage of sufferers of skin diseases, are present in the Suffrage miniature of Anthony added by King Charles V to the Savoy Hours (Fig. 2).

One of the most beloved saints of all times is Francis of Assisi. His intense devotion to Christ and his Passion was sanctioned by God in 1224 when Francis received the stigmata, the imprint of the Savior's wounds on his hands, feet and side, a divine favor granted to very few. This climactic moment in Francis' life is usually the subject of the Suffrage miniatures devoted to him, as is the case with the historiated initial in a Flemish Book of Hours of about 1485 (Fig. 100). Francis kneels in religious ecstasy as he receives the wounds from a vision of the crucified Christ who hovers, supported by angelic wings, in the air before him.

Along with Anthony of Padua, Augustine, and Jerome, who were more popular in Italy than in northern Europe, Walters 328, a Neapolitan Book of Hours of the 1450s, also includes a fourth saint popular in the south, Bernardino of Siena (Fig. 101). Bernardino, a priest and Franciscan monk who became vicar general of the order's Strict Observance in 1430, is shown, as is often the case, as an emaciated old man, a sign of his tireless devotion. He holds up a placard on which is written "I.H.S.," the abbreviation for the name "Ihesus." The saint would raise such a tablet for the crowd's veneration after each of his sermons. Bernardino died in 1444 and was canonized six years later; this manuscript, datable to the 1450s, testifies to the rapidity with which his fame and cult spread.

Daniel does not often appear in Books of Hours, but as this Old Testament prophet was the patron saint of Daniel Rym, a wealthy Ghent burgher, a Suffrage to him was requested for the manuscript Rym commissioned. Daniel's wife, Elizabeth van Munte, is depicted in the book at prayer before Elizabeth of Hungary, and Rym is portrayed before his patron Daniel (Pl. 36). The prophet is incarcerated in the lions' den, but the docility of the tamed beasts makes them appear more like sheep than lions. Outside the prison a guard sleeps through his watch, oblivious to the figure of Habakkuk, carried by an angel, who brings food for Daniel. Rym kneels in the border, his ejaculatory appeal written on the scroll unfurling from his joined hands: "Sancte Daniel: Ora pro nobis" ("Holy Daniel: pray for us"). Medieval people asked their patron saints to perform the role of go-between, or celestial advocate, between them and the Almighty.

Mary Magdalene often heads the Suffrages for female saints. Her religious career, which took her from prostitute to devoted friend of Christ, and the first per-

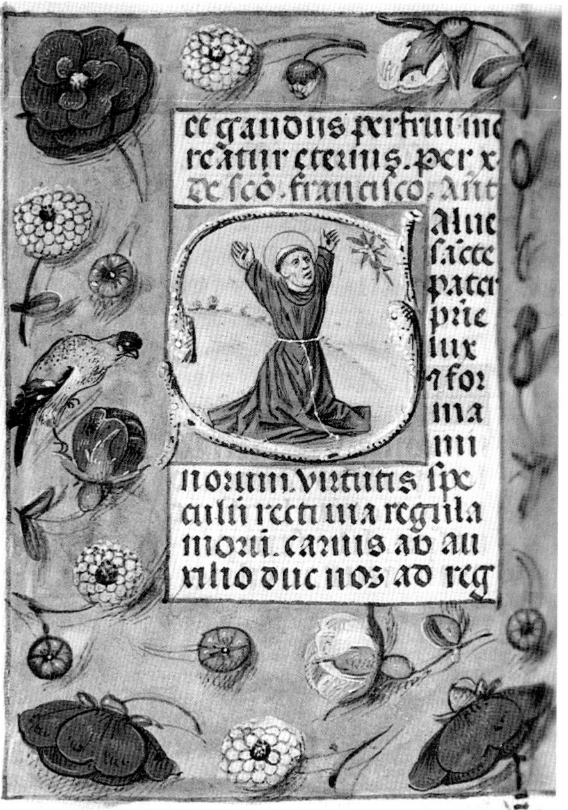

Fig. 100. *Stigmatization of Francis,* Belgium, ca. 1485 (Walters 176, fol. 160v; Cat. No. 100).

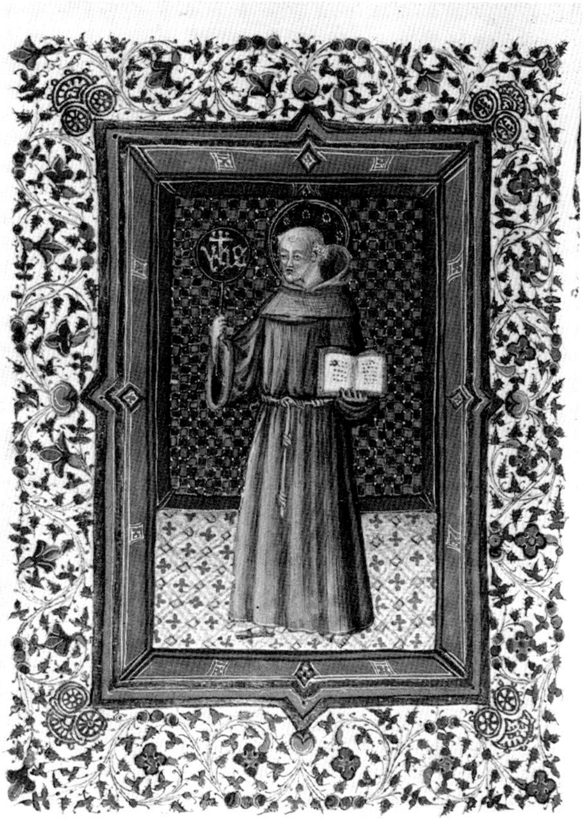

Fig. 101. *Bernardino,* Italy, Naples, ca. 1450s, by Matteo Felice (Walters 328, fol. 171v; Cat. No. 115).

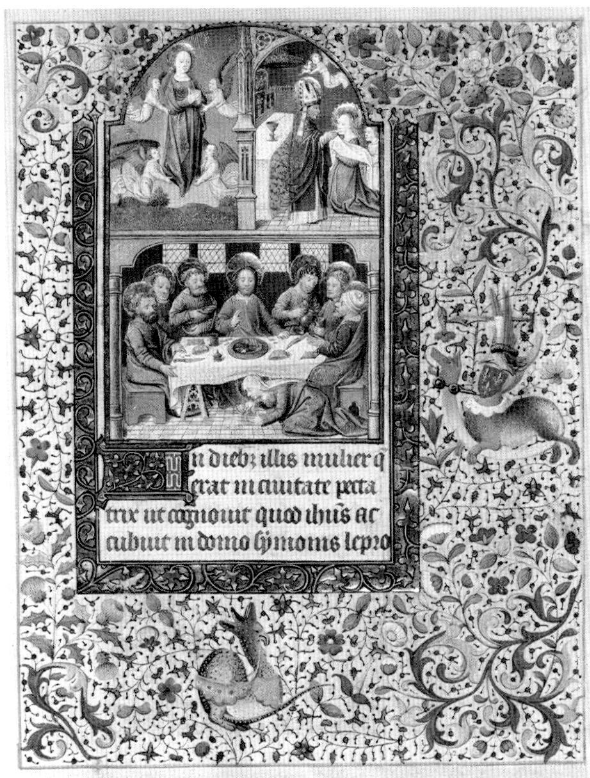

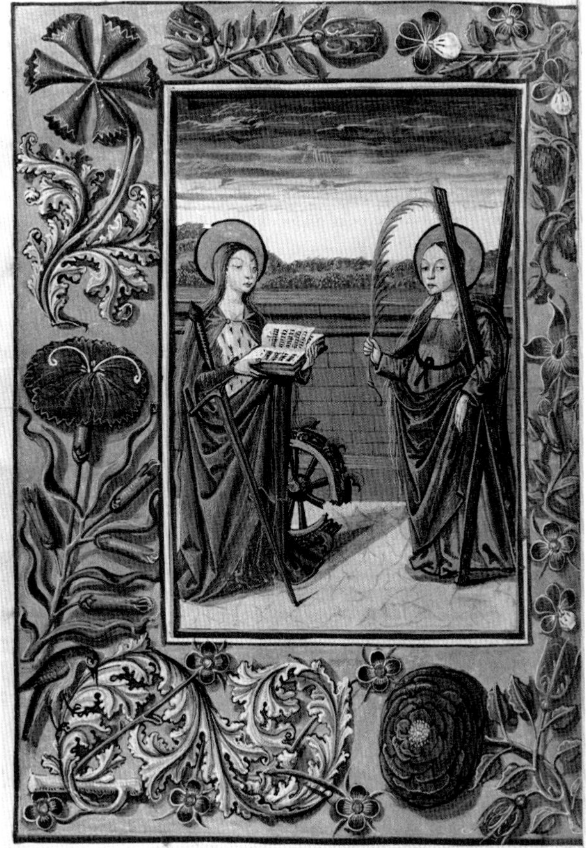

son to whom the Savior revealed himself after the Resurrection, was a perpetual source of hope for even the worst medieval sinner. Indeed, the Magdalene is one of the most popular of all female saints. The intensity of her devotion to Christ was revealed at the dinner before Christ's entry into Jerusalem and his subsequent Passion. Mary washed Christ's feet with her tears, dried them with her hair, and anointed them with expensive fragrant oil. Scandalized by the flagrant waste of money, the apostles castigated Mary; Christ, however, rebuked them and, alluding to forthcoming events, reminded his followers that he would not always be among them. This is the dramatic scene depicted in the Suffrage miniature for Mary Magdalene in a Book of Hours illuminated by the Coëtivy Master (Fig. 102). After Christ's departure from this earth in the Ascension, Mary, her sister Martha, and her brother Lazarus, whom Christ had raised from the dead, traveled, according to legend, to the south of France. There, for the last thirty years of her life, Mary lived in a cave as a hermit. Her time spent in meditation was rewarded by angels who, seven times a day, would lift her to heaven to hear the celestial choirs. At the end of her life, angels transported her to Aix-en-Provence so that she could receive her last Communion from the hands of St. Maximinus. As the miniature, which shows her soul being carried aloft, reveals, Mary expired at this enviable moment.

Catherine of Alexandria can be considered *the* most popular female saint of the Middle Ages. She is the foremost representative of a whole group of early Christian virgin martyrs, known for their beauty, who endured a variety of tortures before eventually dying for their faith. A member of a wealthy third-century patrician family, Catherine was converted to Christianity following a vision of Christ in which the Savior took her as his mystic bride. Christ's rival for the virgin's hand was, however, the Emperor Maxentius. Catherine's refusal to marry the ruler prompted him to sentence the young girl to be killed by torture wheels studded with nails and hooks whose turning would tear the beautiful, but unattainable, flesh from her body. Miraculous lightning destroyed the wheels and saved Catherine from this painful and disfiguring death. The angered emperor then decapitated his would-be bride. Among the many Suffrages in the Almugavar Hours,

Fig. 102. *Mary Magdalene Washing Christ's Feet, Levitated by Angels, Receiving her Last Communion,* France, Angers?, 1460s, by the Coëtivy Master (Henri de Vulcop?) (Walters 274, fol. 193; Cat. No. 42).

Fig. 103. *Catherine and Eulalia of Barcelona,* Spain, Catalonia, 1510–20 (Walters 420, fol. 271v; Cat. No. 118).

an early sixteenth-century Spanish manuscript, is one to Catherine (Fig. 103). She is depicted dressed in ermine (for she was a princess), holding a book and a sword. The former attribute alludes to her scholarship, the latter to the device by which she met her end. At her feet is her ubiquitous attribute, one of the broken torture wheels. Catherine is the patron of young maidens, of wheelwrights and millers, of students and philosophers because of her learning, and of nurses because milk, not blood, flowed from her veins after her beheading. (The text of the Suffrage to Catherine from the Almugavar Hours is given in the Appendix.)

As an economizing feature, some Books of Hours would double up their saints, placing two in one miniature. Such is the case here where, standing next to Catherine, is Eulalia, patroness of the city and cathedral of Barcelona. The governor Dacian, following Diocletian's orders of persecution, tried sharp iron hooks, burning torches, and boiling oil to convince Eulalia to sacrifice to the pagan gods. After a series of brutal tortures, the steadfast girl, twelve or fourteen years old, died by crucifixion. In the miniature she holds a palm of martyrdom and the X-shaped cross (like St. Andrew's) on which she died.

Barbara, another early virgin martyr, was the daughter of an Eastern satrap who had her ensconced in a tower as protection from Christian influences. Managing to receive instruction from a priest who impersonated her doctor, Barbara was baptized and proceeded to pierce a third window in her two-window prison to proclaim her belief in the Trinity. Not amused, her father had Barbara beaten and scourged, and, finally, decapitated her himself—whereupon he was consumed by fire from heaven. In the miniature of Barbara in a Book of Hours illuminated by Loyset Liédet (a Flemish illuminator who rarely painted *Horae*), the virgin, dressed in royal ermine and wearing a gold crown, holds her palm of martyrdom as she studies the pages of a book (Fig. 104). A tower, her principal attribute, looms behind her. Barbara's alterations to the building caused her to be patron of architects, builders, and stonemasons; because of her father's fate, the saint is

Fig. 104. *Barbara,* Belgium, Ghent?, ca. 1470, by Loyset Liédet (Walters 279, fol. 184v; Cat. No. 96).

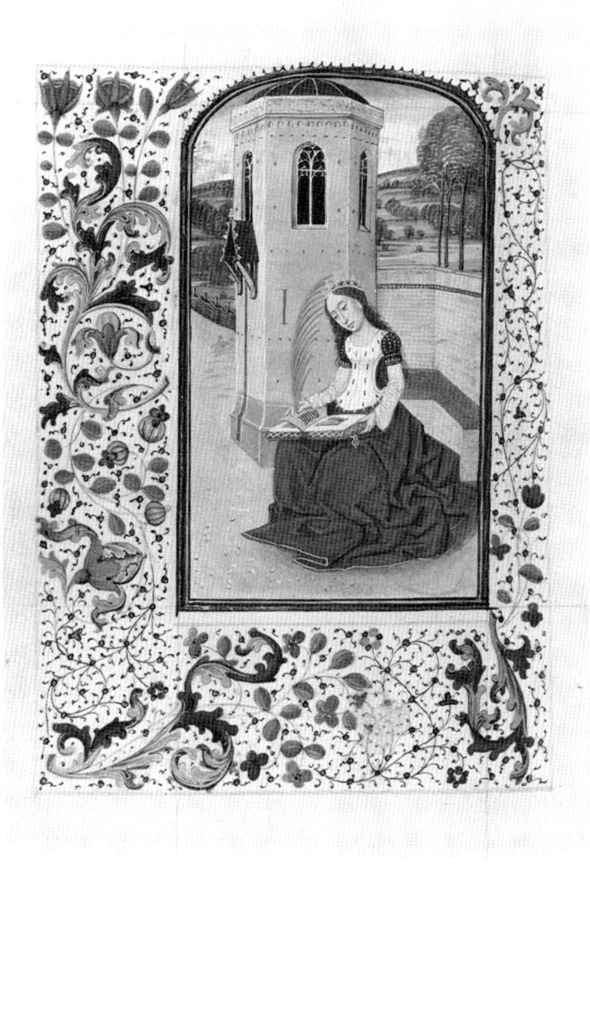

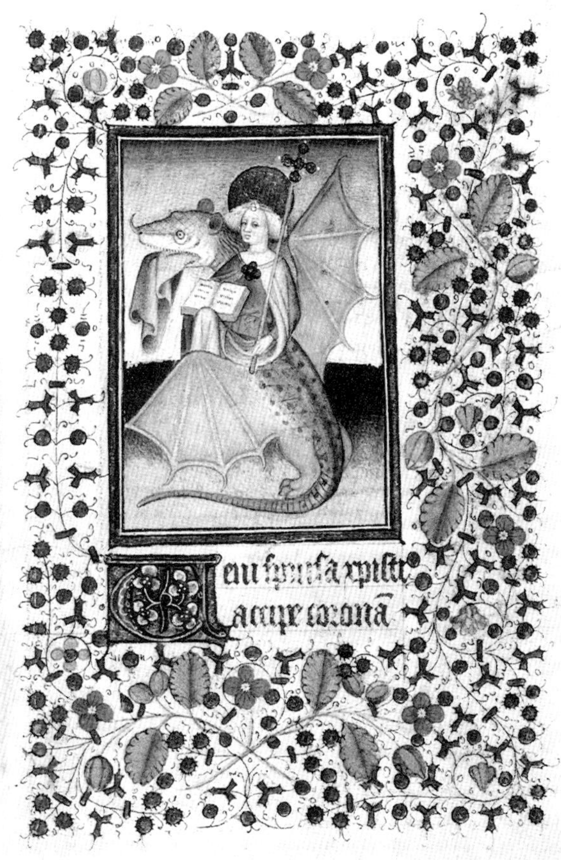

Fig. 105. *Margaret Emerging from the Dragon,* eastern France, 1420s, by the Master of Walters 219 (Walters 219, fol. 257; Cat. No. 32).

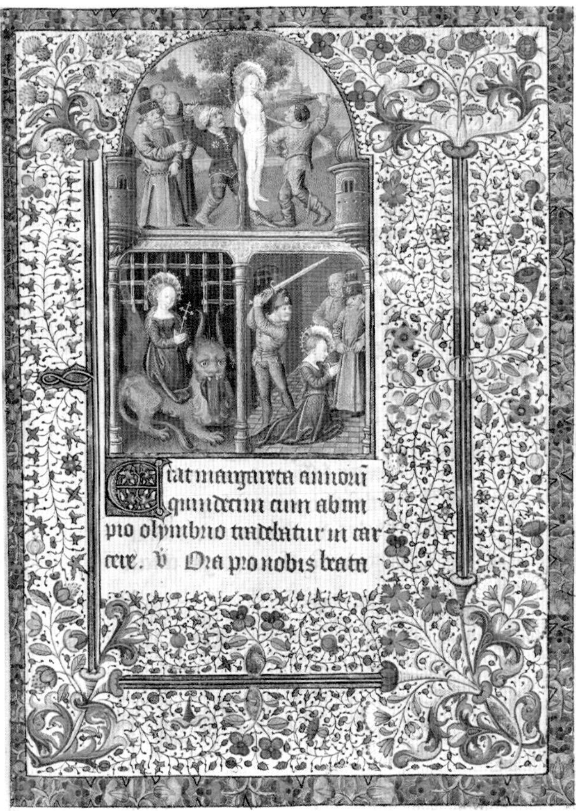

Fig. 106. *Margaret Flagellated, Emerging from the Dragon, Decapitated,* France, Angers?, 1460s, by the Coëtivy Master (Henri de Vulcop?) (Walters 274, fol. 180; Cat. No. 42).

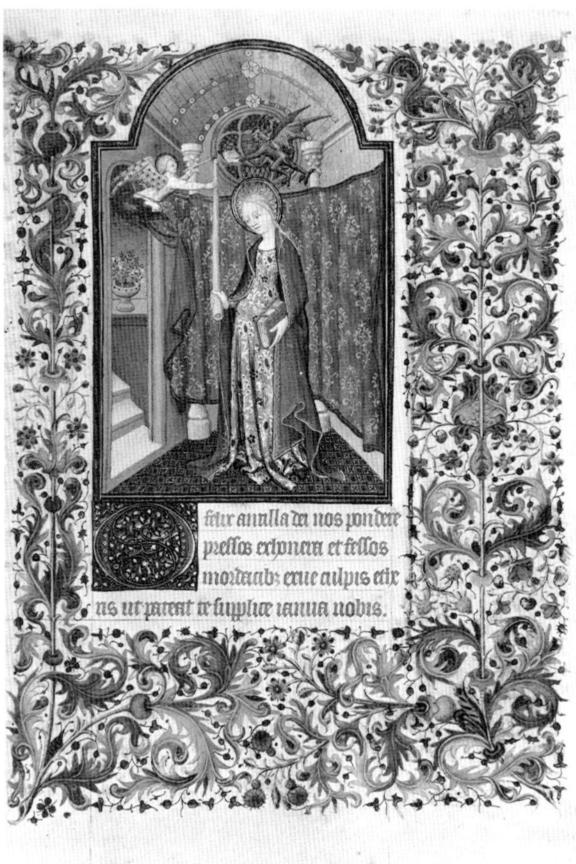

Fig. 107. *Geneviève,* France, Paris, 1420s, by the Master of the Harvard Hannibal (Walters 287, fol. 141; Cat. No. 29).

invoked against fire and lightning.

Margaret, like Catherine and Barbara, was also an extremely popular saint in the late Middle Ages, another of this large group of early Christian virgin martyrs. Attractive, as all of these early saints seem to have been, Margaret caught the eye of the Roman prefect Olybrius who wanted the virtuous girl as his wife or mistress. Rejecting both offers, Margaret was subjected to tortures and thrown into prison where a devil, in the form of a dragon, swallowed her. The cross she carried, however, upset the beast's stomach that then miraculously opened and ejected her to safety. Typical in its iconography is the miniature of Margaret in Walters 219 (Fig. 105). The beautiful virgin, handsomely coiffed, holds her cross and, in this case, a book, and emerges from the winged dragon's stomach even as the monster, a surprised look on its face, continues to swallow Margaret's cloak.

The Book of Hours by the Coëtivy Master also contains a three-part miniature for Margaret (Fig. 106). This picture shows the scourging that Olybrius administered to his reluctant paramour, the saint's emergence from the dragon, and, finally, the decapitation by which she met her martyrdom. Margaret was the patron of pregnant women. This seems to have originated not only from her miraculous deliverance from the stomach of the dragon, but also from the death of her mother and the abandonment by her father at an early age. (The Suffrage to Margaret from Walters 274 is provided in the Appendix.)

Geneviève, patroness of Paris, is illustrated here by a miniature from the Book of Hours by the Master of the Harvard Hannibal (Fig. 107). During her life this fifth-century virgin is credited with twice saving the population of the French capital: once from famine during the long blockade by invading Franks, and the second time when her exhortations to the Parisian citizens to fast and pray averted an attack by Attila the Hun. In the miniature she carries her attribute, a candle, which was continually snuffed out by a small devil with bellows, while Geneviève was on her way to evening prayers, and which an angel would just as continually relight.

Surely the most bizarre saint of the entire Middle

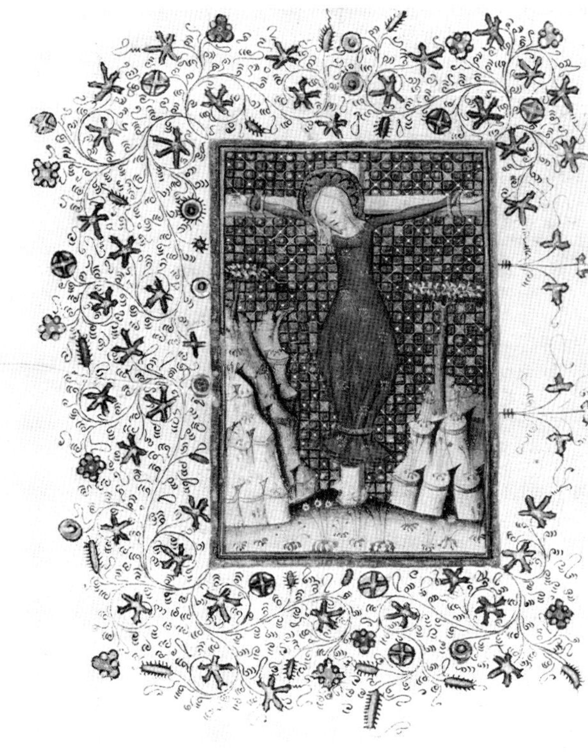

Ages is Wilgefortis, the patron of bearded ladies. The legends surrounding this figure reveal a great deal about the inner workings of the medieval mind. The daughter of a heathen king of Portugal, Wilgefortis (or, Wildefortis, Uncumber, Liberata, etc.) was betrothed against her will to the king of Sicily. To help her keep her vow of chastity, she asked God to disfigure her body. God answered her prayers by causing her to grow a beard and moustache, whereupon her father promptly had the unsuitable bride crucified. Our example (Fig. 108), by a follower of the Master of Guillebert de Mets, is from the same Book of Hours as the St. George discussed above (Pl. 35). (The presence of her relics in Brussels helps account for her popularity in Flemish manuscripts.) The virgin saint owes her existence to medieval misinterpretation of Byzantine crucifixes in which Christ is dressed in long robes; such a crucifix, the "Volto Santo" ("Holy Face"), still exists in Lucca. Mistaking the long-robed, mustachioed Christ for a bearded lady, overactive imaginations invented the steadfast Wilgefortis ("Virgo fortis") and the legend behind her hirsute appearance. Wilgefortis has tantalized storytellers not only of the Middle Ages, but also of today; she plays a pivotal role in *The Manticore,* the second novel of the *Deptford Trilogy* by the Canadian author Robertson Davies.

Fig. 108. *Wilgefortis Crucified,* Belgium, ca. 1430–40, by a follower of the Master of Guillebert de Mets (Walters 170, fol. 174v; Cat. No. 84).

CHAPTER XII

Office of the Dead

Taken in their totality, the miniatures that mark the beginning of the Office of the Dead are the most iconographically varied of all those that appear in Books of Hours. There are more different images for this text than for any other. These miniatures are also among the most fascinating, touching, as they do, on the late medieval fear of and obsession with death.

With but rare exceptions, a Book of Hours contains a single miniature for its Office of the Dead. The usual subject of this picture is what is called a "funeral service" (Pl. 12, Figs. 111, 112). A group of three or four monks, huddled around a lectern or before a large choir book, are shown chanting over a draped coffin. What are these monks singing? It is not the Requiem, the funeral Mass, but the text that the medieval reader is about to begin: the Office of the Dead. The recitation of the Office of the Dead formed an integral part of the medieval funeral, which explains, in part, the popularity of this image. Another reason lies in the identification that the lay reader could have with the ordained clergy officiating at the funeral service. While the Book of Hours can be described as a layman's breviary, with, in general, vastly simplified and reduced texts, with the Office of the Dead this was not the case. The Office to be found in Books of Hours is the same text to be found in the breviary itself. Thus, with the Office of the Dead the lay man in the nave was reciting the same prayers as the ordained man in the choir.

Although the medieval funeral, in its different ritual parts, is the dominant theme for the Office of the Dead, a few Books of Hours illustrate those events preceding the funeral. They show the deathbed. A Book of Hours produced in Bourges about 1470 includes a rare depiction of the administration of the Last Rites (Fig. 109). A priest, dressed in alb and black stole, offers the Eucharist that he has just removed from the pyx, the small receptacle used to transport the host, to a dying man who, with folded hands, receives the wafer with a comforted expression. As is still Catholic practice, Confession and Communion were frequently administered to the sick and dying on the same occasion as Extreme Unction, the sacramental anointing that provided aid and comfort as well as perfect spiritual health to those about to pass from this world to the next. The greatest medieval fear in conjunction with death was, of course, to die in the state of mortal sin thereby damning oneself to the eternity of hell. The perfect death was one that immediately followed the reception of Communion.

A dramatic example of Death's arrival at the bedside of the dying is found in a French Book of Hours of the 1480s (Pl. 37). In his luxuriously draped bed lies an old man attended by two figures, the younger of which, his son, places a candle within his hands. Unseen by the attendants, Death, wielding a lance, has entered the room and placed his hand on the bed. The old man, his eyes closed, has just fallen victim to Death's power. His soul, with pleading, outstretched arms, races up on heavenly beams of light toward his protector St. Michael. The archangel's aid is not lightly invoked, for two devils, glowing red from hell's fires, make the best of their last chance to steal this soul from God.

A few Books of Hours illustrate the Office of the Dead with those pathetic activities that followed immediately upon the loved one's death: distribution of bread to the poor, taking inventory of the deceased man's possessions and reading of the will, or preparation of the dead for burial. For example, in a Flemish Hours of about 1430, a group of men and two women, the one in the center probably the dead man's widow, pray over the corpse (Fig. 110). The body lies on the tile floor of a house and, although nearly skeletal, is probably meant to be the corpse of a man who has just died and has yet to be wrapped in a shroud. The various steps in the preparation of the corpse for burial are represented as border vignettes scattered around the large miniature of a burial in a *Horae* probably from Troyes about 1470 (Fig. 119). In the upper left corner the man is shown on his deathbed with his soul, having just departed, fought over by a devil and an angel. At the upper right two women sew the corpse into a shroud. In the next vignette the body is placed into a coffin. Following these preparations, the corpse is borne, in the first of two processions, to church, and the medieval funeral begins. At the church, monks, sometimes accompanied by lay people and mourners, recite or chant the Office of the Dead over the bier; the fourth vignette, at the lower right, in the French Book of Hours shows two Franciscans and two Dominicans reading the Office.

As mentioned above, a depiction of the recitation or chanting of the Office of the Dead is the single most frequently found image for this text. It is the subject of the miniature in the *Horae* illuminated by the Master of the Munich *Golden Legend* (Pl. 12) as well as in two other Parisian Books of Hours of the early fifteenth century (Figs. 111, 112). These three are representative of innumerable examples that could be cited. Monks in habits and priests in black copes chant the Office from large antiphonals, or, as noted in the border vignette just mentioned, read the service from breviaries over the coffin. The latter is covered by a pall, and either a few candles, or many, incorporated into an elaborate catafalque, burn nearby.

In the medieval funeral the Requiem, the funeral Mass, follows the recitation of the Office of the Dead, either immediately or on the next morning if the body had been carried into church the previous evening and the Office had been said then. The representation of the funeral Mass from a Dutch Book of Hours painted about 1435–40 is typical, with monks and mourners, as in the miniatures we have already seen, gathered around the coffin at the foot of the altar (Fig. 113a). Their attention is turned, however, to the celebrant of the Requiem Mass, his hands brought together in prayer over the altar on which we can detect a missal and a

Fig. 109. *Last Rites,* France, Bourges, ca. 1470, by a follower of the Master of Morgan 96 (Walters 205, fol. 127; Cat. No. 47).

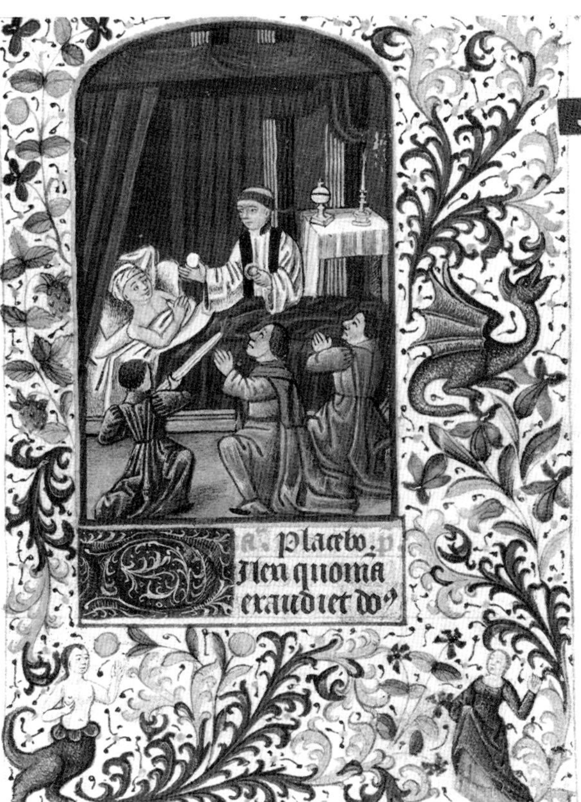

Fig. 110. *Group of Men and Women Praying over a Corpse,* Belgium, Bruges?, ca. 1430, by a painter related to the Gold Scrolls group (Walters 239, fol. 101v; Cat. No. 87).

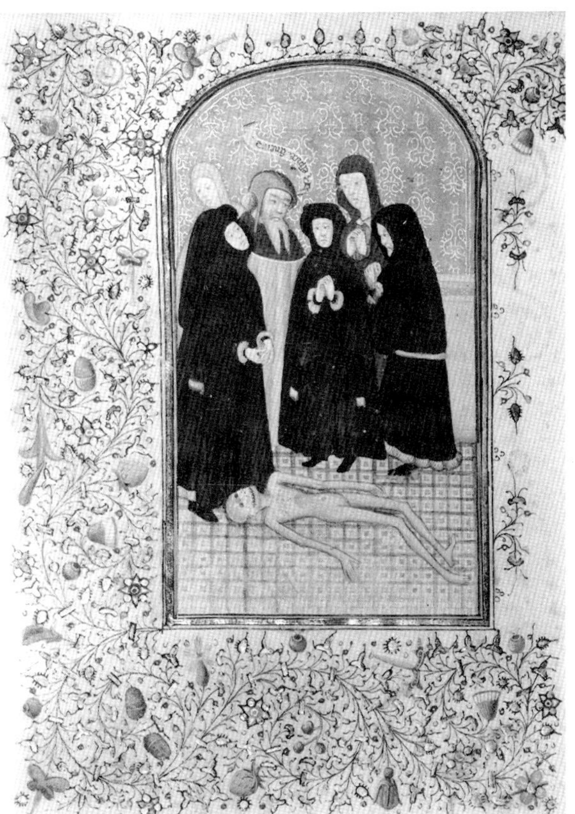

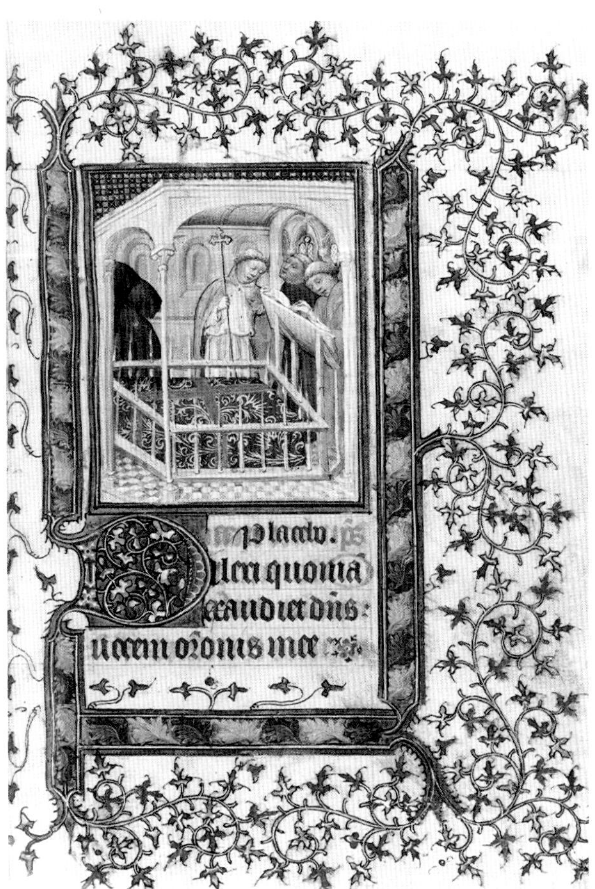

Fig. 111. *Funeral Service,* France, Paris, ca. 1405–10, by the Master of Berry's *Cleres Femmes* (Walters 209, fol. 151; Cat. No. 22).

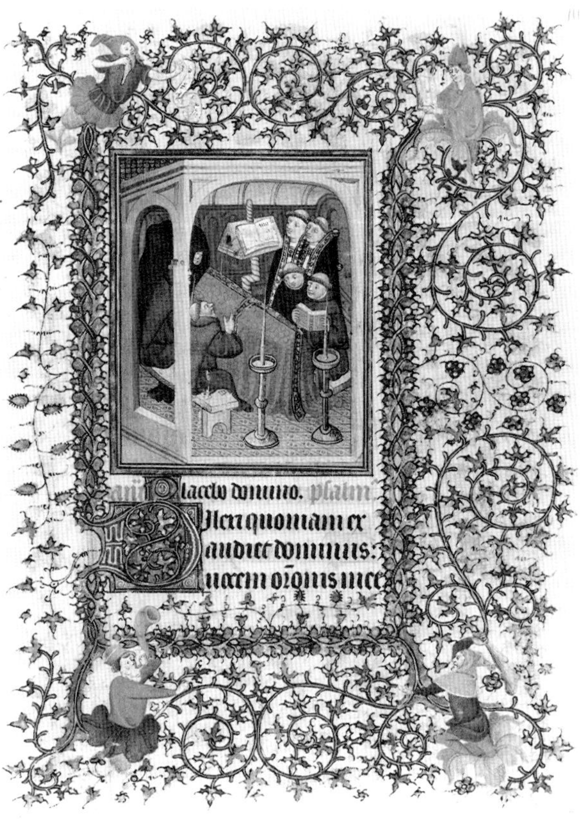

Fig. 112. *Funeral Service,* France, Paris, ca. 1410–20, by a follower of the Boucicaut Master (Walters 276, fol. 111; Cat. No. 27).

chalice covered by a pall, a small square piece of stiffened linen. The purpose of the funeral Mass is made immediately apparent in the leaf facing this miniature (Fig. 113b). Following the opening antiphon "Placebo Domino," the Office begins with Psalm 114, "Dilexi quoniam." In the large historiated "D" are three female souls suffering the purifying flames of purgatory (not, as is sometimes mistakenly thought, of hell). The frailty of human nature was nearly a guarantee that one would yield to sin's temptations during the course of one's life; purgatory cleansed the sinner, making him worthy of eventually enjoying the Beatific Vision of heaven. The faithful who remained on earth could help the departed through prayer, and the Requiem Mass recited upon the death of a loved one was said for his immediate benefit. A miniature in a French Book of Hours by the Coëtivy Master reveals the efficacy of the Requiem Mass in an even more dramatic fashion than in the Dutch manuscript just described. The funeral Mass includes a moving depiction of purgatory placed, as it were, in the basement of the church (Pl. 38). Male and female souls twist and turn in a kind of sleep—their eyes are all shown closed—albeit a slumber spent in intense heat and flame. The purgative sentences for two fortunate souls are completed and we see them being raised out of the fires, with eyes now open, and led to a doorway representing the entrance to heaven.

When the Requiem Mass was completed, the Absolution, the blessing of the bier with both incense and holy water, was performed. The Buves Hours produced in northern France or Flanders in the 1450s includes a representation of this rarely-depicted part of the medieval funeral (Fig. 114). At the left of the miniature we see the celebrant swinging the censer over the draped coffin, the acolyte behind him holding back the folds of his cope. At the back of the church the empty altar is given prominence, an allusion to the Mass the celebrant has just finished.

After the Requiem and the Absolution, the bier is carried from the church to the cemetery in a second, formal procession, another important component of

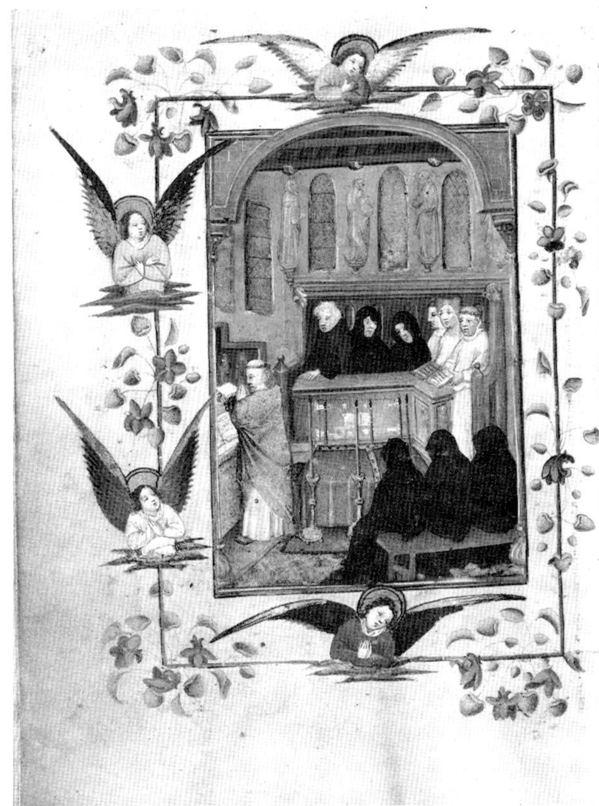

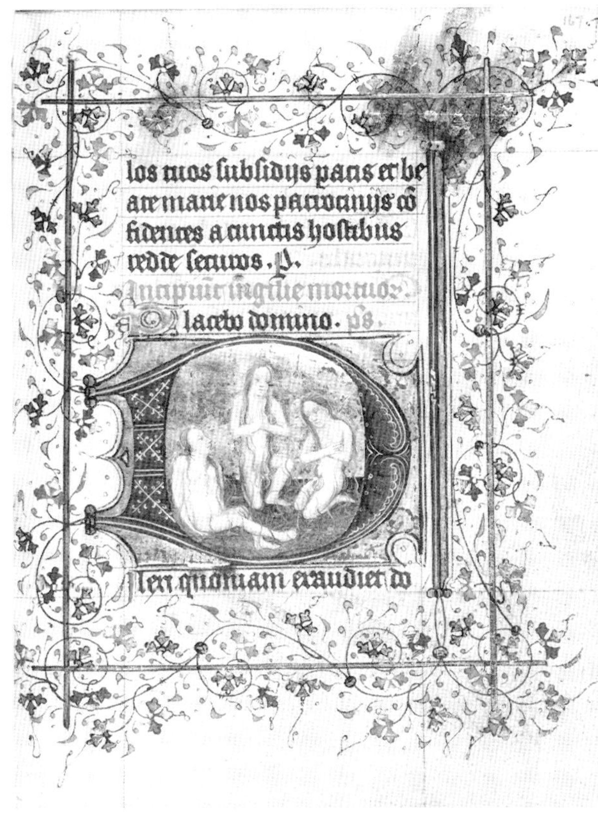

Fig. 113. a) *Funeral Mass;* b) *Souls in Purgatory,* Holland, ca. 1435–40, by one of the Masters of Zweder van Culemborg (Walters 168, fol. 166v–167; Cat. No. 109).

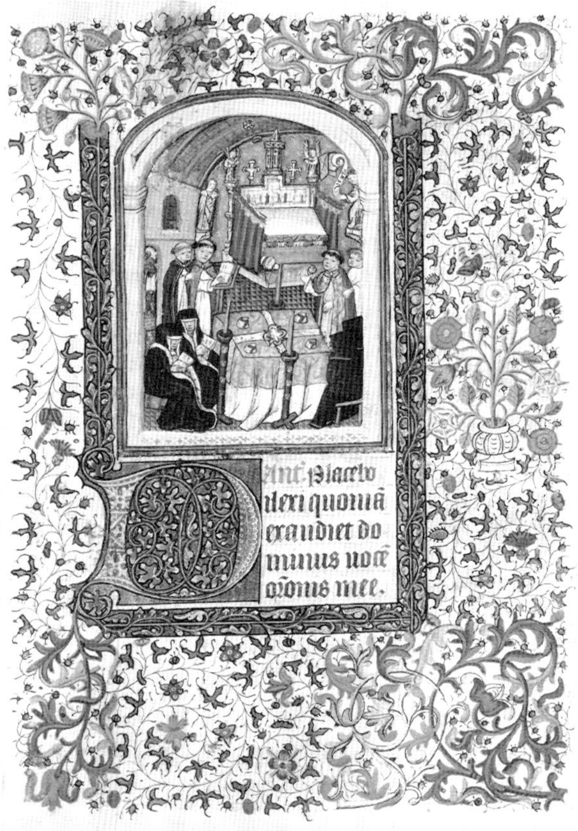

Fig. 114. *Absolution,* northern France or southern Belgium, 1450s (Walters 267, fol. 86; Cat. No. 40).

the medieval funeral. In an early sixteenth-century *Horae,* probably from Rouen, the funeral procession is the subject, rarely treated in this manner, of the Office of the Dead miniature (Fig. 115). A group of torch-bearing monks heads the cortege that includes members of the clergy, mourners dressed in black, pallbearers—two priests and two Franciscans—followed by more torch-bearing mourners. The procession turns the corner of the cemetery and reaches the entrance where an acolyte kneels while blessing the graveyard with holy water. Inside, a hunchback opens the grave.

After being borne to the graveyard, the corpse is laid out to receive its final blessing. Man is here at his most desolate; still bound, in a way, to earth by a body not yet decomposed, his soul is no longer of this world but it is not yet of the next. This sense of being completely alone, of being abandoned by both God and his fellow man, permeates the miniatures that the Rohan Master painted for the Office of the Dead in

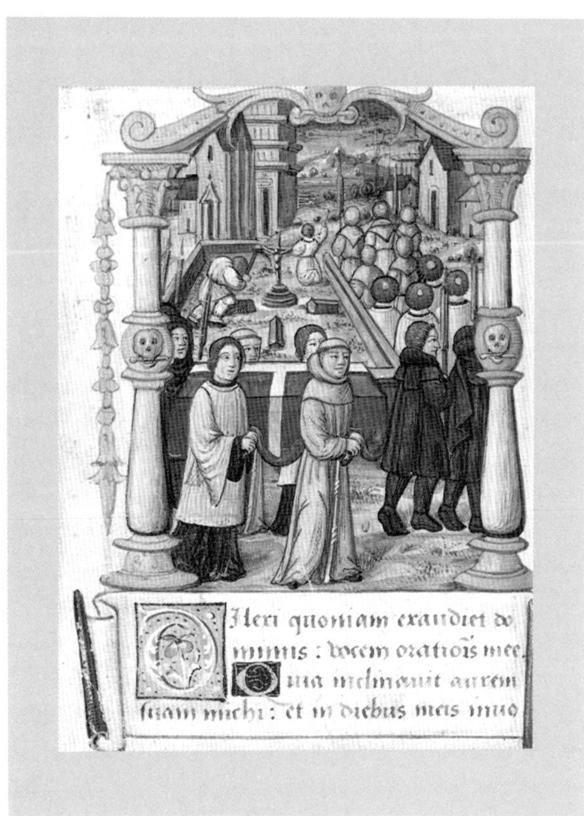

Fig. 115. *Funeral Procession,* France, Rouen?, early 16th century (Walters 424, fol. 62v; Cat. No. 74).

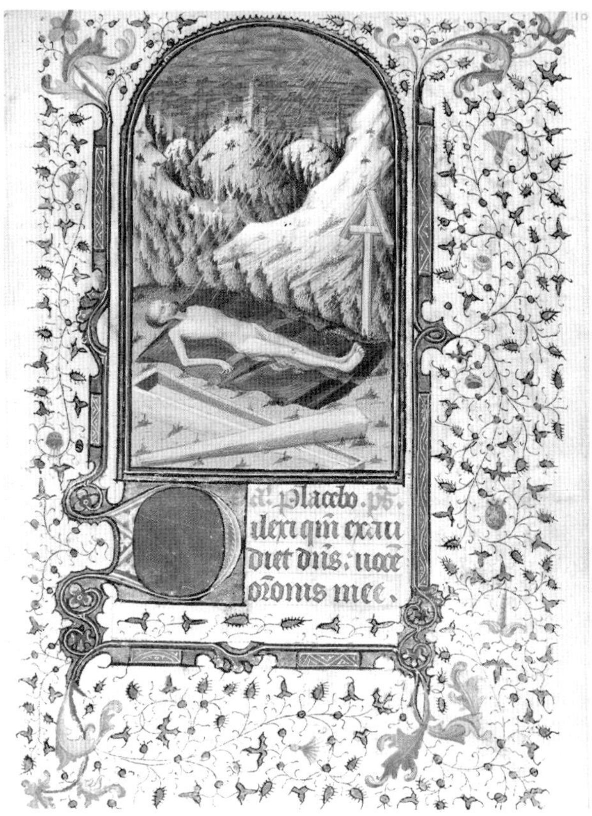

Fig. 116. *Exposed Corpse,* France, Paris? or Troyes?, 1420s by the Rohan Master (Walters 741, fol. 102; Cat. No. 31).

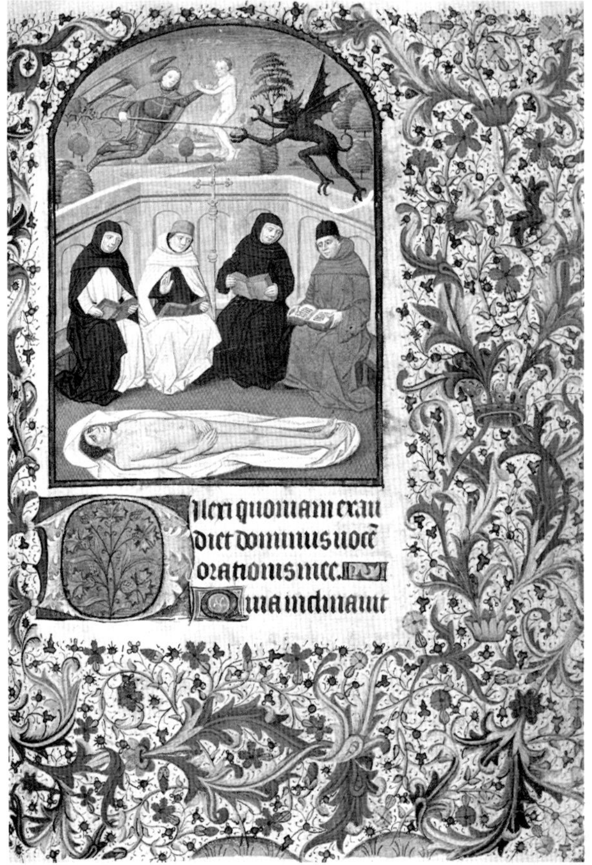

Fig. 117. *Clerics Pray over a Corpse while Michael Battles a Devil for his Soul,* France, Rouen, ca. 1480, by the Master of the Geneva Latini (Walters 284, fol. 85; Cat. No. 60).

Books of Hours of the early fifteenth century (Fig. 116). The treacherous, inhospitable landscape with its rough trees, its cities seen in a distance that alludes to the dead man's separation from life, its lack even of the companionship of other dead (the grave prepared for this corpse seems to be the only one in the cemetery), all embody, in this miniature, the despair with which people in the late Middle Ages anticipated their end. God's forgiving kindness shines down upon this corpse, but, like the light from a distant, although powerful, star, its beams appear faint and ineffectual.

The naked corpse awaiting burial is also the subject of the Office of the Dead miniature in an early fifteenth-century Book of Hours to which paintings were added in Rouen about 1480 by the Master of the Geneva Latini (Fig. 117). Here, the corpse has the comfort of his shroud, a consolation denied to the Rohan Master's figure, and the prayers of the four monks who have gathered together for his aid. Not trying to guess which of the monastic orders might be more pleasing to God, the deceased arranged for a Dominican, a Premonstratensian, a Benedictine, and a Franciscan to pray for the benefit of his soul. Above the monks' heads and, of course, invisible to them, the metaphysical battle over the dead man's soul rages between St. Michael and a devil.

The final blessing of the corpse prior to burial is represented in a Book of Hours painted in Amiens in the 1430s by a follower of the Master of Walters 281 (Fig. 118). Surrounded by mourners, members of his family, and the priest and his assistant, the corpse receives the last sprinkling of holy water. The gravedigger at the bottom of the miniature has encountered the bones of previous inhabitants of the site he opens. In the Middle Ages, the grave, for the common man, was not a place of eternal rest. It was a place of temporary interment where one's sinful flesh was cleansed from the skeleton—graves were dug and redug with an inevitable disturbance of prior occupants.

After the final blessing, the corpse is buried (Pl. 39, Fig. 119). Representations of burial, after those that depict the chanting of the Office of the Dead, constitute the second most frequently found theme accompanying the text of the Office of the Dead. Elements found in these fifteenth-century miniatures, one Flemish and one French, are typical of countless such pictures: a priest, wearing a cope, reading from his service book (called a ritual) or sprinkling holy water with an aspergillum, the priest's assistant and an acolyte with the processional cross, mourners and family members, and, finally, the laborers and the corpse they lower into the ground. In the miniatures the corpse is buried protected only by its shroud. Coffins in the Middle Ages were, in general, only used as a means of transport for the body from home to church and from church to cemetery. Once at the grave, the corpse was removed from its carrier and buried without it. In the French manuscript (Fig. 119), we notice again the bones that have been disturbed by the recent digging; in the Flemish manuscript we see what happens to these bones (Pl. 39). Once removed from the earth, they were not returned to it but, in an effort to save space, were placed in storage areas, called charnel houses, surrounding the graveyard.

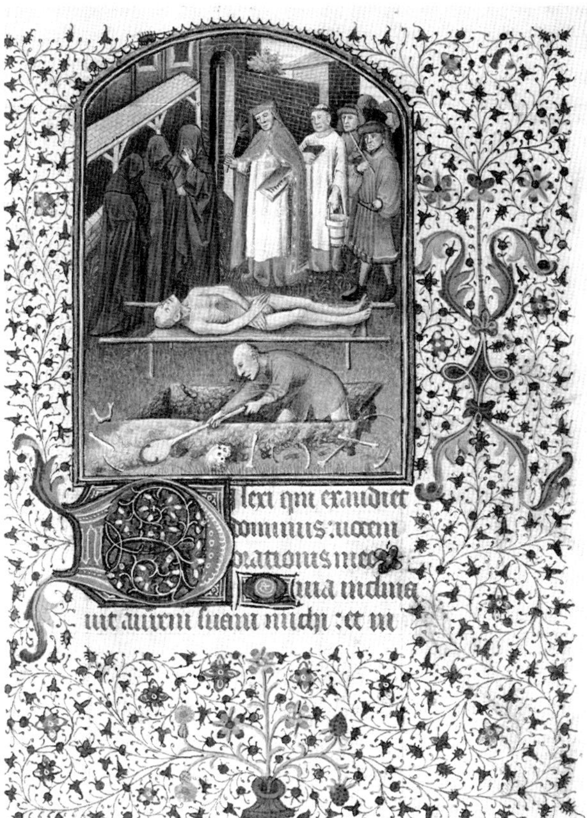

Fig. 118. *Burial Service*, France, Amiens, 1430s, by a follower of the Master of Walters 281 (Walters 262, fol. 90; Cat. No. 36).

The dread with which the late medieval mind anticipated death tolerated few images representing the possible turn of events that took place after burial. It was presumptuous to assume reward and it was depressing to anticipate just deserts. As could be expected, however, images of Christ as Judge or of the Last Judgement do occur. An example of the latter is found in a second Rouen Book of Hours by the Master of the Geneva Latini (Fig. 120). Seated on a rainbow and with the world, literally, at his feet, Christ looks to his

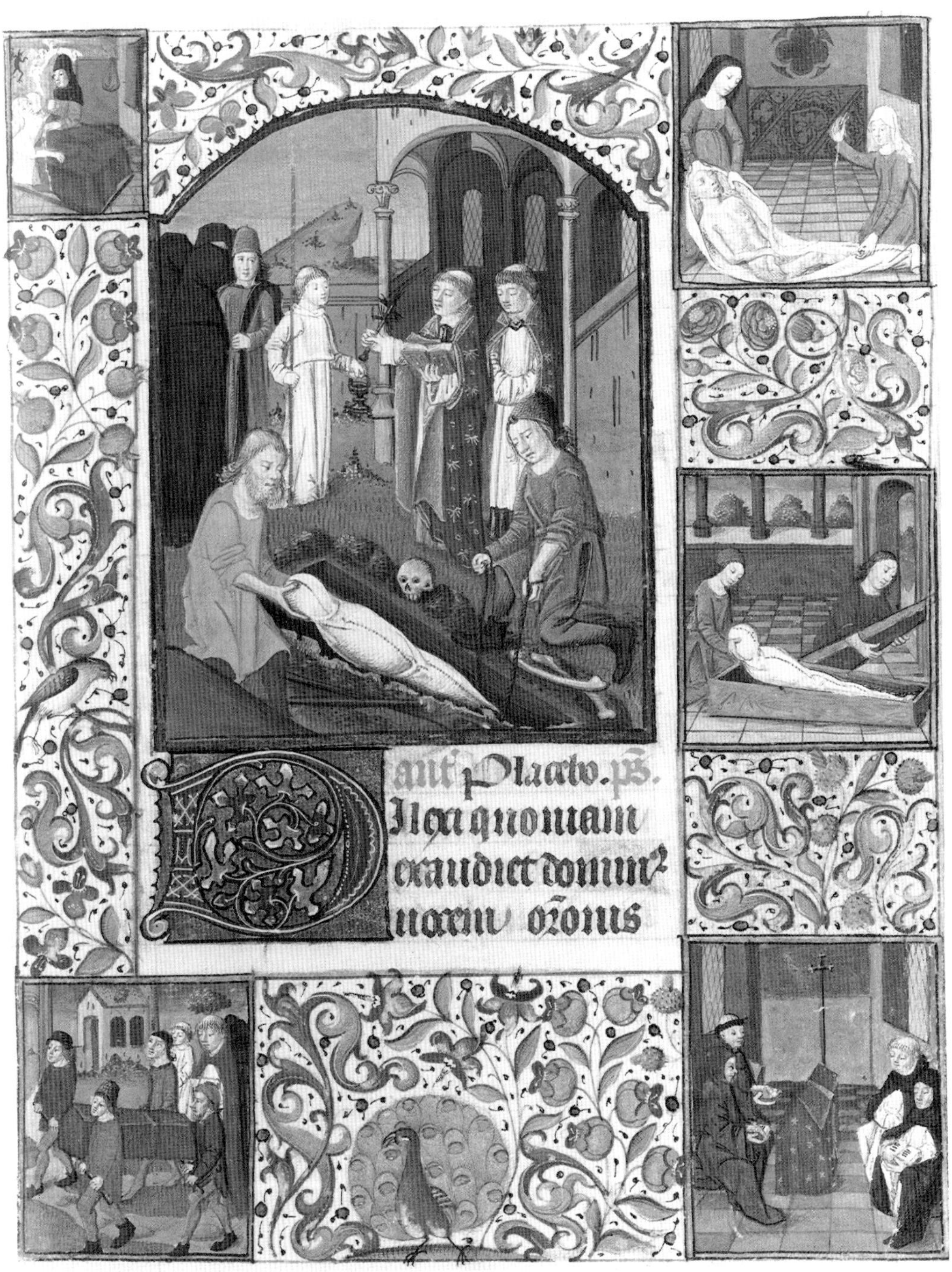

Fig. 119. *Burial Service* with border vignettes, France, Troyes?, ca. 1470 (Walters 249, fol. 119; Cat. No. 49).

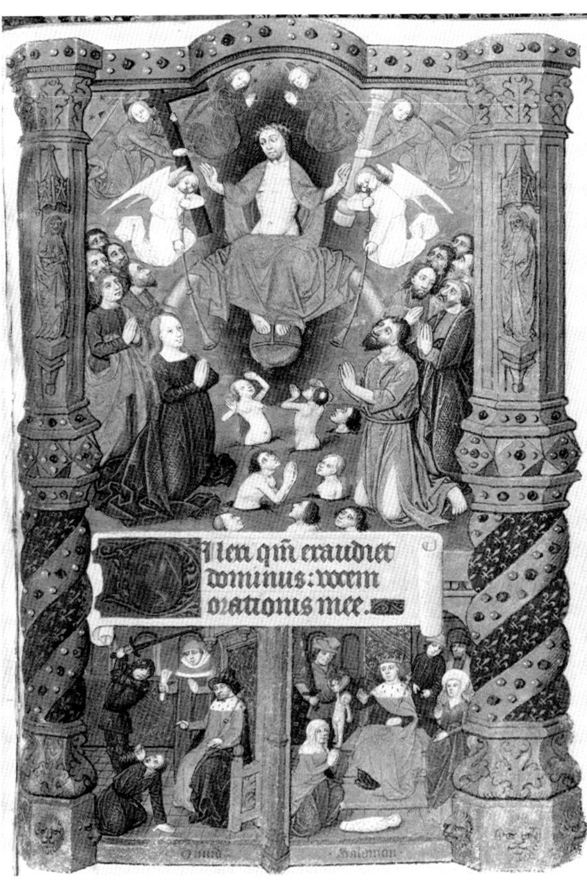

Fig. 120. *Last Judgement,* border: *David Ordering a Decapitation, Judgement of Solomon,* France, Rouen, ca. 1480, by the Master of the Geneva Latini (Walters 233, fol. 98; Cat. No. 59).

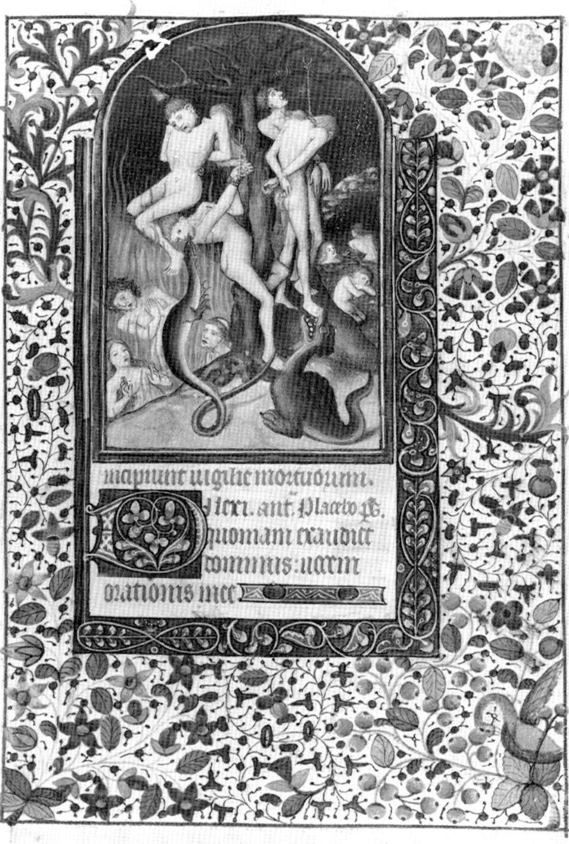

Fig. 121. *Torments of the Damned,* France, Savoy, ca. 1465–70, by an artist of the Hours of Louis de Savoie (Walters 292, fol. 88; Cat. No. 44).

kneeling mother who is first among mankind's intercessors. Blasts from the angels' trumpets call forth the dead who rise timidly, fearfully, from their graves. Two contrasting scenes of judgement, a decapitation, representing justice, and Solomon's wise decision concerning the fate of the child with two mothers, an allusion to mercy, are juxtaposed in the lower border.

The Marescalci Hours contains an unusual subject for its Office of the Dead: the Torments of the Damned (Fig. 121). Five unfortunate souls hang from a bare tree, desperately trying to escape the tongues of the flames and the dragons that lick at their flesh. Other souls suffer in the depths of the fiery pit itself or of the frigid waters of an ice-filled lake. When hell appears in the Office of the Dead its role is usually subsidiary and placed, appropriately enough, in the lower margin of the leaf. Such is the case with Walters 90, an early fourteenth-century Book of Hours from northern France, where the principal illustration consists of a traditional funeral service but the lower border includes a vignette of devils carrying off souls to hell (Cat. No. 7).

The Commendation of Souls, a series of psalms recited after the Office of the Dead, is often found in English Books of Hours or in those manufactured elsewhere (often in Belgium) for use in Great Britain. This text is often accompanied by a hopeful vision of heavenly reward that could not be more different from the nightmare of the Marescalci Hours described above. The miniature in the Mostyn Hours, made in England in the 1460s, is typical (Fig. 122). Departing from the site of the dead man's tomb, two angels gently carry his soul, in the form of a nude child, aloft in a large white cloth. God the Father awaits the newcomer, a large number of souls already enjoying the comfort of his bosom.

Individual figures from both the Old and New Testament whose heroic ability to withstand the specially difficult trials with which life tested them are also pressed into service as spiritual models for readers of

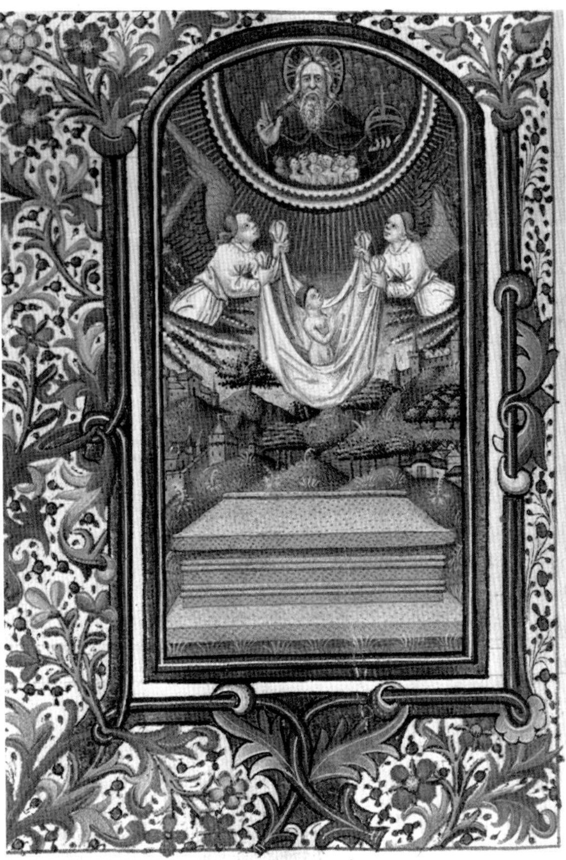

Fig. 122. *Souls Borne to Heaven,* England, ca. 1460–70 (Philadelphia Museum of Art, '45-65-6, fol. 206v; Cat. No. 113).

Books of Hours. Since the nine lessons of the Office are all taken from the Book of Job (see the Appendix), it was inevitable that representations of Job, the biblical model of patience, serve as the visual complement to this text. Towards the late fifteenth century in France images of the Old Testament hero became as popular as the funeral service and burial had been throughout the earlier history of the Book of Hours. A late fifteenth-century *Horae* from the workshop of Jean Poyet provides us with an example of Job on the Dungheap, the episode of the prophet's life most frequently depicted (Fig. 123). In some Books of Hours, as is the case here and in the slightly earlier Walters 245 (Cat. No. 64), instead of a single miniature introducing the entire Office of the Dead, each of the nine lessons is accompanied by a miniature. Cycles of this kind enable the reader to empathize with Job in each of his tribulations, from loss of family and livestock, to ridicule from his wife and friends, to beatings by the devil.

After Job, the second most frequently found hero in miniatures for the Office of the Dead is Lazarus, the brother of Mary and Martha and close friend of Christ. The Raising of Lazarus became an increasingly popular subject for the Office during the course of the fifteenth century, especially among Flemish illuminators. It was the chosen subject in a late fifteenth-century *Horae* painted by the workshop of the Master of Edward IV (Fig. 124). The iconography, with figures of apostles in addition to Mary and Martha, and men holding their noses against the dead man's four-day aroma, is standard, but the expansion of the miniature into the border is symptomatic of the often playful visual games Flemish painters enjoyed. The Raising of Lazarus obviously alludes to mankind's resurrection at the Second Coming, and the subject offers a hopeful prefiguration of God's merciful forgiveness. One of the pairs of responses and versicles in the Office of the Dead makes a direct connection between this historical event and the future one faced by the reader: "You who raised Lazarus fetid from the tomb, You, Lord, give them rest, and a place of pardon. You who are to come to judge the living and the dead, to judge the world by fire, You, Lord." Another factor makes Lazarus an appropriate figure for the Office of the Dead. According to medieval legend Lazarus, once returned from the grave, was able, like Dante, to give a detailed report of all the torments of hell he had witnessed.

The other Lazarus of the Bible is the sore-covered beggar—and patron of lepers in the Middle Ages—who is hero of the parable of the rich man Dives. The first of two episodes involving Lazarus the beggar for the Office of the Dead is the Feast of Dives, as found in the Hours of Florimond Robertet from the second decade of the sixteenth century (Fig. 125). Dives and his wife feast from a generously laid table, apparently oblivious to the supplications of Lazarus who has just entered the room. A servant of Dives', acting as a sort of Renaissance bouncer, raises his arm in a gesture forbidding Lazarus to take a further step. The ailing beggar, who holds, like medieval lepers, a clapper in his hand to warn passersby of his approach, raises his other hand to his head with resigned despair. As mentioned in the biblical text and shown in the miniature, Lazarus' pitiful sores attract the attention of Dives' dogs. The Office of the Dead from another early sixteenth-century Book of Hours illustrates the second episode from the parable (Fig. 126). After his death, Lazarus receives his reward and enjoys the eternal comfort of Abraham's bosom. Dives, burning in hell's undying flames, points to his mouth, beseeching Abraham to "send Lazarus, that he may dip the tip of his finger in water to cool my tongue." Too late, is the message delivered from on high.

Death personified as a living skeleton is the final

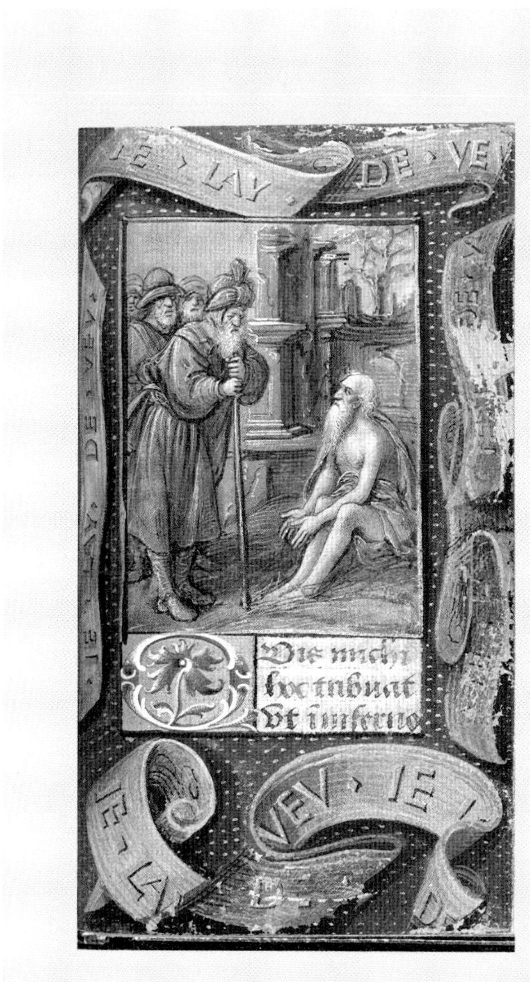

Fig. 123. *Job on the Dungheap,* France, Tours, end of the 15th century, by Jean Poyet and his workshop (Walters 430, fol. 145; Cat. No. 68).

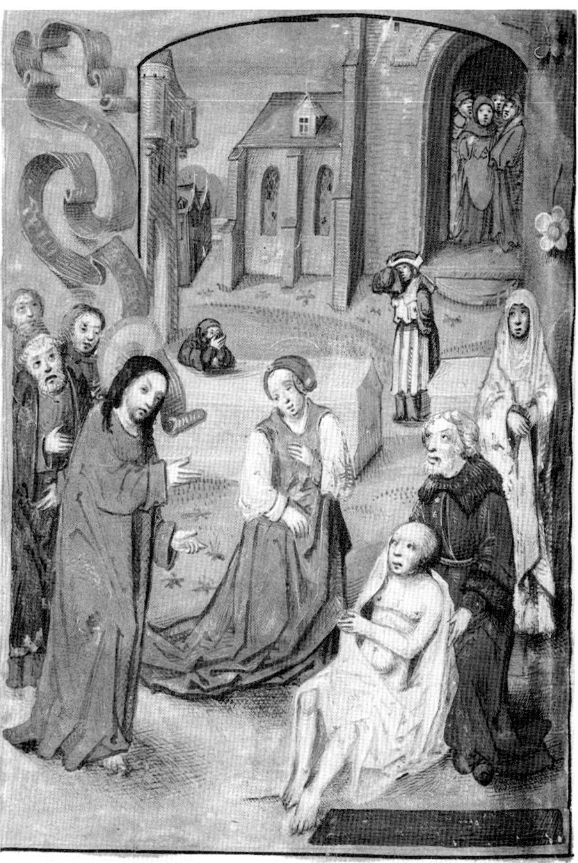

Fig. 124. *Raising of Lazarus,* Belgium, Bruges, late 15th century, by the workshop of the Master of Edward IV (Walters 435, fol. 128v; Cat. No. 102).

category of themes used for the Office of the Dead. These images are among the most moving and horrifying produced in the Middle Ages and Renaissance, as was already seen in the deathbed miniature from the Burgundian Book of Hours discussed above (Pl. 37). This figure of Death has many of the characteristic features that can be found in a great number of similar images: Death carries a lance, ragged pieces of decaying flesh still hang from his bones, his power is wielded by the slightest touch, and his appearance is a cause of surprise to his victim. This element of unpleasant surprise, so characteristic of representations of the Dance of Death, is found in a miniature painted about 1475 by the Maître Francois (Fig. 127). A terrified man, fleeing from Death and his arrow, is about to take his last step over the edge of a dock. His flight is in vain, of course, for either Death's sting will conquer this victim or the deep waters will do the job. The plaque above this struggle reads, "All who are and all who are to be, shall by a fatal step pass away."

Surprise—as well as terror—is central to the power of images of the Three Living and the Three Dead, a theme that becomes popular, especially in France, in the fifteenth century. As illustrated from a Rouen Book of Hours of about 1480, the story tells of three princes, young, carefree, and richly dressed, out for a day's pleasurable hawking (Fig. 128). They pass an ancient graveyard where three corpses, in varying stages of decay, rise up from their tombs and address the frightened youths: "We were once as you are now, and what we are you soon will be." The borders include roundels the theme of which is Death as the Great Equalizer whose victims are from all classes of society.

Death who stalks his victims can be found in other miniatures. In an eerie painting by a follower of Jean Fouquet in the 1470s, a menacing band of skeletons

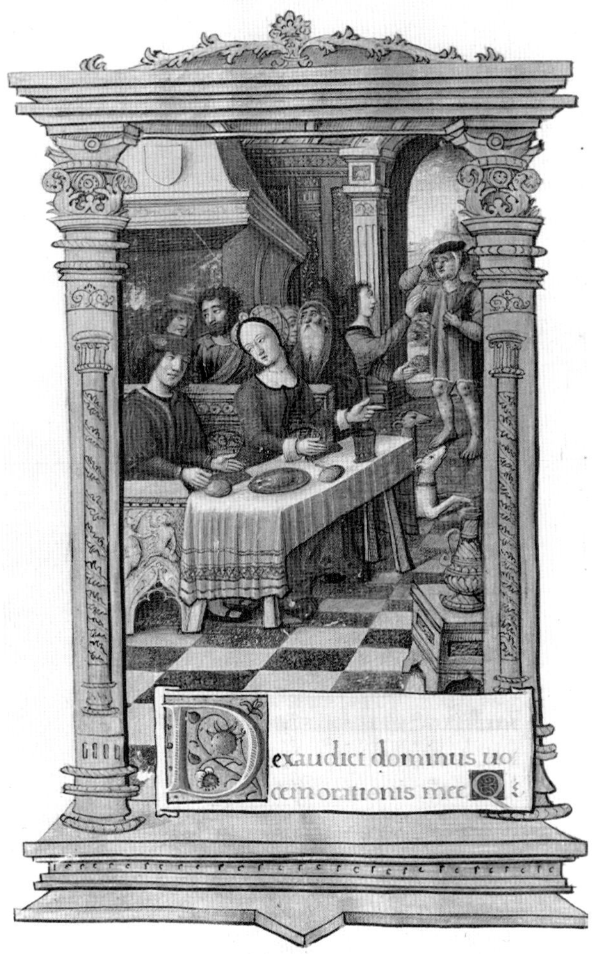

Fig. 125. *Lazarus at the Feast of Dives,* France, Paris, ca. 1510–20, by the Master of Morgan 85 (Walters 452, fol. 113v; Cat. No. 72).

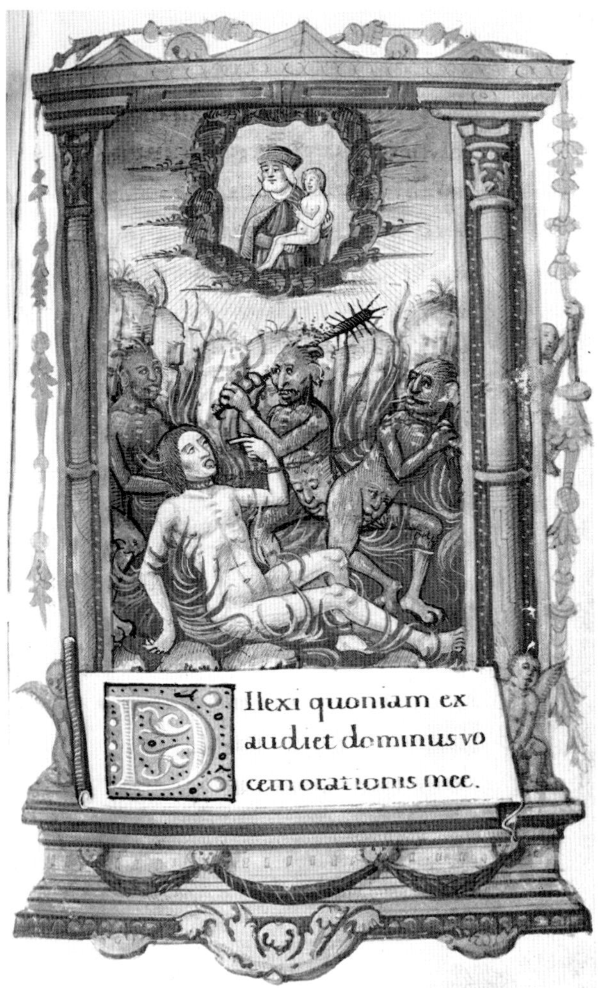

Fig. 126. *Dives in Hell,* France, Paris, early 16th century, by a follower of the Master of Petrarch's Triumphs (Library of Congress, Rosenwald 15, fol. 117; Cat. No. 71).

riding oxen, symbols of death's slow but unrelenting progress, emerges from the dark woods (Fig. 129). They throw their lances at a group of frightened men unable to withstand the attack.

Some illuminators choose to represent but a single figure of Death in their miniatures for the Office of the Dead. The effect can be arresting. Death as the Grim Reaper, the consuming force that mows down all in his path, is the subject of a miniature in an Italian Book of Hours of about 1475 attributed to Girolamo da Cremona (Fig. 130). Death stands in a rocky landscape, his grin, as well as the skull and bone on the ground, attest to both his power and the pleasure it provides him. On his head he wears an elaborate burlet, a type of padded headgear popular with both sexes at the middle of the century. With this, his only garment, Death scoffs at man's vanity and ridicules those trifles that occupy man's attention, distracting him from the care for his own salvation. Another Death, this one holding a mirror, is found in a late fifteenth-century Flemish Book of Hours painted by a follower of Simon Marmion (Fig. 131). The figure of Death is shown in dramatic close-up, a device Marmion exploited to great advantage in his work. The mirror that Death holds, a popular conceit of the late Middle Ages and Renaissance, is the symbol of vanity. In this miniature, however, the mirror is cleverly positioned so that we, the viewer, have no choice but to imagine ourselves reflected on its surface. We are drawn into the miniature itself and Death, literally, holds us in his hand.

Finally, there is the Book of Hours painted by Jean Colombe for Princess Anne of France in the 1470s. This extremely rich production, befitting its royal patron, contains 107 large miniatures. The Office of the Dead, with an elaborate cycle of twenty-four minia-

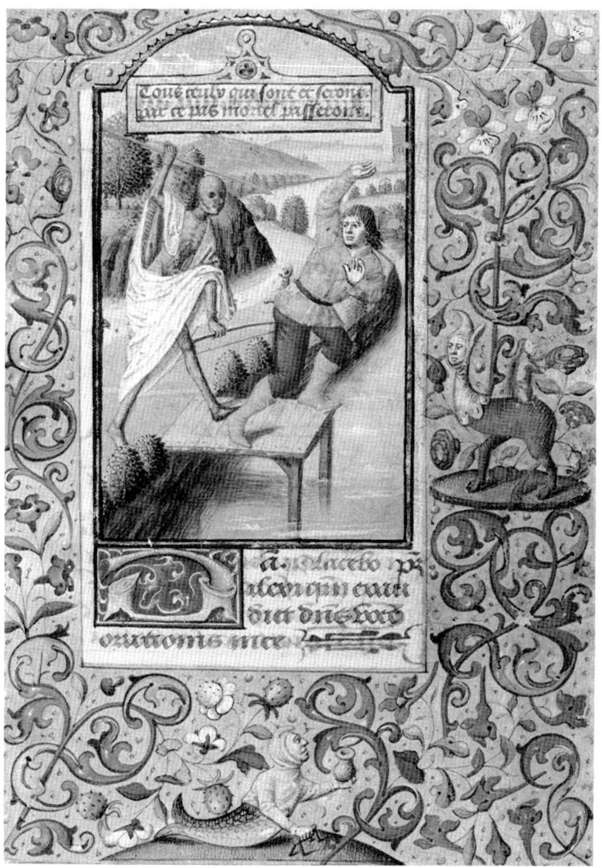

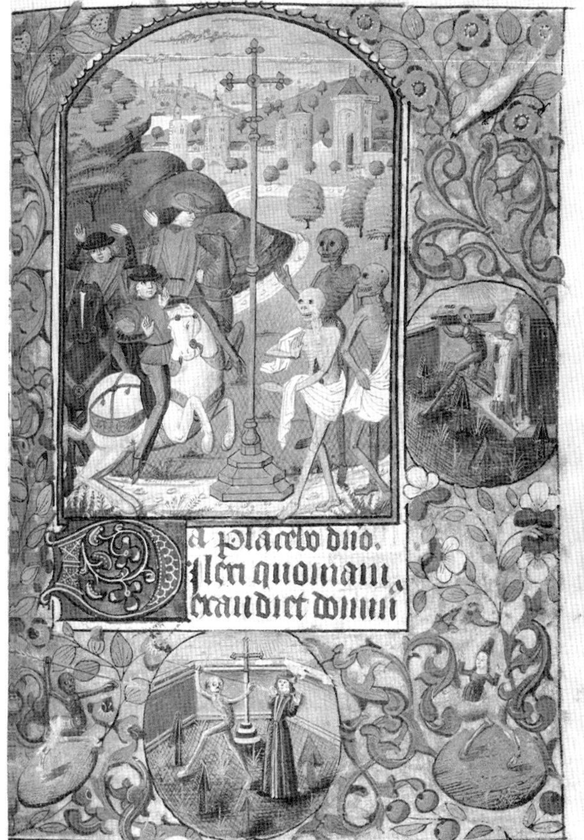

Fig. 127. *Death Attacking a Man,* France, Paris, ca. 1475, by the Maître François (Walters 214, fol. 91; Cat. No. 51).

Fig. 128. *Three Living and Three Dead,* border: *Death Approaching a Pope; Death Attacking a Young Man,* France, Rouen, ca. 1480, by the workshop of the Master of the Geneva Latini (Walters 241, fol. 92; Cat. No. 61).

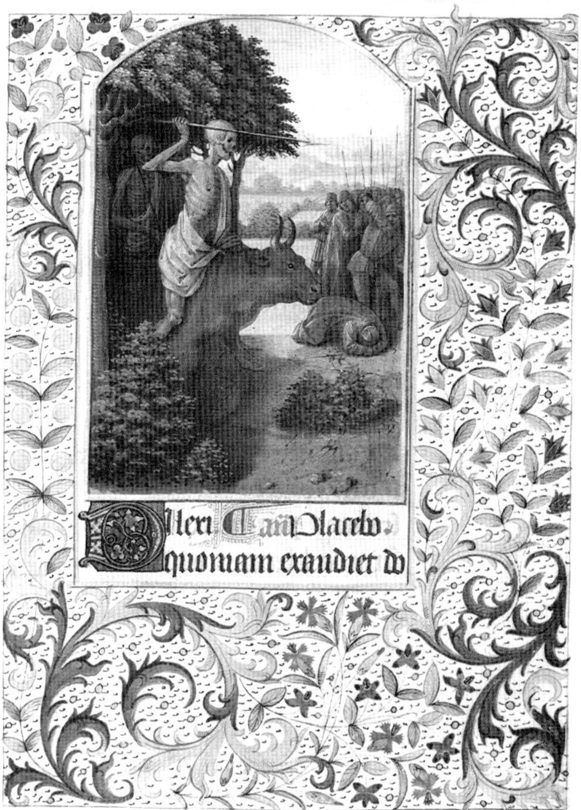

Fig. 129. *Death Riding Oxen,* France, Tours, 1470s, by a follower of Jean Fouquet (Library of Congress 93, fol. 114; Cat. No. 54).

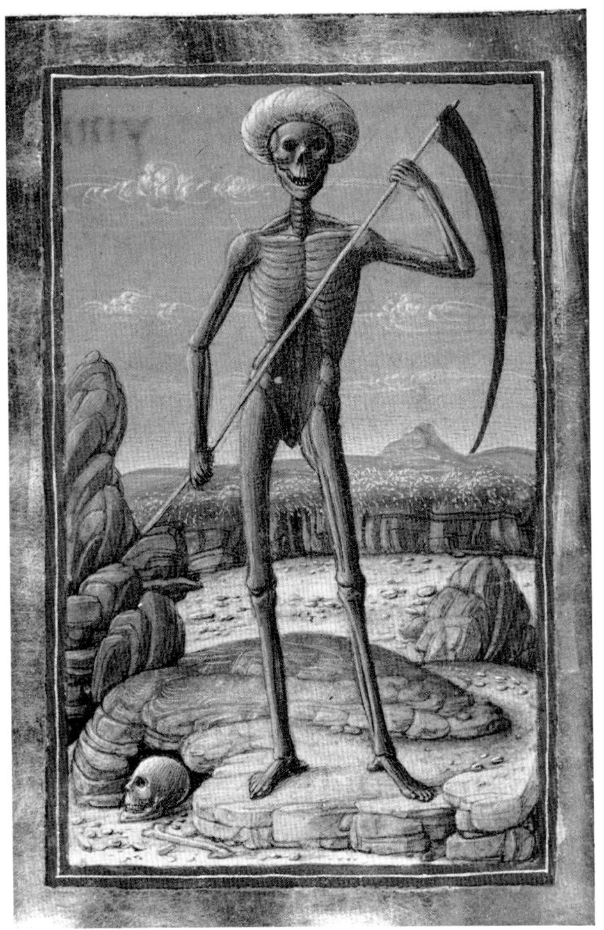

Fig. 130. *Grim Reaper,* Italy, ca. 1475, attributed to Girolamo da Cremona (Philadelphia Free Library, Lewis 118, fol. 95v; Cat. No. 117).

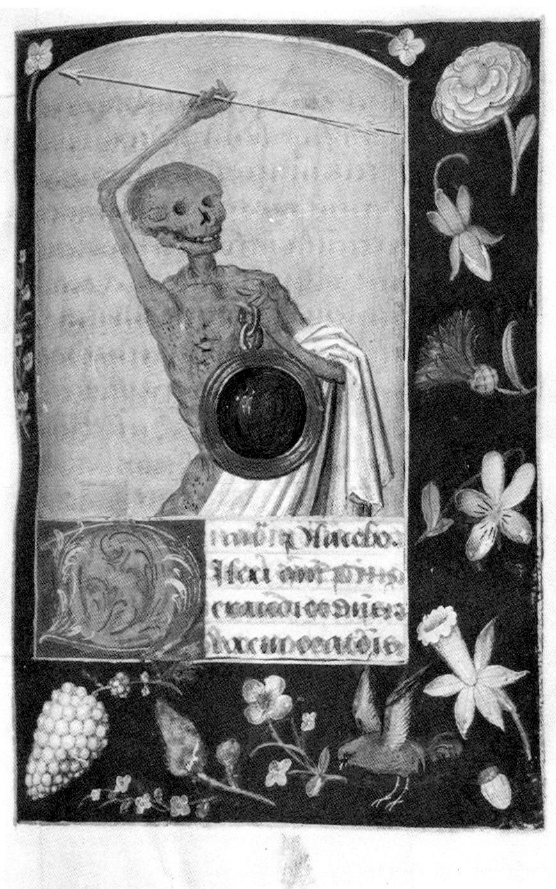

Fig. 131. *Death Holding a Mirror,* Belgium, ca. 1480s, by the Master of Antoine Rolin (Walters 431, fol. 115; Cat. No. 101).

tures, uses many subjects already mentioned, the Feast of Dives, a Funeral Procession, Souls Released from Purgatory, as well as more unusual ones. The long cycle is introduced, however, by a very simple representation of Death, but, perhaps, one of the most terrifying ever painted (Pl. 40). With a head like a huge swollen malignant cyst, Death looms up from his tomb, filling the miniature with his menacing presence. Placed at just a hair's distance from the picture plane, he seems not only capable, but also eager, to reach out and snare us as his next victim.

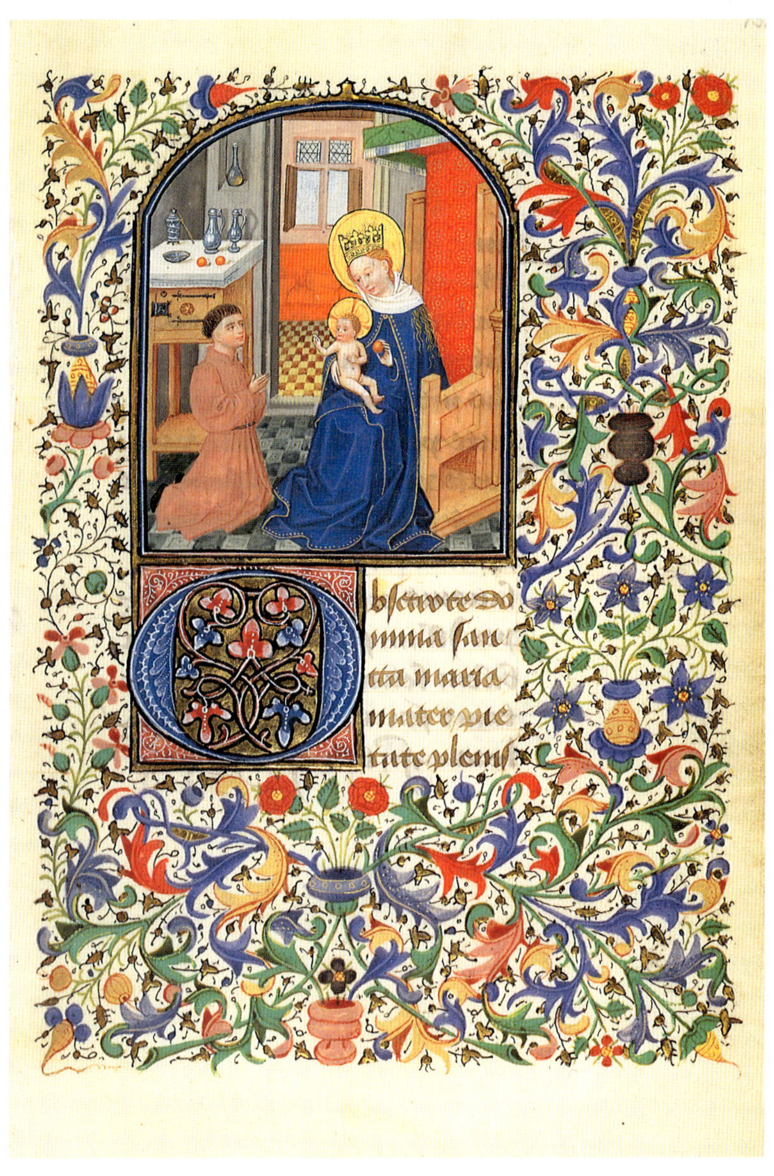

Pl. 29. *Madonna with Kneeling Patron* ("Obsecro te"), Belgium, Bruges, ca. 1450, by Willem Vrelant (Walters 220, fol. 138; Cat. No. 91).

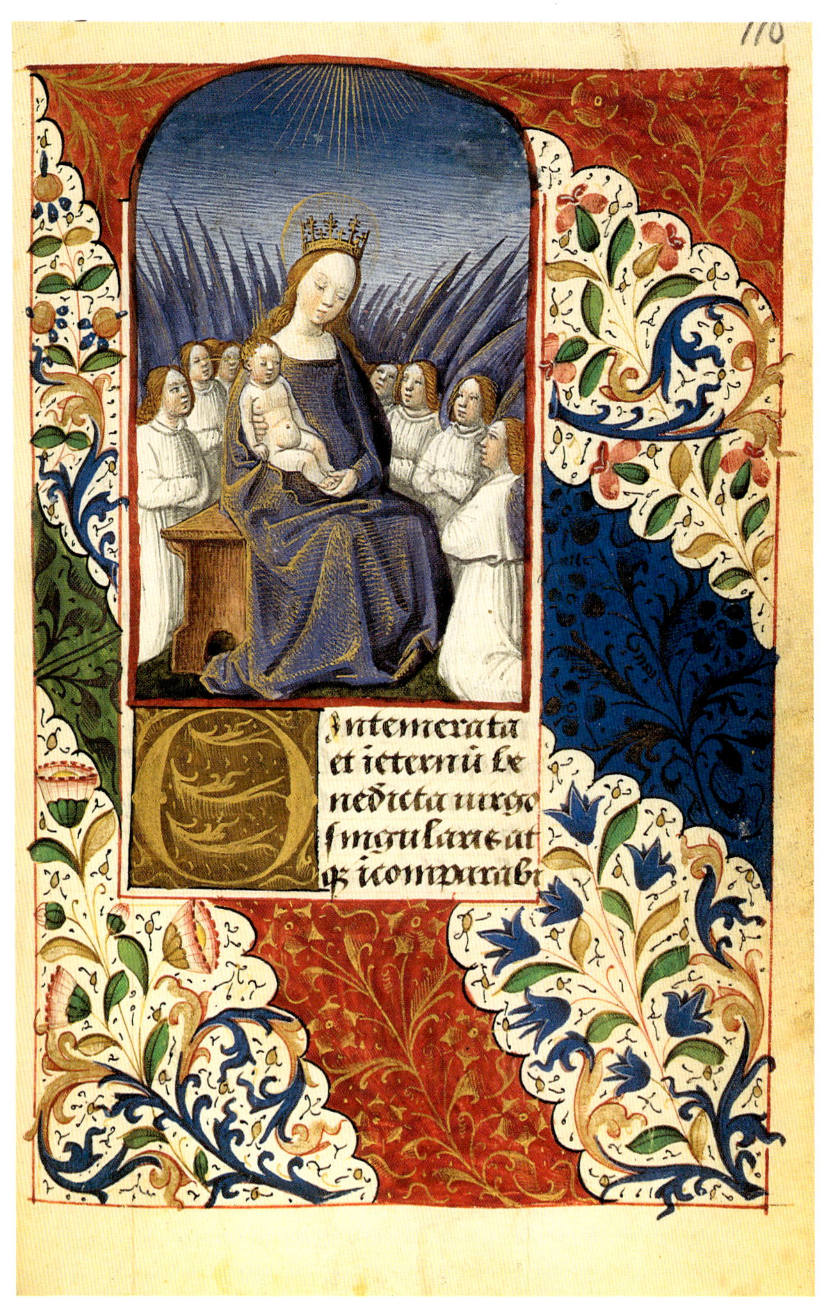

Pl. 30. *Madonna Surrounded by Angels* ("O intemerata"), France, Bourges?, ca. 1480, by Jean Colombe (Walters 213, fol. 110; Cat. No. 56).

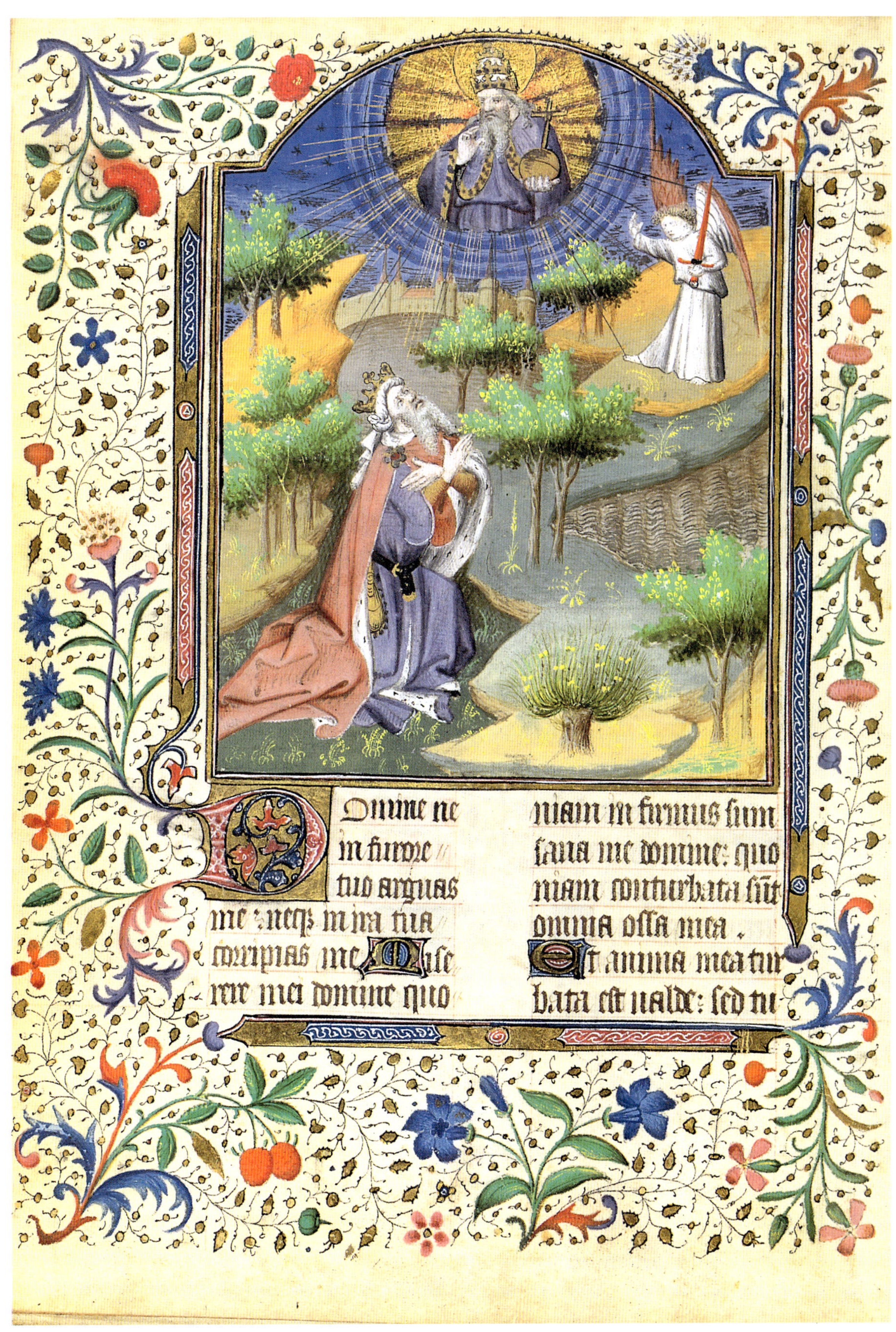

Pl. 31. *David in Prayer* (Penitential Psalms), France, Paris?, ca. 1425–30, by the workshop of the Bedford Master (Walters 289, fol. 94v; Cat. No. 33).

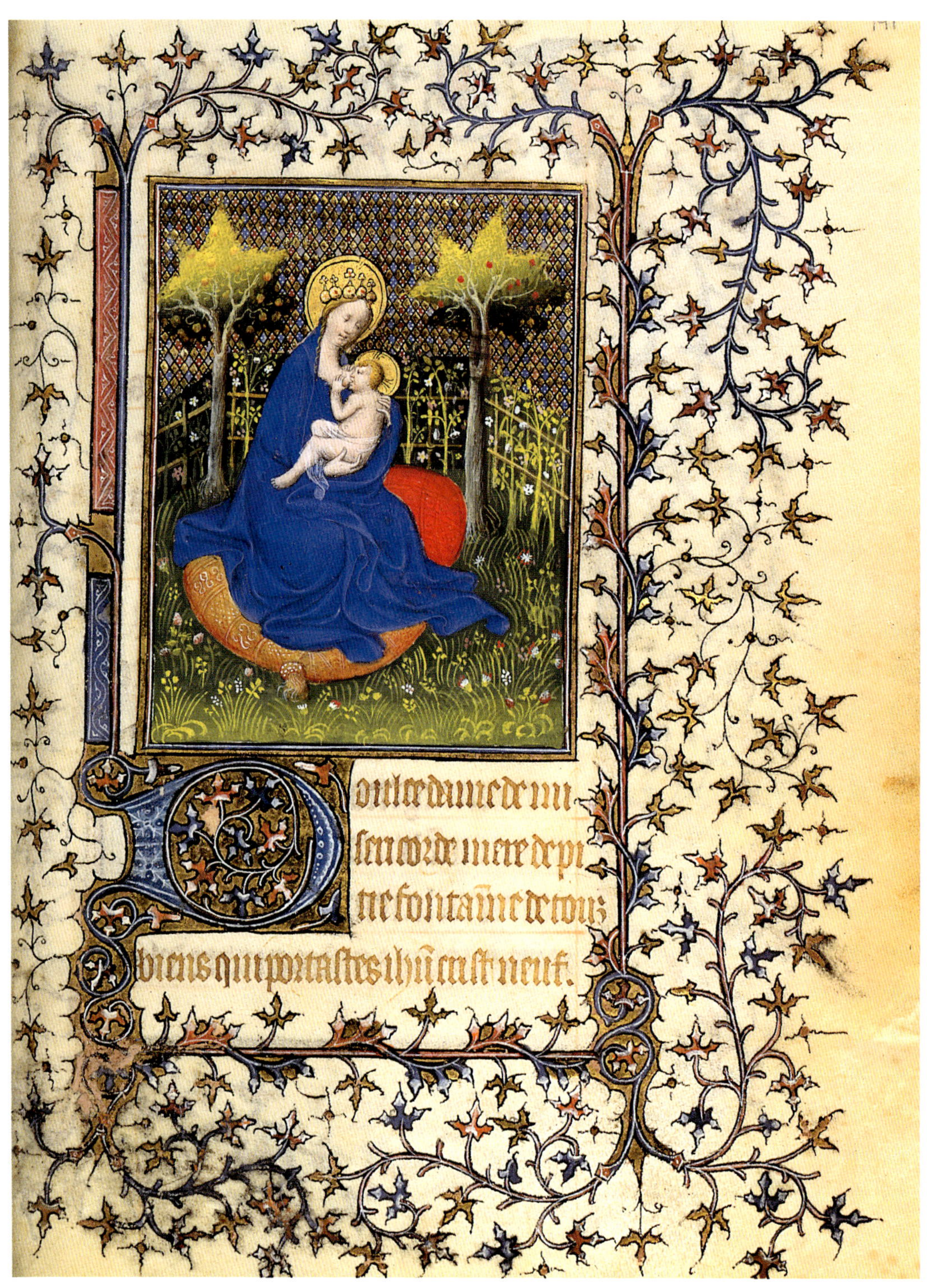

Pl. 32. *Virgo Lactans* (Accessory Text: 15 Joys of the Virgin), France, Paris, ca. 1410, by a follower of the Master of Berry's *Cleres Femmes* (Walters 232, fol. 191; Cat. No. 21).

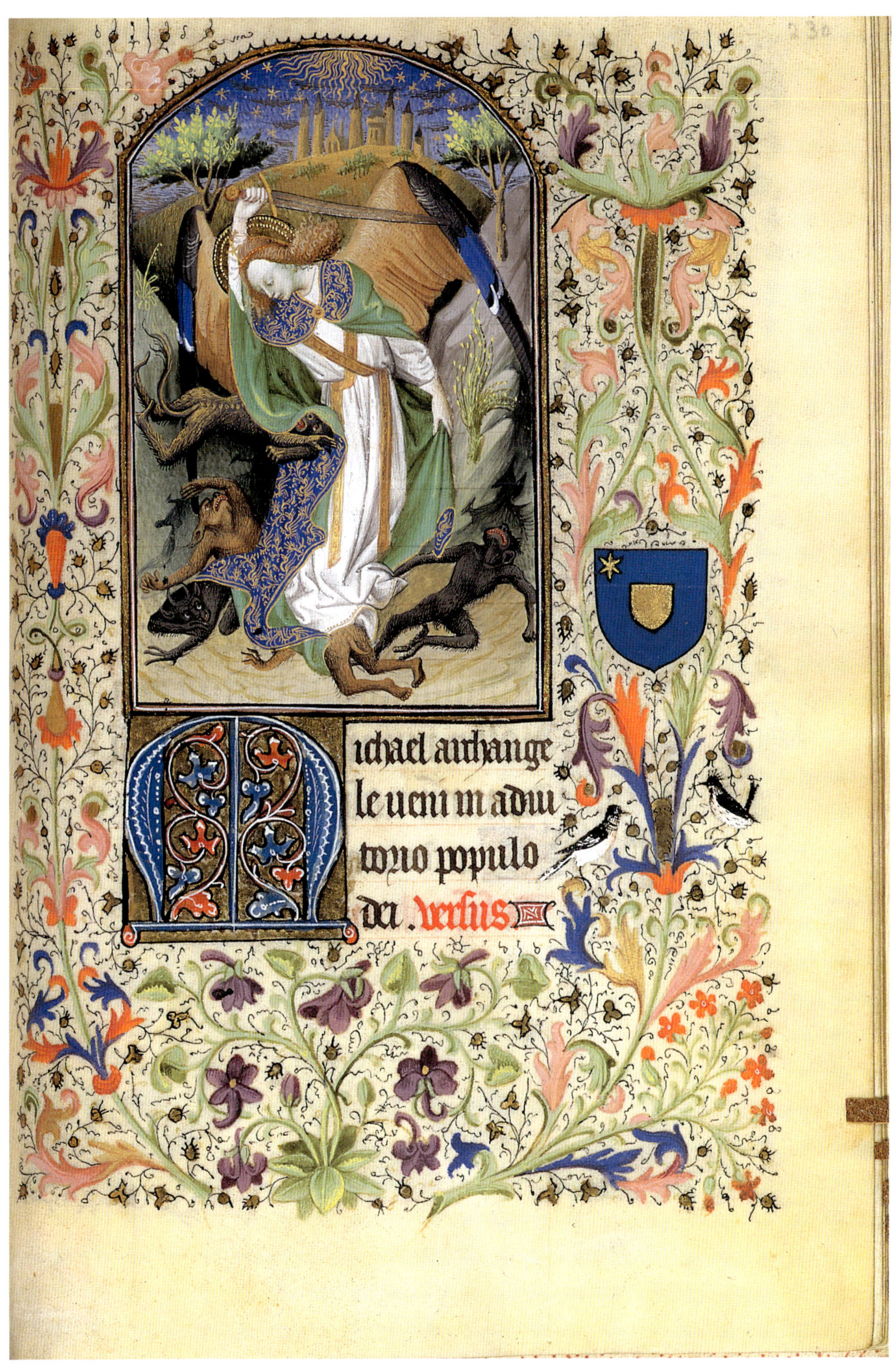

Pl. 33. *Michael Battling Devils* (Suffrage), northern France or Belgium, Tournai, ca. 1430–35, by the Master of Walters 281 (Walters 281, fol. 230; Cat. No. 35).

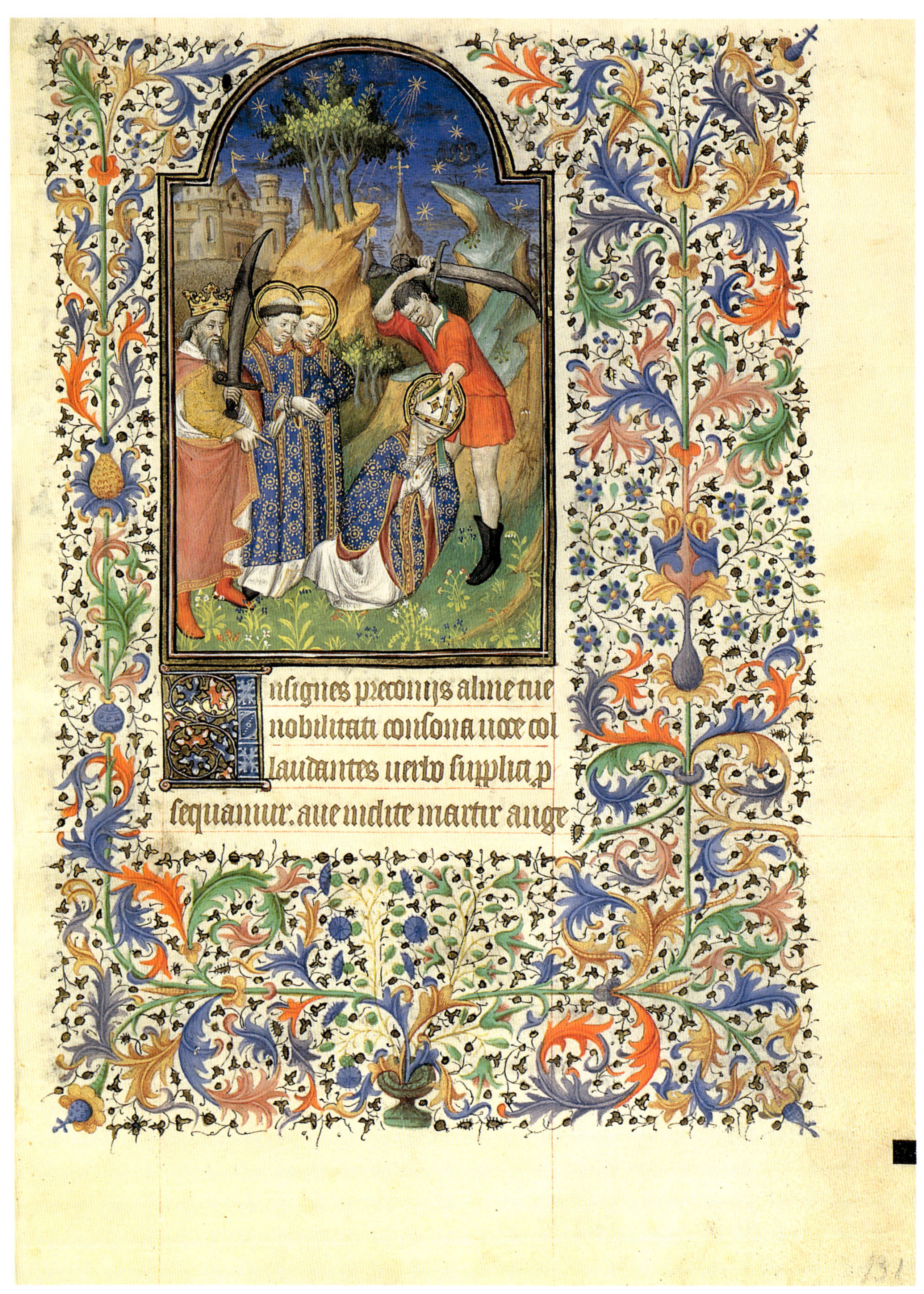

Pl. 34. *Martyrdom of Dennis, Eleutherius, and Rusticus* (Suffrage), France, Paris, 1420s, by the Master of the Harvard Hannibal (Walters 287, fol. 131; Cat. No. 29).

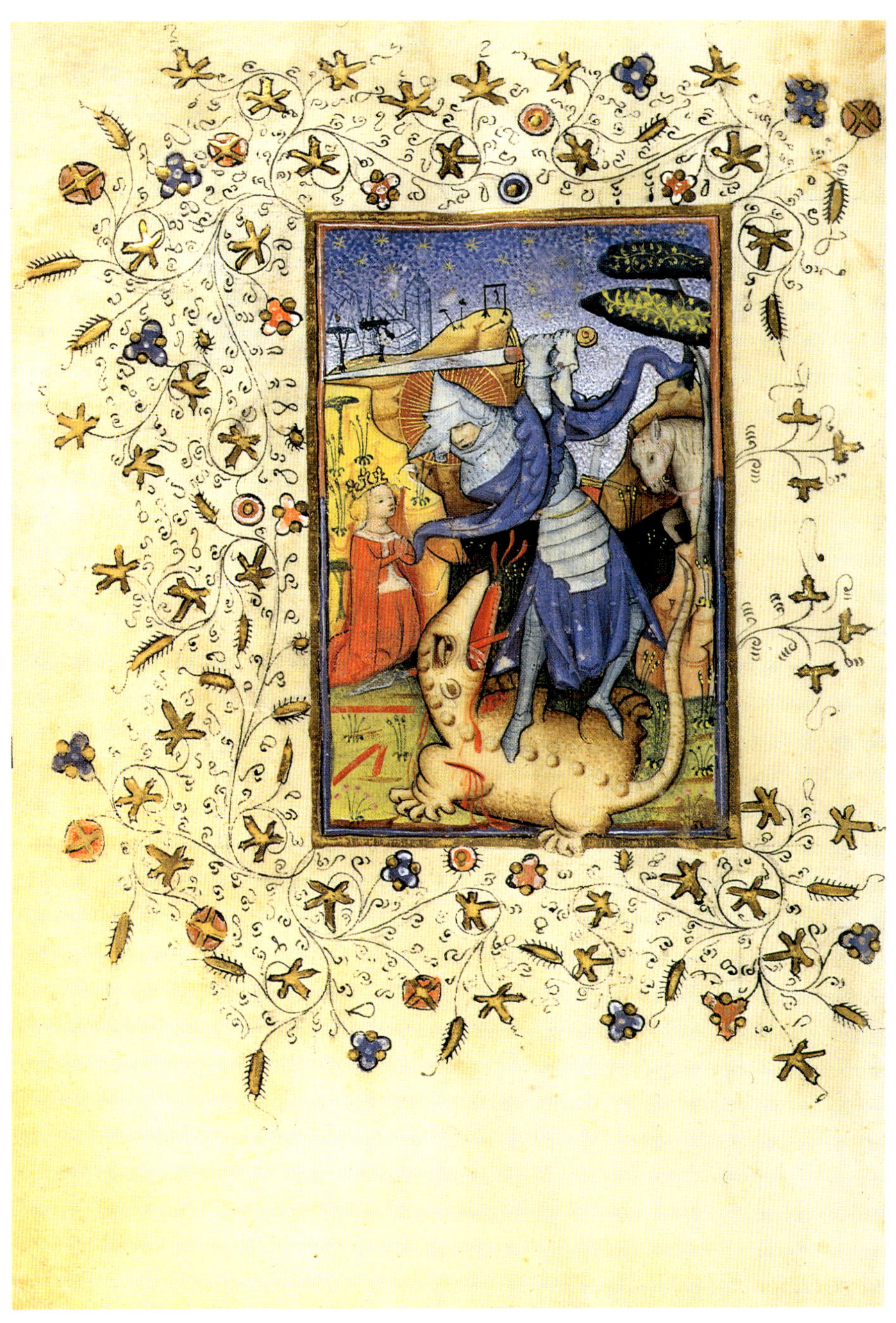

Pl. 35. *George Slaying the Dragon* (Suffrage), Belgium, ca. 1430–40, by a follower of the Master of Guillebert de Mets (Walters 170, fol. 157v; Cat. No. 84).

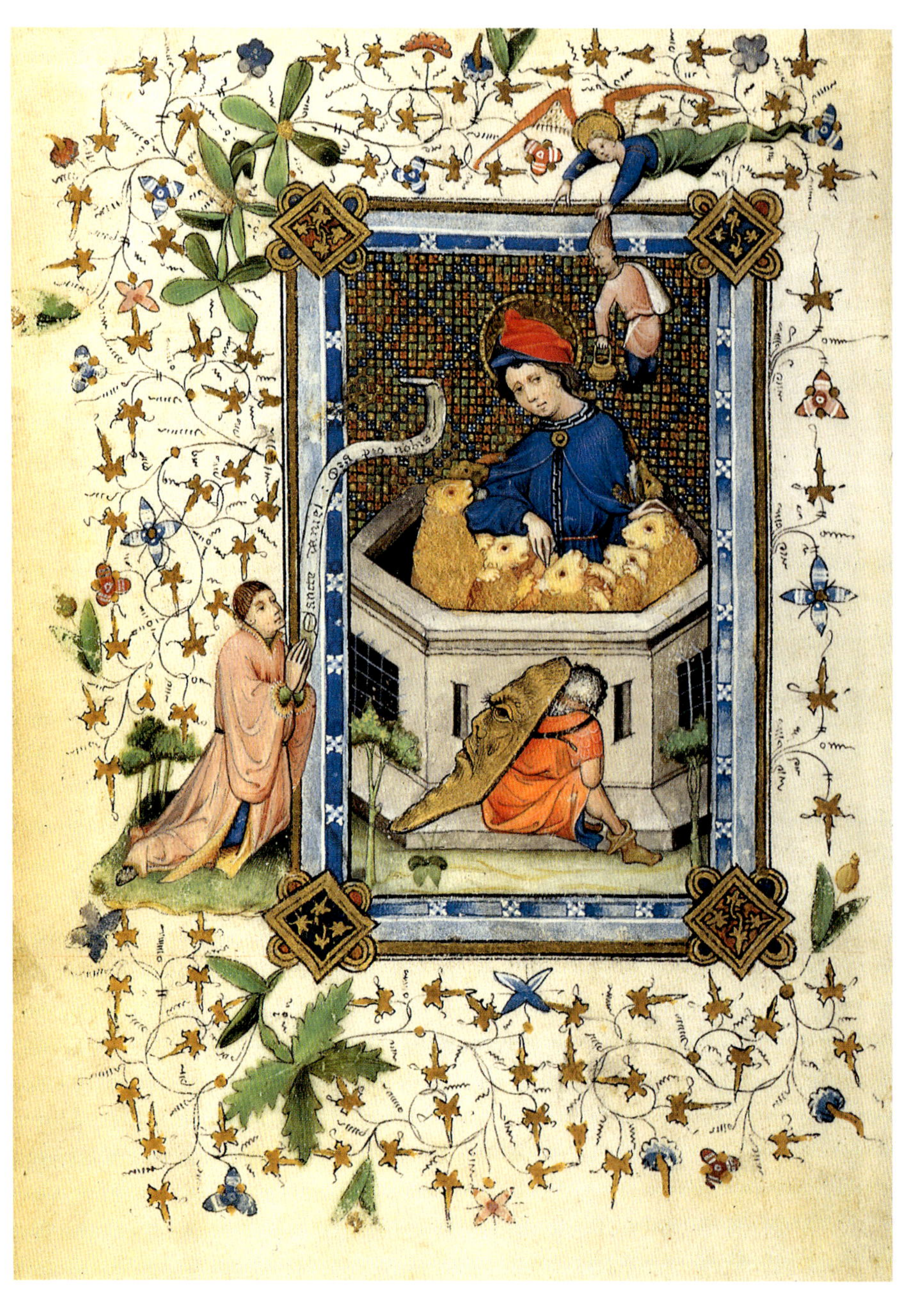

Pl. 36. *Daniel in the Lions' Den, with Kneeling Daniel Rym* (Suffrage), Belgium, Ghent?, late 1420s, by the Master of Guillebert de Mets (Walters 166, fol. 168v; Cat. No. 83).

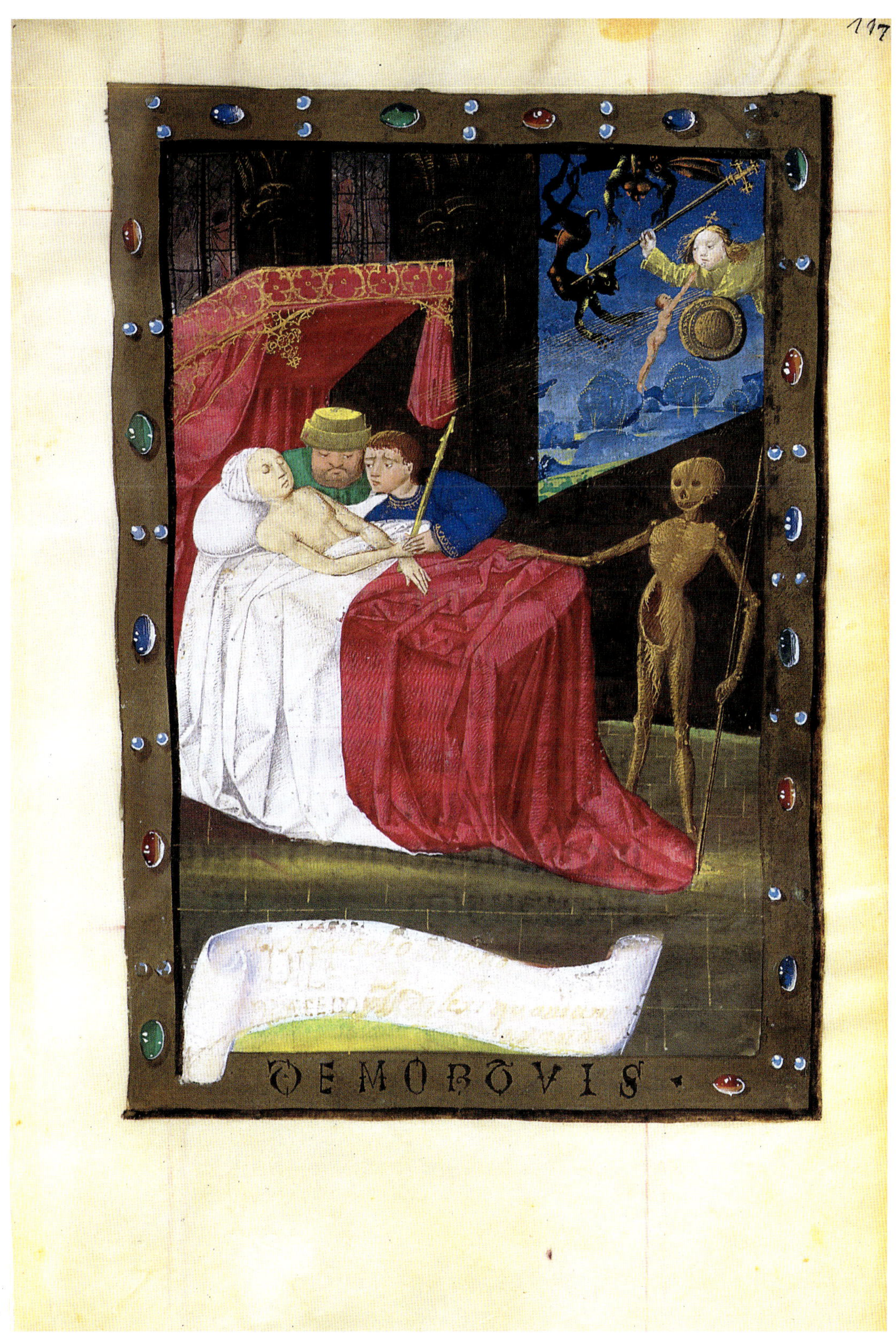

Pl. 37. *Death Approaching the Deathbed and Battle over the Soul* (Office of the Dead), France, Burgundy?, ca. 1480–90 (Walters 457, fol. 117; Cat. No. 63).

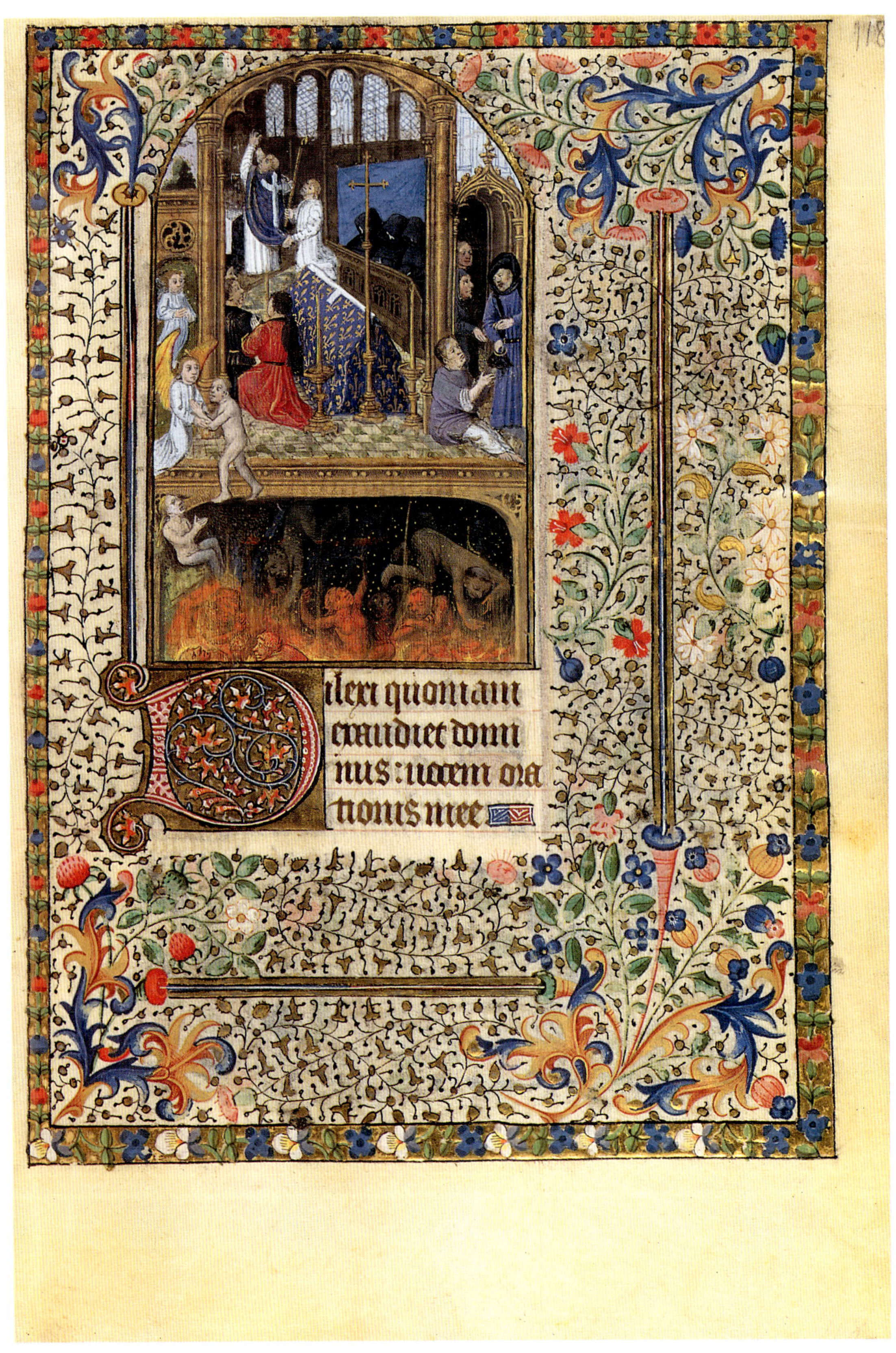

Pl. 38. *Funeral Mass with Souls Released from Purgatory* (Office of the Dead), France, Angers?, 1460s, by the Coëtivy Master (Henri de Vulcop?) (Walters 274, fol. 118; Cat. No. 42).

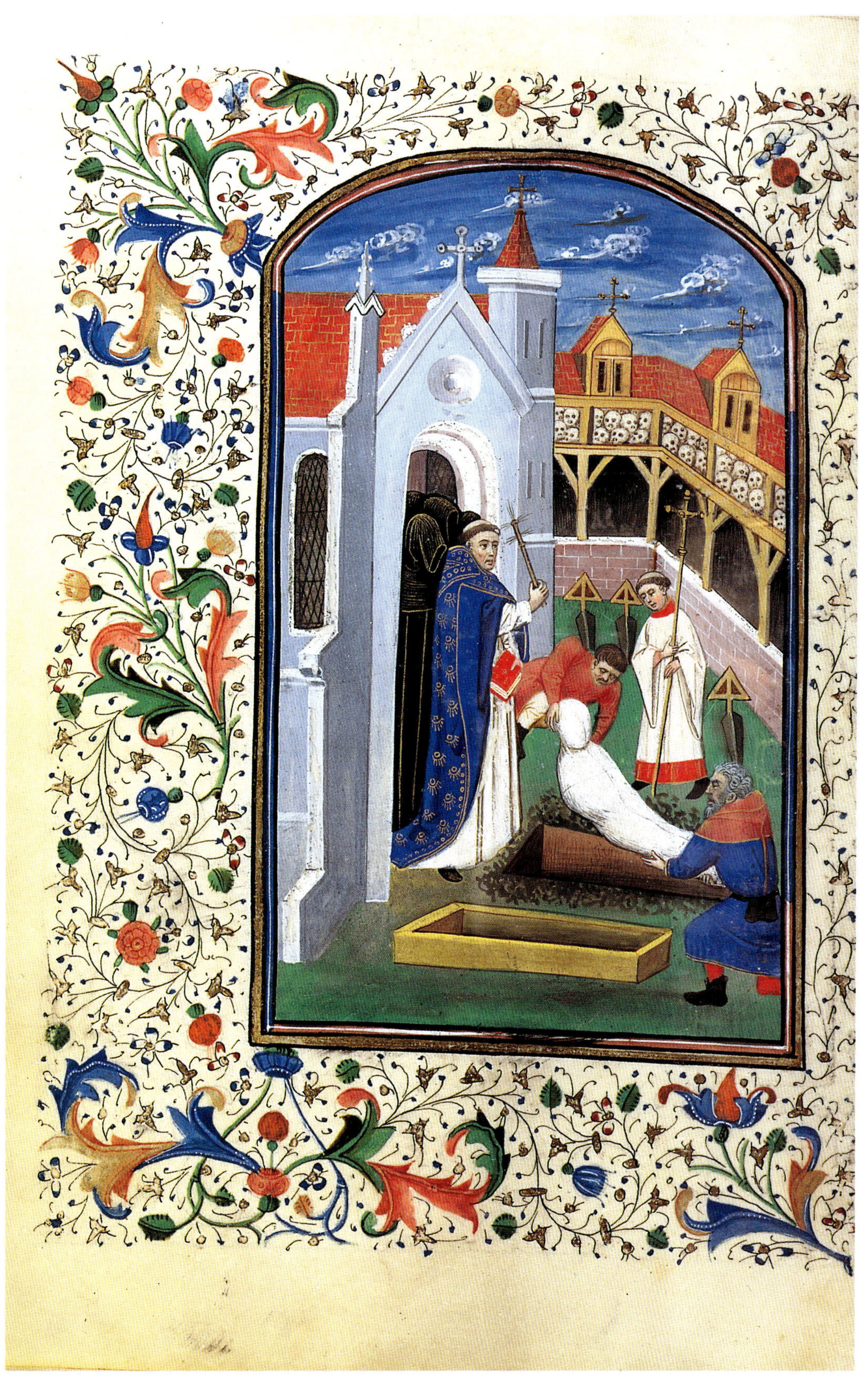

Pl. 39. *Burial Service* (Office of the Dead), Belgium, Bruges, ca. 1460, by Willem Vrelant (Walters 197, fol. 175v; Cat. No. 93).

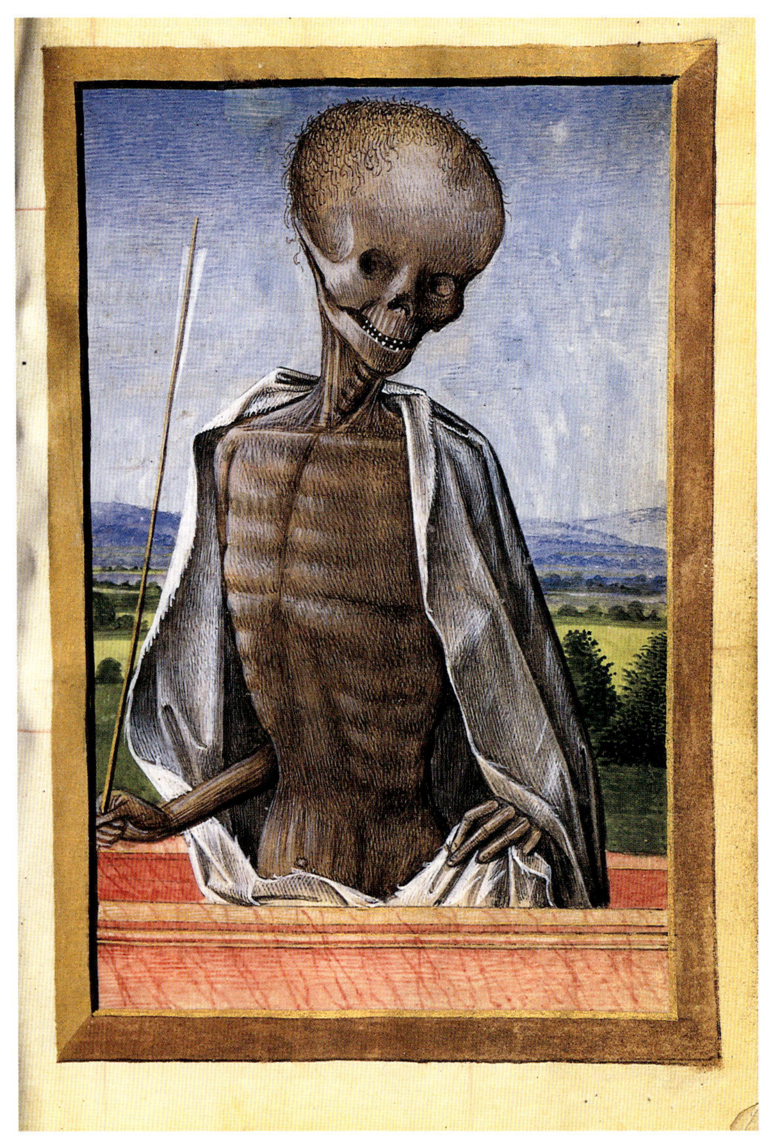

Pl. 40. *Death, with an Arrow, Rising from a Tomb* (Office of the Dead), France, Bourges, late 1470s, by Jean Colombe (Morgan M.677, fol. 245; Cat. No. 55).

CHAPTER XIII

"Use" and "Beyond Use"

For the history of painting in the late Middle Ages, no single class of manuscripts is as important as Books of Hours. This is not only because many artists are known largely or only through their paintings in such books, but also because our knowledge of most local and regional styles of painting depends on our ability to localize these books through their texts. It is customary to determine where such books were written by identifying local use for several of their standard texts: the Calendar, the Hours of the Virgin, the Litany, and the Office of the Dead. The use of these texts is determined through applying various tests, both published and unpublished (discussed in the Appendix with bibliographic tools cited in "Books for Further Reading"); this chapter will focus on the limits of our present tests, their revision, and new ways of determining where Books of Hours were written. What follows is an application of some new methods based on a long-term project, now computerized, that aims at providing more reliable tests for localization than are now available. This project has been christened "Beyond Use."

The most obvious limitation of all the traditional tests is that they may indicate where a Book of Hours was intended to be used, but not where it was made. This is nowhere clearer than with the many French *Horae* written for the use of Paris that were demonstrably made in "provincial" centers, or with the numerous Books of Hours made for export, such as those made for Sarum (English) use, but actually produced in French or Flemish centers. In such cases the use tests are misleading. Another problem arises from the fact that, during the fifteenth century, books were increasingly written according to the use of Rome, thereby hiding their origins. The popularity of this use seems to reflect, in part, a desire for a non-local or universal text that might be used anywhere. Even when the most widely employed test for the Hours of the Virgin, that devised by Falconer Madan (see "Books for Further Reading"), seems to yield clear results, they are sometimes wrong. This test fails to distinguish many different local uses, because too few are identified, too few textual components from the Hours of the Virgin are involved (only the antiphons and capitula of Prime and None), and because the incipits given (the first two or three words thought to define those texts) are too short. My method is to record, in addition to the Madan components, incipits or whole texts for the following: the first lesson and its response at Matins; the first psalm antiphon, the capitulum, and the antiphon for the canticle at Lauds; the antiphons and capitula from Terce and Sext; the first psalm antiphon, capitulum, and antiphon for the canticle at Vespers; and the same for Compline.

Some of the failings of Madan's test are overcome in the unpublished material for determining use in both the Hours of the Virgin and the Office of the Dead compiled by Victor Leroquais and contained in his notebooks housed at the Bibliothèque Nationale in Paris, and a few copies of the notebooks are now available in this country. Leroquais identified many uses, particularly French ones, and recorded more components from the Hours of the Virgin. However, their identifying incipits, as in Madan, are often still too short to distinguish substantially different components beginning with the same words. Again, to avoid this problem, it has been necessary for me to collect either much longer incipits or whole component texts. The same problem occurs in Leroquais' test for the Office of the

Dead (consisting of lessons and their responses), which suffers further because the number of components does not always permit us to distinguish different uses. But until my material (which adds the versicles to the lessons and responses) is published, the Leroquais test has been the only one available for the Office of the Dead. The study by Knud Ottosen (which includes responses and versicles, but not lessons) is now available.

Genuine liturgical Calendars are quite precise, with specific local feasts and a hierarchical grading for each feast indicating how it is to be observed, a grading which may also be peculiar to a particular locale. By and large this is not true for Calendars in Books of Hours that instead tend to be intentionally vague by including mainly widely observed feasts with a combination of local or regional ones pointing in different and conflicting directions, and by having only a rudimentary system of grading by color. In the fifteenth century, this vagueness is particularly evident in what may be called the composite Calendar, of which there are many varieties, but which are completely filled with a feast for every day of the year, unlike truly liturgical Calendars that have many "empty" days. While scholars usually treat such composite Calendars as though they were true liturgical ones, searching them for local or regional feasts, composite Calendars seldom reveal a place or even a specific region for their use. My strategy with these Calendars has been different. I treat them as texts, with their entries as variant readings, in order to differentiate various versions, to form families or groups, and, finally, to localize them.

A consideration of two Walters manuscripts (W.220 and W.240, Cat. Nos. 91, 92) will illustrate my procedures. Both are illustrated by the same artist, who was named the Master of Arsenal 575 by James Douglas Farquhar (*Creation and Imitation: The Work of a Fifteenth-Century Manuscript Illuminator,* Fort Lauderdale, 1976). Since both manuscripts follow the use of Rome in their Hours of the Virgin and Office of the Dead, these texts seem to give little help in localizing the books, but significantly for Walters 220 the same precise form and order of the lessons, responses, and versicles in the Office of the Dead have been found in only one of the 500 or so manuscripts I have recorded, M.493 of the Pierpont Morgan Library, a book almost certainly made around 1470 in Bruges (for its rather spare Calendar includes the local feasts of St. Donatian on October 14 and St. Basil on June 14 written in gold).

Since the use is seemingly useless, Professor Farquhar, after noting that other scholars have localized the Calendar of Walters 220 to Rheims or Bruges, suggests the possibility of Paris as the intended place for its use. This is important to his belief that the artist worked mainly in the region of Paris and Rouen. While this Calendar does have some Parisian feasts, it also includes many saints from the Low Countries, Germany, and elsewhere. But the most telling feasts are those for St. Donatian, a bishop of Rheims and patron of Bruges, written in red on October 14; for the translation of his relics at Bruges on August 30; and for St. Basil, whose relics were in his church at Bruges, written in red on June 14. These feasts, the most specific ones in the Calendar, argue strongly that it was made for use in Bruges, in spite of the many feasts not associated with that city. That much is evident from traditional methods of analysis. Of the 140 Calendars I have recorded so far, mostly from the Low Countries with a smaller number from France, that of Walters 220 agrees in more than 50 percent of its entries only with Calendars connected either with Bruges itself or with the Ghent/Bruges school of illumination. Furthermore, it clearly belongs to a small family of full composite Calendars, all of which have the Bruges features mentioned above, and with which it agrees in about 80 to 90 percent of its entries—a remarkably high agreement considering the carelessness with which such Calendars were often copied. Other identified members of this small family, though still others surely exist, are as follows (all, like the two Walters *Horae* with which we began, conform to the use of Rome except for the as yet unidentified Office of the Dead in M. 285):

89.1 percent: Los Angeles, J. Paul Getty Museum, MS IX.7. The Llangattock Hours, thought to have been made in Bruges and/or Ghent about 1450–60. Its "Obsecro te" agrees most closely with Walters 196 (Vrelant shop, Bruges?, ca. 1470, Cat. No. 94) and Getty IX.8 (Vrelant, Bruges, ca. 1460); its Litany with the Older Prayer Book of Maximilian (Vienna 1907, Bruges, ca. 1490); and its Petitions with Morgan M.59 (Bruges?, ca. 1460).

88.3 percent: A dismembered *Horae,* formerly Philip C. Duschnes, New York. Illustrated about 1445 by an artist of the Gold Scrolls group, which worked mainly in Bruges. Other texts not available.

83.8 percent: Vienna, Österreichische Nationalbibliothek, Cod. 1856. The Black Prayer Book of Galeazzo Maria Sforza, illustrated by the Master of Anthony of Burgundy (sometimes identified with Philippe de Mazerolles), probably at Bruges in the third quarter of the fifteenth century. Its "Obsecro te," Litany, and Petitions agree very closely with Walters 240 and Getty IX.8 (see above).

79.2 percent: New York, Pierpont Morgan Library, M.285. Its "Obsecro te" agrees most closely with the Hastings Hours (London, British

Library, MS Add. 54782, probably Bruges, ca. 1480, by the Master of Mary of Burgundy); its Litany and Petitions with the Older Prayer Book of Maximilian (Vienna 1907).

By comparing all the Calendar feasts in a given manuscript with those in Walters 220, we can derive a ratio of matching to non-matching entries. This number, expressed above as a percentage, is obtained by dividing the number of entries that agree in the two manuscripts by the number of entries that differ. (The number of differences is figured by subtracting the number of agreements from the total number of entries in the two Calendars.)

Most of the discrepancies result merely from the shifting of a feast by a day or two. The striking similarity of these Calendars suggests that a common model lies behind them, a model probably compiled at a slightly earlier date in Bruges and copied there in one or more scriptoria. The appendix to this chapter contains a "normal" version of this Calendar based on the agreements between the individual manuscripts and eliminating the most idiosyncratic entries. In all probability, this version comes close to the common model. This, of course, was not the only kind of full and composite Calendar employed in the scriptoria at Bruges and Ghent. How many versions there were, which manuscripts followed which version, and precisely where each was employed are still undetermined.

The remaining texts in Walters 220 are not much help for localization. Its "Obsecro te" and "O intemerata" do not strongly agree with any of the more than 500 French and Flemish texts recorded, although the former prayer is closest to that in MS 2 of the Getty Museum, illuminated by the Master of Guillebert de Mets and another artist. Its Litany and Petitions are in a form not seen elsewhere and provide only a few inconclusive points of comparison.

In contrast, most of the texts of Walters 240 (Cat. No. 92) are very helpful in localizing the manuscript. Its full, composite Calendar agrees about equally with ones from Flanders (best with Vienna 1856) and others from Brittany and especially Angers and Le Mans; the most likely explanation for this mixture seems to be that it was composed in Bruges for a patron in northwestern France. Otherwise, the texts of Walters 240 have an obvious affiliation with Bruges. Although its Litany contains no special local saints, many components and sequences of its Kyrie, Apostles, Martyrs, and Virgins agree with those in three *Horae* encountered before, Vienna 1856, Getty IX.8, and Vienna 1907, all of which appear to be from Bruges. Even its Kyrie (the seemingly unpromising set of appeals to the persons of the Trinity, to the Virgin, and to angels that is usually ignored by scholars) has one very minor variant (the substitution of *domini* for *dei* in the general appeal to angels and archangels) that has only been found in Vienna 1856 and Getty IX.8. Similarly, its list of Apostles, while unique among my recorded texts, has a sequence of five saints (Matthew, Simon, Jude, Thomas, and Barnabus) found only in the Getty manuscript. As for the Martyrs, they have almost exactly the same choice and pattern as the list in Vienna 1856 and include Erasmus, Lupus, and Donatus as does Vienna 1907, while Getty IX.8 has only the first and last, the only other recorded manuscript to include any two of the three. The Confessors of Walters 240 begin with exactly the same sequence as does Vienna 1856 and have the same four general appeals found there and in a previously mentioned book illuminated in the same shop, also on black vellum, Morgan M.493. The only regional saint among the Confessors of Walters 240 is Gislenus, the saint of the Hainaut who appears in six other manuscripts, among them Walters 220 and Vienna 1856. In the Virgins section, the beginning sequence parallels Vienna 1856, Getty IX.8, and a few French *Horae,* but the ending has a distinctly Netherlandish appeal to *Omnes sancte virgines et/ac vidue (et) continentes,* occurring also in the Llangattock Hours (Getty IX.7) and Vienna 1907, among others.

A series of prayers called Petitions follow the Litany. They are normally divided into three parts: first those beginning with "Ab" (or "A") that appeal for protection from something; second those beginning with "Per" that appeal through various events in the life of Christ; and third those beginning with "Ut" asking that something be or not be. The "Ab" Petitions in Walters 240 follow one distinctly Flemish pattern found in, among other manuscripts, Vienna 1907. Except for three French manuscripts, the appeal "A furore tuo" has been found only in Vienna 1907 and some other Flemish manuscripts; and only Getty IX.8 and Walters 240 reverse the last two words in the common petition "Ab appetitu inanis glorie." While the "Per" Petitions of Walters 240 are not identical with any others, some of them and some of their sequences agree consistently only with Morgan manuscript M.493. Among the most typical "Ut" Petitions is one, "Ut nosmetipsos in tuo sancto servicio confortare digneris," which is uncommon in this precise form but almost exclusively Flemish, occurring in Vienna 1907, Vienna 1856, and six other manuscripts. Following the Petitions are various other prayers that have been tabulated, but in the case of Walters 240 they have proved too common to be useful. In studying the Litanies and Petitions, it should be clear that not only the presence or absence of elements, but also their order and actual wording are essential for determining their relations to other manuscripts and thus their origins.

Whereas the results so far point repeatedly to a small group of closely interrelated manuscripts, they do not allow us to define precisely the relations between the various texts, for these are subject to many variables, such as different liturgical practices, the habits of a particular scribe, the concerns of an "editor" or "publisher," and the personal interests of a patron. Thus, they are not always simple and direct copies, and their interrelations are sometimes obscured. To eliminate these variable factors, one needs to study standard texts, for which the scribe's task is simply one of transcription. For this purpose the two common Latin prayers to the Virgin, the "Obsecro te" and the "O intemerata," have proved ideal, especially the former, as one version is almost universally used, though at least two others exist. The text of this version is published by Victor Leroquais in his *Livres d'Heures* (volume II, pages 346–47) and will be cited here for comparison. (My own "standard" text differs somewhat, since it is based on the normal readings in over 500, mostly French and Flemish manuscripts, while Leroquais' version is transcribed from a single French *Horae.*)

Among the almost 2,000 variants I have recorded in the "Obsecro te," most are either rare readings found in only small groups, or widespread variants found in large groups of both French and Flemish books. However, of the many Flemish readings, a few occur in large numbers, such as the addition of the words *et spes* to *salus* in Leroquais' line 3. Over eighty instances of this reading, all of them Flemish, have been recorded, including Walters 240 and most of its related manuscripts (but not Walters 220).

More telling for the links between Walters 240 and other manuscripts are the small-group readings, of which the following is a sample (the line numbers again referring to the Leroquais text):

line 1—*domina* + *mea* (exclusively Flemish, found also in Getty IX.8 and Vienna 1856)

line 9—*humanam carnem accipere* for *accipere humanam carnem* (almost wholly Flemish, found in Getty and Vienna)

line 23—*auxilium* + *michi* (only in Getty, Vienna, and San Marino, Huntington 1087, a manuscript almost certainly from Bruges)

line 23—*conquestis* for *requestis* (only in Getty)

line 24—*rebus illis* for *illis rebus* (excepting one Rouen book, found only in Flemish texts, including Getty and Vienna)

line 35—*beatam* for *veram* (common Flemish, in Getty and Vienna)

These six variants of the thirty-eight that appear in Walters 240 link it with this small group of manuscripts. Obtaining a fuller and surer measure of its relationship to the other manuscripts requires a comparison of all of its variants, common and uncommon. For these comparisons the computer yields the following results:

87.5 percent: Getty IX.8, which agrees in thirty-five of its thirty-seven variants

83.3 percent: Vienna 1856, which agrees in thirty-five of its thirty-nine variants

72.7 percent: Huntington 1087, which agrees in thirty-two of its thirty-eight variants

66.7 percent: Walters 196, which agrees in twenty-eight of its thirty-two variants

62.2 percent: Morgan M.316, which agrees in twenty-eight of its thirty-five variants

59.1 percent: Getty IX.7, which agrees in twenty-six of its thirty-two variants.

And so on, down to a number of texts with less than 2 percent agreement and one with 0 percent. The best agreements would be even better if one eliminated probable scribal errors, such as the substitution in the Walters manuscript of *meis* for *mei* in line 41, or three of the four unique variants in Vienna 1856. Two readings in Getty IX.8 (the substitution of *aterrimum* for *accerbissimum* in line 15 and the omission of *audisti* in line 18) are genuine since they also occur elsewhere, but both only in Huntington 1087. In general, results might also be improved if a system of ranking the variants according to their significance and length were introduced. Nevertheless, as with the Calendars, the evidence distinctly points to a Bruges version of the "Obsecro te." It is, however, not the only Bruges version, for such a manuscript as Morgan M.285, which has the Bruges Calendar, shares with Walters 240 only nine of its thirty-nine variants (or 13.2 percent).

From all of this evidence, the Litanies, Petitions, and "Obsecro te," a group of three manuscripts (Walters 240, Getty IX.8, and Vienna 1856) with a high percentage of agreement has been isolated, along with a larger family of near relatives, that depend upon the same model and in all probability were written in the same scriptorium over the course of ten to twenty years. Further study of the various versions of texts, along with their palaeographical and codicological evidence, should allow us to distinguish the different scriptoria active in Bruges and to understand their organization and operation, as well as their working arrangements with the artists.

This demonstration shows the effectiveness of such textual studies. While the full evidence should be published at some time and in some form, "Beyond Use" will remain open; new manuscripts will be recorded and additional texts will continue to be added. The data are still too narrowly limited chronologically to the fifteenth century and geographically to France and the Low Countries to be published just yet.

A Bruges Calendar

The Calendar below has been compiled from the following manuscripts:

Walters Art Museum, W.220 (Cat. No. 91)
J. Paul Getty Museum, MS IX.7 (The Llangattock Hours)
Dismembered *Horae*, formerly Philip C. Duschnes, New York
Österreichische Nationalbibliothek, Cod. 1856 (The Black Prayer Book of Galeazzo Maria Sforza)
Pierpont Morgan Library, M.285

No doubt this list is very incomplete, and many other manuscripts will be eventually added. Their addition may require some refinements in this composite Calendar, which is being printed to help identify such additions and thus to enlarge our understanding of the history and geography of this calendrical text.

Most of the following entries occur in all of the above manuscripts. Where they do not all agree, the entry either represents the majority of manuscripts or, lacking a clear majority, the alternative feasts are listed, separated by a slash (/). In spelling, the names and words follow the manuscripts, although some variant spellings (and other variations) are given in parentheses. When major feasts are distinguished by color in the manuscripts, either red or gold, they are signaled by an asterisk (*). The following conventional abbreviations are employed:

abb.	=	abbot
aep.	=	archbishop
ap.	=	apostle
archang.	=	archangel
cf.	=	confessor
diac.	=	deacon
doct.	=	doctor
ep.	=	bishop
evang.	=	evangelist
m.	=	martyr
Oct.	=	octave
pb.	=	priest
pp.	=	pope
proph.	=	prophet
reg.	=	king or queen
subdiac.	=	subdeacon
Transl.	=	translation
v.	=	virgin
vid.	=	widow

JANUARY

1 Circumcisio Domini*
2 Stephani, Oct.
3 Johannis, Oct.
4 Innocentium, Oct.
5 Thome, Oct., aep.
6 Epyphania Domini*
7 Ysodori, m.
8 Gudille, v.
9 Iudoci, ep. cf.
10 Pauli primi heremite
11 Quintini, m.
12 Ciriaci & Zothici, m.
13 Epyphanie, Oct.
14 Felicis in pincis, m.
15 Mauri, abb.
16 Marcelli, pp.
17 Anthonii, abb.
18 Prisce, v.
19 Marii & Marte, m.
20 Fabiani & Sebastiani, m.
21 Agnetis, v.
22 Vincentii, m.*
23 Emerenciane, v.
24 Macharii, m.
25 Conversio Pauli*
26 Policarpi, ep. m.
27 Johannis Crisostomi
28 Agnetis secundo
29 Valerii/Valeriani/Vallerici, ep. cf.
30 Aldegundis, v.
31 Prothi/Iacincti, m.

FEBRUARY

1 Brigide, v.
2 Purificatio Marie*
3 Blasii, ep. m.
4 Geminiani, m./Germani, ep. m.
5 Agathe, v. m.
6 Amandi & Vedasti, ep.*
7 Hereni & Zotici, m.
8 Guillermi/Guilleoni, ep. cf.
9 Appollonie, v. m.
10 Scolastice, v.
11 Domiciani, cf.
12 Victoris, m.
13 Juliani, m.
14 Valentini, m.
15 Guilberti, abb.
16 Juliane, v. m.
17 Pancracii/Pancronii, ep. cf.
18 Appollinaris, m.
19 Galli, abb.
20 Eleutherii, ep.
21 Marcelli, cf. m.
22 Cathedra Petri*
23 Policarpi, ep.
24 Mathie, ap.*
25 Donati, m.
26 Fortunati, m.
27 Alexandri, m.
28 Romani, abb.

MARCH

1 Albini, ep.
2 Supplicii, pp. m.
3 Eusebii, m.
4 Foci, ep. m.
5 Victoris, m.
6 Quiriaci (Quiriani), m.
7 Perpetue & Felicitatis, m.
8 Gay, m.
9 Poncii, m.
10 Gordiani, m.
11 Agapiti, m.
12 Gregorii, pp.
13 Marcedonii, ep.
14 Felicissimi, ep. m.
15 Longini, m.
16 Matrone, v.
17 Ghertrudis, v.
18 Theodorii, m.
19 Landoaldi, cf.
20 Cutberti (Cuberti), ep.
21 Benedicti, abb.
22 Iustini, m.
23 Maximi, ep.
24 Fidelis, ep.
25 Annunciacio Marie*
26 Theodori/Theodorici, ep.
27 Resurrectio Domini
28 Columbani, ep. cf. (v./m.)
29 Saturnini, cf.
30 Quirini, m.
31 Pastoris, ep.

APRIL

1 Poncii, m.
2 Marie Egyptiace
3 Pancracii, m.
4 Ambrosii, ep. cf.
5 Claudiani, m.
6 Celestini, pp.
7 Sixti, pp.
8 Calixti, pp.
9 Theodosie, v.
10 Ezechielis, proph.
11 Leonis, pp.
12 Iulii, ep.
13 Eusebii/Eusebie/Eufemie, v.
14 Tiburcii, m.
15 Olimpiadis, v. m.
16 Paterni, ep.
17 Petri, diac.
18 Ursmari, ep. cf.
19 Eleutherii, ep.
20 Appollini, m.
21 Marcelli, ep.
22 Formati, ep. m./Fortunati, m.
23 Georgii, m.*
24 Eutropis, m.
25 Marci, evang.*
26 Cleti, pp. m.
27 Anastasii, ep. m.
28 Vitalis, m.
29 Petri novi, m.
30 Germani, ep.

MAY

1 Philippi & Iacobi, ap.*
2 Germani, ep. m.
3 Invencio Crucis*
4 Walburgis, v.
5 Gengulphi, m.
6 Iohannis ante Portam Latinam (*)
7 Iuvenalis, cf.
8 Nycholay, Transl., ep.
9 Gordiani, m./Nicolay, ep. (*)
10 Mamerti, ep.
11 Nerei & Accillei, m.
12 Marie ad Martires, (m.)/Pancrace, cf.
13 Servacii, ep. cf.
14 Aquilli (Aquillini), ep.
15 Ysodoris, m.
16 Honorati, ep. cf.
17 Brandani, m. (ep. cf.)
18 Torpetis, v. m.
19 Potenciane, v.
20 Basille, v.
21 Helene, reg.
22 Papie, v.
23 Translatio domini
24 Donatiani (Donati), m.
25 Urbani, pp. m.
26 Augustini, Transl., ep.
27 Seraphionis, pb.
28 Huberti, ep.
29 Eutropii, ep.
30 Peregrini, ep. cf.
31 Petronille, v. (ep. m.)

JUNE

1 Nicomedis, m.
2 Marcellini (Marcelli), m.
3 Celestini, ep.
4 Cypriani, ep.
5 Bonifacii, ep.
6 Gudewali, ep.
7 Luciane, v. m.
8 Medardi, ep.
9 Primi & Feliciani (Felicis), m.

10 Landoaldi, ep.
11 Barnabe, ap.*
12 Ruphi, ep. m.
13 Valeriani/Valerici, ep.
14 Basilii, ep.*
15 Fereoli, pb. (ep. cf.)
16 Viti & Modesti, m.
17 Ciriaci & Julite, m.
18 Marcelliani, m.
19 Gervasii & Prothasii, m.
20 Vitalis, m.
21 Albini (Albani), m.
22 Riquardi, m. (ep. cf.)
23 Vigilia
24 Nativitas Johannis Baptiste*
25 Eligii, ep. cf.*
26 Johannis & Pauli, m.
27 Hilarii (Hilarini), m.
28 Vigilia
29 Petri & Pauli, ap.*
30 Commemoratio Pauli

JULY

1 Johannis Baptiste, Oct.
2 Visitacio Marie
3 Thome, Transl., ap.*
4 Martini, (Transl.) ep. cf.(*)
5 Domiciani/Donatiani/Dominici, (ep. cf. m.)
6 Petri & Pauli, Oct.
7 Nicostrati, m./Domiciani/Petri, subdiac.
8 Kyliani (Kiriani), m.
9 Zenonis/Sevonis/Gevonis, m.
10 Septem Fratrum
11 Benedicti, (Deposito), abb.(*)
12 Cleti, pp. m.
13 Anacieti, pp. m.
14 Amelberge, v.
15 Divisio Apostolorum
16 Monulphi, ep. cf.
17 Alexii, cf.
18 Iusti, ep.
19 Arsenii (Arstini), abb.
20 Margarete, v. m.
21 Praxedis, v. m.
22 Marie Magdalene*
23 Appollinaris, ep. m.
24 Cristine (Xpristine), v.
25 Iacobi, ap. & Xpofori, m.*
26 Anne matris marie
27 Septem Dormientium, m.
28 Panthaleonis, m.
29 Felicis & Simplicis, ep. m.
30 Abdon & Sennen, m.
31 Germani, ep. cf.

AUGUST

1 Petri, Ad Vincula*
2 Stephani, pp. m.
3 Stephani, Inventio
4 Nichomedis, ep. m.
5 Dominici, cf.
6 Walburgis, v.
7 Sixti, pp. cf.
8 Felicissimi, m.
9 Vigilia
10 Laurencii, m.*
11 Gaugerici, ep. cf.
12 Clare, v.
13 Ypolyti, m.
14 Vigilia
15 Assumptio Marie*
16 Arnulphi, ep.
17 Laurencii, Oct.
18 Agapiti, m.
19 Magni, m.
20 Philiberti, ep.
21 Privati, ep. m.
22 Marie Assumptionis, Oct.
23 Thimothei, m.
24 Bartholomei, ap.*
25 Ludovici, reg. (ep.) cf.
26 Herenei & Habundi, m.
27 Bernardi, abb.
28 Augustini, ep. cf. doct.
29 Decollatio Johannis Baptiste*
30 Donaciani, Transl.
31 Paulini, ep. cf.

SEPTEMBER

1 Egidii, abb.*
2 Justi, ep.
3 Remeali, ep.
4 Eleutherii, ep.
5 Bertini, abb.
6 Amandi (Amanti), ep.
7 Enorcii (Evorcii), ep. cf.
8 Nativitas Marie*
9 Gorgonii, m.
10 Prothi & Iacincti, m. (cf.)
11 Guidonis, cf.
12 Hugonis, ep.
13 Philippi, ep.
14 Exaltatio Crucis*
15 Marie, Oct./Nichomedis, m.
16 Eufemie, v.
17 Lamberti, ep. m.
18 Fereoli, m.
19 Columbani, m.
20 Vigilia
21 Mathei, ap. evang.*

22 Mauricii, m. (ep.)
23 Tecle, v. m.
24 Andocii, m.
25 Firmini, ep. m.
26 Merodii, ep. m.
27 Cosme & Damiani, m.
28 Marcealis, m.
29 Michaelis, archang.*
30 Iheronimi, pb. cf.

OCTOBER

1 Bavonis & Remigii, ep. cf.*
2 Leodegarii, ep. m.
3 Euualdorum Duorum, pb.
4 Francisci, cf.
5 Fidis, v. m.
6 Martini, abb. cf./Marci, pp.
7 Marcelli & Epulei, m.
8 Benedicte
9 Dyonisii, m. (ep.)*
10 Gereonis, cf.
11 Augustini, Transl.
12 Venancii, abb. cf.
13 Theophili, m.
14 Donaciani, ep.*
15 Wulfranni, ep. cf.
16 Galli, abb. cf.
17 Luciani, ep. m.
18 Luce, evang.*
19 Pelagie, v.
20 Capracii, m./Cypriani, ep. m.
21 Undecim millium virginum
22 Severii, m.
23 Felicis, m./Severini, cf.
24 Felicis, m./Severini, cf.
25 Crispini & Crispiniani, m.
26 Remoldi, ep.
27 Vigilia
28 Symonis & Iude, ap.*
29 Piati, Transl., (pb./ep.)
30 Saturnini, ep.
31 Quintini, m. & Vigilia

NOVEMBER

1 Omnium Sanctorum*
2 Commemoratio Animarum*
3 Innumerabilium m./Huberti, ep. cf.
4 Eustacii, m.
5 Winnoci, abb.
6 Leonardi, cf.
7 Willibrordi, ep.
8 Coronatorum Quatuor, m.
9 Theodorii, m.
10 Martini, pp.
11 Martini, ep.*
12 Livini, ep.
13 Brictii, m. (ep. cf.)
14 Clementini, m.
15 Machuti, ep.
16 Thiburcii, cf./Gumberti, ep.
17 Omari (Otmari), cf.
18 Martini, Oct.
19 Elizabeth, vid.
20 Edmundi, m.
21 Columbani, abb.
22 Cecilie, v.
23 Clementis, pp.*
24 Grisogoni, m.
25 Katherine, v.*
26 Lini, pp.
27 Martini, pp. m./Maximi, ep. cf.
28 Cezarii, m.
29 Vigilia
30 Andree, ap.*

DECEMBER

1 Eligii, ep.
2 Candide, v. m.
3 Cassiani, m.
4 Barbare, v.
5 Dalmaciani, cf. (m.)
6 Nicholay, ep.*
7 Andree, Oct.
8 Conceptio Marie*
9 Innocenti, pp.
10 Eulalie, v.
11 Damasci, pp.
12 Ouberti, ep.
13 Lucie, v./Clare, v. (m.)
14 Nichasii, ep. m.*
15 Odilde/Oberti, ep./Judoci, cf.
16 Candide, v.
17 Ignatii/Lazari, m.
18 Agricole, m./Alphee, v.
19 Severini, m. (ep. cf.)/Melchiadis, pp.
20 Tecle, v./Mercurii, m.
21 Thome, ap.*
22 Felicis, pp./Theodosie, v.
23 Eugenie, v.
24 Vigilia
25 Nativitas Domini*
26 Stephani, protom.*
27 Johannis, ap. evang.*
28 Innocentium*
29 Thome, aep.*
30 Columbani, ep./Perpetui, ep.
31 Silvestri, pp. cf.

Appendix

1. Calendar (see Chapter IV)

Medieval Calendars contain a number of mysterious-looking columns of numbers, letters, and texts. These require some explanation. The first two columns consist of the Golden Numbers and the Dominical Letters. These are important elements of the medieval Calendar because together they enable the reader to determine the Sunday for Easter, the most important feast of the Christian year, but a movable one whose date depends on both the lunar and solar year. In the year 325 the Council of Nicaea determined that Easter in the Western Church was to be celebrated on the Sunday following the first full moon that falls on or after the vernal equinox (the spring day when day and night are the same length). Should the full moon happen on a Sunday, Easter is then pushed to the following Sunday.

The first column of the Calendar is a series of Roman numerals called the Golden Numbers. These numbers, from "i" through "xix," are distributed in what appears to be random order throughout the entire year. (January 1 is marked by "iii," January 3 by "xi," January 5 by "xix," and so on; see, for example, Figs. 15a, 17.) The Golden Number, which changes every year, indicates the occurrence of new moons and, counting forward fourteen days, full moons throughout the year. To determine the Golden Number of a given year, the following equation was devised: take the year, add one, and divide by nineteen—the resulting remainder is the Golden Number; if the remainder is zero, the Golden Number is nineteen ("xix"). Take as an example the year 1524:

1524 + 1 = 1525
1525 ÷ 19 = 80, remainder 5
"v" = Golden Number for the year 1524.

The second column contains the Dominical Letters. These, representing the days of the week, run A, B, C, D, E, F, and G. For any given year the Dominical Letter will identify all the Sundays of that year. To determine the Dominical Letter for any year from 1 to 1582 (after which date the Julian calendar was altered to the Gregorian) the following formula is used: the year is added to a quarter of itself, with the remainder ignored; the sum is divided by seven; the remainder from this operation is subtracted from three or, if that result produces zero or a negative number, from ten; the result corresponds to the Dominical Letter. Take our example of the year 1524:

1524 + (1524 ÷ 4) = 1524 + 381 = 1905
1905 ÷ 7 = 272, remainder 1
3 − 1 = 2
2 = Dominical Letter B.

Equipped with the Golden Number "v" and the Dominical Letter "B" for the year 1524, we can now find the date of Easter for that year. Turning to a medieval Calendar, we search for the appearance of "v"—the vernal equinox of that year—from March 1 to April 12. (The same Golden Number may appear twice but only one will produce a date for Easter between March 22 and April 25 inclusive.) Finding the first appearance of "v" on March 9 (Fig. 18, for example), we count forward fourteen days (including March 9) to March 22, the date of the first full moon after the vernal equinox. The next appearance of the Dominical Letter "B" is on March 27. Easter Sunday for the year 1524 is thus March 27.

Some owners of Books of Hours requested charts or tables as a supplement to the Calendars to aid them in these complex calculations. Charts for determining both the Golden Number and Dominical Letter precede the Calendar in Walters 170 (Cat. No. 84). Some Books of Hours relieved the reader completely of this unpleasant task and included clear tables listing the year, the date of Easter, the Golden Number, and the Dominical Letter. Such a table occurs in the Hours of Jean de Mauléon (Fig. 132). The table begins with the year 1524 (its Easter date offers contemporaneous confirmation of the calculations performed above) and continues through 1540. The last column in the chart, labelled

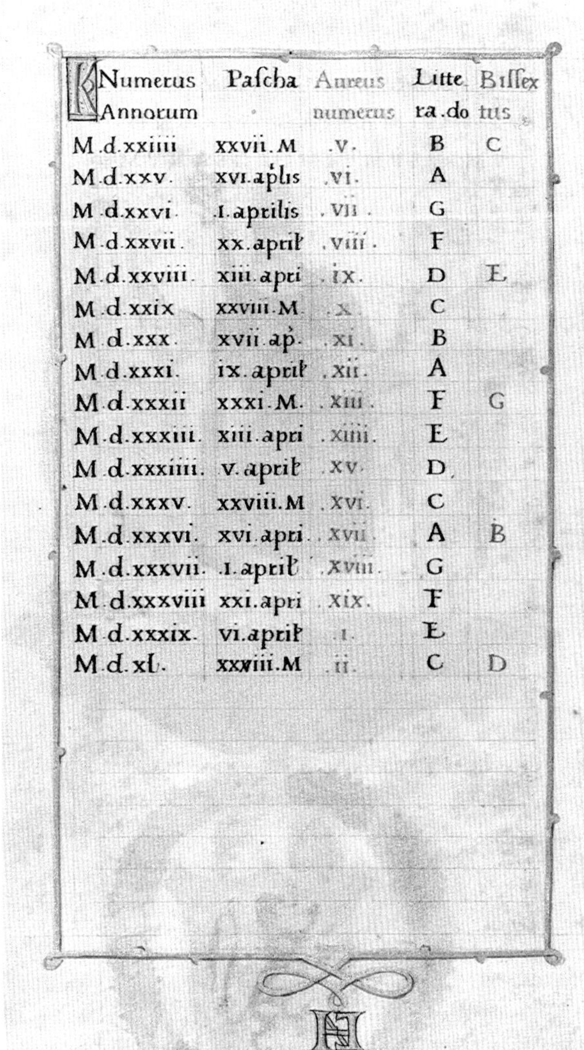

Numerus Annorum	Paſcha	Aureus numerus	Litte ra.do	Biſſex tus
M.d.xxiiii	xxvii.M	.v.	B	C
M.d.xxv.	xvi.aplis	.vi.	A	
M.d.xxvi	.i.aprilis	.vii.	G	
M.d.xxvii.	xx.april	.viii.	F	
M.d.xxviii.	xiii.apri	.ix.	D	E
M.d.xxix	xxviii.M.	.x.	C	
M.d.xxx.	xvii.ap.	.xi.	B	
M.d.xxxi.	ix.april	.xii.	A	
M.d.xxxii	xxxi.M.	.xiii.	F	G
M.d.xxxiii.	xiii.apri	.xiiii.	E	
M.d.xxxiiii.	v.april	.xv.	D	
M.d.xxxv.	xxviii.M	.xvi.	C	
M.d.xxxvi.	xvi.apri.	.xvii.	A	B
M.d.xxxvii.	.i.april	.xviii.	G	
M.d.xxxviii	xxi.apri	.xix.	F	
M.d.xxxix.	vi.april	.i.	E	
M.d.xl.	xxviii.M	.ii.	C	D

Fig. 132. Easter Table for the Years 1524 to 1540, France, Tours?, 1524 (Walters 449, fol. 1v; Cat. No. 77).

"Bissextus," indicates leap years. As revealed by the table, 1524 was a leap year and this meant that the Dominical Letter for the months of January and February fell back to C before jumping up to B.

The next two columns in the medieval Calendar (sometimes conflated into one) contain the Roman calendar, one of the most confusing ways of reckoning time ever devised (Figs. 21, 22, and 25). Each Roman month contained three fixed days; these were known as the Calends (the first of each month, from which we derive our word "Calendar"), the Nones (occurring on the 5th or the 7th of the month), and the Ides (falling on either the 13th or the 15th of the month). All the remaining days of the month were reckoned backwards from these three fixed points. Thus Christmas Day, the 25th of December, was, for the Romans, "viii Kalendas Januarii," or, the 8th day before the Calends of January. In the roughly 250 years spanning the popularity of Books of Hours one can trace the gradual decline and then abandonment of this system. Earlier manuscripts tend to have the complete Roman calendar, while, as time passes, the Roman numbers themselves are dropped but a general reference to the system is retained in the form of the "N's," 'Id's," and "Kl's" that are repeated, if somewhat meaninglessly, in the columns (Fig. 20). Eventually, as in the Calendars of the Hours of Jean de Mauléon (Pl. 15, Figs. 8, 17) and Walters 425 (Fig. 15) the system disappears entirely.

The main part of a Calendar is composed of the 365 feast days of the year. (See, for example, the Calendar provided at the end of Chapter XIII.) The major feasts of the year, written in red or sometimes blue or gold, were standard for the Western Church and therefore appear in all Calendars. Minor feasts or locally venerated saints changed from region to region and thus from manuscript to manuscript. These locally celebrated feasts can be helpful in determining where a particular Book of Hours was intended to be used. This is what is meant by the "use" given in each of the entries in the Catalogue of Manuscripts. (Use indicators are also provided by the Hours of the Virgin and the Office of the Dead.) Since cities, both large and small, produced books for their own market, the use of a Book of Hours can offer evidence pointing to its place of manufacture. The use can be quite specific, with the saints pointing to a single city, but it can also be vague, with the feasts referring to a large area or whole country. In some Books of Hours, Calendars are composites of more than one area, sometimes more than one country, and others are so general that they seem to have been written intentionally to apply to nowhere in particular and anywhere in general at the same time.

References cited in "Books for Further Reading" offer some of the basic sources for determining the use of a Calendar. The task can take hours and, sometimes, yield little or conflicting results.

2. Gospel Lessons (see Chapter V)

Although taken from the Bible, the four Gospel Lessons can more properly be considered extracts from the missal, the service book used by the priest at Mass. They are the Gospel readings for four of the Church's major feasts: Christmas Day (December 25, the reading is taken from the third, or main, Mass of the day); the Feast of the Annunciation (March 25); Epiphany (January 6); and the Feast of the Ascension (a movable feast whose date depended upon that of Easter).

The first Gospel Lesson, from John, acts as a preamble for the entire Book of Hours. Its theme is mankind's need of redemption and God's willingness to provide it. This Lesson, opening with the famous passage, "In principio erat verbum" ("In the beginning was the word"), starts immediately with the theme of Christ's Divinity, then proceeds to the witness of John the Baptist, the Jews' rejection of Christ, the theme of Christians as the new children of God, and the Incarnation.

The Gospel Lesson of Luke describes the Annunciation,

the angel's reference to the conception of John the Baptist, and ends with the Virgin's acceptance of God's will.

Matthew's Lesson, after mentioning the birth of Christ, immediately launches into the story of the Three Magi, their journey, Herod's concerns over the prophecy of the Messiah, the Magi's worship of Christ, their gifts, and, finally, the Magi's return to their homes.

Mark's Gospel Lesson relates Christ's appearance to the eleven apostles after the Resurrection, his command to preach salvation throughout the world, his granting to the apostles miraculous powers, and, finally, the Savior's Ascension.

JOHN (1:1–14, Gospel Lesson for Christmas Day)
"In principio erat verbum . . . plenum gratiae et veritatis."
LUKE (1:26–38, Gospel Lesson for the Feast of the Annunciation)
"In illo tempore: Missus est angelus . . . secundum verbum tuum."
MATTHEW (2:1–12, Gospel Lesson for the Feast of Epiphany)
"In illo tempore: Cum natus est Jesus . . . in regionem suam."
MARK (16:14–20, Gospel Lesson for the Feast of the Ascension)
"In illo tempore: Recumbentibus undecim discipulis . . . sequentibus signis."

3. Hours of the Virgin (see Chapter VI)

Like the Calendar and the Office of the Dead, the Hours of the Virgin had variations in its text—different psalms, antiphons, and capitula ("little chapters"), for example, that were used in different cities or dioceses. This is what is known as their "use." The sources, both published and unpublished, traditionally used by art and textual historians to determine usage are cited in "Books for Futher Reading."

One of the great attractions of the Hours of the Virgin for the lay devotee is their simplicity. This is not the case with the breviary whose complicated texts require an attentive mind schooled in the intricacies of Church liturgy. With a *Horae* in hand, one prayed with the same basic Hours of the Virgin every day. Matins is composed of three Nocturns, the name given to a group of three psalms followed by three lessons that was originally read during the night. As rubrics contained in many Books of Hours tell us, the first Nocturn is for Sundays, Mondays, and Thursdays; the second Nocturn for Tuesdays and Fridays; and the third for Wednesdays and Saturdays.

Some Books of Hours contain textual variations for the two seasons of Advent and Christmastide. In these manuscripts, the basic text of the Hours of the Virgin was for use throughout most of the year, from the day after the Feast of the Purification of the Virgin (that is, on February 3) until the Saturday before the first Sunday of Advent. From the first Sunday of Advent until Christmas Eve variations form what were called the Advent Hours. At Christmastide, from Christmas Day up to and including the Feast of the Purification (February 2), a second set of variations applied.

An "incipit" (opening phrase) outline of the Hours of the Virgin, from Walters 240 (Cat. No. 92), is provided below to offer the reader a means of understanding the structure of the multiple elements that make up this long series of prayers. The Hours are for the use of Rome and include, as is typical of many fifteenth-century *Horae*, three lessons; other Books of Hours, especially earlier ones, have nine lessons (three different ones for each of the Nocturns). The following abbreviations are used:

A. = antiphon
Abs. = absolution
Ben. = benediction
Cant. = canticle
Cap. = capitulum
Inv. = Invitatory
Les. = lesson
Or. = oration
Ps. = psalm
R. = response
V. = versicle

HOURS OF THE VIRGIN

MATINS

V. Domine labia mea aperies
R. Et os meum annuntiabit laudem tuam
V. Deus in adiutorium meum intende
R. Domine ad adiuvandum me festina
Gloria patri . . .
Inv. Ave Maria gratia plena . . .
Ps. Venite exultemus . . . (Ps. 94)
Hymn Quem terra ponthus . . .

(1st Nocturn, for Sunday, Monday, and Thursday:)
A. Benedicta tu
Ps. Domine Dominus noster . . . (Ps. 8)
A. Benedicta tu in mulieribus . . .
A. Sicut myrra
Ps. Celi enarrant . . . (Ps. 18)
A. Sicut myrra electa . . .
A. Ante thorum
Ps. Domini est terra . . . (Ps. 23)
A. Ante thorum huius virginis . . .
V. Difussa est . . .
R. Propterea benedixit . . .
Pater noster . . .

(2nd Nocturn, for Tuesday and Friday:)
A. Specie tua
Ps. Eructavit cor meum . . . (Ps. 44)
A. Specie tua et pulchritudine . . .
A. Adiuvabit eam
Ps. Deus noster . . . (Ps. 45)
A. Adiuvabit eam Deus vultu . . .
A. Sicut letantioum
Ps. Fundamenta eius . . . (Ps. 86)
A. Sicut letantium omnium nostrum . . .

V. Sancta Dei genetrix . . .
R. Intercede pro nobis . . .
Pater noster . . .

(3rd Nocturn, for Wednesday and Saturday:)
A. Gaude Maria
Ps. Cantate Domino . . . (Ps. 95)
A. Gaude Maria virgo . . .
A. Dignare me
Ps. Dominus regnavit . . . (Ps. 96)
A. Dignare me laudare te . . .
A. Post partum
Ps. Cantate Domino . . . (Ps. 97)
A. Post partum virgo . . .
V. Adiuvabit eam . . .
R. Deus in medio . . .
Pater noster . . .
Abs. Precibus et meritis . . .
V. Iube Domine . . .
Ben. Nos cum prole . . .

Les. I: In omnibus requiem . . . (Ecclus. 24:11–13)
R. Sancta et immaculata . . .
V. Benedicta tu . . .
Les. II: Et sic in Syon . . . (Ecclus. 24:15–16)
R. Beata es . . .
V. Ave Maria . . .
Les. III: Quasi cedrus . . . (Ecclus. 24:17–20)
R. Felix namque . . .
V. Ora pro populo . . .
Gloria patri . . .
Cant. Te Deum . . . (Hymn of St. Ambrose)

LAUDS

V. Deus in adiutorium meum intende
R. Domine ad adiuvandum me festina
Gloria patri . . .
A. Assumpta est
Ps. Dominus regnavit . . . (Ps. 92)
A. Assumpta est Maria . . .
A. Maria virgo
Ps. Iubilate Deo . . . (Ps. 99)
A. Maria virgo assumpta est . . .
A. In odorem
Ps. Deus Deus meus . . . (Ps. 62)
Ps. Deus misereatur . . . (Ps. 66)
A. In odorem unguentorum . . .
A. Benedicta
Cant. Benedicite omnia opera . . . (Canticle of the Three Children, Daniel 3:57–88, 56)
A. Benedicta filia tua . . .
A. Pulchra es
Ps. Laudate Dominum . . . (Ps. 148)
Ps. Cantate Domino . . . (Ps. 149)
Ps. Laudate Dominum . . . (Ps. 150)
A. Pulchra es decora . . .
Cap. Viderunt eam . . . (Canticle of Canticles 6:8)
Hymn O gloriosa domina . . .
V. Benedicta tu in mulieribus . . .
R. Et benedictus . . .
A. Beata Dei
Cant. Benedictus Dominus . . . (Canticle of Zachary, Luke 1:68–79)
A. Beata Dei genitrix . . .
Or. Deus qui de beate Marie . . .
A. Sancti Dei omnes . . .
V. Letamini in Domino . . .
R. Et gloriamini . . .
Or. Protege Domine . . .
Or. Omnes sancti . . .
Or. Et pacem tuam . . .

PRIME

V. Deus in adiutorium meum intende
R. Domine ad adiuvandum me festina
Gloria patri . . .
Hymn Memento salutis . . .
A. Assumpta est
Ps. Deus in nomine tuo . . . (Ps. 53)
Ps. Benedixisti Domine . . . (Ps. 84)
Ps. Laudate Dominum . . . (Ps. 116)
A. Assumpta est Maria . . .
Cap. Que est ista . . . (Canticle of Canticles 6:9)
V. Dignare me . . .
R. Da michi virtutem . . .
Or. Deus qui virginalem . . .
A. Sancti Dei omnes . . .
V. Letamini in Domino . . .
R. Et gloriamini . . .
Or. Exaudi nos Deus . . .
Or. Omnes sancti . . .
Or. Et pacem tuam . . .

TERCE

V. Deus in adiutorium meum intende
R. Domine ad adiuvandum me festina
Gloria patri . . .
Hymn Memento salutis . . .
A. Maria virgo
Ps. Ad Dominum . . . (Ps. 119)
Ps. Levavi oculos . . . (Ps. 120)
Ps. Letatus sum . . . (Ps. 121)
A. Maria virgo assumpta est . . .
Cap. Et sic in Syon . . . (Ecclus. 24:15)
V. Difussa est . . .
R. Propterea benedixit . . .
V. Domine exaudi . . .
R. Et clamor meus . . .
Or. Deus qui salutis . . .
A. Sancti Dei omnes . . .
V. Letamini in Domino . . .
R. Et gloriamini . . .
Or. Protege Domine . . .
Or. Omnes sancti . . .
Or. Et pacem tuam . . .

SEXT

V. Deus in adiutorium meum intende
R. Domine ad adiuvandum me festina
Gloria patri . . .
Hymn Memento salutis . . .
A. In odorem
Ps. Ad te levavi . . . (Ps. 122)
Ps. Nisi quia Dominus . . . (Ps. 123)
Ps. Qui confidunt . . . (Ps. 124)
A. In odorem unguentorum . . .
Cap. Et radicavi . . . (Ecclus. 24:16)
V. Benedicta tu . . .
R. Et benedictus fructus . . .
V. Domine exaudi . . .
R. Et clamor meus . . .
Or. Concede misericors Deus . . .
A. Sancti Dei omnes . . .
V. Letamini in Domino . . .
R. Et gloriamini . . .
Or. Exaudi nos Deus . . .
Or. Omnes sancti . . .
Or. Et pacem tuam . . .

NONE

V. Deus in adiutorium meum intende
R. Domine ad adiuvandum me festina
Gloria patri . . .
Hymn Memento salutis . . .
A. Pulchra es
Ps. In convertendo . . . (Ps. 125)
Ps. Nisi Dominus . . . (Ps. 126)
Ps. Beati omnes . . . (Ps. 127)
A. Pulchra es et decora . . .
Cap. In plateis . . . (Ecclus. 24:19–20)
V. Post partum . . .
R. Dei genitrix . . .
V. Domine exaudi . . .
R. Et clamor meus . . .
Or. Famulorum tuorum . . .
A. Sancti Dei omnes . . .
V. Letamini in Domino . . .
R. Et gloriamini . . .
Or. Presta quesumus . . .
Or. Omnes sancti . . .
Or. Et pacem tuam . . .

VESPERS

V. Deus in adiutorium meum intende
R. Domine ad adiuvandum me festina
Gloria patri . . .
A. Dum esset rex
Ps. Dixit Dominus Domino meo . . . (Ps. 109)
A. Dum esset rex in accubitu . . .
A. Leva eius
Ps. Laudate pueri . . . (Ps. 112)
A. Leva eius sub capite . . .
A. Nigra sum
Ps. Letatus sum . . . (Ps. 121)
A. Nigra sum sed formosa . . .
A. Iam enim
Ps. Nisi Dominus . . . (Ps. 126)
A. Iam enim hyems . . .
A. Speciosa
Ps. Lauda Iherusalem . . . (Ps. 147)
A. Speciosa facta es . . .
Cap. Ab initio . . . (Ecclus. 24:14)
Hymn Ave maris stella . . .
V. Diffusa est . . .
R. Propterea benedixit . . .
A. Beata mater
Cant. Magnificat anima mea . . . (Canticle of the Blessed Virgin, Luke 1:46–55)
A. Beata mater et innupta . . .
V. Domine exaudi . . .
R. Et clamor meus . . .
Or. Concede nos famulos tuos . . .
A. Sancti Dei omnes . . .
V. Letamini in Domino . . .
R. Et gloriamini . . .
Or. Protege Domine . . .
Or. Omnes sancti . . .
Or. Et pacem tuam . . .

COMPLINE

V. Converte nos Deus salutaris noster
R. Et averte iram tuam a nobis
V. Deus in adiutorium meum intende
R. Domine ad adiuvandum me festina
Gloria patri . . .
Ps. Sepe expugnaverunt . . . (Ps. 128)
Ps. De profundis . . . (Ps. 129)
Ps. Domine non est exaltatum . . . (Ps. 130)
Cap. Ego mater . . . (Ecclus. 24:24)
Hymn Memento salutis . . .
V. Ora pro nobis . . .
R. Ut digni . . .
A. Sub tuum
Cant. Nunc dimittis . . . (Canticle of Simeon, Luke 2:29–32)
A. Sub tuum presidium . . .
V. Domine exaudi . . .
R. Et clamor meus . . .
Or. Beate et gloriose . . .
A. Sancti Dei omnes . . .
V. Letamini in Domino . . .
R. Et gloriamini . . .
Or. Exaudi nos Deus . . .
Or. Omnes sancti . . .
Or. Et pacem tuam . . .

4. Hours of the Cross, Hours of the Holy Spirit (see Chapter VII)

The Hours of the Cross and the Hours of the Holy Spirit are much shorter than the Hours of the Virgin. They consist of seven, instead of the usual eight, canonical Hours (Matins, Prime, Terce, Sext, None, Vespers, and Compline, without Lauds). The texts are shorter too because each Hour consists primarily of only a hymn and a prayer, with a few versicles and responses sprinkled about. There are no lengthy psalms or long lessons. By contrast, the Hours of the Passion, like the Hours of the Virgin, are actually an Office, and as such it is a much longer text, including all eight canonical Hours. In addition to the hymns, prayers, versicles, and responses that the Hours of the Cross and the Hours of the Holy Spirit contain, the Hours of the Passion, like those of the Virgin, also have psalms, lessons, canticles, and capitula.

Below are given incipit outlines for the Hours of the Cross and the Hours of the Holy Spirit. An outline for the Hours of the Passion is not provided because their structure duplicates much of that of the Hours of the Virgin (an outline for which is provided above in Part 3) and because this text is subject to great variations. The following abbreviations are used:

A. = antiphon
Or. = oration
R. = response
Recom. = recommendation
V. = versicle

HOURS OF THE CROSS

MATINS

V. Domine labia mea aperies
R. Et os meum annuntiabit laudem tuam
V. Deus in adiutorium meum intende
R. Domine ad adiuvandum me festina
Gloria patri . . .
Hymn Patris sapientia . . .
V. Adoramus te . . .
R. Quia per sanctam crucem . . .
Or. Domine Ihesu Christe filii Dei vivi pone passionem . . .

PRIME

V. Deus in adiutorium . . .
R. Domine ad adiuvandum . . .
Gloria patri . . .
Hymn Hora prima ductus est Ihesus ad Pylatum . . .
V. Adoramus te . . .
R. Quia per sanctam crucem . . .
Or. Domine Ihesu Christe . . .

TERCE

V. Deus in adiutorium . . .
R. Domine ad adiuvandum . . .
Gloria patri . . .
Hymn Crucifige clamitant hora tertiarum . . .
V. Adoramus te . . .
R. Quia per sanctam crucem . . .
Or. Domine Ihesu Christe . . .

SEXT

V. Deus in adiutorium . . .
R. Domine ad adiuvandum . . .
Gloria patri . . .
Hymn Hora sexta Ihesus est cruci . . .
V. Adoramus te
R. Quia per sanctam crucem . . .
Or. Domine Ihesu Christe . . .

NONE

V. Deus in adiutorium . . .
R. Domine ad adiuvandum . . .
Gloria patri . . .
Hymn Hora nona Dominus Ihesus expiravit . . .
V. Adoramus te . . .
R. Quia per sanctam crucem . . .
Or. Domine Ihesu Christe . . .

VESPERS

V. Deus in adiutorium . . .
R. Domine ad adiuvandum . . .
Gloria patri . . .
Hymn De cruce deponitur hora vespertina . . .
V. Adoramus te . . .
R. Quia per sanctam crucem . . .
Or. Domine Ihesu Christe . . .

COMPLINE

V. Converte nos . . .
R. Et averte iram . . .
V. Deus in adiutorium . . .
R. Domine ad adiuvandum . . .
Gloria patri . . .
Hymn Hora completorii datur sepulture . . .
V. Adoramus te . . .
R. Quia per sanctam crucem . . .
Or. Domine Ihesu Christe . . .
Recom. Has horas canonicas cum devotione . . .

HOURS OF THE HOLY SPIRIT

MATINS

V. Domine labia mea aperies
R. Et os meum annuntiabit laudem tuam
V. Deus in adiutorium meum intende
R. Domine ad adiuvandum me festina
Gloria patri . . .
Hymn Nobis Sancti Spiritus gratia sit data . . .
A. Veni Sancte Spiritus . . .
V. Emitte Spiritum tuum . . .
R. Et renovabis faciem . . .
Or. Omnipotens sempiterne Deus . . .

PRIME

V. Deus in adiutorium . . .
R. Domine ad adiuvandum . . .
Gloria patri . . .
Hymn De virgine Maria . . .
A. Veni Sancte Spiritus . . .
V. Emitte Spiritum . . .
R. Et renovabis . . .
Or. Omnipotens sempiterne . . .

TERCE

V. Deus in adiutorium . . .
R. Domine ad adiuvandum . . .
Gloria patri . . .
Hymn Suum Sanctum Spiritum . . .
A. Veni Sancte Spiritus . . .
V. Emitte Spiritum . . .
R. Et renovabis . . .
Or. Omnipotens sempiterne . . .

SEXT

V. Deus in adiutorium . . .
R. Domine ad adiuvandum . . .
Gloria patri . . .
Hymn Septiformen gratiam . . .
A. Veni Sancte Spiritus . . .
V. Emitte Spiritum . . .
R. Et renovabis . . .
Or. Omnipotens sempiterne . . .

NONE

V. Deus in adiutorium . . .
R. Domine ad adiuvandum . . .
Gloria patri . . .
Hymn Spiritus paraclitus fuit appellatus . . .
A. Veni Sancte Spiritus . . .
V. Emitte Spiritum . . .
R. Et renovabis . . .
Or. Omnipotens sempiterne . . .

VESPERS

V. Deus in adiutorium . . .
R. Domine ad adiuvandum . . .
Gloria patri . . .
Hymn Dextere Dei digitus . . .
A. Veni Sancte Spiritus . . .
V. Emitte Spiritum . . .
R. Et renovabis . . .
Or. Omnipotens sempiterne . . .

COMPLINE

V. Converte nos . . .
R. Et averte iram . . .
V. Deus in adiutorium . . .
R. Domine ad adiuvandum . . .
Gloria patri . . .
Hymn Spiritus paraclitus nos velit . . .
A. Veni Sancte Spiritus . . .
V. Emitte Spiritum . . .
R. Et renovabis . . .
Or. Omnipotens sempiterne . . .
Recom. Has horas canonicas cum devotione . . .

5. "Obsecro te" and "O intemerata" (see Chapter VIII)

English translations of the "Obsecro te" and "O intemerata" are in the one case difficult, and in the second, impossible, to find. For this reason, and because of their enormous popularity in Books of Hours, the complete texts of both prayers are given here.

"OBSECRO TE"

I beseech you, Mary, holy lady, mother of God, most full of piety, daughter of the greatest king, most glorious mother, mother of orphans, consolation of the desolate, the way for those who stray, salvation for those who hope in you, virgin before giving birth, virgin while giving birth, virgin after giving birth, fountain of pity, fountain of salvation and grace, fountain of piety and joy, fountain of consolation and kindness, through that holy, unutterable joy with which your spirit rejoiced in that hour when the Son of God was announced to you by the archangel Gabriel and was conceived, and through that divine mystery that was then worked by the Holy Spirit; and through that holy unutterable piety, grace, mercy, love, and humility through which your Son descended to accept human flesh in your most venerable womb and which he saw in you when he commended you to St. John the Apostle and Evangelist and when he exalted you over the angels and archangels; and through that holy inestimable humility in which you responded to the archangel Gabriel, 'Behold the handmaiden of the Lord, be it done unto me according to thy word'; and through those most holy fifteen joys that you had in your Son, Our Lord Jesus Christ; and through that holy, great compassion and that most bitter sorrow in your heart that you had when you saw your Son, Our Lord Jesus Christ, nude and lifted up on the cross, hanging, crucified, wounded, thirsty but served gall and vinegar, and you heard him cry 'Eli' and you saw him dying; and through the five wounds of your Son and through the collapse of his flesh because of the great pain of his wounds; and through the sorrow that you had when you saw him wounded; and through the fountains of his blood and through all his suffering; and through all the sorrow of your heart and through the fountains of your tears; with all the saints and elect of God. Come and hasten to my aid and counsel, in all my prayers and requests, in all my difficulties and needs, and in all those things that I will do, that I will say, that I will think, in every day, night, hour, and moment of my life. And secure for me, your servant, from your esteemed Son the fullness of all mercy and consolation, all counsel and aid, all help, all blessings and sanctification, all salvation, peace, and prosperity, all joy and gladness, and an abundance of everything good for the spirit and the body, and the grace of the Holy Spirit so that he might set all things in good order for me, guard my soul, rule and protect my body, lift up my mind, direct my course, preserve my senses, control my ways, approve my actions, fulfill my wishes and desires, instill holy thoughts, forgive the evils I have done in the past, correct those of the present, and temper those of the future, grant me an honest and honorable life, and grant me victory over all the adversities of this world, and true peace for my spirit and body, good hope, charity, and faith, chastity, humility, and patience, rule and protect my five bodily senses, make me fulfill the seven works of mercy, make me firmly believe in and hold to the twelve articles of faith and the Ten Commandments of the law, and from the seven deadly sins keep me free and defend me until my end. And at the end of my life show me your face, and reveal to me the day and hour of my death. Please hear and receive this humble prayer and grant me eternal life. Listen and hear me, Mary, sweetest virgin, Mother of God and of mercy. Amen.

The translation is of the "Obsecro te" from Walters 224 (Cat. No. 58). This example was chosen because the original Latin is nearly identical to the version published by Leroquais (*Livres d'heures,* II, 346–47) to which the reader may turn for comparison. The miniature of the *Virgin of Mercy* accompanying this prayer is reproduced in Fig. 61.

"O INTEMERATA"

O immaculate virgin, blessed for eternity, unique and without equal, virgin Mother of God, Mary, temple of God, most full of grace, gate to the kingdom of heaven, sanctuary of the Holy Spirit, you through whom, after God himself, the whole world lives, turn the ears of your piety towards my unworthy prayers and be kind to me, a sinner, and be a helper in all things. O most blessed John, beloved friend of Christ, who was chosen by Our Lord Jesus Christ to remain a virgin, and, among all the others, was more esteemed and was imbued, before all the others, with the heavenly mysteries, apostle of Christ and most glorious evangelist, I beseech you, with the mother of our Savior, to consider, with her, me worthy of your help. O jewels of the heavens, Mary and John, two divine lamps shining before God, dispel the gloom of my faults with your radiance. Be the two upon whom God the Father, through his own Son, specially built his own house, and be the two in whom the only Son of God the Father, as the reward of your most sincere virginity, confirmed this as his special privilege, thus saying to you, as he was hanging on the cross, 'Woman, behold thy son,' and then to the other, 'Behold thy mother.' By the sweetness of this most sacred love may you be joined by the words of Our Lord as mother and son, you two to whom I, the sinner, commend my body and soul today and every day, so that you might be, at every hour and every moment of my life, inside and outside me, my steadfast guardians and pious intercessors before God. I indeed believe firmly and accept without any doubt that he who wants to be yours will belong to God, and he who does not want to be yours will not belong to God, for you can obtain whatever you ask from God without delay. By virtue of your most powerful worthiness, beg, for me, for the deliverance of my body and soul. I beseech you to offer your glorious prayers so that my heart would be made worthy of being captured, entered, and inhabited by the Holy Spirit who would purify me of all sordid vices and embellish me with sacred virtues, who would help me stand, almost perfectly, in God's favor and make me persevere, and, after the course of my life is over, lead me to the joy of his elect, this most benevolent Paraclete, greatest bestower of grace, who, consubstantial with the Father and Son and co-eternal with them, lives and reigns as God forever and ever, Amen.

The above is translated from the "O intemerata" in Walters 213 (Cat. No. 56). The original Latin is nearly identical to that published by Wilmart (*Auteurs spirituels,* 488–90). The miniature of the *Madonna with Angels* accompanying this prayer is illustrated in Pl. 30.

6. Penitential Psalms (see Chapter IX)

The Penitential Psalms, sometimes preceded by the antiphon "Ne reminiscaris" ("Remember not, O Lord, our offenses"), are as follows:

Psalm 6: Domine ne in furore . . .
Psalm 31: Beati quorum . . .
Psalm 37: Domine ne in furore . . .
Psalm 50: Miserere mei Deus . . .
Psalm 101: Domine exaudi . . .
Psalm 129: De profundis . . .
Psalm 142: Domine exaudi . . .

7. Accessory Texts (see Chapter X)

JOYS OF THE VIRGIN

"Doulce dame de miséricordie . . ." followed by 15 verses, each beginning with "Très doulce dame . . ." or

"Gaude virgo mater Christi . . ." followed by 15 verses beginning with "Gaude . . ."

7 REQUESTS TO OUR LORD

"Quiconques veult estre bien conseillies . . . ," a prologue sometimes preceding the prayer itself that begins:

"Doulz Dieux doulz Père sainte Trinité un Dieu . . ." followed by 7 verses, each beginning "Biau sire Dieux . . ."

PASSION OF CHRIST according to John 18:1–19:42

"Egressus est Ihesus cum discipulis suis . . ."

STABAT MATER

"Stabat mater dolorosa, iuxta crucem lacrimosa . . ."

SALVE SANCTA FACIES

"Salve sancta facies nostri redemptoris in qua nitet species divini splendoris . . ."

WEEKDAY HOURS

The Hours for the Days of the Week are structured like the Hours of the Cross and the Hours of the Holy Spirit and consist of Matins through Compline but no Lauds. Each Hour is short, consisting of a hymn plus a prayer, preceded by versicles and responses, and with a few antiphons; there are no psalms nor lessons. See the incipit outline above in Part 4. Other optional Hours, such as the Hours of St. Catherine, follow this same format.

7 PRAYERS OF ST. GREGORY

"O Domine Ihesu Christe adoro te in cruce pendentem . . ." followed by 6 verses, each beginning "O Domine Ihesu Christe adoro te . . ."

7 VERSES OF ST. BERNARD

"Illumina oculos meos ne unquam obdormiam in morte . . ."

7 LAST WORDS OF OUR LORD

"Domine Ihesu Christe qui septem verba die ultimo vite tue . . ."

PSALTER OF ST. JEROME

"Verba mea auribus percipe Domine . . ."

PRAYER OF BLESSED PETER OF LUXEMBOURG

"Deus Pater qui creasti mundum et illuminasti . . ."

8. Suffrages (see Chapter XI)

Suffrages consist of three short elements—an antiphon, a versicle, and a response—followed by a prayer. Since these prayers are innumerable, what follows is a sampling of four Suffrages to four of the more popular saints of the Middle Ages.

The following abbreviations are used:

A. = antiphon
Or. = oration
R. = response
V. = versicle

SUFFRAGE TO CHRISTOPHER (from Walters 240; see Fig. 92)

A. O Christopher, martyr in honor of the Savior, make our spirit worthy, by means of Christ's most powerful love, of the piety such as you yourself obtained, give the afflicted people the blessings that you secured by your death, bestow comfort, remove the burdens in our minds, and help make the final judgement a merciful one for us all. Amen.

V. O Lord, you have crowned him with glory and honor.

R. And you have placed him above the works of your own hands.

Or. We beseech you, almighty God, through your blessed martyr Christopher whom we commemorate, by virtue of his pious merits and intercessions, that we be free from sudden death, plague, hunger, fear and poverty, and from all the treacheries of our enemies. Through you, Jesus Christ, savior of the world, whom Christopher himself deserved to carry on his shoulders. God who lives and reigns for ever and ever. Amen.

SUFFRAGE TO SEBASTIAN (from Walters 719; see Fig. 93)

A. O Saint Sebastian, protect and keep me always, in the evening, in the morning, at all hours, and at every moment, healthy in mind as I am now, and take away from me, O martyr, infirmity, sickness, and sudden difficulty. In the same manner, defend and guard from the plague me and my friends who, like us, admit their sins, through God, and holy Mary, and you, pious martyr. You, saint of Milan, have the power, if you wish, to stop this pestilence, and to be heard by God because, as we all know, God deems you worthy. This dreadful plague drives the citizens of Milan crazy and the priest is begging God to stop the pestilence. Since you have shown that you could not stop the plague unless a church were built and dedicated to you, may God stop the plague and then the people will rejoice. You cured the mute Zoe, and you transformed Nicostratus, her husband, in a marvellous way. You have comforted martyrs in their agony, and promised them again and again eternal life. O Saint Sebastian, stay with us always, through your merits guard and guide us who are alive now, and protect us from the plague, interceding for us to the Trinity and the holy Virgin Mary. And thus let us end our lives, so we may receive our reward and gain the company of the pious Christian martyrs.

A. O how the celebrated martyr Sebastian shone in grace when, loaded by military honors and pressured by the other soldiers, he comforted weak hearts by the power of God's divine word.

V. Pray for us, Saint Sebastian.

R. That we may be worthy of escaping the epidemic plague and obtaining the promises of Christ.

Or. O God, who strengthened your blessed martyr Sebastian in your faith and love so that no flattery or torments could separate him from your devotion, we beg you for solace in persecution, help in tribulation, relief from this particular plague, and protection for as long as possible in order to avoid courageously all diabolical snares and machinations and to see through, aided by your intercession, all the trials you have authorized for me.

SUFFRAGE TO CATHERINE (from Walters 420; see Fig. 103)

A. Prudent and vigilant virgin, you are in heaven with the spouse who chose you from all the world, so beautiful, rare, radiant, and worthy among all the maidens of Sion and the daughters of Jerusalem. You, daughter, joined to God, rejoice in your royal marriage.

V. Pray for us, blessed Catherine, virgin and martyr.

R. So that we be absolved of our sins.

Or. O God, who handed over to Moses the law at the top of Mount Sinai, and who had the body of blessed Catherine, virgin and martyr, miraculously laid to rest in the same place by your angels, we beseech you, through her merits and intercession, to give us the strength to ascend the mountain where Christ dwells. Through Our Lord, Christ. Amen.

SUFFRAGE TO MARGARET (from Walters 274; see Fig. 106)

A. When Margaret was fifteen years old she was thrown into jail by the ungodly Olybrius.

V. Pray for us, blessed Margaret.

R. So that we may fulfill the promises of Christ.

Or. Hear us, O God, our Savior, we rejoice with the same happiness as did blessed Margaret, your virgin and martyr, so that, like her, we may learn the proper path to devotion.

9. Office of the Dead (see Chapter XII)

The Office of the Dead is one of the longest texts in a Book of Hours. It usually appears towards the end of the manuscript, sometimes as the last text, but often the second-to-last and followed by the Suffrages. As opposed to the eight or seven hours that make up most Offices or Hours, the Office of the Dead consists of only the three hours of Vespers, Matins, and Lauds.

Like the Calendar and the Hours of the Virgin, the text of the Office of the Dead can vary from city to city or region to region and can thus provide an indication of where the Book of Hours was meant to be used; this is what is meant by the "use" given in the catalogue entries. The Office of the Dead outlined below is for the use of Paris and is based on Walters 209 (Cat. No. 22; Fig. 111). The following abbreviations are used:

A. = antiphon
Les. = lesson
Or. = oration
Ps. = psalm
R. = response
V. = versicle

OFFICE OF THE DEAD

VESPERS

A. Placebo
Ps. Dilexi quoniam . . . (Ps. 114)
A. Placebo Domino . . .
A. Heu mihi
Ps. Ad Dominum . . . (Ps. 119)
A. Heu mihi quia . . .
A. Dominus
Ps. Levavi oculos . . . (Ps. 120)
A. Dominus custodit . . .
A. Si iniquitates
Ps. De profundis . . . (Ps. 129)
A. Si iniquitates observaveris . . .
A. Opera
Ps. Confitebor tibi . . . (Ps. 137)
A. Opera manuum . . .
A. Qui Lazarum
Magnificat anima mea . . . (Canticle of the Virgin, Luke 1:46–55)
A. Qui Lazarum resuscitasti . . .
Pater noster
V. Et ne nos . . .
R. Sed libera nos . . .
V. In memoria eterna . . .
R. Ab auditione mala . . .
V. A porta inferi . . .
R. Erue Domine . . .
Ps. Lauda anima mea . . . (Ps. 145)
V. Domine exaudi . . .
R. Et clamor meus . . .
Or. Inclina Domine aurem . . .
Or. Deus qui nos patrem . . .
Or. Deus venie largitor . . .
Or. Fidelium Deus . . .

MATINS

(1st Nocturn:)
A. Dirige
Ps. Verba mea . . . (Ps. 5)
A. Dirige Domine . . .
A. Convertere
Ps. Domine ne in furore . . . (Ps. 6)
A. Convertere Domine . . .
A. Nequando
Ps. Domine Deus meus . . . (Ps. 7)
A. Nequando rapiat . . .
V. A porta inferi . . .
R. Erue Domine . . .
Pater noster
V. Et ne nos . . .
R. Sed libera nos . . .
Les. I: Parce mihi Domine . . . (Job 7:16–21)
R. Qui Lazarum . . .
V. Qui venturus . . .

Les. II: Tedet animam meam . . . (Job 10:1–7)
R. Credo quod . . .
V. Quem visurus . . .
Les. III: Manus tue Domine . . . (Job 10:8–12)
R. Heu mihi . . .
V. Anima mea . . .

(2nd Nocturn:)
A. In loco
Ps. Dominus regit me . . . (Ps. 22)
A. In loco pascue . . .
A. Delicta
Ps. Ad te Domine . . . (Ps. 24)
A. Delicta iuventutis . . .
A. Credo videre
Ps. Dominus illuminatio mea . . . (Ps. 26)
A. Credo videre bona . . .
V. In memoria eterna . . .
R. Ab auditione mala . . .
Pater noster
V. Et ne nos . . .
R. Sed libera nos . . .
Les. IV: Quantas habeo iniquitates . . . (Job 13:22–28)
R. Ne recorderis . . .
V. Amplius lava me . . .
Les. V: Homo natus de muliere . . . (Job 14:1–6)
R. Domine quando . . .
V. Commissa mea . . .
Les. VI: Quis mihi hoc . . . (Job 14:13–16)
R. Peccantem me . . .
V. De profundis . . .

(3rd Nocturn:)
A. Domine
Ps. Exaltabo te . . . (Ps. 29)
A. Domine abstraxisti . . .
A. Complaceat
Ps. Expectans expectavi . . . (Ps. 39)
A. Complaceat tibi . . .
A. Sitivit
Ps. Quemadmodum desiderat . . . (Ps. 41)
A. Sitivit anima . . .
V. Audivi vocem . . .
R. Scribe beati . . .
Pater noster
V. Et ne nos . . .
R. Sed libera nos . . .
Les. VII: Spiritus meus . . . (Job 17:1–3, 11–15)
R. Domine secundum . . .
V. Quoniam iniquitatem . . .
Les. VIII: Pelli meae . . . (Job 19:20–27)
R. Momento mei . . .
V. Et non revertetur . . .
Les. IX: Quare de vulva . . . (Job 10:18–22)
R. Libera me . . .
V. Dies illa dies irae . . .
V. Tremens factus . . .
V. Tremebunt angeli . . .
V. Vix iusti . . .
V. Quid ergo . . .
V. Vox de celis . . .
V. Creator omnium . . .
R. Libera me . . .

LAUDS

A. Exultabunt
Ps. Miserere mei Deus . . . (Ps. 50)
A. Exultabunt Domino . . .
A. Exaudi
Ps. Te decet . . . (Ps. 64)
A. Exaudi Domine . . .
A. Me suscepit
Ps. Deus Deus meus . . . (Ps. 62)
A. Me suscepit dextera . . .
A. A porta inferi
Ego dixi . . . (Canticle of Ezechias, Isaiah 38:10–20)
A. A porta inferi erue . . .
A. Omnis
Ps. Laudate Dominum . . . (Ps. 148)
Ps. Cantate Domino . . . (Ps. 149)
Ps. Laudate Dominum . . . (Ps. 150)
A. Omnis spiritus . . .
A. Credo Domine
Benedictus Dominus . . . (Canticle of Zachary, Luke 1:68–79)
A. Credo Domine Ihesu . . .
Pater noster
V. In memoria eterna . . .
R. Ab auditione mala . . .
V. A porta inferi . . .
R. Erue Domine . . .
V. Credo videre bona . . .
R. In terra . . .
Ps. De profundis . . . (Ps. 129)
V. Requiem eternam . . .
R. Et lux perpetua . . .
V. Domine exaudi . . .
R. Et clamor meus . . .
Or. Inclina Domine . . .
Or. Deus qui nos patrem . . .
Or. Deus venie largitor . . .
Or. Fidelium Deus . . .

Catalogue of Manuscripts

France
1-77

Belgium
78-106

Holland
107-110

England
111-114

Italy
115-117

Spain
118

Germany
119

Only the most recent or most relevant bibliographic citation has been provided for each manuscript.

Brinkmann, B. "Simon Bening." *The Dictionary of Art.* J. Turner, ed., London, 1996, III, 725–27.

Clark, G. T. *Made in Flanders: The Master of the Ghent Privileges and Manuscript Painting in the Southern Netherlands in the Time of Philip the Good.* Turnhout, 2000.

Kanter, L. B., B. D. Boehm, C. B. Strehlke, G. Freuler, C. C. M. Thurman, and P. Palladino. *Painting and Illumination in Early Renaissance Florpence, 1300–1450.* New York, 1994.

Katzenstein, R. "A Neapolitan Book of Hours in the J. Paul Getty Museum." *J. Paul Getty Museum Journal* XVIII, 1990, 69–98.

Los Angeles, J. Paul Getty Museum. "Manuscript Acquisitions: The Ludwig Collection." *J. Paul Getty Museum Journal* XII, 1984, 281–306.

Marrow, J. H. *A Descriptive and Analytical Catalogue of Dutch Illustrated Manuscripts of the 15th and 16th Centuries.* Doornspijk (forthcoming).

Plummer, J., with the assistance of G. Clark. *The Last Flowering: French Painting in Manuscripts, 1420–1530, from American Collections.* New York, 1982.

Randall, L. M. C. "From Cîteaux Onwards: Cistercian-Related Manuscripts in The Walters Art Gallery." *Studies in Cistercian Art and Architecture* III, Kalamazoo, 1987, 111–36.

Randall, L. M. C., assisted by J. Oliver, C. Clarkson, J. Krochalis, and J. Morrish. *Medieval and Renaissance Manuscripts in the Walters Art Gallery. Volume I: France, 875–1420.* Baltimore, 1989.

Randall, L. M. C., assisted by C. Clarkson and J. Krochalis. *Medieval and Renaissance Manuscripts in the Walters Art Gallery. Volume II: France, 1420–1540.* Baltimore, 1992.

Randall, L. M. C., assisted by J. H. Oliver, C. Clarkson, and C. Mark, with J. Plummer and J. H. Marrow, consultants. *Medieval and Renaissance Manuscripts in the Walters Art Gallery. Volume III: Belgium, 1250–1530.* Baltimore, 1997.

Sandler, L. F. *Gothic Manuscripts, 1285–1385.* (A Survey of Manuscripts Illuminated in the British Isles, V) London, 1986.

Schutzner, S. *Medieval and Renaissance Manuscript Books in the Library of Congress: A Descriptive Catalog. Volume I: Bibles, Liturgy, Books of Hours.* Washington, 1989.

Tanis, J. R., with J. A. Thompson, ed., with essays by C. W. Dutschke, J. H. Marrow, W. G. Noel, A. B. Quandt, K. A. Smith, J. R. Tanis, J. A. Thompson, and R. S. Wieck. *Leaves of Gold: Manuscript Illuminations from Philadelphia Collections.* Philadelphia, 2001.

Voelkle, W. M. "Morgan Manuscript M.1001: The Seven Deadly Sins and the Seven Evil Ones." *Monsters and Demons in the Ancient and Medieval Worlds: Papers Presented in Honor of Edith Porada.* Mainz, 1987, 101–14.

Wieck, R. S. *Late Medieval and Renaissance Illuminated Manuscripts, 1350–1525, in the Houghton Library.* Cambridge (Mass.), 1983.

Wieck, R. S. "The Savoy Hours and Its Impact on Jean, Duc de Berry." *Yale University Library Gazette* LXVI/ Supplement 1991, 159–80.

Wieck, R. S., W. M. Voelkle, and K. M. Hearne. *The Hours of Henry VIII: A Renaissance Masterpiece by Jean Poyet.* New York, 2000.

Catalogue of Manuscripts

1 Fig. 3

Walters Art Museum, MS W. 40.

France, Paris, 3rd quarter of the 13th century.

Vellum, 171 leaves, $6\frac{1}{4}$ x $4\frac{1}{4}$ in. (16 x 10.9 cm), 1 column, 14 lines, in Latin with French additions, in *textura,* 20 large miniatures and 12 historiated initials, by the Bari workshop.

Use: Calendar: Rheims; Hours of the Virgin: Paris; Office of the Dead: Paris.

TEXT	IMAGE
Calendar (added in the early 14th century, 1–12v)	
	(Series of prefatory miniatures:)
Various prayers including 15 Joys of the Virgin, 7 Requests to Our Lord, Gospel Lesson of John, O intemerata, Mass of the Virgin, Suffrages for Sts. Louis and Nicholas (added in the early 14th century to the backs of the original 13th-century miniatures, 13–32v)	Annunciation (13v) Visitation (14) Nativity (15v) Annunciation to the Shepherds (16) Adoration of the Magi (17v) Presentation in the Temple (18) Flight into Egypt (19v) Massacre of the Innocents (20) Baptism of Christ (21v) Entry into Jerusalem (22) Betrayal (23v) Christ Mocked (24) Christ before Pilate (25v) Buffeting of Christ (26) Flagellation (27v) Christ Carrying the Cross (28) Crucifixion (29v) Entombment (30) Three Marys at the Tomb (31v) Harrowing of Hell (32)
Hours of the Virgin (33–97v)	
Matins	Madonna Enthroned, in "D" (33)
Lauds	Woman Praying before an Altar, in "D" (57v)
Prime	Woman Praying before an Altar, in "D" (69v)
Terce	Woman, with Book of Hours, Praying before an Altar, in "D" (75)
Sext	Woman Praying before an Altar, in "D" (78v)
None	Woman Praying before an Altar, in "D" (82)
Vespers	Woman Praying before an Altar, in "D" (85v)
Compline	Man Praying before an Altar, in "C" (92)
Penitential Psalms, Litany (97v–115)	Christ Enthroned, in "D" (97v)
15 Gradual Psalms (115–126v)	David in Prayer before an Altar, in "A" (115)
Office of the Dead (127–171v)	
Vespers	Funeral Service, in "D" (127)
Matins and Lauds	Woman Praying before an Altar, in "V" (134v)

BIBLIOGRAPHY: Randall, *Medieval and Renaissance Manuscripts,* I, 68–71, no. 29, figs. 58–60.

❖ ❖ ❖

2 Fig. 48

Walters Art Museum, MS W. 97.

France, Paris, last quarter of the 13th century.

Vellum, 139 leaves, $6\frac{1}{4}$ x $4\frac{1}{4}$ in. (16 x 11 cm), 1 column, 14 lines, in Latin and French, in *textura,* 8 historiated initials and 12 calendar and 12 zodiacal vignettes.

Use: Calendar: Paris; Hours of the Virgin: Paris, altered to Rome in the late 15th or early 16th century; Office of the Dead: Paris.

TEXT	IMAGE
Calendar (1–6v)	Zodiacal sign on each recto and verso
Jan.	Janus Feasting (1)
Feb.	Keeping Warm (1v)
Mar.	Pruning (2)
Apr.	Picking Flowers (2v)
May	Hawking (3)
Jun.	Mowing (3v)
Jul.	Reaping (4)
Aug.	Threshing (4v)
Sept.	Sowing (5)
Oct.	Treading Grapes (5v)
Nov.	Thrashing for Acorns (6)
Dec.	Slaughtering a Pig (6v)
Hours of the Virgin (7–62v)	
Matins	Madonna with Kneeling Patroness, in "D" (7)
Lauds	Betrayal, in "D" (20)
Prime	(Historiated initial missing)
Terce	Flagellation, in "D" (36)
Sext	Christ Carrying the Cross, in "D" (40)
None	Crucifixion, in "D" (44)
Vespers	(Historiated initial missing)
Compline	(Historiated initial missing)
Penitential Psalms, Litany (63–80v)	Christ Enthroned, in "D" (63)
15 Gradual Psalms (81–91v)	Woman Kneeling in Prayer before an Altar, in "A" (81)
Office of the Dead (91v–137)	Funeral Service, in "D" (92)
Suffrages (137–139)	

BIBLIOGRAPHY: Randall, *Medieval and Renaissance Manuscripts,* I, 97–99, no. 41, figs. 85, 86.

❖ ❖ ❖

3 Fig. 37

Walters Art Museum, MS W. 39.

Northern France, late 13th century.

Vellum, 158 leaves, $3\frac{7}{8}$ x $2\frac{5}{8}$ in. (9.7 x 6.8 cm), 1 column, 11 lines, in Latin and French, in *textura,* 12 historiated initials and 11 calendar vignettes.

Use: Calendar: Lille; Office of the Virgin: Collégiale of St. Pierre of Lille.

TEXT	IMAGE
Calendar (1v–12v)	
Jan.	Janus Feasting (1v)
Feb.	Keeping Warm (3)
Mar.	Pruning (3v)
Apr.	Picking Flowers (4v)
May	Hawking (6)
Jun.	Ploughing (6v)
Jul.	Mowing (7v)
Aug.	Reaping (9)
Sept.	Trimming Vines (9v)
Oct.	Thrashing for Acorns (11)
Nov.	Slaughtering an Ox (12)
Dec.	(Vignette missing)

Office of the Holy Spirit (misbound, 13–50v)	
Matins	Pentecost, in "D" (13)
Lauds	Betrayal, in "D" (24)
Prime	Flagellation, in "D" (39)
Terce	(Historiated initial missing)
Sext	Resurrection, in "D" (30)
None	Three Marys at the Tomb, in "D" (33)
Vespers	Noli me tangere, in "D" (36)
Compline	(Historiated initial missing)
Hours of the Virgin (51–124v)	
Matins	(Historiated initial missing)
Lauds	(Historiated initial missing)
Prime	(Historiated initial missing)
Terce	Annunciation to the Shepherds, in "D" (91)
Sext	Adoration of the Magi, in "D" (96v)
None	Presentation in the Temple, in "D" (102)
Vespers	(Historiated initial missing)
Compline	Flight into Egypt, in "C" (118)
Penitential Psalms (125–143v)	Man Praying before an Altar, in "D" (125)
15 Gradual Psalms (144–148v)	David in Deep Water, in "A" (144)
Litany (148–158)	

BIBLIOGRAPHY: Randall, *Medieval and Renaissance Manuscripts,* I, 90–93, no. 39, figs. 79, 80.

❖ ❖ ❖

4 Fig. 40

Walters Art Museum, MS W. 86.

Northeastern France, late 13th century.

Vellum, 174 leaves, 3 ¼ x 2 ¼ in. (8.4 x 5.8 cm), 1 column, 11 lines, in Latin and French, in *textura,* 6 large miniatures and 8 historiated initials.

Use: Calendar: southern Belgium/northern France, with entries pointing to Arras; Hours of the Virgin: Arras.

TEXT	IMAGE
Calendar (1–12v)	
	(Series of prefatory miniatures:)
	Christ Washing the Feet of the Apostles (13v)
	Betrayal (14)
	Christ before Pilate (15v)
	Flagellation (16)
	Crucifixion (17v)
	Three Marys at the Tomb (18)
Hours of the Virgin (19–106v)	
Matins	Annunciation, in "D" (19)
Lauds	Visitation, "D" (50)
Prime	Nativity, in "D" (65v)
Terce	(Historiated initial missing)
Sext	(Historiated initial missing)
None	Presentation in the Temple, in "D" (83)
Vespers	Massacre of the Innocents, in "D" (88v)
Compline	Flight into Egypt, in "C" (99v)
Penitential Psalms, Litany (107–133)	David Harping, in "D" (107)
Office of the Holy Spirit (135–169)	Trinity, in "D" (135)
15 Gradual Psalms (169–172v)	

BIBLIOGRAPHY: Randall, *Medieval and Renaissance Manuscripts,* I, 113–15, no. 47, figs. 96, 97.

5 Fig. 56

Walters Art Museum, MS W. 98.

France, Rheims, end of the 13th century.

Vellum, 121 leaves, 6 x 4 ⅜ in. (15.2 x 11.3 cm), 1 column, 16 lines, in Latin and French, in *textura,* 5 large (fols. 1–95) and 7 small historiated initials and 12 calendar and 12 zodiacal vignettes (in Stockholm).

Use: Calendar: composite, but with many entries relevant to prisoners; Hours of the Virgin: unidentified.

TEXT	IMAGE
Calendar (Stockholm, Nationalmuseum, MS B 1648)	Zodiacal sign on each verso
Jan.	Janus Feasting
Feb.	Tending Sheep
Mar.	Pruning
Apr.	Picking Flowers
May	Hawking
Jun.	Mowing
Jul.	Reaping
Aug.	Threshing
Sept.	Sowing
Oct.	Treading Grapes
Nov.	Keeping Warm
Dec.	Slaughtering a Pig
Hours of the Virgin (1–47v)	
Matins	Madonna with Angels between a Kneeling Nun and Patroness, in "D" (1)
Lauds	(Historiated initial missing)
Prime	(Historiated initial missing)
Terce	(Historiated initial missing)
Sext	Honorina in Prison, in "D" (31)
None	Catherine Confounding the Doctors, in "D" (35)
Vespers	(Historiated initial missing)
Compline	(Historiated initial missing)
Penitential Psalms, Litany (48–63v)	(Historiated initial missing)
15 Gradual Psalms (64–71v)	Leonard Releasing Prisoners, in "A" (64)
Various prayers including O intemerata, Gospel Lesson of John, Suffrages, Litany of the Virgin, Apostles' Creed (misbound, 72–95, 101–113v)	Madonna, with Kneeling Patroness, in "K" (101)
Hours of the Passion (95–100v, 114–121v)	
Matins	Battle of Constantine, in "D" (95)
Lauds	Helena Excavating the True Cross, in "D" (98)
Prime	Finding of the True Cross, in "D" (114)
Terce	(Historiated initial missing)
Sext	Helena Testing the Crosses, in "D" (115v)
None	Heraclius on Horseback, in "D" (117)
Vespers	Heraclius Entering Jerusalem with the True Cross, in "D" (118)
Compline	Queen of Sheba Making the Sign of the Cross, in "C" (120)

BIBLIOGRAPHY: Randall, *Medieval and Renaissance Manuscripts,* I, 119–23, no. 49, pl. Vb, figs. 100, 101.

❖ ❖ ❖

6 Fig. 41

Walters Art Museum, MS W. 93 ("de Bar Hours").

France, Lorraine, early 14th century, produced for a member of the de Bar family.

Vellum, 148 leaves, 4⅞ x 3¾ in. (12.3 x 9.7 cm), 1 column, 12 lines, in Latin and French, in *textura,* 25 large miniatures and 12 zodical vignettes.

Use: Calendar: Verdun; Hours of the Virgin: Châlons-sur-Marne.

TEXT	IMAGE
Calendar (1–12v)	Zodiacal sign on each verso
	(Series of prefatory miniatures:)
	God Creating Adam and Eve (13v)
	God Instructing Adam and Eve (14)
	Temptation of Adam and Eve (15v)
	Expulsion (16)
	Adam and Eve Toiling (17v)
	Sacrifice of Cain and Abel (18)
	Cain Killing Abel (19v)
	Noah Receiving the Dove of Peace (20)
Hours of the Virgin (21–101)	
Matins	Annunciation (21)
Lauds	Visitation (38v)
Prime	Nativity (55v)
Terce	Annunciation to the Shepherds (64v)
Sext	Adoration of the Magi (70v)
None	Presentation in the Temple (76)
Vespers	Massacre of the Innocents (81v)
Compline	Flight into Egypt (93v)
Penitential Psalms, Litany (101v–130)	Christ as Judge (101v)
Hours of the Cross (130v–144)	
Matins	Betrayal (130v)
Prime	Christ Mocked (133)
Terce	Christ Carrying the Cross (134v)
Sext	Crucifixion (136)
None	Crucifixion with Longinus (137v)
Vespers	Deposition (139)
Compline	Entombment (140v)
Prayer to Veronica's Veil, 5 Joys of the Virgin (144–147v)	Head of Christ (147v)

BIBLIOGRAPHY: Randall, *Medieval and Renaissance Manuscripts,* I, 149–52, no. 57, figs. 118, 119.

❖ ❖ ❖

7 Fig. 36

Walters Art Museum, MS W. 90.

Northern France, early 14th century.

Vellum, 254 leaves, 5⅛ x 3¾ in. (13.1 x 9.6 cm), 1 column, 14 lines, in Latin, in *textura,* 7 large miniatures, 24 historiated initials, 12 calendar and 12 zodiacal vignettes, and numerous marginalia.

Use: Calendar: St. Omer; Hours of the Virgin: Thérouanne; Office of the Dead: Dominican.

TEXT	IMAGE
Calendar (2v–14)	Zodiacal sign on each recto
Jan.	Janus Feasting (2v)
Feb.	Keeping Warm (3v)
Mar.	Pruning (4v)
Apr.	Picking Flowers (5v)
May	Hawking (6v)
Jun.	Carrying Wood (7v)
Jul.	Mowing (8v)
Aug.	Reaping (9v)
Sept.	Harvesting Grapes (10v)
Oct.	Sowing (11v)
Nov.	Thrashing for Acorns (12v)
Dec.	Slaughtering a Pig (13v)
	(Series of prefatory miniatures:)
	God Creating the Heavens (15)
	God Creating the Earth and Trees (16)
	God Creating the Animals (17)
	God Creating Adam (18)
	God Creating Eve (19)
	Temptation of Adam and Eve (20)
	God Enthroned (21)
Hours of the Virgin (22–90)	
Matins	Annunciation, in "D" (22)
Lauds	Visitation, in "D" (48v)
Prime	Nativity, in "D" (61v)
Terce	Annunciation to the Shepherds, in "D" (67v)
Sext	Presentation in the Temple, in "D" (71v)
None	Adoration of the Magi, in "D" (75)
Vespers	Massacre of the Innocents, in "D" (78v)
Compline	Flight into Egypt, in "C" (86)
Hours of the Passion (91–134)	
Matins	(Historiated initial missing)
Lauds	Christ before Pilate, in "D" (100)
Prime	Flagellation, in "D" (106v)
Terce	Christ Carrying the Cross, in "D" (109v)
Sext	Crucifixion, in "D" (114v)
None	Deposition, in "D" (119v)
Vespers	Entombment, in "D" (126)
Compline	Resurrection, in "C" (130)
Office of the Holy Spirit (135–162v)	
Matins	Pentecost, in "D"; border: Kneeling Patroness (135)
Lauds	Crucifixion of Peter, in "D" (144v)
Prime	Decapitation of Paul, in "D" (148v)
Terce	James Holding a Monstrance, in "D" (151)
Sext	Flaying Bartholomew, in "D" (153)
None	John the Evangelist Boiled in Oil, in "D" (155)
Vespers	Jude Holding a Hatchet, in "D" (157)
Compline	John the Baptist Preaching, in "D" (160)
Commendation of Souls (163–194v)	(Historiated initial missing?)
Office of the Dead (194v–241)	Funeral Service, in "D"; border: Devils Carrying Souls to Hell (194v)
O intemerata, Athanasian Creed (241v–248)	
Litany (248–253v)	

BIBLIOGRAPHY: Randall, *Medieval and Renaissance Manuscripts,* I, 138–42, no. 54, figs. 112, 113.

❖ ❖ ❖

8 Fig. 72

Walters Art Museum, MS W. 104.

France, probably Arras, early 14th century.

Vellum, 113 leaves, 6⅝ x 4¾ in. (16.8 x 12.1 cm), 1 column, 18 lines, in Latin, in *textura,* 2 large (fol. 1–v) and 5 small miniatures, 5 historiated initials, and borders filled with numerous marginalia.

Use: Hours of the Virgin: Arras, with Parisian elements; Office of the Dead: Paris, with Arras elements.

TEXT	IMAGE
Hours of the Virgin (1v–49v)	
Matins	Crucifixion (1)
	Virgin with Kneeling Patron (1v)
Lauds	Annunciation, in "D" (19)
Prime	Visitation, in "D" (28)
Terce	Nativity, in "D" (32v)
Sext	(Historiated initial missing)
None	(Historiated initial missing)
Vespers	Presentation in the Temple, in "D" (39v)
Compline	Massacre of the Innocents, in "C" (45v)
Penitential Psalms (51–60v)	Three Crowned Musicians (51)
15 Gradual Psalms, followed by various prayers (61–70v)	David Kneeling before Christ (61)
Litany (misbound, 71–73v, 75)	Madonna Enthroned, with Angels; border: Angels (70v)
	Three Monks Chanting; border: Saints (71)
Office of the Dead (74, 76–112)	Funeral Service; border: Clerics with Books (74)

BIBLIOGRAPHY: Randall, *Medieval and Renaissance Manuscripts*, I, 142–45, no. 55, pl. Vc, figs. 114, 115.

❖ ❖ ❖

9 Fig. 71

Los Angeles, J. Paul Getty Museum, MS Ludwig IX.3 ("Ruskin Hours").

Northern France, early 14th century.

Vellum, 128 leaves, 10½ x 7¼ in. (26.5 x 18.5 cm), 1 column, 14 lines, in Latin and French, in *textura*, 11 large (marking, except where missing, the beginning of each of the hours of the Office of the Holy Spirit and Hours of the Virgin) and 102 small historiated initials, 9 oblong Litany miniatures, 12 calendar vignettes, and numerous marginalia.

Use: Calendar: southern Belgium; Hours of the Virgin: Amiens.

TEXT	IMAGE
Hours of the Cross (added slightly later, 1–2)	
(Matins missing)	(Historiated initial missing)
Prime	Christ Mocked, in "D" (1)
Terce	Flagellation, in "D" (1)
Sext	Christ Carrying the Cross, in "D" (1)
None	Crucifixion, in "D" (1v)
Vespers	Deposition, in "D" (1v)
Compline	Resurrection, in "C" (2)
Calendar (2v–14)	
Jan.	Triple-faced Janus Feasting (2v)
Feb.	Keeping Warm (3v)
Mar.	Pruning (4v)
Apr.	Picking Flowers (5v)
May	Hawking (6v)
Jun.	Mowing (7v)
Jul.	Reaping (8v)
Aug.	Picking Grapes (9v)
Sept.	Sowing (10v)
Oct.	Thrashing for Acorns (11v)
Nov.	Slaughtering a Pig (12v)
Dec.	Baking Bread (13v)
Office of the Holy Spirit (15–36)	
Matins	Betrayal, in "D"; Virgin Praying to God, in "D" (15)
	Two Men with a Scroll, in "V" (15v)
	Bishop with Dove of Holy Spirit, in "V" (17)
	Virgin, in "B" (18)
	Bishop before a Fire, in "S"; Peter and the Virgin, in "O" (19v)
	Apostle and the Virgin, in "V" (20)
	Bishop with Two Assistants, in "T" (20v)
Lauds	Christ Mocked, in "D"; Two Men with a Scroll, in "L" (23)
	Two Men with a Scroll, in "C" (24v)
	Two Men with a Scroll, in "L" (25v)
	Peter, in "G" (26)
	Peter and the Virgin, in "T" (26v)
	Christ before Herod, in "B" (27)
	Christ in Prayer, in "D" (28v)
Prime	Christ before Caiaphas, in "D"; Virgin with the Apostles, in "D"; border: Kneeling Soldier (29)
	Peter's Denial, in "T" (30)
	John the Evangelist and the Virgin, in "S" (30v)
(Terce, Sext, None, and beginning of Vespers missing)	(4 large historiated initials missing)
Vespers	Ascension, in "D" (32)
Compline	Pentecost, in "D" (32)
	Peter, in "S" (32v)
	Paul, in "N"; Peter, in "V" (33v)
	Peter with Apostles, in "N" (33)
	Virgin with Apostles, in "D" (35v)
Salve regina (37)	
Hours of the Virgin (37v–102)	
Matins	Annunciation, in "D"; Man Praying, in "D" (37v)
	Monks Chanting, in "V" (38)
	Christ Blessing Plants, in "Q" (39)
	Woman Praying, in "D" (40)
	Madonna, in "C" (41)
	Man before God the Father, in "D" (42v)
	Madonna with Kneeling Man and Woman, in "S" (44)
	Christ as Judge with the Virgin, in "S" (45)
	Christ as Judge with the Virgin and a Man, in "S" (45v)
	John the Evangelist and the Virgin, in "E" (46)
	Deposition, in "D" (48v)
	Madonna with Male Saint, in "M" (50)
	Virgin and Christ, in "B" (51v)
	Madonna, in "S"; border: Kneeling Patron (52v)
	Virgin with Walking Christ Child, in "G" (53)
	Nativity, in "F" (54v)
	Monk Preaching to a Crowd, in "C" (55)
	Christ as Judge, in "C" (56v)
	Man, Attacked by a Devil, Appealing to the Madonna, in "O" (58)
	Virgin and Christ with a Kneeling Man, in "O" (59)
	Christ (?) Preaching, in "O" (60)
	Male Saint Baptized by Cleric Saint, in "T" (61)
Lauds	Visitation, in "D"; Enthroned Christ, in "D" (63v)

	David Harping, with Kneeling Men, in "I" (64v)
	Man Praying, in "D" (65v)
	Saint Preaching, in "D" (66v)
	Three Clerics in the Fiery Furnace, in "B" (67v)
	Earth and Angels in Heaven, in "L"; border: David in Prayer (69v)
	Monks Chanting, in "C" (71)
	Musicians with Kneeling Man, in "L" (72)
	Virgin, in "I" (72v)
	Madonna, in "O" (73)
	John the Baptist (?) Preaching, in "B" (73v)
	Virgin, in "D"; border: Kneeling Man (75)
Prime	Nativity, in "D"; Praying Man, in "V" (76)
	Goliath, in "B"; border: David (76v)
	Christ (?) Preaching, in "Q" (77v)
	Man Praying, in "V" (79)
	Virgin with Cleric, in "H" (80v)
	Woman Praying, in "F" (81)
Terce	Annunciation to the Shepherds, in "D"; Man Praying, in "V" (81v)
	Praying Man Attacked by Devil, in "A" (82)
	Christ with Praying Woman, in "L" (82v)
	David Addressing an Angel, in "L" (83v)
	Virgin Opening Gate of Heaven, in "P" (84v)
	Priest Giving Communion, in "D" (85)
Sext	Herod with a Soldier, in "D"; Monks Chanting, in "V"; border: Massacre of the Innocents (85v)
	Woman Praying, in "A" (86)
	Man with Donkey and Two Devils, in "N" (86v)
	Tower Flanked by Female Saint and Devil, in "Q" (87v)
	Virgin Pointing to Burning Books, in "G" (88)
	Monk Chanting, in "B" (88v)
None	Adoration of the Magi, in "D" (89)
	Harrowing of Hell, in "I" (90)
	God Blessing a Tower, in "N" (90v)
	Diners Surprised by the Hand of God, in "B" (91)
	Virgin Resurrecting a Dead Man, in "P" (92)
	Holy Spirit Resurrecting a Dead Man, in "G" (92v)
Vespers	(Large historiated initial missing)
	Monks Chanting, in "L" (93)
	Clerics Chanting, in "L" (93v)
	Christ Blessing a Church, in "N" (94v)
	Christ Preaching to a Crowd, in "L" (95)
	Virgin Holding Flowers, in "E" (96)
	Annunciation, in "A" (96)
	Madonna with Male Saint, in "M" (97)
	Annunciation, in "D" (98)
Compline	Flight into Egypt, in "D" (98v)
	Man Brandishing a Cross at Two Devils, in "S" (99v)
	Man Praying, in "D" (100)
	Virgin with Young Christ, in "S" (100v)
	Virgin with Kneeling Woman, in "V" (101)
	Madonna with Male Saint, in "N" (101v)
	Crucifixion with Kneeling Man, in "G" (102)
Litany, Prayers (102v–108v)	Christ Enthroned Flanked by Angels; Seraphim; Two Kneeling Angels; Christ with Kneeling Man; Flagellation (102v)
	Bishop Saint and Prophet; Peter; Paul; Andrew; James (103)
	John the Evangelist; Incredulity of Thomas; James; Philip; Bartholomew (103v)
	Matthew; Simon Preaching; Judas Thadias; Matthias; Angel (104)
	Luke; Barnabas; Apostles and Evangelists; Disciples; Massacre of the Innocents (104v)
	Confessors; Monks and Hermits; Noli me tangere; Felicitas; Perpetua (105)
	Martyrdom of Agatha; Agnes; Cecilia; Lucy; Catherine (105v)
	Anastasia; Petronilla; Benedicta; Brigida; Gertrude (106)
	Margaret Emerging from the Dragon; Barbara; Christine; All Virgins; Female Saints (106v)
	Christ Enthroned, in "O" (108v)
Penitential Psalms, Prayers (added slightly later, 109–125)	

BIBLIOGRAPHY: Los Angeles, J. Paul Getty Museum, "Manuscript Acquisitions: The Ludwig Collection," 292, no. 52, illus.

❖ ❖ ❖

10 Fig. 55

Walters Art Museum, MS W. 38.

Northern France, 1310–20.

Vellum, 227 leaves, 4½ x 3¼ in. (11.6 x 8.2 cm), 1 column, 12 lines, in Latin and French, in *textura*, 25 historiated initials.

Use: Calendar: northern France (Somme/Oise/Aisne area); Hours of the Virgin: Amiens; Office of the Dead: Soissons.

TEXT	IMAGE
Calendar (1v–13)	
Hours of the Virgin (14–96v)	
Matins	Madonna, with Two Kneeling Patronesses, in "D" (14)
Lauds	Annunciation, in "D" (45)
Prime	Visitation, in "D" (60v)
Terce	Nativity, in "D" (68)
Sext	Annunciation to the Shepherds, in "D" (72v)
None	Adoration of the Magi, in "D" (77)
Vespers	Flight into Egypt, in "D" (81v)
Compline	Massacre of the Innocents, in "C" (90v)
Hours of the Holy Spirit (98–117v)	
Matins	Trinity, in "D" (98)
Prime	Peter with Dove of Holy Spirit, in "D" (104)

Terce	God Holding Orb, with Dove, in "D" (106v)
Sext	God Creating the Stars, with Dove, in "D" (109)
None	God Creating Birds and Plants, with Dove, in "D" (111)
Vespers	God Creating Fish and Seas, with Dove, in "D" (113)
Compline	God Expelling Adam and Eve, with Dove, in "C" (115)
Hours of the Passion (118–142v)	
Matins	Betrayal, in "D" (118)
Lauds	Christ before Pilate, in "D" (122)
Prime	Christ Buffeted, in "D" (126v)
Terce	Christ before Pilate, in "D' (129v)
Sext	Christ Carrying the Cross, in "D" (132)
None	Crucifixion, in "D" (134v)
Vespers	Deposition, in "D" (137)
Compline	Noli me tangere, in "D" (140)
Penitential Psalms, Litany (144–165v)	David in Prayer before an Altar, in "D" (144)
Office of the Dead (166–224)	Funeral Service, in "D" (166)

BIBLIOGRAPHY: Randall, *Medieval and Renaissance Manuscripts*, I, 153–55, no. 58, figs. 120, 121.

❖ ❖ ❖

11

Figs. 1, 2

New Haven, Yale University, Beinecke Rare Book and Manuscript Library, MS 390 ("Savoy Hours").

France, Paris, 2nd quarter of the 14th century, produced for Blanche of Burgundy, Countess of Savoy, with additions of ca. 1370 for King Charles V of France.

Vellum, 26 leaves (all that remain of an original ca. 282 leaves), 7⅞ x 5¾ in. (20.1 x 14.7 cm), 1 column, 26 lines, in Latin and French, in *textura*, 50 miniatures (all that remain of at least 245 miniatures) by the workshop of Jean Pucelle and the workshop of the Master of the Bible of Jean de Sy.

(*Use:* Calendar: Paris; Hours of the Virgin: Paris.)

(Note: Sections destroyed in the 1904 fire at the Biblioteca Nazionale of Turin are in parentheses; surviving leaves are marked with an asterisk.)

TEXT	IMAGE
[Commissioned by Blanche of Burgundy:]	
(Calendar)	(Labor of the month and zodiacal vignette for each month)
(Psalter)	(At least 8 miniatures?)
(Office of the Trinity)	
(Matins)	(Trinity)
(Lauds)	(Trinity Creating Man)
(Prime)	(Trinity Appearing to a Prophet)
(Terce)	(Christ Enthroned)
(Sext)	(Baptism of Christ)
(None)	(Christ or Holy Spirit Adored by Moses and Aaron)
(Vespers)	(Apostle Preaching)
(Compline)	(Holy Spirit Adored by Jews)
(Office of the Holy Spirit)	
(Matins)	(Baptism of Christ)
(Lauds)	(Pentecost)
(Prime)	(Trinity)
(Terce)	(Peter Preaching)
(Sext)	(Saint Preaching)
(None)	(Peter and Paul Baptizing)
(Vespers)	(Peter Celebrating Mass)
(Compline)	(Pope Inspired by Holy Spirit)
(Prayer to the Virgin, in pseudo-Greek)	
(Hours of the Virgin)	
(Matins)	(Annunciation)
(Lauds)	(Visitation)
(Prime)	(Nativity)
(Terce)	(Annunciation to the Shepherds)
(Sext)	(Adoration of the Magi)
(None)	(Presentation in the Temple)
(Vespers)	(Flight into Egypt)
(Compline)	(Coronation of the Virgin)
(Prayers in pseudo-Greek)	
(Hours of the Passion)	
(Matins)	(Betrayal)
(Lauds)	(Christ before Pilate)
(Prime)	(Flagellation)
(Terce)	(Christ Carrying the Cross)
(Sext)	(Crucifixion)
(None)	(Deposition)
(Vespers)	(Entombment)
(Compline)	(Resurrection)
(Office of John the Baptist)	
(Matins)	(Zacharias in Temple)
(Lauds)	(Visitation)
(Prime)	(Birth of John the Baptist)
(Terce)	(John the Baptist in the Desert)
(Sext)	(Baptism of Christ)
(None)	(Arrest of John the Baptist)
(Vespers)	(Dance of Salome)
(Compline)	(Head of John the Baptist Presented to Herodias)
(Office of the Angels)	
(Matins)	(Michael Battling a Devil)
(Lauds)	(Angel Weighing Souls)
(Prime)	(Two Angels Appearing to Abraham)
(Terce)	(Jacob Wrestling the Angel)
(Sext)	(Subject unknown)
None	*Angels Protecting a Soldier (5)
Vespers	*Angels Administering to Christ after his Temptation (12v)
(Compline)	(John the Evangelist? Writing)
(Prayers to the Virgin)	(Virgin with Kneeling Blanche of Burgundy)
	(Virgin, in an initial)
(Office of John the Evangelist)	
(Matins)	(John the Evangelist Writing)
(Lauds)	(John Boiled in Oil)
(Prime)	(John in the Desert)
(Terce)	(John Healing a Sick Man)
(Sext)	(John Holding the Poisoned Chalice)
(None)	(John Performing a Marriage?)
(Vespers)	(Subject unknown)
(Compline)	(John, Amid Flames, Adoring the Host)
(Office of St. Louis)	
(Matins)	(Louis Enthroned, Surrounded by Angels; border: Consecration of Louis)
(Lauds)	(Louis Flagellated)
(Prime)	(Louis Carrying Relics)
(Terce)	(Louis Carrying the Cross)
(Sext)	(Louis Sailing to War)
(None)	(Louis' Breviary Miraculously Returned)
(Vespers)	(Louis Burying the Bones of Crusaders)
(Compline)	(Louis Feeding a Leprous Monk)
(Office of St. Louis of Toulouse)	
(Matins)	(Louis of Toulouse Returning his Crown to the Pope)
(Lauds)	(Louis Joins the Franciscans)
(Prime)	(Louis Feeding the Poor)

(Terce)	(Louis Resuscitating the Dead)
(Sext)	(Louis Giving His Cloak to a Poor Man)
(None)	(Burial of Louis)
(Vespers)	(Infant Healed by Louis)
(Compline)	(Woman Delivered from a Demon by Louis)
(Office of Mary Magdalene)	
(Matins)	(Mary Magdalene Washing Christ's Feet)
(Lauds)	(Noli me tangere)
(Prime)	(Subject unknown)
(Terce)	(Subject unknown)
(Sext)	(Mary Magdalene Chasing Demons)
(None)	(Levitation of Mary Magdalene Seen by a Priest)
(Vespers)	(Mary Magdalene Receiving Her Last Communion)
(Compline)	(Apparition of Mary Magdalene)
(Suffrages)	(Crucifixion)
	(Angels)
	(Angels Kneeling)
	(Michael Weighing Souls)
	(Saints)
	(Trinity)
(Office of the Dead)	(Funeral Service)
(Penitential Psalms, Litany)	(Christ in Majesty)
(15 Gradual Psalms)	(Blanche of Burgundy Kneeling before a Vision of the Crucifixion)
	(Annunciation)
(Suffrages)	(Nativity)
	(Adoration of the Magi)
	(Presentation in the Temple)
	(Christ among the Doctors)
	(Entry into Jerusalem)
	(Last Supper)
	(Agony in the Garden)
	(Flagellation)
	(Christ Led to Calvary)
	(Crucifixion)
	(Deposition)
	(Entombment)
	(Resurrection)
	(Resurrection)
	(3 Marys at the Tomb)
	(Ascension)
	(Pentecost)
	(Assumption of the Virgin)
	(Apostles)
	*All Apostles (11)
	*John the Evangelist with Kneeling Blanche of Burgundy (11v)
	*Andrew with Kneeling Blanche (6)
	*James with Kneeling Blanche (6v)
	(Maurice)
	(Nicasius)
	(Stephen)
	(Lambert with Kneeling Blanche of Burgundy)
	(Christopher with Kneeling Blanche)
	(Lawrence)
	(George)
	(Martyrdom of Thomas Becket)
	(Vincent)
	(Clement)
	*Decapitation of Martyrs (3)
	*Louis with Kneeling Blanche of Burgundy (3v)
	(Leodegar)
	(Dominic with Kneeling Blanche of Burgundy)

	*Silvester with Kneeling Blanche (13)
	*Augustine with Kneeling Blanche (13v)
	*Martin Dividing His Cloak (14)
	*Remigius with Kneeling Blanche (14v)
	*Eligius with Kneeling Blanche (15)
	*Anthony with Kneeling Blanche (15v)
	*Leonard with Two Prisoners (16)
	*Gregory with Kneeling Blanche (16v)
	*Benedict with Kneeling Blanche (7)
	*All Confessors (7v)
	*Romaric with Kneeling Blanche (17)
	*Agnes Slain (17v)
	*Agatha's Breasts Removed (defaced, 18)
	*Coronation of Cecilia and Valerian (18v)
	*Lucy with Kneeling Blanche of Burgundy (19)
	*Ursula with Kneeling Blanche (19v)
	*Visitation (20)
	*Geneviève with Kneeling Blanche (20v)
	*Gertrude with Kneeling Blanche (21)
	*Barbara with Kneeling Blanche (21v)
	*Mary Magdalene with Kneeling Blanche (8)
	*Catherine with Kneeling Blanche (8v)
	*Margaret Emerging from the Dragon (9)
	*All Virgins (9v)
	*Clare with Kneeling Blanche (22)
	*Pope and All Clergy (22v)
	*Kings and Princes (23)
	*Laborers (23v)
	(Suffrage for those in mortal sin: subject unknown)
	(Suffrage for those in danger at sea: subject unknown)
	(Suffrage for prisoners: subject unkown)
	*Givers of Alms (24)
	*Blanche of Burgundy Praying before an Altar for Her Parents and Friends (24v)
	*Blanche Praying before an Altar for Herself (25)
	*Souls Released from Purgatory (25v)
Suffrages, Prayer of St. Peter Martyr, 5 Joys of the Virgin (2, 10, 26)	*Trinity with Kneeling Blanche (2)
	*Angels (2v)
	*All Saints (10)
	*Celebrant at Mass Kissing the Pax, Blanche of Burgundy Attending (10v)
[Added by Charles V:]	
(Suffrages:)	(Trinity)
	(Annunciation)
	(Crucifixion)
	(Charles V Worshiping Relics)
	(Angels)
	(John the Baptist)
	*John the Evangelist Writing (1)
	*James Called by Christ (1)
	*All Apostles (1v)

TEXT	IMAGE
	(Evangelists' Symbols)
	(Decapitation of Dennis)
	(Cosmas and Damian)
	(Lawrence)
	(All Martyrs)
	(Remigius with Kneeling Charles V)
	*Anthony with Kneeling Charles V (4)
	*Julian the Hospitaller in a Boat (4)
	*Leonard Freeing Prisoners (4v)
	(Louis with Kneeling Charles V)
	(Louis of Toulouse with Kneeling Charles V)
	(Gile with the Hind)
	(Charlemagne)
	(Confessors)
	(Mary Magdalene)
	(Catherine Confounding the Doctors)
	(Apollonia)
	(Agnes with Kneeling Charles V)
	(Ursula and 11,000 Virgins)
	(All Virgins)
	(Charles V Praying)
	(Saints)
	(Charles V Praying)
(Prayers to God, for Mass, when going to bed and waking up, to the Cross, St. Dennis, St. Louis, for Communion, to the Trinity, God, when waking up, to John the Evangelist)	(Charles V Praying)
	(Charles V Praying to Christ)
	(Charles V Praying to Trinity)
	(Charles V Praying to the Virgin)
	(Charles V Praying to a Crucifix)
	(Charles V Praying to Statue of Christ)
	(Presentation in the Temple)
	(Entombment, with Charles V Kissing Hand of Christ)
	(Charles V Praying to the Trinity)
	(Charles V Praying)
	(Crucifixion, with Charles V)
	(Charles V Praying)
	(Charles V Assisting at Mass)
	(Charles V Praying to God)
	(Charles V Praying)
	(Charles V Kissing a Cross)
	(Charles V Praying to a Statue of Dennis, Rusticus, and Eleutherius)
	(Charles V Praying to a Statue of Louis)
	(Charles V Receiving Communion)
	(Charles V Praying to a Statue)
	(Charles V before Christ)
	(Charles V before a Vision of Christ)
	(Charles V Assisting at Mass)
	(Charles V Praying in Bed)
	(John the Evangelist Writing)
(Mass of the Trinity, of St. Dennis, of the Dead, of St. Louis, of Angels, of the Holy Spirit, of the Cross, of Relics, of the Virgin)	(Trinity)
	(Dennis Carrying His Head)
	(Funeral Mass)
	(Louis Burying the Dead)
	(Angels)
	(Pentecost)
	(Charles V Kissing a Cross)
	(Charles V Praying before Relics)
	(Charles V Praying to the Virgin)
(Suffrages)	(Peter and Paul with Charles V and Jeanne de Bourbon)
(Psalter of St. Jerome)	(Jerome Writing)
(Ex-libris of Jean, Duc de Berry, and list of contents, written by Jean Flamel)	

BIBLIOGRAPHY: Wieck, "The Savoy Hours and Its Impact and Jean, Duc de Berry."

12 Fig. 39

Walters Art Museum, MS W. 84.

Northern France, ca. 1360.

Vellum, 244 leaves, 2¼ x 1¾ in. (5.9 x 4.5 cm), 1 column, 10 lines, in Latin and French, in *textura*, 8 miniatures and 2 historiated initials.

Use: Calendar: general, with one entry pointing to Rheims; Hours of the Virgin: Rheims; Office of the Dead: Rheims.

TEXT	IMAGE
Calendar (1–12v)	
Hours of the Virgin (13–115)	
Matins	Annunciation (13)
Lauds	Visitation, in "D" (34v)
Prime	Nativity (55)
Terce	Annunciation to the Shepherds (66v)
Sext	Adoration of the Magi (74v)
None	Presentation in the Temple (81v)
Vespers	Massacre of the Innocents (89)
Compline	Flight into Egypt (104v)
Penitential Psalms, Litany (117–148v)	Christ as Judge, in "D" (117)
Office of the Dead (149v–242)	Funeral Service (149v)

BIBLIOGRAPHY: Randall, *Medieval and Renaissance Manuscripts*, I, 184–86, no. 69, fig. 139.

❖ ❖ ❖

13 Fig. 43

Washington, D.C., Library of Congress, Edith G. Rosenwald Hours.

France, Paris, ca. 1360.

Vellum, 163 leaves, 2⅝ x 2 in. (6.6 x 4.9 cm), 1 column, 10 lines, in Latin, in *textura*, 23 miniatures and 11 calendar and 12 zodiacal vignettes, by the Master of the *Livre du Sacre de Charles V.*

Use: Calendar: Bruges; Hours of the Virgin: Rome.

TEXT	IMAGE
Calendar (1v–13)	Zodiacal sign on each recto
Jan.	Feasting (modern replacement, 1v)
Feb.	Keeping Warm (2v)
Mar.	Pruning (3v)
Apr.	Picking Flowering Branches (4v)
May	Hawking (5v)
Jun.	Mowing (6v)
Jul.	Reaping (7v)
Aug.	Threshing (8v)
Sept.	Sowing (9v)
Oct.	Treading Grapes (10v)
Nov.	Thrashing for Acorns (11v)
Dec.	Slaughtering a Pig (12v)
	(Series of prefatory miniatures:)
	Virgo Lactans (14)
	John the Baptist (15)
	James (16)
	Christopher Carrying Christ (17)
	Anthony (18)
	Catherine (19)
	Barbara (?) (20)
	Geneviève (21)
	Margaret Emerging from the Dragon (22)
Hours of the Virgin (23–120v)	
Matins	Birth of the Virgin (23)
Lauds	(Miniature missing)
Prime	Annunciation (60v)
Terce	Visitation (77v)

Sext	Nativity (84)
None	(Miniature missing)
Vespers	Presentation in the Temple (97v)
Compline	Flight into Egypt (111v)
Penitential Psalms, Litany (121–150v)	Last Judgement (121)
Hours of the Cross (151–163)	
Matins	Betrayal (151)
Prime	Christ before Pilate (153v)
Terce	Flagellation (155)
Sext	Crucifixion (156v)
None	Deposition (158)
Vespers	Entombment (159v)
Compline	Resurrection (161)

BIBLIOGRAPHY: Schutzner, *Medieval and Renaissance Manuscript Books,* 283–86, MS 45, pl. XVII.

❖ ❖ ❖

14 Fig. 6

Walters Art Museum, MS W. 89 ("Hours of Isabelle de Coucy").

France, Paris, ca. 1380, made for Isabelle de Coucy, wife of Raoul II de Raineval.

Vellum, 161 leaves, 4½ x 3¼ in. (11.5 x 8.3 cm), 1 column, 11 lines, in French and Latin, in *textura,* 3 large miniatures, 9 armorial initials, and numerous marginalia, by the Master of the *Rational des divins offices.*

Use: Hours of the Virgin: Paris.

TEXT	IMAGE
	(Series of prefatory miniatures:)
	Catherine (1v)
	Margaret Emerging from the Dragon (2v)
	Madonna with Kneeling Isabelle de Coucy; border: Coucy arms (3v)
Hours of the Virgin (4–134v)	
Matins	Raineval/Coucy arms, in "D" (4)
Lauds	Raineval arms, in "D" (36v)
Prime	Coucy arms, in "D" (66v)
Terce	Raineval arms, in "D" (79)
Sext	Coucy arms, in "D" (86v)
None	Raineval arms, in "D" (94)
Vespers	Raineval arms, in "D" (103)
Compline	Coucy arms, in "D" (122)
Penitential Pslams (135–160)	Raineval arms, in "D" (135)

BIBLIOGRAPHY: Randall, *Medieval and Renaissance Manuscripts,* I, 194–95, no. 73, figs. 146, 147.

❖ ❖ ❖

15 Pl. 19

Walters Art Museum, MS W. 96.

France, Paris, ca. 1390.

Vellum, 348 leaves, 6⅛ x 4⅜ in. (15.6 x 11.2 cm), 1 column, 16 lines, in Latin and French, in *textura,* 14 large miniatures by followers of Jacquemart de Hesdin.

Use: Calendar: Paris; Hours of the Virgin: Paris; Office of the Dead: Paris.

TEXT	IMAGE
Calendar (1–12v)	
Gospel Lessons (13–16v)	
O Maria piissima, Obsecro te, O intemerata (two versions), Stabat mater (17–27)	
Passion according to John (27–28v)	
Hours of the Virgin (30–90v)	
Matins	Annunciation (30)
Lauds	Visitation (50)
Prime	Nativity (60)
Terce	Annunciation to the Shepherds (65v)
Sext	Adoration of the Magi (70)
None	Presentation in the Temple (74)
Vespers	Flight into Egypt (78v)
Compline	Coronation of the Virgin (85v)
Penitential Psalms, Litany (92–108)	Christ in Majesty (92)
Hours of the Cross (108v–111v)	Crucifixion (108v)
Hours of the Holy Spirit (112–115)	Pentecost (112)
Hours of the Conception of the Virgin (115v–118v)	Meeting at the Golden Gate (115v)
15 Joys of the Virgin (119–122v)	(Miniature missing)
7 Requests to Our Lord (123–126v)	Christ as Judge (123)
Mass of the Holy Spirit, of the Virgin, of the Dead (127–135v)	
5 Joys of the Virgin, followed by various prayers (135v–137v)	
Office of the Dead (138–202v)	Funeral Service (138)
Suffrages (204–215v)	
Various prayers including those recited when waking up, to the Eucharist, when going to bed, 7 Verses of St. Bernard (216–348v)	

BIBLIOGRAPHY: Randall, *Medieval and Renaissance Manuscripts,* I, 205–09, no. 76, figs. 153–55.

❖ ❖ ❖

16 Fig. 35

Walters Art Museum, MS W. 94.

France, Paris, end of the 14th century.

Vellum, 186 leaves, 5⅜ x 4⅛ in. (13.6 x 10.5 cm), 1 column, 15 lines, in Latin and French, in *textura,* 11 large miniatures by the workshop of Pseudo-Jacquemart de Hesdin.

Use: Calendar: Paris; Hours of the Virgin: Paris; Office of the Dead: Paris.

TEXT	IMAGE
Calendar (1–12v)	
Gospel Lessons (13–17v)	
Hours of the Virgin (19–80)	
Matins	(Miniature missing)
Lauds	Visitation (40v)
Prime	Nativity (51v)
Terce	Annunciation to the Shepherds (57v)
Sext	Adoration of the Magi (61v)
None	Presentation in the Temple (retouched, 65v)
Vespers	Flight into Egypt (69v)
Compline	(Miniature missing)
Hours of the Cross (80v–83v)	Crucifixion (80v)
Hours of the Holy Spirit (84–87)	Trinity (84)
Penitential Psalms, Litany (89–107v)	(Miniature missing)
Office of the Dead (108–153)	Funeral Service (108)
15 Joys of the Virgin (153v–159)	Madonna with Kneeling Patroness (153v)
7 Requests to Our Lord (159–161v)	Last Judgement (159)
Obsecro te, O intemerata (163–169v)	
Mass of the Holy Spirit, of the Cross, of the Virgin, of the Dead (169v–179v)	

Suffrages (179v–186v)
BIBLIOGRAPHY: Randall, *Medieval and Renaissance Manuscripts,* I, 202–05, no. 75, figs. 151, 152.

❖ ❖ ❖

17 Pl. 28

Walters Art Museum, MS W. 237.

France, Avignon, ca. 1400.

Vellum, 190 leaves, 6⅞ x 4½ in. (16 x 11.5 cm), 1 column, 14 lines, in Latin, in *textura,* 18 miniatures.

Use: Calendar: general; Hours of the Virgin: Rome; Office of the Dead: Rome.

TEXT	IMAGE
Calendar (1–12v)	
Gospel Lessons (13–17v)	
Hours of the Virgin (18–93v)	
Matins	Annunciation (18)
Lauds	Visitation (30v)
Prime	Nativity (43v)
Terce	Annunciation to the Shepherds (48v)
Sext	Adoration of the Magi (53v)
None	Presentation in the Temple (58)
Vespers	Massacre of the Innocents (63)
Compline	Flight into Egypt (71v)
Hours of the Cross (94–104)	
Matins	Betrayal (94)
Prime	Christ Mocked (95v)
Terce	Christ Carrying the Cross (97)
Sext	Crucifixion (98v)
None	Christ's Side Pierced (100)
Vespers	Deposition (101v)
Compline	Entombment (103)
Hours of the Holy Spirit (104v–107v)	Trinity (104v)
Penitential Pslams, Litany (110–131)	Christ Enthroned (110)
Office of the Dead (131v–180v)	Funeral Service (131v)
Obsecro te, Prayer of Charlemagne, and other prayers (added later, 182–190)	

BIBLIOGRAPHY: Randall, *Medieval and Renaissance Manuscripts,* I, 210–13, no. 78, pl. VId, fig. 156.

❖ ❖ ❖

18 Fig. 63

Walters Art Museum, MS W. 99.

Northern France, early 15th century.

Vellum, 181 leaves, 6¾ x 4¾ in. (17.3 x 12.1 cm), 1 column, 13 lines, in Latin and French, in *textura,* 8 large miniatures.

Use: Calendar: northern France/southern Belgium, with entries pointing to Soissons; Hours of the Virgin: Soissons (variant); Office of the Dead: Soissons.

TEXT	IMAGE
Calendar (1–12v)	
Gospel Lessons (13–18v)	
Hours of the Virgin (19–78v)	
Matins	Annunciation (19)
Lauds	Visitation (32)
Prime	(Miniature missing)
Terce	(Miniature missing)
Sext	Adoration of the Magi (55)
None	Presentation in the Temple (60)
Vespers	(Miniature missing)
Compline	Coronation of Virgin (73)
Penitential Pslams, Litany (79–100)	Christ Enthroned between the Eucharist and Tablets of the Law (79)
Office of the Dead (101–152)	Funeral Service (101)
Hours of the Cross (153–156)	(Miniature missing)
Glorieuse vierge royne (157–167)	Madonna with Kneeling Patron (157)
O intemerata, Obsecro te (169–178v)	
Suffrages (178v–181)	

BIBLIOGRAPHY: Randall, *Medieval and Renaissance Manuscripts,* I, 257–59, no. 92, fig. 177.

❖ ❖ ❖

19 Pl. 24

Walters Art Museum, MS W. 231.

France, Paris, ca. 1405.

Vellum, 163 leaves, 7¼ x 5 in. (18.3 x 12.9 cm), 1 column, 16 lines, in Latin and French, in *textura,* 20 large miniatures by the Luçon Master and his workshop.

Use: Calendar: Paris; Hours of the Virgin: Paris; Office of the Dead: Paris.

TEXT	IMAGE
(Text erased)	Madonna (1)
Calendar (2–13v)	
Gospel Lessons (John only, 15; 16 added later)	John Writing, Matthew Examining Pen, Mark Sharpening Pen, Luke Contemplating (14v)
Hours of the Virgin (17–72v)	
Matins	Annunciation (17)
Lauds	Visitation (37)
Prime	Nativity (46)
Terce	Annunciation to the Shepherds (51)
Sext	Adoration of the Magi (54v)
None	Presentation in the Temple (58)
Vespers	Flight into Egypt (62)
Compline	Coronation of the Virgin (68)
Weekday Hours (73–88)	
Salve regina misericordie, Concede nos famulos tuos (89–v)	Madonna with Kneeling Patroness Presented by John the Baptist and Catherine (89)
15 Joys of the Virgin? (original text erased, 90–91)	First Bath of Christ (90)
Prayer for Assumption of the Virgin (92)	Death of the Virgin (91v)
Penitential Psalms, Litany (93–108v)	David in Prayer (93)
Passion according to John? (original text erased, 109v)	Betrayal (109v)
Hours of the Cross (110–115v)	Christ Carrying the Cross (110)
Stabat mater (ending with later addition, 116v–118v)	Crucifixion (116v)
7 Requests to Our Lord (original text erased, 119–v)	Man of Sorrows (119)
Hours of Holy Spirit (120–124v)	Pentecost (120)
Office of the Dead (125–163v)	Last Judgement (125)

BIBLIOGRAPHY: Randall, *Medieval and Renaissance Manuscripts,* I, 228–32, no. 84, figs. 164–66.

❖ ❖ ❖

20 Fig. 16

Walters Art Museum, MS W. 103.

France, Paris, 1400–10.

Vellum, 149 leaves, 7¼ x 5⅝ in. (19.8 x 14.2 cm), 1 column, 17 lines, in Latin and French, in *textura,* 22 small miniatures, 1 historiated initial, and 12 calendar vignettes, by the workshop of the Luçon Master.

Use: Calendar: mainly Paris, but with some entries pointing to St. Omer; Hours of the Virgin: Avranches; Office of the Dead: Nantes.

TEXT	IMAGE
Calendar (1–12v)	
Jan.	Feasting (1)
Feb.	Keeping Warm (2)
Mar.	Pruning (3)
Apr.	Picking Flowers (4)
May	Hawking (5)
Jun.	Mowing (6)
Jul.	Reaping (7)
Aug.	Threshing (8)
Sept.	Treading Grapes (9)
Oct.	Sowing (10)
Nov.	Thrashing for Acorns (11)
Dec.	Slaughtering a Pig (12)
Gospel Lessons (14–19)	John on Patmos (14)
	Luke Examining Pen (15v)
	Matthew Writing (17)
	Mark Writing (18v)
Prayers to guardian angel, St. Michael, St. Firminus (19v–20v)	Angel with Kneeling Patroness (19v)
Hours of the Virgin (22–79v)	
Matins	Annunciation (22)
Lauds	Visitation, in "D" (30v)
Matins of the Hours of the Cross	Betrayal (41)
Prime	Nativity (43)
Prime of the Cross	Christ before Pilate (48)
Terce	Annunciation to the Shepherds (49v)
Terce of the Cross	Christ Carrying the Cross (53v)
Sext	Adoration of the Magi (55)
Sext of the Cross	Crucifixion (59)
None	Presentation in the Temple (60v)
None of the Cross	Crucifixion with Longinus (64v)
Vespers	Flight into Egypt (66)
Vespers of the Cross	Deposition (72)
Compline	Coronation of the Virgin (73v)
Compline of the Cross	Entombment (78)
7 Requests to Our Lord, Je te salue Maria (80–85v)	
Penitential Psalms, Litany (86–101v)	David in Prayer (86)
Suffrages (102–117v)	
Office of the Dead (118–148)	Funeral Service (118)
Prayer to St. Christopher (148v–149v)	Christopher Carrying Christ (148v)

BIBLIOGRAPHY: Randall, *Medieval and Renaissance Manuscripts,* I, 225–28, no. 83, figs. 162, 163.

❖ ❖ ❖

21 — Pl. 32, Fig. 83

Walters Art Museum, MS W. 232.

France, Paris, ca. 1410.

Vellum, 212 leaves, 6¾ x 5⅛ in. (17.2 x 13 cm), 1 column, 14 lines, in Latin and French, in *textura,* 16 large miniatures by the Luçon Master and a follower of the Master of Berry's *Cleres Femmes.*

Use: Calendar: Paris; Hours of the Virgin: Paris; Office of the Dead: Paris.

TEXT	IMAGE
Calendar (1–12v)	
Gospel Lessons, Salve regina (13–18)	
Hours of the Virgin (19–85)	
Matins	Annunciation (19)
Lauds	Visitation (42v)
Prime	Nativity (53v)
Terce	Annunciation to the Shepherds (59v)
Sext	Adoration of the Magi (64)
None	Presentation in the Temple (68v)
Vespers	Flight into Egypt (73)
Compline	Coronation of the Virgin (80)
Hours of St. Catherine (85v–92v)	Catherine Confounding the Doctors (85v)
Prayer of Blessed Peter of Luxembourg, Prayer of St. Augustine (93–104v)	Peter Kneeling before a Vision of the Crucifixion (93)
Penitential Psalms, Litany (105–124)	David in Prayer (105)
Hours of the Cross (124v–132)	Crucifixion (124v)
Hours of the Holy Spirit (132v–138v)	Pentecost (132v)
Office of the Dead (139–183v)	Funeral Service (139)
Obsecro te, O intemerata (183v–190v)	
15 Joys of the Virgin (191–196)	Virgo Lactans (191)
7 Requests to Our Lord (196v–199)	Last Judgement (196v)
Mass of the Virgin, of the Holy Spirit, of the Cross, of the Dead (199v–209)	

BIBLIOGRAPHY: Randall, *Medieval and Renaissance Manuscripts,* I, 232–35, no. 85, pl. VIIb, figs. 167, 168.

❖ ❖ ❖

22 — Fig. 111

Walters Art Museum, MS W. 209.

France, Paris, ca. 1405–10.

Vellum, 263 leaves, 5⅜ x 3⅜ in. (13.5 x 8.6 cm), 1 column, 13 lines, in Latin and French, in *textura,* 12 miniatures by the Master of Berry's *Cleres Femmes* and his workshop.

Use: Calendar: Paris; Hours of the Virgin: Paris; Office of the Dead: Paris.

TEXT	IMAGE
Calendar (1–12v)	
Gospel Lessons (13–19v)	
Obsecro te, O intemerata, 7 Verses of St. Bernard, followed by various prayers including the Passion according to Matthew (19v–36v)	
Hours of the Virgin (37–109v)	
Matins	Annunciation (37)
Lauds	Visitation (51v)
Prime	Nativity (66v)
Terce	Annunciation to the Shepherds (75)
Sext	Adoration of the Magi (81v)
None	Presentation in the Temple (87)
Vespers	Flight into Egypt (92v)
Compline	Coronation of the Virgin (102)
Penitential Psalms, Litany (110–133)	God the Father in Majesty (110)
Hours of the Cross (133v–142)	Crucifixion (133v)
Hours of the Holy Spirit (142v–150v)	Pentecost (142v)
Office of the Dead (151–215v)	Funeral Service (151)
Mass of the Holy Spirit, of the Cross, of the Virgin, of the Dead (216–230v)	
Suffrages (230v–239)	
Various prayers including the 5 Joys of the Virgin (240–263v)	

BIBLIOGRAPHY: Randall, *Medieval and Renaissance Manuscripts,* I, 235–38, no. 86, pl. VIIc, fig. 169.

23

Pl. 16

Walters Art Museum, MS W. 265.

France, Paris, ca. 1410–20.

Vellum, 247 leaves, 7⅜ x 4⅞ in. (18.8 x 12.4 cm), 1 column, 13 lines, in Latin and French, in *textura*, 15 large miniatures by an artist related to the Master of Berry's *Cleres Femmes*.

Use: Calendar: Paris; Hours of the Virgin: Paris; Office of the Dead: Paris.

TEXT	IMAGE
Calendar (3–14v)	
Gospel Lessons (15–22)	John on Patmos (15)
	Luke Writing (17)
	Matthew Writing (19)
	Mark Writing (21)
Transfiguration according to Mark, Apostles' Creed, 10 Commandments, 7 Works of Mercy, 7 Sacraments, 7 Gifts of the Holy Spirit, 3 Theological Virtues, 4 Cardinal Virtues, 7 Last Words of Our Lord (22v–30v)	Transfiguration (22v)
Hours of the Virgin (31–104)	
Matins	(Miniature missing)
Lauds	Visitation (56v)
Prime	Nativity (69)
Terce	(Miniature missing)
Sext	Adoration of the Magi (80)
None	Presentation in the Temple (85)
Vespers	Flight into Egypt (90)
Compline	Coronation of the Virgin (98)
Penitential Psalms, Litany (105–127v)	David in Prayer (105)
Hours of the Cross (128–135v)	Crucifixion (128)
Hours of the Holy Spirit (136–141v)	(Miniature missing)
Office of the Dead (142–193)	Funeral Service (142)
15 Joys of the Virgin (194–200)	Madonna Enthroned, with Kneeling Patroness (194)
7 Requests to Our Lord, followed by numerous prayers including Obsecro te, O intemerata, 5 Joys of the Virgin, Athanasian Creed, prayers said before and after receiving Communion, 5 Joys of St. Catherine, Prayer of St. Theophilus (201–247v)	(Miniature missing)

BIBLIOGRAPHY: Randall, *Medieval and Renaissance Manuscripts*, I, 238–42, no. 87, pl. VIId, fig. 170.

❖ ❖ ❖

24

Fig. 54

Walters Art Museum, MS W. 271.

France, Paris (?), early 15th century.

Vellum, 252 leaves, 8 x 5½ in. (20.5 x 14 cm), 1 column, 15 lines, in Latin and French, in *textura*, 20 large miniatures by a follower of the Boucicaut Master and other painters.

Use: Calendar: Paris, but with some entries pointing to southern Belgium; Hours of the Virgin: Paris; Office of the Dead: Paris.

TEXT	IMAGE
Calendar (1–12v)	
Obsecro te, O intemerata, Salve regina, Omnipotens sempiterne Deus (13–21v)	
Gospel Lessons, preceded by various prayers (incomplete, 21v–25v)	
Hours of the Virgin (26–92)	
Matins	Annunciation (26)
Lauds	Visitation (50)
Prime	Nativity (61v)
Terce	Annunciation to the Shepherds (67v)
Sext	Adoration of the Magi (72v)
None	Presentation in the Temple (77)
Vespers	Flight into Egypt (81v)
Compline	(Miniature missing)
Penitential Psalms, Litany (93–110)	David in Prayer (93)
Hours of the Cross (110v–116)	Helena Excavating the True Cross (110v)
Hours of the Trinity (117–120v)	Trinity (117)
Hours of the Holy Spirit (121–122)	(Miniature missing)
Office of the Dead (121v–167)	Funeral Service (121v)
15 Joys of the Virgin (168–173)	Madonna with Kneeling Patroness Presented by Catherine (168)
7 Requests to Our Lord (173v–177)	Christ as Judge, with Evangelists' Symbols (173v)
Hours of the Passion (178–220v)	
Matins	Betrayal (178)
Lauds	Christ Mocked (185v)
Prime	Flagellation (191v)
Terce	Christ Carrying the Cross (195)
Sext	Christ Nailed to the Cross (200v)
None	Crucifixion (205v)
Vespers	Deposition (212v)
Compline	(Miniature missing)
7 Last Words of Our Lord, followed by various prayers including those recited to the Eucharist, before and after receiving Communion, against Thunder (221–236v)	
Suffrages (237–252v)	

BIBLIOGRAPHY: Randall, *Medieval and Renaissance Manuscripts*, I, 267–70, no. 95, figs. 181, 182.

❖ ❖ ❖

25

Fig. 57

Walters Art Museum, MS W. 238.

France, Paris, ca. 1412.

Vellum, 170 leaves, 7¼ x 5¼ in. (18.4 x 13.4 cm), 1 column, 16 lines, in Latin and French, in *textura*, 13 large miniatures by the workshop of the Boucicaut Master.

Use: Calendar: Paris; Hours of the Virgin: Paris; Office of the Dead: Paris.

TEXT	IMAGE
Calendar (1–12v)	
Gospel Lessons (13–17)	
Passion according to John (17–19)	
Obsecro te, O intemerata (19–24v)	
Hours of the Virgin (25–79v)	
Matins	Annunciation (25)
Lauds	Visitation (45)
Prime	Nativity (54v)
Terce	Annunciation to the Shepherds (59v)
Sext	(Miniature missing)
None	Presentation in the Temple (65v)
Vespers	Flight into Egypt (69)
Compline	Coronation of the Virgin (75)
Hours of the Cross (79v–82)	Crucifixion (79v)
Hours of the Holy Spirit (82v–85)	Pentecost (82v)
Penitential Psalms, Litany (86–103v)	David in Prayer (86)
15 Joys of the Virgin (104–109)	Madonna Enthroned, with Angel (104)
7 Requests to Our Lord (109–112)	Christ as Judge (109)

Office of the Dead (112v–152)	Funeral Service (112v)
Suffrages (152–169v)	
Prayer to the Eucharist (added somewhat later, 170–v)	

BIBLIOGRAPHY: Randall, *Medieval and Renaissance Manuscripts,* I, 252–54, no. 90, fig. 174.

❖ ❖ ❖

26 Pl. 25, Fig. 73

Walters Art Museum, MS W. 260.

France, Paris, ca. 1415.

Vellum, 250 leaves, 7¼ x 5⅝ in. (19.6 x 14.4 cm), 1 column, 14 lines, in Latin and French, in *textura,* 13 large and 4 small (Gospel Lessons) miniatures, 24 historiated initials, 12 calendar and 12 zodiacal vignettes, and border figures throughout, by the workshop of the Boucicaut Master and another painter.

Use: Calendar: Paris; Hours of the Virgin: Paris; Office of the Dead: Paris.

TEXT	IMAGE
Calendar (1–12v)	Zodiacal sign on each recto
Jan.	Triple-faced Woman Feasting (1)
Feb.	Keeping Warm (2)
Mar.	Pruning (3)
Apr.	Picking Flowers (4)
May	Hawking (5)
Jun.	Carrying Produce (6)
Jul.	Sharpening a Scythe (7)
Aug.	Reaping (8)
Sept.	Treading Grapes (9)
Oct.	Sowing (10)
Nov.	Thrashing for Acorns (11)
Dec.	Slaughering a Pig (12)
Gospel Lessons (13–17v)	John on Patmos (13)
	Luke Writing (14)
	Matthew Examining Pen (15v)
	Mark Writing (17)
Obsecro te, O intemerata, 7 Verses of St. Bernard (18–26v)	Madonna, in "O" (18)
	Virgin with a Book, in "O" (21v)
Hours of the Virgin (27–97v)	
Matins	Annunciation (27)
Lauds	Visitation (51v)
Prime	Preparation of Christ's Bath (63v)
Terce	Annunciation to the Shepherds (70)
Sext	Adoration of the Magi (75)
None	Presentation in the Temple (80)
Vespers	Flight into Egypt (84v)
Compline	Death of the Virgin (92)
Penitential Psalms, Litany (98–115v)	(Miniature missing)
Hours of the Cross (116–122v)	Crucifixion (116)
Hours of the Holy Spirit (123–128v)	Pentecost (123)
Office of the Dead (129–176v)	Funeral Service (129)
Athanasian Creed, followed by various prayers including 7 Last Words of Our Lord (177–194v)	(Miniature missing?)
O intemerata, Stabat mater, 25 Joys of the Virgin, Suffrages, Passion according to John, various prayers (195–216v)	
15 Joys of the Virgin (217–223)	Madonna with Christ Playing a Psaltery (217)
7 Requests to Our Lord (223v–227v)	Christ as Judge (223v)
Suffrages (227v–237)	Trinity, in "T" (227v)
	Madonna, in "S" (228)
	Michael, in "M" (229)
	John the Baptist, in "I" (229v)
	James, in "A" (230)
	Andrew, in "A" (230v)
	John the Evangelist, in "V" (231)
	Simon and Jude, in "T" (231v)
	Lapidation of Stephen, in "T" (232)
	Grilling of Lawrence, in "L" (232v)
	Christopher Carrying Christ, in "X" (233)
	Martin Dividing His Cloak, in "D" (233v)
	Nicholas Resuscitating the Three Boys, in "B" (234)
	Maurus, in "I" (234v)
	Mary Magdalene, in "M" (235)
	Catherine, in "V" (235v)
	Margaret Emerging from the Dragon, in "A" (236)
	All Saints, in "G" (236v)
Mass of the Holy Spirit (237–241v)	Priest Celebrating Mass, in "S" (237)
Mass of the Virgin (242–243v)	Virgin at Mass, in "S" (242)
Mass of the Dead (244–246v)	Funeral Service, in "R" (244)
Mass of the Trinity (247–250v)	Priest Celebrating Mass, in "B" (247)

BIBLIOGRAPHY: Randall, *Medieval and Renaissance Manuscripts,* I, 261–66, no. 94, fig. 180.

❖ ❖ ❖

27 Fig. 112

Walters Art Museum, MS W. 276.

France, Paris, ca. 1410–20.

Vellum, 158 leaves, 8⅛ x 5¼ in. (20.5 x 14.8 cm), 1 column, 15 lines, in Latin, in *textura,* 14 large miniatures by the Guise Master and other followers of the Boucicaut Master.

Use: Hours of the Virgin: Paris; Office of the Dead: Paris.

TEXT	IMAGE
Gospel Lessons (2–6v)	
Obsecro te (7–10)	
Hours of the Virgin (11–78v)	
Matins	Annunciation (11)
Lauds	Visitation (35)
Prime	Nativity (47v)
Terce	Annunciation to the Shepherds (53v)
Sext	Adoration of the Magi (58)
None	Presentation in the Temple (62)
Vespers	Flight into Egypt (66v)
Compline	Coronation of the Virgin (73v)
Penitential Psalms, Litany (79–96v)	David in Prayer (79)
Hours of the Cross (97–104)	Crucifixion (97)
Hours of the Holy Spirit (104v–110v)	Pentecost (104v)
Office of the Dead (111–154v)	Funeral Service (111)
Suffrages (155–158)	Nicholas Resuscitating the Three Boys (155)
	Mary Magdalene (156)

BIBLIOGRAPHY: Randall, *Medieval and Renaissance Manuscripts,* I, 259–61, no. 93, figs. 178, 179.

❖ ❖ ❖

28 Fig. 26

Walters Art Museum, MS W. 254.

France, Paris, ca. 1420.

Vellum, 193 leaves, 7⅜ x 5¼ in. (18.7 x 14.5 cm), 1 column, 14 lines, in Latin and French, in *textura,* 20 large miniatures by a follower of the Boucicaut Master.

Use: Calendar: mainly Paris; Hours of the Virgin: Paris; Office of the Dead: Paris.

TEXT	IMAGE
Calendar (1–12v)	
Obsecro te, O intemerata (13–20v)	Virgin Standing (13)
	Virgin Weaving (17)
Gospel Lessons (misbound, 22–25v, 50–53)	John on Patmos (50)
	Luke Writing (22)
	Matthew Sharpening Pen (24)
	Mark Writing (52)
Hours of the Virgin (26–49v, 54–94)	
Matins	Annunciation (26)
Lauds	Visitation (48v)
Prime	Nativity (63)
Terce	Annunciation to the Shepherds (69)
Sext	Adoration of the Magi (74)
None	Presentation in the Temple (78)
Vespers	Flight into Egypt (82)
Compline	Coronation of the Virgin (89)
Penitential Psalms, Litany (96–113v)	David in Prayer (96)
Hours of the Cross (114–121v)	Crucifixion (114)
Hours of the Holy Spirit (122–128v)	Pentecost (122)
Office of the Dead (130–172v)	Burial Service (130)
15 Joys of the Virgin (173–178v)	Madonna Serenaded by an Angel (173)
7 Requests to Our Lord (179–182)	Last Judgement (179)
Suffrages (182–193v)	

BIBLIOGRAPHY: Randall, *Medieval and Renaissance Manuscripts*, II, 3–6, no. 101, fig. 191.

❖ ❖ ❖

29 Pls. 18, 34, Figs. 29, 88, 107

Walters Art Museum, MS W. 287.

France, Paris, 1420s.

Vellum, 200 leaves, 8⅞ x 6½ in. (22.6 x 16.5 cm), 1 column, 16 lines, in Latin and French, in *textura*, 40 large, and 12 calendar and 12 zodiacal vignettes, by the Master of the Harvard Hannibal.

Use: Calendar: Paris; Hours of the Virgin: Paris; Office of the Dead: Paris.

TEXT	IMAGE
Calendar (1–12v)	Zodiacal sign on each verso
Jan.	Feasting (1)
Feb.	Keeping Warm (2)
Mar.	Pruning (3)
Apr.	Picking Flowering Branches (4)
May	Hawking (5)
Jun.	Mowing (6)
Jul.	Reaping (7)
Aug.	Threshing (8)
Sept.	Sowing (9)
Oct.	Treading Grapes (10)
Nov.	Thrashing for Acorns (11)
Dec.	Slaughtering a Pig (12)
Gospel Lessons (14–21)	John on Patmos (14)
	Luke Writing (16)
	Matthew Writing (18)
	Mark Writing (20)
Passion according to John (21v–23)	Flagellation (21v)
Hours of the Virgin (24–85v)	
Matins	Annunciation (24)
Lauds	Visitation (46)
Prime	Nativity with Annunciation to the Shepherds (57)
Terce	Adoration of the Magi (63)
Sext	(Miniature missing)
None	Annunciation to the Shepherds (70)
Vespers	Flight into Egypt (74v)
Compline	Coronation of the Virgin (81)
Penitential Psalms, Litany (86–107v)	David in Prayer (86)
Hours of the Cross (108–116v)	Crucifixion (108)
Hours of the Holy Spirit (117–124v)	Pentecost (117)
Suffrages (125–148v)	Trinity (125)
	Michael Battling a Devil (126)
	John the Baptist (127)
	Peter (128)
	Paul (129)
	John the Evangelist (130)
	Martyrdom of Dennis, Eleutherius, and Rusticus (131)
	Sebastian Shot with Arrows (132)
	Claude of Besançon (133)
	Martin Dividing His Cloak (134)
	Nicholas Resuscitating the Three Boys (135)
	Anthony (136)
	Firminus of Amiens (137)
	Mary Magdalene (138)
	Anne with the Virgin (139)
	Decapitation of Catherine (140)
	Geneviève (141)
	Margaret Emerging from the Dragon (142)
	Gabriel and Other Angels (143)
	George Slaying the Dragon (144)
	Gervase and Protase (145)
	(Christopher missing)
	Maurus (147)
Office of the Dead (149–192)	Funeral Mass (149)
15 Joys of the Virgin (192v–197v)	Madonna Enthroned, Crowned and Serenaded by Angels (192v)
7 Requests to Our Lord (198–200v)	Last Judgement (198)

BIBLIOGRAPHY: Randall, *Medieval and Renaissance Manuscripts*, II, 10–17, no. 103, pl. IXb, figs. 193, 194.

❖ ❖ ❖

30 Fig. 87

Walters Art Museum, MS W. 259.

France, Paris, 1420s.

Vellum, 168 leaves, 7¼ x 5⅞ in. (19.6 x 14.9 cm), 1 column, 15 lines, in Latin and French, in *textura*, 16 miniatures by the workshop of the Master of the Harvard Hannibal.

Use: Calendar: Paris; Hours of the Virgin: Rouen; Office of the Dead: Rouen.

TEXT	IMAGE
Calendar (1–12v)	
Gospel Lessons (13–17v)	
Obsecro te, O intemerata (17v–24v)	
Hours of the Virgin (25–78v)	
Matins	Annunciation (25)
Lauds	Visitation (36v)
Prime	Nativity (49)
Terce	Annunciation to the Shepherds (55)
Sext	Adoration of the Magi (59)
None	Presentation in the Temple (63)
Vespers	Flight into Egypt (67)
Compline	Coronation of the Virgin (73v)
Suffrages (79–80v)	Peter (79)
	Andrew (80)
Penitential Psalms, Litany (81–101v)	David in Prayer (81)
Hours of the Cross (102–109v)	Crucifixion (102)

Hours of the Holy Spirit (110–115v)	Pentecost (110)
15 Joys of the Virgin (116–121)	Madonna Enthroned, Crowned (116)
7 Requests to Our Lord (121v–125)	Christ as Judge (121v)
Office of the Dead (125v–168v)	Funeral Service (125v)

BIBLIOGRAPHY: Randall, *Medieval and Renaissance Manuscripts*, II, 6–10, no. 102, pl. IXa, fig. 192.

❖ ❖ ❖

31 Fig. 116

Walters Art Museum, MS W. 741.

France, Paris (?) or Troyes (?), 1420s.

Vellum, 169 leaves, 7 x 5⅛ in. (17.8 x 13 cm), 1 column, 15 lines, in Latin and French, in *textura*, 10 miniatures by the Rohan Master and his workshop.

Use: Calendar: Troyes, but with some entries pointing to the neighboring cities of Châlons-sur-Marne and Auxerre; Hours of the Virgin: Troyes; Office of the Dead: Troyes.

TEXT	IMAGE
Calendar (1–12v)	
Gospel Lessons, Matthew only (incomplete, 13v)	Matthew Writing (mistakenly given Luke's attribute, 13)
Hours of the Virgin (14–67v)	
Matins	(Miniature missing)
Lauds	Visitation (24)
Prime	Annunciation to the Shepherds (35v)
Terce	Nativity (41v)
Sext	Adoration of the Magi (46)
None	Presentation in the Temple (50)
Vespers	Flight into Egypt (54)
Compline	(Miniature missing)
Penitential Psalms, Litany (68–93v)	David in Prayer (68)
15 Joys of the Virgin (missing, only rubrics remaining)	(Miniature missing?)
Hours of the Holy Spirit (94–97)	(Miniature missing)
Hours of the Cross (97v–101v)	Crucifixion (97v)
Office of the Dead (102–147v)	Exposed Corpse (102)
Obsecro te, O intemerata (148–156)	
Suffrages (156v–167v)	

BIBLIOGRAPHY: Randall, *Mediaval and Renaissance Manuscripts*, II, 29–35, no. 107, figs. 199, 200.

❖ ❖ ❖

32 Fig. 105

Walters Art Museum, MS W. 219.

Eastern France, 1420s.

Vellum, 265 leaves, 5⅜ x 3⅞ in. (13.6 x 10 cm), 1 column, 12 lines, in Latin and French, in *textura*, 26 large miniatures by the Master of Walters 219 and the Master of the Breviary of Jean sans Peur.

Use: Calendar: Paris; Hours of the Virgin: Rome; Office of the Dead: Rome.

TEXT	IMAGE
Calendar (4–15v)	
Gospel Lessons (16–25)	Creation of Eve (16)
	Marriage of the Virgin (18v)
	Massacre of the Innocents (21)
	John the Evangelist Resuscitating Two Condemned Men (23v)
Hours of the Virgin (26–128v)	
Matins	Virgin Weaving in the Temple (26)
Lauds	David Cutting Out the Tongue of Goliath (55)
Prime	Kiss of Justice and Peace (74)
Terce	Deathbed Scene with Michael Battling for the Soul (80v)
Sext	Death Invading a Garden Party (86v)
None	Christ Giving Adam and Eve the Spade and Spindle (92)
Vespers	Crossing of the Red Sea (98)
Compline	Flagellation (109v)
Penitential Psalms, Litany (130–157v)	Last Judgement (130)
Hours of the Cross (158–164v)	Crucifixion (158)
Hours of the Holy Spirit (165–171)	Trinity (165)
Office of the Dead (171v–233)	Raising of Lazarus (171v)
Obsecro te (234–240)	Madonna Enthroned, with Kneeling Patron Presented by Bishop Saint (234)
Prayers of the Indulgence (240v–244v)	Mass of St. Gregory (240v)
Suffrages (245–258)	Nicholas Saving the Sinking Ship (245)
	Temptation of Anthony (246v)
	Catherine Confounding the Doctors (248)
	John the Baptist (249v)
	Christopher Carrying Christ (251)
	Martyrdom of Dennis, Eleutherius, and Rusticus (253)
	Sebastian Shot with Arrows (255)
	Margaret Emerging from the Dragon (257)

BIBLIOGRAPHY: Randall, *Medieval and Renaissance Manuscripts*, I, 280–85, no. 100, figs. 189, 190.

❖ ❖ ❖

33 Pl. 31

Walters Art Museum, MS W. 289.

France, Paris (?), ca. 1425–30.

Vellum, 201 leaves, 9 x 6⅜ in. (23 x 16.1 cm), 2 columns, 23 lines, in Latin and French, in *textura*, 16 large miniatures by the workshop of the Bedford Master.

Use: Calendar: composite, but with entries pointing to Poitiers; Hours of the Virgin: Rome; Office of the Dead: Paris.

TEXT	IMAGE
Calendar (1–6v)	
Gospel Lessons, Passion according to John, 7 Last Words of Our Lord, Obsecro te, Anima Christi sanctifica me, and various prayers (7–14v)	
Hours of the Virgin (15–51v)	
Psalms for the Hours	Patroness Kneeling before a Sculpture of the Crucifixion (15)
Matins through Compline	Christ Appearing to His Mother (34)
Office of the Conception of the Virgin (52–59v)	Meeting at the Golden Gate (52)
Office of the Birth of the Virgin (60–66)	Birth of the Virgin (60)
Office of the Annunciation (66v–72)	Annunciation (66v)
Office of the Purification of the Virgin (72v–78)	Presentation in the Temple (72v)

Office of the Assumption of the Virgin (78v–87)	Assumption of the Virgin (78v)
Office of Christmas (87v–94)	Nativity (87v)
Penitential Psalms, Litany (94v–104v)	David in Prayer (94v)
Office of Easter (106–111)	Resurrection (106)
Office of the Pentecost (111v–121v)	Pentecost (111v)
Office of the Birth of John the Baptist (122–134v)	Birth of John the Baptist (122)
Office of All Saints (135–155)	Coronation of the Virgin, surrounded by All Saints (135)
Office of the Dead (156–180v)	Burial Service with Michael Battling a Devil for the Soul (156)
Hours of the Cross (181–186)	Crucifixion (181)
Hours of the Holy Spirit (186v–191)	Baptism of Christ (186v)
Obsecro te, 7 Verses of St. Bernard, Suffrages, O intemerata, other prayers (191–201v)	

BIBILIOGRAPHY: Randall, *Medieval and Renaissance Manuscripts*, II, 54–61, no. 111, pl. XIb, figs. 204–06.

❖ ❖ ❖

34 Pls. 1–12

Walters Art Museum, MS W. 288.

France, Paris, ca. 1425–30.

Vellum, 177 leaves, 8¾ x 6⅜ in. (22.3 x 16.2 cm), 1 column, 16 lines, in Latin and French, in *textura*, 12 large miniatures and 42 border roundels, by the Master of the Munich *Golden Legend*.

Use: Calendar: composite, with many Parisian entries; Hours of the Virgin: Paris; Office of the Dead: Paris.

TEXT	IMAGE
Calendar (1–12v)	
Gospel Lessons of John and Luke (13–15v)	
Hours of the Virgin (17–87v)	
Matins	Annunciation; border: Sacrifice of Joachim and Anne, Meeting at the Golden Gate, Birth of the Virgin, Virgin Praying in the Temple, Virgin Weaving, Marriage of the Virgin (17)
Lauds	Visitation; border: Birth of John the Baptist, Circumcision and Naming of John the Baptist, John the Baptist Entering the Wilderness (41)
Prime	Nativity; border: Angel Playing Lute, Fall of the Temple of Peace, Augustus and the Tiburtine Sibyl (52v)
Terce	Annunciation to the Shepherds; border: Shepherds Dancing, Adoration of the Shepherds, Shepherds Journey to Bethlehem (59)
Sext	Adoration of the Magi; border: Magi in Observation Tower, Magi Journey to Bethlehem, Magi before Herod (64)
None	Presentation in the Temple; border: Annunciation, Nativity, Annunciation to a Shepherd (68v)
Vespers	Flight into Egypt; border: Herod Commanding Soldiers, Soldier Questioning Farmer, Massacre of the Innocents (73v)
Compline	Coronation of the Virgin; border: Presentation in the Temple, Flight into Egypt, Fall of the Idols (81)
Penitential Psalms, Litany (89–107v)	David and Uriah; background: David in Prayer; border: Uriah Kisses Bathsheba Goodbye, Uriah Riding to Battle, Uriah Slain (89)
Hours of the Cross (108–116v)	Crucifixion; border: Agony in the Garden, Betrayal, Christ before Caiaphas, Flagellation, Christ Carrying the Cross, Entombment (108)
Hours of the Holy Spirit (117–124)	Pentecost; border: Ascension, Apostle Baptizing, Apostle Preaching (117)
Office of the Dead (124–171v)	Funeral Service; border: Man Placing Corpse in Coffin, Funeral Procession, Man Praying at Grave Site (124v)
7 Last Words of Our Lord, followed by various prayers (171v–176v)	

BIBLIOGRAPHY: Randall, *Medieval and Renaissance Manuscripts*, II, 40–45, no. 109, fig. 202.

❖ ❖ ❖

35 Pls. 17, 33, Fig. 34

Walters Art Museum, MS W. 281.

Northern France or Belgium, Tournai, ca. 1430–35.

Vellum, 242 leaves, 7⅞ x 5¾ in. (20.2 x 14.5 cm), 1 column, 14 lines, in Latin, in *textura*, 27 large miniatures, many with border figures, by the Master of Walters 281 and possibly the Master of Morgan 453.

Use: Calendar: northern France; Hours of the Virgin: Rome; Office of the Dead: Rome.

TEXT	IMAGE
Calendar (1v–13)	
Gospel Lessons (15–22)	John on Patmos (15) Luke Painting the Virgin (17) Matthew Writing and Seeing Vision of the Madonna (19) Mark Writing (21)
Obsecro te, O intemerata (22v–29v)	
Hours of the Virgin (31–118v)	
Matins	Marriage of the Virgin; border: Virgin Weaving (added somewhat later, 30v) Annunciation (31)
Lauds	Visitation (64)
Prime	Nativity (79)
Terce	Annunciation to the Shepherds (85)
Sext	Adoration of the Magi (91)
None	Presentation in the Temple (97)
Vespers	Flight into Egypt (103)
Compline	Coronation of the Virgin (112)
Penitential Psalms, Litany (119–142v)	David in Prayer (119)
Hours of the Cross (143–154v)	Crucifixion (143)
Hours of the Holy Spirit (155–166v)	Pentecost (155)
Office of the Dead (167–227v)	Funeral Mass (167)
Suffrages (228–242v)	Trinity (228) Michael Battling Devils (230) John the Baptist (231) John the Evangelist (232) Bartholomew with Kneeling Patron (233)

	Christopher Carrying Christ (234)
	Anthony Nourished by an Angel (236)
	Mary Magdalene Levitated by Angels (237)
	Catherine (239)
	Avia Given Communion by the Virgin (241)

BIBLIOGRAPHY: Randall, *Medieval and Renaissance Manuscripts,* II, 61–68, no. 112, pl. XIc, figs. 207, 208.

❖ ❖ ❖

36 Fig. 118

Walters Art Museum, MS W. 262.

France, Amiens, 1430s.

Vellum, 142 leaves, 7 1/4 x 5 1/4 in. (19.7 x 14.6 cm), 1 column, 17 lines, in Latin and French, in *textura,* 14 large miniatures by a follower of the Master of Walters 281.

Use: Calendar: Amiens; Hours of the Virgin: Amiens; Office of the Dead: Amiens.

TEXT	IMAGE
Calendar (1–12v)	
Gospel Lessons (13–16v)	
Hours of the Virgin (17–60v)	
Matins	Annunciation (17)
Lauds	Visitation (27)
Prime	Nativity (36)
Terce	Annunciation to the Shepherds (41)
Sext	Adoration of the Magi (44v)
None	Presentation in the Temple (47v)
Vespers	Flight into Egypt (51)
Compline	Coronation of the Virgin (57)
Penitential Psalms, Litany (61–75v)	David in Prayer (61)
Hours of the Cross (76–78v)	Crucifixion (76)
Hours of the Holy Spirit (79–81v)	Pentecost (79)
Suffrages (82–88v)	Margaret Emerging from the Dragon (87)
7 Verses of the St. Bernard (89–v)	
Office of the Dead (misbound: this and next text originally followed Hours of Holy Spirit, 90–128v)	Burial Service (90)
5 Joys of the Virgin (129–v)	
Obsecro te, O intemerata (130–134v)	
15 Joys of the Virgin (135–139v)	Madonna Enthroned, with Patroness Presented by John the Baptist (135)
7 Requests to Our Lord (139–142v)	

BIBLIOGRAPHY: Randall, *Medieval and Renaissance Manuscripts,* II, 79–83, no. 115, pl. XIIa, fig. 211.

❖ ❖ ❖

37 Fig. 60

Philadelphia, Philadelphia Museum of Art, MS 1945–65–4 ("Collins Hours").

France, Amiens, or Belgium, Bruges, ca. 1440.

Vellum, 188 leaves, 7 7/8 x 5 1/2 in. (20 x 14 cm), 1 column, 17 lines, in Latin, in *textura,* 26 large miniatures by the Master of the Collins Hours.

Use: Calendar: composite; Hours of the Virgin: Rome; Office of the Dead: Rome.

TEXT	IMAGE
Calendar (1–12v)	
Hours of the Cross (14–26)	
Matins	Betrayal (13v)
Prime	Flagellation (15v)
Terce	Christ Carrying the Cross (17v)
Sext	(Miniature missing)
None	Entombment (20v)
Vespers	Resurrection (22v)
Compline	Harrowing of Hell (24v)
Gospel Lessons (28–36v)	John on Patmos (27v)
	Luke Writing (29v)
	Matthew Reading (32v)
	Mark Writing (35v)
Mass of the Virgin (38–42v)	Virgo Lactans (37v)
Hours of the Virgin (44–105v)	
Matins	Annunciation (43v)
Lauds	Visitation (61v)
Prime	Nativity (73v)
Terce	Annunciation to the Shepherds (78v)
Sext	Presentation in the Temple (83v)
None	Adoration of the Magi (88v)
Vespers	Flight into Egypt (93v)
Compline	Coronation of the Virgin (101v)
Penitential Psalms, Litany (108–127v)	David in Prayer (107v)
Office of the Dead (129–169)	Absolution (128v)
O intermerata, Obsecro te (171–176v)	Madonna Enthroned, with Angel (170v)
	Virgin Weaving (173v)
Stabat mater, various prayers (177–181v)	(Patroness Kneeling before an Altar; 1 of 3 miniatures missing)
Suffrages (183–187)	Destruction of Catherine's Torture Wheels (182v)
	Mary Magdalene (184v)
	Christ Speaking to the Woman Taken in Adultery (186v)

BIBLIOGRAPHY: Tanis et al., *Leaves of Gold,* 78–81, no. 19, illus. p. 79, fig. 19-1, frontispiece.

❖ ❖ ❖

38 Fig. 85

Walters Art Museum, MS W. 257.

France, Paris (?), mid-1440s.

Vellum, 221 leaves, 7 1/8 x 5 1/4 in. (18.6 x 13.5 cm), 1 column, 14 lines, in Latin and French, in *textura,* 13 large miniatures.

Use: Calendar: Paris; Hours of the Virgin: Rome; Office of the Dead: Dominican.

TEXT	IMAGE
Calendar (1–12v)	
Gospel Lessons (13–19)	
Obsecro te, O intemerata, 7 Last Words of Our Lord (19–30v)	
Hours of the Virgin (31–120)	
Matins	Annunciation (31)
Lauds	Visitation (44v)
Prime	Nativity (59)
Terce	Annunciation to the Shepherds (65)
Sext	Adoration of the Magi (71)
None	Presentation in the Temple (77)
Vespers	Flight into Egypt (83)
Compline	Coronation of the Virgin (93)
Penitential Psalms, Litany (121–141v)	David in Prayer (121)
Hours of the Cross (142–145v)	Crucifixion (142)
Hours of the Holy Spirit (146–149v)	Pentecost (146)
Office of the Dead (150–203v)	Burial Service (150)

TEXT	IMAGE
Suffrages, Salve sancta facies, 8 Verses of St. Bernard, Suffrages (204–221)	Trinity (204)

BIBLIOGRAPHY: Randall, *Medieval and Renaissance Manuscripts,* II, 112–16, no. 123, figs. 222, 223.

❖ ❖ ❖

39 — Fig. 53

Walters Art Museum, MS W. 251.

France, Paris, ca. 1450.

Vellum, 168 leaves, 7½ x 5⅜ in. (19.1 x 13.7 cm), 1 column, 15 lines, in Latin and French, in *textura,* 12 miniatures and 10 border vignettes, by the Master of Jean Rolin II.

Use: Calendar: mainly Paris; Hours of the Virgin: Paris; Office of the Dead: Paris.

TEXT	IMAGE
Calendar (2–13v)	
Gospel Lessons (14–19)	
Obsecro te, O intemerata (19–25v)	
Hours of the Virgin (26–92v)	
Matins	Annunciation; border: Birth of the Virgin, Marriage of the Virgin, Virgin Weaving; Presentation of the Virgin (26)
Lauds	Visitation (49v)
Prime	Nativity (61)
Terce	Annunciation to the Shepherds (67)
Sext	Adoration of the Magi (72)
None	Presentation in the Temple (76)
Vespers	Flight into Egypt (80v)
Compline	Coronation of the Virgin (87v)
Penitential Psalms, Litany (93–108v)	David in Prayer (93)
Hours of the Cross (109–114v)	Crucifixion; border: Agony in the Garden, Betrayal, Christ before Pilate, Christ Carrying the Cross, Deposition, Entombment (109)
Hours of the Holy Spirit (115–120v)	Pentecost (115)
Office of the Dead (121–168v)	Burial Service (121)

BIBLIOGRAPHY: Randall, *Medieval and Renaissance Manuscripts,* II, 128–32, no. 127, pl. XIIb, figs. 227, 228, 393.

❖ ❖ ❖

40 — Pl. 14, Figs. 12, 89, 114

Walters Art Museum, MS W. 267 ("Buves Hours").

Northern France or southern Belgium, 1450s, possibly produced for a woman of the Picard Buves Family.

Vellum, 188 leaves, 7⅞ x 5⅝ in. (20.1 x 14.4 cm), 1 column, 17 lines, in Latin and French, in *textura,* 21 large miniatures.

Use: Calendar: Hainault, with entries pointing to Mons and Cambrai; Hours of the Virgin: unidentified; Office of the Dead: unidentified.

TEXT	IMAGE
Calendar (1v–12)	
Prayer to guardian angel (12v–13)	
Hours of the Virgin (13v–85v)	
Matins	Gabriel Presenting a Kneeling Patroness (13v)
	Virgin Annunciate (14)
Lauds	Visitation (38)
Prime	Nativity with Preparation of Christ's Bath (49v)
Terce	Annunciation to the Shepherds (59v)
Sext	Adoration of the Magi (64)
None	Massacre of the Innocents (68v)
Vespers	Flight into Egypt (73)
Compline	Coronation of the Virgin (80v)
Office of the Dead (86–133v)	Absolution (86)
Penitential Psalms, Litany, followed by various prayers recited before, while, and after receiving Communion (135–159)	David in Prayer (134v)
Hours of the Cross (159v–169v)	Crucifixion (159v)
Hours of the Holy Spirit (170–177)	Pentecost (170)
Suffrages (177v–183)	John Baptizing Christ (177v)
	John the Evangelist (178v)
	Sebastian Shot with Arrows (179v)
	Anthony (180v)
	Barbara (181v)
	Margaret Emerging from the Dragon (182v)
O intemerata (184–188v)	Last Judgement (183v)
	Madonna with Angel Presenting a Flower (184)

BIBLIOGRAPHY: Randall, *Medieval and Renaissance Manuscripts,* III, 226–34, no. 246, pl. XXXIIIb, fig. 474.

❖ ❖ ❖

41 — Fig. 98

Walters Art Museum, MS W. 269.

Northern France, ca. 1460.

Vellum, 156 leaves, 7¼ x 5¼ in. (18.4 x 13.5 cm), 1 column, 16 lines, in Latin and French, in *textura,* 18 miniatures and 1 historiated initial.

Use: Calendar: Rheims; Hours of the Virgin: Rheims; Office of the Dead: Rheims.

TEXT	IMAGE
Various prayers (added somewhat later, 1–3v)	
Calendar (4–15v)	
Hours of the Virgin (16–57)	
Matins	Annunciation; border: Making Music and Playing Backgammon (16)
Lauds	Visitation (25)
Prime	Nativity (34)
Terce	Annuncation to the Shepherds (38v)
Sext	Adoration of the Magi (42)
None	Presentation in the Temple (45)
Vespers	Flight into Egypt (48)
Compline	Coronation of the Virgin (53v)
7 Verses of St. Bernard, 5 Joys of the Virgin, various prayers (57v–59v)	
Penitential Psalms, Litany, followed by Gospel Lesson of John (60–75v)	Last Judgement (60)
15 Joys of the Virgin (76–80v)	Madonna with Kneeling Patroness (76)
7 Requests to Our Lord (81–83v)	
Hours of the Cross (84–86v)	Crucifixion; Pelican Feeding Her Young, in "D" (84)
Hours of the Holy Spirit (87–89v)	Pentecost (87)
Obsecro te in French, Passion according to Luke, various prayers including some to the Eucharist, Suffrages (89v–100v)	
Hours of St. Catherine, various prayers, Suffrages (101–108v)	
Suffrages (110–114v)	Laetus (110)
	Remy (111)
	Nicholas Resuscitating the Three Boys (112)

	Christopher Carrying Christ (113)
	Catherine (114)
Office of the Dead (116–150)	Death of the Virgin (116)
Prayers to the Virgin, against thunder, to the Eucharist, to guardian angel (added somewhat later, 150v–156v)	

BIBLIOGRAPHY: Randall, *Medieval and Renaissance Manuscripts*, II, 139–44, no. 129, figs. 231, 232, 3097.

❖ ❖ ❖

42

Pl. 38, Figs. 13, 102, 106

Walters Art Museum, MS W. 274.

France, Angers (?), 1460s.

Vellum, 203 leaves, 8⅝ x 5⅞ in. (21.9 x 15 cm), 1 column, 15 lines, in Latin and French, in *textura*, 22 large miniatures, 1 historiated initial, 12 calendar and 12 zodiacal vignettes, by the Coëtivy Master (Henri de Vulcop?), and other painters, with some miniatures retouched in the 16th century.

Use: Calendar: mainly Paris; Hours of the Virgin: Paris; Office of the Dead: Paris.

TEXT	IMAGE
Calendar (1–12v)	Zodiacal sign on each verso
Jan.	Feasting (1)
Feb.	Keeping Warm (2)
Mar.	Pruning (3)
Apr.	Courting and Making Flower Wreaths (4)
May	Hawking (5)
Jun.	Mowing (6)
Jul.	Reaping (7)
Aug.	Threshing (8)
Sept.	Treading Grapes (9)
Oct.	Sowing (10)
Nov.	Thrashing for Acorns (11)
Dec.	Slaughtering a Pig (12)
Gospel Lessons (13–18)	John on Patmos, Matthew Writing, Mark Writing, Luke Writing (13)
Obsecro te, O intemerata (18v–26v)	Madonna, Pietà, Mass of St. Gregory (18v)
	Virgo Lactans, in "O" (22v)
Hours of the Virgin (27–93v)	
Matins	Annunciation to Joachim, Meeting at the Golden Gate, Birth of the Virgin, Marriage of the Virgin, Annunciation (27)
Lauds	Virgin Walking, Visitation, Birth and Naming of John the Baptist (51v)
Prime	Annunciation to the Shepherds, Nativity with Adoration of the Shepherds (63v)
Terce	Meeting of the Magi at the Crossroads, Magi before Herod, Adoration of the Magi (69v)
Sext	Holy Family Walk to Temple, Presentation in the Temple (74)
None	Herod Ordering Soldiers, Joseph Warned by the Angel, Massacre of the Innocents, Flight into Egypt (78)
Vespers	Holy Family Returns from Egypt, Virgin and Joseph Enter the Temple, Christ among the Doctors (82)
Compline	Coronation of the Virgin, Death at the Virgin's Door, Death of the Virgin (16th-century replacement, 88v)
Penitential Psalms, Litany (94–110v)	David and Goliath, David Leading a Procession of the Ark (94)
Hours of the Cross (111–114)	Betrayal, Christ Carrying the Cross, Crucifixion (111)
Hours of the Holy Spirit (114v–117v)	Baptism of Christ, Christ Healing a Demoniac, Pentecost (114v)
Office of the Dead (118–164)	Funeral Mass with Souls Released from Purgatory (118)
15 Joys of the Virgin (164v–169v)	Virgin of the Apocalypse, Entombment (164v)
7 Requests to Our Lord (170–173)	Trinity (170)
Suffrages (174–199v)	Preaching and Martyrdom of James the Less (176)
	Margaret Flagellated, Emerging from the Dragon, Decapitated (180)
	Amator Remonstrates Germain of Auxerre's Hanging a Tree with Trophies of the Chase, Amator Burns the Tree, Germain Distributes Alms, Germain Receives Alms (186)
	Death of Lazarus, Mary and Martha Beseech Christ's Aid, Raising of Lazarus (189)
	Coronation of Charlemagne by Leo III, Death of Charlemagne (191v)
	Mary Magdalene Washing Christ's Feet, Levitated by Angels, Receiving Her Last Communion (193)
7 Verses of St. Bernard, prayer for Communion (199v–203v)	

BIBLIOGRAPHY: Randall, *Medieval and Renaissance Manuscripts*, II, 157–66, no. 132, pl. XIIIb, figs. 235–38, 403.

❖ ❖ ❖

43

Fig. 33

New York, Pierpont Morgan Library, MS M. 1003.
(Gift of Mr. and Mrs. Landon K. Thorne, Jr.)

France, Paris, or eastern France (?), ca. 1465.

Vellum, 255 leaves, 9⅛ x 6⅝ in. (23.1 x 16.7 cm), 1 column, 14 lines, in Latin and French, in *textura*, 16 large miniatures, 3 historiated borders, 39 border vignettes, and 12 calendar and 12 zodiacal vignettes, by the Master of Jacques de Luxembourg.

Use: Calendar: mainly Paris; Hours of the Virgin: Paris; Office of the Dead: Paris.

TEXT	IMAGE
Calendar (1–12v)	Zodiacal sign on each recto
Jan.	Feasting (1)
Feb.	Keeping Warm (2)
Mar.	Pruning (3)
Apr.	Picking Flowering Branches (4)
May	Hawking (5)
Jun.	Mowing (6)
Jul.	Reaping (7)
Aug.	Threshing (8)
Sept.	Sowing (9)
Oct.	Treading Grapes (10)
Nov.	Thrashing for Acorns (11)
Dec.	Slaughtering a Pig (12)
Gospel Lessons (13–19v)	Last Supper; border: John on Patmos (13)
	God Sending Christ Child to the Virgin; border: Old Testament Souls Awaiting Redemption, Luke Writing (miniature missing)
	Magi before Herod; border: Magi Traveling; Matthew Writing

	(mistakenly given Mark's attribute) (16)
	Ascension; border: Mark Writing (mistakenly given Matthew's attribute) (18v)
Obsecro te, O intemerata (20–29)	Lamentation; border: Betrayal, Christ Carrying the Cross, Christ Nailed to the Cross (20)
	(Miniature missing)
Hours of the Virgin (31–112)	
Matins	Annunciation; border: Presentation of the Virgin in the the Temple, Virgin Weaving, Marriage of the Virgin, flanked by Kneeling Patron and Patroness (31)
Lauds	Visitation; border: Annunciation, Virgin Traveling, Birth of John the Baptist (61)
Prime	Nativity; border: Joseph Reproving the Virgin, Angel Appearing to Joseph, Virgin and Jospeh Travel to Bethlehem (75)
Terce	Annunciation to the Shepherds; border: Shepherds Travel to Bethlehem, Adoration of the Shepherds, Shepherds Making Music (82v)
Sext	Adoration of the Magi; border: Magus Traveling, Magus Traveling, Magi Meeting at the Crossroads (87)
None	Presentation in the Temple; border: Angel Appearing to the Holy Family, Angel with Joseph, Holy Family Travel to Temple (92v)
Vespers	(Miniature missing)
Compline	Coronation of the Virgin; border: Death of the Virgin, Funeral Procession of the Virgin, Assumption of the Virgin (105v)
Penitential Psalms, Litany (113–136v)	David in Prayer; border: David and Uriah, David with Bathsheba, Death of Uriah (113)
Hours of the Cross (137–145v)	Crucifixion; border: Flagellation, Christ Mocked, Christ Stripped of His Garments (137)
Hours of the Holy Spirit (146–153)	Pentecost; border: Noli me tangere, Christ Appearing to Thomas, Christ on Road to Emmaus (146)
Office of the Dead (153v–211)	Raising of Lazarus; border: Administration of Last Rites, Funeral Service, Burial (153v)
15 Joys of the Virgin (211v–217v)	Madonna Enthroned, Serenaded by Angels; border: Christ among the Doctors, Miracle at Cana, Multiplication of Loaves and Fishes (211v)
7 Requests to Our Lord (218–223)	(Miniature missing)
Suffrages (223v–236v)	
Mass of the Trinity, of the Holy Spirit, of the Virgin, of the Dead (237v–254v)	

BIBLIOGRAPHY: Plummer, *Last Flowering*, 60–61, no. 80, pl. 80.

❖ ❖ ❖

44 Figs. 51, 121

Walters Art Museum, MS W. 292 ("Marescalci Hours").
France, Savoy, ca. 1465–70.

Vellum, 186 leaves, 8⅞ x 6⅛ in. (22.7 x 16.3 cm), 1 column, 16 lines, in Latin, in *textura*, 13 large miniatures and 14 historiated initials, by an artist of the Hours of Louis de Savoie.

Use: Calendar: general, but with entries pointing to Burgundy/ Franche-Comté; Hours of the Virgin: unidentified; Office of the Dead: Rome.

TEXT	IMAGE
Calendar (1–12v)	
Mass of the Virgin (13–15v)	Madonna, in "S" (13)
Gospel Lessons (15v–20)	John on Patmos with the Beast of the Apocalypse, in "I" (15v)
	Luke Writing, in "I" (17)
	Matthew Writing, in "C" (18)
	Luke Writing, in "I" (19v)
Hours of the Virgin (21–87v)	Madonna Enthroned with Kneeling Patron and Patroness Presented by John the Baptist and Catherine (added in the 1490s, 20v)
Matins	Creation of Eve (21)
Lauds	Cain Killing Abel (38v)
Prime	Animals Entering Noah's Ark (50v)
Terce	Sacrifice of Isaac (55)
Sext	Judith Decapitating Holofernes (59v)
None	Job on the Dungheap Tormented by His Wife and the Devil (63)
Vespers	Moses Presenting the Tablets of the Law to the Israelites (67v)
Compline	Moses' Rod Turned into a Snake (75)
Office of the Dead (88–131)	Torments of the Damned (88)
Obsecro te, O intemerata (131–136v)	Virgin, in "O" (131)
	Coronation of the Virgin, in "O" (134v)
Stabat mater (137–138v)	Lamentation, in "S" (137)
Domine Iesu Christe redemptor mundi (139–141v)	Christ Seated on Rainbow, in "D" (139)
Suffrages (141v–146)	Claude of Besançon, in "D" (142)
	Christopher Carrying Christ, in "D" (143)
	Temptation of Anthony, in "D" (144)
7 Last Words of Our Lord (146v–149)	Crucifixion, in "D" (146v)
Passion according to John (149–151v)	Flagellation, in "I" (149)
Penitential Psalms, Litany (152–171v)	David in Prayer, with Kneeling Patron Presented by George (152)
Hours of the Cross (172–178v)	Crucifixion, with Kneeling Patroness (172)
Hours of the Holy Spirit (179–184v)	Pentecost, with Kneeling Patroness (179)
Obit of Jacobus Marescalci (added in 1493, 185v)	

BIBLIOGRAPHY: Randall, *Medieval and Renaissance Manuscripts*, II, 184–90, no. 137, pl. XIVd, figs. 247–49.

❖ ❖ ❖

45 Figs. 7, 78

Walters Art Museum, MS W. 222 ("Tourotte Hours").
France, Poitiers, ca. 1465.

Vellum, 101 leaves, 6½ x 4⅞ in. (16.4 x 12.4 cm), 1 column, 20 lines, in Latin and French, in *littera batarda*, 10 large and 1 small (fol. 93v) miniatures by the Master of Walters 222, a second artist, and a third who added and retouched miniatures in the early 16th century.

Use: Calendar: composite, but mainly Brittany; Hours of the Virgin: Poitiers; Office of the Dead: Poitiers.

TEXT	IMAGE
Domine Iesu Christi qui dixisti, Royne des cieulx glorieuse (added in the early 16th century, 1-v)	Tourotte Family Praying, with Anthony and Peter (added in the early 16th century, 1v)
	God with Christ and the Virgin Interceding for the Tourottes (added in the early 16th century, 2)
Calendar (3–14v)	
Hours of the Virgin (15–51)	
Matins	Annunciation (15)
Lauds	
Matins of the Hours of the Cross	Crucifixion (28v)
Matins of the Hours of the Holy Spirit	Pentecost (29v)
Matins of the Hours of St. Catherine	Catherine in Her Study (30v)
Prime	
Prime of the Cross	
Prime of the Holy Spirit	
Prime of St. Catherine	
Terce	
Terce of the Cross	
Terce of the Holy Spirit	
Terce of St. Catherine	
Sext	
Sext of the Cross	
Sext of the Holy Spirit	
Sext of St. Catherine	
None	
None of the Cross	
None of the Holy Spirit	
None of St. Catherine	
Vespers	
Vespers of the Cross	
Vespers of the Holy Spirit	
Vespers of St. Catherine	
Compline	
Compline of the Cross	
Compline of the Holy Spirit	
Compline of St. Catherine	
Obsecro te (51v–54)	Madonnna Enthroned with Mme. Tourotte Presented by Clare (patroness retouched in the early 16th century, 51v)
Penitential Psalms, Litany (55–66)	David in Prayer (55)
Office of the Dead (66v–86)	Job on the Dungheap (66v)
Gospel Lesson of John, Suffrages, 7 Verses of St. Bernard (87–93v)	
Salve sancta facies (93v–94v)	Veronica Holding Her Veil (93v)
Je vous supli très glorieuse (added in the early 16th century, 96–98)	Anne with the Virgin and Child, with Mme. Tourotte Presented by Barbara (added in the early 16th century, 96)

BIBLIOGRAPHY: Randall, *Medieval and Renaissance Manuscripts*, II, 207–12, no. 142, p. XVIa, fig. 255.

❖ ❖ ❖

46

Pl. 22, Fig. 44

Walters Art Museum, MS W. 223.

France, probably Poitiers, 1460s.

Vellum, 162 leaves, $5\frac{1}{4}$ x 4 in. (14.5 x 10.1 cm), 1 column, 15 lines, in Latin, in *textura*, 19 large miniatures and 8 historiated borders, by the Master of Walters 222 and a follower of the Masters of Morgan 96 and 366.

Use: Calendar: general, but with some entries pointing to southern France and Poitiers; Hours of the Virgin: Rome; Office of the Dead: Rome.

TEXT	IMAGE
Calendar (1–12v)	
Gospel Lesson of John (13–15)	John on Patmos (13)
Obsecro te (15v–19v)	Madonna Enthroned, Crowned by Angels (15v)
Hours of the Virgin (20–89v)	
Matins	(Miniature missing)
Lauds	Visitation; border: Birth of John the Baptist, John the Baptist Preaching to a Crowd (40v)
Prime	Nativity; border: Shepherds Dancing (54)
Terce	Annunciation to the Shepherds; border: Shepherds Tending Their Flock (58v)
Sext	Adoration of the Magi; border: Journey of the Magi (62v)
None	Presentation in the Temple; border: Circumcision (66v)
Vespers	(Miniature missing)
Compline	Coronation of the Virgin; border: Death of the Virgin, Assumption of the Virgin (76)
Penitential Psalms, Litany (90–110)	David and Goliath; border: David as Shepherd, David in Prayer (90)
Office of the Dead (111–149)	Last Judgement; border: Hell (111)
Suffrages (149v–161)	Trinity (149v)
	Michael Battling a Devil (150v)
	Christopher Carrying Christ (151v)
	Sebastian Shot with Arrows (153)
	Anthony (155)
	George Slaying the Dragon (156v)
	Margaret Emerging from the Dragon (157v)
	Mary Magdalene (158v)
	All Saints (160)
Prayer to the Virgin (added later, 161v–162v)	

BIBLIOGRAPHY: Randall, *Medieval and Renaissance Manuscripts*, II, 212–16, no. 143, pl. XVIb, figs. 256, 257.

❖ ❖ ❖

47

Fig. 109

Walters Art Museum, MS W. 205.

France, Bourges, ca. 1470.

Vellum, 202 leaves, $4\frac{1}{4}$ x $3\frac{1}{4}$ in. (11.1 x 8.3 cm), 1 column, 17 lines, in Latin and French, in *textura*, 49 large miniatures by a follower of the Master of Morgan 96.

Use: Calendar: northern France; Hours of the Virgin: Rome; Office of the Dead: Bourges.

TEXT	IMAGE
Calendar (2–13v)	
Gospel Lessons (14–21)	John on Patmos (14)
	Luke Painting the Virgin (16)
	Matthew Writing (18)
	Mark Examining Pen (20)
Obsecro te, O intemerata (22–29v)	Virgo Lactans (22)
	Pietà (26)
Hours of the Virgin (30–93)	
Matins	Annunciation (30)
Lauds	Visitation (41v)
Prime	Nativity (53v)
Terce	Annunciation to the Shepherds (58)

Sext	Adoration of the Magi (62)
None	Presentation in the Temple (65v)
Vespers	Flight into Egypt (69v)
Compline	Coronation of the Virgin (77)
Hours of the Cross (94–104)	
Matins	Betrayal (94)
Prime	Flagellation (95v)
Terce	Christ Crowned with Thorns (97)
Sext	Crucifixion: Christ Offered Vinegar (98v)
None	Crucifixion: Christ's Side Pierced (100)
Vespers	Deposition (101v)
Compline	Entombment (103)
Hours of the Holy Spirit (105–109)	Pentecost (105)
Penitential Psalms, Litany (110–126v)	David in Prayer (110)
Office of the Dead (127–167v)	Last Rites (127)
Stabat mater (168–170)	Virgin Praying before a Crucifix (168)
Suffrages (171–197v)	Peter and Paul (171)
	John the Baptist Preaching (172)
	John the Evangelist Drinking from the Poisoned Cup (173)
	Andrew (174)
	Thomas (175)
	Matthew (176)
	Bartholomew (177)
	Simon and Jude (178)
	James and Philip (179)
	James (180)
	Matthias (181)
	Luke (182)
	Mark (183)
	Sebastian Shot with Arrows (184)
	Michael Battling a Devil (187)
	Lapidation of Stephen (188)
	Christopher Carrying Christ (189)
	Mass of St. Gregory (190)
	Nicholas Resuscitating the Three Boys (191)
	Temptation of Anthony (192)
	Claude of Besançon (193)
	Decapitation of Catherine (195)
	Margaret Emerging from the Dragon (196)
	Barbara (197)
Prayer of St. Augustine (added later, 198–202v)	

BIBLIOGRAPHY: Randall, *Medieval and Renaissance Manuscripts*, II, 228–33, no. 146, figs. 260, 261.

❖ ❖ ❖

48 Fig. 27

Cambridge, Mass., Harvard University, Houghton Library, MS Richardson 7 ("Habert du Berry d'Artois—Hoe Hours").

France, Troyes (?), ca. 1470.

Vellum, 237 leaves, 10½ x 7½ in. (26.6 x 18.4 cm), 1 column, 16 lines, in French and Latin, in *textura*, 29 large miniatures, 9 border roundels, 2 historiated initials, and 12 calendar and 12 zodiacal vignettes.

Use: Calendar: Troyes; Hours of the Virgin: Sens; Office of the Dead: Troyes.

TEXT	IMAGE
Calendar (1–12v)	Zodiacal sign on each recto
Jan.	Feasting (1)
Feb.	Keeping Warm (2)
Mar.	Pruning (3)
Apr.	Picking Flowering Branches (4)
May	Hawking (5)
Jun.	Mowing (6)
Jul.	Reaping (7)
Aug.	Threshing (8)
Sept.	Treading Grapes (9)
Oct.	Sowing (10)
Nov.	Thrashing for Acorns (11)
Dec.	Slaughtering a Pig (12)
Gospel Lessons (13–20v)	John on Patmos (13)
	Matthew Writing (15)
	Luke Painting the Virgin (17)
	Mark Writing (19)
Hours of the Cross (21–36v)	
Matins	Betrayal; border: Agony in the Garden, Christ before Annas, Christ before Caiaphas, Apostles (21)
Prime	Christ before Pilate (23)
Terce	Flagellation (25)
Sext	Christ Carrying the Cross (27)
None	Crucifixion (29)
Vespers	Deposition (31)
Compline	Entombment (33)
Passion according to John	
Hours of the Holy Spirit (37–45v)	Pentecost (37)
Hours of the Virgin (47–126)	
Matins	Annunciation; border: Marriage of the Virgin, Virgin Weaving, Birth of the Virgin, Joachim Praying; Meeting at the Golden Gate, in "D" (47)
Lauds	Visitation (63)
Prime	Nativity (77v)
Terce	Annunciation to the Shepherds (86v)
Sext	Adoration of the Magi (93)
None	Presentation in the Temple (99)
Vespers	Flight into Egypt (106)
Compline	Coronation of the Virgin (116)
Penitential Psalms, Litany (127–145v)	David in Prayer (127)
Obsecro te, O intemerata, other prayers (146v–155v)	Madonna with Kneeling Patron and Patroness Presented by William of Aquitaine (?) and Catherine (146v)
	Pietà (151)
Suffrages, followed by prayers to the Eucharist, the Virgin, and St. Catherine (156–182)	Michael Battling a Devil (156)
	Noli me tangere (158)
	Christopher Carrying Christ (160v)
	Sebastian Shot with Arrows (162)
	Border: Madonna (173v)
	Decapitation of Catherine (178)
8 Verses of St. Bernard, followed by various prayers, including many to the Eucharist (183–199v)	Head of Christ, in "S" (188v)
Office of the Dead (201–237)	Burial Service (201)

BIBLIOGRAPHY: Wieck, *Late Medieval and Renaissance Illuminated Manuscripts*, 28–29, no. 13, illus.

❖ ❖ ❖

49 Fig. 119

Walters Art Museum, MS W. 249.

France, Troyes (?), ca. 1470.

Vellum, 180 leaves, 7 x 5⅜ in. (17.8 x 13.8 cm), 1 column, 15 lines, in Latin and French, in *textura*, 17 large and 58 border miniatures, and 2 historiated initials.

Use: Calendar: Troyes; Hours of the Virgin: Troyes; Office of the Dead: Troyes.

TEXT	IMAGE
Calendar (5–16v)	
Gospel Lessons (17–24)	John on Patmos; border: John Preaching, Directing the Digging of His Grave, Praying from His Grave, Assumed into Heaven, Miracles at John's Grave Site (17)
	Luke Writing (19)
	Matthew Reading (21)
	Mark Sharpening Pen (23)
Hours of the Cross (25–30v)	Crucifixion: border; Agony in the Garden, Christ before Pilate, Flagellation, Christ Crowned with Thorns, Christ Carrying the Cross (25)
Hours of the Holy Spirit (31–36v)	Pentecost; border: Deposition, Entombment, Resurrection, Noli me tangere, Ascension (31)
Hours of the Virgin (37–91)	
Matins	Annunciation; border: Meeting at the Golden Gate, Education of the Virgin, Presentation of the Virgin, Virgin Weaving, Virgin in Prayer before the Ark (37)
Lauds	Visitation; border: Virgin in Prayer, Angel Appears to Joseph, Virgin with Joseph, Joseph and the Virgin Travel to Bethlehem (48v)
Prime	Nativity; border: Joseph and the Virgin Enter Bethlehem, They Seek Shelter, They Are Refused Shelter, They Tie Up in a Stable (60v)
Terce	Annunciation to the Shepherds; border: Shepherds Eating, Annunciation to the Shepherds, They Travel to the Stable, Adoration of the Shepherds (66v)
Sext	Adoration of the Magi; border: Magus Follows the Star, Meeting of Two Magi, Meeting of Three Magi, Magi Enter Bethlehem (71)
None	Circumcision; border: Handmaiden Presents Christ to the Virgin, First Bath of Christ, Angels Tend to Christ, Adoration of the Christ Child (75)
Vespers	Massacre of the Innocents; border: Herod Orders His Soldiers, Massacre, Massacre, Soldiers Report to Herod (79)
Compline	Flight into Egypt; border: Holy Family Encounters a Sower, Soldiers Question Sower, Holy Family Reaches Egypt, Angel Bids Them to Return to Israel (86)
Obsecro te, O intemerata (91–97v)	Pietà, in "O" (91)
	Madonna, in "O" (95)
Penitential Psalms, Litany (99–118v)	David in Prayer; border: David as Shepherd, David and Goliath, David Presenting Goliath's Head to Saul, David Enthroned, David Harping (99)
Office to the Dead (119–163)	Burial Service; border: Deathbed, Corpse Sewn into Shroud, Placed in a Coffin, Monks Pray over Coffin, Coffin Carried to the Cemetery (119)
Suffrages (165–176)	Nicholas Resuscitating the Three Boys, with Kneeling Patroness (169)

BIBLIOGRAPHY: Randall, *Medieval and Renaissance Manuscripts,* II, 194–99, no. 139, figs. 251, 252.

❖ ❖ ❖

50 Figs. 14, 81, 90

Walters Art Museum, MS W. 285 ("Hours of Pope Leo X").

France, Paris (?) and/or Loire region (?), ca. 1470, with a calendar of ca. 1430.

Vellum, 115 leaves, 8⅛ x 5¾ in. (20.6 x 14.7 cm), 1 column, 14 lines, in Latin and French, in *textura,* 3 large (fols. 2, 16, 89) and 10 small miniatures, 2 coats-of-arms, and 12 calendar and 12 zodiacal miniatures, by a follower of the Bedford Master, the Master of Jean Rolin II, the Maître François (?), and the Master of Adélaïde de Savoie.

Use: Calendar: mainly Paris; Office of the Dead: Paris.

TEXT	IMAGE
	Arms of Leo X (added in the early 16th century, 1)
	Crucifixion (added, probably from a missal, 2)
Calendar (4–15v)	Zodiacal sign on each recto
Jan.	Janus Feasting (4v)
Feb.	Keeping Warm (5v)
Mar.	Pruning (6v)
Apr.	Picking Flowering Branches (7v)
May	Hawking (8v)
Jun.	Mowing (9v)
Jul.	Reaping (10v)
Aug.	Threshing (11v)
Sept.	Treading Grapes (12v)
Oct.	Sowing (13v)
Nov.	Thrashing Acorns (14v)
Dec.	Slaughtering a Pig (15v)
Hours of the Holy Spirit (misbound, 16–17v, 24–27v)	Pentecost (16)
Hours of the Cross (18–23v)	(Miniature missing)
Office of the Dead (28–78v)	(Miniature missing)
15 Joys of the Virgin (79–84v)	(Miniature missing)
7 Requests to Our Lord (85–86v)	(Miniature missing)
Suffrage, Ave cuius concepcio, Suffrages, Stabat mater, 7 Verses of St. Bernard, Crucem tuam adoramus, O bone Iesu, Suffrages, and other prayers (87–115)	(Miniature missing)
	Visitation (87v)
	Paul and Peter (89)
	Crucifixion of Andrew (90)
	Margaret Emerging from the Dragon (91)
	Radegundis (91v)
	(Miniature missing)
	Crucifixion (94)
	Bernard in His Study (100)
	Cross in a Niche (106)
	Christ with Kneeling Patroness (107)
	Geneviève (109v)
	Mary Magdalene Carried by Angels (110)
	Coat-of-Arms (added in the early 16th century, 115v)

BIBLIOGRAPHY: Randall, *Medieval and Renaissance Manuscripts,* II, 174–80, no. 135, pls. XIVa–b, figs. 244, 245.

❖ ❖ ❖

51 Fig. 127

Walters Art Museum, MS W. 214.

France, Paris, ca. 1475.

Vellum, 185 leaves, 5⅝ x 3⅞ in. (14.2 x 9.7 cm), 1 column, 21 lines, in Latin and French, in *littera batarda,* 5 large (fols. 28, 67–91) and 78 small miniatures by the Maître François.

Use: Calendar: mainly Paris; Hours of the Virgin: Bourges; Office of the Dead: Bourges.

TEXT	IMAGE
Calendar (1–12v)	
Gospel Lessons (13–17v)	John on Patmos (13)
	Luke Writing (14)
	Matthew Writing (15v)
	Mark Reading (17)
Passion according to John (18–27)	Betrayal (18)
Hours of the Virgin (28–66)	
Matins	Annunciation (28)
Lauds	Visitation (37v)
Prime	Nativity (47)
Terce	Annunciation to the Shepherds (51v)
Sext	Adoration of the Magi (54v)
None	Presentation in the Temple (57v)
Vespers	Massacre of the Innocents (60)
Compline	Coronation of the Virgin (62v)
Penitential Psalms, Litany (67–83)	David in Prayer (67)
Hours of the Cross (84–87)	Crucifixion (84)
Hours of the Holy Spirit (88–90v)	Pentecost (88)
Office of the Dead (91–118)	Death Attacking a Man (91)
Litany to the Virgin, Prayers (119–150)	Madonna Surrounded by All Saints (119)
O domina sanctissima Maria mater	Virgin Reading While Christ Learns to Walk (121)
Salve mater salvatoris	Madonna in Glory (122)
Salve stella maris	Madonna on Crescent Moon, Serenaded by Angels (124)
Salve mater salvatoris	Madonna in a Ship (125v)
7 Joys of the Virgin	Madonna Surrounded by Cherubim (127)
Obsecro te	Madonna Seated (128v)
O intemerata	Madonna with Reading Christ (132)
Per illud que tormentum	Lamentation (135v)
7 Verses of St. Bernard	Bernard Reading (136)
Ave Domine Ihesu Christe verbum patris	Salvator Mundi (137v)
Adoro te Deum Patrem et Filium et Spiritum	Trinity (138)
O bone Ihesu	Man of Sorrows (139v)
7 Last Words of Our Lord	Crucifixion, with Kneeling Patron (141)
O dulcissime Domine	Christ Child with Instruments of the Passion (142v)
Passion according to John	Christ Carrying the Cross (145v)
Deus qui manus tuas	Christ Crowned with Thorns (147)
Domine Ihesu Christe qui hanc sacratissimam carnem	Salvator Mundi (147v)
Domine Ihesu Christe qui hora matutinali	Flagellation (148)
Gratias ago tibi domine	God Blessing (148v)
Domine Ihesu Christe qui me creasti	Christ Blessing Kneeling Patron (149)
Hours of St. Catherine (151–157v)	
Matins	Mystic Marriage of Catherine (151)
Prime	Catherine Confounding the Doctors (151v)
Terce	Catherine Flagellated (152)
Sext	Catherine Converts Empress Faustina and Porphyrius (153)
None	Catherine's Torture Wheels Destroyed by an Angel (154)
Vespers	Decapitation of Catherine (154v)
Compline	Catherine's Body Transported by Angels (154v)
Gaude virgo Katherina	Catherine in her Study (156v)
Suffrages (157v–184)	Baptism of Christ (157v)
	Pentecost (158)
	Worshipers Kissing a Cross (158v)
	Michael Battling a Devil (159)
	Peter, as Pope, Blessing a Man (159v)
	Decapitation of Paul (160)
	Andrew (160v)
	James (161)
	John the Baptist (161v)
	Lapidation of Stephen (162)
	5 Plague Saints (162v)
	Temptation of Anthony (163v)
	Sebastian Shot with Arrows (164)
	Christopher (166)
	Eutropius Blessing a Cripple (167)
	Nicholas Resuscitating the Three Boys (167v)
	Fiacre (168)
	Julian the Hospitaller in a Boat (168v)
	Cosmas and Damian Blessing (169)
	Gatian Blessing (169v)
	Martin Dividing His Cloak (170v)
	Avertinus Blessing (171)
	Lawrence (171v)
	Claude of Besançon Blessing a Cripple (172)
	Mathurin Blessing a Prisoner (173)
	Cornelius and Cyprian (174)
	Martyrdom of Thomas Becket (174v)
	Pope Saint Blessing (175)
	Anne Instructing the Virgin (175v)
	Noli me tangere (176)
	Margaret Emerging from the Dragon (176v)
	Barbara (177)
	Apollonia (177v)
	Radegund (178v)
	Trinity (179)
	Three Worshipers at an Altar (182v)
	Pentecost (183v)

BIBLIOGRAPHY: Randall, *Medieval and Renaissance Manuscripts,* II, 275–82, no. 158, pl. XVIIIb, figs. 276, 277, 402.

❖ ❖ ❖

52 Fig. 59

Walters Art Museum MS W. 800.

(Gift of Eleanor P. Spencer)

France, Paris, 1470s.

Vellum, 292 leaves, 3¾ x 2⅝ in. (9.6 x 6.8 cm), 1 column, 12 lines, in Latin, in *littera batarda,* 14 large miniatures by the Maître François.

Use: Calendar: mainly Paris; Hours of the Virgin: Paris; Office of the Dead: Paris.

TEXT	IMAGE
Calendar (1–12v)	
Gospel Lessons, Passion according to John (misrubricated Luke) followed by various prayers (13–28)	John on Patmos (13)
Passion according to John, followed by various prayers (29–59v)	Betrayal (29)
Hours of the Virgin (61–176v)	
Matins	Annunciation (61)

Lauds	Visitation (101)
Prime	Nativity (120)
Terce	Annunciation to the Shepherds (130)
Sext	Adoration of the Magi (137)
None	Presentation in the Temple (144)
Vespers	Flight into Egypt (151)
Compline	Coronation of the Virgin (165)
Penitential Psalms, Litany (177–209)	David in Prayer (177)
Hours of the Cross (210–217)	(Miniature missing)
Hours of the Holy Spirit (218–226)	Pentecost (218)
Office of the Dead (227–287v)	Burial Service (227)
Obsecro te (288–292v)	Madonna Enthroned, Serenaded by Angels (288)

BIBLIOGRAPHY: Randall, *Medieval and Renaissance Manuscripts,* II, 266–70, no. 156, pl. XVIIIa, figs. 273, 274.

❖ ❖ ❖

53 Fig. 68

New York, Pierpont Morgan Library, MS M. 1001.

France, Poitiers, ca. 1475.

Vellum, 165 leaves, 5⅞ x 4¼ in. (14.8 x 10.8 cm), 1 column, 16 lines, in Latin, in *littera batarda,* 38 large and 1 small (fol. 17v) miniatures, and 20 historiated borders, attributed to Robinet Testard.

Use: Calendar: Poitiers; Hours of the Virgin: Rome; Office of the Dead: Rome.

TEXT	IMAGE
Calendar (1–12v)	
Gospel Lessons (13–17)	John on Patmos, Matthew Examining Pen, Luke Writing, Mark Examining Pen; border: Martyrdom of Mark (13)
	Miraculous Bleeding Host of Dijon (17v)
Hours of the Virgin (18–74v)	
Matins	Annunciation; border: Presentation of the Virgin, Virgin Weaving, Virgin Brought Food by an Angel, Marriage of the Virgin (18)
Lauds	Visitation; border: Birth of John the Baptist, John the Baptist Preaching (34)
Prime	Nativity; border: Shepherds Tending Sheep, Shepherds Dancing (44)
Terce	Annunciation to the Shepherds; border: Shepherds Tending Goats and Cattle (48)
Sext	Adoration of the Magi; border: Journey and Meeting of the Magi (51)
None	Presentation in the Temple; border: Virgin Kneeling with Christ Child before an Altar, Circumcision (54)
Vespers	Flight into Egypt; border: Massacre of the Innocents (57)
Compline	Coronation of the Virgin; border: Apostles Gather around the Virgin, Death of the Virgin (62)
Hours of the Cross (76–79v)	Crucifixion; border: Veronica Displaying Her Veil, Quarrel over Christ's Robe (76)
Hours of the Holy Spirit (80–83)	Pentecost; border: Christ on the Road to Emmaus, Ascension (80)
Penitential Psalms, Litany (84–107v)	Pride Riding a Lion; border: Lucifer and the Proud (84)
	Envy Riding a Camel; border: Beelzebub and Envious Men Eye the Riches of the Wealthy (86)
	Anger Riding a Leopard Watched by Leviathan; border: Men and Women Fighting (88)
	Avarice Riding a Wolf Watched by Mammon (?); border: the Avaricious, with Purses, Hoarding (91)
	Gluttony Riding a Pig; border: Berich and a Gluttonous Feast (94)
	Sloth Riding an Ass; border: Astarot and Sleeping Cobblers (97)
	Lust Riding a Goat; border: Asmodeus with Men and Women Cavorting (98)
Office of the Dead (109–137)	
Vespers	Last Judgement; border: Sinners Transported to Hell (109)
Matins and Lauds	Job on the Dungheap; border: Raising of Lazarus (114)
Obsecro te, O intemerata (139–144v)	Madonna Serenaded by Angels (139)
Suffrages (145–154)	Sebastian (145)
	Anthony (146)
	Christopher Carrying Christ (147)
	Trinity (148v)
	Michael Battling a Devil (149v)
	John the Baptist (150v)
	Stephen (151v)
	Lawrence (152v)
	George Slaying the Dragon (153v)
5 Prayers of St. Gregory (154v–155v)	Mass of St. Gregory (154v)
Suffrages (156–162v)	Martin Dividing His Cloak (156)
	Mary Magdalene (157)
	Apollonia (158)
	Catherine (159)
	Margaret Emerging from the Dragon (160)
	Barbara (161)
	All Saints (162)

BIBLIOGRAPHY: Voelkle, "Morgan Manuscript M. 1001."

❖ ❖ ❖

54 Fig. 129

Washington, D.C., Library of Congress, MS 93.

France, Tours, 1470s.

Vellum, 145 leaves, 7¾ x 5½ in. (19.7 x 14 cm), 1 column, 13 lines, in Latin, in *textura,* 4 large miniatures by a follower of Jean Fouquet.

Use: Calendar: Tours; Hours of the Virgin: Tours; Office of the Dead: Paris? (abbreviated).

TEXT	IMAGE
Athanasian Creed (1–5)	
Calendar (6–17v)	
Obsecro te (18–22v)	Madonna (18)
Gospel Lesson of John, followed by prayers (23–25v)	
Hours of the Virgin (26–78)	Annunciation (26)
Hours of the Cross (78v–81v)	
Hours of the Holy Spirit (82–85v)	
O intemerata (86–89v)	
Penitential Psalms, Litany (90–112)	David and Goliath (90)
Office of the Dead (114–145v)	Death Riding a Bull (114)

BIBLIOGRAPHY: Shutzner, *Medieval and Renaissance Manuscript Books,* 345–47, MS 57.

55 Pl. 40

New York, Pierpont Morgan Library, MS M. 677 ("Hours of Anne of France").

France, Bourges, late 1470s, produced for Princess Anne of France.

Vellum, 333 leaves, 5¾ x 4¼ in. (14.7 x 10.9 cm), 1 column, 10 lines, in Latin and French, in *littera batarda,* 107 large miniatures and 12 calendar and 12 zodiacal vignettes, by Jean Colombe and his workshop.

Use: Calendar: composite, but with Ursinus of Bourges in red; Hours of the Virgin: Rome; Office of the Dead: unidentified.

TEXT	IMAGE
Calendar (1–6v)	Zodiacal sign of each recto and verso
Jan.	Feasting (1)
Feb.	Breaking Ground (1v)
Mar.	Pruning (2)
Apr.	Walking (2v)
May	Riding (3)
Jun.	Mowing (3v)
Jul.	Reaping (4)
Aug.	Sowing (4v)
Sept.	Treading Grapes (5)
Oct.	Thrashing for Acorns (5v)
Nov.	Baking (6)
Dec.	Slaughtering a Pig (6v)
Prayers and meditations of the rosary (8–26)	Annunciation (7v)
	Entry into Jerusalem (11v)
	Christ Crowned with Thorns (15v)
	Crucifixion (19)
	Harrowing of Hell (22v)
Gospel Lessons (27v–37)	John on Patmos (27)
	Luke Painting the Virgin (29v)
	Matthew Writing (32v)
	Mark Writing (35v)
Stabat mater (38v–42)	Man of Sorrows (37v)
	Virgin Praying (38)
Hours of the Virgin (43v–185v)	
Matins	Annunciation, with Kneeling Princess Anne of France (42v–43)
	God Instructing Adam and Eve (46v)
	Eve Tempting Adam (48v)
	God in the Firmament (51)
	Youth Praying to Christ (54v)
	David Speaking to a Man (57)
	Earth Engulfing Abiram, Korah, and Dathan (61)
	Transfiguration (63v)
	Transporting the Ark (65v)
	Uzziah Smitten (68v)
	Ark Carried into Temple (71v)
	God Adored by Mankind (77v)
Lauds	Visitation (81v)
	David and Nathan in Temple (82v)
	Samuel Called by God (84v)
	David and Shimei (86)
	Three Hebrews in the Fiery Furnace (89v)
	God in the Firmament Adored (93)
	Madonna (98)
	John the Baptist among Ruins (99v)
Prime	Nativity (104)
	Virgin in Prayer, with Joseph (105)
	God Asking Abraham to Sacrifice Isaac (106)
	Jacob Wrestling with the Angel (108)
	God in the Heavens Adored (110v)
Terce	Annunciation to the Shepherds (114)
	Esau Bringing Food to Isaac (115v)
	Jacob Receiving Food from Rebecca (117)
	Battle (119)
Sext	Adoration of the Magi (123v)
	David Offering His Soul to God (125)
	Shepherd Watering Sheep (126v)
	Outdoor Banquet and Celebration (128v)
None	Presentation in the Temple (132v)
	Exodus (134)
	David Admonished by Nathan (135v)
	Dancing in the Street (137)
Vespers	Flight into Egypt (141)
	God the Father and Son (142)
	David Exhorting Boys (144)
	Procession to Church (146)
	David Forbidden by Nathan to Build the Temple (148)
	David Exhorting Children (149v)
	Madonna in Heaven Serenaded by Angels (152)
Compline	Death of the Virgin (157v)
	Annunciation of the Virgin's Death (158v)
	Entombment of the Virgin (160v)
	Assumption of the Virgin (162v)
	Virgin and Christ Enthroned (165)
Hours of the Cross (186v–200)	
Matins	Agony in the Garden (186)
Prime	Christ before Pilate (188)
Terce	Christ Buffeted (190)
Sext	Christ Carrying the Cross (192)
None	Crucifixion (194)
Vespers	Deposition (196)
Compline	Entombment (198)
Hours of the Holy Spirit (201–210v)	
Matins	Resurrection (200v)
Prime	Ascension (202v)
Terce	Pentecost (204)
Sext	Virgin's Farewell to Peter (205v)
None	Peter Baptizing (207)
Vespers	Peter Reproving Ananias and Sapphira (208)
Compline	Death of Ananias (209v)
Penitential Psalms, Litany (211v–244v)	Bathsheba at Her Bath (211)
	Bathsheba before David (213v)
	David and Uriah (216v)
	Uriah Leading Army (221)
	Uriah's Body Carried to Camp (225)
	Nathan Admonishes a Repenting David (230v)
	David in Prayer (232v)
	Virgin and Christ Enthroned Surrounded by All Saints (236)
Office of the Dead (245v–332v)	
Vespers	Death, with an Arrow, Rising from a Tomb (245)
	David Approaching Saul Hiding in a Cave (247)
	Jacob's Ladder (249)
	Purgatory (250v)
	Maidens Led to Church (252v)
	Funeral Procession Entering Church (255)
	Dying Man Attended by Monks (257)
Matins	Funeral Service (261v)
	David Steals Saul's Armor (264)
	David in Prayer (267)
	David in Prayer (269v)
	Lazarus at the Feast of Dives (277)
	Deaths of Dives and Lazarus (279)

	David Anointed by Samuel (283)
	Man Who Fell among Thieves (290v)
	Man Preaching to a Crowd (295)
	Good Samaritan Brings the Victim to an Inn (298)
Lauds	David Praying at the Brink of Hell (307)
	Elijah in the Fiery Chariot (311)
	David and Nathan Dispatch Laborers (314)
	Isaiah Ministered by an Angel (317v)
	Priest Praying before an Altar (321)
	Decapitation of John the Baptist (326)
	Souls Rescued from Purgatory (329)

BIBLIOGRAPHY: Plummer, *Last Flowering,* 53–54, no. 70, pls. 70a–70c.

❖ ❖ ❖

56

Pl. 30

Walters Art Museum, MS W. 213.

France, Bourges (?), ca. 1480.

Vellum, 142 leaves, 5⅞ x 4 in. (15 x 10 cm), 1 column, 19 lines, in Latin and French, in *littera batarda,* 30 large and 3 small (fols. 12–15) miniatures by Jean Colombe and his workshop.

Use: Calendar: mainly Paris; Hours of the Virgin: Rome; Office of the Dead: Rome.

TEXT	IMAGE
Calendar (4–9v)	
Gospel Lessons (10v–15v)	John on Patmos (10v)
	Luke Painting the Virgin (12)
	Matthew Writing (13v)
	Mark Sharpening Pen (15)
Hours of the Virgin (16–56)	
Matins	Annunciation (16)
Lauds	Visitation (25v)
Prime	Nativity (36)
Terce	Annunciation to the Shepherds (39v)
Sext	Adoration of the Magi (42v)
None	Presentation in the Temple (45v)
Vespers	Flight into Egypt (48v)
Compline	Coronation of the Virgin (53v)
Hours of the Cross (58–60v)	Crucifixion (58)
Hours of the Holy Spirit (61–63v)	Pentecost (61)
Penitential Psalms, Litany (64–77v)	David and Goliath (64)
Office of the Dead (78–103v)	Job on the Dungheap (78)
Obsecro te, O intemerata (106–112v)	Virgin Praying (106)
	Madonna Surrounded by Angels (110)
Passion according to John (113–123)	Agony in the Garden (113)
Suffrages (123v–137)	John the Baptist (123v)
	John the Evangelist (124v)
	Peter and Paul (125v)
	James (126v)
	Lapidation of Stephen (127v)
	Sebastian Shot with Arrows (128v)
	Lawrence (129v)
	Anthony (130v)
	Nicholas Resuscitating the Three Boys (131v)
	Fiacre (132v)
	Eutropius (133v)
	Eligius (134v)
	Martin Dividing His Cloak (135v)
	Dennis (136v)

BIBLIOGRAPHY: Randall, *Medieval and Renaissance Manuscripts,* II, 282–87, no. 159, pl. XVIIIc, figs. 278, 279, 400.

57

Fig. 32

Walters Art Museum, MS W. 445.

France, Bourges (?), late 1480s.

Vellum, 140 leaves, 4¼ x 3 in. (10.7 x 7.6 cm), 1 column, 21 lines, in Latin, in *littera batarda,* 35 large miniatures, 11 historiated borders, 12 calendars and 12 zodiacal vignettes, by Jean Colombe and his workshop.

Use: Calendar: northern France/southern Belgium; Hours of the Virgin: Rome; Office of the Dead: Rome.

TEXT	IMAGE
Calendar (1–12v)	Zodiacal sign on each verso
Jan.	Feasting (1)
Feb.	Breaking Ground (2)
Mar.	Pruning (3)
Apr.	Picking Flowers (4)
May	Riding (5)
Jun.	Shearing Sheep (6)
Jul.	Mowing (7)
Aug.	Reaping (8)
Sept.	Sowing (9)
Oct.	Treading Grapes (10)
Nov.	Slaughtering a Pig (11)
Dec.	Baking Bread (12)
Obsecro te, O intemerata (13–17v)	Madonna, with Kneeling Patron, Serenaded by Angels (13)
	Lamentation (16)
Gospel Lessons (18–24v)	John the Evangelist Led to Tub of Boiling Oil; border: Eagle (18)
	Luke Preaching to a Large Crowd; border: Ox (20)
	Matthew Vanquishing Two Dragons with Sign of the Cross; border: Angel (21v)
	Mark's Body Dragged through the Streets of Alexandria; border: Lion (23v)
Hours of the Virgin (25–77v)	
Matins	(Miniature missing)
Lauds	Jethro Meeting Moses (37v)
Suffrages	
Matins of the Hours of the Cross	Abner Slain by Joab (43v)
Matins of the Hours of the Holy Spirits	Gideon and the Miraculous Fleece (44v)
Prime	Moses and the Burning Bush (45v)
Prime of the Cross	Daniel in Prison (48)
Prime of the Holy Spirit	Miraculous Flowering of Aaron's Rod (49)
Terce	David Receives Abner (50)
Terce of the Cross	Abraham and Isaac Journey to Their Sacrifice (52v)
Terce of the Holy Spirit	Moses Receiving the Tablets of the Law (53v)
Sext	Solomon Receiving the Queen of Sheba (54v)
Sext of the Cross	Tubalcain Working His Forge (56v)
Sext of the Holy Spirit	Elijah Calls Down Fire from Heaven (57v)
None	Presentation of Samuel in the Temple (58v)
None of the Cross	Moses and the Brazen Serpent (61)
None of the Holy Spirit	Eating the Paschal Lamb (62)
Vespers	David Escapes from Saul's Soldiers (63)
Vespers of the Cross	King of Hai Taken Down from the Cross (66v)
Vespers of the Holy Spirit	Noah Building the Ark (67v)
Compline	Solomon and Bathsheba Enthroned (68v)
Compline of the Cross	Jonah Thrown to the Whale (70v)

Compline of the Holy Spirit	Israelites Led by a Column of Fire (71v)
Hours of St. Agatha (78–80v)	Agatha's Breasts Cut Off; border: Decapitation of Agatha (78)
Hours of St. Joseph (81–83v)	Joseph Traveling; border: Joseph in Prayer (81)
Hours of John the Baptist (84–87v)	Decapitation of John the Baptist; border: Burning of the Bones of John the Baptist (84)
Hours of Mary Magdalene (88–90)	Noli me tangere; border: Angels Mourning Mary Magdalene (88)
Hours of St. Catherine (90v–91v)	Catherine Saved from the Wheel; border: Decapitation of Catherine (90v)
O bone Iesu, O piissime Iesu, O dulcissime Iesu, 7 Last Words of Our Lord, and other prayers to Christ (92–96)	Mass of St. Gregory; border: Arma Christi (92)
Penitential Psalms, Litany (97–115)	David, with Head of Goliath, Received in Triumph (97)
Office of the Dead (115v–131v)	Job on the Dungheap; border: Beggar (115v)
Various Prayers (added somewhat later, 132–140v)	

BIBLIOGRAPHY: Randall, *Medieval and Renaissance Manuscripts,* II, 375–82, no. 177, pl. XIXc, figs. 309, 310.

❖ ❖ ❖

58 Figs. 30, 52, 61

Walters Art Museum, MS W. 224.

France, Rouen, ca. 1480.

Vellum, 81 leaves, 6⅝ x 4½ in. (16.9 x 11.4 cm), 1 column, 26 lines, in Latin and French, in *littera batarda,* 13 large miniatures by the Master of the Geneva Latini.

Use: Calendar: Rouen; Hours of the Virgin: Rouen; Office of the Dead: Rouen.

TEXT	IMAGE
Calendar (1–6v)	
Gospel Lessons (7–10)	John on Patmos, Matthew Writing, Mark Examining Pen, Luke Writing; border: John Boiled in Oil (7)
Obscero te, O intemerata (10v–16)	Virgin of Mercy; Virgin, in "O"; border: Madonna flanked by Patron and Patroness (retouched ca. 1500, 10v)
	Lamentation; Virgin, in "O"; border: Angels with Instruments of the Passion (13v)
Hours of the Virgin (17–41v)	
Matins	Moses and the Burning Bush; Gideon and the Miraculous Fleece, in "D"; border: Annunciation (17)
Lauds	Dream of Pharaoh's Butler; Virgin Walking, in "D"; border: Visitation (22v)
Suffrages	
Prime	Augustus and the Tiburtine Sibyl; Shepherd, in "D"; border: Nativity (30)
Terce	Jacob's Ladder; Shepherd, in "D"; border: Annunciation to the Shepherds (33)
Sext	Magi Worshiping Christ as the Star of Bethlehem; Massacre of the Innocents, in "D"; border: Adoration of the Magi (35)
None	Sacrifice of Isaac; Baptism of Christ, in "D"; border: Presentation in the Temple (37)
(Vespers missing)	(Miniature missing)
Compline	Solomon Receives the Queen of Sheba; Virgin Praying, in "C"; border: Coronation of the Virgin (39)
Penitential Psalms, Litany (43–54v)	Bathsheba at Her Bath; David in Prayer, in "D"; border: Uriah Slain (43)
Hours of the Cross (55–56v)	Isaiah Sawn Asunder; Suicide of Judas, in "D"; border: Crucifixion (55)
Hours of the Holy Spirit (57–58v)	Building of the Tower of Babel; Moses Receiving the Tablets of the Law, in "D"; border: Pentecost (57)
Office of the Dead (59–73)	(Miniature missing)
Passion according to John, and various prayers including those said while passing a cross, when passing a cemetery, to the Eucharist (74–80v)	

BIBLIOGRAPHY: Randall, *Medieval and Renaissance Manuscripts,* II, 308–13, no. 165, pl. XVIIId, figs. 287–89.

❖ ❖ ❖

59 Fig. 120

Walters Art Museum, MS W. 233.

France, Rouen, ca. 1480.

Vellum, 136 leaves, 6⅞ x 4⅝ in. (17.5 x 11.8 cm), 1 column, 17 lines, in Latin and French, in *textura,* 11 large and 12 small (fols. 92v–95) miniatures, 12 calendar and 12 zodiacal vignettes, by the Master of the Geneva Latini.

Use: Calendar: Rouen; Hours of the Virgin: Rouen; Office of the Dead: Rouen.

TEXT	IMAGE
Calendar (1–12v)	Zodiacal sign on each verso
Jan.	Feasting (1)
Feb.	Keeping Warm (2)
Mar.	Pruning (3)
Apr.	Picking Flowers (4)
May	Hawking (5)
Jun.	Mowing (6)
Jul.	Reaping (7)
Aug.	Threshing (8)
Sept.	Sowing (9)
Oct.	Treading Grapes (10)
Nov.	Thrashing for Acorns (11)
Dec.	Slaughtering a Pig (12)
Gospel Lessons (13–17)	John on Patmos, Matthew Writing, Mark Writing, Luke Examining Pen, Christ Child with Cross (13)
Obsecro te, O intemerata (18–24)	(2 miniatures missing)
Hours of the Virgin (25–73)	
Matins	Annunciation; border: Temptation, Gideon and the Miraculous Fleece (25)
Lauds	Visitation (35)
Suffrages	
Prime	Nativity (49)
Terce	Annunciation to the Shepherds (54)
Sext	Adoration of the Magi (57v)
None	Presentation in the Temple (60v)

Vespers	Flight into Egypt with Massacre of the Innocents (64)
Compline	Coronation of the Virgin (69v)
Penitential Psalms, Litany (75–91v)	David Admonished by Nathan, David and Goliath in backround; border: Isaiah at Bedside of Ezechias, Jonah Admonishing King Sennacherib (75)
Hours of the Cross (92–95v)	
Matins	(Miniature missing)
Prime	Flagellation (92v)
Terce	Christ Carrying the Cross (93)
Sext	Christ Nailed to the Cross (93v)
None	Crucifixion (94)
Vespers	Deposition (94v)
Compline	Entombment (95)
Hours of the Holy Spirit (96–97v)	(Miniature missing)
Office of the Dead (98–136)	Last Judgement; border: David Ordering a Decapitation, Judgement of Solomon (98)

BIBLIOGRAPHY: Randall, *Medieval and Renaissance Manuscripts*, II, 304–08, no. 164, fig. 286.

❖ ❖ ❖

60 Fig. 117

Walters Art Museum, MS W. 284.

Northwestern France, 1420s, with miniatures painted in Rouen ca. 1480 when the manuscript was completed for a lady said to be of the Movy en Beauvaisie and Bazan de Flamanville (Caen) family.

Vellum, 140 leaves, 8½ x 5⅝ in. (21.7 x 14.2 cm), 1 column, 16 lines, in Latin and French, in *textura*, 13 large miniatures by the Master of the Geneva Latini.

Use: Calendar: Coutances; Hours of the Virgin: Coutances; Office of the Dead: Coutances.

TEXT	IMAGE
Calendar (1–12v)	
Gospel Lessons, Passion according to John, various prayers including Salve regina, Regina celi (13–20v)	
Hours of the Virgin (21–60v)	
Matins	Annunciation (21)
Lauds	Visitation (29v)
Prime	Nativity (38)
Terce	Annunciation to the Shepherds (42)
Sext	Adoration of the Magi (45v)
None	Presentation in the Temple (48v)
Vespers	Flight into Egypt (52)
Compline	Coronation of the Virgin (57)
Hours of the Cross (61–63v)	Crucifixion (61)
Hours of the Holy Spirit (64–68v)	Pentecost (64)
Penitential Psalms, Litany (69–84v)	David Admonished by Nathan (69)
Office of the Dead (85–118v)	Clerics Pray over a Corpse While Michael Battles a Devil for His Soul (85)
Suffrages (118v–125v)	
Obsecro te, O intemerata, various prayers including 15 Joys of the Virgin (126–139)	
Prayer to John the Evangelist (139v–140)	John the Evangelist with Kneeling Patroness (139v)

BIBLIOGRAPHY: Randall, *Medieval and Renaissance Manuscripts*, II, 294–300, no. 162, figs. 283, 284, 396.

61 Fig. 128

Walters Art Museum, MS W. 241.

France, Rouen, ca. 1480.

Vellum, 136 leaves, 7⅜ x 5⅛ in. (18.7 x 12.9 cm), 1 column, 15 lines, in Latin and French, in *textura*, 14 large miniatures, 6 border vignettes, and 12 calendar vignettes, by the workshop of the Master of the Geneva Latini.

Use: Calendar: Rouen; Hours of the Virgin: Rouen; Office of the Dead: Rouen.

TEXT	IMAGE
Calendar (1–12v)	
Jan.	Feasting (1)
Feb.	Keeping Warm (2)
Mar.	Pruning (3)
Apr.	Picking Flowers and Making Wreaths (4)
May	Hawking (5)
Jun.	Mowing (6)
Jul.	Reaping (7)
Aug.	Threshing (8)
Sept.	Treading Grapes (9)
Oct.	Sowing (10)
Nov.	Thrashing for Acorns (11)
Dec.	Slaughtering a Pig (12)
Gospel Lessons (13–18v)	John on Patmos, Matthew Writing, Mark Examining Pen, Luke Writing (13)
Hours of the Virgin (19–67)	
Matins	Annunciation; border: Virgin Weaving; Marriage of the Virgin (19)
Lauds	Visitation (29v)
Prime	Nativity (43)
Terce	Annunciation to the Shepherds (48)
Sext	Adoration of the Magi (51)
None	Presentation in the Temple (54)
Vespers	Flight into Egypt (57)
Compline	Coronation of the Virgin (63)
Hours of the Cross (67v–70v)	Crucifixion (67v)
Hours of the Holy Spirit (71–74)	Pentecost (71)
Penitential Psalms, Litany (75–91v)	David Admonished by Nathan; border: David and Goliath; David, Carrying Goliath's Head, Received in Triumph (75)
Office of the Dead (92–120)	Three Living and Three Dead; border: Death Approaching a Pope; Death Attacking a Young Man (92)
15 Joys of the Virgin, 7 Requests to Our Lord (121–128v)	Madonna Enthroned, with Kneeling Patroness (121)
Obsecro te, O intemerata (128v–136)	

BIBLIOGRAPHY: Randall, *Medieval and Renaissance Manuscripts*, II, 300–04, no. 163, figs. 285, 405.

❖ ❖ ❖

62 Figs. 74, 80

Walters Art Museum, MS W. 291 ("Hours of Ogier Bénigne").

France, Burgundy (Dijon?), ca. 1480.

Vellum, 145 leaves, 9¼ x 6¼ in. (23.6 x 16 cm), 1 column, 19 lines, in Latin and French, in *textura*, 15 large and 23 small (fols. 29–37v, 133–140) miniatures and 4 border vignettes.

Use: Calendar: composite, but with many entries pointing to northern France and southern Belgium, with specific entries pointing to the Burgundian area of Dijon/Langres/Besançon; Hours of the Virgin: Rome; Office of the Dead: Rome.

TEXT	IMAGE
Bénigne family records (mid-16th century, 2–3v)	
Calendar (5–16v)	
O salutaris hostia (added ca. 1500, 18)	Miraculous Bleeding Host of Dijon (added ca. 1500, 17v)
Passion according to John (20–26v)	Agony in the Garden; border: Betrayal, Christ before Caiaphas, Flagellation, Christ Crowned with Thorns (19v)
Gospel Lessons (28–31v)	John on Patmos (28)
	Luke Writing (29)
	Matthew Writing (30)
	Mark Writing (31)
Obsecro te, O intemerata (32–36)	Pietà (32)
	Madonna (34v)
Suffrages (36–38)	John the Baptist (36)
	John the Evangelist (36v)
	Lawrence (37)
	Nicholas Resuscitating the Three Boys (37)
	Mary Magdalene (37v)
Hours of the Virgin (38v–83v)	
Matins	Annunciation (38v)
Lauds	Visitation (52v)
Prime	Nativity (61)
Terce	Annunciation to the Shepherds (64v)
Sext	Adoration of the Magi (68)
None	Presentation in the Temple (71v)
Vespers	Flight into Egypt (75)
Compline	Coronation of the Virgin (80v)
Hours of the Cross (84–86v)	Crucifixion (84)
Hours of the Holy Spirit (87–89)	Pentecost (87)
Penitential Psalms, Litany (90–101v)	David in Prayer (90)
Office of the Dead (102v–132v)	Job on the Dungheap (102)
Suffrages (133–140v)	Christ Blessing (133)
	Michael Battling a Devil (133v)
	Peter and Paul (134)
	Stephen (134v)
	Christopher Carrying Christ (134v)
	Sebastian Shot with Arrows (135v)
	Claude of Besançon (136v)
	Anthony (137v)
	Anne Instructing the Virgin (138)
	Catherine (138v)
	Margaret Emerging from the Dragon (139)
	Barbara (139v)
	Apollonia (140)
Bénigne family records (mid-16th century, 141v–144v)	

BIBLIOGRAPHY: Randall, *Medieval and Renaissance Manuscripts*, II, 393–400, no. 180, pl. XXa, figs. 316–18.

❖ ❖ ❖

63 Pl. 37

Walters Art Museum, MS W. 457.

France, Burgundy (?), ca. 1480–90.

Vellum, 155 leaves, 8 x 5⅝ in. (20.5 x 14.2 cm), 1 column, 14 lines, in Latin and French, in *textura*, 12 large miniatures.

Use: Calender: northern France; Hours of the Virgin: Rome; Office of the Dead: Rome.

TEXT	IMAGE
Calendar (Feb. and Mar. missing, 2–11v)	
Gospel Lessons (13–18v)	John on Patmos (13)
Obsecro te (19–22v)	Pietà (19)
Hours of the Virgin (24–87v)	
Matins	Annunciation (24)
Lauds	Visitation (36a)
Prime	(Miniature missing)
Terce	Annunciation to the Shepherds (55v)
Sext	Adoration of the Magi (59v)
None	Presentation in the Temple (63v)
Vespers	Flight into Egypt (67v)
Compline	(Miniature missing)
Hours of the Cross (88–90v)	Crucifixion (88v)
Hours of the Holy Spirit (91–94v)	Pentecost (91)
Penitential Psalms, Litany (97–116v)	David in Prayer (97)
Office of the Dead (117–154)	Death Approaching the Deathbed and Battle over the Soul (117)

BIBLIOGRAPHY: Randall, *Medieval and Renaissance Manuscripts*, II, 356–61, no. 174, fig. 304.

❖ ❖ ❖

64 Figs. 31, 79

Walters Art Museum, MS W. 245.

France, mid-1480s.

Vellum, 90 leaves, 6½ x 4⅝ in. (16.7 x 11.6 cm), 2 columns, 26 lines, in Latin and French, in *littera batarda*, 16 large (fols. 5, 8, 13, 14, 15, 18, 20v, 22v, 24v, 27, 31, 39, 58, 62, 63, 67) and 79 small miniatures, 16 historiated borders, and 12 calendar and 12 zodiacal vignettes.

Use: Calendar: composite; Hours of the Virgin: Angers; Office of the Dead: Angers.

TEXT	IMAGE
Calendar (1v–4)	Zodiacal signs accompany each vignette
Jan. and Feb.	Feasting and Keeping Warm (1v)
Mar. and Apr.	Pruning and Picking Flowers (2)
May and Jun.	Hawking and Carrying Sheep (2v)
Jul. and Aug.	Mowing and Reaping (3)
Sept. and Oct.	Sowing and Treading Grapes (3v)
Nov. and Dec.	Slaughtering a Pig and Baking Bread (4)
Hours of the Virgin (5–29v)	
Matins	Annunciation; border: Tree of Jesse, Isaiah, Kneeling Patroness (5)
	Two Kneeling Men Praying (5v)
	Temptation of Eve (6v)
	Moses and the Burning Bush (6v)
	Gideon and the Miraculous Fleece (7v)
Lauds	Visitation; border: Meeting at the Golden Gate, Annunciation to Anne, Annunciation to Joachim (8)
	Salvator Mundi (8v)
	Christ Healing a Sick Woman (8v)
	Priest Hearing Confession (?) (9)
	Three Hebrews in the Fiery Furnace (9v)
	David in Prayer with Animals of Creation (10v)
	Zacharius Writing (11v)
Matins of the Hours of the Cross	Crucifixion; border: Flagellation, Christ Carrying the Cross (13)
Matins of the Hours of the Holy Spirit	Pentecost; border: Baptism of Christ, Temptation of Christ (14)
Prime	Nativity; border: Virgin and Joseph Approach the Inn (15)

	Dream of Pharaoh's Butler (15v) Augustus and the Tiburtine Sibyl (16) Joseph's Rod (16)
Prime of the Cross Prime of the Holy Spirit	
Terce	Annunciation to the Shepherds; border: Adoration of the Shepherds; Shepherds Dancing (18) Shepherd in Prayer (18v) Shepherd Speaking with Two Men (18v) Shepherds Drawing Water from a Well (19)
Terce of the Cross Terce of the Holy Spirit	
Sext	Adoration of the Magi; border: Magi before Herod (20v) Three Soldiers Offer Water to David (21) Solomon Enthroned (21) Magi Worshiping Christ as the Star of Bethlehem (21v)
Sext of the Cross Sext of the Holy Spirit	
None	Presentation in the Temple; border: Holy Family Leaving Temple, Simeon (?) (22v) Flowering of Aaron's Rod (23) Menorah (23) Presentation of Samuel (23v)
None of the Cross None of the Holy Spirit	
Vespers	Massacre of the Innocents; border: Flight into Egypt, Soldier with Speared Child (24v) Egyptians' Statue of the Virgin and Child (25) Moses Breaking Pharaoh's Crown (25) Nebuchadnezzar's Dream (25)
Vespers of the Cross Vespers of the Holy Spirit	
Compline	Coronation of the Virgin; border: Death of the Virgin (27) Ark of the Covenant (27v) Virgin of the Apocalypse (27v) Virgin with Christ (28)
Penitential Psalms, Litany (31–37v)	Bathsheba at Her Bath; border: Death of Uriah, David and Goliath (31) David Admonished by Nathan (31v) David Harping (32v) David with the Angel (33v) David with a Dragon (34) David in Prayer (35) David in Prayer with Kneeling Patroness (35v)
Office of the Dead (39–52v)	
Vespers	Three Living and Three Dead; border: Hermit (39)
Matins and Lauds	Job with his Family (42v) Destruction of Job's Family (42v) Job Loses His Livestock (43) Job Tormented by the Devil (45v) Job Beaten by the Devil (46) Job Tormented by His Friends (46) Job Tormented by His Wife (49v) Job Tormented by His Friends (50) Job, Restored, Addressing Group of Men (50v)
Passion according to John (53–57v)	Agony in the Garden (53) Betrayal (53v) Pilate Washing His Hands (54v) Christ Crowned with Thorns (55) Christ Nailed to the Cross (56) Crucifixion (56v) Deposition (57v)
Prayers to the Trinity, God the Father, Christ, and the Holy Spirit (58–61v)	Trinity; border: Angels (58) God the Father (59) Man of Sorrows (60) Pentecost (61v)
7 Prayers of St. Gregory (62–v)	Mass of St. Gregory; border: Arma Christi (62)
Gospel Lessons (63–66)	John Boiled in Oil; border: John on Patmos, John with the Cup of Poison (63) Luke Writing (64) Matthew Writing (64v) Mark Writing (65v)
Obsecro te, O intemerata, Stabat mater, Ave cuius conceptio, and other prayers (67–79v)	Lamentation; border: Two Thieves, Preparation of the Tomb (67) Madonna (69) Virgin at Foot of the Cross (76v) Anne with Virgin in Her Womb (77v)
Suffrages (80–87v)	Michael Slaying the Dragon (80) John the Baptist (80) John the Evangelist (80v) Peter and Paul (80v) James (81) Stephen (81v) Christopher Carrying Christ (81v) Lawrence (82v) Sebastian Shot with Arrows (82v) Dennis (83) Nicholas Resuscitating the Three Boys (83v) Martin Dividing His Cloak (84) Claude of Besançon (84) Anthony (85) Anne Instructing the Virgin (85) Mary Magdalene (85v) Catherine (86) Margaret Emerging from the Dragon (86) Barbara (86v) Apollonia (87)
Hours of the Trinity (added later, 87v–90v)	

BIBLIOGRAPHY: Randall, *Medieval and Renaissance Manuscripts,* II, 321–28, no. 168, figs. 294–96.

❖ ❖ ❖

65 Fig. 23

Walters Art Museum, MS W. 227.

France, Tours (?), ca. 1490.

Vellum, 137 leaves, 6½ x 4¼ in. (16.2 x 11.1 cm), 1 column, 22 lines, in Latin, in *littera batarda,* 9 large and 16 small (fols. 9–16v, 128–133v) miniatures, and 12 calendar and 12 zodiacal vignettes, by a follower of Jean Bourdichon.

Use: Calendar: general for northern France/southern Belgium; Hours of the Virgin: Rome; Office of the Dead: Rome.

TEXT	IMAGE
Calendar (3–8v)	Zodiacal sign on each recto and verso
Jan.	Feasting (3)
Feb.	Breaking Ground and Pruning (3v)

Mar.	Pruning (4)
Apr.	Making Flower Wreaths (4v)
May	Courting (5)
Jun.	Shearing Sheep (5v)
Jul.	Mowing and Reaping (6)
Aug.	Threshing (6v)
Sept.	Treading Grapes (7)
Oct.	Ploughing and Sowing (7v)
Nov.	Baking Bread (8)
Dec.	Slaughtering and Roasting Pigs (8v)
Gospel Lessons (9–13v)	John Writing (9)
	Luke Examining Pen (10)
	Matthew Writing (11v)
	Mark Writing (12v)
Obsecro te, O intemerata (13v–18)	Virgo Lactans (13v)
	Lamentation (16v)
Hours of the Virgin (19–73v)	
Matins	Annunciation (19)
Lauds	Visitation (34)
Prime	Nativity (43v)
Terce	Annunciation to the Shepherds (47v)
Sext	(Miniature missing)
None	Presentation in the Temple (54)
Vespers	Flight into Egypt (58)
Compline	Coronation of the Virgin (64)
Penitential Psalms, Litany (74–87v)	David Anointed by Samuel (74)
Hours of the Cross (88–89v)	(Miniature missing)
Hours of the Holy Spirit (90–91v)	(Miniature missing)
Office of the Dead (92–127v)	Job on the Dungheap (92)
Suffrages (128–134v)	Trinity (128)
	Michael (128v)
	James (129)
	Sebastian Shot with Arrows (129v)
	Claude of Besançon (130)
	Anthony (131v)
	Mary Magdalene (132)
	Catherine (132v)
	Geneviève (133)
	Barbara (133v)

BIBLIOGRAPHY: Randall, *Medieval and Renaissance Manuscripts*, II, 454–58, no. 196, pl. XXIb, figs. 343, 344.

❖ ❖ ❖

66 Fig. 62

Walters Art Museum, MS W. 294.

France, end of the 15th century.

Vellum, 92 leaves, 9 ¼ x 6 ⅜ in. (24.7 x 16.2 cm), 1 column, 24 lines, in Latin and French, in *littera batarda*, 10 large and 8 small (fols. 5v–17) miniatures.

Use: Calendar: general; Hours of the Virgin: Rome; Office of the Dead: Rome.

TEXT	IMAGE
Calendar (1–3v)	
Gospel Lessons (5–8)	John on Patmos (4v)
	Luke Reading (5v)
	Matthew Contemplating (6v)
	Mark Writing (7v)
Obsecro te, O intemerata, Stabat mater, 7 Prayers of St. Gregory, various other prayers (8–15v)	Madonna (8) Pietà (10)
Suffrages, various prayers including those said while and after receiving Communion, 7 Verses of St. Bernard (15v–18v)	Michael Battling a Devil (15v) Christopher Carrying Christ (16) Mary Magdalene (17)
Hours of the Virgin (19–56v)	
Matins	Annunciation (19)
Lauds	Visitation (25)
Prime	Nativity (31v)
Terce	Annunciation to the Shepherds (34)
Sext	Adoration of the Magi (37)
None	Presentation in the Temple (39v)
Vespers	Flight into Egypt (42)
Compline	Coronation of the Virgin (46)
Penitential Psalms, Litany (57–66v)	(Miniature missing)
Hours of the Cross (67–v)	(Miniature missing)
Hours of the Holy Spirit (68–69v)	Pentecost (68)
Office of the Dead (70–92)	(Miniature missing)

BIBLIOGRAPHY: Randall, *Medieval and Renaissance Manuscripts*, II, 458–62, no. 197, pl. XXIIa, figs. 345, 346.

❖ ❖ ❖

67 Pl. 20

Walters Art Museum, MS W. 295.

France, Tours, late 15th century, possibly produced for a La Tour d'Auvergne, seigneur d'Oliergues, comte de Beaufort, vicomte de Turenne.

Vellum, 60 leaves, 12 ¼ x 8 ¼ in. (32.3 x 21.1 cm.), 1 column, 23 lines, in Latin, in *textura*, 12 miniatures by Jean Poyet and his workshop.

Use: Calendar: Saintes; Hours of the Virgin: Saintes; Office of the Dead: Rome.

TEXT	IMAGE
Calendar (3–8v)	
Hours of the Virgin (9–31v)	
Matins	Annunciation (9)
Lauds	Visitation (16)
Prime	Nativity (20v)
Terce	Annunciation to the Shepherds (22)
Sext	Adoration of the Magi (24)
None	Presentation in the Temple (25v)
Vespers	Flight into Egypt (27)
Compline	Coronation of the Virgin (30)
Hours of the Cross (31v–33)	Christ Carrying the Cross (31v)
Hours of the Holy Spirit (33–34v)	Pentecost (33)
Penitential Psalms, Litany (34v–42)	David in Prayer (35)
Office of the Dead (42–59v)	Job on the Dungheap (42v)
	Arms of La Tour d'Auvergne (59v)

BIBLIOGRAPHY: Randall, *Medieval and Renaissance Manuscripts*, II, 410–13, no. 185, pl. XXb, fig. 325.

❖ ❖ ❖

68 Fig. 123

Walters Art Museum, MS W. 430.

France, Tours, end of the 15th century.

Vellum, 166 leaves, 4 ¼ x 2 ½ in. (10.8 x 6.4 cm), 1 column, 16 lines, in Latin and French, in *littera batarda*, 21 large miniatures by Jean Poyet and his workshop.

Use: Calendar: general; Hours of the Virgin: Rome; Office of the Dead: Rome.

TEXT	IMAGE
Calendar (1–12v)	
Hours of the Virgin (13–83v)	
Matins	Annunciation (13)
Lauds	Visitation (36v)
Prime	(Miniature missing)
Terce	Annunciation to the Shepherds (55)

Sext	(Miniature missing)
None	(Miniature missing)
Vespers	Flight into Egypt (68)
Compline	(Miniature missing)
Penitential Psalms, Litany (83v–113v)	David Anointed by Samuel (84)
	David and Goliath (86)
	David Harping (88)
	Bathsheba at Her Bath (91v)
	David and Uriah (94v)
	David Admonished by Nathan (98)
	David in Prayer (99v)
Office of the Dead (114–162v)	
Vespers	Death Riding a Bull (114)
Matins and Lauds	Job with His Family (131)
	Job Tormented by the Devil (132v)
	Job Loses His Livestock (134)
	Destruction of Job's Family (142)
	Job Tormented by His Friends (143v)
	Job on the Dungheap (145)
	Job Tormented by the Devil (153v)
	Job Beaten by the Devil (155)
	(Miniature missing)
Stabat mater (163–164v)	(Miniature missing)
Suffrages (165–166v)	Peter of Luxembourg Praying before a Crucifix (165v)

BIBLIOGRAPHY: Randall, *Medieval and Renaissance Manuscripts*, II, 440–44, no. 192, pl. XXd, figs. 338, 339.

❖ ❖ ❖

69

Fig. 67

Walters Art Museum, MS W. 454.

France, Tours, ca. 1500, produced for L. de Blanry.

Vellum, 115 leaves, 7⅛ x 4⅝ in. (18 x 11.5 cm), 1 column, 21 lines, in Latin, in *littera batarda*, 13 large and 18 small (fols. 8v–11v, Suffrages) miniatures by a follower of Jean Poyet.

Use: Calendar: northern France; Hours of the Virgin: Rome; Office of the Dead: Rome.

TEXT	IMAGE
Calendar (1–6v)	
Gospel Lessons (7v–11)	John on Patmos (7)
	Luke with Ox (8v)
	Matthew with Angel (9v)
	Mark Examining Pen, with Lion (10v)
Obsecro te (11v–14)	Madonna (11v)
Hours of the Virgin (15v–66v)	
Matins	Annunciation (15)
Lauds	Visitation (28v)
Matins of the Hours of the Cross	Crucifixion (37)
Matins of the Hours of the Holy Spirit	Pentecost (38)
Prime	Nativity (39)
Terce	Annunciation to the Shepherds (42v)
Sext	Adoration of the Magi (46)
None	Presentation in the Temple (49)
Vespers	Flight into Egypt (52)
Compline	Coronation of the Virgin (56v)
Penitential Psalms, Litany (67v–82)	David and Uriah (67)
Office of the Dead (83v–106)	Job on the Dungheap (83)
Suffrages (107–114v)	Trinity (107)
	Michael (107v)
	John the Baptist (108)
	John the Evangelist (108v)
	Peter and Paul (109)
	Stephen (109v)
	Lawrence (110)
	Christopher Carrying Christ (110v)
	Sebastian (111v)
	Nicholas Resuscitating the Three Boys (112v)
	Anthony (112v)
	Anne with the Virgin (113)
	Mary Magdalene (113v)
	Catherine (114)

BIBLIOGRAPHY: Randall, *Medieval and Renaissance Manuscripts*, II, 400–04, no. 181, figs. 319, 320.

❖ ❖ ❖

70

Fig. 96

New York, Pierpont Morgan Library, MS H. 8 ("Cumberland Hours" or "Hours of Henry VIII").

(Dannie and Hettie Heineman Collection, Gift of The Heineman Foundation, 1977)

France, Tours, ca. 1500.

Vellum, 200 leaves, 10⅛ x 7 in. (25.7 x 18 cm), 1 column, 17 lines, in Latin and French, in *littera batarda*, 14 large (fols. 13, 30v–170) and 29 half-page miniatures, and 12 half-page calendar illustrations, all with an historiated border, by Jean Poyet.

Use: Calendar: mainly Franciscan and Augustinian; Hours of the Virgin: Rome; Office of the Dead: Rome.

TEXT	IMAGE
Calendar (1–6v)	Zodiacal sign on each recto and verso; each monochrome border is filled with specific or generic saints or events commemorated in the calendar
Jan.	Feasting and Keeping Warm (1)
Feb.	Keeping Warm (1v)
Mar.	Pruning (2)
Apr.	Picking Flowers and Making Wreaths (2v)
May	Picking Branches (3)
Jun.	Mowing (3v)
Jul.	Reaping (4)
Aug.	Threshing (4v)
Sept.	Treading Grapes (5)
Oct.	Sowing and Ploughing (5v)
Nov.	Thrashing for Acorns (6)
Dec.	Roasting Slaughtered Pigs (6v)
Gospel Lessons (7–12v)	John on Patmos; border: John Boiled in Oil (7)
	Luke Writing; border: Annunciation (9)
	Matthew Writing; border: Magi Meeting at the Crossroads (10v)
	Mark Contemplating; border: Christ Preaching to a Crowd (12)
Passion according to John (13–21v)	Ego Sum (13)
Obsecro te, O intemerata (21v–25v)	Holy Family; border: Angels Making Music (21v)
	(Miniature missing)
Stabat mater, Mass of the Virgin (26–29v)	Lamentation; border: Deposition (26)
	(Miniature missing)
Hours of the Virgin (31–93v)	
Matins	Annunciation (30v)
Lauds	Visitation (40v)
Prime	Nativity (51v)
Terce	Annunciation to the Shepherds (56v)
Sext	Adoration of the Magi (61v)
None	Presentation in the Temple (65v)
Vespers	Massacre of the Innocents (69v)
Compline	(Miniature missing)

Hours of the Cross (95–101)	Christ Carrying the Cross (94v)
Hours of the Holy Spirit (102–106v)	Pentecost (101v)
Penitential Psalms, Litany (107v–127)	David and Uriah (108v)
Office of the Dead (127v–167v)	
Vespers	Job on the Dungheap (127v)
Matins and Lauds	Feast of Dives; border: Dives in Hell (134v)
7 Prayers of St. Gregory (168v–169v)	Mass of St. Gregory (168)
Suffrages (170v–193)	Jerome in Penance (170)
	Trinity; border: Angels (171)
	Michael Battling a Devil; border: Fall of the Rebel Angels (172)
	Baptism of Christ; border: John the Baptist Preaching (173)
	John the Evangelist Descending into His Grave; border: John and the Beast of the Apocalypse (174)
	Fall of Simon Magus; border: Decapitation of Paul and Crucifixion of Peter (175)
	James with Hermogenes; border: Decapitation of James (176)
	Philip Vanquishing Idols and Devils; border: Philip Baptizing (177)
	Conversion of Christopher; border: Christopher Carrying Christ (178)
	Sebastian, Shot with Arrows, Abandoned by Archers; border: Sebastian's Body Cast into the Sewer (179)
	Claude of Besançon Resuscitating a Dead Man; border: Pilgrims Kneeling before Claude's Shrine (180v)
	Martyrdom of Adrian; border: Christians in Prison (181v)
	Nicholas Giving Gold to the Three Maidens; border: Nicholas Resuscitating the Three Boys (182v)
	Temptation of Anthony; border: Anthony in the Wilderness (183v)
	Stigmatization of Francis; border: Francis in the Fiery Chariot (184v)
	Anthony of Padua Showing the Host to the Kneeling Mule; border: Anthony Preaching (185v)
	Anne Instructing the Virgin; border: Presentation of the Virgin in the Temple (186v)
	Mary Magdalene Washing the Feet of Christ; border: Levitation of Mary Magdalene (187v)
	Catherine Rescued from the Torture Wheels; border: Decapitiation of Catherine (188v)
	Margaret and Olybrius; border: Margaret and the Dragon (189v)
	Decapitation of Barbara; border: Barbara before Her Tower (190v)
	Martha Taming the Tarasque; border: Martha Preaching (191v)
	All (Male) Saints; border: All (Female) Saints (192v)
Various Prayers including those recited when waking up, when leaving the house, when entering a church, before a crucifix, at the Elevation, followed by the Athanasian Creed (194–199v)	

BIBLIOGRAPHY: Wieck et al., *The Hours of Henry VIII.*

71

Fig. 126

Washington D.C., Library of Congress, MS Rosenwald 15.
France, Paris, early 16th century.
Vellum, 181 leaves, $5\frac{7}{8}$ x $3\frac{5}{8}$ in. (14.2 x 9.3 cm), 1 column, 18 lines, in Latin with later French additions, in *littera humanistica rotunda,* 16 large and 25 small (fols. 14v–17, 30v, 156v–172v) miniatures by a follower of the Master of Petrarch's Triumphs.
Use: Calendar: Bourges; Hours of the Virgin: Bourges; Office of the Dead: Bourges.

TEXT	IMAGE
Calendar (1–12)	
Gospel Lessons (13–17v)	John on Patmos (12v)
	Luke Writing (14v)
	Matthew Examining Pen (15v)
	Mark Writing (17)
Passion according to John (17v–26v)	Agony in the Garden (18)
Obsecro te, O intemerata (27–32)	Madonna Enthroned, Serenaded by Angels (27)
	Pietà (30v)
Hours of the Virgin (32v–100v)	
Matins	Annunciation (32v)
Lauds	Visitation (49)
Matins of the Hours of the Cross	Crucifixion (59)
Matins of the Hours of the Holy Spirit	Pentecost (60v)
Prime	Nativity (62)
Prime of the Cross	
Prime of the Holy Spirit	
Terce	Annunciation to the Shepherds (69)
Terce of the Cross	
Terce of the Holy Spirit	
Sext	Adoration of the Magi (74v)
Sext of the Cross	
Sext of the Holy Spirit	
None	Presentation in the Temple (80)
None of the Cross	
None of the Holy Spirit	
Vespers	Flight into Egypt (86)
Vespers of the Cross	
Vespers of the Holy Spirit	
Compline	Coronation of the Virgin (94)
Compline of the Cross	
Compline of the Holy Spirit	
Penitential Psalms, Litany (100v–116v)	David in Prayer (101)
Office of the Dead (116v–157v)	Dives in Hell (117)
	Burial Service (156v)
Suffrages, 7 Prayers of St. Gregory, Suffrages (158–172v)	Trinity (158)
	God the Father (159)
	Christ (159v)
	Holy Spirit as a Youth (160)
	Veronica Holding Her Veil (160v)
	Bernardino (162)
	Mass of St. Gregory (163v)
	Michael Battling a Devil (165)
	John the Baptist (165v)
	John the Evangelist (166)
	Peter and Paul (166v)
	James (167v)
	Grilling of Lawrence (168)
	Nicholas Resuscitating the Three Boys (168v)
	Temptation of Anthony (169)
	Mary Magdalene in Her Cave (169v)
	Decapitation of Catherine (170v)
	Margaret Emerging from the Dragon (171)
	Barbara (171v)
	All Saints (172v)

Various prayers, including those said before, while, and after receiving Communion, and to the Virgin (added somewhat later, 173–181)

BIBLIOGRAPHY: Schutzner, *Medieval and Renaissance Manuscript Books*, 330–34, MS 54, illus.

❖ ❖ ❖

72 Fig. 125

Walters Art Museum, MS W. 452 ("Hours of Florimond Robertet").

France, Paris, ca. 1510–20, produced for Florimond Robertet.

Vellum, 155 leaves, 6⅞ x 4¼ in. (17.5 x 10.8 cm), 1 column, 22 lines, in Latin, in *littera humanistica rotunda*, 15 large and 3 small (fols. 47–49) miniatures by the Master of Morgan 85.

Use: Calendar: Franciscan; Hours of the Virgin: Rome; Office of the Dead: Rome.

TEXT	IMAGE
Calendar (1–12v)	
Passion according to John (13v–20v)	Entry into Jerusalem, Expulsion of the Merchants from the Temple, Last Supper, Christ Washing the Feet of the Apostles (13)
	Agony in the Garden, Betrayal, Christ before Pilate, Christ Crowned with Thorns (13v)
	Flagellation, Ecce Homo, Christ Carrying the Cross, Crucifixion (14)
Passions according to Matthew, Mark, Luke (21–45)	
Gospel Lessons (45v–49v)	John on Patmos (45v)
	Luke Examining Pen (47)
	Matthew Writing (48)
	Mark Writing (49)
Hours of the Virgin (51–94)	
Matins	Annunciation (51)
Lauds	Visitation (62)
Prime	Nativity (69)
Terce	(Miniature missing)
Sext	Adoration of the Magi (73v)
None	Presentation in the Temple (76v)
Vespers	Flight into Egypt (79v)
Compline	Death of the Virgin (84)
Hours of the Cross (94–97)	Crucifixion (94v)
Hour of the Holy Spirit (97v–99v)	Pentecost (97v)
Penitential Psalms, Litany (100v–112v)	David Decapitating Goliath (100v)
Office of the Dead (113v–135)	Lazarus at the Feast of Dives (113v)
Suffrages (135v–145)	
Obsecro te, O intemerata, followed by various prayers, including 7 Joys of the Virgin (145–154v)	

BIBLIOGRAPHY: Randall, *Medieval and Renaissance Manuscripts*, II, 521–26, no. 208, pl. XXIIIc, figs. 368–72.

❖ ❖ ❖

73 Fig. 28

Walters Art Museum, MS W. 455.

France, Rouen (?), early 16th century.

Vellum, 177 leaves, 8⅛ x 5⅝ in. (20.7 x 14 cm), 1 column, 15 lines, in Latin and French, in *textura*, 21 miniatures by a follower of the Master of Morgan 85.

Use: Calendar: composite, but with many entries pointing to northern France; Hours of the Virgin: Rome (with Lauds variant); Office of the Dead: unidentified.

TEXT	IMAGE
Calendar (3–14v)	
Gospel Lessons (16–23)	John on Patmos (16)
	Luke Writing (18)
	Matthew Writing (20)
	Mark Writing (22)
Obsecro te (24–27v)	(Miniature missing)
Hours of the Virgin (28–94v)	
Matins	Annunciation (28)
Lauds	Visitation (48v)
Prime	Nativity (60v)
Terce	Annunciation to the Shepherds (66)
Sext	Adoration of the Magi (71)
None	Presentation in the Temple (75v)
Vespers	Flight into Egypt (80v)
Compline	Assumption of the Virgin (89v)
Anima Christi sanctifica me (95–v)	Elevation of the Host (95)
Suffrages (96–99v)	Michael Slaying the Dragon (96)
	All Saints (97)
	Angels Holding a Pax (98v)
Penitential Psalms, Litany (100–117v)	David in Prayer (100)
Hours of the Cross (118–121v)	Crucifixion (118)
Hours of the Holy Spirit (122–125v)	Pentecost (122)
Office of the Dead (126–177)	
Vespers	Funeral Service (126)
Matins and Lauds	Raising of Lazarus (135)

BIBLIOGRAPHY: Randall, *Medieval and Renaissance Manuscripts*, II, 535–40, no. 210, pl. XXIVa, fig. 379.

❖ ❖ ❖

74 Fig. 115

Walters Art Museum, MS W. 424.

France, Rouen (?), early 16th century.

Vellum, 87 leaves, 3⅜ x 2⅜ in. (8.6 x 6.1 cm), 1 column, 20 lines, in Latin, in *littera gotica antiqua*, 15 large and 5 small (Suffrages) miniatures, and 1 armorial device.

Use: Hours of the Virgin: Rome; Office of the Dead: Rome.

TEXT	IMAGE
Gospel Lesson of John (1–2v)	John the Evangelist Boiled in Oil (1)
Passion according to John (3–4v)	Christ Carrying the Cross (3)
Hours of the Virgin (5–48)	
Matins	Annunciation (5)
Lauds	Visitation (17v)
Matins of the Hours of the Cross	Agony in the Garden (26)
Matins of the Hours of the Holy Spirit	Pentecost (27)
Prime	Nativity (28)
Prime of the Cross	
Prime of the Holy Spirit	
Terce	Annunciation to the Shepherds (31)
Terce of the Cross	
Terce of the Holy Spirit	
Sext	Adoration of the Magi (34)
Sext of the Cross	
Sext of the Holy Spirit	
None	Presentation in the Temple (37)
None of the Cross	
None of the Holy Spirit	
Vespers	Flight into Egypt (40)
Vespers of the Cross	
Vespers of the Holy Spirit	

Compline	Death of the Virgin (44v)
Compline of the Cross	
Compline of the Holy Spirit	
Penitential Psalms, Litany (48–62)	David in Prayer (48v)
Office of the Dead (62–82)	Funeral Procession (62v)
Stabat mater (83–84v)	Armorial device (added somewhat later, 82v)
	Lamentation, with Arma Christi (83)
Suffrages (84v–87v)	Margaret Emerging from the Dragon (84v)
	Anne Instructing the Virgin (85)
	Barbara (85v)
	Catherine (86v)
	Susanna at Her Bath (87)

BIBLIOGRAPHY: Randall, *Medieval and Renaissance Manuscripts,* II, 497–501, no. 205, fig. 365.

❖ ❖ ❖

75 Fig. 4

Walters Art Museum, MS W. 446.

France, Tours or Bourges, ca. 1510–20, made for Jean Lallemant le Jeune.

Vellum, 96 leaves, 6 x 3⅝ in. (15.2 x 9.3 cm), 1 column, 25 lines, in Latin, in *littera humanistica cursiva,* 14 large and 6 small (fols. 7v–8v, 92v–94) miniatures.

Use: Calendar: Franciscan; Hours of the Virgin: Rome; Office of the Dead; Rome.

TEXT	IMAGE
Calendar (1–6v)	
Gospel Lessons (7–9)	Hair Shirt Seen through Torn Curtain (7v)
	Sealed Book (8)
	Hair Shirt Seen through Torn Curtain (8v)
Passion according to John (10–13v)	Seraph Holding Sealed Book, Crucifix (9v)
Obsecro te, Spes anime mee (13v–15)	
Hours of the Virgin (16–47v)	
Matins	Hair Shirt and Madonna Seen through Torn Curtain (15v)
Lauds	Seraph Holding Sealed Book, Visitation (24)
Prime	Hair Shirt and Nativity Seen through Torn Curtain (29v)
Terce	Seraph Holding Sealed Book, Annunciation to the Shepherds (32)
Sext	Hair Shirt and Adoration of the Magi Seen through Torn Curtain (34)
None	Seraph Holding Sealed Book, Presentation in the Temple (35v)
Vespers	Hair Shirt and Flight into Egypt Seen through Torn Curtain (37v)
Compline	Seraph Holding Sealed Book, Assumption of the Virgin (41)
Hours of the Cross (48–49v)	Hair Shirt and Cross Seen through Torn Curtain (48)
Hours of the Holy Spirit (50–52)	Seraph Holding Sealed Book, Dove of the Holy Spirit (50)
Penitential Psalms, Litany (53–62)	Hair Shirt and David in Prayer Seen through Torn Curtain (52v)
Office of the Dead (63–81)	Seraph Holding Sealed Book, Christ as Judge (62v)
	Border: Skull (63, 66, 68, 68v, 71, 71v, 74v, 75)
Suffrages, various prayers including O intemerata, and those said before and after receiving Communion (81v–92)	Hair Shirt and All Saints Seen through Torn Curtain (81v)
Psalm 90 recited against enemies and various tribulations (92v–93)	Seraph Holding Sealed Book (92v)
7 Verses of St. Bernard (93–93v)	Hair Shirt Seen through Torn Curtain (93)
Hours of the Sacrament (94–96v)	Seraph Holding Sealed Book (94)

BIBLIOGRAPHY: Randall, *Medieval and Renaissance Manuscripts,* II, 540–49, no. 211, pl. XXIVb, fig. 380.

❖ ❖ ❖

76 Fig. 18

Walters Art Museum, MS W. 451.

France, early 16th century, with miniatures added, in Bourges (?), ca. 1535–37 for Jean Lallemant le Jeune.

Vellum, 169 leaves, 7⅛ x 4⅞ in. (18.1 x 12.3 cm), 1 column, 20 lines, in Latin, in *littera batarda,* 7 miniatures, 12 calendar and 12 zodiacal vignettes, and 2 coats of arms.

Use: Calendar: composite; Hours of the Virgin: Rome; Office of the Dead: Rome.

TEXT	IMAGE
Lallemant family obits and other early inscriptions (1v–3)	Arms of Jean Lallemant le Jeune (3v)
Calendar (4–9v)	Zodiacal sign on each recto and verso
Jan.	Keeping Warm (4)
Feb.	Feasting (4v)
Mar.	Pruning and Breaking Ground (5)
Apr.	Courting and Making Flower Wreaths (5v)
May	Riding (6)
Jun.	Mowing (6v)
Jul.	Reaping (7)
Aug.	Storing Wheat (7v)
Sept.	Treading Grapes and Making Wine (8)
Oct.	Sowing (8v)
Nov.	Thrashing for Acorns (9)
Dec.	Slaughtering a Pig (9v)
Gospel Lessons (11–15)	Emblematic Tower with Prisoner Praying to Evangelists' Symbols (10v)
Obsecro te, O intemerata (15–20v)	
Passion according to John (20v–26v)	
Hours of the Virgin (27–75v)	Emblematic Tower with Prisoner Praying to the Madonna (27)
Hours of the Cross (77–78v)	Emblematic Tower with Prisoner Praying to a Crucifix (76v)
Hours of the Holy Spirit (80–81v)	Emblematic Tower with Prisoner Praying to Dove of the Holy Spirit (79v)
Penitential Psalms, Litany (82–97v)	Emblematic Tower with Prisoner Praying to God with a Sword (82)
Office of the Dead (98–129v)	Emblematic Tower with Prisoner Praying to Christ as Judge (98)
Suffrages, Salve santa facies, Stabat mater, 7 Verses of St. Bernard, Passion according to John, 7 Prayers of St. Gregory, and other prayers including those said before, while, and after receiving Communion (131–168)	Emblematic Tower with Prisoner Praying to All Saints (130v)
	Coat-of-arms (169)

BIBLIOGRAPHY: Randall, *Medieval and Renaissance Manuscripts,* II, 552–61, no. 213, pl. XXVb, figs. 382, 383.

77 Pl. 15, Figs. 8, 17, 132

Walters Art Museum, MS W. 449 ("Hours of Jean de Mauléon").

France, Tours (?), datable to 1524, made for Jean de Mauléon, Bishop of St.-Bernard-de-Comminges.

Vellum, 170 leaves, 6⅝ x 3⅞ in. (17 x 10 cm), 1 column, 23 lines, in Latin, in *littera humanistica rotunda*, 16 large and 5 small (fols. 17v–19v, 125, 141v) miniatures, and 12 calendar and 12 zodiacal vignettes, by the 1520s Hours Workshop.

Use: Calendar: mainly Toulouse and southeastern France; Hours of the Virgin: Toulouse; Office of the Dead: Toulouse.

TEXT	IMAGE
	Bertrand between John the Baptist and John the Evangelist (1)
Easter Table (1v)	
Domine deus omnipotens (2)	
Calendar (2v–14)	Zodiacal sign on each verso
Jan.	Playing Dice (2v)
Feb.	Cooking and Feasting (3v)
Mar.	Pruning (4v)
Apr.	Hawking (5v)
May	Making Music (6v)
Jun.	Shearing Sheep (7v)
Jul.	Mowing (8v)
Aug.	Reaping (9v)
Sept.	Ploughing and Sowing (10v)
Oct.	Making Wine (11v)
Nov.	Thrashing for Acorns (12v)
Dec.	Slaughtering a Pig (13v)
7 Prayers of St. Gregory, Suffrage for St. Susanna (14v–16)	
Gospel Lessons (17–20)	John on Patmos (16v)
	Luke Writing (17v)
	Matthew Writing (18v)
	Mark Examining Pen (19v)
Passion according to John (20–26)	Agony in the Garden (21)
Stabat mater, followed by other prayers (26–31v)	
Hours of the Virgin (33–75v)	
Matins	Annunciation (32v)
Lauds	Visitation (40v)
Suffrages	
(Prime missing)	(Miniature missing)
Terce	(Miniature missing)
Sext	(Miniature missing)
None	Presentation in the Temple (55)
Vespers	Flight into Egypt (57v)
Compline	Assumption of the Virgin (63v)
Penitential Psalms, Litany (75v–90)	Bathsheba at Her Bath (76)
Office of the Dead (91–115v)	
Vespers	Lazarus at the Feast of Dives (90v)
Matins and Lauds	Dives in Hell Beseeching Lazarus in the Bosom of Abraham (95)
Hours of the Cross (115v–119)	Crucifixion (116)
Hours of the Holy Spirit (119–122)	Pentecost (119v)
Hours of St. Barbara (122–125)	
Hours of the Cross (125–129)	Ecce Homo (125)
Suffrages (129–141v)	
Hours of the Conception of the Virgin (141v–146)	Virgin Surrounded by Her Symbols (141v)
Passion according to Matthew (146–154)	Entry into Jerusalem (146v)
Passion according to Mark (155–161)	Last Supper (154v)
Passion according to Luke (162–168v)	Christ Washing the Feet of the Apostles (161v)

BIBLIOGRAPHY: Randall, *Medieval and Renaissance Manuscripts*, II, 526–35, no. 209, color frontispiece, figs. 373–78.

78 Fig. 49

Walters Art Museum, MS W. 85.

Southern Belgium, ca. 1300.

Vellum, 116 leaves, 2⅝ x 1¾ in. (6.8 x 4.9 cm), 1 column, 9 lines, in Latin, in *textura*, 2 historiated initials, numerous initials enclosing heads and standing and seated figures representing Christ, evangelists, saints, and each folio decorated with marginalia.

Use: Hours of the Virgin: Dominican.

TEXT	IMAGE
(The manuscript is in very fragmentary condition.)	
Hours of the Virgin (1–68v)	
(Matins missing)	(Historiated initial missing)
Lauds	(Historiated initial missing)
Prime	(Historiated initial missing)
Terce	(Historiated initial missing)
(Sext missing)	(Historiated initial missing)
None	Crucifixion, in "D" (32)
Vespers	Entombment, in "D" (42)
Compline	(Historiated initial missing)
Penitential Psalms, Litany (69–116)	(Historiated initial missing)

BIBLIOGRAPHY: Randall, *Medieval and Renaissance Manuscripts*, III, 65–67, no. 221, fig. 427.

❖ ❖ ❖

79 Fig. 22

Walters Art Museum, MS W. 37.

Belgium, Huy, ca. 1300–10.

Velllum, 197 leaves, 3⅝ x 2¾ in. (9.3 x 6.9 cm), 1 column, 13 lines, in Latin and French, in *textura*, 14 large miniatures, 11 large and numerous small historiated initials, and 12 calendar and 12 zodiacal vignettes.

Use: Calendar: Liège; Hours of the Virgin: Liège; Office of the Dead: Liège.

TEXT	IMAGE
Calendar (3–8v)	Zodiacal sign on each recto and verso
Jan.	Feasting (3)
Feb.	Pruning (3v)
Mar.	Breaking Ground (4)
Apr.	Picking Flowers (4v)
May	Making Music (5)
Jun.	Picking Flowers (5v)
Jul.	Mowing (6)
Aug.	Reaping (6v)
Sept.	Treading Grapes (7)
Oct.	Sowing (7v)
Nov.	Carrying a Pig (8)
Dec.	Slaughtering an Ox (8v)
	(Series of prefatory miniatures:)
	Nativity (9v)
	Presentation in the Temple (10v)
	Christ among the Doctors (11v)
	Entry into Jerusalem (12v)
Hours of the Nativity of the Virgin (13–100)	
Matins	(Miniature and historiated initial missing)
Lauds	Betrayal (32v)
	Judas Receiving Payment, in "D" (33)
Prime	Christ before Pilate (48v)
	Denial of Peter, in "D" (49)

Terce	(Miniature missing)
	Two Jews, in "D" (63)
Sext	Christ Carrying the Cross (69v)
	Lapidation of Stephen, in "D" (70)
None	Crucifixion with *Ecclesia* and *Synagoga* (76v)
	Crucifixion with Two Thieves, in "D" (77)
Vespers	Deposition (83v)
	Entombment, in "D" (84)
Compline	Three Marys at the Tomb (92v)
	Two Nuns, in "C" (93)
Penitential Psalms (101–115)	Noli me tangere (100v)
	Transfiguration, in "D" (101)
15 Gradual Psalms (116–127)	Martyrdom of Lambert (115v)
	Dominic Raising Napoleon Orsini from the Dead, in "A" (116)
Litany, followed by various prayers (127–134)	
Hours of the Holy Spirit (135–147v)	Ascension (134v)
	Pentecost, in "D" (135)
Office of the Dead (149–197)	Harrowing of Hell (148v)
	God Holding Souls to His Bosom above a Damned Soul, in "D" (149)

BIBLIOGRAPHY: Randall, *Medieval and Renaissance Manuscripts*, III, 56–64, no. 220, pl. XXXVIIIa, figs. 425, 426, 597.

❖ ❖ ❖

80 Figs. 21, 25

Walters Art Museum, MS W. 88.

Belgium, Cambrai (?), early 14th century.

Vellum, 202 leaves, 4¼ x 3 in. (10.9 x 7.1 cm), 1 column, 13 lines, in Latin and French, in *textura*, 1 large historiated initial, 24 calendar vignettes, and marginalia on every leaf.

Use: Calendar: Cambrai; Hours of the Virgin: unidentified; Office of the Dead: Cambrai.

TEXT	IMAGE
Calendar (3v–15)	
Jan.	Janus Feasting (3v)
	Hunting (4)
Feb.	Cooking (4v)
	Tending Bellows (5)
Mar.	Pruning (5v)
	Breaking Ground (6)
Apr.	Picking Flowers (6v)
	Making Flower Wreaths (7)
May	Hawking (7v)
	Training a Falcon (8)
Jun.	Carrying Wood (8v)
	Training a Falcon (9)
Jul.	Mowing (9v)
	Mowers Flirting (10)
Aug.	Reaping (10v)
	Reaper Drinking (11)
Sept.	Sowing (11v)
	Harrowing (12)
Oct.	Threshing (12v)
	Winnowing (13)
Nov.	Slaughtering a Pig (13v)
	Feeding Pigs (14)
Dec.	Baking Bread (14v)
	Making Dough (15)
Hours of the Virgin (16–107)	
Matins and Lauds	(Historiated initial missing)
Prime	(Historiated initial missing)
Terce	(Historiated initial missing)
Sext	(Historiated initial missing)
None	(Historiated initial missing)
Vespers	(Historiated initial missing)
Compline	Resurrection in "D"; border: Kneeling Patroness (100v)
Litany, followed by various prayers (107v–116v)	
5 Joys of the Virgin, followed by various prayers (117–120v)	
Office of the Dead (121–179v)	(Historiated initial missing)
Various Prayers to the Virgin (180–196v)	

BIBLIOGRAPHY: Randall, *Medieval and Renaissance Manuscripts*, III, 67–72, no. 222, figs. 428, 429.

❖ ❖ ❖

81 Fig. 91

Walters Art Museum, MS W. 215.

Southern Belgium or northern France, early 15th centrury.

Vellum, 181 leaves, 5⅛ x 3⅞ in. (13.8 x 9.8 cm), 1 column, 14 lines, in Latin, in *textura*, 24 small miniatures and 5 historiated initials.

Use: Calendar: northern France; Hours of the Virgin: St.-Pierre, Lille; Office of the Dead: Premonstratensian (with mistaken first response).

TEXT	IMAGE
Calendar (1v–12v)	
Our Father, Apostles' Creed, Confiteor, 5 Joys of the Virgin, various other prayers (14–19v)	
Hours of the Virgin (20–73v)	
Matins and Lauds	Madonna, in "D" (20)
Suffrages	John the Baptist (39)
	Nicholas (39v)
	Mary Magdalene (40v)
	Apostles (41)
Prime	
Suffrages	Archangels (46v)
	John the Evangelist (47)
Terce	
Suffrages	Priest Celebrating Mass (50v)
	Andrew (51v)
Sext	
Suffrages	Crucifixion (54v)
	Martyrs (55)
None	
Suffrages	Peter and Paul (58v)
	Catherine (59v)
Vespers	
Suffrages	Lapidation of Stephen (65v)
	Christopher Carrying Christ (66)
	Margaret Emerging from the Dragon (67)
	Confessors (67v)
	Virgins (68v)
Compline	
Suffrages	Sebastian Shot with Arrows (72v)
	All Saints (73)
Office of the Dead (74–101)	Funeral Service (74)
Hours of the Holy Spirit (102–119v)	Trinity, in "D" (102)
Hours of the Cross (120–125v)	Christ Carrying the Cross, in "D" (120)
Penitential Psalms, Litany (126–139)	Christ as Judge, in "D" (126)
Various prayers including Passion according to John, to the	

Eucharist, Confiteor, Obsecro te, O intemerata, Athanasian Creed (140–157v)	
Gospel Lessons (157v–163)	Luke's Ox (157v)
	Matthew's Angel (159)
	Mark's Lion (160v)
	John's Eagle (161v)
Salve regina misericordie, followed by other prayers (164–181v)	Pietà, in "S" (164)

BIBLIOGRAPHY: Randall, *Medieval and Renaissance Manuscripts*, III, 91–97, no. 227, figs. 437, 438.

❖ ❖ ❖

82 Fig. 94

Walters Art Museum, MS W. 164.

Belgium, 1430s.

Vellum, 185 leaves, 5⅛ x 4 in. (13.9 x 10.1 cm), 1 column, 13 lines, in Latin and French, in *textura*, 48 large miniatures.

Use: Calendar: Belgium; Office of the Dead: Liège.

TEXT	IMAGE
Calendar (1–12v)	
Doulz Dieux Ihesucrist (13v–14)	
Hours of the Passion (16–71)	
Matins	Agony in the Garden (15v)
Lauds	Betrayal (26)
Prime	Pilate Washing His Hands (33v)
Terce	Flagellation (38)
Sext	Christ Carrying the Cross (45)
None	Crucifixion (52)
Vespers	Deposition (60)
Compline	Entombment (65)
Office of the Dead (75–136v)	Funeral Service (74v)
Passion according to John (139–141)	John on Patmos (138v)
Suffrages (141v–184)	George Slaying the Dragon (141v)
	Ascension (142v)
	Pentecost (143v)
	Trinity (144v)
	Helena with the True Cross (145v)
	Michael Battling a Devil (147)
	John the Baptist (148)
	Peter and Paul (149)
	Andrew (150)
	John the Evangelist (151)
	James (152)
	Two Apostles (153)
	Stephen (154)
	Margaret Emerging from the Dragon (155v)
	Anne with the Virgin and Christ (156v)
	Two Virgins (158)
	Maurus (159)
	Relics above an Altar Incensed by Worshiper (160)
	Martydom of Thomas Becket (161)
	Decapitation of Numerous Martyrs (162)
	Martin Dividing His Cloak (163v)
	Nicholas Resuscitating the Three Boys (164v)
	Francis (165v)
	Louis (166v)
	Two Confessors (167v)
	Mary Magdalene (168v)
	Catherine (170)
	Decapitation of Dennis (171)
	Lawrence (172v)
	Nicasius (173v)
	Vincent (175)
	Clement (176)
	All Saints (177)
	Kiss of Peace (178)
	Gile Protecting the Hind (178bv)
	Lupus (179)
	Decapitation of Desiderius (180)
	Julian in a Boat (183v)

BIBLIOGRAPHY: Randall, *Medieval and Renaissance Manuscripts*, III, 132–39, no. 232, pl. XXXa, figs. 448, 566.

❖ ❖ ❖

83 Pl. 36

Walters Art Museum, MS W. 166 ("Hours of Daniel Rym").

Belgium, Ghent (?), late 1420s, produced for Daniel Rym and his wife, Elizabeth van Munte.

Vellum, 186 leaves, 6¼ x 4⅝ in. (15.9 x 11.8 cm), 1 column, 16 lines, in Latin and Dutch, in *textura*, 13 large miniatures, 1 historiated initial, 1 figural border and numerous marginalia, by the Master of Guillebert de Mets.

Use: Hours of the Virgin: Bruges (?)

TEXT	IMAGE
Hours of the Virgin (2–40v)	Annunciation (1v)
Penitential Psalms, Litany (42–60)	Last Judgement (41v)
	David in Prayer, in "D" (42)
Obsecro te, O intemerata, both in Dutch, followed by various prayers including Stabat mater, Salve regina, 7 Joys of the Virgin (62–105)	Virgo Lactans (61v)
	Border: Elizabeth van Munte Kneeling before Elizabeth of Hungary (62)
Hours of Cross (107–119v)	
Matins	Betrayal (106v)
Prime	Man of Sorrows Surrounded the Arma Christi (109v)
Terce	Flagellation (111v)
Sext	Christ Carrying the Cross (113v)
None	Crucifixion (115v)
Vespers	Deposition (117v)
Compline	(Miniature missing)
Precor te piissime Domine Ihesu Christe, 7 Last Words of Our Lord, followed by various prayers including Gospel Lesson of John, 7 Verses of St. Bernard (120–167)	
Suffrages (159–183v)	John the Baptist and Peter (158v)
	Christopher Carrying Christ, and Anthony (160v)
	Cornelius and Livinus (165v)
	Daniel in the Lions' Den, with Kneeling Daniel Rym (168v)

BIBLIOGRAPHY: Randall, *Medieval and Renaissance Manuscripts*, III, 112–23, no. 230, pl. XXIXb, figs. 441–45, 564, 587.

❖ ❖ ❖

84 Pl. 35, Fig. 108

Walters Art Museum, MS W. 170.

Belgium, ca. 1430–40.

Vellum, 182 leaves, 6⅜ x 4¼ in. (16.4 x 12 cm), 1 column, 16 lines, in Latin and Dutch, in *textura*, 27 large miniatures and 8 historiated initials (fols. 9–45) by a follower of the Master of Guillebert de Mets.

Use: Calendar: England, but with some entries for southern

Belgium; Hours of the Virgin: Rome; Office of the Dead: Rome? (text incomplete).

TEXT	IMAGE
Charts for determining Dominical Letters and Golden Numbers (1v)	
Calendar (2–7v)	
Hours of the Virgin (9–48)	
Matins	Madonna with Kneeling Patron (8v)
	Kneeling Patron, in "D" (9)
Lauds	Visitation, in "D" (17v)
Prime	Annunciation to the Shepherds, in "D" (27)
Terce	Nativity, in "D" (30)
Sext	Adoration of the Magi, in "D" (33)
None	Presentation in the Temple, in "D" (35v)
Vespers	Massacre of the Innocents, in "D" (39)
Compline	Flight into Egypt, in "D" (should be "C," 45)
Hours of the Cross (50–60v)	
Matins	Betrayal (49v)
Prime	Christ before Pilate (51)
Terce	Flagellation (53v)
Sext	Christ Carrying the Cross (55v)
(None missing)	(Miniature missing)
Vespers	Deposition (57v)
Compline	Entombment (59v)
Mass of the Virgin, followed by Gospel Lessons (62–71)	Death of the Virgin (61v)
Obsecro te, followed by other prayers (73–80)	Adoration of the Magi (72v)
Penitential Psalms, Litany (82–97v)	Last Judgement (81v)
Office of the Dead (99–112)	Funeral Service (98v)
Salve sancta facies (added somewhat later, 113–114)	
Suffrages, and various other prayers (116–126)	Trinity (115v)
5 Joys of the Virgin, followed by various prayers including O intemerata, Stabat mater (128–136v)	Annunciation (127v)
Suffrages (138–143v)	Michael Battling a Devil (137v)
	John the Baptist (140v)
	Daniel in the Lions' Den (142v)
7 Last Words of Our Lord (145–147)	Resurrection (144v)
Precor te piisime Domine Ihesu Christe, followed by various prayers (149–151v)	Man of Sorrows Surrounded by the Arma Christi (148v)
Suffrages (152–164v)	Christopher Carrying Christ (154v)
	George Slaying the Dragon (157v)
	Cornelius (159v)
	Sebastian Shot with Arrows (161v)
	Anthony (163v)
Gaude pia Magdalena, Gaude virgo Katherina, Gaude Barbara regina (166–173)	Mary Magdalene with Kneeling Patron (165v)
	Catherine (168v)
	Barbara (171v)
Suffrages, followed by various prayers (175–178v)	Wilgefortis Crucified (174v)
Hours of the Holy Spirit (added later, 179–182)	

BIBLIOGRAPHY: Randall, *Medieval and Renaissance Manuscripts*, III, 123–32, no. 231, pl. XXIXc, figs. 446, 447, 565, 599.

❖ ❖ ❖

85 Pl. 27

Walters Art Museum, MS W. 172 ("Hours of Jan Eggert").

Belgium, ca. 1440, probably produced for Jan Eggert.

Vellum, 121 leaves, 8¾ x 6⅜ in. (22.2 x 16.2 cm), 1 column, 19 lines, in Latin, in *textura*, 11 large miniatures and 9 historiated initials, by Master of the Ghent Privileges and the workshop of the Master of Guillebert de Mets.

Use: Calendar: Utrecht, with Augustinian entries; Hours of the Virgin: Windesheim Congregation; Office of the Dead: Windesheim Congregation.

TEXT	IMAGE
Calendar (1–6v)	
Hours of the Virgin (8–50v)	
Matins	Agony in the Garden (7v)
	Annunciation (8)
Lauds	Betrayal (20v)
	Visitation, in "D" (21)
Prime	Christ before Pilate (28v)
	Annunciation to the Shepherds, in "D" (29)
Terce	Flagellation (32v)
	Nativity, in "D" (33)
Sext	Christ Carrying the Cross (35v)
	Adoration of the Magi, in "D" (36)
None	Crucifixion (38v)
	Presentation in the Temple, in "D" (39)
Vespers	Deposition (41v)
	Flight into Egypt, in "D" (42)
Compline	Entombment (46v)
	Massacre of the Innocents, in "C" (47)
Hours of the Cross, Suffrages, 15 Gradual Psalms (52–60v)	Madonna (51v)
Penitential Psalms, Litany (61–80v)	David in Prayer, in "D" (61)
Office of the Dead (82–112)	Priest Celebrating Mass While Souls Are Released from Purgatory (81v)
	Raising of Lazarus, in "D" (82)
Prayers recited before and after receiving Communion (112v–117v)	

BIBLIOGRAPHY: Clark, *Made in Flanders*, 189–91 (additional references on p. 491), color figs. 10–11, figs. 93–104.

❖ ❖ ❖

86 Fig. 93

Walters Art Museum, MS W. 719 ("Egmont Hours").

Belgium, ca. 1440, produced for a member of the Egmont family.

Vellum, 194 leaves, 6 x 4½ in. (15.3 x 11.2 cm), 1 column, 13 lines, in Latin and French, in *textura*, 19 large miniatures by the Master of the Ghent Privileges and his workshop.

Use: Calendar: Liège; Hours of the Virgin: unidentified; Office of the Dead: Liège.

TEXT	IMAGE
Calendar (1–12v)	
Hours of the Virgin (14–67)	
Matins	Virgo Lactans; border: Kneeling Patron (13v)
Lauds	Annunciation (25)
Prime	Visitation (36v)
Terce	Nativity (41v)
Sext	Adoration of the Magi (45v)
None	Presentation in the Temple (49v)
Vespers	Flight into the Egypt (53v)
Compline	Death of the Virgin (61v)
Office of the Dead (68–122)	Raising of Lazarus (67v)
Hours of the Compassion of the Virgin, followed by various prayers (123–128v)	Crucifixion (122v)
Suffrages, followed by various	Peter (129v)

prayers including Salve regina, Stabat mater (130–142)	James (131) Simon (132) Anthony (133) Sebastian Shot with Arrows (134)
Penitential Psalms, Litany, followed by numerous prayers including Salve sancta facies (144–182v)	Last Judgement (143v) Veronica with Her Veil (182bv)
Gospel Lesson of John (183–184)	
Suffrages (186–188v)	Catherine (185v) Barbara (187v)
Athanasian Creed (189–193)	

BIBLIOGRAPHY: Clark, *Made in Flanders*, 195–97 (additional references on p. 491), color fig. 17, figs. 139–50.

❖ ❖ ❖

87 Fig. 110

Walters Art Museum, MS W. 239.

Belgium, Bruges (?), ca. 1430.

Vellum, 131 leaves, 6⅝ x 4⅞ in. (16.7 x 12.3 cm), 1 column, 17 lines, in Latin, in *textura*, 13 large miniatures, 3 historiated initials, and 1 figural border, by a painter related to the Gold Scrolls group.

Use: Calendar: mainly Bruges; Hours of the Virgin: Rome; Office of the Dead: Rome.

TEXT	IMAGE
Calendar (1–6v)	
Suffrages (8–12)	Armorial miniature (7v) Margaret Emerging from the Dragon; Margaret as Shepherdess, in "G" (8) Sebastian Shot with Arrows; Sebastian Holding Bow and Arrows, in "O" (9v) Anthony; Temptation of Anthony, in "O" (11)
Hours of the Cross (14–16v)	Crucifixion; border: Evangelists' Symbols (13v)
Mass of the Virgin, followed by Gospel Lessons (misbound, 17–21, 23–24v, 29–v)	
Hours of the Virgin (misbound, 22–v, 25–84v)	
Matins	(Miniature missing)
Lauds	(Miniature missing)
Prime	Nativity (49v)
Terce	Annunciation to the Shepherds (54v)
Sext	Massacre of the Innocents (59v)
None	Adoration of the Magi (63v)
Vespers	Presentation in the Temple (67v)
Compline	(Miniature missing)
Advent Hours	Coronation of the Virgin (78v)
Penitential Psalms, Litany (86–100v)	Last Judgement (85v)
Office of the Dead (102–131v)	Group of Men and Women Praying over a Corpse (101v)

BIBLIOGRAPHY: Randall, *Medieval and Renaissance Manuscripts*, III, 157–63, no. 235, pl. XXXIa, figs. 454, 455, 568.

❖ ❖ ❖

88 Figs. 76, 77

Walters Art Museum, MS W. 211.

Belgium, Bruges, ca. 1440.

Vellum, 234 leaves, 4⅝ x 3½ in. (11.8 x 8.9 cm), 1 column, 17 lines in Latin and French, in *textura*, 21 large miniatures by a painter within the Gold Scrolls group.

Use: Calendar: Utrecht, but with some entries pointing to Belgium and northern France; Hours of the Virgin: Rouen; Office of the Dead: Rome.

TEXT	IMAGE
Calendar (1v–13)	
Sunday Hours and Mass of the Trinity (15–22)	Trinity (14v)
Monday Hours and Mass of the Dead (24–29v)	Souls in Purgatory Comforted by Angels (23v)
Tuesday Hours and Mass of the Holy Spirit (31–36)	Pentecost (30v)
Wednesday Hours and Mass of All Saints (38–44)	All Saints (37v)
Thursday Hours and Mass of the Holy Sacrament (46–51)	Adoration of the Eucharist (45v)
Friday Hours and Mass of the Cross (53–58)	Crucifixion (52v)
Saturday Hours and Mass of the Virgin, followed by Gospel Lessons, Passion from the service on Good Friday, Passion according to John (60–81)	Virgo Lactans, Crowned (59v)
Salve sancta facies, followed by various prayers including two sets of the 5 Joys of the Virgin, Stabat mater, 7 Joys of the Virgin, 7 Last Words of Our Lord, O intemerata, Obsecro te (83–111)	Veronica with Her Veil (82v)
Hours of the Virgin (113–159v)	
Matins	Annunciation (112v)
Lauds	Visitation (122v)
Suffrages	
Prime	Nativity (136v)
Terce	Adoration of the Christ Child (139v)
Sext	Circumcision (143v)
None	Presentation in the Temple (147v)
Vespers	Adoration of the Magi (151v)
Compline	Rest on the Flight into Egypt (155v)
Suffrages (160–163v)	Jodocus (160) Christopher Carrying Christ (161v)
Prayer of Blessed Peter of Luxembourg, Suffrages, other prayers (165–176)	Peter of Luxembourg Kneeling before a Crucifix (164v)
8 Verses of St. Bernard, 15 Joys of the Virgin, 7 Requests to Our Lord (176v–184)	
Penitential Psalms, Litany (186–201)	Last Judgement (185v)
Office of the Dead (203–234v)	Funeral Service (202v)

BIBLIOGRAPHY: Randall, *Medieval and Renaissance Manuscripts*, III, 147–57, no. 234, pl. XXXc, figs. 451–53.

❖ ❖ ❖

89 Fig. 45

Walters Art Museum, MS W. 173.

Belgium, Bruges, 1440s.

Vellum, 106 leaves, 10⅛ x 6⅞ in. (25.7 x 17.5 cm), 1 column, 19 lines, in Latin and French, in *textura*, 17 large miniatures and 8 historiated initials, by a painter within the Gold Scrolls group.

Use: Calendar: Bruges; Hours of the Virgin: Rome.

TEXT	IMAGE
Calendar (1–6v)	
Gospel Lessons (8–14v)	John Sharpening Pen (7v) Luke Writing (9v) Matthew Writing (11v) Mark Examining Pen (13v)
Hours of the Cross (16–20)	Crucifixion (15v)
Hours of the Holy Spirit (22–25v)	Pentecost (21v)

Hours of the Virgin (26–67v)	
Matins	Agony in the Garden; Annunciation in "D" (26)
Lauds	Betrayal; Visitation, in "D" (34)
Prime	Christ before Pilate; Nativity, in "D" (43)
Terce	Flagellation; Annunciation to the Shepherds, in "D" (47)
Sext	Christ Carrying the Cross; Adoration of the Magi, in "D" (51)
None	Crucifixion; Presentation in the Temple, in "D" (55)
Vespers	Deposition; Massacre of the Innocents, in "D" (59)
Compline	Entombment; Flight into Egypt, in "C" (64)
Suffrages, 7 Last Words of Our Lord (68–75)	Nicholas (71v) Francis (73v)
Penitential Psalms, Litany (78–90)	Last Judgement (77v)
15 Joys of the Virgin, 7 Requests to Our Lord, Obsecro te, O intemerata, Salve regina, 7 Verses of St. Bernard, and other prayers (91–106v)	

BIBLIOGRAPHY: Randall, *Medieval and Renaissance Manuscripts,* III, 186–93, no. 240, figs. 463, 464.

❖ ❖ ❖

90 — Fig. 64

Walters Art Museum, MS W. 246.

Belgium, Bruges, ca. 1445

Vellum, 148 leaves, 6¾ x 5⅛ in. (17.2 x 13 cm), 1 column, 18 lines, in Latin, in *textura,* 24 large miniatures by a painter within the Gold Scrolls group.

Use: Calendar: Bruges; Hours of the Virgin: Rome; Office of the Dead: Rome.

TEXT	IMAGE
Calendar (3–8v)	
Hours of the Trinity (10–12)	Trinity (9v)
Una hora non potuistis vigilare (14–v)	Agony in the Garden (13v)
Hours of the Cross (16–28v)	
Matins	Betrayal (15v)
Prime	Christ before Pilate (17v)
Terce	Flagellation (19v)
Sext	Christ Carrying the Cross (21v)
None	Crucifixion (23v)
Vespers	Deposition (25v)
Compline	Entombment (27v)
Hours of the Holy Spirit (30–32)	Pentecost (29v)
Mass of the Virgin, followed by Gospel Lessons (34–40v)	Madonna in a Garden (33v)
Mass of the Holy Sacrament (42–44)	Last Supper (41v)
Mass of the Ascension (46–48)	Ascension (45v)
Hours of the Virgin (50–87v)	
Matins	Annunciation (49v)
Lauds	Visitation (57v)
Prime	Nativity (66v)
Terce	Annunciation to the Shepherds (70v)
Sext	Adoration of the Magi (73v)
None	Presentation in the Temple (76v)
Vespers	Massacre of the Innocents (79v)
Compline	Flight into Egypt (84v)
Penitential Psalms, Litany (89–104v)	Last Judgement (88v)
Office of the Dead (106–127v)	Funeral Service (105v)
Psalter of St. Jerome (129–141)	Jerome Writing (128v)
Suffrages (141–147v)	

BIBLIOGRAPHY: Randall, *Medieval and Renaissance Manuscripts,* III, 163–69, no. 236, pl. XXXIb, figs. 456, 569.

❖ ❖ ❖

91 — Pl. 29, Figs. 11, 86

Walters Art Museum, MS W. 220.

Belgium, Bruges, ca. 1450.

Vellum, 231 leaves, 6 x 4⅛ in. (15.3 x 10.3 cm), 1 column, 14 lines, in Latin, in *littera batarda,* 18 large miniatures by Willem Vrelant.

Use: Calendar: Bruges; Hours of the Virgin: Rome; Office of the Dead: Rome.

TEXT	IMAGE
Calendar (1–12v)	
Gospel Lessons, followed by various prayers, (14–23)	John Writing, Matthew Writing, Mark Writing, Luke Writing (14)
Hours of the Cross (24–27v)	Christ Crowned with Thorns (24)
Hours of the Holy Spirit (28–32)	Pentecost (28)
Mass of the Virgin, followed by Salve mater dolorosa (32–42)	
Hours of the Virgin (43–112)	
Matins	Annunciation (42v)
Lauds	Visitation (64)
Prime	Nativity (77)
Terce	Annunciation to the Shepherds (84)
Sext	Adoration of the Magi (89)
None	Presentation in the Temple (94)
Vespers	Massacre of the Innocents (99)
Compline	Coronation of the Virgin (108)
Hours of the Compassion of the Virgin (113–137)	Lamentaion (113)
Obsecro te, O intemerata (138–145)	Madonna with Kneeling Patron (138)
Salve Sancta facies (146–147v)	Portrait of Christ (146)
Suffrages, followed by various prayers including some to the Eucharist (148–157v)	John the Baptist (148) Catherine Presenting Patroness to Christ (150v)
Penitential Psalms, Litany (158–186)	David in Prayer (158)
Office of the Dead, Mass of the Dead (187–231v)	Burial Service (187)

BIBLIOGRAPHY: Randall, *Medieval and Renaissance Manuscripts,* III, 210–19, no. 244, pl. XXXIIc, figs. 469–71, 571.

❖ ❖ ❖

92 — Pl. 21, Figs. 10, 82, 92

Walters Art Museum, MS W. 240.

Belgium, Bruges, ca. 1450s.

Vellum, 410 leaves, 6⅞ x 4⅞ in. (17.5 x 12.3 cm), 1 column, 17 lines, in Latin, in *textura,* 33 large miniatures by Willem Vrelant.

Use: Calendar: composite, with many entries pointing to southern Belgium and northern France; Hours of the Virgin: Rome; Office of the Dead: Rome.

TEXT	IMAGE
Calendar (2–13v)	
Sunday Hours and Mass of the Trinity, Prayer to the Trinity (15–34v)	Trinity Surrounded by Evangelists' Symbols (14v)
Monday Hours and Mass of the Dead (36–53v)	Raising of Lazarus (35v)
Tuesday Hours and Mass of the Holy Spirit (55–66)	Pentecost (54v)

TEXT	IMAGE
Wednesday Hours and Mass of All Saints (68–81v)	All Saints (67v)
Thursday Hours and Mass of the Holy Sacrament (83–97v)	Adoration of the Host (82v)
Friday Hours of the Cross, 7 Last Words of Our Lord, Stabat mater, Mass of the Cross (99–121)	Crucifixion (98v)
Saturday Hours of the Virgin, O gloriosissima et precellentissima, Obsecro te, Mass of the Virgin, Gospel Lessons (123–145)	Madonna Attended by Angels (122v)
Prayer before Mass (146–147)	
Mass of St. Michael (149–154v)	Michael Battling Three Devils (148v)
Mass of the Conception of the Virgin (156–161v)	Meeting at the Golden Gate (155v)
Mass of the Virgin (163–166v)	Annunciation (162v)
Hours of the Virgin (168–234v)	
Matins	Annunciation (167v)
Lauds	Visitation (183v)
Prime	Nativity (193v)
Terce	Annunciation to the Shepherds (198v)
Sext	Adoration of the Magi (203v)
None	Presentation in the Temple (208v)
Vespers	Massacre of the Innocents (213v)
Compline	Flight into Egypt (220v)
Advent Office	Death of the Virgin (226v)
Prayer before the Penitential Psalms (235–237v)	
Penitential Psalms, interspersed with prayers against the 7 Deadly Sins, prayer after the Psalms, Litany (239–262v)	Last Judgement (238v)
Mass for Remission of Sins (263–265v)	
Office of the Dead (268–303v)	Funeral Mass (267v)
Psalter of St. Jerome (305–320)	Jerome Removing the Lion's Thorn (304v)
Suffrages (321–335v)	John the Baptist (320v)
	Christopher Carrying Christ (322v)
	George Slaying the Dragon (324v)
	Sebastian Shot with Arrows (326v)
	Andrew (328v)
	Augustine (330v)
	Stigmatization of Francis (332v)
	Bernardino; border: Kneeling Patron (334v)
Psalms (336–345v)	
Hours of the Passion (346–372)	
Passion according to Matthew (374–386v)	Matthew Writing (373v)
Passion according to Mark (388–398v)	Mark Writing (387v)
Passion according to Luke (400–410v)	Luke Writing (399v)

BIBLIOGRAPHY: Randall, *Medieval and Renaissance Manuscripts,* III, 240–50, no. 248, pls. XXXIVb–c, figs. 477–79, 573.

❖ ❖ ❖

93 Pl. 39, Fig. 99

Walters Art Museum, MS W. 197.

Belgium, Bruges, ca. 1460.

Vellum, 268 leaves, 8⅜ x 6 in. (21.2 x 15.2 cm), 1 column, 13 lines, in Latin in *textura,* 24 large miniatures, 1 historiated initial, and 11 calendar and 11 zodiacal vignettes, by Willem Vrelant.

Use: Calendar: general for Holland and Belgium, but also with entries pointing to France; Hours of the Virgin: Rome; Office of the Dead: Rome (abbreviated).

TEXT	IMAGE
Calendar (1–11v)	Zodiacal sign on each recto
(Jan. missing)	(Vignette missing)
Feb.	Chopping Wood (1)
Mar.	Breaking Ground (2)
Apr.	Picking Flowers (3)
May	Hawking (4)
Jun.	Mowing (5)
Jul.	Reaping (6)
Aug.	Threshing (7)
Sept.	Treading Grapes (8)
Oct.	Sowing (9)
Nov.	Thrashing for Acorns (10)
Dec.	Slaughtering a Pig (11)
Suffrages (13–33v)	John the Baptist (12v)
	Christopher Carrying Christ (14v)
	Anthony (16v)
	Nicholas Resuscitating the Three Boys (18v)
	Adrian (20v)
	Quentin (22v)
	Stigmatization of Francis (24v)
	Blaise (26v)
	Margaret Emerging from the Dragon (28v)
	Geneviève (30v)
	Barbara (32v)
Hours of the Cross (35–42v)	Crucifixion (34v)
Hours of the Holy Spirit (43–49)	(Miniature missing)
Mass of the Virgin (51–56)	Madonna Enthroned, Serenaded by Angels (50v)
Gospel Lessons (56v–61v)	
Hours of the Virgin (63–145v)	
Matins	Annunciation (62v)
Lauds	Visitation (76v)
Prime	Nativity (92v)
Terce	Annunciation to the Shepherds (99v)
Sext	Adoration of the Magi (106v)
None	Presentation in the Temple (112v)
Vespers	Massacre of the Innocents (118v)
Compline	Flight into Egypt (128v)
Advent Hours	Coronation of the Virgin (135v)
Penitential Psalms, Litany (147–174)	Last Judgement (146v)
Office of the Dead (176–209v)	Burial Service (175v)
Passion according to John, 7 Last Words of Our Lord, followed by various prayers (210–219v)	
Salve sancta facies, followed by various prayers to the Eucharist, including those said while and after receiving Communion, and when leaving church (219v–236)	Portrait of Christ, in "S" (219v)
O intemerata, Obsecro te, followed by various prayers to the Virgin (236–249v)	
Psalms and various prayers including the Athanasian Creed (250–268v)	

BIBLIOGRAPHY: Randall, *Medieval and Renaissance Manuscripts,* III, 251–62, no. 250, pl. XXXVa, figs. 481–84, 574, 590.

❖ ❖ ❖

94 Fig. 58

Walters Art Museum, MS W. 196.

Belgium, Bruges, ca. 1470.

Vellum, 187 leaves, 8⅛ x 5½ in. (20.7 x 14 cm), 1 column, 21 lines, in Latin, in *textura,* 24 large miniatures, 9 historiated initials, and 12 calendar and 12 zodiacal vignettes, by the workshop of Willem Vrelant.

Use: Calendar: general, but with entries pointing to Belgium and Holland, and with Franciscan entries; Hours of the Virgin: Rome; Office of the Dead: Rome.

TEXT	IMAGE
Calendar (1–13)	Zodiacal sign on each recto
Jan.	Keeping Warm (1v)
Feb.	Pruning (2v)
Mar.	Breaking Ground (3v)
Apr.	Picking Flowering Branches (4v)
May	Hawking (5v)
Jun.	Mowing (6v)
Jul.	Reaping (7v)
Aug.	Threshing (8v)
Sept.	Treading Grapes (9v)
Oct.	Thrashing for Acorns (10v)
Nov.	Sowing (11v)
Dec.	Stunning a Bull (12v)
Hours of the Cross (15–26v)	
Matins	Betrayal (14v)
Prime	Christ before Pilate (16v)
Terce	Flagellation (18v)
Sext	Christ Carrying the Cross (20v)
None	(Miniature missing)
Vespers	Deposition (23v)
Compline	Entombment (25v)
Hours of the Holy Spirit (28–39v)	
Matins	David Receiving the Holy Spirit (27v)
Prime	(Miniature missing)
Terce	Holy Spirit Hovering over the Earth (30v)
Sext	Baptism of Christ (32v)
None	Apostles Blessing a Group (34v)
Vespers	Christ Appearing to the Apostles (36v)
Compline	Pentecost (38v)
Mass of the Virgin (40–43)	(Miniature missing)
Gospel Lessons (45–51v)	John Writing (44v)
	Luke Writing (46v)
	Matthew Writing (48v)
	Mark Contemplating (50v)
Obsecro te, O intemerata (52–55v)	
Hours of the Virgin (56–129)	
Matins	(Miniature missing)
Lauds	Visitation (68v)
(Prime missing)	(Miniature missing)
(Terce missing)	(Miniature missing)
Sext	(Miniature missing)
None	Presentation in the Temple (78v)
Vespers	Massacre of the Innocents (82v)
Compline	Flight into Egypt (88v)
Advent Hours	
Vespers	Rejection of Joachim's Offering (93v)
Compline	Annunciation to Joachim, in "C" (98v)
Matins	Meeting at the Golden Gate, in "D" (101)
Lauds	Birth of the Virgin, in "D" (113)
Prime	Presentation of the Virgin in the Temple, in "D" (119v)
Terce	Marriage of the Virgin, in "D" (122)
Sext	Death of the Virgin, in "D" (124v)
None	Coronation of the Virgin, in "D" (126v)
Advent Mass of the Virgin (129–134)	Augustus and Tiburtine Sibyl, in "R" (129)
Hours of the Conception of the Virgin (134–137v)	Virgin of the Apocalypse, in "D" (134)
Stabat mater, Athanasian Creed (139–142v)	Lamentation (138v)
Penitential Psalms, Litany (144–157)	David in Prayer (143v)
Office of the Dead (159–185)	Raising of Lazarus (158v)

BIBLIOGRAPHY: Randall, *Medieval and Renaissance Manuscripts,* III, 318–26, no. 264, pl. XXXVIa, figs. 500, 584, 591, 592.

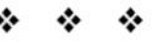

95 Fig. 46

Walters Art Museum, MS W. 195.

Belgium, Bruges, ca. 1470.

Vellum, 121 leaves, 7¼ x 5⅛ in. (18.5 x 13 cm), 1 column, 15 lines, in Latin and French, in *textura,* 13 large miniatures and 2 historiated initials by the workshop of Willem Vrelent; 12 calendar vignettes (as part of the calendar added in the 1480s) by a northern French painter.

Use: Calendar: (added in France in the 1480s): Bayeux; Hours of the Virgin: Rome.

TEXT	IMAGE
Calendar (1–12v)	
Jan.	Feasting (1)
Feb.	Keeping Warm (2)
Mar.	Pruning (3)
Apr.	Picking Flowers (4)
May	Riding (5)
Jun.	Shearing Sheep (6)
Jul.	Mowing (7)
Aug.	Reaping (8)
Sept.	Sowing (9)
Oct.	Treading Grapes (10)
Nov.	Slaughtering a Pig (11)
Dec.	Baking Bread (12)
Hours of the Cross (14–19v)	Christ with Angels (13v)
Hours of the Virgin (21–75v)	
Matins	Agony in the Garden (20v)
Lauds	Betrayal (31v)
Prime	Christ before Pilate (43v)
Terce	Flagellation (48v)
Sext	Christ Carrying the Cross (53v)
None	Crucifixion (58v)
Vespers	Deposition (63v)
Compline	Entombment (71v)
Penitential Psalms, Litany (77–92v)	Last Judgement (76v)
5 Prayers of St. Gregory, Domine Iesu Christe redemptor mundi (94–97v)	Mass of St. Gregory (93v)
Obsecro te, 7 Joys of the Virgin, Salve regina, 8 Verses of St. Bernard, and other prayers (99–107v)	Madonna Enthroned, with Angels (98v)
Suffrages, followed by various prayers (107v–116)	Anthony, in "V" (108v)
	John (110v)
	Catherine, in "V" (111v)

BIBLIOGRAPHY: Randall, *Medieval and Renaissance Manuscripts,* III, 326–31, no. 265, figs. 501, 502, 585.

❖ ❖ ❖

96 Fig. 104

Walters Art Museum, MS W. 279.

Belgium, Ghent (?), ca. 1470.

Vellum, 193 leaves, 8⅛ x 5½ in. (20.5 x 14 cm), 1 column, 14 lines, in Latin and French, in *littera batarda,* 11 large miniatures and 12 historiated initials, by Loyset Liédet and his workshop.

Use: Calendar: composite of northern France, Belgium, and Holland; Hours of the Virgin: Rome; Office of the Dead: Rome (abbreviated).

TEXT	IMAGE
Calendar (1–12v)	
Gospel Lessons (13–19v)	
Obsecro te, O intemerata (20–28v)	Madonna, in "O" (20)
	Madonna, in "O" (25)
Hours of the Cross (31–34v)	(Miniature missing)
Hours of the Virgin (38–112)	
Matins	(Miniature missing)
Lauds	Visitation (52v)
Prime	Nativity (37v)
Terce	Annunciation to the Shepherds (75v)
Sext	Presentation in the Temple (82v)
None	Circumcision (88v)
Vespers	Flight into Egypt (95v)
Compline	Coronation of the Virgin (106v)
Penitential Psalms, Litany (113–136)	David in Prayer (112v)
Office of the Dead (139–173)	Burial Service (138v)
Suffrages (177–189)	Christopher Carrying Christ (176v)
	Sebastian Shot with Arrows, in "O" (177v)
	John the Baptist, in "I" (179)
	Paul and Peter, in "P" (180)
	James, in "O" (180v)
	Anthony, in "C" (181v)
	All Saints, in "O" (183v)
	Barbara (184v)
	Margaret Emerging from the Dragon, in "C" (186v)
	Apollonia, in "I" (187v)
	Mary Magdalene, in "I" (188v)
Ave virgo graciosa (190–193v)	Madonna, in "A" (190)

BIBLIOGRAPHY: Randall, *Medieval and Renaissance Manuscripts*, III, 342–48, no. 269, pl. XXXVIb, figs. 507, 508, 593.

❖ ❖ ❖

97 Pl. 23, Figs. 38, 42

Walters Art Museum, MS W. 272.

Belgium, Bruges (?), ca. 1470s.

Vellum, 212 leaves, 8 x 6¼ in. (20.4 x 16 cm), 1 column, 14 lines, in Latin and French, in *textura*, 12 large and 20 small (fols. 30, 31v, Suffrages) miniatures, by a follower of the Master of Anthony of Burgundy (Philippe de Mazerolles?).

Use: Calendar: Mons, Convent of St. Waltrudis; Hours of the Virgin: unidentified; Office of the Dead: Mons, Convent of St. Waltrudis.

TEXT	IMAGE
Calendar (1–12v)	
Hours of the Cross (14–22)	Crucifixion (13v)
Hours of the Holy Spirit (23–30)	Pentecost (22v)
Gospel Lessons of John and Luke (30–33)	John and Mark Writing (30)
	Luke Painting the Virgin (31v)
Hours of the Virgin (34–110v)	
Matins	Annunciation (33v)
Lauds	Visitation (62v)
Prime	Nativity (75v)
Terce	Annunciation to the Shepherds (81v)
Sext	Adoration of the Magi (86v)
None	Presentation in the Temple (91v)
Vespers	Flight into Egypt (96v)
Compline	Massacre of the Innocents (104v)
O intemerata (111–113v)	
Penitential Psalms, Litany (115–136)	David in Prayer (114v)
7 Last Words of Our Lord, 8 Verses of St. Bernard, followed by various prayers (136–142v)	
Suffrages (142v–157)	Michael Battling a Devil (142v)
	John the Baptist (143v)
	Peter (144)
	John the Evangelist (144v)
	Martyrdom of Quentin (145)
	Sebastian Shot with Arrows (146)
	Nicholas with the Three Boys and Three Maidens (146v)
	Anthony (147v)
	Stigmatization of Francis (148)
	Bernard (149)
	5 Plague Saints (150)
	Noli me tangere (151)
	Waltrudis (151v)
	Apollonia (152v)
	Anne with the Virgin and Christ Child (153)
	11,000 Virgins (154)
	Catherine with Other Virgin Saints (155)
	All Saints (156)
Office of the Dead (158–212v)	Raising of Lazarus (157v)

BIBLIOGRAPHY: Randall, *Medieval and Renaissance Manuscripts*, III, 392–401, no. 277, pl. XXXIXa, figs. 520, 521.

❖ ❖ ❖

98 Figs. 5, 97

Walters Art Museum, MS W. 439 ("Hours of Adolph of Cleves and La Marck").

Belgium, ca. 1480, produced for Adolph of Cleves and La Marck.

Vellum, 302 leaves, 6⅝ x 4¾ in. (16.8 x 12.2 cm), 1 column, 12 lines, in Latin and French, in *littera batarda*, 14 large miniatures, 24 historated initials, and 3 historiated borders.

Use: Calendar: Dominican; Hours of the Virgin: Dominican.

TEXT	IMAGE
Calendar (1–12v)	
Obsecro te (15–22)	Adolph of Cleves and La Marck, Kneeling in Prayer (13v)
	Madonna (14)
	Arms of Adolph (14v)
O intemerata (23–27v)	Pietà (22v)
Stabat mater, followed by various prayers to the Virgin (28–39v)	Crucifixion; border scenes: Agony in the Garden, Betrayal, Christ before Pilate, Flagellation, Christ Carrying the Cross, Entombment (28)
5 Joys of the Virgin, followed by various prayers (40–51)	Annunciation, in "G" (40)
Suffrages (51v–80)	Claude of Besançon, in "O" (51v)
	Sebastian Shot with Arrows, in "O"; border: Archers' Practice (54)
	Adrian, in "O" (58)
	Temptation of Anthony, in "V" (59)
	Michael Weighing Souls and Battling a Devil, in "M" (60v)
	George Slaying the Dragon, in "O" (62v)
	Nicholas Resuscitating the Three Boys, in "D"; border: Two Women Buying Jewelry (64)
	Christopher Carrying Christ, in "D" (65)

	Evisceration of Erasmus, in "A" (69v)
	Anne with the Virgin and Christ, in "D" (70v)
	Margaret Emerging from the Dragon, in "D" (72)
	Catherine, in "D" (73v)
	Barbara, in "D" (75)
	Augustine Praying, in"D" (76)
O beatissima virgo maria, followed by various prayers to the Virgin (80v–87v)	Madonna with Kneeling Adolph of Cleves and La Marck, in "O" (80v)
Gospel Lessons (88–98v)	John on Patmos, in "I" (88)
	Matthew Writing, in "C" (90v)
	Luke Writing, in "I" (94)
	Mark Writing, in "I" (97)
Hours of the Virgin (100–203)	
Matins	Annunciation (99v)
Lauds	Visitation (121)
Prime	Nativity (145v)
Terce	Annunciation to the Shepherds (153)
Sext	Presentation in the Temple (161v)
None	Adoration of the Magi (168v)
Vespers	Massacre of the Innocents (176)
Compline	Flight into Egypt (194)
Penitential Psalms, Litany (205–245v)	David in Prayer (204v)
Passion according to John (246–266)	Man of Sorrows, in "I"; border: Arma Christi (246)
7 Last Words of Our Lord, followed by various prayers (266v–288v)	Crucifixion, in "D" (266v)
Vrai dieu en trois personnes, followed by various prayers (289–295v)	Trinity, in "V" (289)
Suffrages (296–297v)	
7 Prayers of St. Gregory, Mon Dieu j'ai pechie (298–302v)	Mass of St. Gregory, in "D" (298)

BIBLIOGRAPHY: Randall, *Medieval and Renaissance Manuscripts,* III, 423–36, no. 281, pls. XLa–b, figs. 526–28, 602.

❖ ❖ ❖

99

Fig. 84

Washington, D.C., Library of Congress, MS Rosenwald 9.

Belgium, Bruges, 1480s.

Vellum, 135 leaves, 5⅞ x 3⅞ in. (15.1 x 10.1 cm), 1 column, 20 lines, in Latin, in *littera batarda,* 21 large and 24 small (fols. 106v–134) miniatures by the Master of the Prayer Book of ca. 1500.

Use: Calendar: Bruges; Hours of the Virgin: Rome; Office of the Dead: Rome (abbreviated).

TEXT	IMAGE
Calendar (1–12v)	
Gospel Lessons (13v–19)	John on Patmos (13v)
	Luke Writing (15)
	Matthew Writing (16v)
	Mark Writing (18)
Hours of the Cross (21–23v)	Crucifixion (21)
Hours of the Holy Spirit (24–26)	Pentecost (24)
Hours of the Virgin (27–60v)	
Matins	Annunciation (27)
Lauds	Visitation (35)
Prime	Nativity (43v)
Terce	Annunciation to the Shepherds (46v)
Sext	Adoration of the Magi (49v)
None	Presentation in the Temple (52)
Vespers	Flight into Egypt (54v)
Compline	Massacre of the Innocents (58v)
Penitential Psalms, Litany (62–74v)	David in Prayer (63)
Office of the Dead (75–85)	Raising of Lazarus (75)
Prayer recited when waking up followed by other prayers (87–93v)	Patron Praying at Bedside (87)
7 Joys of the Virgin, followed by various prayers (94–96v)	Virgo Lactans (94)
Prayers to Mary Magdalene, including 7 Joys of Mary Magdalene (97–100v)	Mary Magdalene in Her Cave (97)
Prayers to the Trinity, followed by other prayers including those said at the Elevation (101–104v)	Trinity (101)
Prayers said at the Elevation of the Host and of the Chalice (105–106)	Patron Praying at the Transubstantiation (105)
Salve sancta facies (106v–108v)	Head of Christ (106v)
Suffrages, with various prayers interspersed including those recited before, while, and after receiving Communion, 7 Verses of St. Bernard, to the Virgin, Passion according to John, while passing a cemetery (108v–135)	Raising of Lazarus (108v)
	God the Father (109)
	Man of Sorrows (109v)
	Dove of the Holy Spirit (110)
	Anne Instructing the Virgin (110v)
	Geneviève (112)
	Apollonia (112v)
	Anne with the Virgin in Her Womb (114v)
	Madonna (115)
	All Saints (116)
	Michael Battling Devils (116v)
	Stephen (117)
	Anthony (117v)
	Hubert Kneeling before the Miraculous Deer (118)
	Dove of the Holy Spirit (118v)
	Sebastian Shot with Arrows (119v)
	Bernard Vanquishing the Devil (121v)
	Madonna (122v)
	Patron Praying in a Cemetery (128v)
	Patron Praying to God the Father (131)
	Christopher Carrying Christ (132v)
	Barbara (133v)
	Claude of Besançon (134)

BIBLIOGRAPHY: Schutzner, *Medieval and Renaissance Manuscript Books,* 312–17, MS 51, pl. 20, illus.

❖ ❖ ❖

100

Fig. 100

Walters Art Museum, MS W. 176.

Belgium, ca. 1485.

Vellum, 164 leaves, 2⅞ x 2 in. (7.5 x 5.1 cm), 1 column, 15 lines, in Latin, in *textura,* 9 miniatures, 14 historiated initials, and 10 calendar and 10 zodiacal vignettes.

Use: Calendar: Utrecht; Hours of the Virgin: Rome.

TEXT	IMAGE
Calendar (1v–11)	Zodiacal sign on each recto
Jan.	Feasting (1v)
Feb.	Pruning (2v)
Mar.	Breaking Ground (3v)
Apr.	Picking Flowering Branches (4v)
May	(Leaf missing)
Jun.	Mower Drinking (5v)
Jul.	Reaping (6v)
Aug.	Threshing (7v)
Sept.	Treading Grapes (8v)
Oct.	Sowing (9v)
Nov.	Thrashing for Acorns (10v)
Dec.	(Leaf missing)

Mass of the Virgin, followed by Gospel Lessons (12–27)	(Miniature missing)
Hours of the Virgin (29–143v)	
Matins	Annunciation (28v)
Lauds	Visitation (56v)
Prime	Nativity (74v)
Terce	Annunciation to the Shepherds (82v)
Sext	Adoration of the Magi (89v)
None	Presentation in the Temple (96v)
Vespers	Massacre of the Innocents (103v)
Compline	Flight into Egypt (115v)
Advent Hours	Coronation of the Virgin (124v)
O intemerata (144–148)	Virgin and John the Evangelist, in "O" (144)
O bone Iesu (149–151v)	Infant Christ, in "O" (149)
Suffrages (152–164v)	Michael Battling a Devil, in "M" (152)
	John the Baptist, in "I" (153)
	Peter and Paul, in "P" (154)
	James, in "O" (155)
	Christopher Carrying Christ, in "A" (156)
	Sebastian, in "B" (157)
	Blaise, in "A" (158)
	Anthony of Padua, in "S" (159v)
	Stigmatization of Francis, in "S" (160v)
	Catherine, in "V" (161v)
	Barbara, in "A" (162v)
	Mary Magdalene, in "M" (163v)

BIBLIOGRAPHY: Randall, *Medieval and Renaissance Manuscripts,* III, 465–70, no. 287, pl. XLIIc, figs. 536, 537.

❖ ❖ ❖

101 — Figs. 75, 131

Walters Art Museum, MS W. 431.

Belgium, 1490s.

Vellum, 146 leaves, 4½ x 3½ in. (11.4 x 8.8 cm), 1 column, 16 lines, in Latin, in *littera batarda,* 8 large miniatures and 13 border vignettes (Suffrages), by the workshop of the Master of Antoine Rolin.

Use: Calendar: Cambrai; Hours of the Virgin: Rome; Office of the Dead: Rome.

TEXT	IMAGE
Calendar (2–13v)	
Triple Prayer of Jean Gerson (14–v)	
Gospel Lessons (18–22v)	John on Patmos (17v)
Hours of the Cross (23–26)	Crucifixion (23)
Hours of the Holy Spirit (26v–29v)	Pentecost (26v)
Hours of the Virgin (30–77)	Annunciation (30)
Stabat mater (78–80)	Pietà (77v)
Penitential Psalms, Litany (82–97v)	David in Prayer (82)
Obsecro te, O intemerata (98–105v)	Madonna (98)
Suffrages (105v–114)	Michael Slaying a Dragon (106v)
	John the Baptist (107)
	Peter and Paul (107v)
	Christopher Carrying Christ (108)
	Sebastian (108v)
	Adrian (109v)
	Anthony (110)
	Nicholas with the Three Boys and Three Maidens (110v)
	Martyrdom of Quentin (111)
	Mary Magdalene (111v)
	Barbara (112)
	5 Plague Saints (112v)
	5 Virgin Saints (113v)
Office of the Dead (115–146)	Death Holding a Mirror (115)

BIBLIOGRAPHY: Randall, *Medieval and Renaissance Manuscripts,* III, 455–59, no. 285, pls. XLIb–c, figs. 532, 533, 603.

❖ ❖ ❖

102 — Fig. 124

Walters Art Museum, MS W. 435.

Belgium, Bruges, late 15th century.

Vellum, 188 leaves, 5⅞ x 4⅛ in. (14.7 x 10.4 cm), 1 column, 15 lines, in Latin and French, in *littera batarda,* 12 large, 25 small (Gospel Lessons, Suffrages) miniatures, and numerous figural borders, by the workshop of the Master of Edward IV.

Use: Calendar: Belgium, in general, with some entries pointing to Tournai; Hours of the Virgin: Rome; Office of the Dead: Rome (abbreviated).

TEXT	IMAGE
Easter Table (added somewhat later?, 1v–3)	
Calendar (4–15v)	
Gospel Lessons (17–24)	John on Patmos (17),
	Luke Writing (19)
	Matthew Writing (21)
	Mark Writing (23)
Hours of the Cross (26–34v)	Crucifixion (25v)
	Border: Arma Christi (26)
Hours of the Holy Spirit (36–42)	Pentecost (35v)
Hours of the Virgin (44–106v)	
Matins	Annunciation (43v)
Lauds	Visitation (56v)
Prime	Nativity (69v)
Terce	Annunciation to the Shepherds (75v)
Sext	Adoration of the Magi (81v)
None	Presentation in the Temple (87v)
Vespers	Flight into Egypt (92v)
Compline	Coronation of the Virgin (101v)
Penitential Psalms, Litany (108–127v)	David in Prayer; border: David Decapitating Goliath (107v)
	Border: David, with Goliath's Head, Received in Triumph (108)
Office of the Dead (129–160v)	Raising of Lazarus (128v)
Suffrages, followed by various prayers, many to the Eucharist (161–188v)	Michael Slaying a Dragon (161)
	John the Baptist (161v)
	John the Evangelist (162v)
	Peter and Paul (163)
	James (164)
	Stephen (165)
	Lawrence (165v)
	Christopher Carrying Christ (166v)
	Sebastian Shot with Arrows (168)
	Nicholas Resuscitating the Three Boys (169v)
	Claude of Besançon (170)
	Jerome in Penance (171v)
	Stigmatization of Francis (172v)
	Temptation of Anthony (173)
	Adrian (174)
	Anne (175)
	Mary Magdalene (176)
	Decapitation of Catherine (176v)
	Margaret Emerging from the Dragon (177v)
	Barbara (178)
	Apollonia (179v)

BIBLIOGRAPHY: Randall, Medieval and Renaissance Manuscripts, III, 447–55, no. 284, pl. XLIa, figs. 531, 605.

103

Fig. 66

Walters Art Museum, MS W. 427.

Belgium, Bruges (?), ca. 1500.

Vellum, 219 leaves, 3¾ x 2½ in. (9.5 x 6.5 cm), 1 column, 16 lines, in Latin, in *littera gotica rotunda,* 14 large and 5 small (Gospel Lessons; fol. 206) miniatures, and 12 calendar and 12 zodiacal vignettes.

Use: Calendar: composite, with entries pointing to both Bruges and Utrecht; Hours of the Virgin: Rome; Office of the Dead: Rome.

TEXT	IMAGE
Calendar (2v–14)	Zodiacal sign on each recto
Jan.	Feasting (2v)
Feb.	Pruning (3v)
Mar.	Ploughing (4v)
Apr.	Tending Sheep (5v)
May	Courting (6v)
Jun.	Shearing Sheep (7v)
Jul.	Mowing (8v)
Aug.	Reaping (9v)
Sept.	Sowing (10v)
Oct.	Treading Grapes (11v)
Nov.	Stunning an Ox (12v)
Dec.	Slaughtering a Pig (13v)
Salve sancta facies (16–17v)	Salvator Mundi (15v)
Hours of the Cross (19–25v)	Crucifixion (18v)
Hours of the Holy Spirit (27–32v)	Pentecost (26v)
Mass of the Virgin (33–38v)	(Miniature missing)
Gospel Lessons (39–47)	John on Patmos (39)
	Luke Writing (41)
	Matthew Writing (43)
	Mark Contemplating (46)
Hours of the Virgin (49–132)	
Matins	Annunciation (48v)
Lauds	Visitation (69v)
Prime	Nativity (83v)
Terce	Annunciation to the Shepherds (89v)
Sext	Adoration of the Magi (95v)
None	Presentation in the Temple (100v)
Vespers	Massacre of the Innocents (106v)
Compline	Flight into Egypt (115v)
Advent Hours	Coronation of the Virgin (122v)
Penitential Psalms, Litany (134–159)	Bathsheba at Her Bath (133v)
Office of the Dead (159–205v)	Raising of Lazarus (158v)
Obsecro te, O intemerata,	Pietà (206)
Athanasian Creed (206–218)	

BIBLIOGRAPHY: Randall, *Medieval and Renaissance Manuscripts,* III, 480–86, no. 290, pl. XLIIIb, figs. 541–43.

❖ ❖ ❖

104

Fig. 24

Walters Art Museum, MS W. 428.

Belgium, Bruges (?), ca. 1500.

Vellum, 222 leaves, 3¾ x 2¾ in. (9.6 x 6.9 cm), 1 column, 16 lines, in Latin and Italian, in *littera gotica rotunda,* 17 large and 4 small (Gospel Lessons) miniatures, 1 historiated initial, 1 historiated border, and 12 calendar and 12 zodiacal vignettes.

Use: Calendar: general, but with entries pointing to both Bruges and Utrecht; Hours of the Virgin: Rome; Office of the Dead: Rome.

TEXT	IMAGE
Calendar (1v–13)	Zodiacal sign on each recto
Jan.	Keeping Warm and Feasting (1v)
Feb.	Chopping Wood (2v)
Mar.	Pruning (3v)
Apr.	Hawking (4v)
May	Making Music (5v)
Jun.	Mowing (6v)
Jul.	Reaping (7v)
Aug.	Threshing (8v)
Sept.	Treading Grapes (9v)
Oct.	Sowing (10v)
Nov.	Thrashing for Acorns (11v)
Dec.	Roasting a Pig (12v)
Salve sancta facies (15–16)	Salvator Mundi (14v)
Hours of the Cross (18–24v)	Crucifixion (17v)
	Border: Arma Christi (18)
Hours of the Holy Spirit (26–31v)	Pentecost (25v)
Mass of the Virgin (33–38)	Madonna (32v)
Gospel Lessons (38v–44v)	John on Patmos (38v)
	Luke Writing (40)
	Matthew Writing (41v)
	Mark Examining Pen (43v)
Hours of the Virgin (46–131v)	
Matins	Annunciation (45v)
Lauds	Visitation (67v)
Prime	Nativity (81v)
Terce	Annunciation to the Shepherds (87v)
Sext	Adoration of the Magi (93v)
None	Presentation in the Temple (99v)
Vespers	Massacre of the Innocents (105v)
Compline	Flight into Egypt (114v)
Advent Hours	Coronation of the Virgin (121v)
Penitential Psalms, Litany (133–154)	Bathsheba at Her Bath (132v)
Office of the Dead (156–198v)	Raising of Lazarus (155v)
Obsecro te, O intemerata (199–205v)	Pietà, in "O" (199)
Athanasian Creed (206–210)	
O gloriosissima verace virgine Maria (212–213v)	Madonna (211v)
O dulcissima Domine Iesu Christe (215–221v)	Crucifixion (214v)

BIBLIOGRAPHY: Randall, *Medieval and Renaissance Manuscripts,* III, 474–80, no. 289, pl. XLIIIa, figs. 539, 540, 601.

❖ ❖ ❖

105

Fig. 15

Walters Art Museum, MS W. 425.

Belgium, early 16th century.

Vellum, 58 leaves, 3½ x 2½ in. (9 x 6.4 cm), 1 column, 13 lines, in Latin, in *littera gotica rotunda,* 21 large miniatures and 12 calendar and 12 zodiacal vignettes.

Use: Calendar: composite? (second half of each month is missing); Hours of the Virgin: too fragmentary to be identified.

TEXT	IMAGE
Calendar (1–12v)	Zodiacal sign on each recto
Jan.	Keeping Warm and Feasting (1)
Feb.	Pruning and Splitting Wood (2)
Mar.	Breaking Ground (3)
Apr.	Planting (4)
May	Riding (5)
Jun.	Mowing (6)
Jul.	Reaping (7)
Aug.	Threshing (8)
Sept.	Ploughing (9)
Oct.	Treading Grapes and Making Wine (10)
Nov.	Slaughtering a Pig (11)
Dec.	Throwing Snowballs (12)

(From this point the contents are bound in much confusion; what follows is essentially a list of the miniatures arranged in a reconstructed order juxtaposed to the existing or putative texts.)

TEXT	IMAGE
Deus propitius esto mihi et custos mei	Trinity (13)

Hours of the Virgin	
(Matins missing)	(Miniature missing)
Lauds	Visitation (17v)
Prime	Nativity (15v)
(Terce missing)	Annunciation to the Shepherds (40v)
(Sext missing)	(Miniature missing)
(None missing)	(Miniature missing)
Vespers	Flight into Egypt (50)
(Compline missing)	(Miniature missing)
(Penitential Psalms, Litany missing)	David in Prayer (26v)
15 Joys of the Virgin	(Miniature missing)
7 Prayers of St. Gregory	Mass of St. Gregory (23v)
Suffrages	God the Father (57v)
	Anne with the Virgo Lactans (19v)
	Michael Battling a Devil (27)
	John the Baptist (38)
	Margaret Emerging from the Dragon (41)
	Sebastian Shot with Arrows (43v)
	Jerome in Penance (45v)
	Catherine (47v)
	Roch Displaying His Sore (49v)
	Andrew (53)
	Mary Magdalene (54v)
	Christopher Carrying Christ (55)
	Elizabeth of Hungary Distributing Alms (56v)
(?)	Bernard Receiving Milk from the Virgin (30v)

BIBLIOGRAPHY: Randall, *Medieval and Renaissance Manuscripts,* III, 531–39, no. 297, pl. XLIVc–d, fig. 558.

❖ ❖ ❖

106

Fig. 19

New York, Pierpont Library, MS M. 399 ("Da Costa Hours"). Belgium, Bruges (?), ca. 1515.

Vellum, 388 leaves, 6 ¾ x 5 in. (17.1 x 12.6 cm), 1 column, 17 lines, in Latin, in *littera gotica rotunda,* 67 large and 14 small (fols. 21v–33, 42, 199, 374v–385v) miniatures, 16 historiated borders, 12 full-page calendar illustrations and 12 zodiacal vignettes, and 1 coat-of-arms, by Simon Bening.

Use: Calendar: composite; Hours of the Virgin: Rome; Office of the Dead: Rome.

TEXT	IMAGE
	Da Costa Coat-of-Arms (1v)
Calendar (3–14)	Zodiacal sign on each recto
Jan.	Keeping Warm and Feasting (2v)
Feb.	Pruning (3v)
Mar.	Breaking Ground (4v)
Apr.	Tending Sheep, Milking (5v)
May	Courting (6v)
Jun.	Shearing Sheep (7v)
Jul.	Mowing (8v)
Aug.	Reaping (9v)
Sept.	Ploughing and Sowing (10v)
Oct.	Selling an Ox (11v)
Nov.	Scutching Flax (12v)
Dec.	Slaughtering a Pig (13v)
Hours of the Passion (16–35)	
Matins	Betrayal (15v)
Lauds	Christ before Annas (21v)
Prime	Christ before Pilate (23v)
Terce	Ecce Homo (25v)
Sext	Christ Nailed to the Cross (27v)
None	Crucifixion (29)
Vespers	Deposition (31)
Compline	Entombment (33)
Mass of the 5 Wounds of Our Lord (37–41v)	Mass; border: Men Praying (36v)
St. Gregory's Prayer to the 5 Wounds (42–43)	Man of Sorrows (42)
Passion according to Matthew, Mark, Luke, John (45–91v)	Flagellation (44v)
	Christ Crowned with Thorns (58v)
	Ecce Homo (70v)
	Veronica Wipes the Face of Christ (82v)
Hours of the Compassion of the Virgin, followed by the 15 "O's" (93–110)	Mater Dolorosa, surrounded by the 7 Sorrows of the Virgin: Presentation in the Temple, Flight into Egypt, Christ among the Doctors, Christ Carrying the Cross, Crucifixion, Lamentation, Entombment (92v)
Gospel Lessons (112–120v)	John on Patmos; border: Men Transporting a Pillar in a Boat (111v)
	Border: Man on Horseback (112)
	Luke Writing and, in background, Painting the Virgin (113v)
	Matthew Writing (116v)
	Mark Writing; border: Making Music in a Boat (119v)
Suffrages (122–128)	John the Evangelist (121v)
	Mark (123v)
	Matthew (125v)
	Luke (127v)
Hours of the Virgin (130–182)	
Matins	Annunciation (129v)
Lauds	Visitation; border: Landscape (140v)
Prime	Nativity (151v)
Terce	Annunciation to the Shepherds; border: Landscape (157v)
Sext	Adoration of the Magi (162v)
None	Circumcision; border: Landscape (166v)
	Border: Children Spinning Tops (167)
Vespers	Flight into Egypt; border: Landscape (170v)
Compline	Coronation of the Virgin; border: Landscape (176v)
Hours of the Cross (184–188)	Crucifixion (183v)
Hours of the Holy Spirit (190–193)	Pentecost (189v)
Salve sancta facies (195–196)	Salvator Mundi; border: Angels (194v)
	Border: Landscape (195)
Ave vulnus lateris nostri redemptoris (198–v)	Man of Sorrows with Virgin and John the Evangelist; border: Patron Praying (197v)
Ave sanctissima maria mater dei (199–v)	Madonna of the Apocalypse (199)
Antiphons and prayers for different seasons (200–v)	
Penitential Psalms, Litany (203–225)	David and Goliath; border: David Decapitating Goliath (202v)
Office of the Dead (227–270)	Raising of Lazarus; border: Skulls (226v)
Suffrages (272–339v)	Michael Battling a Devil (271v)
	Decapitation of John the Baptist (273v)
	Peter and Paul (275v)
	Andrew (277v)
	James (279v)
	Thomas (281v)
	All Apostles (283v)
	Lapidation of Stephen (285v)
	Lawrence (287v)

	Sebastian Shot with Arrows (289v)
	Christopher Carrying Christ (291v)
	George Slaying the Dragon (293v)
	All Martyrs (295v)
	Jerome in Penance (297v)
	Augustine (299v)
	Bernard Embracing the Crucified Christ (301v)
	Benedict Praying amidst Thorns (304v)
	Stigmatization of Francis (306v)
	Anthony of Padua Preaching to the Fish (308v)
	Dominic (310v)
	Bernardino (312v)
	Onuphrius Praying (314v)
	Roch Displaying His Wound (316v)
	All Confessors (318v)
	Three Magi (320v)
	Anne with the Virgin and Child (322v)
	Catherine (324v)
	Mary Magdalene (326v)
	Elizabeth of Hungary Distributing Bread (328v)
	Helena (330v)
	Apollonia (332v)
	Lucy (334v)
	Ursula (336v)
	Martyrdom of the 11,000 Virgins (338v)
Sunday Hours of the Trinity 341–350)	Trinity (340v)
Hours of the Conception of the Virgin (352–359)	Anne with Virgin in Her Womb (351v)
15 prayers to the wounds of Christ (361–368)	Agony in the Garden (360v)
Mass of the Virgin (370–374)	Mass; border: Courting (369v)
	Border: Jousting (370)
Stabat mater (374v–376)	Virgin and John the Evangelist in Mourning (374v)
Obsecro te, O intemerata (376v–382)	Madonna (376v)
	Lamentation (380)
Conditor celi et terrae rex (382v–385)	God the Father in Heaven (382v)
O dulcissime Domine Iesu Christe (385v–389v)	Christ Child Surrounded by Angels, Holding the Arma Christi (385v)

BIBLIOGRAPHY: Brinkmann, "Simon Bening," 727 (mistakenly cited as M. 311).

❖ ❖ ❖

107 Pl. 26

Walters Art Museum, MS W. 185.

Holland, ca. 1410–15.

Vellum, 286 leaves, 5 x 3¼ in. (12.7 x 9.6 cm), 1 column, 12 lines, in Latin and Dutch, in *textura,* 12 large miniatures and 1 historiated initial.

Use: Calendar: Utrecht; Hours of the Virgin: Windesheim Congregation, but with some variations of Geert Grote; Office of the Dead: Utrecht/Windesheim Congregation (abbreviated).

TEXT	IMAGE
Calendar (1–12v)	
Hours of the Virgin (15–102)	Annunciation (13v)
Matins and Lauds	Betrayal (14v)
	Madonna, in "D" (15)
Prime	Pilate Washing His Hands (49v)
Terce	Flagellation (58v)
Sext	Christ Carrying the Cross (65v)
None	Crucifixion (72v)
Vespers	Lamentation (79v)
Compline	Entombment (91v)
Hours of the Holy Spirit (104–136v)	Pentecost (103v)
Penitential Psalms, Litany (139–170)	Last Judgement (138v)
Office of the Dead (172–215)	Souls in the Bosom of God (171v)
Various prayers including 7 Verses of St. Bernard, Obsecro te (216–224v)	
Hours of Eternal Wisdom (226–278v)	Trinity (225v)
Ex-libris of Françoise de Doffinnes, dated 1584 (283v)	

BIBLIOGRAPHY: Marrow, *Descriptive and Analytical Catalogue of Dutch Illustrated Manuscripts* (forthcoming).

❖ ❖ ❖

108 Fig. 50

Walters Art Museum, MS W. 188.

Holland, ca. 1435.

Vellum, 256 leaves, 5⅝ x 4 in. (14.3 x 10.1 cm), 1 column, 14 lines, in Dutch, in *textura,* 18 historiated initials by one of the Masters of Zweder van Culemborg.

Use: Calendar: Utrecht; Hours of the Virgin: Geert Grote; Office of the Dead: Geert Grote.

TEXT	IMAGE
Easter tables for years 1435–1516 (1–3)	
Calendar (4–15v)	
Hours of the Virgin (16–88)	
Matins	Betrayal, in "H" (16)
Lauds	Christ Crowned with Thorns, in "G" (31v)
Prime	Christ before Pilate, in "G" (47)
Terce	Flagellation, in "G" (53)
Sext	Christ Carrying the Cross, in "G" (59)
None	Crucifixion, in "G" (65)
Vespers	Deposition, in "G" (71)
Compline	Entombment, in "B" (81v)
Hours of the Holy Spirit (89–121v)	
Matins	Trinity, in "O" (89)
Prime	Visitation, in "G" (96)
Terce	Nativity, in "G" (100)
Sext	Annunciation to the Shepherds, in "G" (104)
None	Adoration of the Magi, in "G" (108)
Vespers	Flight in Egypt, in "G" (112)
Compline	Presentation in the Temple, in "B" (117v)
Hours of the Cross (122–140v)	Harrowing of Hell, in "O" (122)
Penitential Psalms, Litany (141–174v)	Michael with the Scales of Judgement, in "H" (141)
Office of the Dead (175–256v)	Souls in Purgatory, in "M" (175)

BIBLIOGRAPHY: Marrow, *Descriptive and Analytical Catalogue of Dutch Illlustrated Manuscripts* (forthcoming).

❖ ❖ ❖

109 Fig. 113

Walters Art Museum, MS W. 168.

Holland, ca. 1435–40, with sections added in Belgium, Bruges, ca. 1460s.

Vellum, 223 leaves, 6¼ x 4½ in. (15.8 x 11.5 cm), 1 column, 15 lines, in Latin, in *textura,* 11 large miniatures and 5 historiated initials by one of the Masters of Zweder van Culemborg, and 15 historiated initials by the workshop of Willem Vrelant.

Use: Calendar: Utrecht; Hours of the Virgin: Rome; Office of the Dead: unidentified.

TEXT	IMAGE
Calendar (3–14v)	
Hours of the Cross (16–22v)	Crucifixion, in "D" (16)
Mass of the Virgin (23–29)	Madonna Enthroned, Serenaded by Angels, in "I" (23)
Gospel Lessons (29–34)	
Obsecro te, O intemerata, Stabat mater, 7 Last Words of Our Lord, and other prayers (34v–50v)	Lamentation, in "O" (34v)
Hours of the Virgin (53–107)	
Matins and Lauds	Betrayal (52v)
	Madonna, in "D" (53)
Prime	Christ before Pilate (76v)
Terce	Flagellation (81v)
Sext	Christ Carrying the Cross (85v)
None	Crucifixion (90v)
Vespers	Deposition (94v)
Compline	Entombment (102v)
Hours of the Holy Spirit (109–127v)	Trinity (108v)
	Pentecost, in "D" (109)
Hours of the Cross (129–147)	Man of Sorrows Surrounded by the Arma Christi (128v)
	Nativity, in "D" (129)
Penitential Psalms, Litany (149–167)	Last Judgement (148v)
	Salvator Mundi, in "D" (149)
Office of the Dead (167–211v)	Funeral Mass (166v)
	Souls in Purgatory, in "D" (167)
Suffrages (213–223)	John the Baptist, in "I" (213)
	James, in "O" (213v)
	Christopher Carrying Christ, in "A" (214v)
	Sebastian Shot with Arrows, in "O" (215v)
	Adrian, in "A" (216v)
	George Slaying a Dragon, in "G" (217v)
	Ghislain, in "S" (218v)
	Catherine, in "I" (219)
	Barbara, in "A" (220)
	Apollonia, in "V" (221)
	Margaret Emerging from the Dragon, in "A" (222)
	Anne Instructing the Virgin, in "C" (222v)

BIBLIOGRAPHY: Marrow, *Descriptive and Analytical Catalogue of Dutch Illustrated Manuscripts* (forthcoming).

❖ ❖ ❖

110 Fig. 69

Walters Art Museum, MS W. 782 ("Van Alfen Hours").

Holland, 1440s.

Vellum, 240 leaves, 5¾ x 4⅜ in. (14.5 x 11.1 cm), 1 column, 17 lines, in Dutch, in *textura,* 8 historiated initials by the workshop of the Master of Catherine of Cleves.

Use: Calendar: Utrecht; Hours of the Virgin: Geert Grote; Office of the Dead: Geert Grote.

TEXT	IMAGE
Calendar (3–14v)	
(From this point the manuscript is misbound; what follows is based on a reconstruction by James Marrow of the original sequence. Numerous large miniature preceding the major texts are probably missing.)	
Hours of the Virgin	Madonna, in "H" (15)
Hours of Eternal Wisdom	Christ Blessing, in "M" (57)
Matins	Veronica's Veil, in "H" (58)
Mass of the Virgin	Tiburtine Sibyl, in "W"; border: Ara Coeli (92)
Mass of the Holy Spirit	Dove of the Holy Spirit, in "D" (99v)
Mass of the Dead	
Hours of the Holy Spirit	(Historiated initial missing)
Hours of the Passion	Man of Sorrows, with Kneeling Patroness, in "H" (109)
Penitential Psalms, Litany	Souls Tormented by Devils in Hell, in "H" (113)
Office of the Dead	Souls in Purgatory, in "M" (200)
Suffrages	
Prayers to the Eucharist	
Various prayers, including 8 Verses of St. Bernard	

BIBLIOGRAPHY: Marrow, *Descriptive and Analytical Catalogue of Dutch Illustrated Manuscripts* (forthcoming).

❖ ❖ ❖

111 Fig. 70

Walters Art Museum, MS W. 102.

England, end of the 13th century.

Vellum, 105 leaves, 10½ x 7¼ in. (26.4 x 18.5 cm), 1 column, 19 lines, in Latin and French, in *textura,* 33 historiated initials, numerous marginal figures including 17 composing a narrative cycle of Renard the Fox, numerous line fillers including 8 large vignettes in the Litany, numerous pen-work grotesques, and 1 pen drawing (fol. 105v).

Use: Hours of the Virgin: Rome? (text incomplete); Office of the Dead: Rome.

TEXT	IMAGE
(The manuscript is bound in much confusion; the following reconstruction is based on that by Florence McCulloch:)	
Hours of the Virgin	
(Matins missing)	(Historiated initials missing)
Lauds	(Historiated initial missing)
Prime	Woman Kneeling in Prayer, in "D" (88v)
Terce	Woman, with Book of Hours, Kneeling in Prayer, in "D" (92v)
Sext	Woman Kneeling in Prayer before an Altar, in "D" (16)
(None, Vespers, and Compline missing)	(Historiated initials missing)
Hours of the Holy Spirit	
Matins	Two Clerics, with Book of Hours, Praying before an Altar, in "D" (22)
Prime	Woman Praying, in "D" (24v)
Terce	Man Praying, in "D" (25v)
Sext	Woman Praying, in "D" (26v)
None	Woman Praying, in "D" (85v)
Vespers	Woman Praying, in "D" (35v)
Compline	Woman Praying, in "D" (42)
Penitential Psalms, Litany	Christ with Cleric Holding a Book, in "D" (43)
	Elephant and Castle (28)

	Adam Holding the Apple (28v)
	Head of Christ/St. Stephen (29)
	Chess Game (29)
	Romulus and Remus (29v)
	Ape Riding a Bear (29v)
	Nude Man (30)
	Margaret (?) Swallowed by the Dragon (30v)
15 Gradual Psalms	Decapitation, in "A" (39)
Office of the Dead	
Matins and Lauds	Two Monks Chanting, in "V" (51)
	Funeral Service, in "P" (55)
Vespers	Two Men Kneeling in Prayer, in "D" (70)
Hours of Christ Crucified	
Matins	Betrayal, in "D" (73v)
Lauds	Flagellation, in "D" (74)
Prime	Christ Carrying the Cross, in "D" (76)
Terce	Crucifixion, in "D" (77v)
Sext	Deposition, in "D" (79v)
None	Entombment, in "D" (81v)
Vespers	Resurrection, in "D" (83)
Compline	Tree of Jesse, in "D" (2)

(On the last leaf of the Office of the Dead and throughout most of the Hours of Christ Crucified is a marginal cycle of the Funeral Procession of Renard the Fox:)

	Sheep Ringing Bells (73)
	Elephant as Pilgrim (73v)
	Bull Blowing Horn (74)
	Horse Playing Drum and Flute (74v)
	Ass Playing Recorder and Bell (75)
	Dog Playing Bagpipes (75v)
	Ape Family (76)
	Brichemer the Stag and Tibert the Cat Carrying Renard's Bier (76v–77)
	Chantecler the Cock Swinging a Censer (77v)
	Ysengrin the Wolf as Bishop (78)
	Cat Beating Cymbal (?) (78v)
	Goat Carrying Crucifix (79)
	Bear Blowing Horn (79v)
	Ram, with Situla, Sprinkling Holy Water with an Aspergillum (80)
	Boar Digging Grave (80v)
	Rabbit Tolling Church Bells (81)
Prayers to the Crucified Christ, prayer for priest before Mass	Crucifixion, in "V" (4)
	Christ Carrying the Cross, in "D" (5)
	Crucifixion with Longinus, in "D" (6)
	Trinity, in "D" (6v)
	Three Marys at the Tomb, in "D" (7v)
	Harrowing of Hell, in "D" (8)
	Christ Child Blessing Kneeling Patron and Patroness, in "G" (9)
	Christ with David, in "D" (10v)
	Christ with Kneeling Patroness, in "C" (12)
Office of St. Catherine	Maxentius Interviewing the Doctors, in "M" (13v)
Prayer for travelers, Suffrage, prayers when waking up and going to bed	
Prayers (added somewhat later)	Grilling of Lawrence (added somewhat later, 105v)

BIBLIOGRAPHY: Sandler, *Gothic Manuscripts*, I, 42, figs. 26–28, 31; II, 20, 22, 24–26, 54, no. 15.

112

Pl. 13, Fig. 95

Walters Art Museum, MS W. 105 ("Butler Hours").

England, ca. 1340, produced for the Butler family of Wem, Salop.

Vellum, 56 leaves, 8¼ x 5⅝ in. (21 x 14.4 cm), 1 column, 13 lines, in Latin and French, in *textura*, 13 large miniatures and 16 historiated initials (2 others in Stockholm and 1 on the art market).

Use: Calendar: Sarum; Hours of the Virgin: Sarum.

TEXT	IMAGE

(The manuscript is presently unbound. The following order reflects its original appearance; the old foliation has been retained.)

	(Series of prefatory miniatures:)
Suffrages for Thomas Becket, Thomas of Lancaster, and other prayers	Resurrected Christ (7)
	Annunciation (7v)
	Annunciation to the Shepherds (8)
	Journey of the Magi (8v)
	Death of the Virgin (9)
	Tree of Vices (9v)
	Crucifixion (10)
	Head of Christ Surrounded by Evangelists' Symbols and Tree with Birds (10v)
	Peter and Paul (11)
	Martyrdom of Thomas Becket (14)
	Butler Family at Mass (15)
	John the Baptist and John the Evangelist (13)
	Helena and Mary Magdalene (12)
Calendar	
Hours of the Virgin	
Matins	Madonna, in "D" (17)
Lauds	Visitation, in "D" (41v)
	Man in Prayer, in "C" (43)
Suffrages	Christ with Dove of the Holy Spirit, in "D" (43v)
	Christ as Judge, in "O" (38)
	(Historiated initial cut out, 38v)
	Lawrence, in "D" (39)
	John the Baptist, in "P" (39v)
	Nicholas Resuscitating the Three Boys, in "D" (32)
	Margaret Emerging from the Dragon, in "D" (32v)
	Catherine, in "D" (33)
	Man Writing, in "O" (33v)
	Christ (?), in "D" (34)
Matins of the Hours of the Cross	Head of Christ, in "P" (34v)
Prime	Betrayal, in "D" (35)
Prime of the Cross	Judas, in "H" (Newton, Mass., The Rendells, Inc., *The Medieval World*, Cat. 146, 1979, no. 79, illus.)
Terce	Christ before Pilate, in "D" (48)
(Terce of the Cross missing)	(Historiated initial missing)
(Sext Missing)	(Historiated initials missing)
(None missing)	(Historiated initials missing)
Vespers	Crucifixion, in "D" (Stockholm, Nationalmuseum, MS B 1727)
Vespers of the Cross	Head of Christ, in "D" (51)
Compline	(Historiated initial missing)
Compline of the Cross	Head of Christ, in "H" (Stockholm, MS B 1726)
Prayer to the Virgin (added somewhat later)	
Prayer to the Eucharist	
(Penitential Psalms and Litany missing)	
(15 Gradual Psalms missing)	

BIBLIOGRAPHY: Sandler, *Gothic Manuscripts*, I, 34, figs. 305, 306; II, 130–31, 132, 133, no. 117.

113

Fig. 122

Philadelphia, Philadelphia Museum of Art, MS 1945–65–6 ("Mostyn Hours").

England, ca. 1460–70.

Vellum, 279 leaves, 5⅞ x 4¼ in. (14.5 x 10.3 cm), 1 column, 15 lines, in Latin, in *textura,* 14 large miniatures.

Use: Calendar: England; Hours of the Virgin: Sarum; Office of the Dead: Sarum.

TEXT	IMAGE
Calendar (1–6v)	
Ave virgo virginum (7v–8)	
Hours of the Virgin (9–116v)	
Matins	Annunciation (8v)
Lauds	Betrayal (19v)
Prime	Christ before Pilate (51v)
Terce	Flagellation (60v)
Sext	Christ Carrying the Cross (68v)
None	Crucifixion (75v)
Vespers	Deposition (82v)
Compline	Entombment (102v)
Penitential Psalms, Litany (118–143v)	Last Judgement (117v)
15 Gradual Psalms (145–158)	David in Prayer (144v)
Office of the Dead (159–205v)	Funeral Service (158v)
Commendation of Souls (207–227)	Souls Borne to Heaven (206v)
Passion Psalms (228–243)	Mass of St. Gregory (227v)
Hours of the Passion (244–277)	Agony in the Garden (243v)

BIBLIOGRAPHY: Tanis et al., *Leaves of Gold,* 85–86, no. 22, illus.

❖ ❖ ❖

114

Fig. 47

Cambridge, Mass., Harvard University, Houghton Library, MS Richardson 34.

England, ca. 1470.

Vellum, 150 leaves, 11⅜ x 8 in. (29 x 20 cm), 1 column, 18 lines, in Latin, in *textura,* 12 large miniatures.

Use: Calendar: Sarum; Hours of the Virgin: Sarum; Office of the Dead: Sarum.

TEXT	IMAGE
Calendar (1–6v)	
7 Prayers of St. Gregory (7–8)	
Hours of the Virgin (13–65v)	
Matins	Annunciation (12v)
Lauds	Betrayal (19v)
Suffrages	
Prime	Pilate Washing His Hands (32v)
Terce	Flagellation (37v)
Sext	Christ Carrying the Cross (41v)
None	Crucifixion (45v)
Salve regina, 5 Joys of the Virgin, other prayers	
Vespers	Deposition (51v)
Suffrages	
Compline	Entombment (61v)
Penitential Psalms, 15 Gradual Psalms, Litany (67–87v)	David in Prayer (66v)
Office of the Dead (89–118)	Funeral Service (88v)
Psalms of Commendation (120–131)	Souls Taken Up to Heaven (119v)
Passion Psalms (132–141)	Man of Sorrows Surrounded by the Arma Christi (131v)
7 Last Words of Our Lord, 8 Verses of St. Bernard, prayers to the Eucharist, Stabat mater, and other prayers (141v–150v)	

BIBLIOGRAPHY:: Wieck, *Late Medieval and Renaissance Illuminated Manuscripts,* 92–93, no. 45, illus.

115

Fig. 101

Walters Art Museum, MS W. 328.

Italy, Naples, ca. 1450s.

Vellum, 220 leaves, 6⅞ x 5 in. (17.5 x 12.7 cm), 1 column, 15 lines, in Latin, in *littera gotica rotunda,* 7 large miniatures and 6 historiated initials by Matteo Felice.

Use: Calendar: general; Hours of the Virgin: Rome; Office of the Dead: Rome.

TEXT	IMAGE
Calendar (1–6v)	
Hours of the Virgin (9–77)	Annunciation, in "D" (9)
Penitential Psalms, Litany (79–100v)	David in Prayer, in "D" (79)
Hours of the Cross (101–108)	Man of Sorrows with the Arma Christi, in "D" (101)
Hours of Corpus Christi (109–115v)	Christ with the Eucharist and Cross, in "D" (109)
Office of the Dead (117–152)	Funeral Service, in "D" (117)
Gospel Lessons (152v–157v)	
Mass of the Virgin (159–164)	Madonna (158v)
9 Joys of the Virgin, Exposition on the Ave Maria (165–169v)	Annuciation, in "G" (165)
Suffrages, Prayer of St. Augustine, Suffrages (170–181)	Anthony of Padua (170v)
	Bernardino (171v)
	Augustine (173v)
	Jerome and the Lion (178v)
	Mary Magdalene (179v)
	Catherine (180v)
Athanasian Creed, Passion according to John, Stabat mater, followed by numerous other prayers, including some to the Eucharist (181v–217)	

BIBLIOGRAPHY: Katzenstein, "A Neapolitan Book of Hours in the J. Paul Getty Museum," 90–92, 94, figs. 31, 32.

❖ ❖ ❖

116

Fig. 65

Walters Art Museum, MS W. 767 ("Adimari Hours").

Italy, Florence, early 1460s, made for a member of the Florentine Adimari family.

Vellum, 278 leaves, 5¼ x 3⅝ in. (13.5 x 9.3 cm), 1 column, 12 lines, in Latin, in *littera gotica rotunda,* 5 large miniatures, 12 historiated initials, and 4 historiated borders, by Zanobi Strozzi.

Use: Calendar: general; Hours of the Virgin: Rome; Office of the Dead: Rome.

TEXT	IMAGE
Calendar (2–13v)	
Hours of the Virgin (15–122v)	
Matins	Annunciation (14v)
	Nativity, in "D"; border: Angels (15)
Lauds	Flight into Egypt, in "D" (45v)
Prime	Presentation in the Temple, in "D" (64)
Terce	Adoration of the Magi, in "D" (71)
Sext	Christ among the Doctors, in "D" (78)
None	Death of the Virgin, in "D" (84)
Vespers	Assumption of the Virgin, in "D" (90v)
Compline	Coronation of the Virgin, in "C" (102)
Hours of the Passion (124–161v)	Crucifixion (123v)
	Agony in the Garden, in "D"; border: Sleeping Apostles, Prophets (124)

Hours of the Cross (163–168)	Lamentation (162v)
	Helena with the True Cross, in "P"; border: Helena Testing the True Cross (163)
Penitential Psalms, Litany (170–203v)	David and Goliath (169v)
	David in Prayer, in "D"; border: Hermit Saints (170)
Office of the Dead (205–277v)	Funeral Service (204v)
	Grim Reaper, in "D"; border: Monks Holding a Skull (205)

BIBLIOGRAPHY: Kanter et al., *Painting and Illumination in Early Renaissance Florence*, 352–56, no. 53. illus.

❖ ❖ ❖

117 Fig. 130

Philadelphia, Philadelphia Free Library, MS Lewis 118.

Italy, ca. 1475.

Vellum, 155 leaves, 5 x 3½ in. (12.7 x 9 cm), 1 column, 13 lines, in Latin, in *littera humanistica rotunda,* 3 large miniatures attributed to Girolamo da Cremona.

Use: Calendar: Dominican; Hours of the Virgin: Rome; Office of the Dead: Rome.

TEXT	IMAGE
Calendar (2–13v)	
Hours of the Virgin (15–91)	(Miniature missing)
Hours of the Cross (92–95)	Man of Sorrows (91v)
Office of the Dead (96–131v)	Grim Reaper (95v)
Penitential Psalms, Litany (133–155)	David in Prayer (132v)

BIBLIOGRAPHY: Tanis et al., *Leaves of Gold*, 100–01, no. 30, illus. p. 100, figs. 30–1, 30–2.

❖ ❖ ❖

118 Fig. 103

Walters Art Museum, MS W. 420 ("Almugavar Hours").

Spain, Catalonia, 1510–20, produced for a member of the Almugavar family.

Vellum, 301 leaves, 7⅞ x 5⅜ in. (19.9 x 13.6 cm), 1 column, 12 lines, in Latin with Spanish additions, in *textura,* 26 large miniatures and 3 borders with historiated vignettes.

Use: Calendar: Barcelona; Hours of the Virgin: Rome; Office of the Dead: Rome.

TEXT	IMAGE
Calendar (1–12v)	
Magnificat, followed by 4 Psalms (14–22)	Presentation of the Virgin in the Temple (13v)
	Border: Resurrection, Ascension (14)
Hours of the Virgin (24–124v)	
Matins	Annunciation (23v)
Lauds	Visitation (40v)
Prime	Nativity (57v)
Terce	Annunciation to the Shepherds (65v)
Sext	(Miniature missing)
None	Adoration of the Magi (79v)
Vespers	Presentation in the Temple (84v)
Compline	Coronation of the Virgin (94v)
Mass of the Virgin, followed by Gospel Lesson of John (126–135v)	Christ among the Doctors (125v)
Office of the Dead (136v–201v)	
Vespers	(Miniature missing)
Matins and Lauds	Burial Service (146v)
Penitential Psalms, Litany, followed by numerous prayers (204–235v)	Man of Sorrows Surrounded by the Arma Christ and Saints; border: Prophets (203v)
Obsecro te, Athanasian Creed (237–248v)	Virgin Enthroned, Serenaded by Angels (236v)
Suffrages (251–283v)	Benedict and Bernard (252v)
	Onuphrius and Mary of Egypt (254v)
	Francis and Anthony of Padua (256v)
	Michael Battling a Devil and Raphael with Tobias (260v)
	Guardian Angels (263v)
	Sebastian Shot with Arrows and Anne Instructing the Virgin and Christ Child (266v)
	George Slaying the Dragon (269v)
	Catherine and Eulalia of Barcelona (271v)
	Mary Magdalene and Margaret Emerging from the Dragon (274v)
	Jerome in Penance and Anthony (276v)
	Cosmas and Damian (278v)
	Christopher Carrying Christ and Helena; border: Prophet (280v)
Salve sancta facies (285–288v)	Veronica with Her Veil (284v)
Hours of the Cross (290–295)	Three Crosses of Calvary (289v)
Hours of the Holy Spirit (296–301)	(Miniature missing)

BIBLIOGRAPHY: Randall, "From Cîteaux Onwards," 135, no. 28.

❖ ❖ ❖

119 Fig. 20

Los Angeles, J. Paul Getty Museum, MS Ludwig IX. 16.

Germany, Strassburg, early 16th century.

Vellum, 239 leaves, 5½ x 4⅛ in. (13.7 x 10.7 cm), 1 column, 20 lines, in Latin, in *littera batarda,* 19 large miniatures and 12 calendar and 12 zodiacal vignettes.

Use: Calendar: Strassburg; Hours of the Virgin: unidentified; Office of the Dead: Order of St. John of Jerusalem.

TEXT	IMAGE
Calendar (1–12v)	Zodiacal sign on each recto
Jan.	Feasting (1)
Feb.	Keeping Warm (2)
Mar.	Pruning (3)
Apr.	Hawking (4)
May	Riding (5)
Jun.	Mowing (6)
Jul.	Reaping (7)
Aug.	Threshing (8)
Sept.	Sowing (9)
Oct.	Treading Grapes (10)
Nov.	Thrashing for Acorns (11)
Dec.	Baking Bread (12)
Sunday Office of the Trinity (14–35)	Trinity (13v)
Passion according to Matthew (36–43v)	Matthew Writing (35v)
Monday Office of the Angel, Obsecro te, Gaudeant alii de sua innocencia, Suffrages (45–59)	Michael Battling a Devil (44v)
Tuesday Office of Holy Wisdom (60–70)	Salvator Mundi (59v)
Passion according to Mark, Ave sanctissima et immaculata semper virgo, 7 Sorrows of the Virgin,	Mark Examining Pen (70v)

Suffrages (71–83)	
Wednesday Office of the Sorrow of Our Lord (84–94)	Man of Sorrows (83v)
Passion according to Luke, O intemerata, In manus tuas sancta et immaculata virgo, Suffrages (95–107)	Luke Writing (94v)
Thursday Office of the Holy Spirit, various prayers to the Virgin, Suffrages (108–127)	Pentecost (107v)
Friday Office of the Passion (128–141)	Betrayal (127v)
Passion according to John, various prayers including Stabat mater, Suffrages (142–153)	John on Patmos (141v)
Saturday Office of the Virgin (155–188)	
Matins and Lauds	Annunciation (154v)
Prime	Visitation (165v)
Terce	Nativity (168v)
Sext	Circumcision (171v)
None	Adoration of the Magi (174v)
Vespers	Presentation in the Temple (177v)
Compline	Coronation of the Virgin (182v)
Suffrages	
Various prayers to the Virgin, Office of the Compassion of the Virgin, 7 Psalms to the Virgin (188v–207)	
Office of the Dead (208–226)	Raising of Lazarus (207v)
Penitential Psalms, Litany (227–239v)	David in Prayer (226v)

BIBLIOGRAPHY: Los Angeles, J. Paul Getty Museum, "Manuscript Acquisitions: The Ludwig Collection," 294, no. 65.

Concordance

MANUSCRIPT	CATALOGUE NUMBER		
Baltimore, Walters Art Museum			
W.37	79	W.215	81
W.38	10	W.219	32
W.39	3	W.220	91
W.40	1	W.222	45
W.84	12	W.223	46
W.85	78	W.224	58
W.86	4	W.227	65
W.88	80	W.231	19
W.89	14	W.232	21
W.90	7	W.233	59
W.93	6	W.237	17
W.94	16	W.238	25
W.96	15	W.239	87
W.97	2	W.240	92
W.98	5	W.241	61
W.99	18	W.245	64
W.102	111	W.246	90
W.103	20	W.249	49
W.104	8	W.251	39
W.105	112	W.254	28
W.164	82	W.257	38
W.166	83	W.259	30
W.168	109	W.260	26
W.170	84	W.262	36
W.172	85	W.265	23
W.173	89	W.267	40
W.176	100	W.269	41
W.185	107	W.271	24
W.188	108	W.272	97
W.195	95	W.274	42
W.196	94	W.276	27
W.197	93	W.279	96
W.205	47	W.281	35
W.209	22	W.284	60
W.211	88	W.285	50
W.213	56	W.287	29
W.214	51	W.288	34

W.289 33
W.291 62
W.292 44
W.294 66
W.295 67
W.328 115
W.420 118
W.424 74
W.425 105
W.427 103
W.428 104
W.430 68
W.431 101
W.435 102
W.439 98
W.445 57
W.446 75
W.449 77
W.451 76
W.452 72
W.454 69
W.455 73
W.457 63
W.719 86
W.741 31
W.767 116
W.782 110
W.800 52

Cambridge (Mass.), Harvard University, Houghton Library

Richardson 7 48
Richardson 34 114

Los Angeles, J. Paul Getty Museum

Ludwig IX.3 9
Ludwig IX.16 119

New Haven, Yale University, Beinecke Rare Book and Manuscript Library

MS 390 11

New York, Pierpont Morgan Library

H.8 70
M.399 106
M.677 55
M.1001 53
M.1003 43

Philadelphia, Philadelphia Free Library

Lewis 118 117

Philadelphia, Philadelphia Museum of Art

1945-65-4 37
1945-65-6 113

Washington, D.C., Library of Congress

MS 93 54
Edith G. Rosenwald Hours 13
Rosenwald 9 99
Rosenwald 15 71

Books for Further Reading

Chapter II: Social History and the Book of Hours

Ariès, P. *The Hour of Our Death.* New York, 1981.

Aston, M. *Lollards and Reformers: Images and Literacy in Late-Medieval Religion.* London, 1984.

Bois, G. *The Crisis of Feudalism: Economy and Society in Eastern Normandy c. 1300–1550.* Cambridge, 1984.

Hansen, W. *Kalenderminiaturen der Stundenbücher: Mittelalterliches Leben im Jahreslauf.* Munich, 1984.

Herlihy, D., and C. Klapisch-Zuber. *Tuscans and Their Families: A Study of the Florentine Catasto of 1427.* New Haven, 1985.

Hilton, R. H., and T. H. Aston, eds. *The English Rising of 1381.* Cambridge, 1984.

Huizinga, J. *The Autumn of the Middle Ages.* Chicago, 1996.

Keen, M. *Chivalry.* New Haven, 1984.

Kirshner, J., and S. F. Wemple, eds. *Women of the Medieval World: Essays in Honor of John H. Mundy.* Oxford, 1985.

Mollat, M., ed. *Histoire de Rouen.* Toulouse, (1982).

Mollat, M., and P. Wolff. *The Popular Revolutions of the Late Middle Ages.* London, 1973.

Panofsky, E. *Tomb Sculpture: Its Changing Aspects from Ancient Egypt to Bernini.* London, 1964.

Ziegler, P. *The Black Death.* London, 1969.

Chapter III: Prayer and the Book of Hours

Belting, H. *Das Bild und sein Publikum im Mittelalter.* Berlin, 1981.

Bossy, J. *Christianity in the West, 1400–1700.* Oxford, 1985.

Brown, P. *The Cult of the Saints: Its Rise and Function in Latin Christianity.* Chicago, 1981.

Delaruelle, E. *La piété populaire au moyen âge.* Turin, 1980.

Galpern, A. N. *The Religions of the People in Sixteenth-Century Champagne.* Cambridge (Mass.), 1976.

Goughaud, L. *Devotional and Ascetic Practices in the Middle Ages.* London, 1927.

Graef, H. *Mary: A History of Doctrine and Devotion.* London, 1963.

Jacobus de Voragine. *The Golden Legend.* New York, 1969.

Leclercq, J. *The Love of Learning and the Desire for God: A Study of Monastic Culture.* New York, 1982.

LeGoff, J. *Time, Work & Culture in the Middle Ages.* Chicago, 1980.

Meiss, M. *Painting in Florence and Siena after the Black Death.* Princeton, 1951.

Panofsky, E. "'Imago Pietatis': Ein Beitrag zur Typengeschichte des 'Schmerzensmanns' und der 'Maria Mediatrix'." *Festschrift für Max J. Friedländer zum 60. Geburtstage.* Leipzig, 1927, 261–308.

Pantin, W. A. "Instruction for a Devout and Literate Layman." *Medieval Learning and Literature: Essays Presented to Richard William Hunt.* Oxford, 1976, 398–422.

Purtle, C. J. *The Marian Paintings of Jan van Eyck.* Princeton, 1982.

Raitt, J., ed. *Christian Spirituality: High Middle Ages and Reformation.* New York, 1987.

Reinburg, V. *Practices of Prayer in Late Medieval and Reformation France.* Princeton (forthcoming).

Rézeau, P. *Les prières aux saints en francais à la fin du moyen âge.* Geneva, 1982–83.

Ringbom, S. "Devotional Images and Imaginative Devotions: Notes on the Place of Art in Late Medieval Private Piety." *Gazette des beaux-arts* LXXIII, 1969, 159–70.

Ringbom, S. *Icon to Narrative: The Rise of the Dramatic Close-up in Fifteenth-Century Devotional Painting.* Doornspijk, 1984.

Saenger, P. "Silent Reading: Its Impact on Late Medieval Script and Society." *Viator* XIII, 1982, 367–414.

Thurston, H. *Familiar Prayers: Their Origin and History.* Westminster (Md.), (1953).

Turner, V., and E. Turner. *Image and Pilgrimage in Christian Culture: Anthropological Perspectives.* Oxford, 1978.

Warner, M. *Alone of All Her Sex: The Myth and the Cult of the Virgin Mary.* New York, 1976.

Wilmart, A. *Auteurs spirituels et textes dévots du moyen âge latin.* Paris, 1932.

Chapters IV–XII: The Book of Hours and Medieval Art

Avril, F., and N. Reynaud. *Les manuscrits à peintures en France, 1440–1520.* Paris, 1993.

Backhouse, J. *Books of Hours.* London, 1985.

Bartz, G., and E. König. "Die Illustration des Totenoffiziums in Stundenbüchern." *Im Angesicht des Todes. Liturgie als Sterbe- und Trauerhilfe: Ein interdisziplinäres Kompendium.* (Pietas Liturgica, III & IV). St. Ottilien, 1987, 487–528.

Books of Hours. London, 1996.

Caen, Bibliothèque municipale. *Livres d'heures de basse-Normandie. Manuscrits enluminés et livres à gravures XIVe–XVIe siècles.* Caen, 1985.

Calkins, R. G. *Illuminated Books of the Middle Ages.* Ithaca (N.Y.), 1983; see Chapter 8, "The Book of Hours."

De Hamel, C. *A History of Illuminated Manuscripts.* Boston, 1986 (London, 1994, second edition); see Chapter 6, "Books for Everybody."

Defoer, H. L. M., et al. *The Golden Age of Dutch Manuscript Painting.* New York, 1990.

Delaissé, L. M. J. "The Importance of Books of Hours for the History of the Medieval Book." *Gatherings in Honor of Dorothy Miner.* Baltimore, 1974, 203–25.

Donovan, C. *The de Brailes Hours: Shaping the Book of Hours in Thirteenth-Century Oxford.* London, 1991.

Duffy, E. *The Stripping of the Altars: Traditional Religion in England, c. 1400–c. 1580.* New Haven, 1992; see Section C, "Prayers and Spells."

Harthan, J. *The Book of Hours, with a Historical Survey and Commentary.* New York, 1977.

König, E., and G. Bartz. *Das Stundenbuch: Perlen der Buchkunst, Gattung in Handshriften der Vaticana.* Stuttgart, 1998.

Leroquais, V. *Les livres d'heures manuscrits de la Bibliothèque nationale.* Paris, 1927; *Supplément aux Livres d'heures manuscrits de la Bibliothèque nationale (acquisitions récentes et donation Smith-Lesouëf).* Mâcon, 1943.

Littlehales, H., ed. *The Prymer, or, Lay Folks' Prayer Book.* London, 1891–97 (Early English Text Society, CIX); includes E. Bishop's introduction, "On the Origin of the Prymer."

Marrow, J. H. *The Hours of Margaret of Cleves.* Lisbon, 1995.

Plotzek, J. M. *Andachtsbücher des Mittelalters aus Privatbesitz.* Cologne, 1987.

Plummer, J., with an introduction by A. Strittmatter. *Liturgical Manuscripts for the Mass and the Divine Office.* New York, 1964.

Taunton, E. L. *The Little Office of Our Lady: A Treatise Theoretical, Practical & Exegetical.* London, 1903.

Wieck, R. S. *Painted Prayers: The Book of Hours in Medieval and Renaissance Art.* New York, 1997 (1999, second printing).

Wieck, R. S. "The Book of Hours." *The Liturgy of the Medieval Church.* T. J. Heffernan and E. A. Matter, eds., Kalamazoo, 2001, 473–513.

Wieck, R. S. "The Death Desired: Books of Hours and the Medieval Funeral." *Death and Dying in the Middle Ages.* E. E. DuBruck and B. I. Gusick, eds., New York, 1999, 431–76.

van Wijk, N. *Het getijdenboek van Geert Grote, naar het Haagse Handschrift 133 E 21.* Leiden, 1940.

Wordsworth, C., ed. *Horae Eboracenses: The Prymer or Hours of the Blessed Virgin Mary, According to the Use of the Illustrious Church of York, with Other Devotions as They Were Used by the Lay-Folk in the Northern Province in the XVth and XVIth Centuries.* London, 1920 (Publications of the Surtees Society, CXXXII).

(Readers may also consult the slightly more specialized citations listed on page 170.)

Determining Use:

For Calendars:

Grotefend, H. *Taschenbuch der Zeitrechnung des deutschen Mittelalters und der Neuzeit.* Hannover, 1982.

Grotefend, H. *Zeitrechnung des deutschen Mittelalters und der Neuzeit.* Hannover, 1891–92.

Guérin, P. *Les petits Bollandistes, ou Vies des saints.* Paris, 1876.

Holweck, F. G. *A Biographical Dictionary of the Saints.* St. Louis, 1924.

Perdrizet, P. *Le calendrier parisien à la fin du moyen âge d'après le bréviaire et les livres d'heures.* Paris, 1933.

Réau, L. *Iconographie de l'art chrétien.* Paris, 1955–59.

Roeder, H. *Saints and Their Attributes, with a Guide to Localities and Patronage.* London, 1955.

Strubbe, E. I., and L. Voet. *De chronologie van de middeleeuwen en de moderne tijden in de Nederlanden.* Antwerp, 1960.

For the Hours of the Virgin:

Leroquais, V. Unpublished notebooks (Paris, Bibliothèque nationale de France, MS nouv. acq. lat. 1.3162–63) containing tests for the localization of the Hours of the Virgin can be consulted in copies or microfilm in some major research libraries.

Madan, F. "Hours of the Virgin (Tests for Localization)." *Bodleian Quarterly Record* III, 1920, 2nd Quarter, 40–44; updated in "The Localization of Manuscripts." *Essays in History Presented to Reginald Lane Poole.* Oxford, 1927, 5–29.

For the Office of the Dead:

Leroquais, V. Unpublished notebooks (Paris, Bibliothèque nationale de France, MS nouv. acq. lat. 1.3162–63) containing tests for the localization of the Office of the Dead can be consulted in copies or microfilm in some major research libraries.

Ottosen, K. *The Responsories and Versicles of the Latin Office of the Dead.* Aarhus, 1993.

INDEX OF ARTISTS

Bari Workshop: Cat. No. 1.
Bening, Simon: Cat. No. 106.
Bourdichon, Jean: Cat. No. 65.
Colombe, Jean: Cat. Nos. 55–57.
1520s Hours Workshop: Cat. No. 77.
Fouquet, Jean: Cat. No. 54.
Girolamo da Cremona: Cat. No. 117.
Gold Scrolls Group: Cat. Nos. 87–90.
Jacquemart de Hesdin: Cat. No. 15.
Liédet, Loyset: Cat. No. 96.
Maître François: Cat. Nos. 50–52.
Master, Bedford: Cat. Nos. 33, 50.
Master, Boucicaut: Cat. Nos. 24–28.
Master, Coëtivy: Cat. No. 42.
Master, Guise: Cat. No. 27.
Master, Luçon: Cat. Nos. 19–21.
Master, Rohan: Cat. No. 31.
Master of Adélaïde de Savoie: Cat. No. 50.
Master of Anthony of Burgundy: Cat. No. 97.
Master of Antoine Rolin: Cat. No. 101.
Master of Berry's *Cleres Femmes:* Cat. Nos. 21–23.
Master of Catherine of Cleves: Cat. No. 110.
Master of Edward IV: Cat. No. 102.
Master of Guillebert de Mets: Cat. Nos. 83–85.
Master of Jacques de Luxembourg: Cat. No. 43.
Master of Jean Rolin II: Cat. Nos. 39, 50.
Master of Morgan 85: Cat. Nos. 72, 73.
Master of Morgan 96: Cat. Nos. 46, 47.
Master of Morgan 366: Cat. No. 46.
Master of Morgan 453: Cat. No. 35.
Master of Petrarch's Triumphs: Cat. No. 71.
Master of the Bible of Jean de Sy: Cat. No. 11.
Master of the Breviary of Jean sans Peur: Cat. No. 32.
Master of the Collins Hours: Cat. No. 37.
Master of the Geneva Latini: Cat. Nos. 58–61.
Master of the Ghent Privileges: Cat. Nos. 85, 86.
Master(s) of the Gold Scrolls: Cat. Nos. 87–90.
Master of the Harvard Hannibal: Cat. Nos. 29, 30.
Master (artist) of the Hours of Louis de Savoie: Cat. No. 44.
Master of the *Livre du Sacre de Charles V:* Cat. No. 13.
Master of the Munich *Golden Legend:* Cat. No. 34.
Master of the Prayer Book of ca. 1500: Cat. No. 99.
Master of the *Rational des divins offices:* Cat. No. 14.
Master of Walters 219: Cat. No. 32.
Master of Walters 222: Cat. Nos. 45, 46.
Master of Walters 281: Cat. Nos. 35, 36.
Master(s) of Zweder van Culemborg: Cat. Nos. 108, 109.
Matteo Felice: Cat. No. 115.
de Mazerolles, Philippe: Cat. No. 97.
Poyet, Jean: Cat. Nos. 67-70.
Pseudo-Jacquemart de Hesdin: Cat. No. 16.
Pucelle, Jean: Cat. No. 11.
Strozzi, Zanobi: Cat. No. 116.
Testard, Robinet: Cat. No. 53.
Vrelant, Willem: Cat. Nos. 91–95, 109.
de Vulcop, Henri: Cat. No. 42.